The Elements of Modern Architecture

Understanding Contemporary Buildings

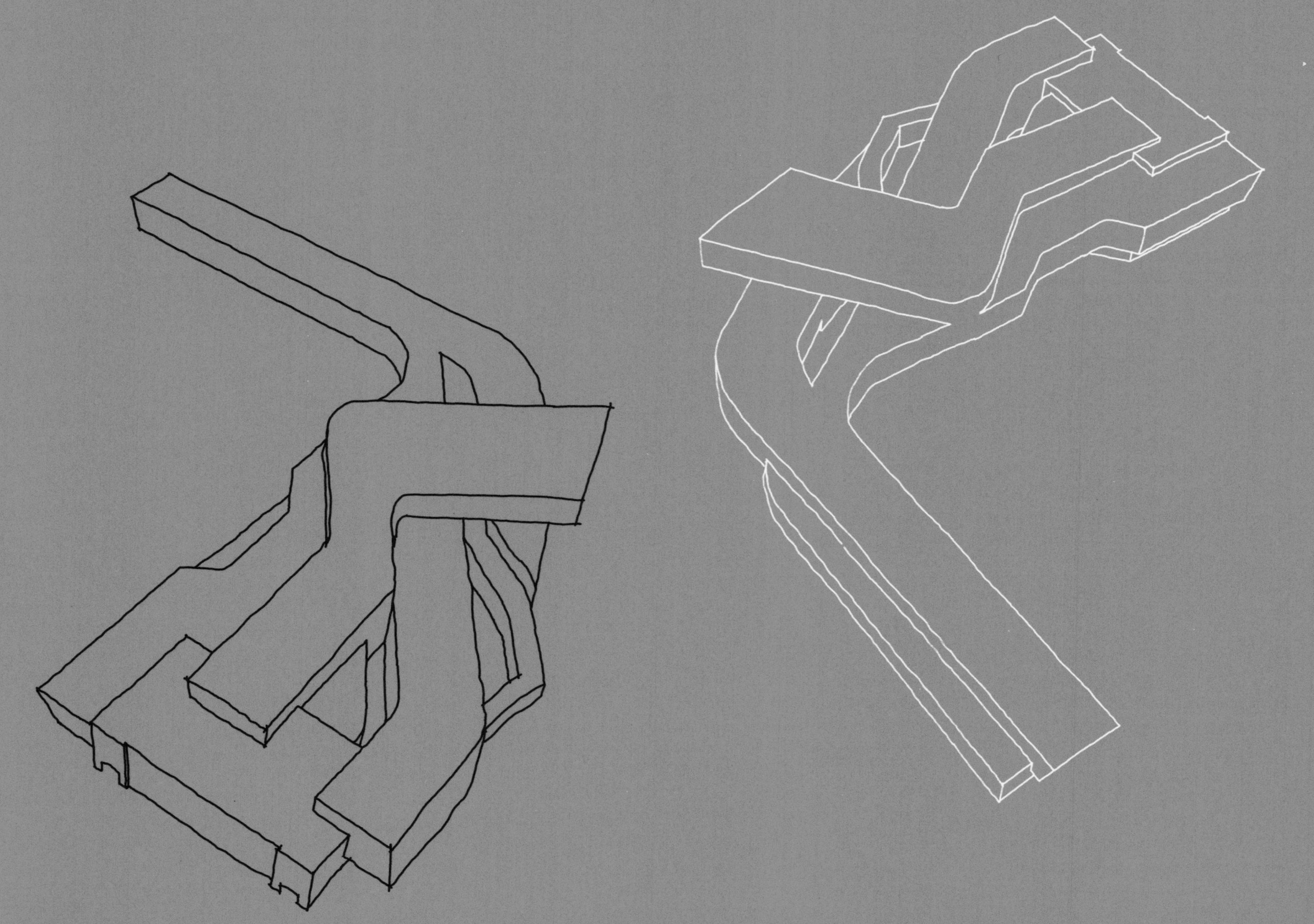

The Elements of Modern Architecture

Understanding Contemporary Buildings

Antony Radford, Selen Morkoç and Amit Srivastava

With over 2,500 illustrations

Thames & Hudson

On the cover: Louisiana Museum of Modern Art (1956–58) The brick-and-timber design of the new building exemplifies responsive cohesion between building, art and landscape (project 7).

Frontispiece: MAXXI (1998–2009) The museum lies like a coiled snake with its head lifted to rest on its body, looking out beyond the site (project 50).

First published in the United Kingdom in 2014 by Thames & Hudson Ltd, 181A High Holborn, London WC1V 7QX

Reprinted 2015

Designed by Adam Hay Studio

British Library Cataloguing-in-Publication Data
A catalogue record for this book is available from the British Library

ISBN 978-0-500-34295-4

Printed and bound in China by Shanghai Offset Printing Products Limited

Contents

Modern Art Museum of Fort Worth | 1996–2002
Views from the interior of the building look out towards the pond. Reflection from the water increases the impact of natural light within and around the building (project 38).

Architectural Analyses: A Visual Guide to Fifty Buildings 1950–2010

This book is about how the elements of contemporary architecture respond to their various physical, social, cultural and environmental contexts. The book examines fifty influential architectural works, all built since 1950. Its aim is to present a concise analysis of their designs that will supplement photographs, descriptions, virtual-reality experiences and real-world visits.

Any architectural work is a complex cultural product that results from many ambitions. Some (very few) of these works are internationally famous buildings that are continually cited as exemplars in the discourses of architecture. We know them through professionally taken photographs, almost always devoid of people. They are typically published as isolated objects excised from their physical, social and environmental contexts. Although these images are often accompanied by plans and text, we rarely get to see a section, and even more rarely any kind of analytical diagrams. Where detail is offered it is usually aimed at a specialist reader. The representation of architecture through isolated fields of specialized knowledge is a distinctly modern phenomenon that widens the gap between contextual reality and produced images.

For architecture, nothing replaces physical reality: the sensory combination of sight, sound, smell and feel, the kinaesthetic experience of moving through a building, the emotional response of a human to her or his occupation of space. Even the immersive environments of 3D digital media are weak substitutes. Yet compared with the numbers that know famous buildings from iconic photographs, very few people can visit and experience one in its physical reality. Paintings and sculptures can tour, but buildings are fixed in (often private) place.

Analysis and interpretation

The pleasure of experiencing architecture is both a direct sensory pleasure grounded in embodiment and a considered intellectual pleasure (Scruton 1979: 73; Pallasmaa, 2011: 28). An intellectual pleasure relies on interpretation and understanding, and if we do not understand we miss much of the enjoyment (a reason, of course, why enthusiasts in any field get far more enjoyment out of the objects of their attention than do outsiders). An analysis opens up the way to an interpretation that seeks to contribute to understanding.

Understanding is not only for pleasure. Any discipline thrives on critical reflection, discussion and debate about its products. The past provides patterns and precedents for future work, and understanding the past helps to make a better future. This transcends the transition from traditional to digital media in design during the sixty years that separate the earliest and most recent buildings in this book. Indeed, digital design media facilitate the adaptation of successful design patterns from the past as well as the exploration of new form (Bruton and Radford 2012).

Analyses offer the means to learn about the 'how' of buildings: how details relate to one another; how a building relates to its urban or rural setting, to its climate and to the society it serves; how materials are used. An analysis can address 'why' questions through interpretation: why a building takes a particular form, why certain materials are selected and why a precedent is referred to in a design.

The analyses in this book aim to offer interpretations akin to those of reviewers or critics, with no claim that we have access to the minds of the architects. Finnish architect and theorist Juhani Pallasmaa emphasizes that the role of responsible architectural criticism is to create and defend the 'sense of the real' in a world that is 'increasingly fictionalized by an architecture of the commercialized image' (Pallasmaa, 2011: 22–23). As critics, the analysers observe, read the available literature (certainly including the words of the architects where published) and present their interpretation of the work. This is particularly significant for the 'why' questions. In some cases architects have described how building form arose during design, while in other cases there is little information about the reasoning behind the building.

As in a review of a book, film or restaurant, the credibility of the analysis depends on it being sufficiently complete to tell a coherent story true to the sense of the real, and on that story being thought-provoking to a reader, encouraging new interpretations. Like a review, too, the aim

Civil Justice Centre | 2001–7
The building form can be described as a layered assembly of components (project 44).

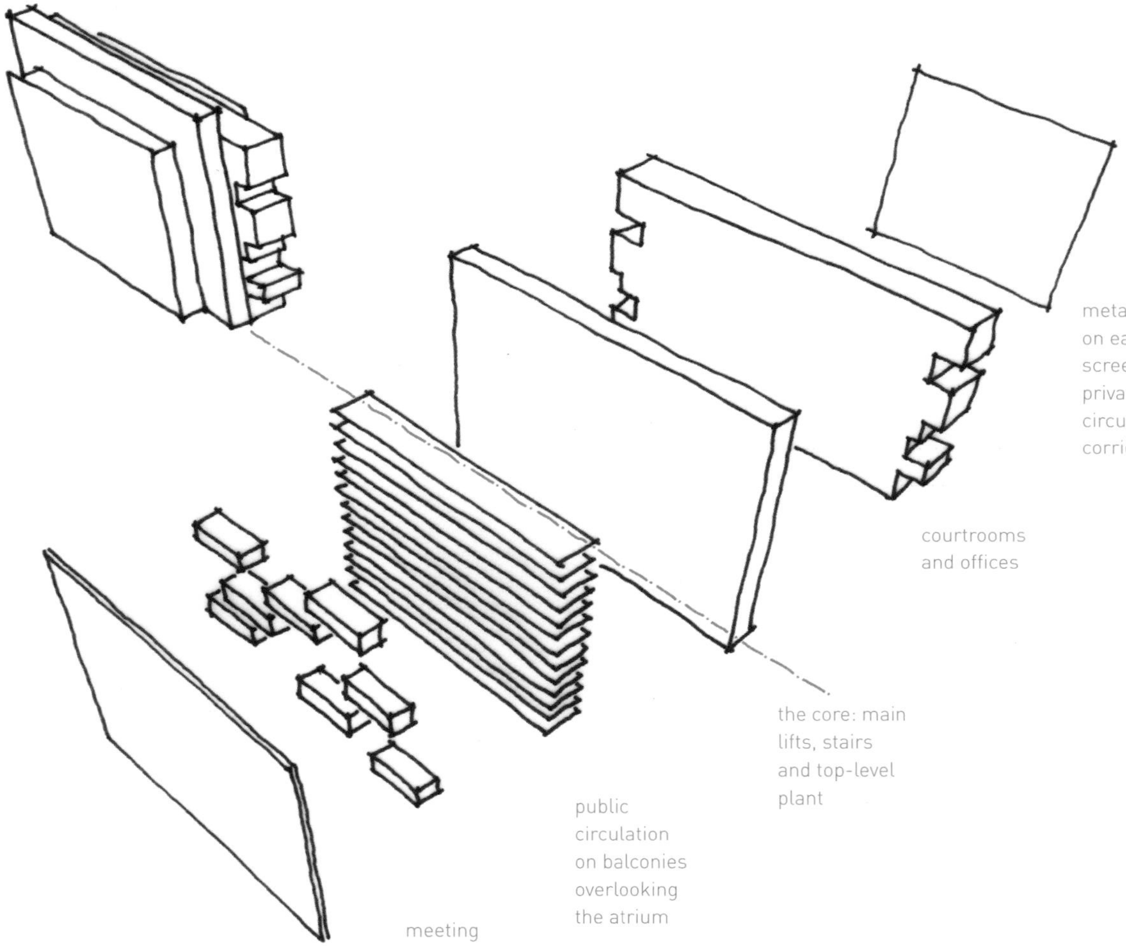

double-skin glass wall on west façade

meeting and waiting rooms suspended in the atrium

public circulation on balconies overlooking the atrium

the core: main lifts, stairs and top-level plant

courtrooms and offices

metal panels on east façade screening private circulation corridors

Guggenheim Museum Bilbao | 1991–97
The tips of the dynamic and sculptural form rise above the city and shimmer in the sunlight, acting as a beacon (project 28).

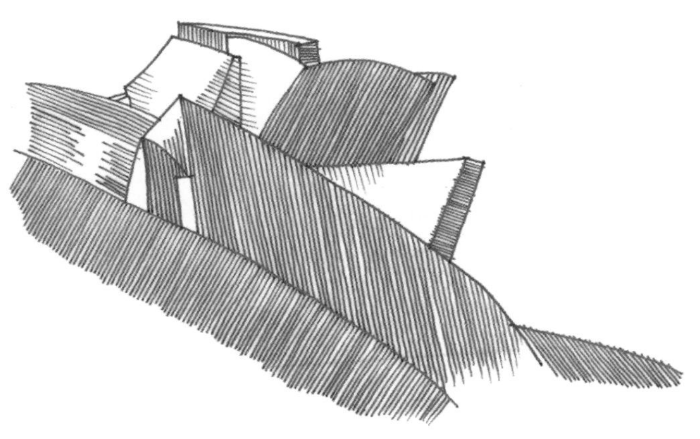

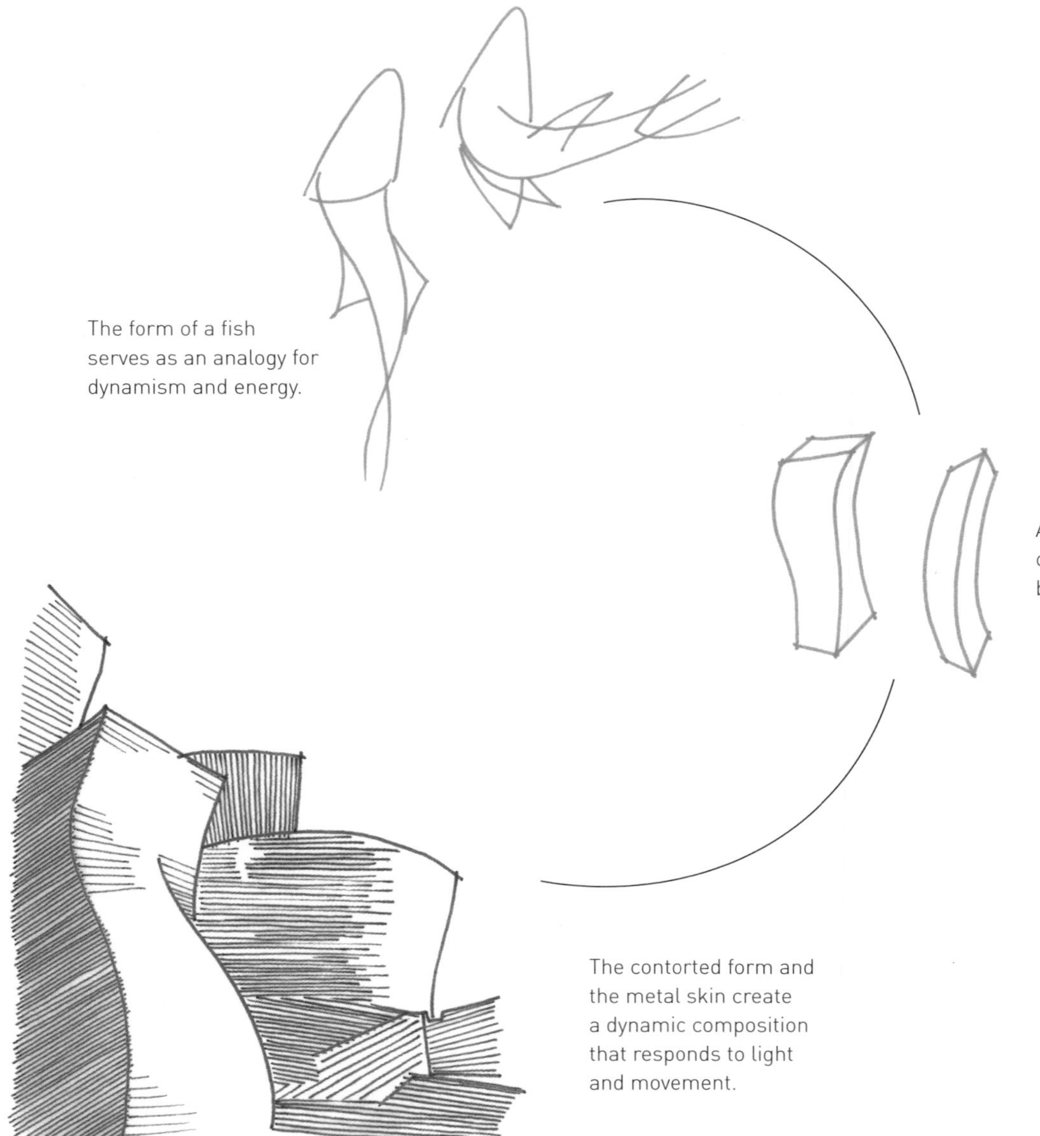

The form of a fish serves as an analogy for dynamism and energy.

Abstraction creates dynamic building form.

The contorted form and the metal skin create a dynamic composition that responds to light and movement.

of these analyses is to offer selected insights that have value, not to exhaustively cover every aspect. The analysis of a work of architecture should prompt readers to look for further ways to analyse the building, and even to disagree with the interpretations of the authors. Because the projects selected here are generally well known, readers are likely to come to them with preconceptions that may or may not be challenged. We want to prompt new interpretations, and a questioning of old interpretations.

Why annotated diagrams?

The analyses are presented as annotated diagrams. For most purposes, drawings are more concise and precise than words for representing ideas about architecture. Nevertheless, sometimes a 'language of words' works better than a 'language of drawings', so short blocks of text supplement diagrams. The format, then, is highly visual. As a collection, the annotated drawings are intended to be sampled rather than read sequentially, both in the selection of buildings that a reader chooses and in the parts of the analyses that are studied in any reading. The collection is a resource to be examined and re-examined. In the hermeneutical model of learning, we come to understand through a cycle of returning to the same topics but with a different and richer background understanding each time. We build our learning by relating new knowledge to our existing knowledge. In an Endnote to this book, some common themes are flagged that are apparent in the collection (see page 330). A reader may choose to start rather than end with this Endnote.

Annotated sketches and diagrams have a long history in architecture, with many architects (and other designers) keeping a personal journal or notebook in which they record ideas and note what they see that might be relevant for their future work. The archives of famous architects also reveal their sketches during their design processes, and how they use sketches to analyse and understand situations and to make proposals for responding to those situations. The act of criticism has been seen as an imitation of the act of creation. The French writer Paul Valéry connected explanation and making: '"To explain" is never anything more than to describe a way of making: it is merely to remake in thought. The why and the how, which are only ways of expressing the implications of this idea, inject themselves into every statement, demanding satisfaction at all costs' (Valéry 1956: 117). We shall understand the design works of others better if we 'remake in thought'.

Wholes, parts and responsive cohesion

Architects are not free to create at will according to their personal desires; architecture is always subject to the contingencies of its time and place. In these analyses we are particularly interested in manifestations of what environmental philosopher Warwick Fox calls 'responsive cohesion' between buildings and parts of buildings and their many contexts (Fox 2006, Radford 2009).

Responsive cohesion is a quality of the relations between the internal components of a 'thing' (Fox also uses the terms 'organization' and 'structure') and between the 'thing' and its contexts (for example a building and its contexts of street, region, climate, society and so on). In formal language, Fox writes that the relational quality of responsive cohesion exists 'whenever the elements or salient features of things can be characterised in terms of interacting (either literally or metaphorically) with each other in mutually modifying ways such that these mutually modifying interactions serve (at least functionally if not intentionally) to generate or maintain an overall cohesive order – an order that "hangs together" in one way or another' (Fox 2006: 72). Thus the parts answer to each other in such a way as to generate, maintain or contribute to the overall cohesion of the whole. Further, according to Fox's 'Theory of Contexts', achieving responsive cohesion between a 'thing' and its larger contexts is always more important than achieving responsive cohesion among its internal components.

Responsive cohesion contrasts with two other basic forms of organization: fixed cohesion (referring to fixed, unyielding relationships), and discohesion (referring to a lack of any relationships). We might find that different aspects of a building, as a composite object, exhibit

Quadracci Pavilion | 1994–2001
Glazed horizontal openings frame views between their divisions that emphasize the repetition of structural elements (project 32).

Lloyd's of London Office Building | 1978–86
The supporting service towers recall the towers and battlements of medieval castles (project 19).

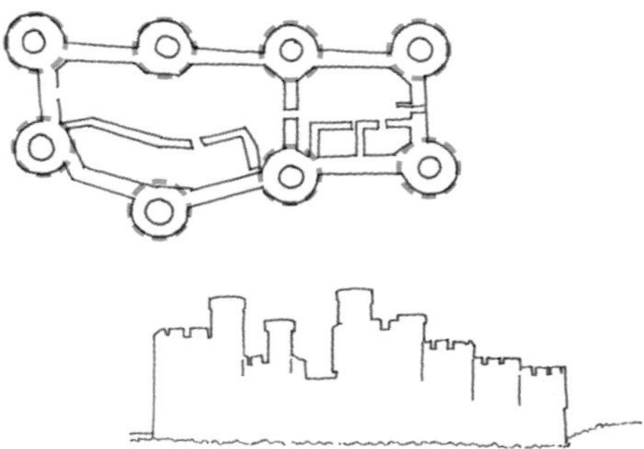

Conwy Castle, Wales (13th century)

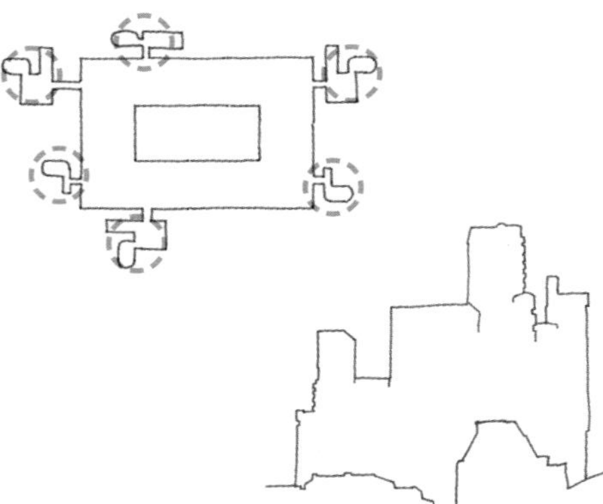

Lloyd's building with service towers (20th century)

instances of any of these three basic forms of organization. Fox argues that not only do informed critics in any field tend to prefer instances of responsive cohesion, but also that this same kind of organization characterizes all beneficial systems (Fox 2011).

A perfect building would respond with a convincing answer to any question about the benefits of its internal and contextual relations at local and global levels, but even famous works of architecture are far from perfect. The discourse of architecture lauds many buildings that are accepted as failing in serious functional, environmental or other ways. We can usually see, though, that certain relations in these buildings exhibit exceptional responsive cohesion, even if others do not. Many of the buildings in this book have aspects that are exemplary and worth emulating, without as a whole being general models for other buildings. In our analyses we shall concentrate on the positive aspects, showing how they demonstrate responsive cohesion in ways that can inform the design of architecture.

In analysing a building we can trace outwards from the building to its immediate contexts, and then to the contexts of those contexts. In this way, we can infer relationships between the building and global concerns such as environmental and cultural sustainability. Overall, analyses of buildings in terms of responsive cohesion emphasize connections rather than objects. We can see that buildings or building elements that exhibit high degrees of responsive cohesion are not marked by uniformity or blandness, because they should always add value to their contexts and this requires much more than simply 'fitting in'.

What to look for

We can list some broad categories of analysis and an order in which to tackle the task. A useful checklist is: place/environment, then people/culture, and then technology/tectonics, sometimes shortened to the more memorable triple of 'place, people, stuff' (Williamson, Radford and Bennetts 2003). Turning this checklist into questions, an analyser/critic can ask:

Place: Where is the building? How does the design respond to global and local environmental concerns, climate and microclimate, sun and noise, flora and fauna? How does it relate to neighbouring and nearby built form?

People: How do people approach, enter and move through the building? How do they experience the building form, its spaces and its symbolism? How does the building function? How does it respond to the ergonomics of human activities? How does it respond to children, the elderly and people with impaired mobility, vision or hearing? How does it respond to the particular regional culture? How does it respond to local and international architectural culture?

Technology: What are key aspects and/or principles in the tectonics of the building? How does the building structure relate to the building as a whole? How do details relate to the whole? What are the chosen materials and why have they been chosen? How does the building section relate to the building plan?

Other questions typical of critical reviews are: How does this design relate to other designs by the same architect, or by other architects? What is the place of the design in architectural discourse, and why is it worth analysing? In short, what is 'special' about the building? In *Design Strategies in Architecture: An Approach to the Analysis of Form* (1989), Geoffrey Baker concentrates on the generation of form, the relations between formal elements and the ways in which a building is approached and entered. In *Analysing Architecture* (2003), Simon Unwin focuses on elements, space and place. Both Baker's and Unwin's work can be interpreted in terms of concepts of responsive cohesion.

Analysis as design

Making an analysis of this kind is like designing – indeed, it involves designing an analysis. It is a creative act in itself. Like designing, it is a reflective practice in which processes of investigating, proposing and

Jewish Museum Berlin | 1988–99

The formal qualities of the zigzag plan form have been used to argue for a literal dismantling of the symbolic marker of Judaism – the Star of David – in developing the overall building form. Other comparisons relate it to the expression of a tortured landscape (project 31).

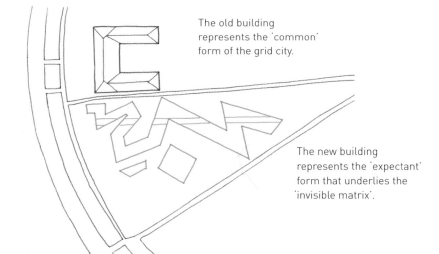

The distorted Star of David functions as a symbolic form generator.

A continuous but tortured history of Berlin intertwines with a straight but ruptured history of the Jewish experience.

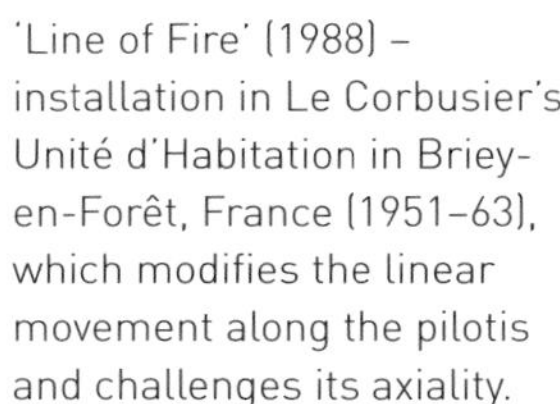

'Line of Fire' (1988) – installation in Le Corbusier's Unité d'Habitation in Briey-en-Forêt, France (1951–63), which modifies the linear movement along the pilotis and challenges its axiality.

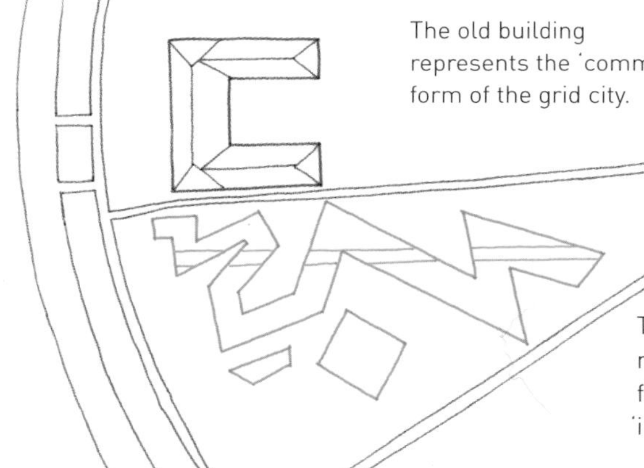

The old building represents the 'common' form of the grid city.

The new building represents the 'expectant' form that underlies the 'invisible matrix'.

The rectilinear forms and oblique cuts of the new building are in sharp contrast to the old Kollegienhaus building.

Eastgate | 1991–96
The building form responds to contexts of climate, culture, function and construction. Silver crowns evocative of African ceremonial headwear mark the entrances to the atrium (project 26).

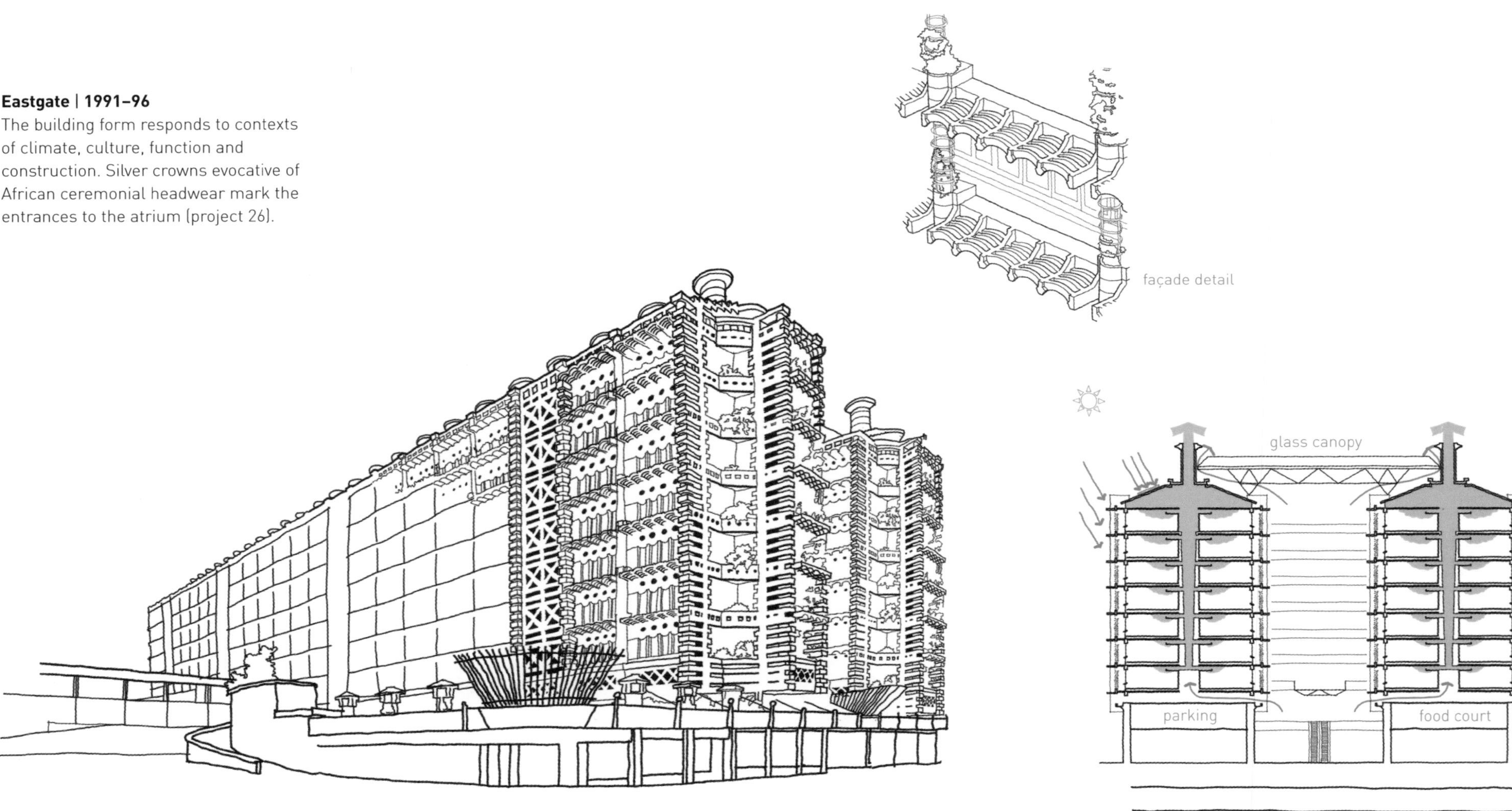

testing take place in a cycle that leads to increasing understanding and confidence. As in designing, we need to undertake research to discover what is already known, in this case what is available in writing, photographs, and models and drawings of and about the building. Once this information is assembled, we then need to find a way to show in annotated drawings answers to the questions about place, people and technology that are suggested above, and other questions that come to mind as the analysis and its representation proceed. We should aim for clarity in presentation and insight in what is presented, remembering that there is a difference between merely describing (reproducing design drawings and photographs, with descriptive text) and the intellectual challenge of critical analysis.

The criterion for success in these analyses is whether they add value (pleasure and knowledge) for someone either visiting the buildings themselves or experiencing them through the partial surrogates of digital models, photographs and conventional descriptive texts. We hope that readers will take these analyses with them on visits to the buildings, will use them to compare buildings, and will use them in conjunction with other representations of the buildings. In doing so, the 'ideal readers' will add their own notes to the pages, contributing their own interpretations of the works.

References

Baker, Geoffrey H., *Design Strategies in Architecture: An Approach to the Analysis of Form*, London: Van Nostrand Reinhold (1989)

Bruton, Dean, and Radford, Antony, *Digital Design: A Critical Introduction*, London: Berg (2012)

Fox, Warwick, *A Theory of General Ethics: Human Relationships, Nature, and the Built Environment*, Cambridge, MA: MIT Press (2006)

Fox, Warwick, 'Foundations of a General Ethics: Selves, Sentient Beings, and Other Responsively Cohesive Structures', in Anthony O'Hear (ed), *Philosophy and the Environment* (Royal Institute of Philosophy Supplement: 69), pp. 47–66, Cambridge: Cambridge University Press (2011)

Pallasmaa, Juhani, T*he Embodied Image: Imagination and Imagery in Architecture*, AD Primer Series, West Sussex: Wiley (2011)

Radford, Antony, 'Responsive Cohesion as the Foundational Value in Architecture', *The Journal of Architecture* 14 (4), pp. 511–32 (2009)

Scruton, Roger, *The Aesthetics of Architecture*, London: Methuen (1979) (republished by Princeton: Princeton University Press, 1980)

Unwin, Simon, *Analysing Architecture*, Abingdon and New York: Routledge (2003)

Valéry, Paul, 'Man and the Sea Shell', in *The Collected Works of Paul Valéry*, vol. 1, selected with an introduction by J. R. Lawler, Princeton: Princeton University Press (1956)

Williamson, Terence, Radford, Antony, and Bennetts, Helen, *Understanding Sustainable Architecture*, London and New York: Spon Press (2003)

Sarabhai House | 1951–55

Le Corbusier

Ahmedabad, India

01

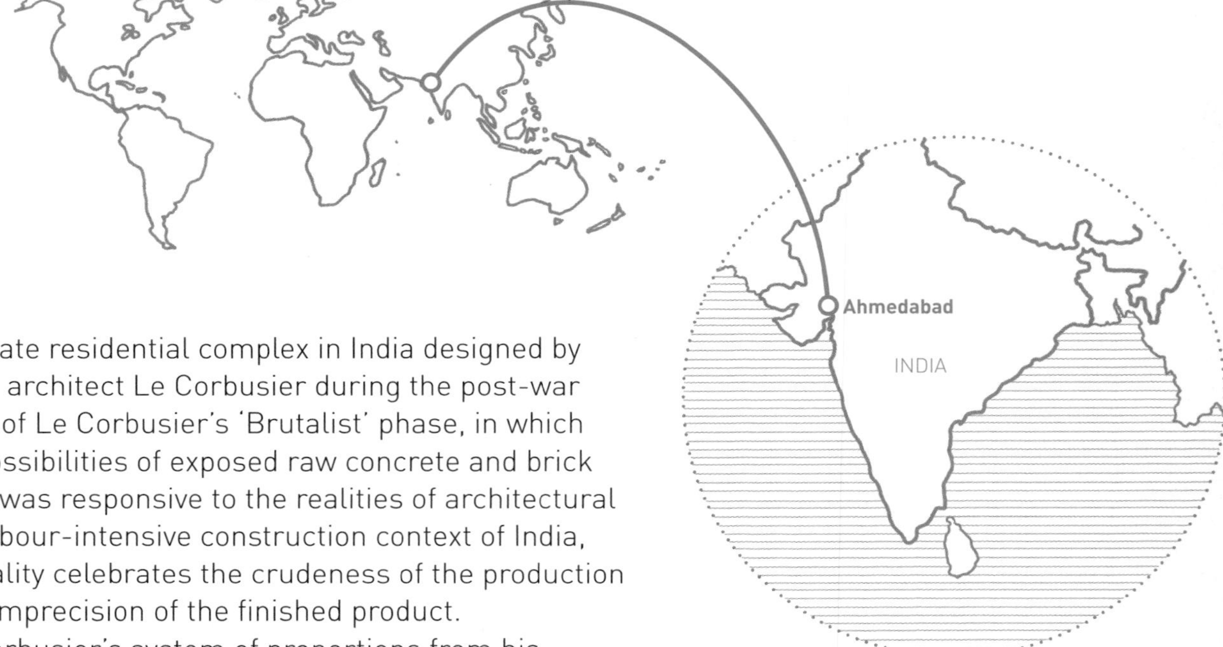

The Sarabhai house is a private residential complex in India designed by the illustrious Swiss-French architect Le Corbusier during the post-war years. It is an early example of Le Corbusier's 'Brutalist' phase, in which he experimented with the possibilities of exposed raw concrete and brick to develop an approach that was responsive to the realities of architectural production. Applied to the labour-intensive construction context of India, such an approach to materiality celebrates the crudeness of the production process by highlighting the imprecision of the finished product.

The design engages Le Corbusier's system of proportions from his Modulor concept, together with climatic features such as brise-soleil, to develop a building that is suited to its programme and to climatic conditions. In addition to the masterly application of these Modernist and universal themes, the design offers a culturally sensitive response to the daily rituals and practices of a wealthy Indian household through a series of spaces that allow for the continuation of traditional patterns of living. This balance of the modern and universal with the traditional and local allows residents to find a cohesive identity that is reflective of the postcolonial context.

Adam Fenton, Rumaiza Hani Ali, Amit Srivastava and Alix Dunbar

01

01 Sarabhai House | 1951–55

Le Corbusier

Ahmedabad, India

Response to urban context

The Sarabhai house is a private residence on a large 8-hectare (20-acre) estate in the city of Ahmedabad. Nestled among the greenery of the estate, the house does not have direct contact with the city's urban fabric. Accordingly, the design responds to the natural elements and the needs of the family. The building complex is composed of a main house for the patrons and ancillary servants' quarters, which spread around the landscape as connected blocks enclosing a series of open spaces between them.

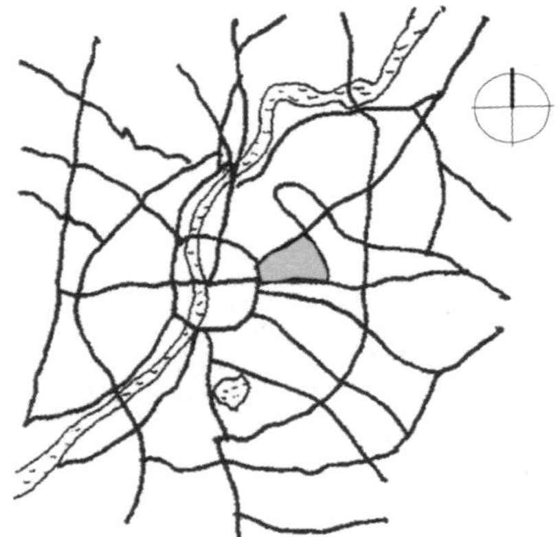

The Sarabhai estate in Ahmedabad

The building is oriented to align with the south-west monsoon winds, allowing it to make maximum use of the cooling winds that are so essential in Ahmedabad's hot climate. The Z-shaped organization of plan elements creates a distinction between the open areas for public use towards the north and the open areas for private use towards the south. The building thus works with the landscape and generates a cohesive whole as a residential environment.

The combination of the built block and the surrounding vegetation creates barriers and thresholds that define the public and private nature of various spaces and control access.

public – private axis

public entry court

main house

servants' quarters

private court

The buildings are oriented so as to capture the south-west monsoon winds.

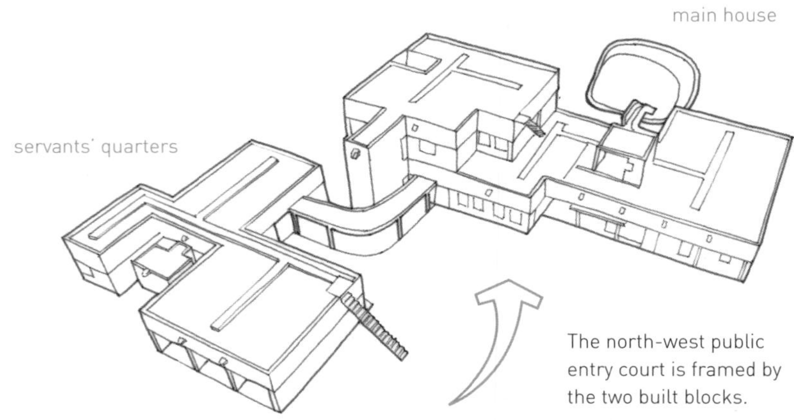

The north-west public entry court is framed by the two built blocks.

The aesthetic connections with the surrounding landscape are carried through into the treatment of the elevations, with the use of simple materials and forms. The use of straight line elements accentuates the contrasting organic nature of the surrounding landscape, and the two forms complement each other.

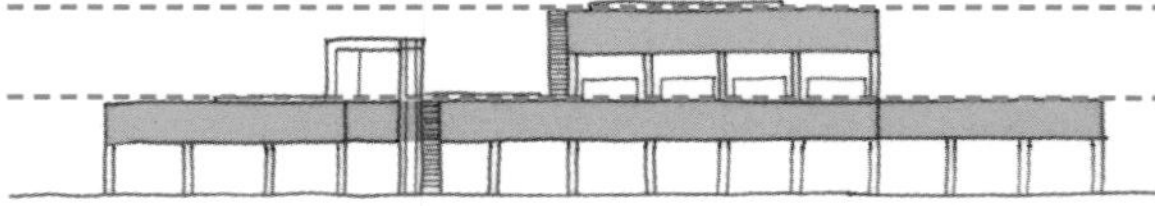

The concrete bands capture the flat and horizontal character of the site.

The thin brick piers capture the vertical accents of the surrounding trees.

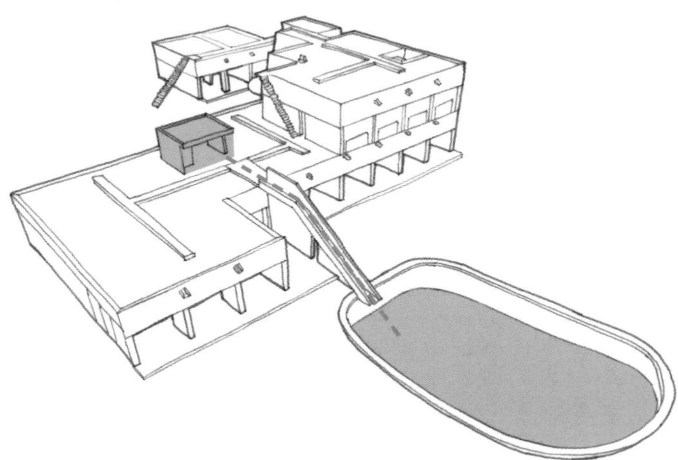

Response to programme

The residential facilities were intended for Manorama Sarabhai, a widow, and her two sons. Accordingly the design provides for a series of different semi-private and private spaces that can address the various needs of the family. The main house can be seen as two private blocks that can be completely closed down to form private spaces for retreat. These constitute the sleeping quarters for the elder son on the west and the mother and younger son on the east. The two blocks are surrounded by a series of semi-private spaces that open up towards the private courts in the south and west. The shared area in the middle forms a connection between this private realm and the more public entrance and living areas towards the north of the building.

The structure is conceived as a series of vaults that bring south-west monsoon winds to all areas while maintaining privacy.

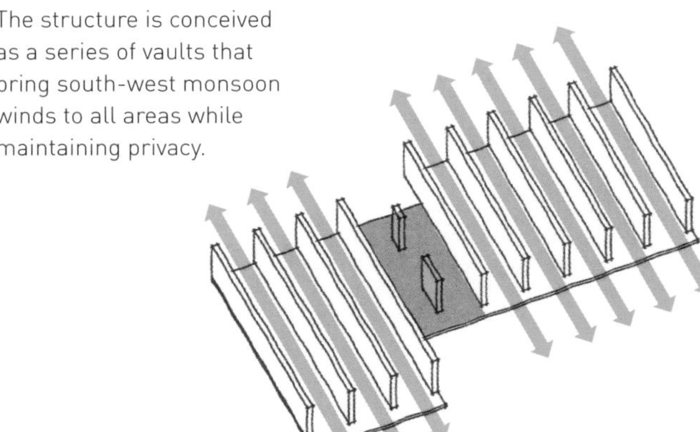

The private areas along the south-west of the building are defined by an axis that connects the rooftop pavilion with the large organic-shaped swimming pool. These elements form the ideal landscape for activities in the summer and connect the built form to this private landscape. Sitting in the rooftop pavilion in the evening breeze, the residents can observe the inviting pool water and the greenery beyond. On a hot summer evening they could even venture down the slide and take a dip in the cooling water. This connection to the lush southern landscape is also maintained through the series of balconies that lines the southern façade of the building.

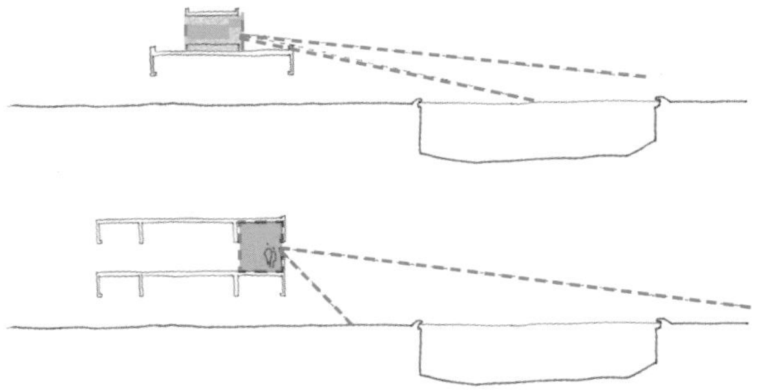

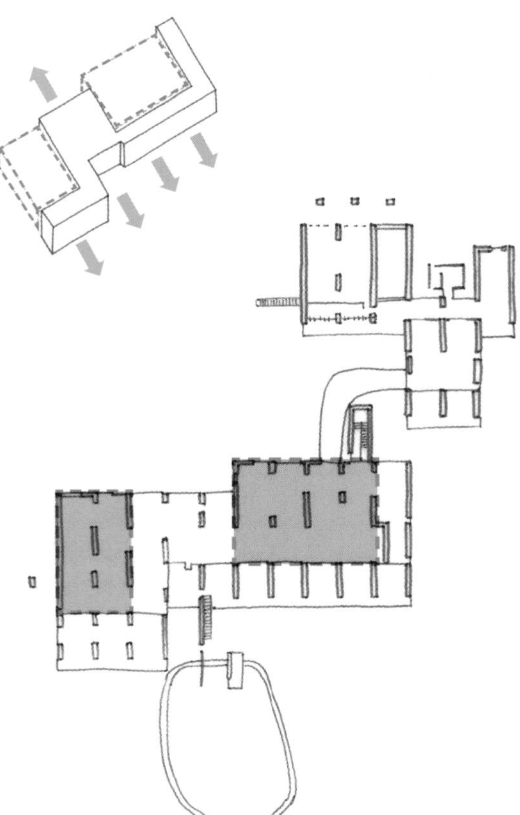

The continuity of the vaults towards the south is interrupted by semi-private verandas.

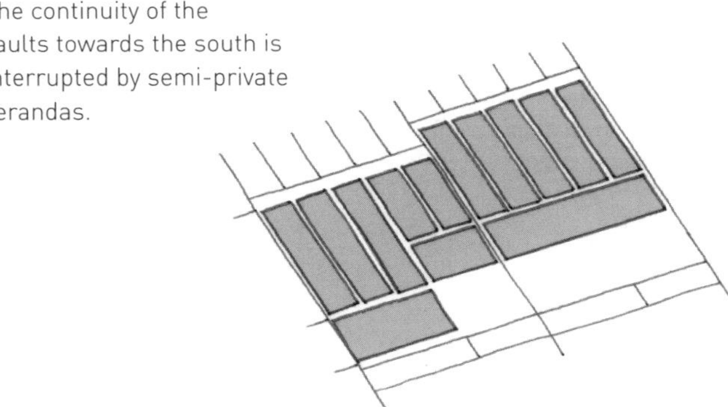

Access to the two private wings continues from the connecting north–south section that acts as the pivotal axis.

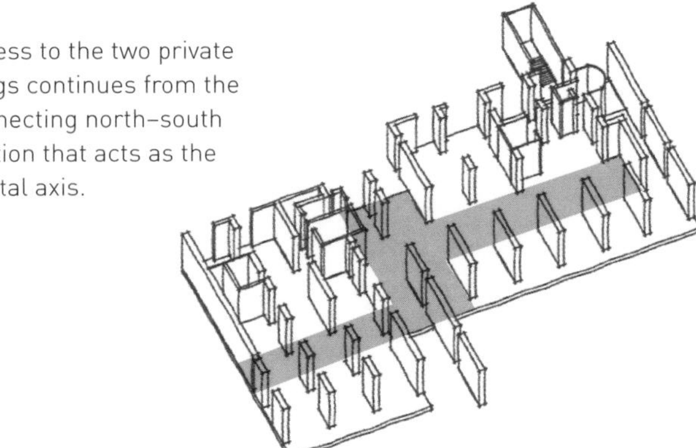

Form and materiality

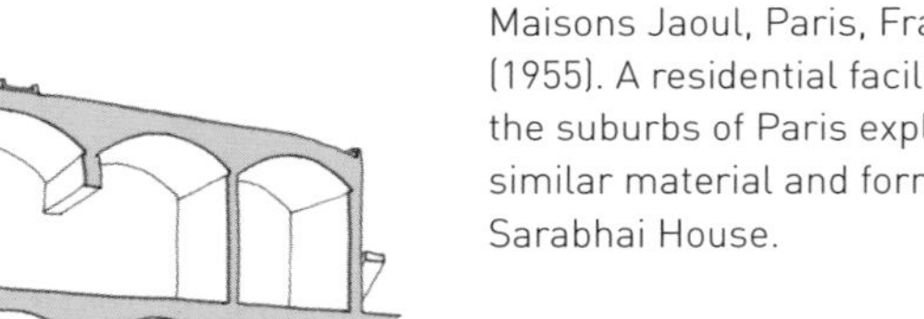

Maisons Jaoul, Paris, France (1955). A residential facility in the suburbs of Paris explores similar material and forms to Sarabhai House.

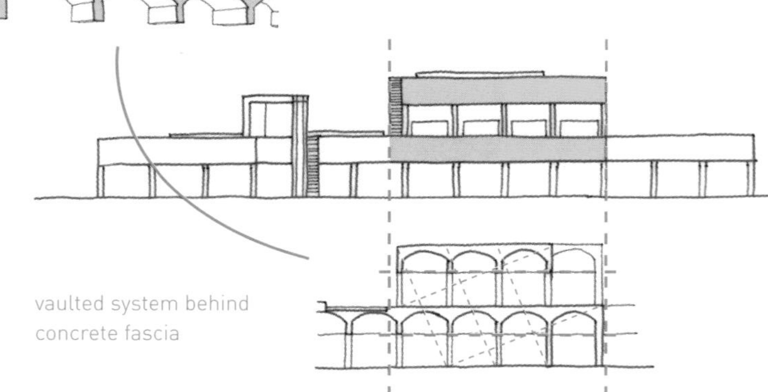

Shodhan House, Ahmedabad (1956). Located like the Sarabhai house in Ahmedabad, this private residence explores the potential of the concrete brise-soleil for the local climate.

The design of the Sarabhai house reflects a combination of the fundamental building materials of brick and concrete. The surfaces remain unadorned and the truth of the material as well as its construction is worn on the exterior façade. The harmony between these two contrasting materials also reflects a desire to marry the traditional with the modern.

As also conceived in other projects of the same time, the design offers a series of concrete vaults as the roof structure, which are supported by exposed brick walls. At the Sarabhai house the concrete vaults are combined with the language of brise-soleil to create a hybrid structure that is well suited to both the climate and the construction industry in India. The series of vaults running along the depth of the building is capped with a concrete band that acts as another layer of sun barriers. The vaulted bays further help in defining the divisions of the interior space without use of walls.

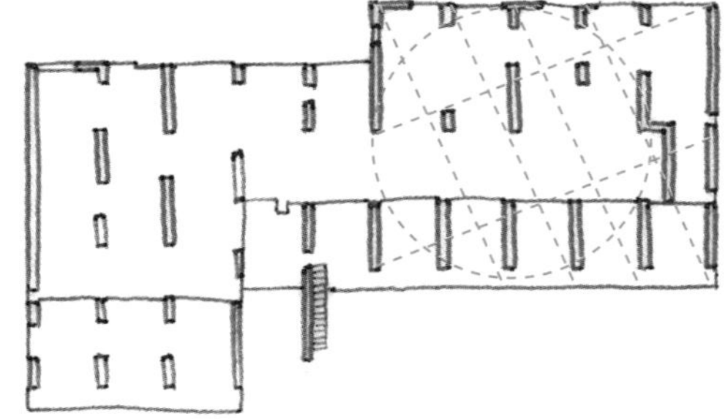

A simple proportional system defines the organization of the various plan and sectional elements. In the internal sections the height of the spaces is developed in relation to the width of the vaults. This system further defines the depth of the internal and external spaces framed by these vaults, bringing the whole composition to cohere as one.

All aspects of the house, from the elements of the window to the distribution of doors and windows along a wall, as well as the Madras stone flooring pattern, are governed by a singular proportional system defined by Le Corbusier's 'Modulor' (top left).

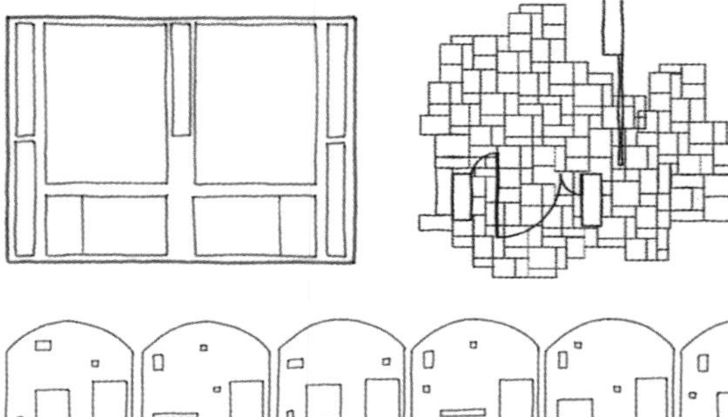

Response to climate

The vaulted systems used for the building also offer opportunities for controlling the internal climate. The undulating tops of the concrete vaults are filled with soil to create a rooftop garden, which increases thermal mass and reduces heat gain. The vaulted interiors further allow for easy flow of cool monsoon air through the interior. In addition, the shaded verandas and cool black Madras stone add to the passive cooling system.

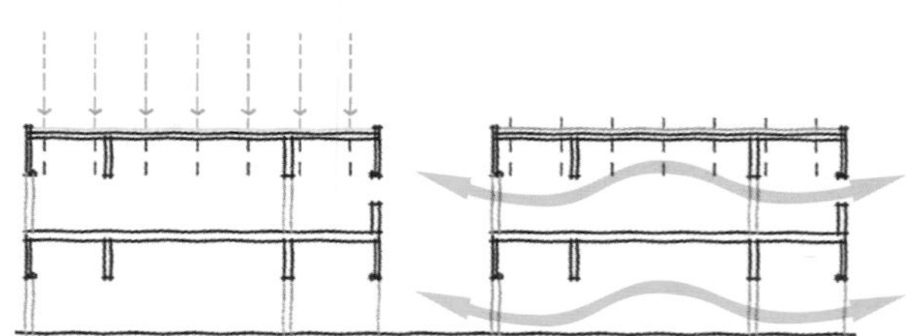

Response to local culture and patterns

The giant slide along the southern edge that connects the rooftop pavilion and the pool reflects the formal qualities of the iconic Jantar Mantar (eighteenth-century architectural-scale astronomical instruments in northern India.)

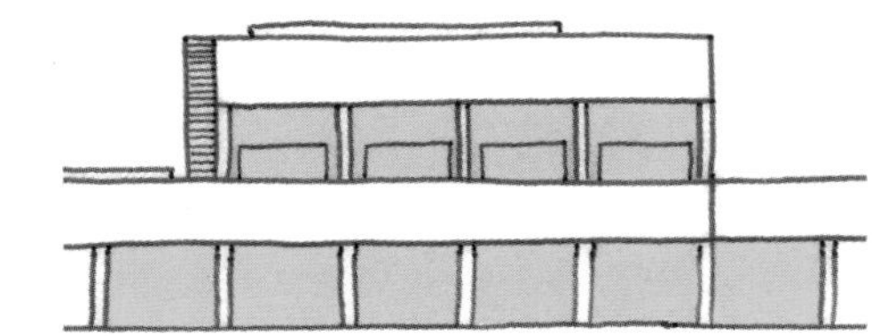

The scale and nature of the brise-soleil on the southern façade reflect the qualities of the shaded arcades of Fatehpur Sikri and other similar traditional Indian structures.

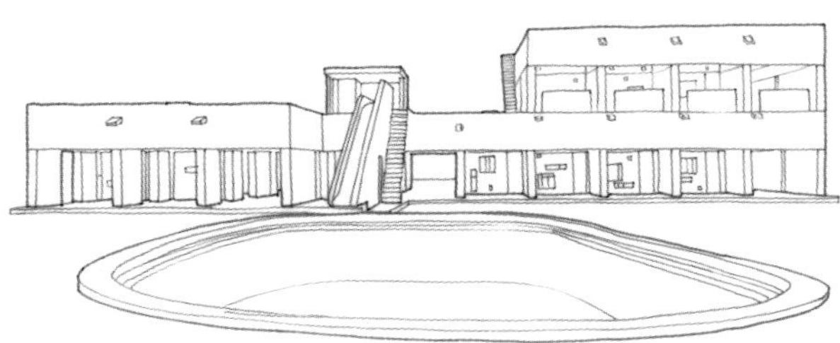

The swimming pool offers respite from the heat.

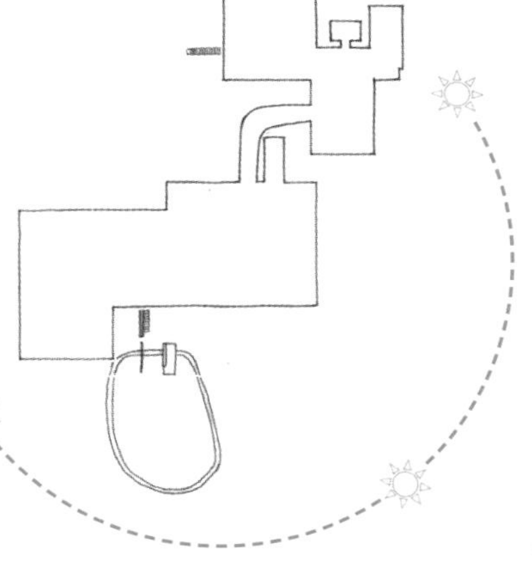

The morning light penetrates the dining room and helps to start the new day.

The various elements of the design come together to address the lifestyle of the occupants based on cultural patterns. The ability to redefine the spaces throughout the day allows for various activities to proceed and the house to serve as an integral part of this daily routine.

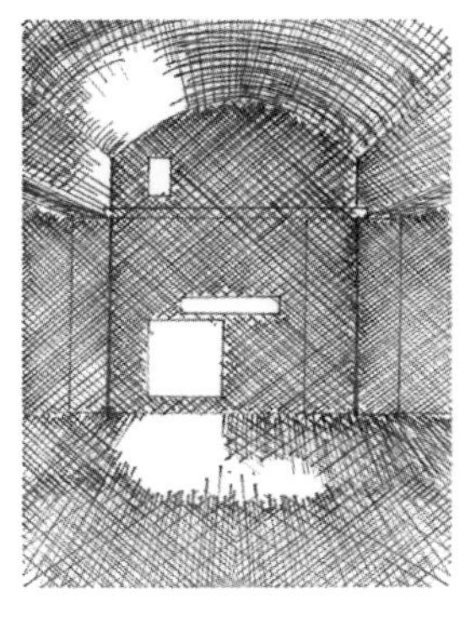

The opening of the doors in the evening allows a cool breeze to flow through the sleeping areas.

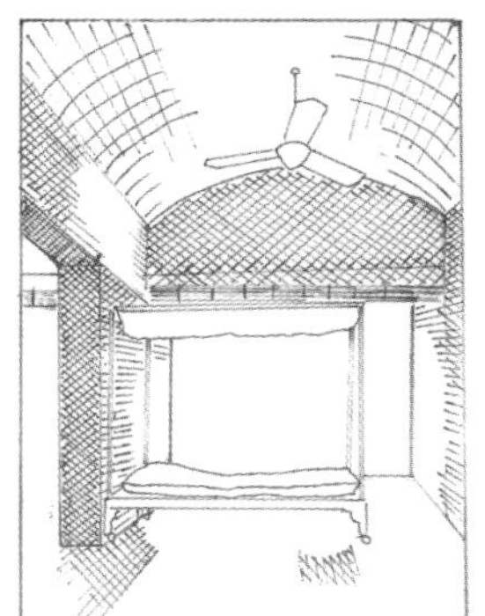

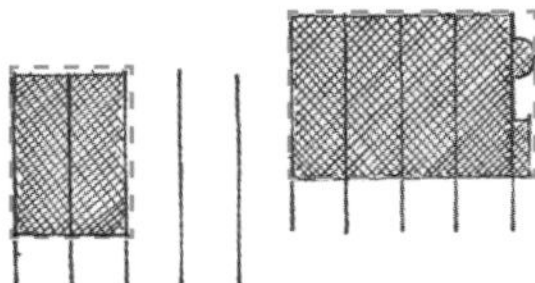

The vaults are closed off during the afternoon, creating a refuge, the effect of which is enhanced by the contrasting light of the window.

02 Canova Museum | 1955–57

Carlo Scarpa

Possagno, Treviso, Italy

The Canova Museum is a concise and powerful interplay of natural light, space and form. It exhibits plaster casts made as a stage in the production of marble sculptures by Antonio Canova (1757–1822), a leading exponent of Italian Classicism. Carlo Scarpa was commissioned in 1955 to design a small extension to the early 1830s basilica hall that originally housed the collection. The basilica remains an integral part of the museum, its symmetry, size and dominance an anchor for the precision and delicacy of the addition. There is responsive cohesion in the unlikely juxtaposition of grand Neoclassical architecture with an intimate, asymmetrical Modern addition.

Antony Radford, Michelle Male and Mun Su Mei

02

02 **Canova Museum | 1955–57**

Carlo Scarpa
Possagno, Treviso, Italy

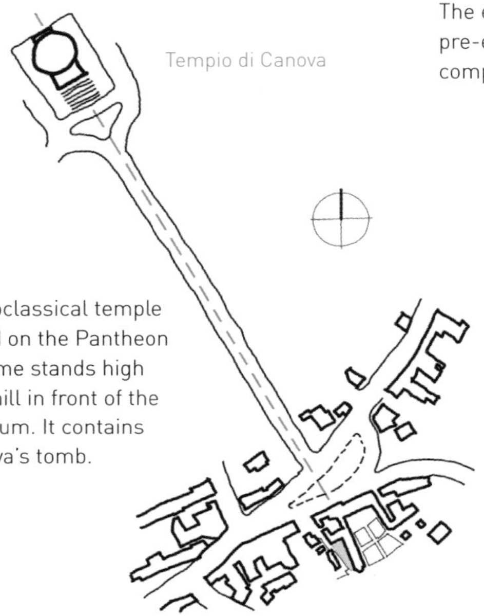

Tempio di Canova

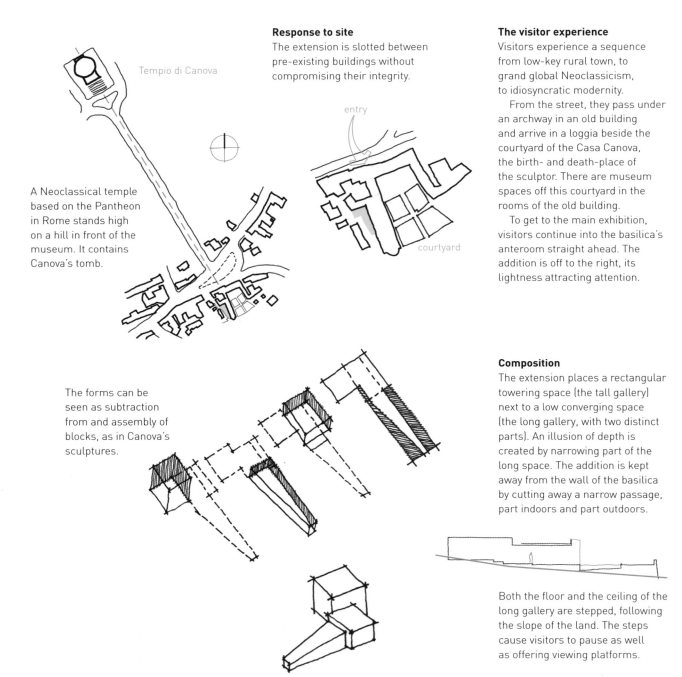

A Neoclassical temple based on the Pantheon in Rome stands high on a hill in front of the museum. It contains Canova's tomb.

Response to site
The extension is slotted between pre-existing buildings without compromising their integrity.

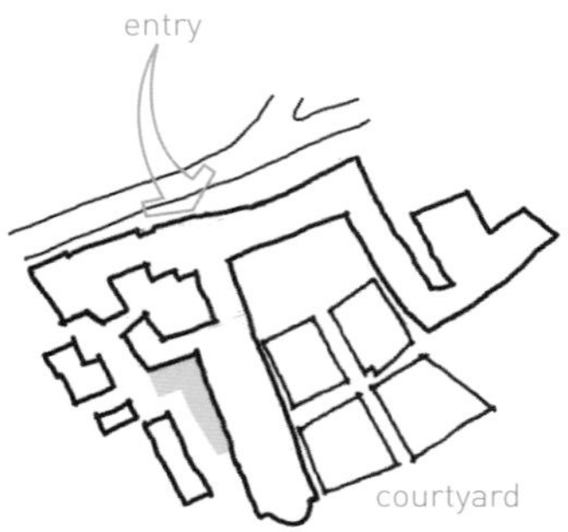

entry

courtyard

The visitor experience
Visitors experience a sequence from low-key rural town, to grand global Neoclassicism, to idiosyncratic modernity.

From the street, they pass under an archway in an old building and arrive in a loggia beside the courtyard of the Casa Canova, the birth- and death-place of the sculptor. There are museum spaces off this courtyard in the rooms of the old building.

To get to the main exhibition, visitors continue into the basilica's anteroom straight ahead. The addition is off to the right, its lightness attracting attention.

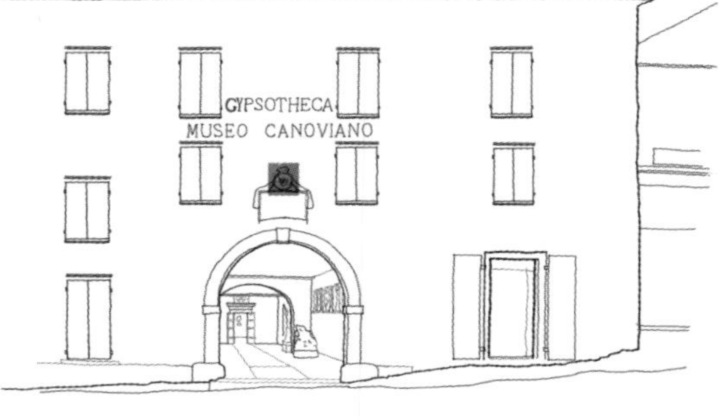

The forms can be seen as subtraction from and assembly of blocks, as in Canova's sculptures.

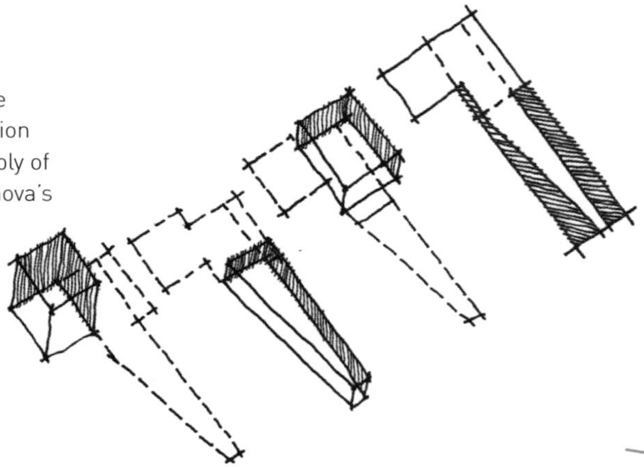

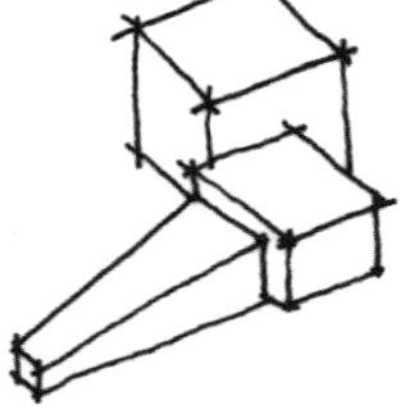

Composition
The extension places a rectangular towering space (the tall gallery) next to a low converging space (the long gallery, with two distinct parts). An illusion of depth is created by narrowing part of the long space. The addition is kept away from the wall of the basilica by cutting away a narrow passage, part indoors and part outdoors.

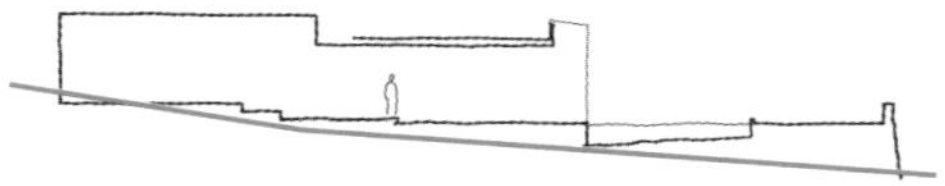

Both the floor and the ceiling of the long gallery are stepped, following the slope of the land. The steps cause visitors to pause as well as offering viewing platforms.

Whiteness
Plaster is a matt white amorphous material and the casts come to life only in light. The conventional approach in museums is to place casts against darker walls so that they stand out. The Neoclassical basilica originally had such walls. Scarpa argued that the casts needed a highly luminous environment that could best be achieved with white walls.

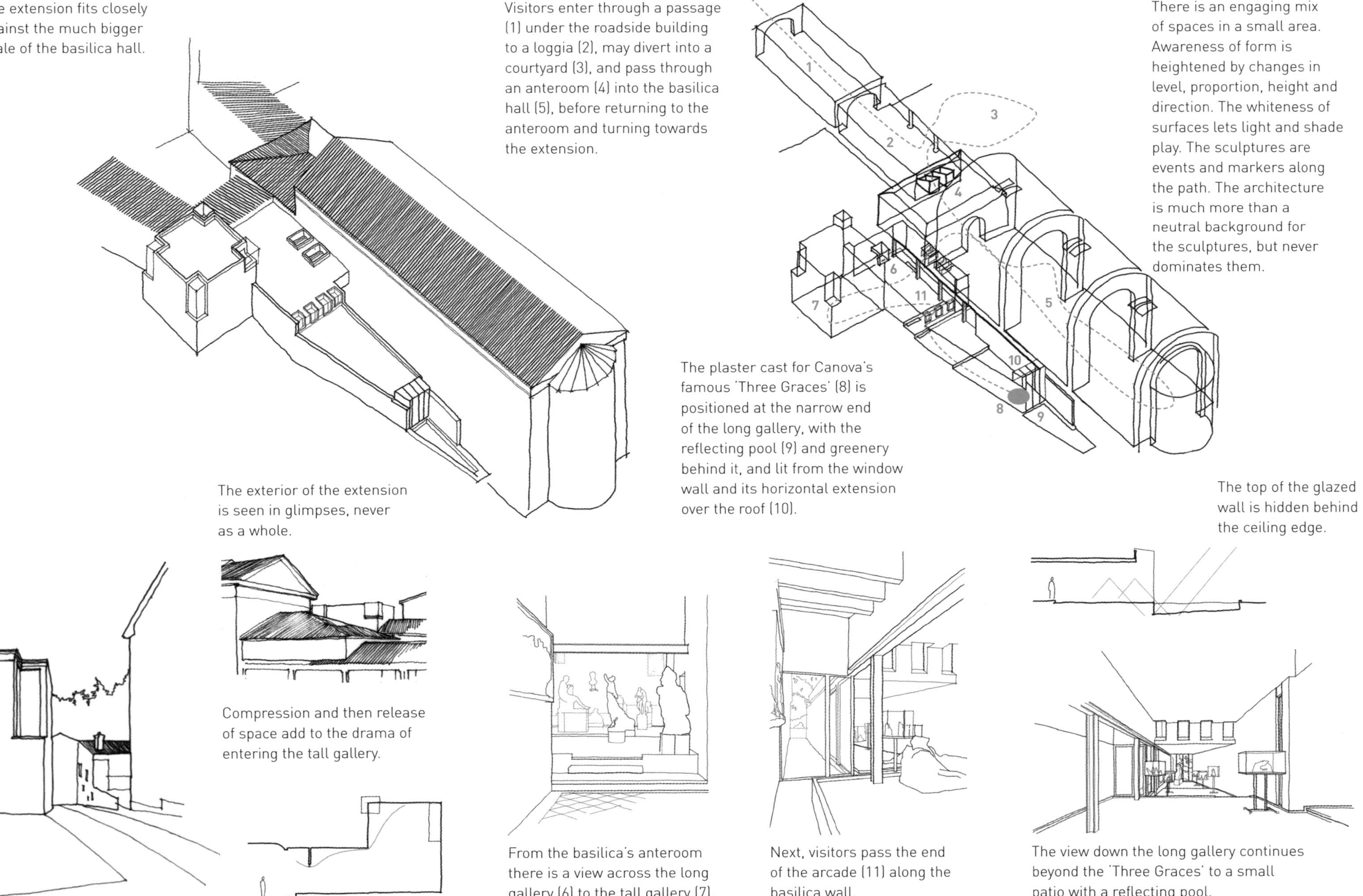

The extension fits closely against the much bigger scale of the basilica hall.

Visitors enter through a passage (1) under the roadside building to a loggia (2), may divert into a courtyard (3), and pass through an anteroom (4) into the basilica hall (5), before returning to the anteroom and turning towards the extension.

There is an engaging mix of spaces in a small area. Awareness of form is heightened by changes in level, proportion, height and direction. The whiteness of surfaces lets light and shade play. The sculptures are events and markers along the path. The architecture is much more than a neutral background for the sculptures, but never dominates them.

The plaster cast for Canova's famous 'Three Graces' (8) is positioned at the narrow end of the long gallery, with the reflecting pool (9) and greenery behind it, and lit from the window wall and its horizontal extension over the roof (10).

The exterior of the extension is seen in glimpses, never as a whole.

The top of the glazed wall is hidden behind the ceiling edge.

Compression and then release of space add to the drama of entering the tall gallery.

From the basilica's anteroom there is a view across the long gallery (6) to the tall gallery (7).

Next, visitors pass the end of the arcade (11) along the basilica wall.

The view down the long gallery continues beyond the 'Three Graces' to a small patio with a reflecting pool.

02 Canova Museum | 1955-57

Carlo Scarpa

Possagno, Italy

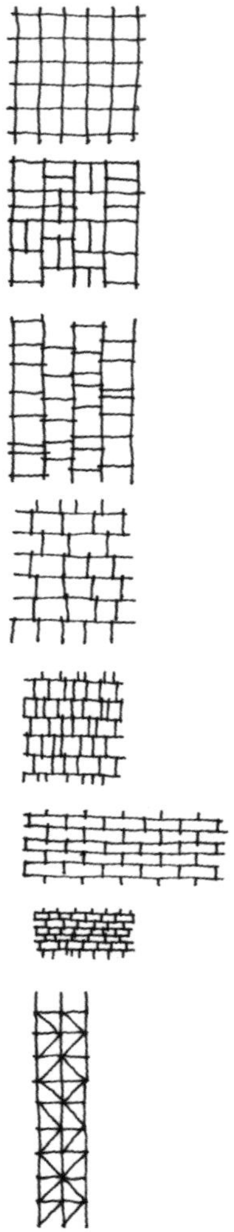

Textures

The extension uses a strictly limited palette of materials. Its exterior is stucco-rendered masonry, with concrete bands around the windows and dividing wall surfaces, as on the old buildings. Inside, rough plaster rendering has been left in its natural state, its roughness contrasting with the smooth surfaces of the plaster casts.

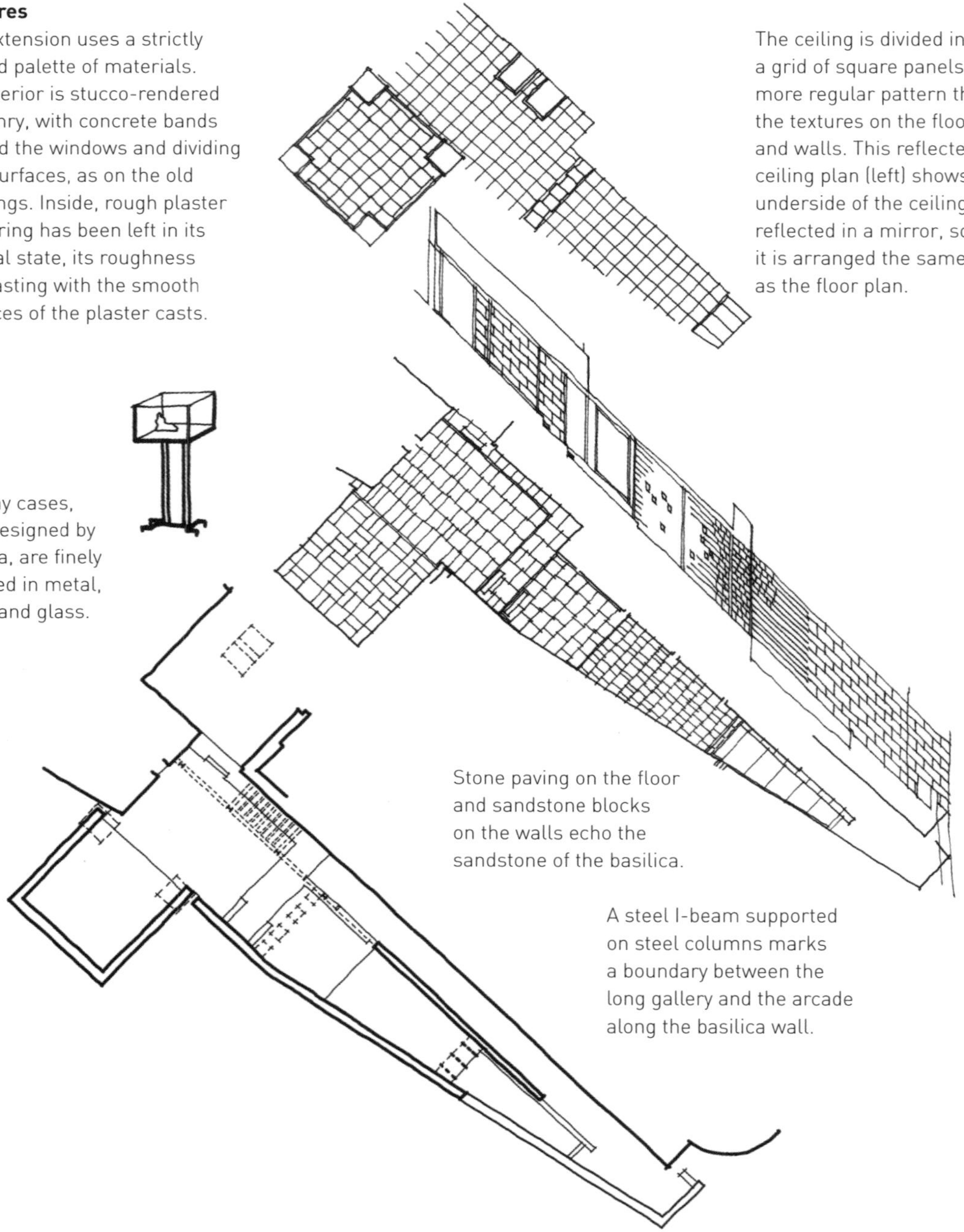

Many different patterns are used on the interior surfaces.

Display cases, also designed by Scarpa, are finely detailed in metal, wood and glass.

The ceiling is divided into a grid of square panels, a more regular pattern than the textures on the floor and walls. This reflected ceiling plan (left) shows the underside of the ceiling as if reflected in a mirror, so that it is arranged the same way as the floor plan.

Stone paving on the floor and sandstone blocks on the walls echo the sandstone of the basilica.

A steel I-beam supported on steel columns marks a boundary between the long gallery and the arcade along the basilica wall.

Borders

Narrow baseboards of black metal mark the junction between wall and floor, like lines drawn over the corners of the white surfaces.

The junction between the ceiling and the wall in the tall gallery is set back in a groove, so that the ceiling appears to float over the walls.

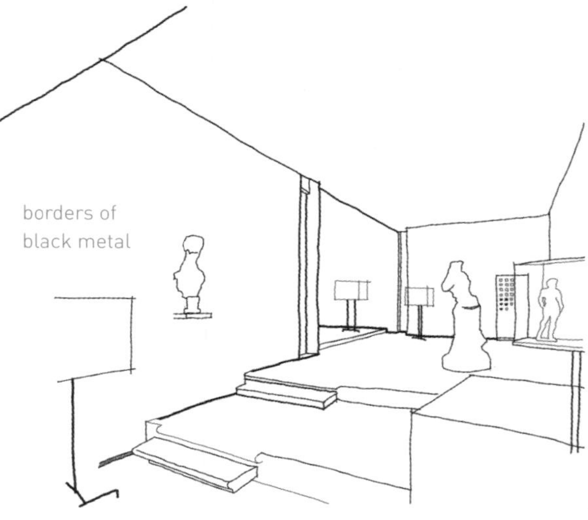

Steps are undercut, so they appear as unsupported platforms floating over the lower floor level.

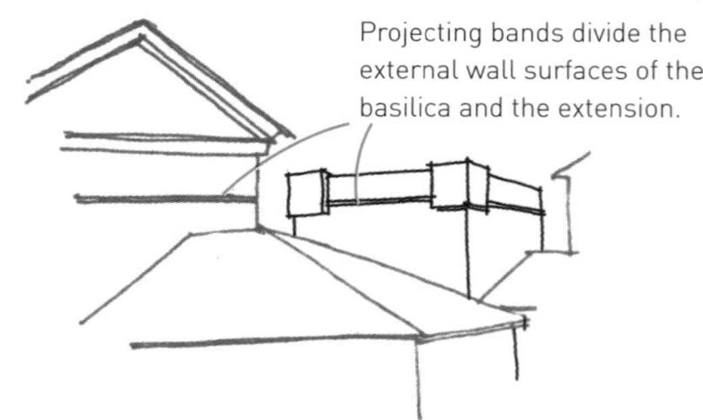

Projecting bands divide the external wall surfaces of the basilica and the extension.

Natural light
Unlike paintings and drawings, the casts do not deteriorate in bright light and sunshine, so Scarpa could use strong direct sunlight to animate the space and the work. The result is a large range of tonal variation in the white interiors to combine legibility with a soft, sensual quality to the visual field.

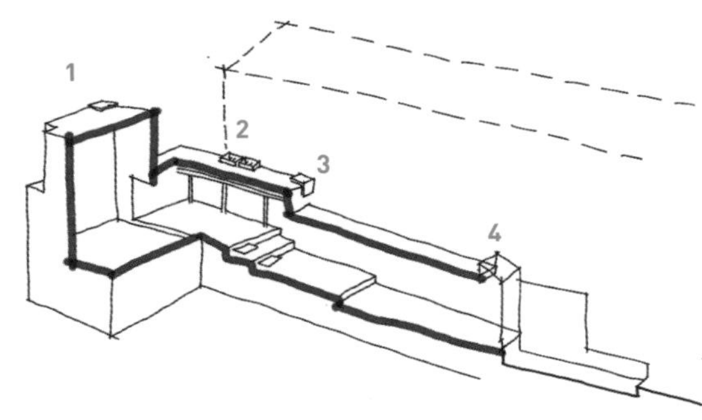

1. High-level glazed corners
In the tall gallery, composite high-level windows and skylights occupy all four upper corners. On the east side, square units sit outside the roof and wall surfaces with horizontal glass at their tops. On the west side, oblong units penetrate the room volume with horizontal glass at their bottoms. Direct shafts of sunlight might penetrate one or more of these corner windows, highlighting square patches of the floor or walls that move with the sun, while the others offer diffuse light reflected off the walls. Visually the corners are undefined, lost in the brightness.

A narrow strip of glass fits between the edges of the vertical panes, blurring the divisions at the corners.

2. Baffled skylights
A horizontal skylight over the arcade between the original basilica wall and the museum extension has large vertical baffles, so that the skylights themselves are outside the field of view in this narrow space. Light directly illuminates the fresco hanging on the basilica wall, and reflected light illuminates the adjacent room. The polished white floor surface distributes the light.

3. Composite skylight-clerestories
Four clerestory lights are inserted into the gap between higher and lower roofs in the long gallery and extend over the roof, lighting the rear part of the room. Although the back of the room faces south, glare is mitigated by the interior brightness of the reflective white surfaces of the room and the competing brightness in the visual field of the glass wall ahead.

4. The glazed end wall
There is a full-height glass wall at the narrow end of the long gallery. Trees screen the view, reducing the glare that would result from a direct view of the sky. A small pool outside the window wall moderates reflected light compared with hard paving, and transforms it to a cooler tone. The angled wall smoothes off the luminance gradient, an elongated version of the splayed sides of a traditional window in a thick wall.

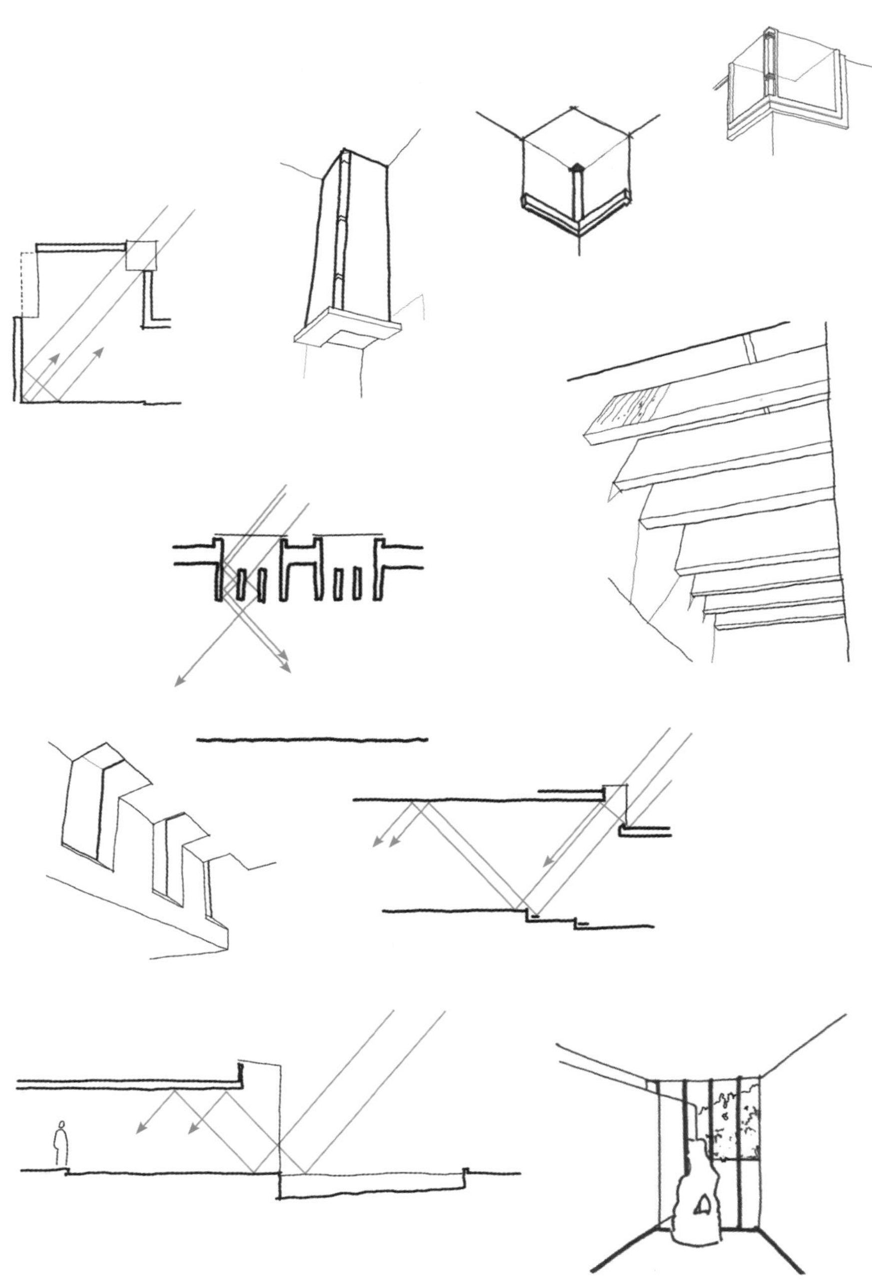

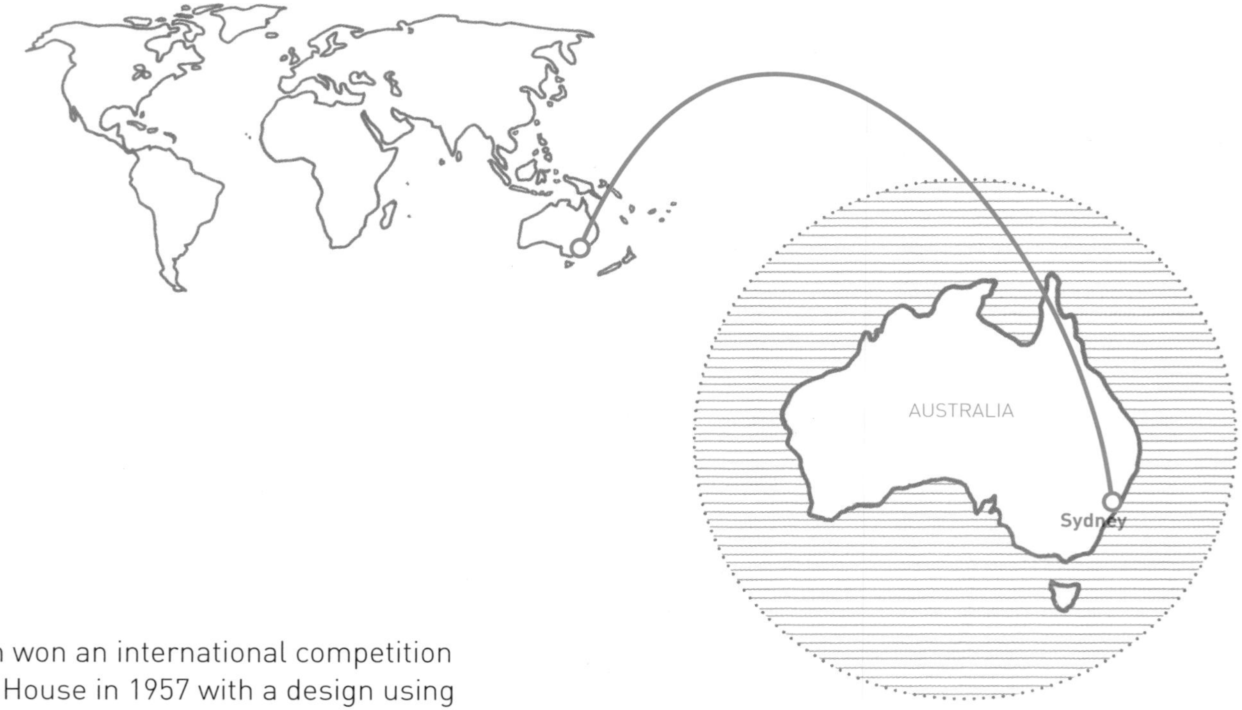

03 Sydney Opera House | 1957–73

Jørn Utzon

Sydney, Australia

AUSTRALIA

Sydney

Danish architect Jørn Utzon won an international competition to design the Sydney Opera House in 1957 with a design using free-form concrete shells. These were structurally ambitious for the time, and Utzon changed the forms to be segments of spheres that could be analysed and constructed. The building is a complex modern monument with a poetic and expressive form that responds brilliantly to its prominent location on a peninsula jutting out into Sydney Harbour.

From the initiation of its construction to its completion, the Opera House was a controversial project. Today, the building is a world-famous symbol of Sydney and of Australian culture.

Selen Morkoç, Thuy Nguyen and Amy Holland

03

Sydney Opera House | 1957–73

Jørn Utzon
Sydney, Australia

Concept ideas

The white forms of the roof echo the sails of yachts in the harbour and clouds lingering overhead.

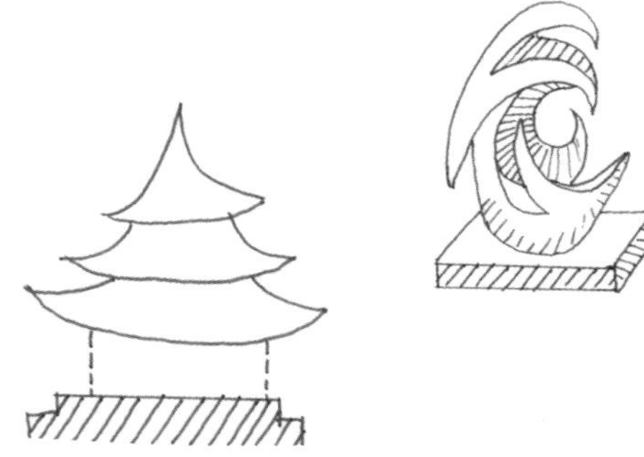

The relation of the roof and base evokes an Asian temple and the free-flowing form of an abstract sculpture fixed on a flat base.

The stepped platform was inspired by ancient pre-Columbian temples that are located on artificial mountain-like raised platforms.

Form generation: roof

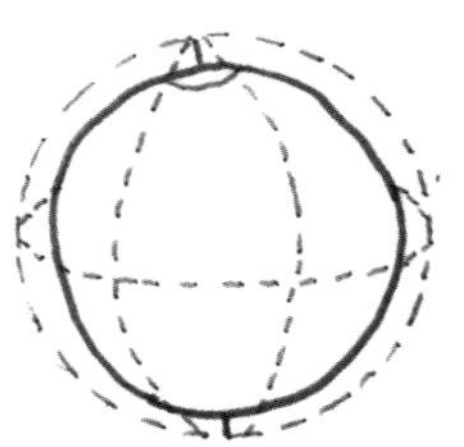

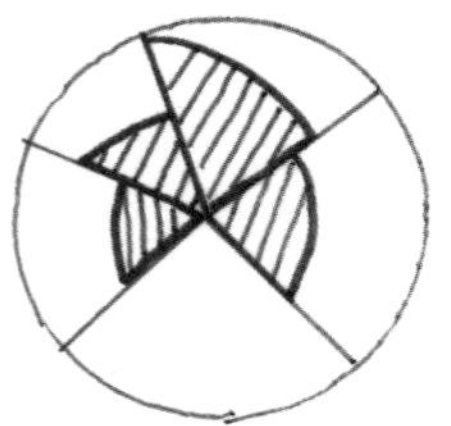

The 1957 competition drawings show free-form thin shells that proved impossible to build at the time. The shapes were rationalized to use spherical geometry.

The shapes of the roof derive from the centre of a sphere. They are taken into the three-dimensional like peel cut from an orange.

The shells are positioned along an axis to form a roof assembly. They are not true shells, but made up of precast-concrete ribbed elements.

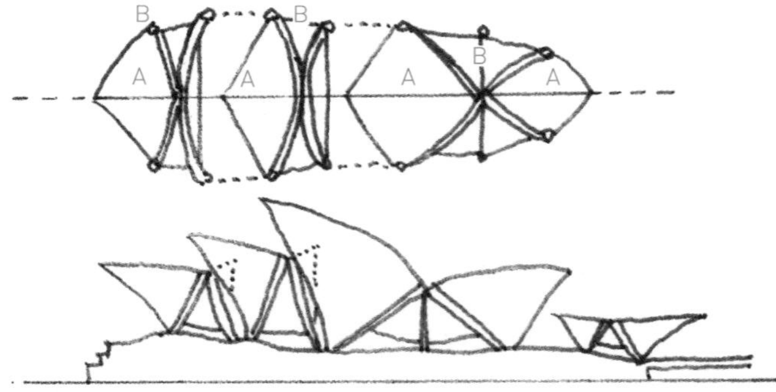

The composition of the spherical scheme of the major hall shell is a combination of main vault A accompanied by a pair of infill vaults B. This sequence is for the three shell assemblies in the building.

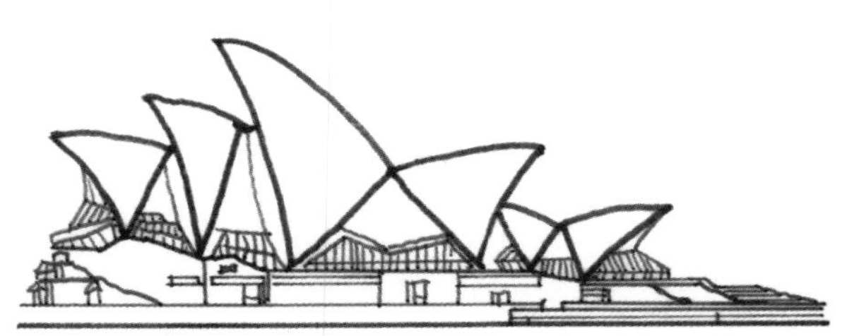

The spaces between the shells and the base are filled by glass walls.

Form generation: platform

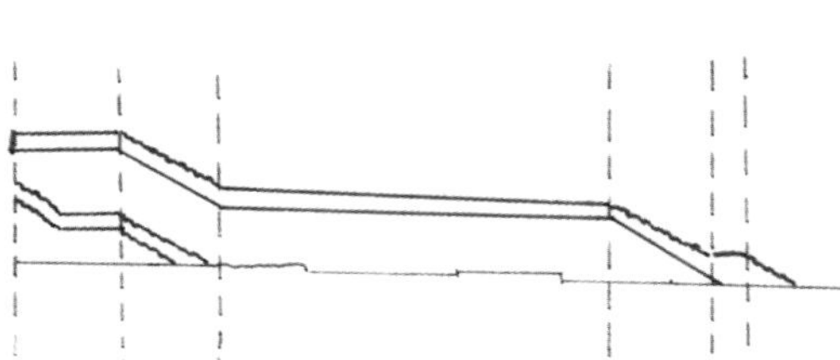

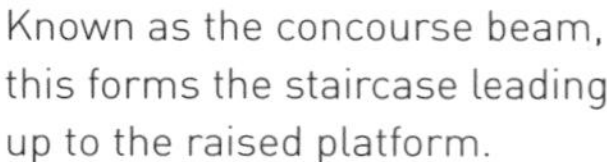

Known as the concourse beam, this forms the staircase leading up to the raised platform.

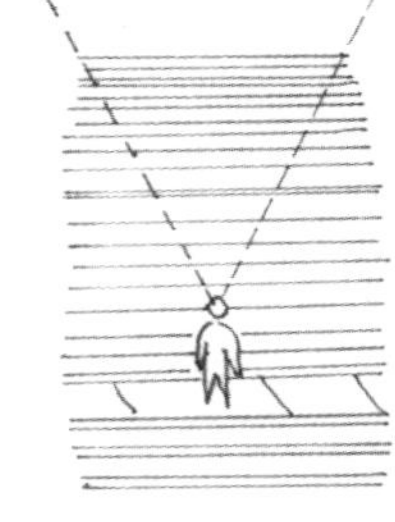

The cone of vision rises as the visitor climbs up the staircase and the Opera House reveals itself slowly.

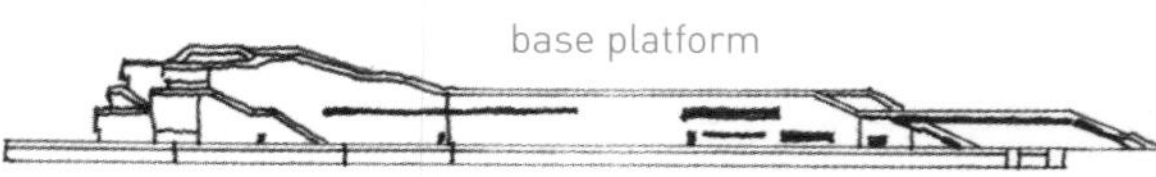

The elevated base platform creates a dominant appearance over the harbour through a visual continuity that separates the building from its surroundings.

Context

The Opera House is located at Bennelong Point in Sydney Harbour.

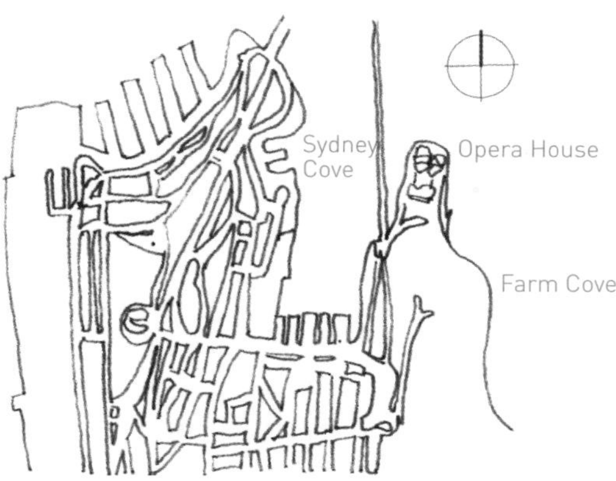

The site is bordered on three sides by the sea. The platform and raised roof shells dominate the context, while the solid platform with its few openings acts as an artificial peninsula.

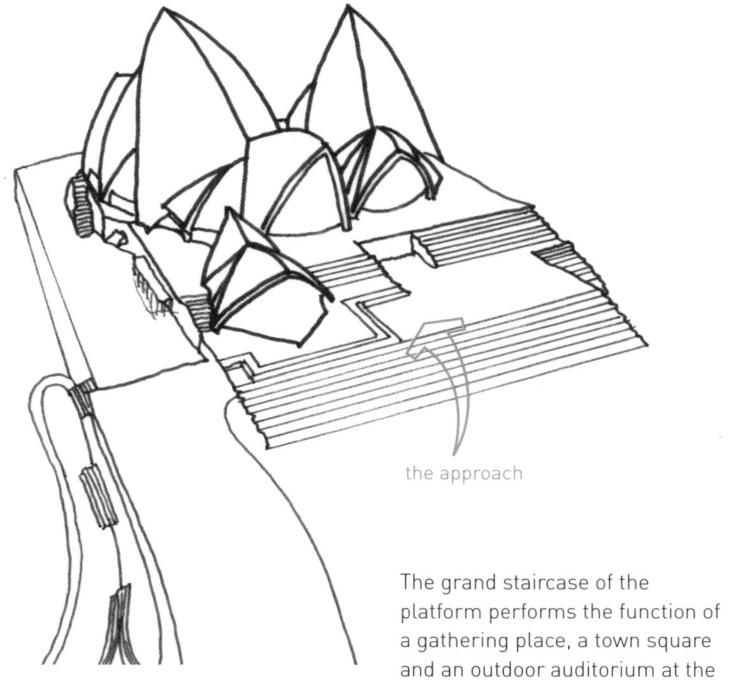

the approach

The grand staircase of the platform performs the function of a gathering place, a town square and an outdoor auditorium at the same time.

The nearby Botanical Gardens capture the most impressive view of the Opera House in its urban context, with the harbour and the Harbour Bridge structure in the background.

Movement

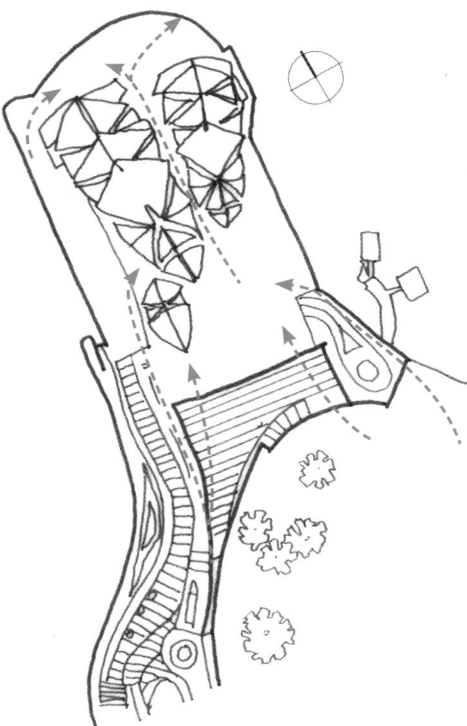

The platform creates open spaces that allow big crowds to gather around the building, as well as offering multiple views of the roof shells from outside.

Boundaries are defined by water and the sandstone cliffs at the edge of the Botanical Gardens. Since completion of the building, the urban design of the area has been redesigned to improve pedestrian and vehicle access.

Planning

Basement

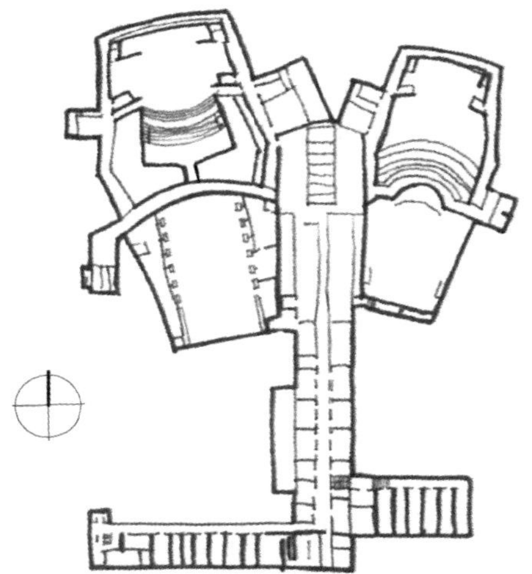

Ground floor

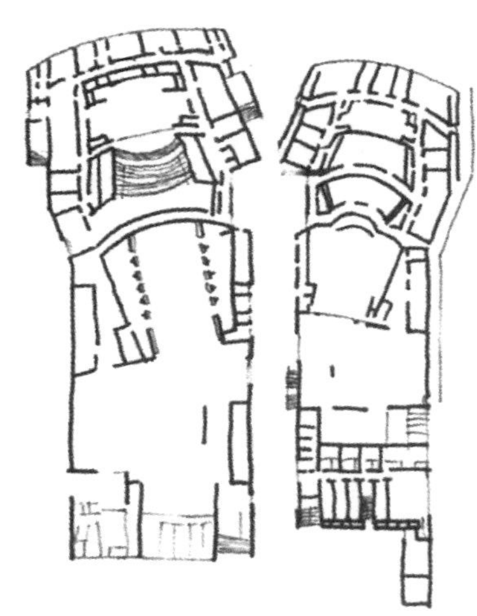

First floor

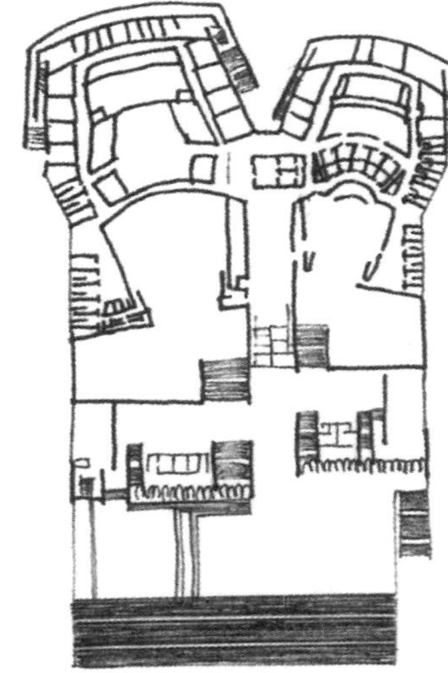

Second floor

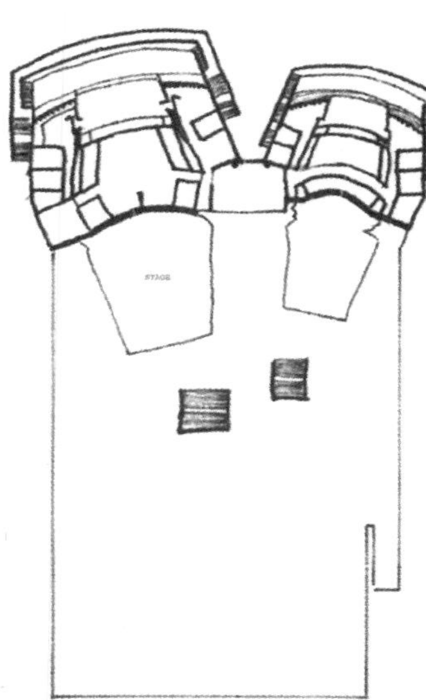

The inaugural plaque and the grid system

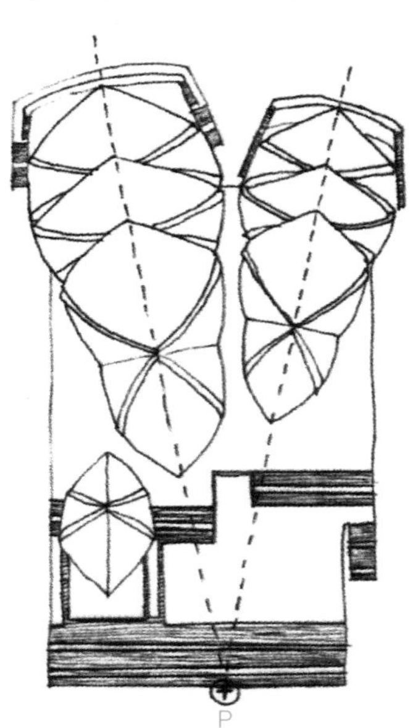

North elevation

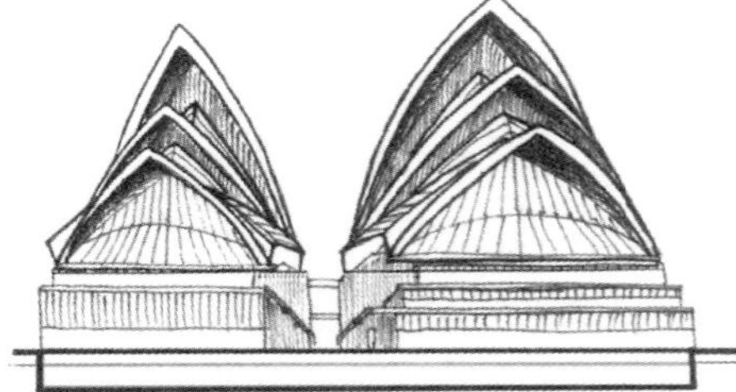

The studio and storage facilities are placed underground to reduce the number of visible floors.

A plaque (P) locates the point of intersection of the axes of the two main building clusters, the basic reference point for setting out the design.

West elevation

The building has limited openings in the base. This allows the artificial platform to maintain its solidity. The mass of the horizontal platform is in striking contrast with the white roof shells.

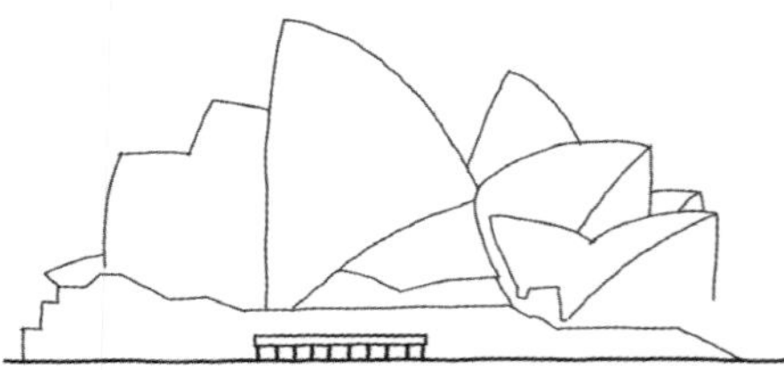

In the early 2000s Utzon with his son Kim Utzon designed a small addition and interior changes to mark and improve the entrance to the drama theatre in the podium.

The in-between spaces

The space between the two halls and the enveloping roofs is occupied by stairs and foyers. These are dramatic spaces characterized by the underside of the roof, sweeping glass and spectacular views of the harbour.

The wall and ceiling structures create a dynamic space within and around the building that allows one to orient oneself inside the building despite the constant change of interior forms.

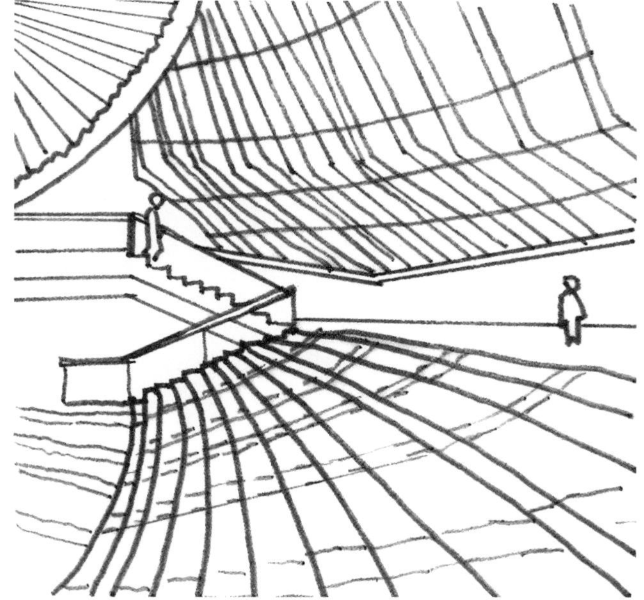

Stairways are dynamic paths that lead to different functions and adapt their form to the changing shapes of the structure.

Lighting

Sydney has a mild climate and there is sunshine on most days. The sunlight brightens the white tiles of the roof and is reflected around the raised platform. Natural light reaches only the edges of the building interior, and artificial light is used in its core.

An icon for Sydney

The view of the Opera House with the Harbour Bridge in the background has become the iconic image of Sydney. The vertical, exposed structural steel frame of the bridge contrasts with the shiny white curvilinear surfaces of the building's roof shells and rock-like mass of its platform base.

Form generation: Utzon's designs for the halls as proposed in 1962

Minor hall Movement of water forming the ridges of a wave inspired the design of the minor hall.

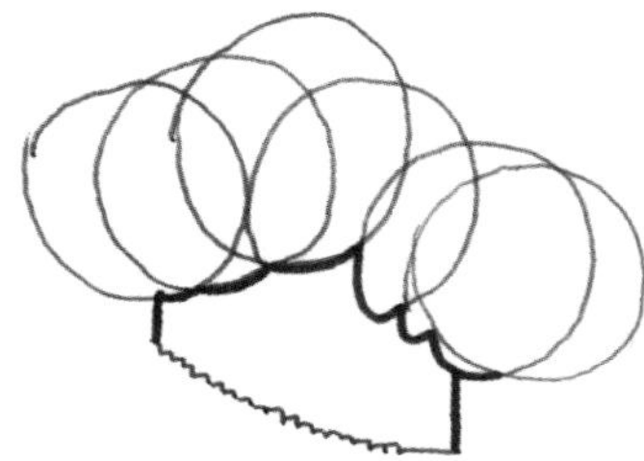

In order to achieve this in the ceiling form, Utzon used convex curves based on successive circle grids.

The drawing shows the overlapping of geometrical convex curves that form the ceiling pattern.

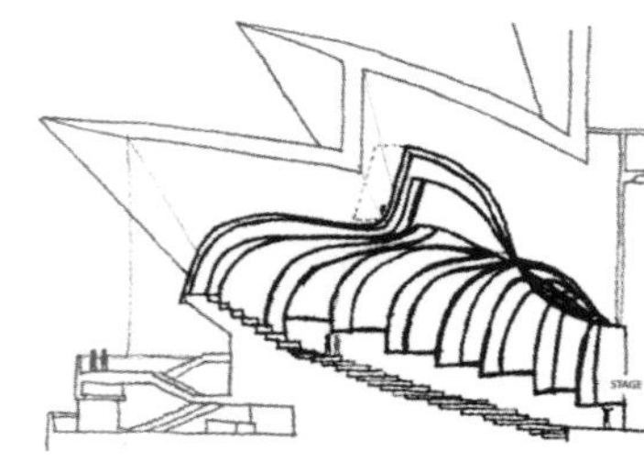

The convex curve structure of the ceiling also serves the function of diffusion of sound.

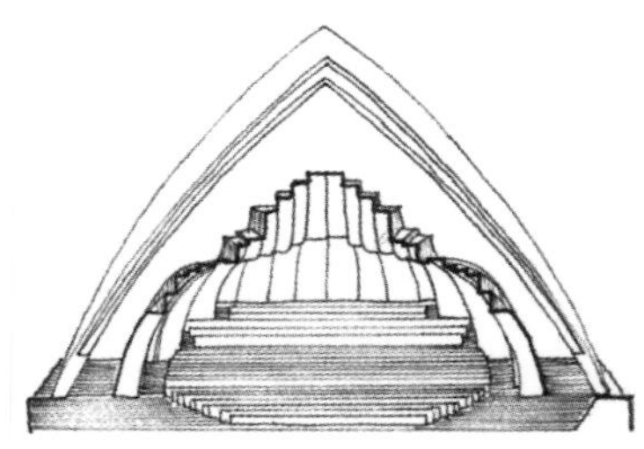

The outside shell vault and the symmetrical structure of the ceiling waves form a double shell.

Major hall The branches of a beech tree as seen from below inspired the idea of the major hall ceiling.

The abstract forms of the branches create a triangular reticulation

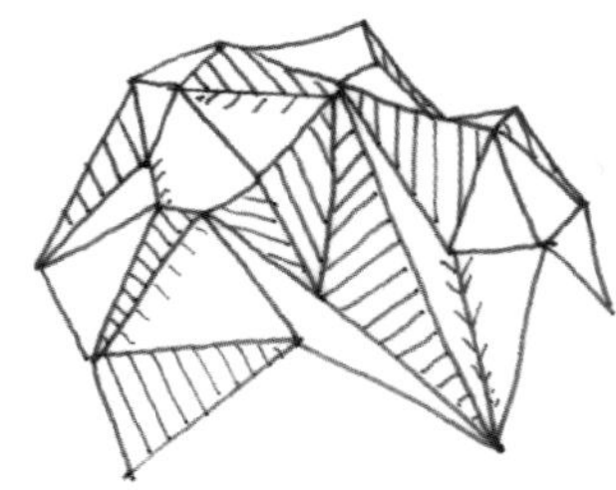

Utzon created the multifaceted ceiling planes based on the triangular forms.

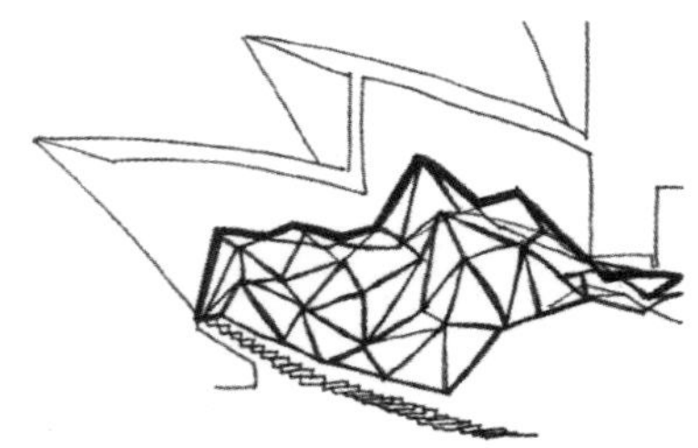

The shape of the ceiling was designed to utilize the space under the shell roof as much as possible, helping to secure the largest possible volume.

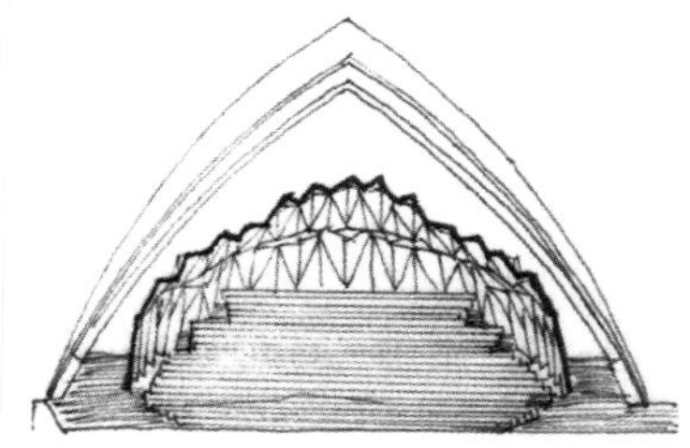

The system of triangulation allowed the ceiling to follow the form of the roof and was useful in achieving the relatively long reverberation time needed for music.

Utzon's plans were altered during the construction process. The larger hall was initially intended for opera as well as concerts but later became a single-purpose concert hall. An orchestral pit was installed in the smaller drama theatre, which was modified to become the opera theatre. This allowed much larger audiences for concerts, but meant that the opera theatre had restricted stage tower and side wings. A rehearsal room in the podium became a small drama theatre.

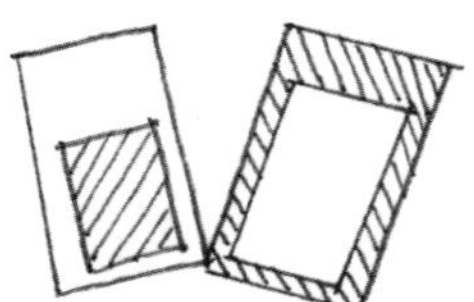

Utzon resigned from the project before its completion. Peter Hall with Lionel Todd and David Livermore led the interior design of the halls. The execution is very different from Utzon's proposals.

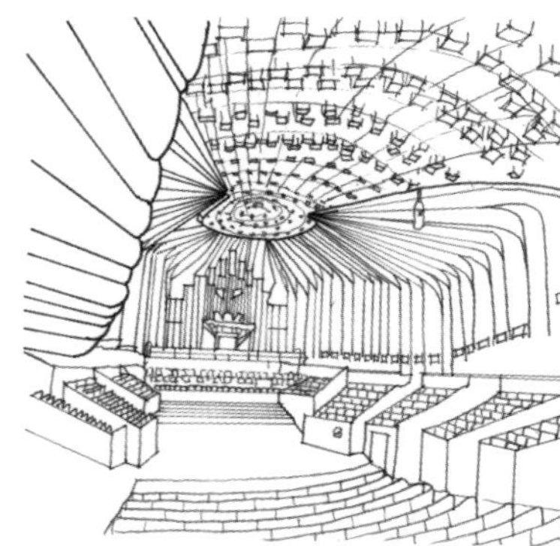

Materials

South elevation

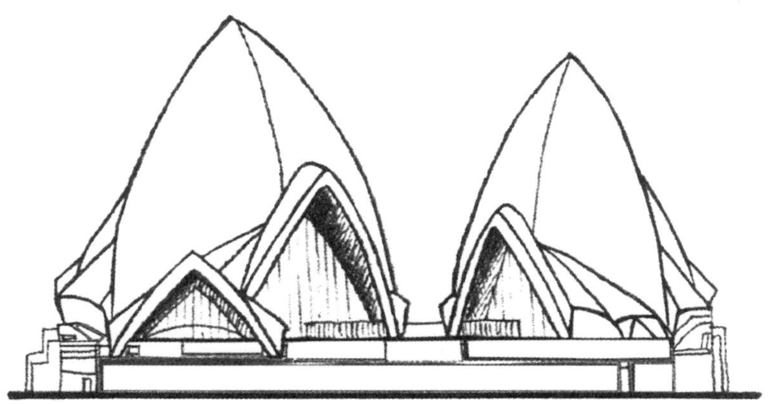

The ground and first floors are clad so that they appear as one surface from the outside. Functional necessities do not compromise the symbolic sculptural effect.

Glass and textured timber come together in the structural shell of concrete in the interior. The ribs of the precast-concrete roof elements are clearly visible. Textured timber and plywood soften the brutality of concrete.

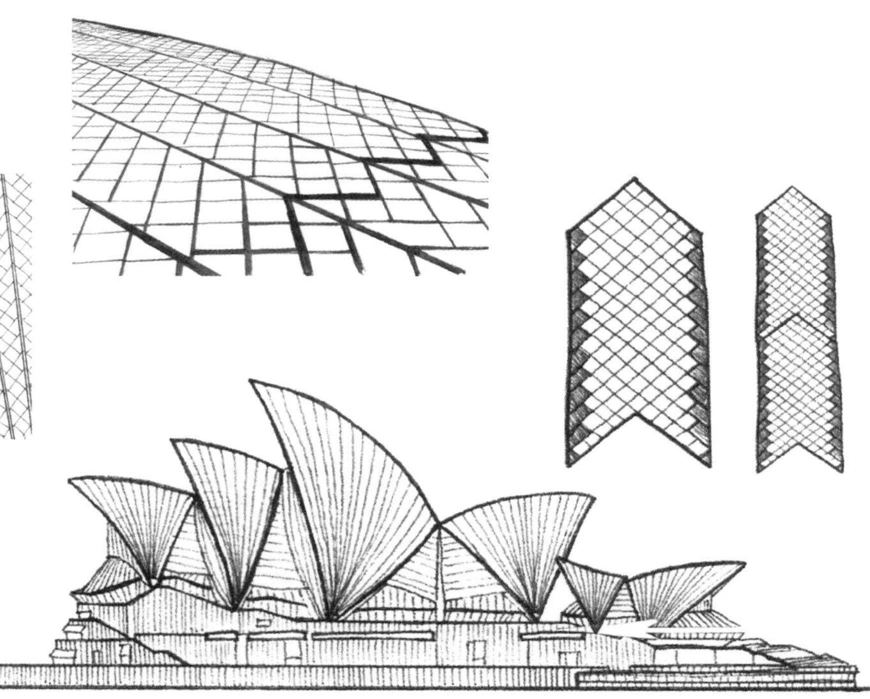

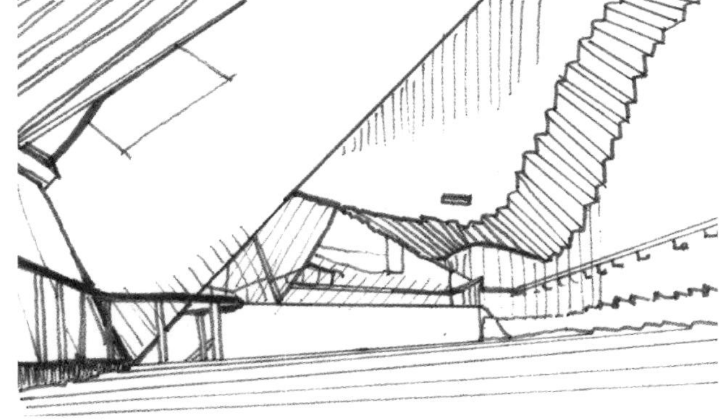

The shells of the roof are clad in white ceramic tiles. The concrete structure of the platform is clad in precast panels with an aggregate of local sandstone. The white tiles emphasize the sculptural character of the building within the context of the harbour.

Solomon R. Guggenheim Museum | 1943–59

Frank Lloyd Wright
New York, USA

04

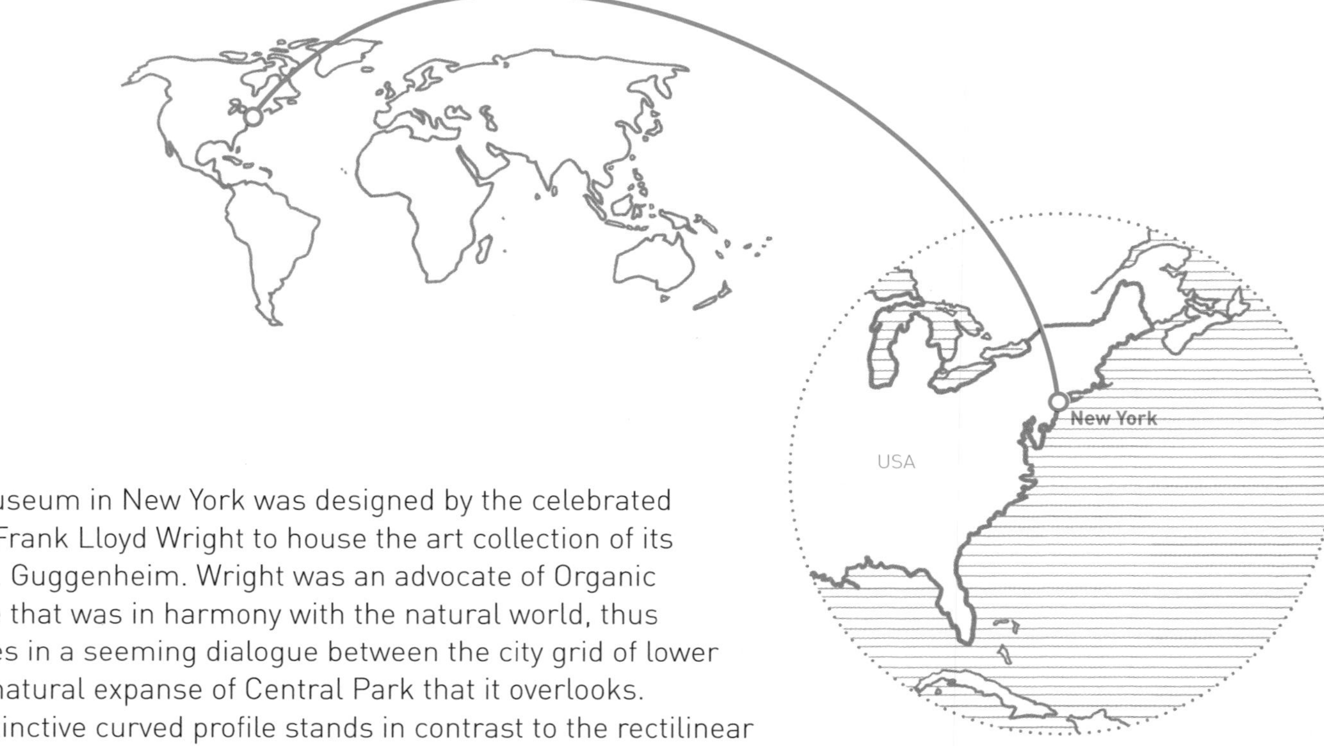

The Guggenheim Museum in New York was designed by the celebrated American architect Frank Lloyd Wright to house the art collection of its founder, Solomon R. Guggenheim. Wright was an advocate of Organic Modern architecture that was in harmony with the natural world, thus the museum engages in a seeming dialogue between the city grid of lower Manhattan and the natural expanse of Central Park that it overlooks.

The building's distinctive curved profile stands in contrast to the rectilinear patterns of its neighbourhood, enlivening the rigidity of the city grid and achieving a landmark character suited to its role as a cultural institution. In keeping with the organic theme, the design engages the analogy of a shell to rethink the organization of a gallery display. It breaks away from the traditional format of differentiated spaces developed as separate display rooms, impeding the continuous flow of movement. Instead, a large ramped interior allows visitors to look through the entire set of displays in one continuous movement. The large, light-filled atrium helps to orient them and binds the entire design into a single cohesive experience.

Amit Srivastava, Katherine Holford, Matthew Bruce McCallum and Lana Greer

THE SOLOMON R GUGGENHEIM MUSEUM

04

Solomon R. Guggenheim Museum | 1943–59

Frank Lloyd Wright

New York, USA

Response to urban context

The building for the Guggenheim Museum is sited in the dense urban context of Manhattan, New York City, but the site is located on an edge facing Fifth Avenue and overlooking Central Park. The design for the museum takes full advantage of this edge condition to develop a structure that complements rather than emulates the surrounding urban context, and the building has become an iconic structure that defines the neighbourhood.

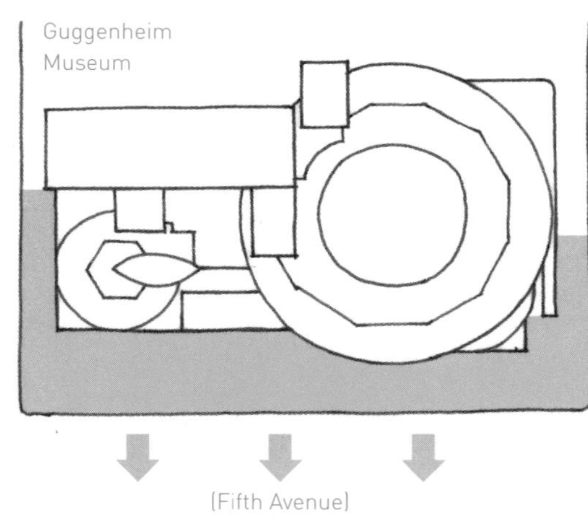

CENTRAL PARK

The overall plan of the building slowly shifts from the rectilinear forms facing the existing buildings to the organic shapes that define its street edge and reflect the organic shapes in the park. The organic frontage is set back from the actual street edge to allow for a public space. With the curved forms of the building on one side and the openness of Central Park on the other, this is a valuable open space within the dense urban fabric of Manhattan.

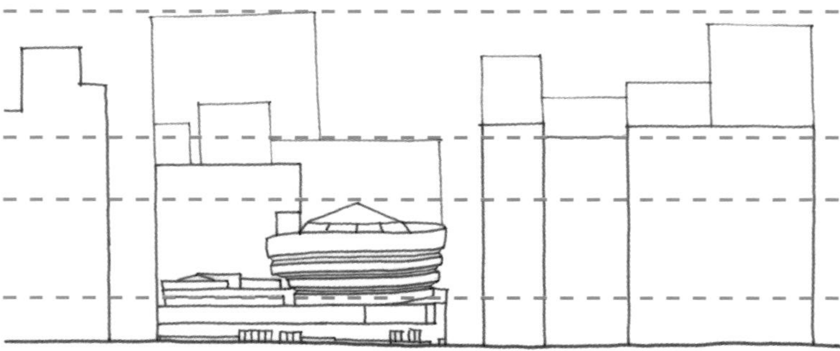

The organic forms interrupt the rhythm of the city grid to create a pause and welcome people to this public institution.

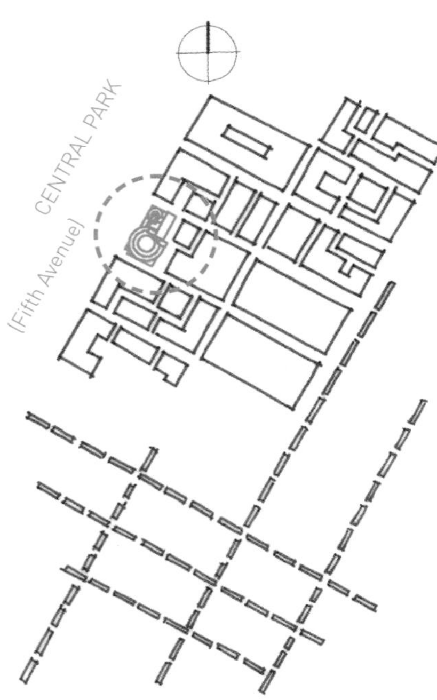

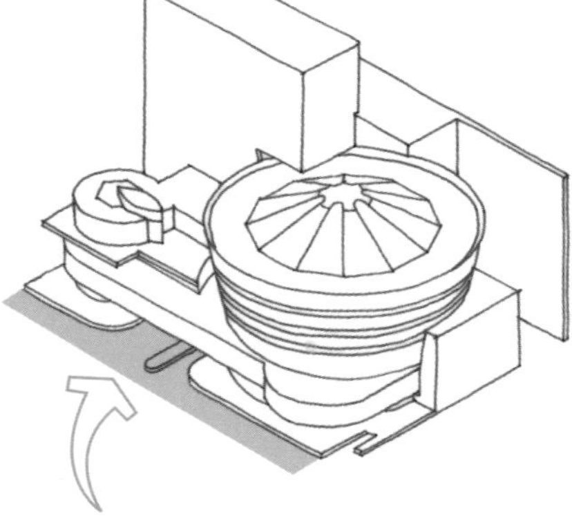

The original design allowed for vehicles to enter the complex for dropping off passengers.

The forms of the building stand in contrast to the rectilinear forms of the surrounding buildings, but the overall composition allows these forms to coexist as a part of a single whole in which the curved and straight lines complement and enhance one another. The limited height of the museum offers the illusion of a gateway into the realm of the high-rise structures in the background.

The scale of the structure is carefully considered in relation to its surroundings to allow the curved forms to be iconic but not to dominate their surroundings. The structure at around 30 metres (98 feet) in height is tall enough to sit comfortably within the towering high-rise neighbourhood without losing its impact. On the other hand, the limited height, along with the layered elevation, complements the human scale and helps the building to connect with the pedestrians on the street. The outward-leaning form also helps the building to extend to the edges, reinforcing its height and providing a clear top edge for the people at street level.

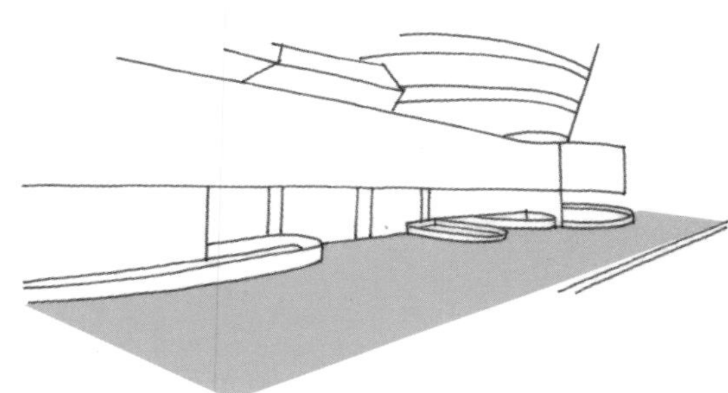

The front entrance now acts as an extended public plaza where the horizontal bandings reinforce the human scale.

Organicism and iconic form

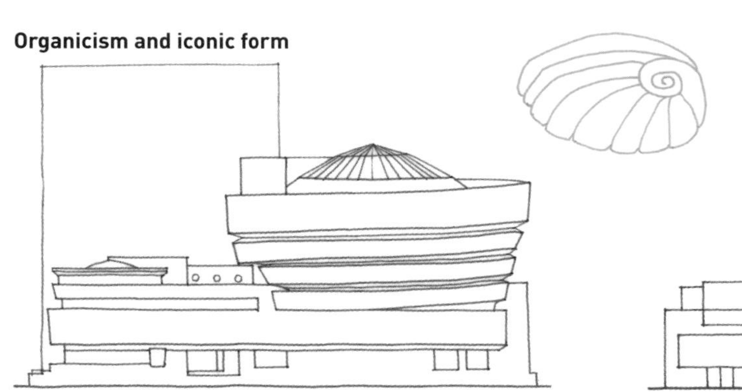

The design engages the idea of a continuous shell-like form to provide for the needs of the art gallery. The idea is based on the architect Frank Lloyd Wright's insistence on an 'Organic Modernism', where the architectural form reflects the symbiotic ordering system of nature. Accordingly, the analogy of the shell is carried through in all aspects of the design, from the external spiral form to the internal sectional elements, bringing the entire design together as an organic whole.

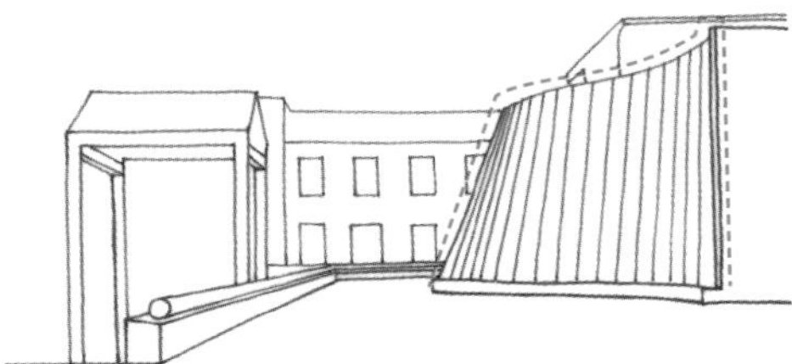

Neue Staatsgalerie by James Stirling (1984)

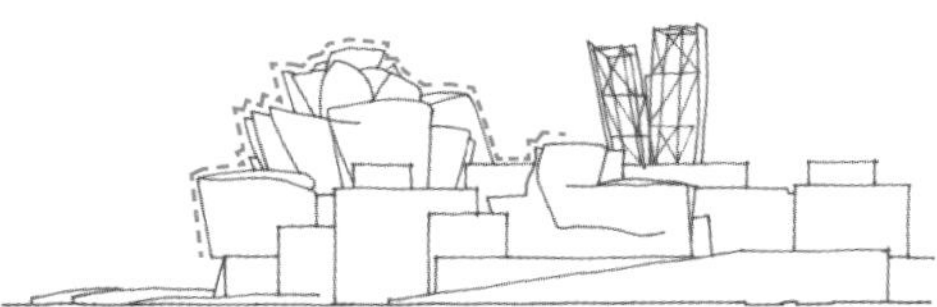

Guggenheim Museum Bilbao by Frank Gehry (1997)

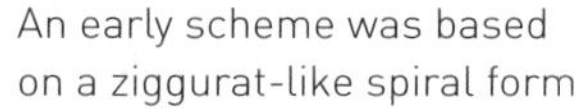

An early scheme was based on a ziggurat-like spiral form.

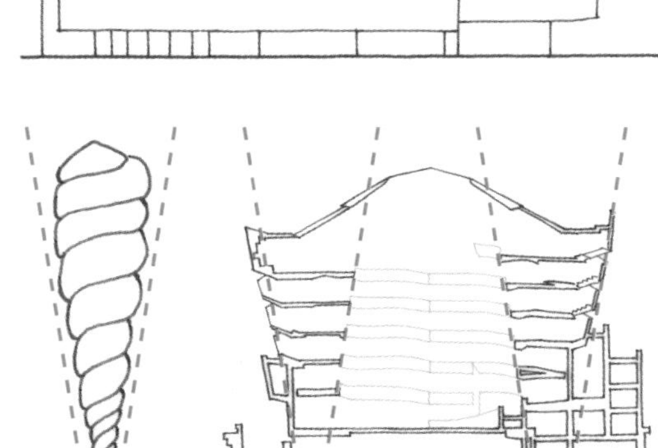

The use of the shell analogy not only serves the functional requirements of the programme but also helps to develop the art gallery as a sculptural form in itself. The use of this unusual sculptural form allowed this public institution to become an icon for the city and promote the disciplines of art and culture. This idea of a museum as a sculptural form that stands out in contrast to the city fabric has since become common in museum design, and many important museum structures around the world follow this strategy. The contrasting forms are placed in the context of the existing fabric of the city and the composition allows the museum structure to act as both a critique and a celebration of the city it is in, thereby fulfilling the role of an art piece and itself becoming a sculpture – but this is successful only with a very high quality of architecture.

Hierarchy of spaces

The overall plan of the museum building offers a combination of forms that are aggregated around a central circular structure. This circular structure is the most important public space and thus acts as a pivotal point for the building. As a visitor walks up or down its ramp, the accesses to the ancillary spaces are gradually revealed, allowing for various different plan forms to emerge. Since the central volume acts as the gallery and the other structures serve various administrative roles, this hierarchical relationship brings the focus back to the central purpose of the building – the display of art.

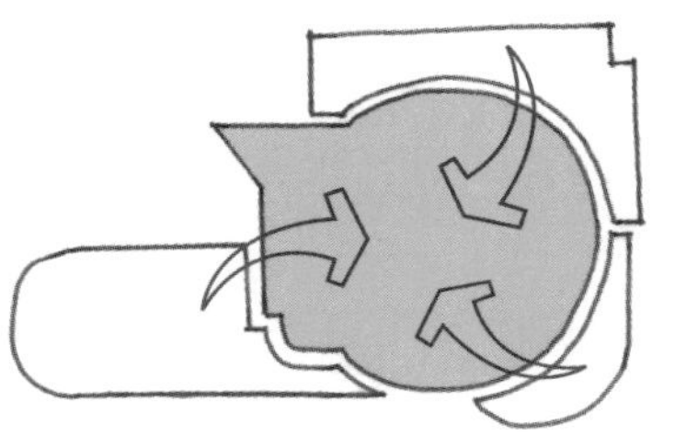

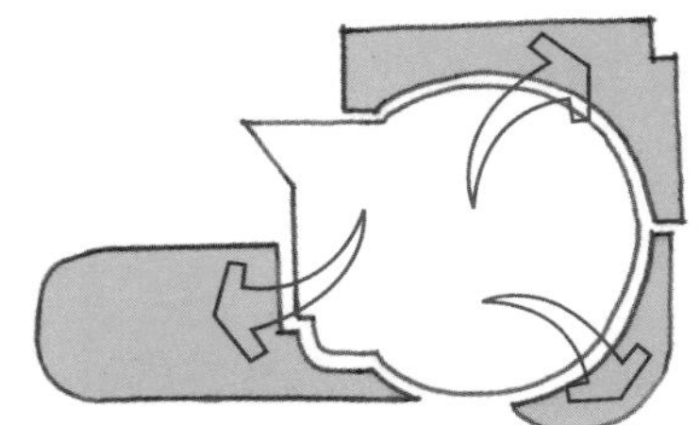

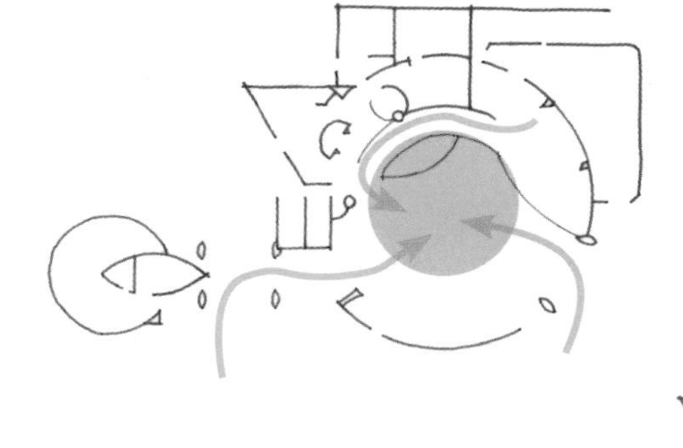

The central atrium on the ground floor acts as a gathering space and attracts people.

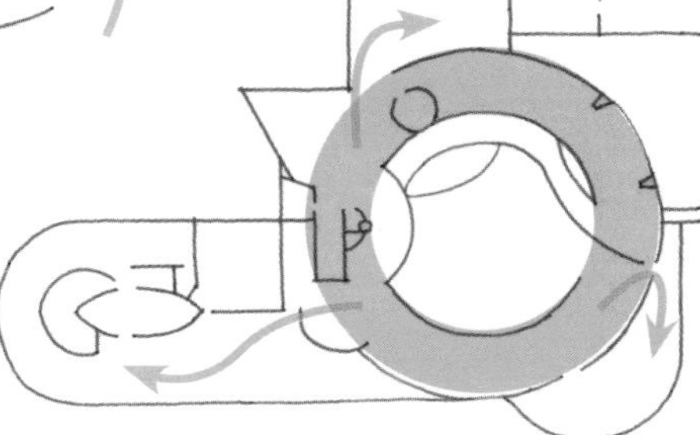

On the upper floor, paths lead off from the centre to secondary functions.

Response to programme

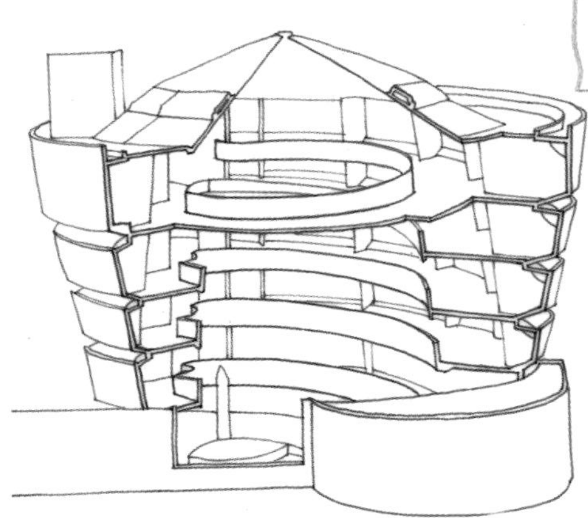

The programmatic needs of a gallery space have been interpreted as a single continuous journey rather than a series of fragmented experiences based on the division of the exhibits to fit different rooms, as in a traditional building. Accordingly, the display spaces of the building are organized around a single, spiralling ramp that allows the visitor to experience all the exhibits in one single journey. Visitors are led up to the top floor and slowly descend the big spiral ramp to view all the exhibits on their way to the base. This type of spatial arrangement also offers the possibility for an exhibition to be curated as a single experience that has been carefully defined by the curator.

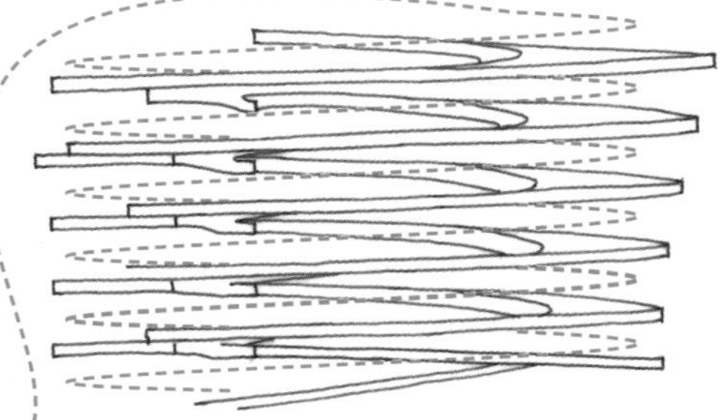

The visitors start viewing the exhibits from the top and slowly descend down the spiralling ramp to the base.

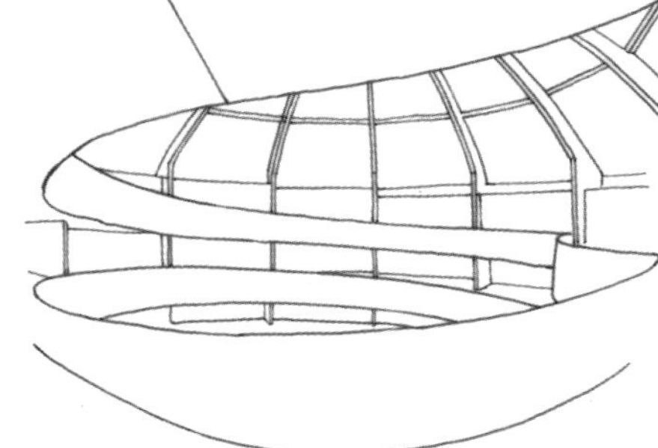

Public entrance areas below are separated from exhibition spaces above, but visual continuity is maintained.

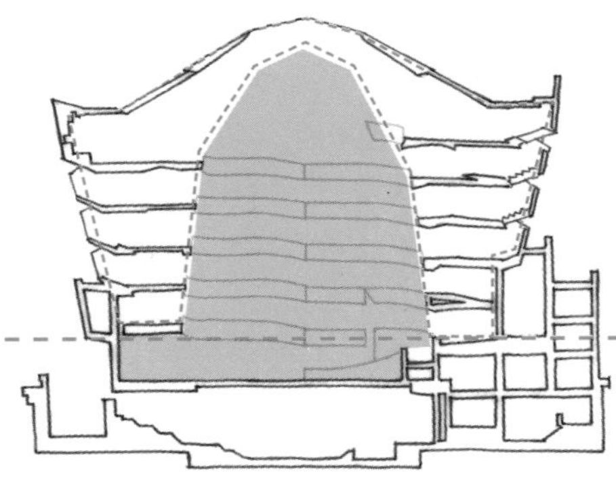

The single volume and the spiral access add to the experience of an exhibition in two specific ways. First, the visual connection between the patrons in the atrium below and those in the gallery spaces above act as cues to participate in the event. Second, the visual connections with the other displays in the exhibition, which can be seen across the atrium, allow for a better appreciation of the overall extent and variety of the exhibits.

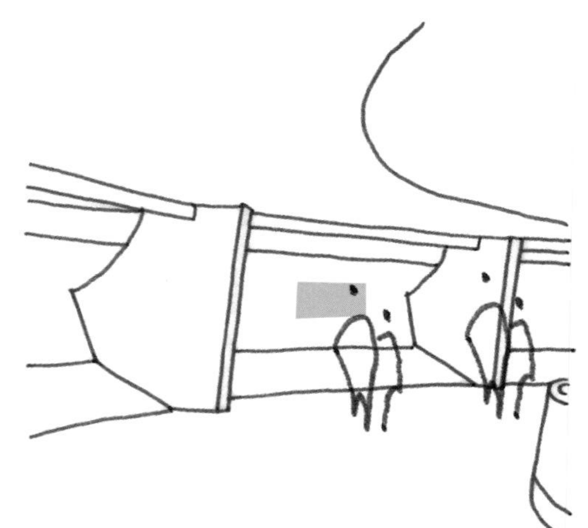

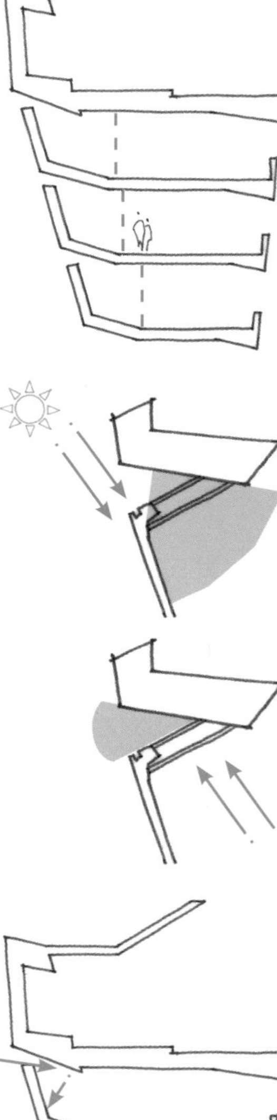

Aside from the experiential aspects of the central spiral circulation pattern, the unique formal composition also allows for several other innovations in terms of addressing the needs of display. The sloping floor along the wall edge creates a psychological barrier between the visitors and the display without the need for railings, while the vertical separators allow for enough privacy to observe the artworks without being disturbed. Furthermore, the angled floor and ceiling work together with a clerestory window to provide diffused natural light to illuminate the artworks.

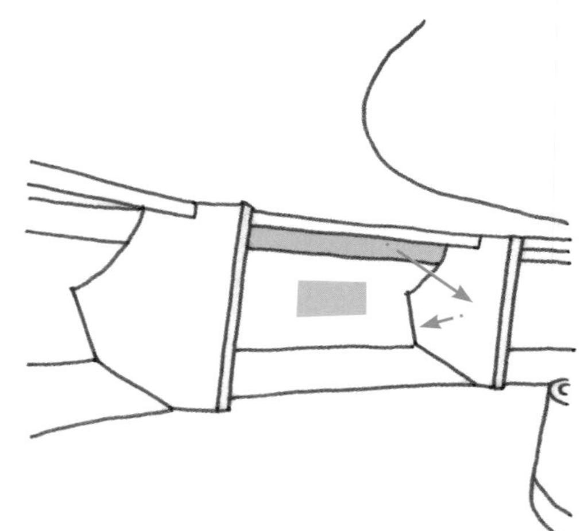

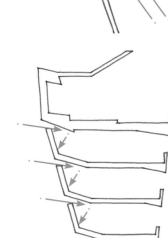

The monumental volume of the atrium helps to connect the various spaces and activities into one experience.

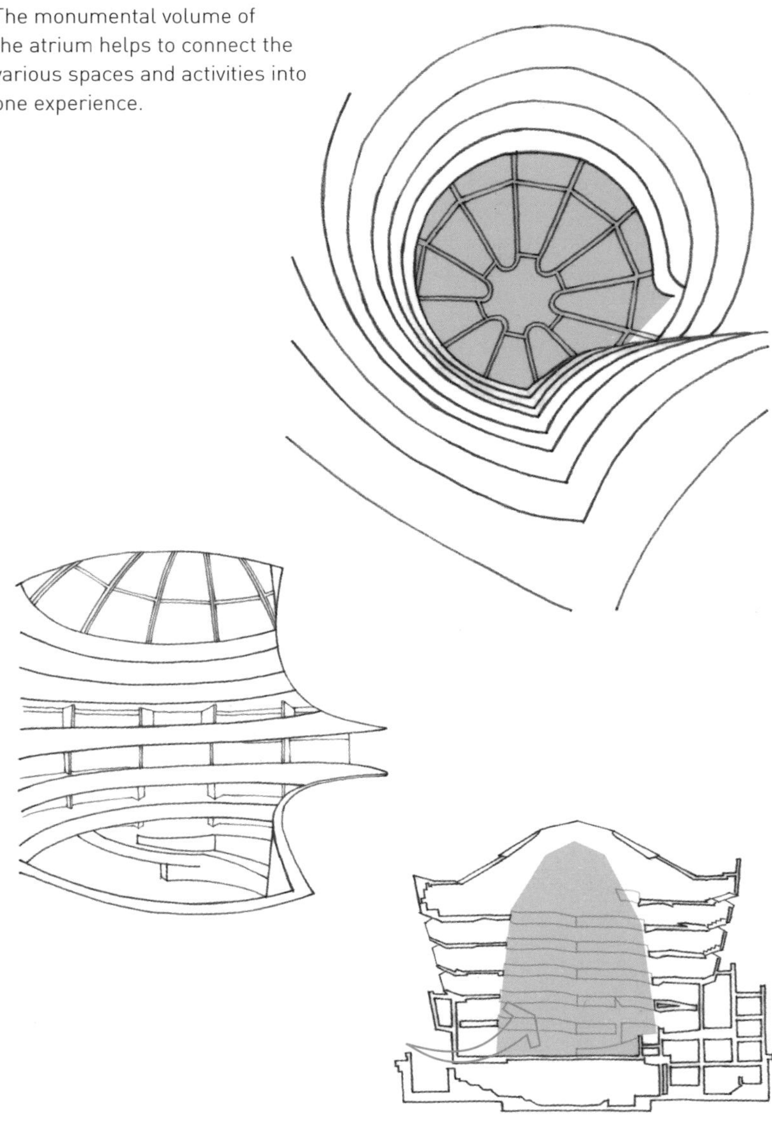

Response to user experience
The treatment of the central atrium space is based on an architectural technique often used by Frank Lloyd Wright, where a visitor is taken through a compressed space before being released into an awe-inspiring monumental interior. Accordingly, here, the visitor enters the structure through a single-storey space before arriving in the monumental interior of the central atrium. As he or she looks up into the light-filled atrium the entire experience of the gallery spaces and the movement of the other visitors become apparent, and the visitor instantaneously becomes part of this shared experience.

As visitors continue upon their journeys along the spiralling ramp and look at the exhibits, they are still tied into the original experience through a continuous connection with the atrium space. Even as they may pause to look at the artworks on display they can immediately return to the shared public realm embodied by the atrium space.

The spiralling curved form also allows for interesting views to be framed as the visitor proceeds along the path around the atrium. The curves are further reflected on the outside of the building, and exterior views are framed from certain vantage points.

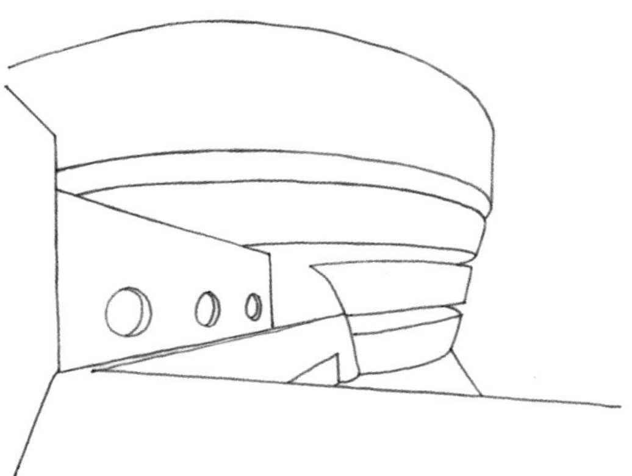

The curved forms offer distinctive views of both the interior and exterior of the building.

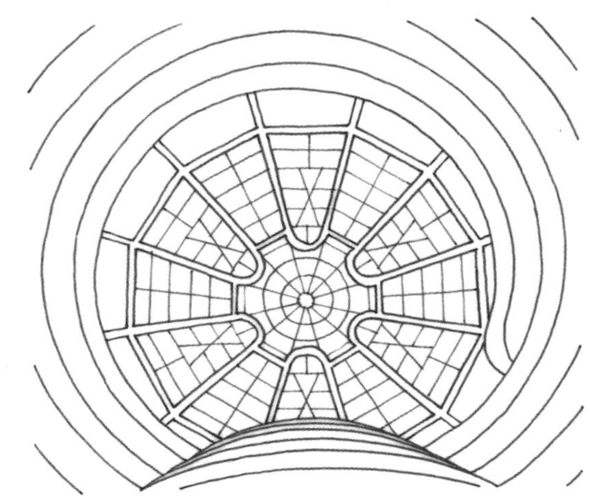

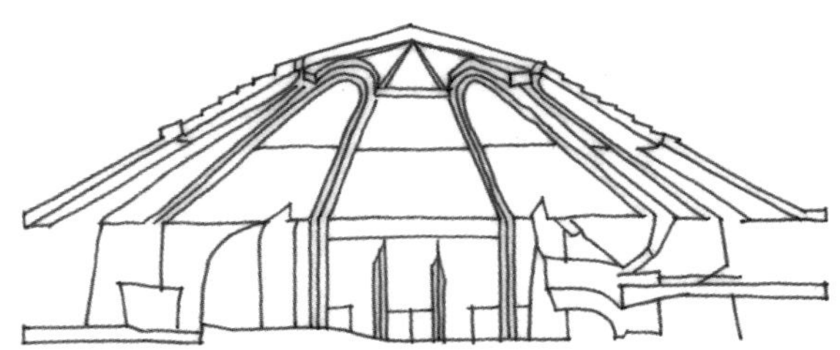

The white interior is topped by a massive skylight that bathes the entire atrium with light. The experience of the great light-filled volume is already a dramatic experience, but the configuration also draws the visitor's eye to the central feature of the skylight itself. The structural members of the skylight are arranged so as to form an ornate structure, which offers a single source of opulence in an otherwise simple and monochromatic interior space. When seen by someone standing in the atrium and looking up, the skylight itself becomes a work of art and generates a sense of awe.

Leicester Engineering Building | 1959–63

Stirling & Gowan

Leicester, England

05

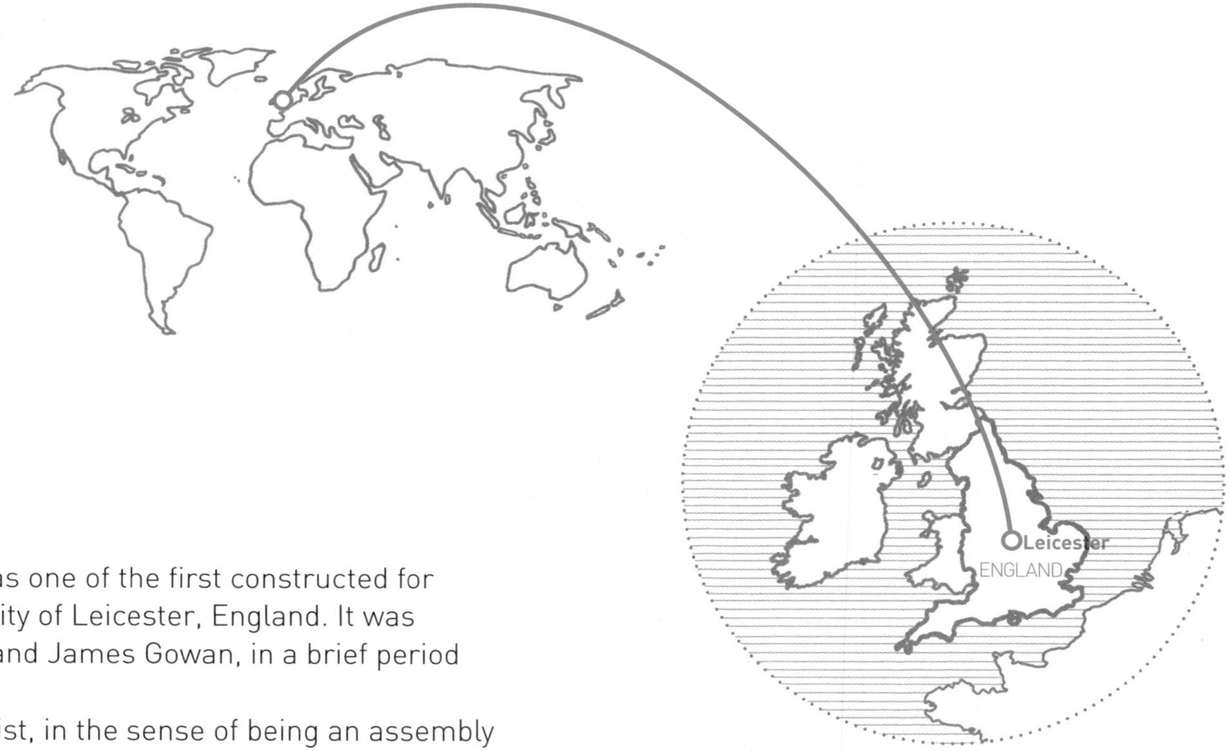

Leicester

ENGLAND

The Engineering Building was one of the first constructed for Leicester University, in the city of Leicester, England. It was designed by James Stirling and James Gowan, in a brief period of fruitful collaboration.

The building is Functionalist, in the sense of being an assembly of identifiable components that fit their different functions and loudly express this functionality in their external form. It has also been called Postmodern, because of its deliberately picturesque composition and exposed services. The form is logical, but it is also poetic, like an intense sculpture. It not only responds to but exploits the variety of activities in the building. It also exploits the possibilities that emerge when forms are put together, as in the cascading glass walls around the circulation space between the building's towers.

Antony Radford and William Morris

05

05 Leicester Engineering Building | 1959–63

Stirling & Gowan

Leicester, England

The Leicester University campus is on the south side of the city centre next to Victoria Park. The site was small for the size of the building. The planning authority relaxed the three-storey height limit that had applied to buildings along the edge the park.

North lighting is traditionally preferred for workshops in the northern hemisphere. The roof lights over the workshop therefore run diagonally across the rectangular workshop plan. The planning of the building adopts this functional combination of elements at 45 degrees to one another as a design theme.

The formal entrance is up a ramp that leads to a 'piano nobile' with terrace and doorway. The more-used ground-level entrances follow the edge of the workshop under the two lecture theatres and into the podium.

The offices, like the workshops, originally had industrial low-cost patent glazing, unifying the scheme. This has since been replaced by more thermally efficient aluminium curtain walling. The change has altered but not significantly detracted from the aesthetics of the building.

A glass-walled spiral staircase allows latecomers to arrive at the back of the large lecture theatre.

The podium houses the lower entrances, the lavatories and access to the workshop.

Most of the site is occupied by a large rectangular workshop with its sides aligned with the site boundary.

On the park side is a set of stacked offices, laboratories and lecture theatres with the stair and lift towers that serve them. Four small labs are stacked over the smaller lecture theatre, and seven floors of offices over the larger one. Over the office stack is a large water tank.

The building is clad in horizontal red brick, vertical red tiles and glass. In-situ fair-faced concrete is exposed at columns and beams.

The lavatories are ventilated through a snorkel at the apex of the podium's triangular base, making a sculptural object out of a mundane necessity.

The windows of the laboratories project out to allow cross-ventilation through horizontal louvres at the base of their triangular cross-section.

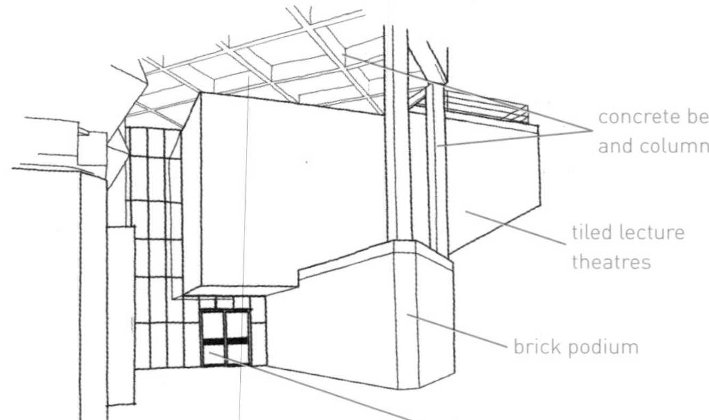

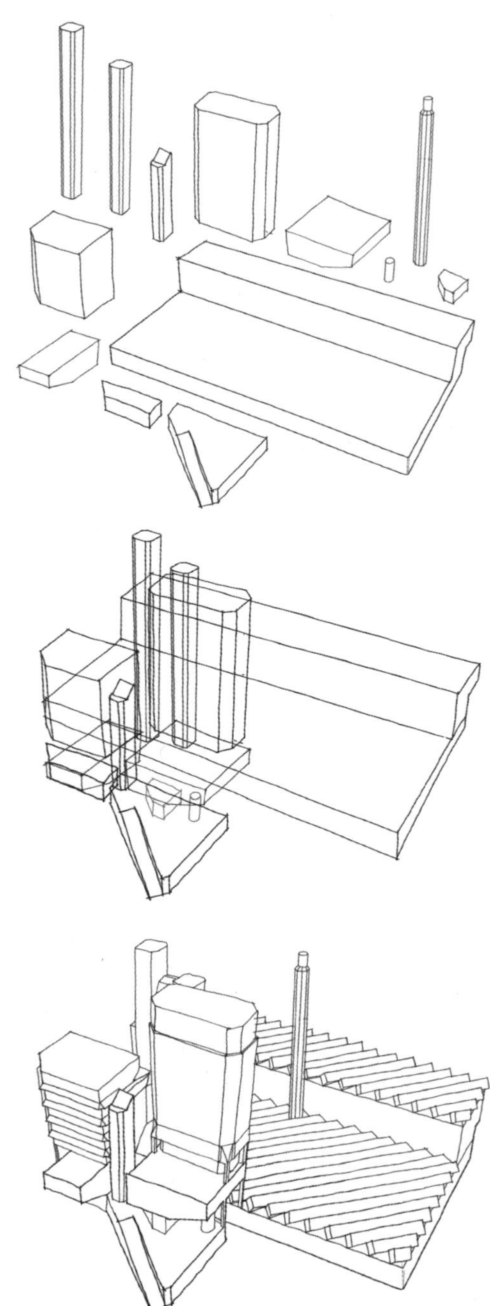

Volumetric reductions

Volumes are reduced to fit the exact spaces required for activities. The corners of the stair and lift towers are chamfered, the top of the stair tower is sloped to match the top flight of stairs, and the unused spaces under the lecture-room seats are cut away.

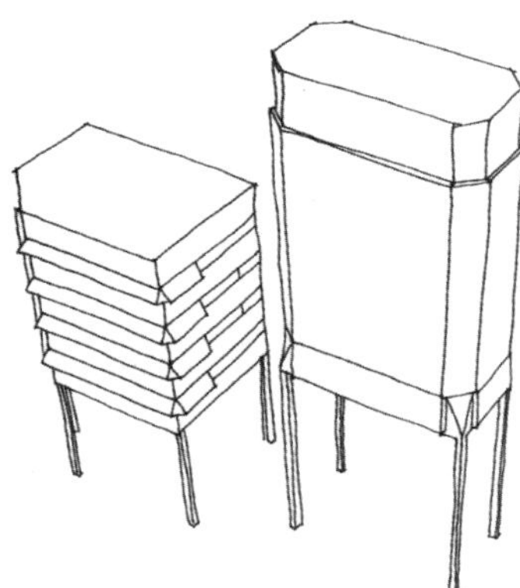

The circulation area in the tower decreases in line with reduced need on each floor. The glass wall of the tower tapers to suit them, making what has been called 'a crystal waterfall'. This is another example of volumetric reduction.

Glass as an object

In Modernist architecture glass was mainly considered in terms of its transparency filling a void between elements, not as an object in its own right. In the Leicester Engineering Building, glass is used as a sculptural material able to form a separate individual volume.

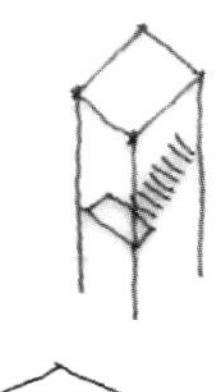

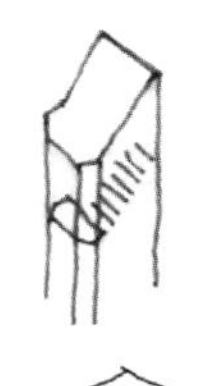

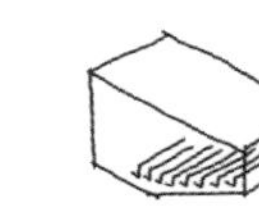

On the corners of lowest floor of the office stack, concrete elements make an elegant transition from the offices' chamfered corners to single columns.

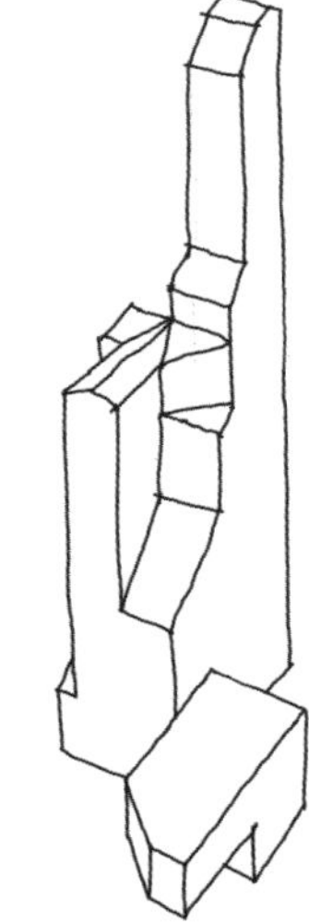

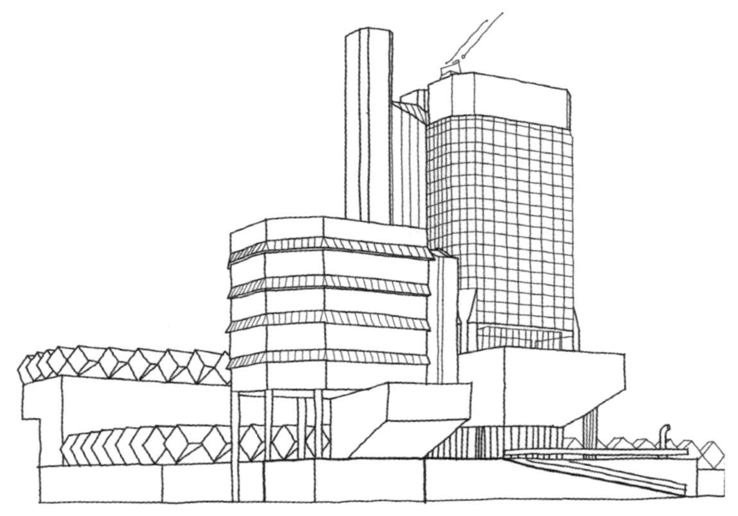

The office tower can be seen as filling in between the structure needed to hold up a water tank at the top of the tower. This idea is emphasized by the glass skin wrapped around the offices with chamfered corners, contrasting with the mass of the tank. The water is delivered down pipes flanking the main staircase.

Trees along the edge of Victoria Park mask much of the lower part of the building, especially in summer. The offices look over this screen.

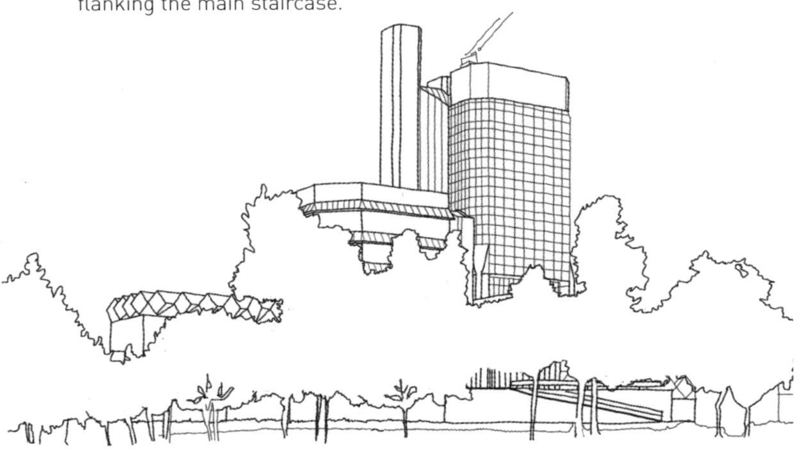

Leicester Engineering Building | 1959–63

Stirling & Gowan
Leicester, England

The internal circulation spaces are treated like 'outside', with the same surfaces and railings.

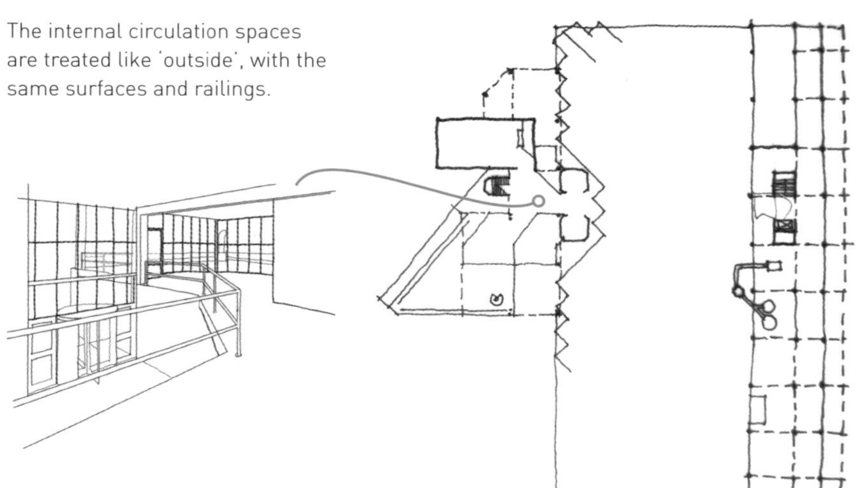

Aerodynamics and electrical workshops are stacked over the ground-level boiler house and maintenance room. The roof lights, service pipes and roof structure continue over the workshop corridor.

The stacking of laboratories is good for services and access. The main vertical duct is in the adjacent lift tower.

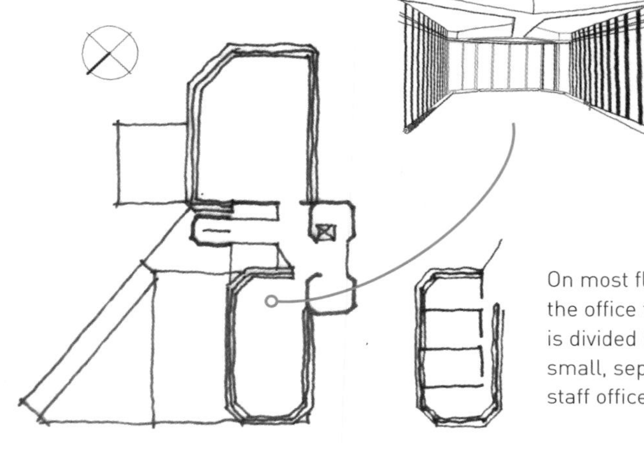

On most floors the office tower is divided into small, separate staff offices.

Workshops

The ground-level workshop is an open-plan shed in which research experiments can be set up and later changed.

The relative sizes of the male (M) and female (F) student lavatories shows expectations about the proportion of male to female engineering students in the late 1950s.

Spaces used by students are grouped on the lower floors so that they can be easily reached by stairs, reducing the load on the single lift.

The upper-level workshop extends over a service road as a propped cantilever high above ground. This allows machinery to be raised from lorries directly into these workshops, through their floors.

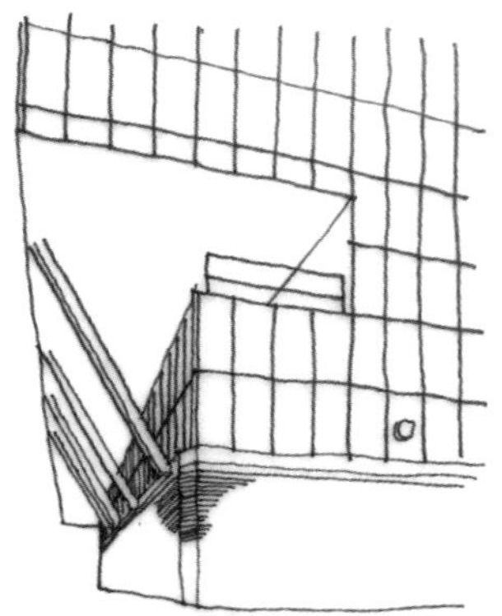

Lecture theatres

The small lecture theatre holds 100 people and cantilevers longways, so that the sloping underside of the seating sticks out. The theatre's elongated form works well for the external composition, but not so well for students sitting in the back rows, who are distant from the lecturer.

The large lecture theatre holds 200 people and cantilevers sideways from the columns of the tower, the mass of the cantilever balanced by the stack of offices above.

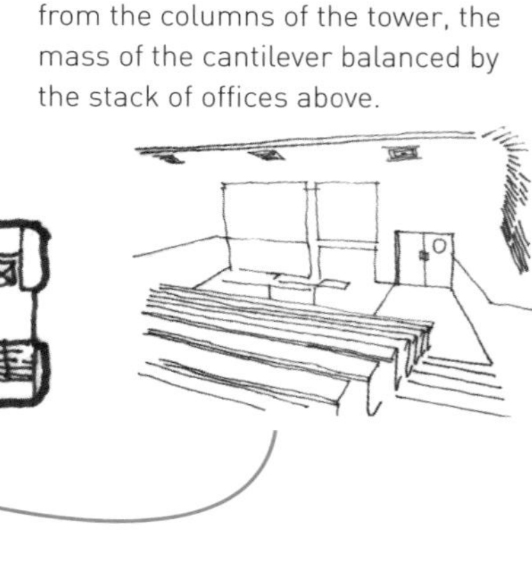

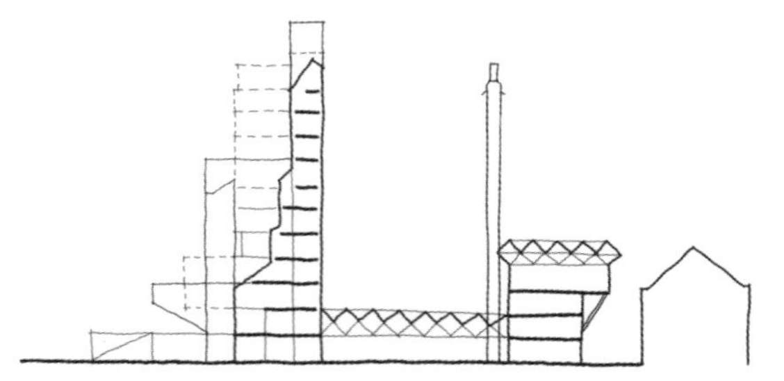

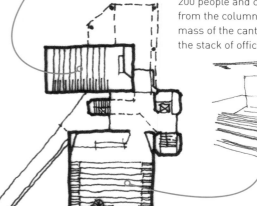

Form from construction

The laboratory tower has deep floors with an egg-crate diagonal structure between edge beams.

The office tower has shallower floors supported by a single star beam.

Instead of the saw-tooth roof traditionally used on factories with strips of north-facing vertical glazing joined by sloping monopitched roofs, this has sloping sides facing south and ends as a line of diamonds over a windowless brick-faced wall.

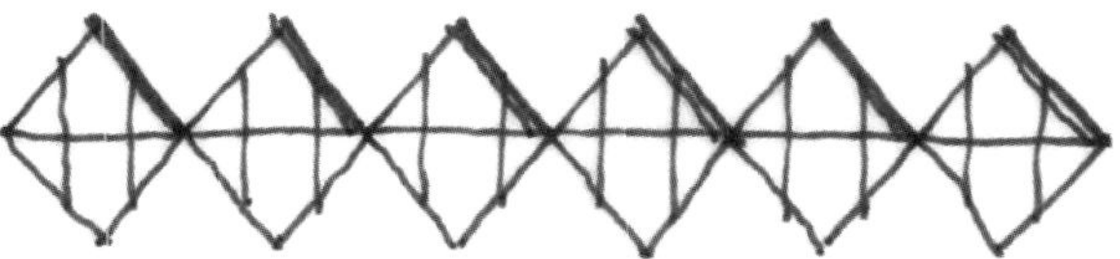

The north-facing glazing is in Plyglass, a fibreglass sheet sandwiched between two sheets of clear glass. On the south-facing side there is an additional aluminium layer in the sandwich to block and reflect light and sun.

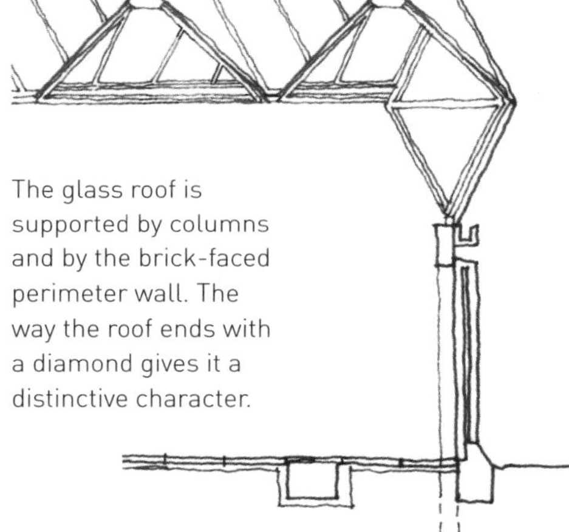

The glass roof is supported by columns and by the brick-faced perimeter wall. The way the roof ends with a diamond gives it a distinctive character.

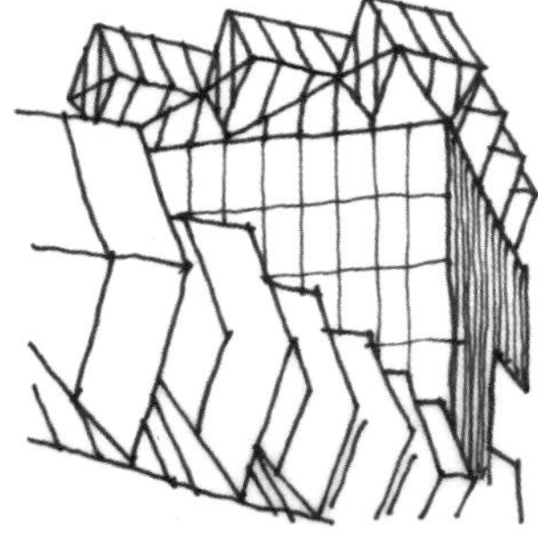

Where the glass roof meets a corner the transition between the grid of the roof and the grid of the walls is managed by triangular planes.

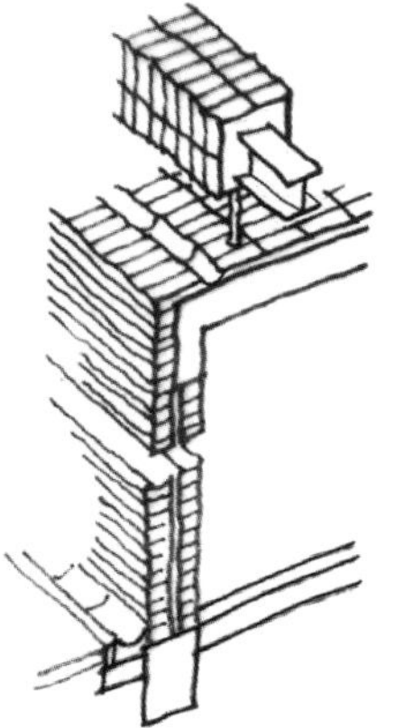

The podium has red clay brick walls and a concrete roof paved in red clay tiles, the consistency emphasizing its reading as a coherent object. A balustrade is similarly tiled, making a band that seems to float above the podium, supported only by thin steel tubes.

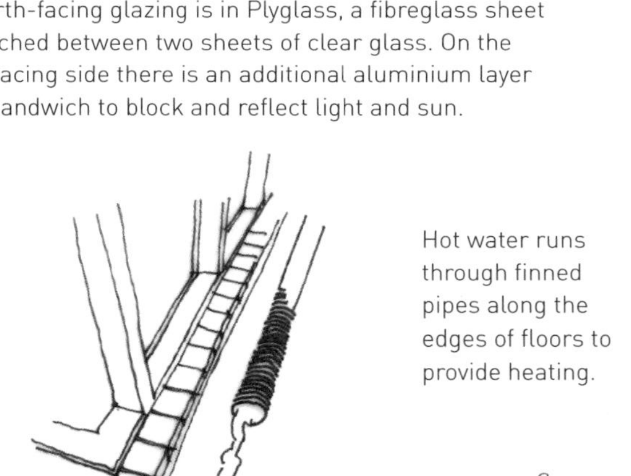

Hot water runs through finned pipes along the edges of floors to provide heating.

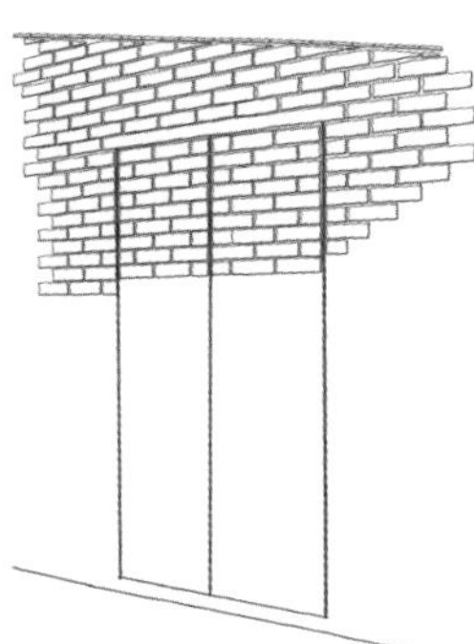

Under the side of the ramp a steel service door is clad in thin bricks to maintain the material consistency of the podium.

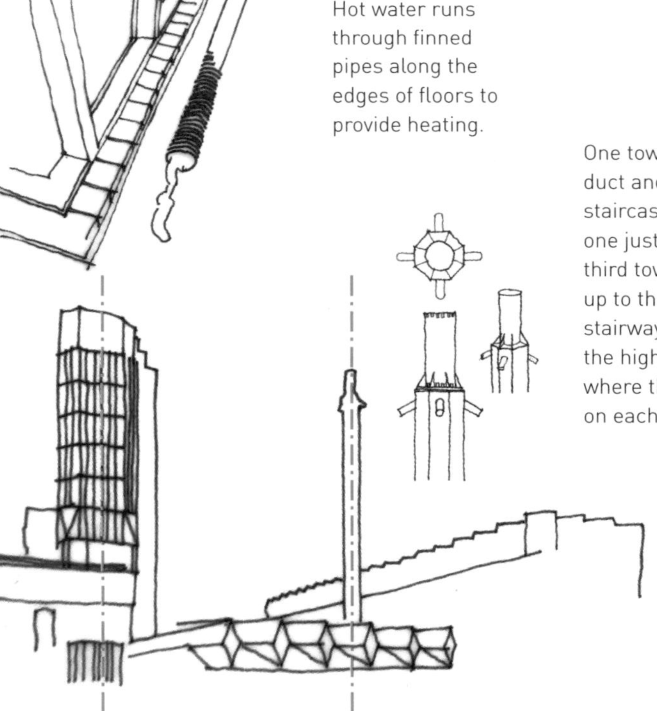

The chimney from the boiler is a slender echo of the main vertical elements at the front of the building. It is a sculptural object, with refined top and side vents to improve airflow.

One tower has a lift, duct and lavatory, one a staircase and ducts, and one just a staircase. This third tower extends only up to the top lab; one stairway was sufficient for the higher office floors, where there are few people on each floor.

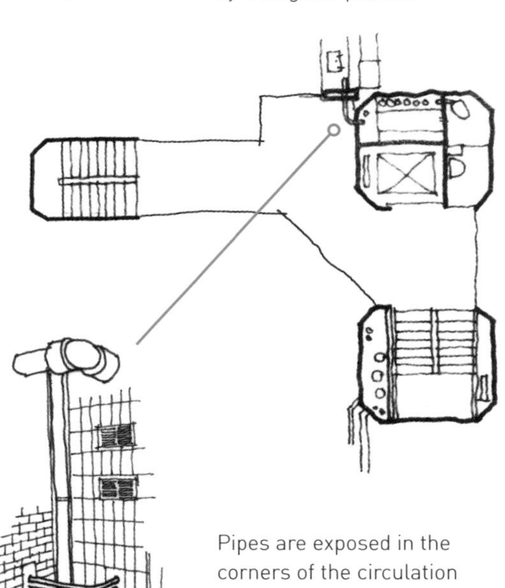

Pipes are exposed in the corners of the circulation spaces, where the pipes connect the laboratories with the vertical ducts in the towers.

Salk Institute for Biological Studies | 1959–66

Louis Khan

La Jolla, California, USA

06

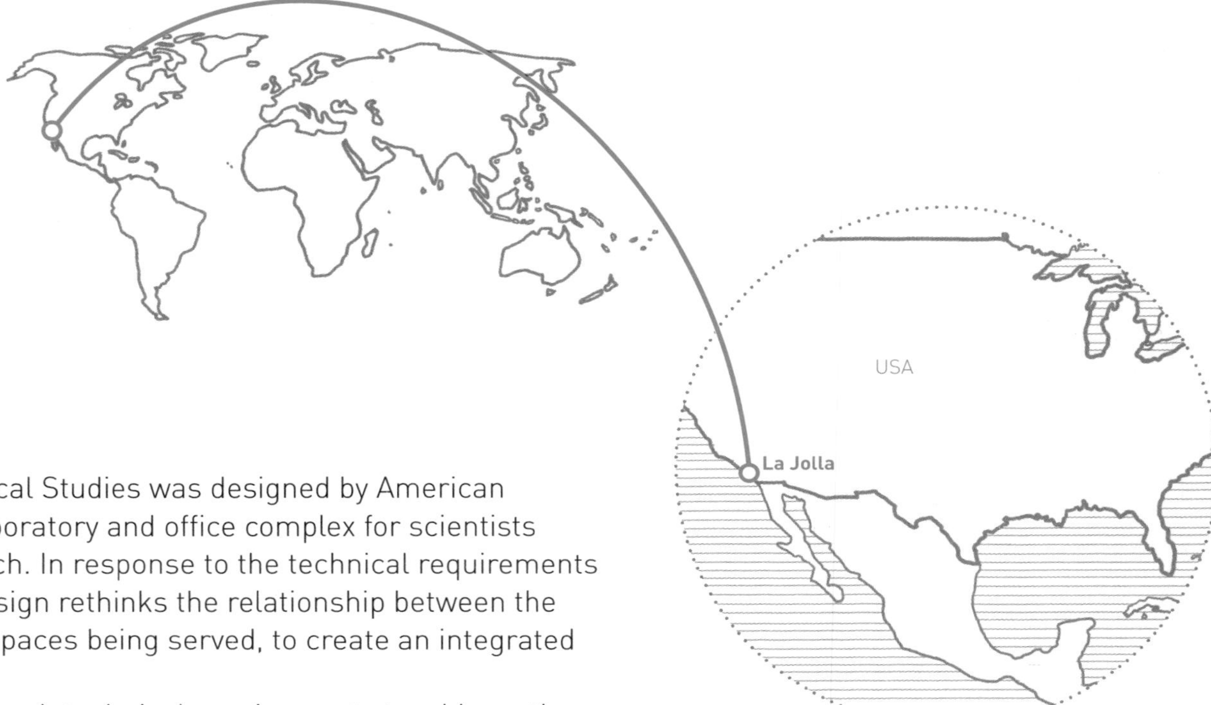

The Salk Institute for Biological Studies was designed by American architect Louis Kahn as a laboratory and office complex for scientists engaged in biological research. In response to the technical requirements of a laboratory facility the design rethinks the relationship between the services and the laboratory spaces being served, to create an integrated research environment.

The building goes beyond such technical requirements to address the Institute founder Jonas Salk's desire to create a complex that transcends the cultural gap between the sciences and the humanities. Its design is developed as a dialogue between the technical spaces of the scientific laboratory and the meditative – almost mystical – spaces of the central plaza, with the researchers' offices suspended in the middle offering a calm place for thinking. Through the interplay of monumental concrete forms in the strong California sun, a series of transition spaces helps to bind the empirical processes of the laboratories with the contemplative task of research thinking in the offices.

Amit Srivastava, Yifan Li, Stavros Zacharia and Lana Greer

06

Salk Institute for Biological Studies | 1959–66

Louis Khan
La Jolla, California, USA

Response to site

La Jolla is a hilly seaside neighbourhood just north of the city of San Diego. The site for the Salk Institute is on a cliff overlooking the Pacific Ocean to the west. Accordingly, the buildings proposed for the new complex were aligned to capture the best views to the west. While the laboratory facilities were sited close to the public access road to the east, the more private areas relating to the residential facilities and the social gathering halls – both unbuilt – were proposed for rocky outcrops right by the ocean's edge.

Sciences

Humanities

area of overlap – 'meeting'

One aim was to create a place that lies in the overlap between the sciences and the humanities.

The design for the Salk Institute was developed in discussion with the founder, Jonas Salk, who wanted the facilities to help to overcome the perceived divide between the 'two cultures' of the sciences and the humanities identified by the British scientist and novelist C. P. Snow. Kahn's approach sought to make these two realms respond to each other by focusing on the transition space in between, leading to a tripartite approach to planning.

views towards the Pacific Ocean over the cliff edge

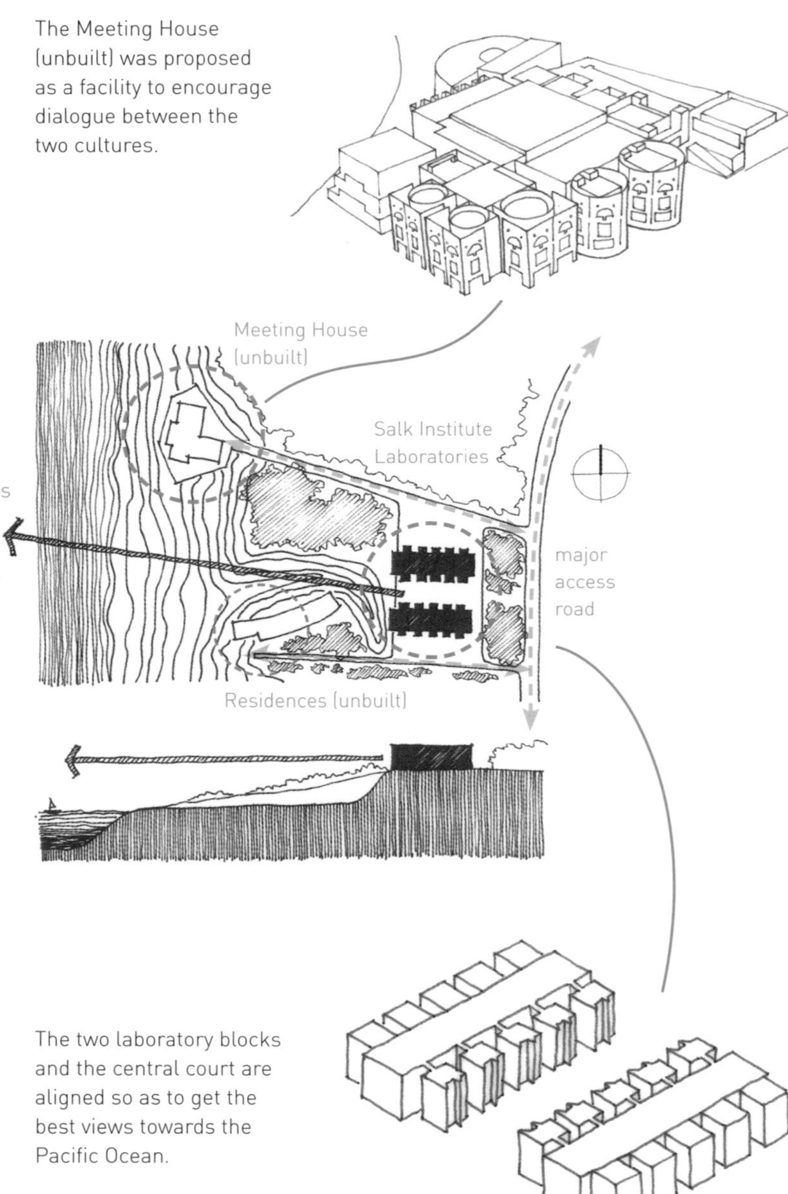

The Meeting House (unbuilt) was proposed as a facility to encourage dialogue between the two cultures.

The two laboratory blocks and the central court are aligned so as to get the best views towards the Pacific Ocean.

Response to formal archetypes

The Salk Institute is undoubtedly a piece of Modernist architecture, but the treatment of the built and open spaces integrates references to various formal archetypes that add richness to the experience.

In the treatment of the central court, the strong focus on axiality towards the Pacific Ocean is similar to that of a basilica. The repetitive office-block elements act as a set of colonnades defining the experience of this court as a 'nave' focusing on the divine light of the altar, recreated here by the setting sun.

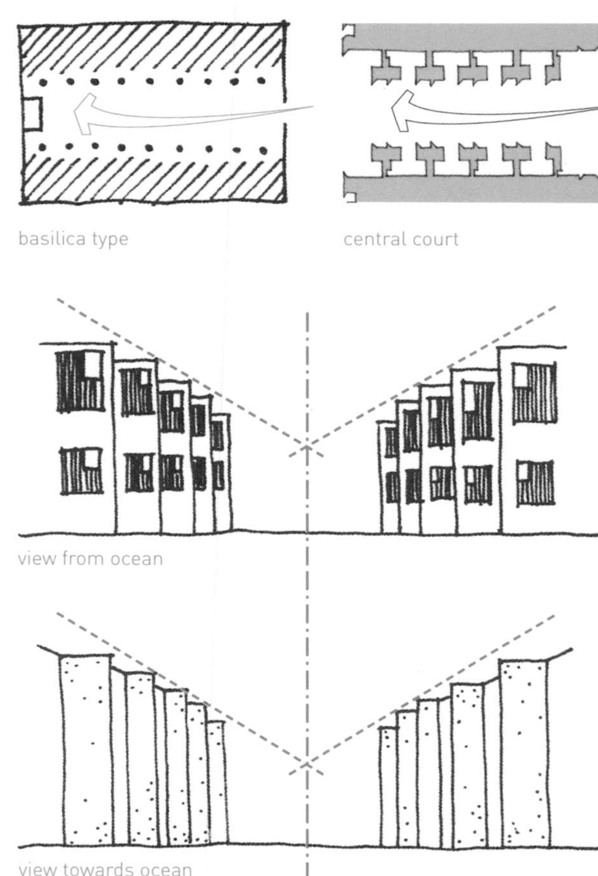

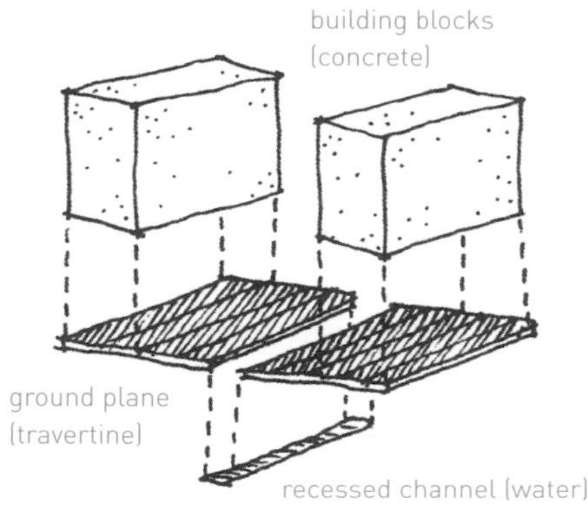

Symbolism and mystical experience

Although originally conceived as a tree-lined courtyard, which would provide respite from the hot summer sun, the central court was subsequently developed as a stone plaza. This hardscape plaza, which intensifies rather than counters the experience of the sun, turns this court into an empty centre, creating opportunities for silent meditation and mystical experiences.

A shallow channel runs along the middle of the court.

The central plaza is developed as a plane of travertine – called by Mexican architect Luis Barragán 'a façade to the sky'.

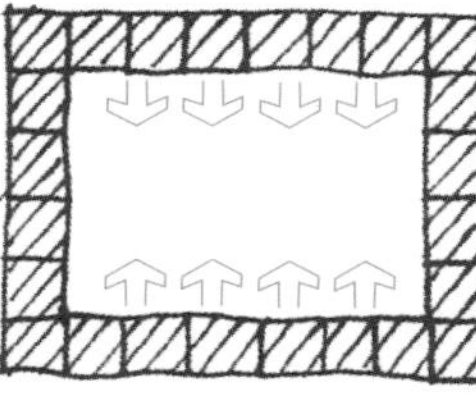

courtyard type

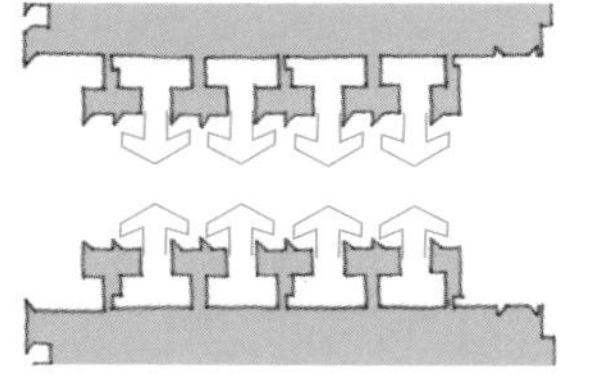

central court

If the central court is considered in relation to the vegetation on the east edge and the cliff face on the west, it can be seen as an enclosed and private sanctuary corresponding to the courtyard type. Here the office blocks suspended from the rest of the building recreate the experience of a monastic cell looking into this meditative central space.

The archetypal relationship between the two rectilinear building blocks and the horizontal datum of the central court is enhanced through the material treatment of these surfaces. The entire plaza is developed as a plane of travertine and is in contrast to the exposed concrete blocks, which seem to hover lightly over this expansive plane. The experience of the vertical blocks is countered by a recessed water channel that runs the length of the plaza parallel to the building blocks.

The channel ends at a trough and cascades through a 'cubic gargoyle' into a lower basin towards the Pacific Ocean.

The water for the channel originates from a small square basin at the east end of the plaza.

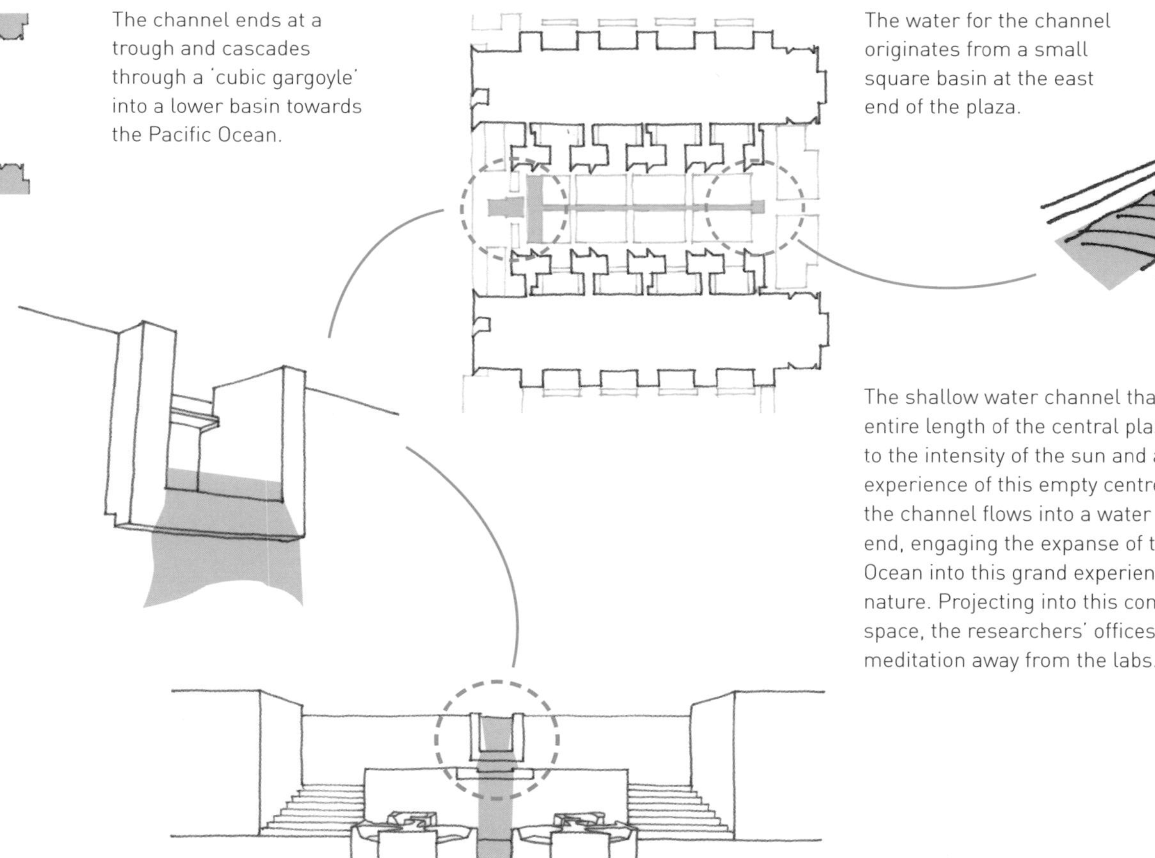

The shallow water channel that runs along the entire length of the central plaza stands in contrast to the intensity of the sun and adds to the mystical experience of this empty centre. The water from the channel flows into a water basin at its western end, engaging the expanse of the entire Pacific Ocean into this grand experience of connecting with nature. Projecting into this contemplative court space, the researchers' offices allow for silent meditation away from the labs.

Salk Institute for Biological Studies | 1959–66

Louis Khan
La Jolla, California, USA

Programme – processal realm

The programmatic requirements of a research institute are considered through two different types of physical environment, relating respectively to the laboratory processes of empirical research and the intellectual processes of conceptualization and theorization. The 'processal' realm is defined by the laboratory spaces and the service cores, which form the rear of the two building blocks.

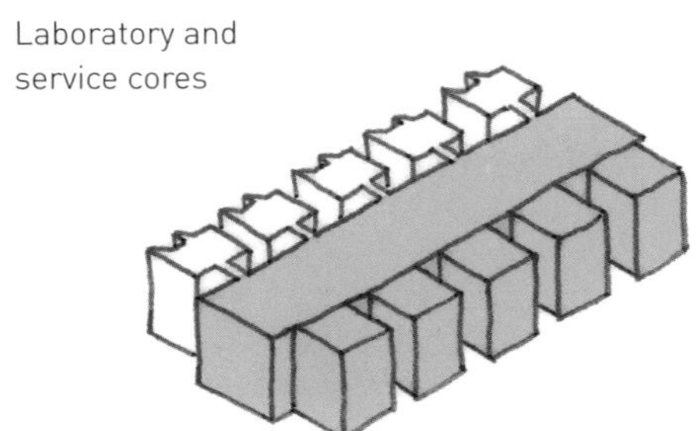

Laboratory and service cores

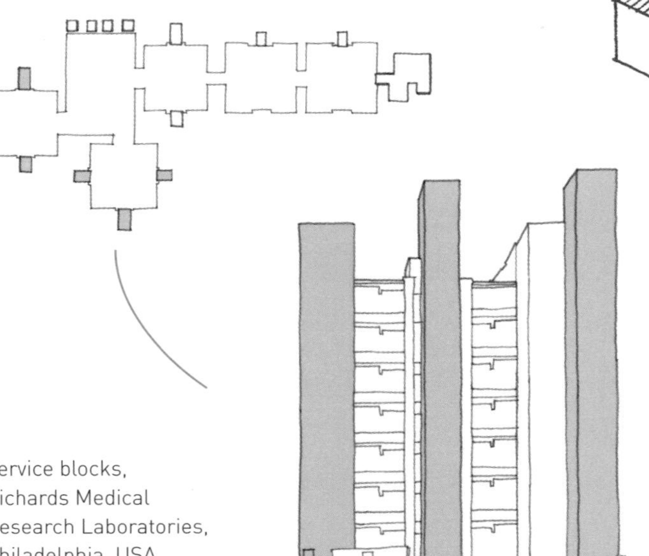

Service blocks, Richards Medical Research Laboratories, Philadelphia, USA (1957–62)

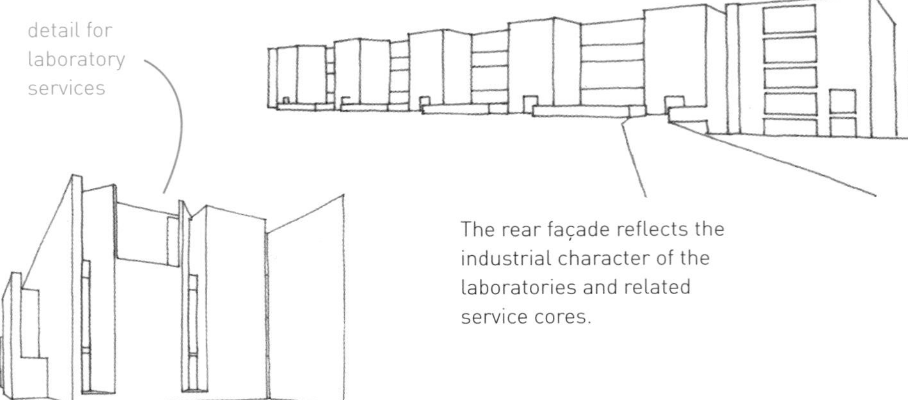

detail for laboratory services

The rear façade reflects the industrial character of the laboratories and related service cores.

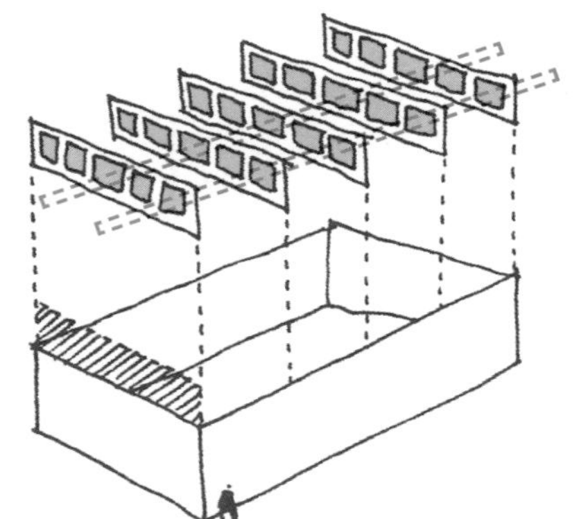

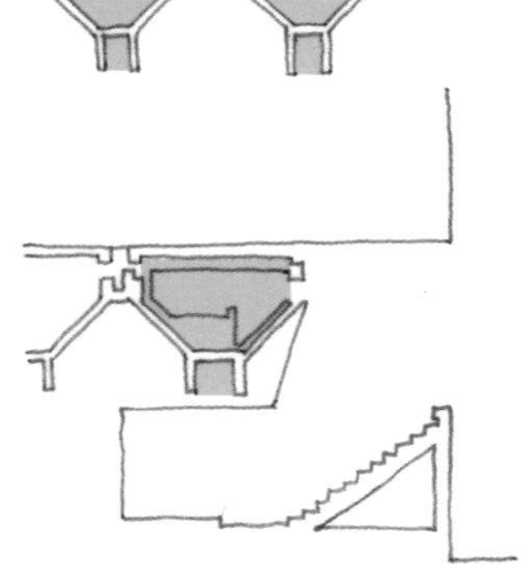

The laboratory spaces require access to numerous mechanical and electronic services and these often end up cluttering the actual work space. Kahn had already attempted a clear separation of the services from the served space in his project for the Richards Medical Research Laboratories, but at the Salk Institute this was further integrated into the section of the building.

The original proposal involved a structural system comprised of box-truss girders and folded plates that would enclose a human-height service core running the span of the building. As built, the structural system was changed to a Vierendeel truss, but it still allowed for an interstitial space that would house all the required services. Slots in the slab allow these services to be dropped to the work areas below as required.

Programme – intellectual realm

The other aspect of the research environment requires researchers to extract themselves from the immediacy of the empirical process and meditate on the process. This aspect is served by the office spaces facing the central court. These small study cells are separated from the laboratory spaces by a short corridor and float away from the building block into the silent and meditative realm of the central court.

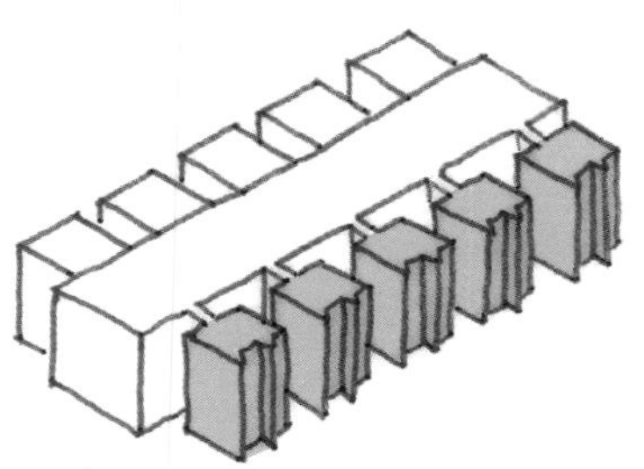

Study cells project out into the central court.

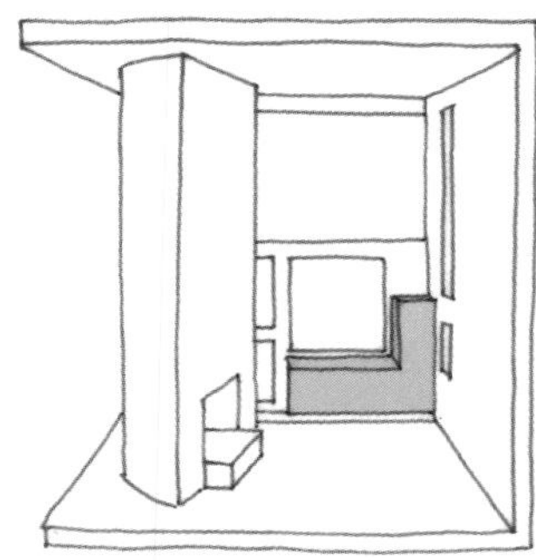

The cypress-clad window seat in Khan's Fisher House (1967) expresses the warmth and intimacy afforded by wood in the context of a private residence. These qualities are mobilized for the Salk Institute study cells.

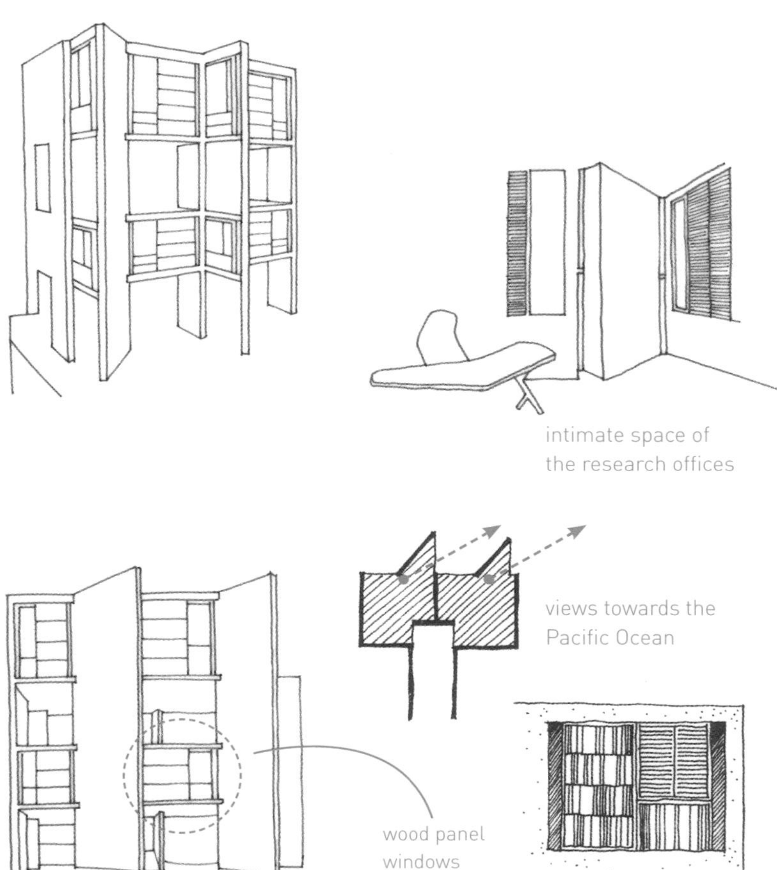

In order to create a space conducive to thinking, the study cells are treated as places of retreat where researchers can separate themselves from the immediacy of the laboratory environment and lose themselves in a different, larger reality.

The physical separation from the laboratory block not only reduces noise but also symbolically brings the researcher into the larger mystical realm of the central plaza. This connection is supported by each study cell's direct view of the plaza and the ocean, while the angled windows restrict views of other rooms. The treatment of these cells in wood contrasts with the exposed concrete of the rest of the building and helps to generate a warm and intimate environment appropriate for thinking.

Permeability of light and vision

The design for the unbuilt Meeting House engaged double-layered walls to allow a play of light and visual transparency.

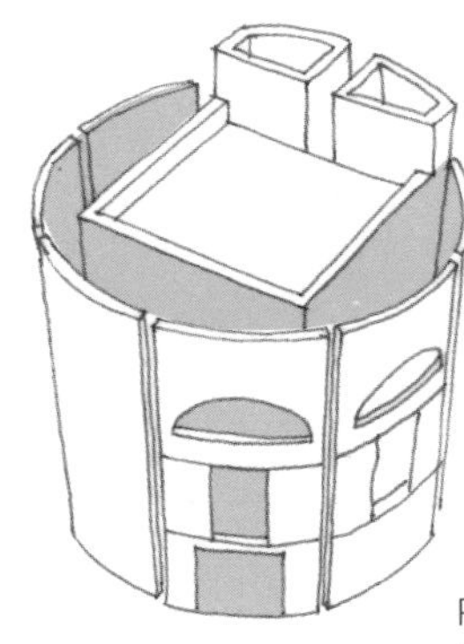

Part of the Meeting House (unbuilt)

While the vision for the Meeting House was never realized, the design for the laboratory block also reflects sensitivity to these issues. The corridor spaces that run along the inner face of the laboratory facilities are separated from the central court by the researchers' office blocks, but the alternating levels of the two blocks are arranged so as to provide a visual connection to the court. This layered encounter adds to the visual interest through the play of light and shadow.

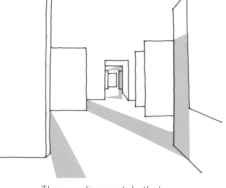

The receding portals that define the connecting bridges between the researchers' offices and the laboratory filter light in interesting patterns.

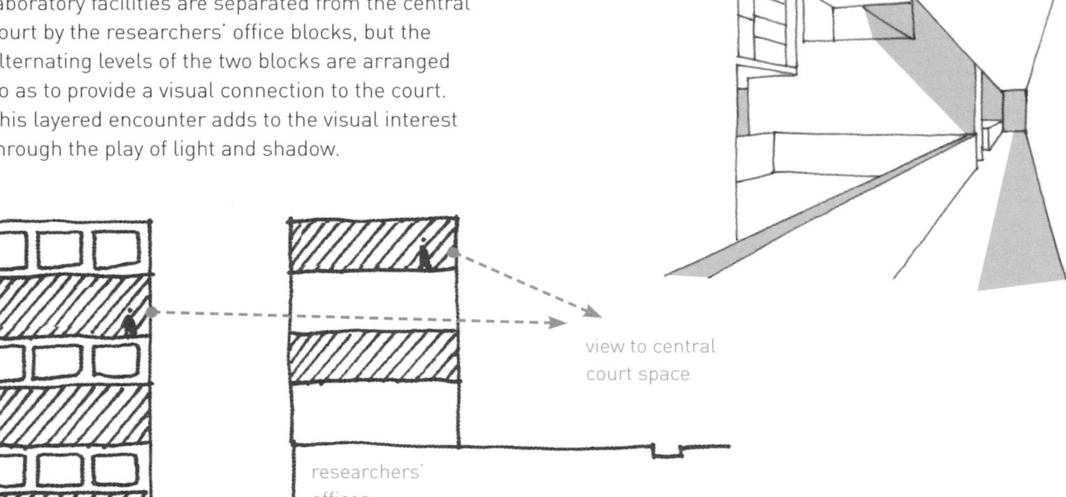

The alternating floors of the laboratory and office blocks help to frame views of the central court.

07 Louisiana Museum of Modern Art | 1956–58

Jørgen Bo and Wilhelm Wohlert

Humlebaek, Denmark

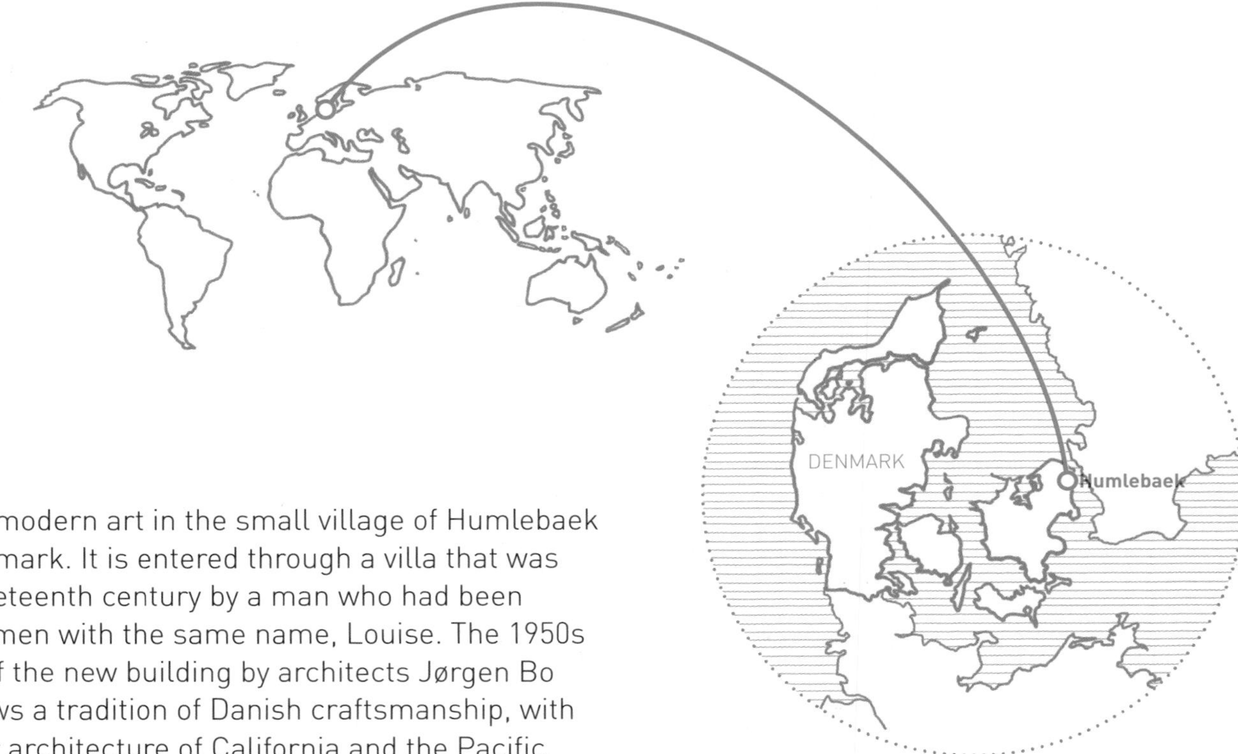

Louisiana is a museum of modern art in the small village of Humlebaek north of Copenhagen, Denmark. It is entered through a villa that was built and named in the nineteenth century by a man who had been married three times to women with the same name, Louise. The 1950s brick-and-timber design of the new building by architects Jørgen Bo and Wilhelm Wohlert follows a tradition of Danish craftsmanship, with influences from the timber architecture of California and the Pacific, particularly Japan.

Louisiana exemplifies responsive cohesion between building, art and landscape – and food, in its delightful café. Each part supports and benefits from the others. The building also demonstrates how straightforward construction, common materials and restraint can result in great architecture.

This analysis concentrates on the gallery as it first opened in 1958. Later extensions designed between 1966 and 1998 by the offices of Bo and/or Wohlert Arkitekter substantially increased its size.

Antony Radford, Charles Whittington and Megan Leen

Louisiana Museum of Modern Art | 1956–58
Jørgen Bo and Wilhelm Wohlert
Humlebaek, Denmark

Visitors can walk through the gallery or through the parklike gardens. Sculptures are positioned both inside and outside. A large Henry Moore sculpture sits on the skyline.

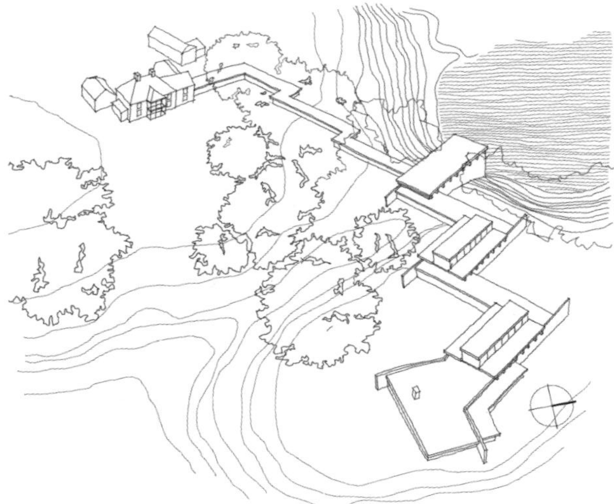

The ordered horizontality of the roof planes emphasizes the trees and lush vegetation of the park. The building skirts the edge of the site, offering a warm, protected path from which to view the gardens and outdoor sculptures. In winter, snow unifies the scene.

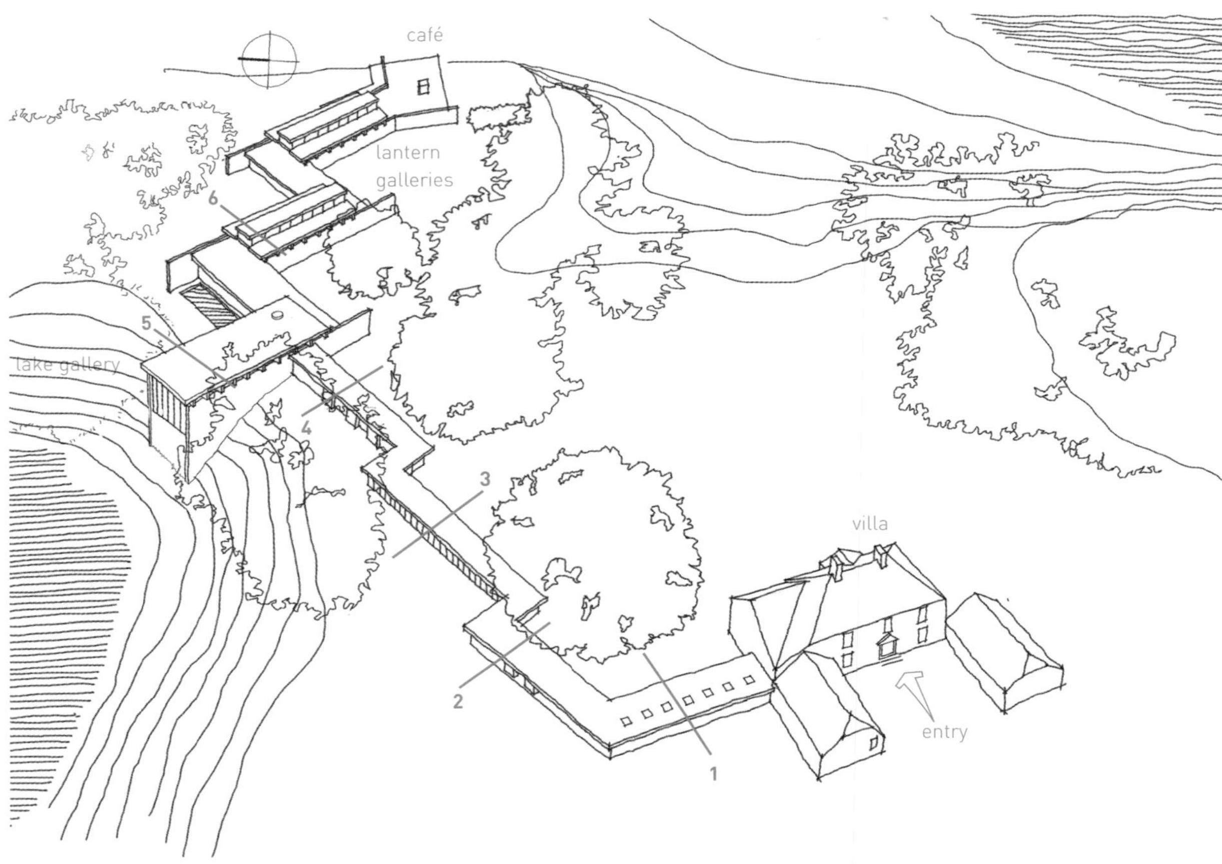

The museum's founder, Knud Jensen, wanted the entrance to remain through the house's front door, as if a visitor were coming to a private house. He also asked the architects for a room overlooking a lake about 200 metres (655 feet) north of the house, and a café on a bluff another 100 metres (330 feet) further on, looking over the sea towards Sweden.

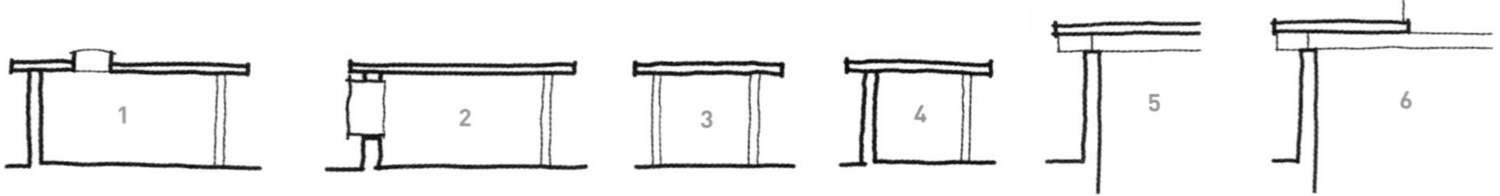

Cross sections show a range of views and daylighting.

The route

Only the original villa can be seen from the street. Visitors arrive through the old gate and move on to the front door, which is inviting and homely. They pass through the entrance hall and three other rooms in formal enfilade before turning and descending some steps to the new galleries, where they find a marked difference in style. The house has painted timber panels, cornices, pedimented doors and small-paned windows; it is a building of separate rooms with openings punched through enclosing walls. By contrast, the extension is a brick-and-timber building of continuous space channelled by intersecting planes of brick or glass.

The journey through the gallery is an unpredictable adventure following long and short axes through distinct spatial experiences. Near the house the corridor turns around an enormous beech tree with a close-up view of its massive trunk, as beautiful as the works of art. The first large gallery, on two levels, has a window wall framing a view of the lake. The second and third large galleries are enclosed top-lit spaces with narrow views at the corners. At the end is a domestic-scale open fireplace and a panoramic vista over the sea to the Swedish coast.

Paintings are seen at the side of the visitor's path on the white side-walls or ahead at the end of a view along a corridor. In the galleries they can be mounted on screens, with visitors weaving around them.

Sculptures are often positioned in front of glass so that they have a backdrop of landscape. Tree cover and roof overhangs reduce glare. Some sculptures are outside in the park, seen through windows or visible only from garden paths.

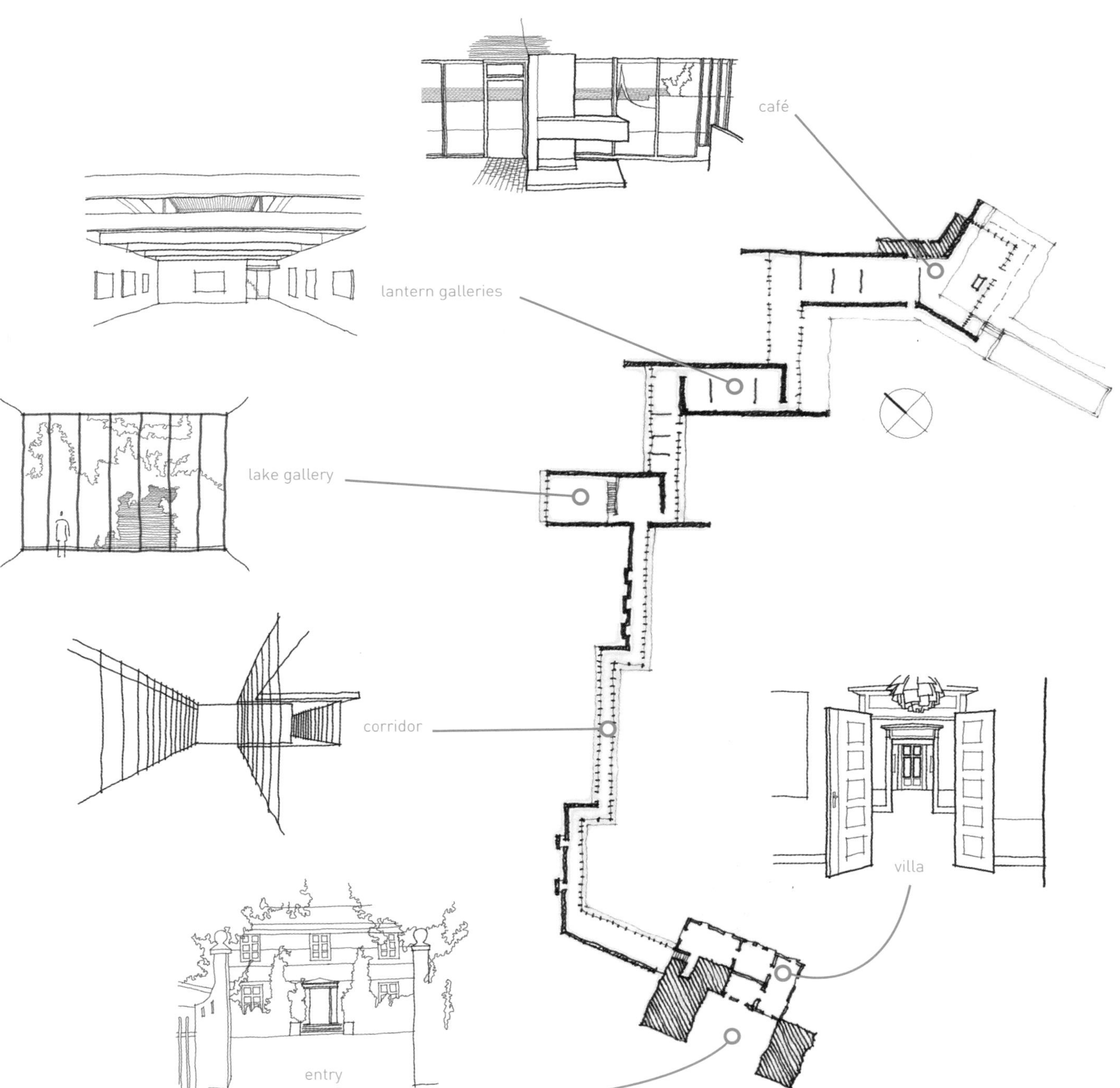

Louisiana Museum of Modern Art | 1956–58

Jørgen Bo and Wilhelm Wohlert

Humlebaek, Denmark

The corridor

The simplest structure is the corridor. A light timber frame sits on a concrete base. Double glazing fits directly into dark-stained laminated timber posts and a slot in the natural timber-boarded ceiling. The floor is of dark-red, brick-sized tiles. Outside, the projecting roof and ceiling and a strip of brick pavers matching the tiles seem to extend the corridor into the landscape. The roof is drained through downpipes that span from soffit to ground. White-painted, unplastered brick walls replace glass on one side of the corridor in some sections.

The lake gallery

The corridor leads to the balcony of a larger, more enclosed gallery, where a group of slender Giacometti figures is lit by a lone circular skylight. To the left, a timber screen and the tall mullions of the window modulate a framed view of the lake. Stairs behind this screen lead down to a lower double-height level. Behind the stairs is an intimate, low-ceilinged gallery.

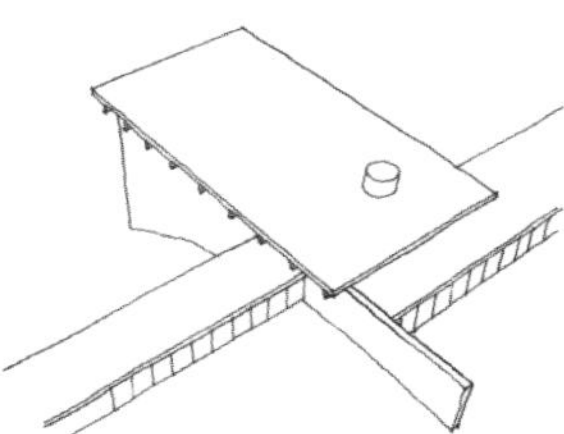

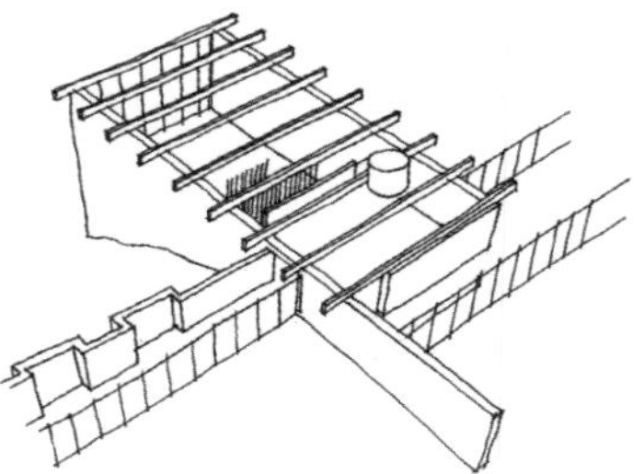

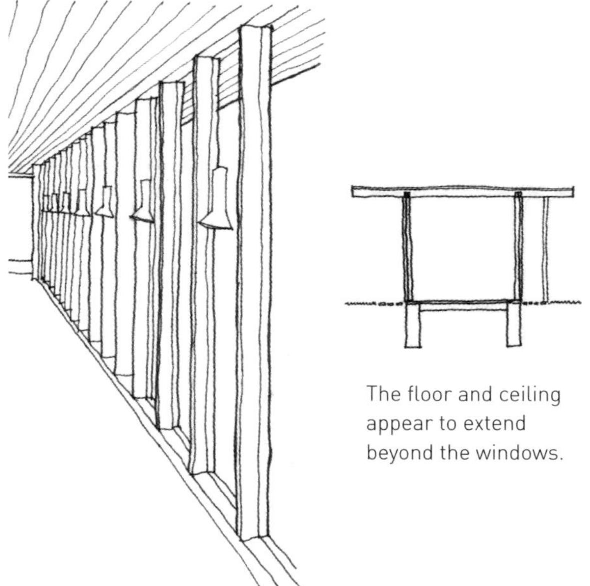

The floor and ceiling appear to extend beyond the windows.

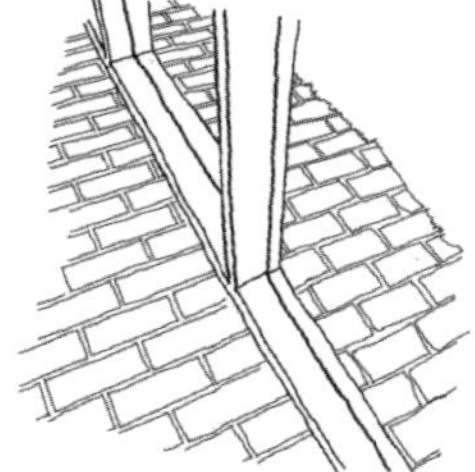

The tile joints inside are regular and consistent, the brick joints outside loose and merging into the grass.

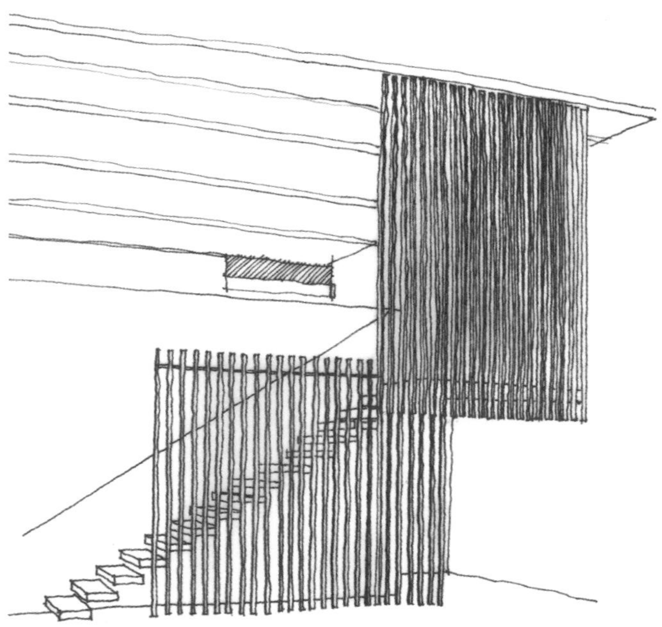

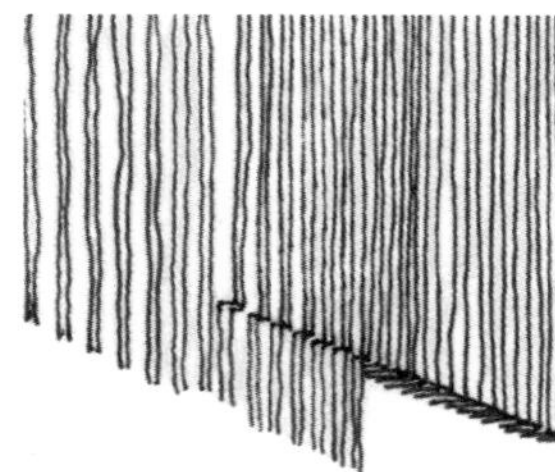

The upper slats project beyond the lower ones so they appear as two rectangles.

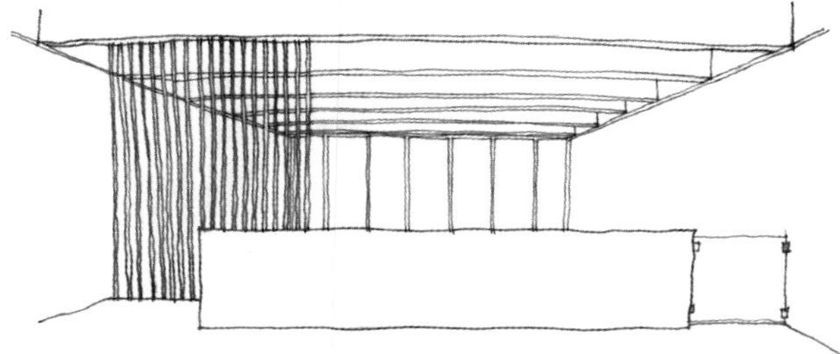

The view is modulated through the screen and the window mullions.

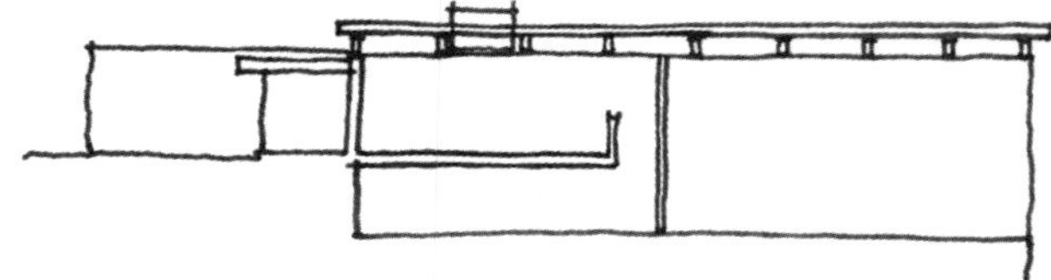

The upper double-height and the lower galleries each have very different spatial characters.

The lantern gallery
The next, wider, section of corridor leads to the first of two top-lit galleries. Laminated timber beams lie over the white brick walls with fixed glass between the beams. They project beyond the walls. Two more beams span over them. Where they cross, a slender laminated timber post rises to support the roof of a large lantern rooflight. The legibility of the structure is not compromised by window frames, skirtings or cornices. As in the corridors, the floors are brick-sized tiles and the ceilings are lined with timber boards.

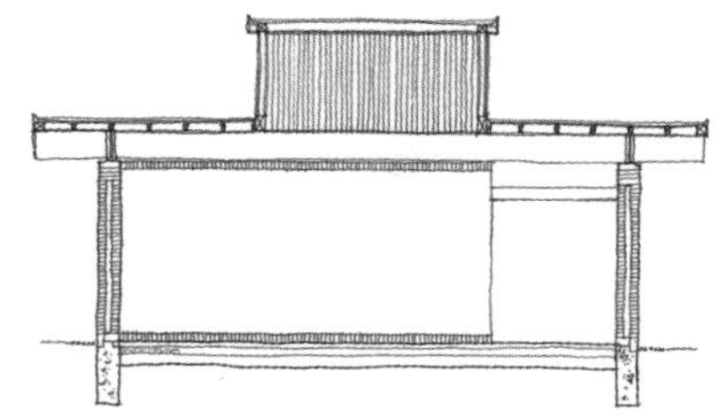

The café
After the culture is a reward: coffee and Danish pastry (*vienerbrød*), seated by an open fire, at the windows, or out on the terrace looking at the yachts and ships and over to the Swedish coast. The roof structure is hidden behind the timber ceiling. The height of the room is increased to suit the big space by lowering most of the floor down two steps, so that tables around the back walls look over the lower area to the view. The feeling evoked is reminiscent of a large but comfortable living room. Later alterations enlarged this space to meet demand – good design but inevitably losing the intimacy of the original.

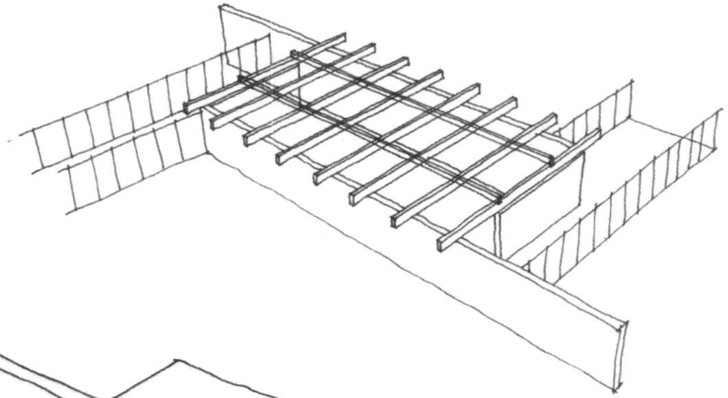

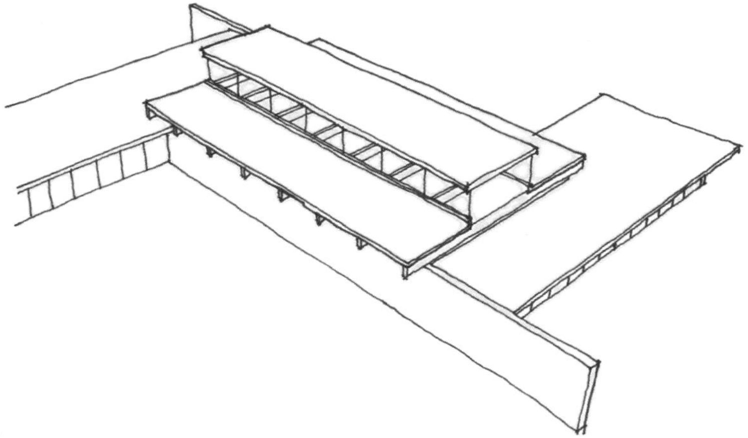

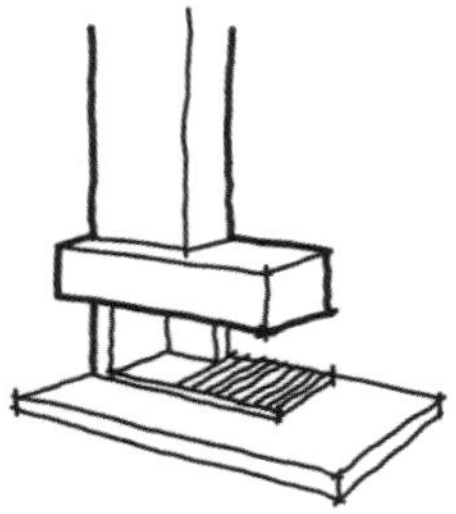

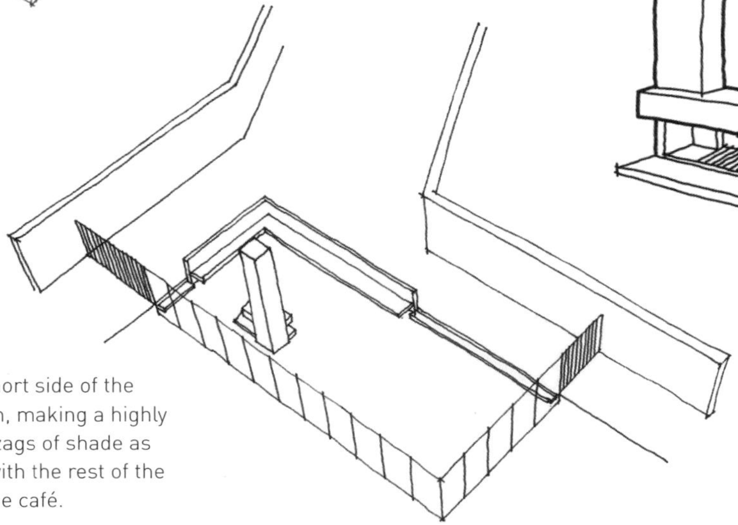

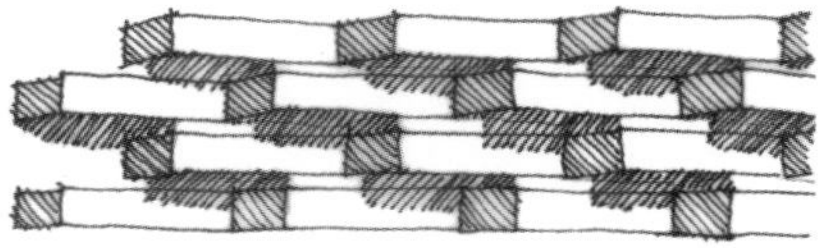

Bricks in the outer leaf of the wall on the short side of the café are laid in a staggered diagonal pattern, making a highly textured surface that displays changing zigzags of shade as the sun moves overhead. The bricks align with the rest of the plan before the crank of the junction with the café.

Louisiana Museum of Modern Art | 1956–58
Jørgen Bo and Wilhelm Wohlert
Humlebaek, Denmark

Extensions
Soon after opening, the museum was extended; further extensions were carried out until 1991.

1855
The original villa.

1958
The original villa with the gallery and café when the museum first opened.

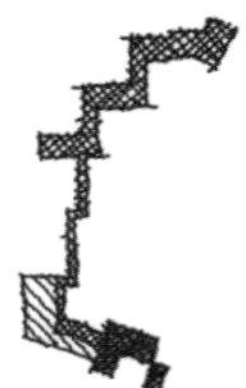

1966
A space for temporary exhibitions is added near the house. The palette of materials and the style are the same as for in the original gallery.

1971
The 1966 extension is enlarged, with more gallery space and a small basement cinema.

1976
A hall for music and talks is added at the far end, next to the café, with stepped seating for 400 people. The style is similar to that of the original gallery but adapted for the new kind of space. Instead of laminated timber beams, timber trusses with steel tie rods span in both directions to carry the roof.

1 Brick-and-timber style maintained in 1971 gallery and 1976 hall

2 Stepped seating in the new performance hall in 1976

3

Eye-level close to ground level in 1982 link – a different view of the world

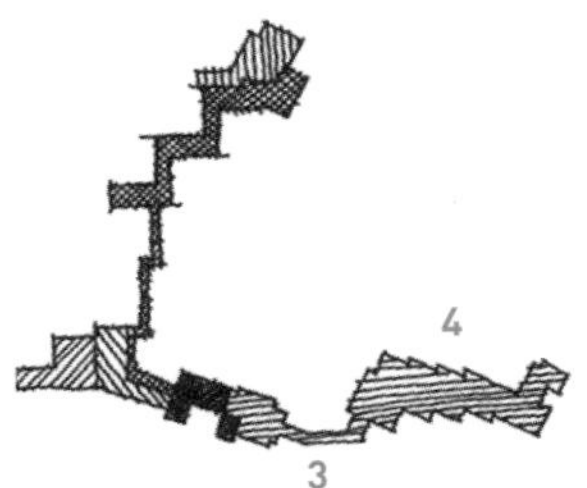

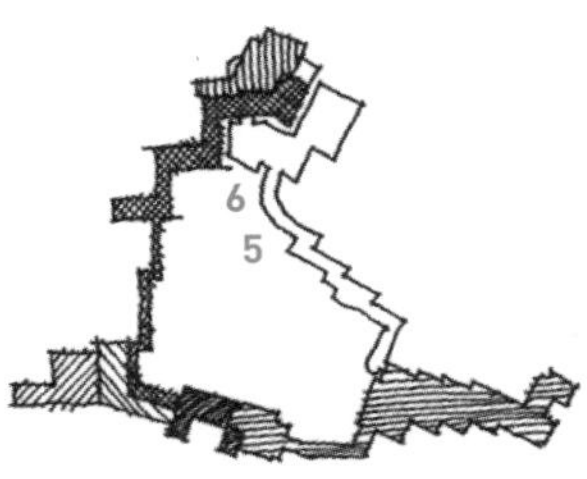

1982

A new ticket counter and shop are attached to the old house, and a new wing of galleries added. The museum is no longer a single route ending in the café. Instead, the 'head' of the house has two 'arms' embracing the garden. The style of the second arm is different to that of the first: a floor of grey marble with white-painted unplastered walls that are smoother than in the original gallery, and white ceilings. The major spaces are less connected to the outside than the original galleries are, and are lit from above through a ceiling of translucent glass-fibre cloth. The new wing ends in a small gazebo.

1991

Underground galleries link the ends of the arms and complete the circle. They have no daylight, allowing controlled low lighting for the display of drawings, textiles and other light-sensitive objects. A steel-and-glass gazebo-like pavilion covers stairs leading up from these underground spaces. Instead of the destination at the end of a visit to a small museum, the café becomes a mid-way stop in a tour of a much larger museum. The potential for exhibitions is enhanced, but the visitor experience is not quite as special and delightful.

4 Top-lit 1982 galleries

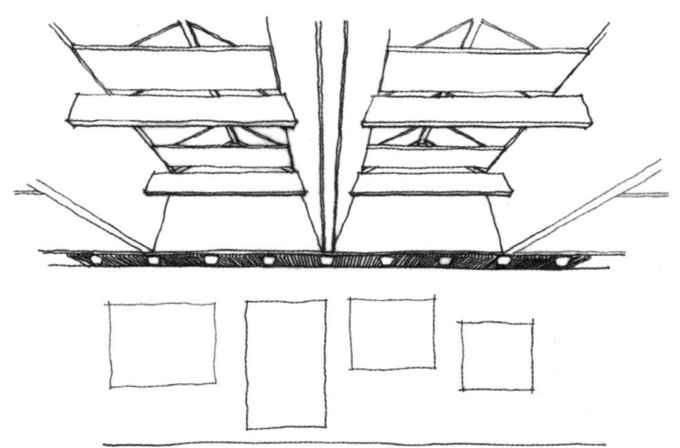

5 White-painted concrete in 1991 underground link

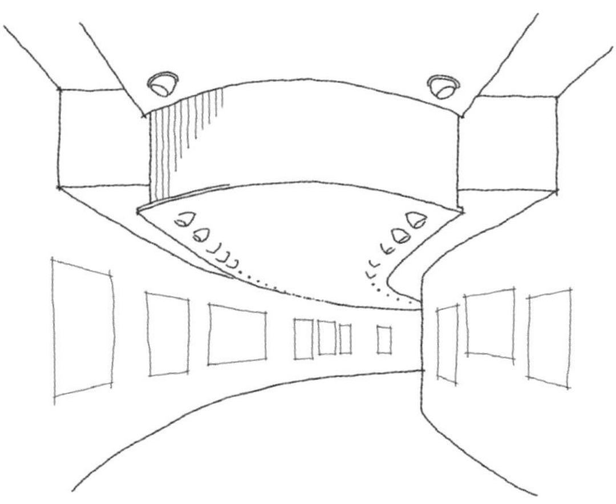

6 Glass vaults in 1991 gazebo

Yoyogi National Gymnasium | 1961–64

Kenzo Tange

Tokyo, Japan

08

The Yoyogi National Gymnasium was developed for the 1964 Tokyo Olympic Games, and contains swimming and diving pools in one building and a smaller sports arena in another building. Olympic Games bring with them international attention and are often treated by cities and nation states as an opportunity to proclaim their modern national identity. This had particular relevance for post-war Japan.

Kenzo Tange's project weds formal qualities of traditional Japanese architecture with innovative modern structural systems. The design extends the connection with the past by aligning itself with the Meiji Shrine, the Shinto shrine dedicated to Emperor Meiji, who oversaw the industrialization and modernization of Japan that led the country into the twentieth century.

Peiman Mirzaei, Chun Yin Lau and Amit Srivastava

08

08 Yoyogi National Gymnasium | 1961–64

Kenzo Tange

Tokyo, Japan

Response to urban context

As large-scale public infrastructure, the gymnasium opens up to its urban context. The sweeping plans of the two buildings that make up the gymnasium deny the distinction between front or back sides, and their alignment within the complex creates opportunities for developing a civic space around them. Accordingly, the complex can be approached from any direction and offers several entrances.

The alignment with the axis of the Meiji Shrine not only offered a symbolic link with the past but also provided a framework for potential future developments of Tokyo city.

Response to traditional vocabulary

Although the gymnasium uses a flexible suspended roof system, it chooses to express it like the solid grand roofs of traditional Japanese buildings such as the nearby Meiji Shrine and other Shinto shrines.

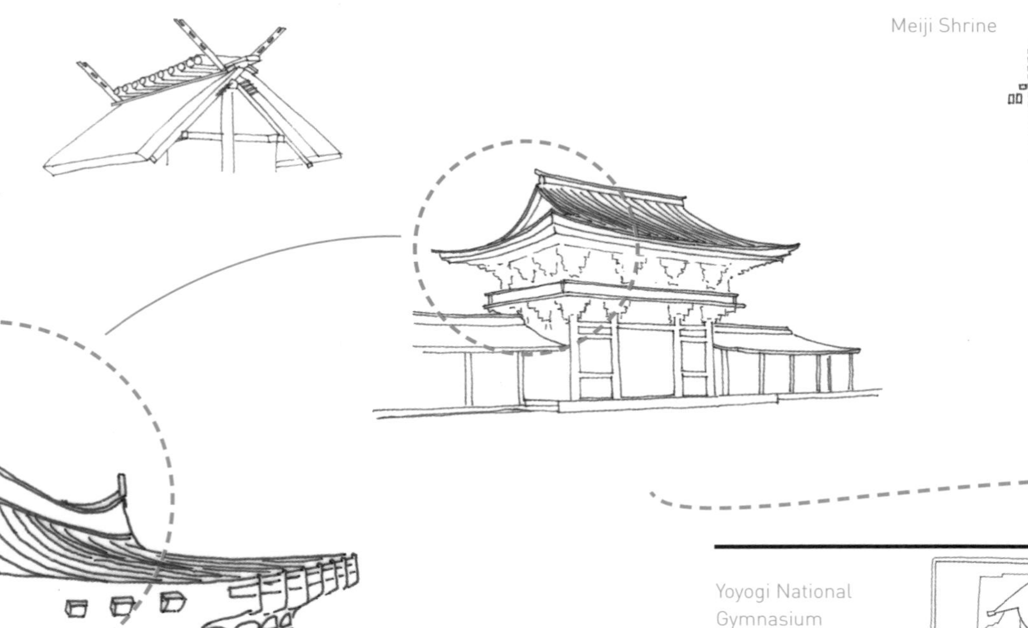

Meiji Shrine

axis

transport

transport

Yoyogi Park (open green)

residential neighbourhood

transport

The two buildings have multiple equally important entry points.

The gymnasium aligns with the axis of the Meiji Shrine, generating a framework for a potential future urban development of Tokyo.

New transport networks including trains and monorail were introduced to showcase modern infrastructure.

Response to technological developments

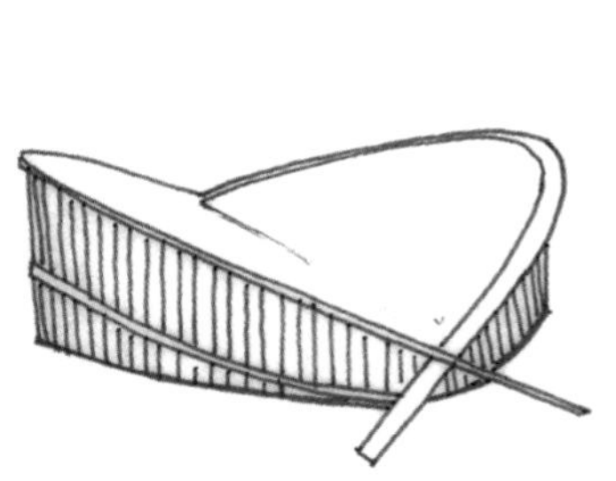

Dorton Arena, Raleigh, North Carolina, USA, by Matthew Niwicki (1953)

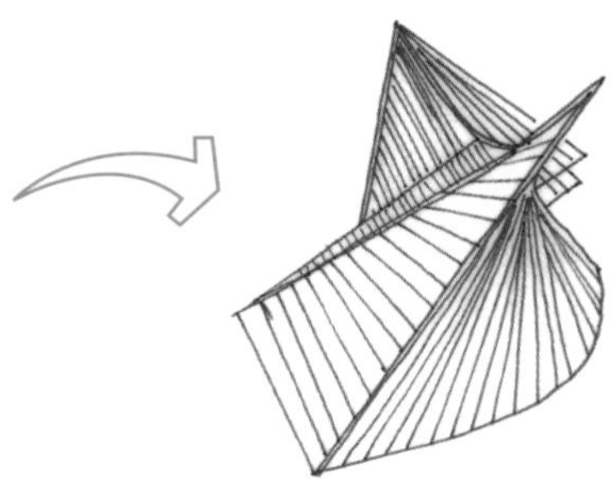

Philips Pavilion, Brussels, Belgium, by Le Corbusier (1958)

Yale Hockey Rink, New Haven, Connecticut, USA, by Eero Saarinen (1958)

Yoyogi National Gymnasium, Tokyo, by Kenzo Tange (1964)

Kenzo Tange, along with other Japanese architects of the time, chose to revise the vocabulary of traditional Japanese building with an eye on innovative, path-breaking technologies. The Yoyogi National Gymnasium uses a structural system that was first employed only a decade earlier and develops it to generate the largest suspended roof of its time. The larger structure consists of two 4-metre (13-foot) steel cables suspended from two concrete supports, forming a catenary that allows the rest of the roof to be suspended from it, while the smaller structure is conceived as a shell-like spiral in which one end of all the hanging beams is supported from a single column in an unwinding fashion.

wide curves

repetitive elements

mesh surfaces

The formal composition is very much a product of its time and engages materials and techniques that defined mid-century experiments in form and structure, such as hyperbolic paraboloid forms and repetitive structural elements.

The larger structure has two 4m (13ft) cables suspended between two concrete supports.

The smaller structure has a spiral of radiating beams.

The curved roof profile showcased technological advances in construction and provided appropriate solutions to problems of wind resistance and snow build-up. Wind can reach hurricane speeds in this area, and the aerodynamic form allows it to safely flow over the structure. The curvature of the roof prevents the build-up of snow across the large roof span and provides for a simple solution for the disposal of rain and snow.

The structural system thus responds to global aspirations and to an understanding of local conditions and building needs.

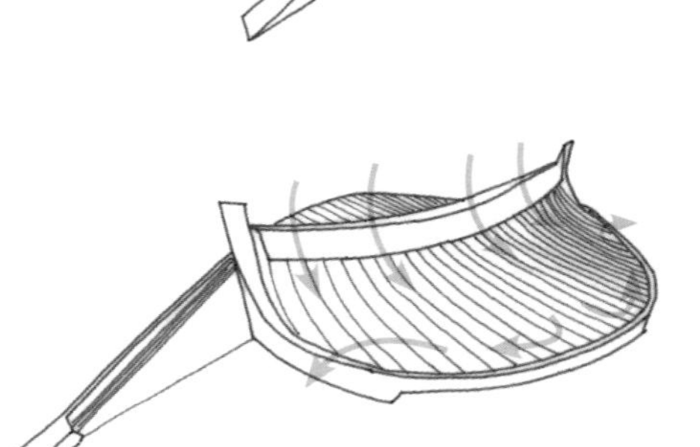

08 Yoyogi National Gymnasium | 1961–64

Kenzo Tange

Tokyo, Japan

Response to programme

Through a simple manipulation of basic geometric forms and a responsive interplay between the two structures, the design is an original response to the programmatic needs for an Olympic arena. The simple circular geometry allows spectator seating to be organized on all sides of the sporting arena, thereby providing everyone in a large audience with an unrestricted view of the event. A simple shifting of the geometry creates opportunities for large entrances and exits in order to allow smooth movement for large crowds.

The large opposing entry and exit allow for easy flow of visitors.

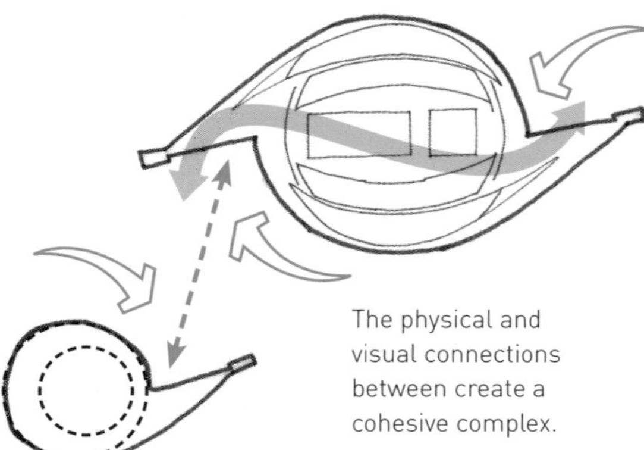

The physical and visual connections between create a cohesive complex.

The shifted geometries of the two buildings respond to each other and create an interactive plaza-like space between them. The physical and visual connections allow spectators to move easily between the venues, and make the entire complex come together as a cohesive whole. Within the buildings themselves, the slightly different shape and size allow for accommodation of different sporting events based on their relationship to the audience. While the large structure allows for views along a rectilinear pool for a swimming event, the smaller structure accommodates sports that can be viewed from all directions, such as boxing.

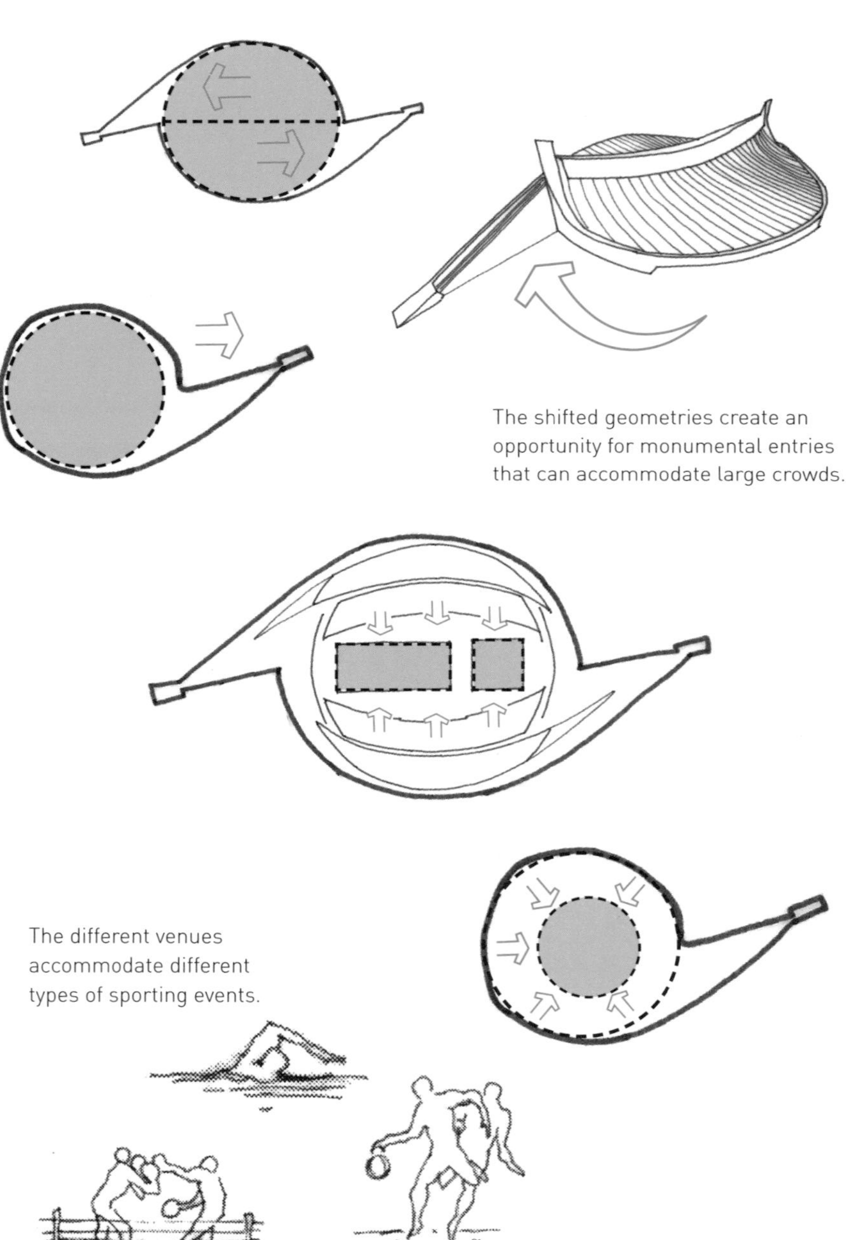

The shifted geometries create an opportunity for monumental entries that can accommodate large crowds.

The different venues accommodate different types of sporting events.

Response to materiality and structure

The combination of two construction systems allows the structure to respond to the two separate programmatic needs of amphitheatre seating and large uninterrupted roofing. The concrete base structure uses a compressive system to allow for multi-tiered seating supported from the ground, while the suspended cable roofing uses a tensile system to generate an umbrella-like covering held from above.

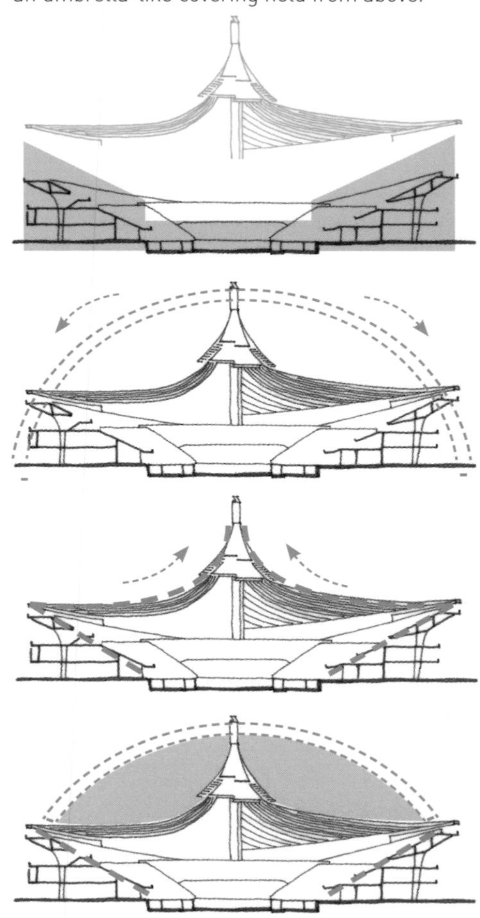

The suspended cable roofing also reduces the overall volume and the associated costs of heating and cooling.

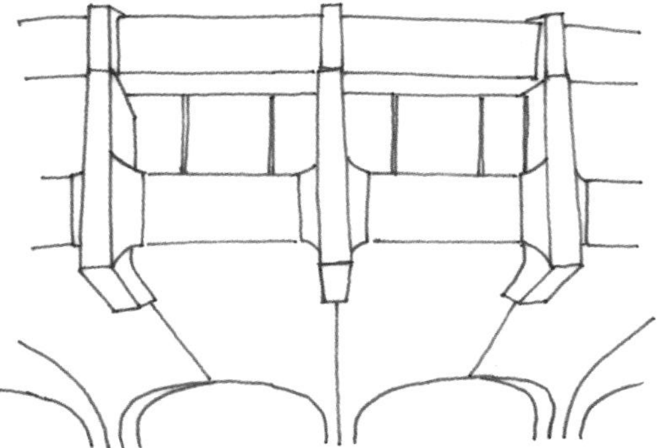

Even where the structure uses raw concrete, this is cantilevered over a series of arched entrances to highlight the lightness of the overall form.

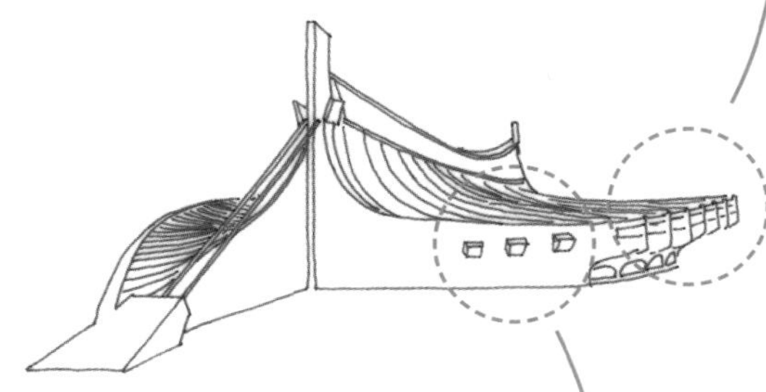

Fenestrations are articulated as separate metal forms that sit in contrast with the concrete base.

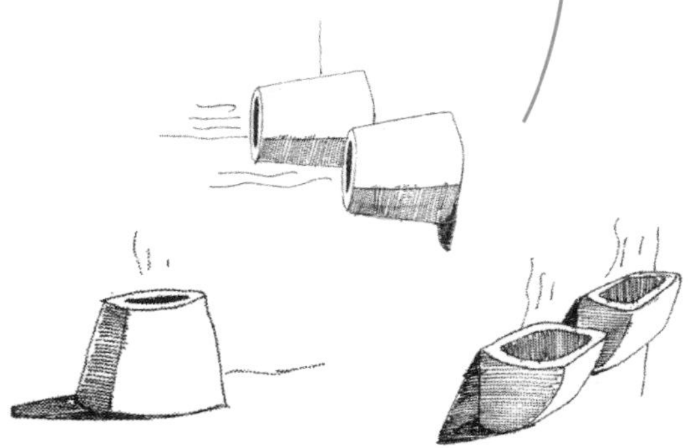

Response to user experience

In addition to welcoming and accommodating large crowds, as required for an Olympic Games event, the structure also creates a remarkable and memorable experience for the users through its engagement with lighting and composition. The structures of both buildings use the points of suspension of the roofs to provide for skylights that allow diffused light to wash over the interior spaces. This further reinforces the relationship between the structures and binds the compositions into a cohesive whole.

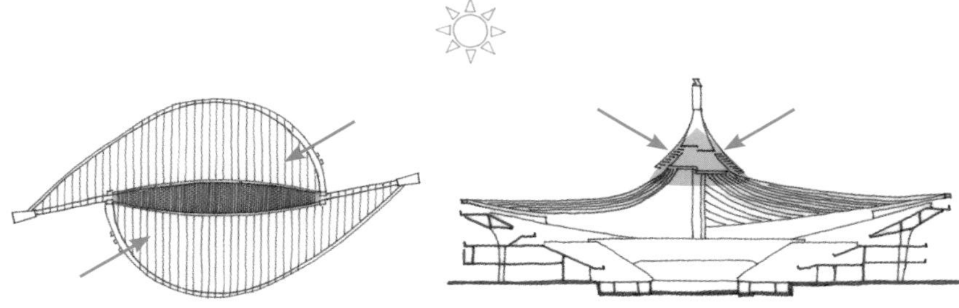

In the larger building the skylight runs along the entire length of the central arena and brings the focus back to the centre of activity within the swimming pools. The centralized light source further allows for artificial lighting to be incorporated in a way that has a similar effect at night. The curved roof structure enables the diffused light to travel along the entire width of the structure and reinforces awareness of its monumental span.

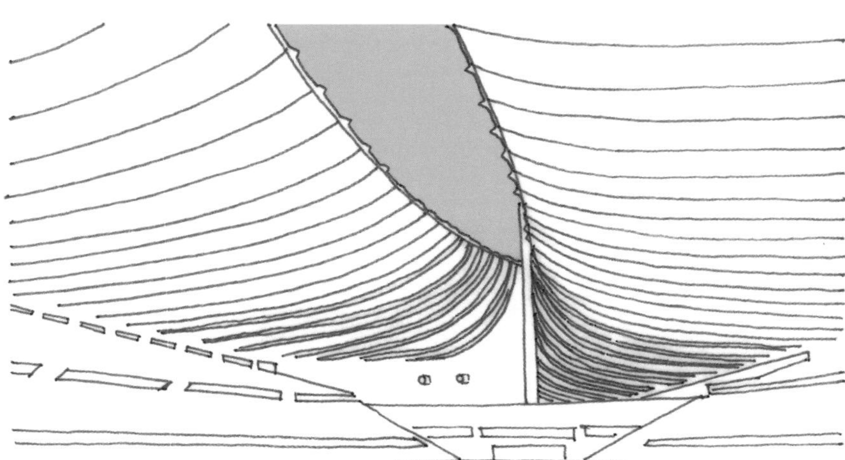

The curved roof and the central skylight draw the eye to the monumental span.

The skylight for the smaller structure wraps around the central support column.

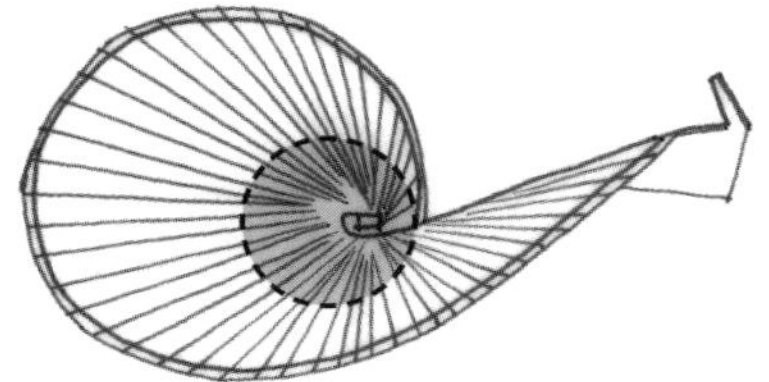

The combination of the central skylight and radiating structural members works to enhance the monumentality of the interior. The radiating cables rising to a central mast literally and symbolically hold the audience, bringing them together in the experience of the event. This idea of a shared experience is an integral part of the Olympic Games, which is an event of global peace and harmony.

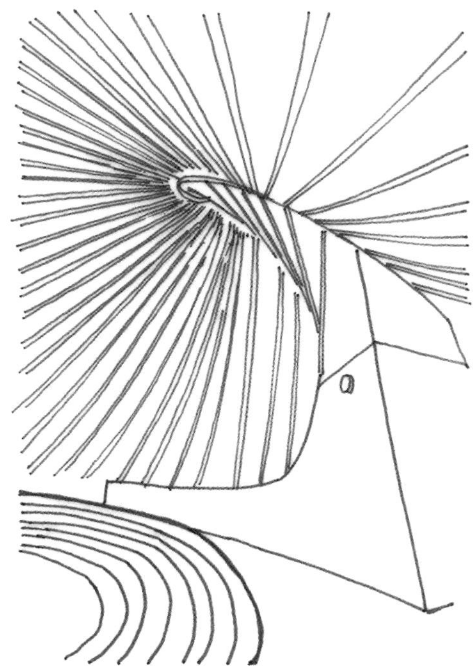

Cables radiate from the centre.

09

Seinäjoki Town Hall | 1958–65

Alvar Aalto

Seinäjoki, Ostrobothnia, Finland

Seinäjoki, a town on the Seinäjoki River about 350 kilometres (220 miles) north-west of Helsinki in Finland, is the site of the major completed example of a civic group designed by Alvar Aalto. Aalto was commissioned to design the building in 1958 and it was built between 1963 and 1965. An annex in the same style was added to the office wing in 1973–74. The remainder of the civic centre includes a library, a theatre, an administration building and a church with a tall bell tower.

The town hall is in Aalto's humanist-rationalist style, in which he links the rationalism of twentieth-century Modernism with his sensitivity to human scale and interpretation. The building is dignified but not oppressive.

Antony Radford, Nigel Reichenbach, Tarkko Oksala and Susan McDougall

09

09

Seinäjoki Town Hall | 1958–65

Alvar Aalto

Seinäjoki, Ostrobothnia, Finland

A 'head and tail' building

The building is organized with a 'head' formed by the council chamber and a 'tail' formed by offices. The head is sculptural and clad in blue ceramic tiles that sparkle in the sun, a landmark in the townscape. The council chamber is raised one floor above the street on pilotis, creating a loggia underneath. The tail is straightforward, with a central corridor, and wraps around an artificial hill on the sunny south side of the building.

The hill was created using soil from the excavations. The building nestles close to this hill, and grass steps lead up to the council chamber, where there is a formal entrance. The hill slopes steeply down to the edge of the office wing, leaving a slot to one side so that ground-floor windows look out on to a planted bank.

Timelessness and ruins

The council chamber can be seen as a carved block, like a large sparkling gem sitting on a rectangular plinth. Aalto's buildings often give an impression of having parts removed. The result is a sense of incompleteness (the missing parts are yet to be added) or ruination (the missing parts have fallen away).

Ceramic tiles do not show signs of age, and white-painted cement render is easily recoated to look new. These elements contrast with other materials such as the copper roof and timber window grilles that – like humans – do change with time.

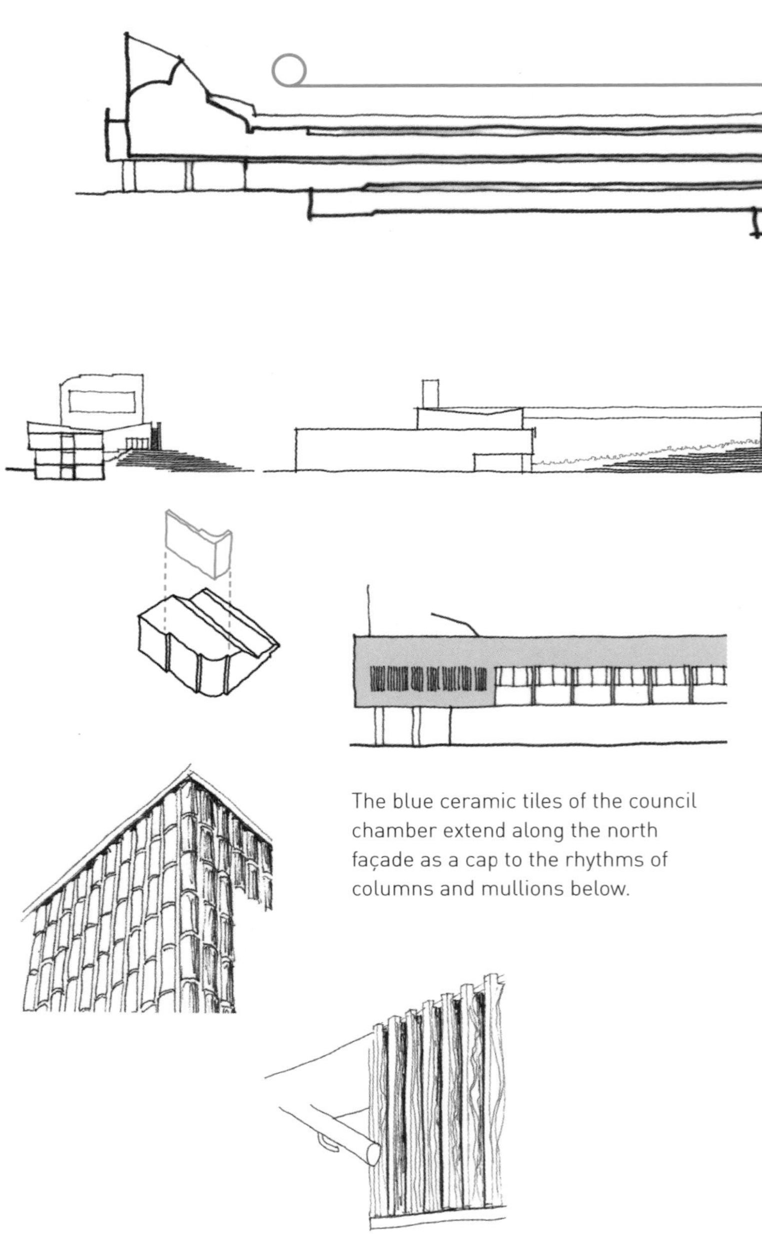

The blue ceramic tiles of the council chamber extend along the north façade as a cap to the rhythms of columns and mullions below.

Reference and action

In plan, the straight edges along the east, north and west sides of the building contrast with the hill and articulation on the south side. In elevation, the rectangular mass of the office block and its extension as the plinth of the council chamber provide a reference for the wedge-shaped block above. Aalto's buildings often have ordered parts that provide a reference for more expressive parts.

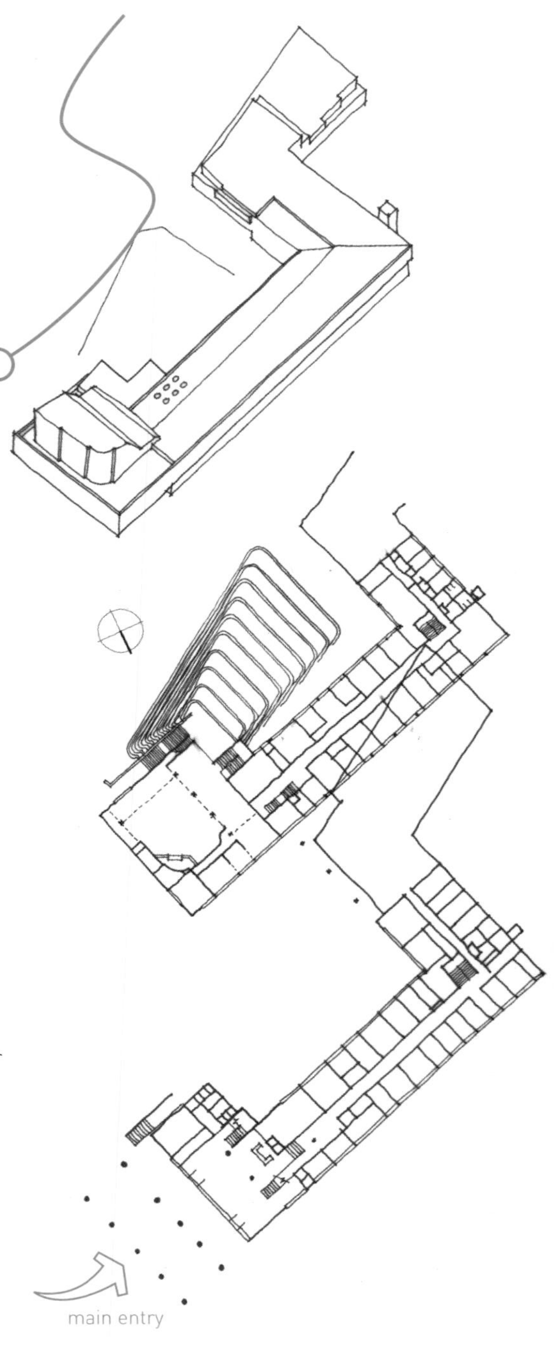

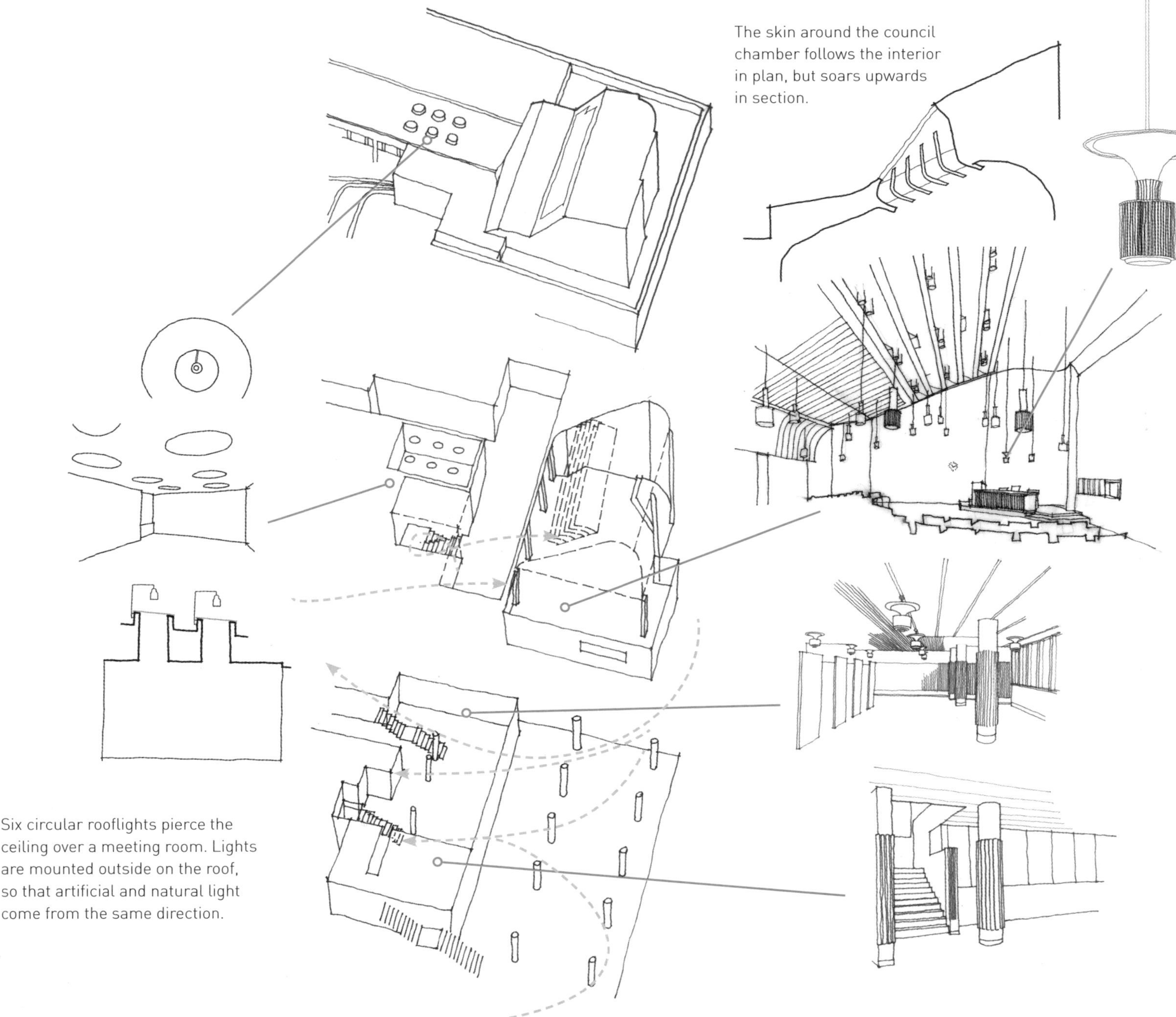

The skin around the council chamber follows the interior in plan, but soars upwards in section.

Six circular rooflights pierce the ceiling over a meeting room. Lights are mounted outside on the roof, so that artificial and natural light come from the same direction.

The council chamber

The town hall was the second building of the civic centre to be completed, after the church. Later additions designed by Alvar Aalto's office are a library, an office building (which contained the police station) and a theatre. Planning of the theatre began in 1961 but its final form was designed in 1984–87 after Aalto's death, when his widow, Elissa Aalto, led the office.

The main entrance to the town hall is reached through the colonnade. The white and grey columns are evocative of a Finnish birch forest with its white-trunked trees. Inside the entrance foyer, the warm timber surfaces and textures suggest a clearing in the woods. The blue ceramic tiles are used on indoor surfaces, providing colour and continuity.

Facing the doors inside is a reception desk, a corridor leading to the administrative offices, and stairs up to the council chamber. Before the building of the theatre the council chamber was intended for cultural events as well as council meetings.

The council chamber is at the top of the grass-stepped hill, and the chairperson's desk is placed on a podium positioned almost in line with the rising steps.

A large rooflight over the council chamber delivers reflected light, avoiding glare. Pendant lamps are irregularly dispersed below, like stars in a night sky. Over the chairperson's table one of these lamps is gold, signifying the importance of the position.

09 Seinäjoki Town Hall | 1958–65

Alvar Aalto

Seinäjoki, Ostrobothnia, Finland

The town hall is in Seinäjoki's administrative and cultural centre. This is close to but not part of the town's commercial centre. The road from the centre of Seinäjoki leads to the north-east corner of the town hall, its distinctive profile and blue-tiled walls acting as a marker.

The five buildings of the civic centre make a fine example of responsive cohesion in urban design. Each has its own distinctive form but follows the same design language. They respond to one another, like a gathering of like-minded people.

1. commercial centre
2. civic centre

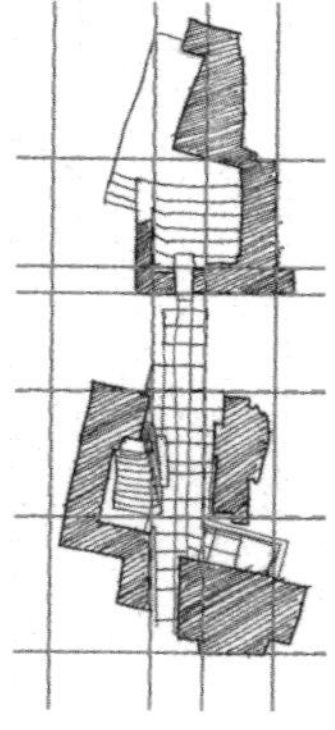

Many urban civic centres have rigid, formal geometries. The complex at Seinäjoki is informal. The rectangular pattern of the paving in the pedestrian plaza provides a reference for its irregular and angled edges.

The spine of the civic plaza is traffic-free, with parking allocated around the outer perimeter. A major road separates the church from the rest of the group.

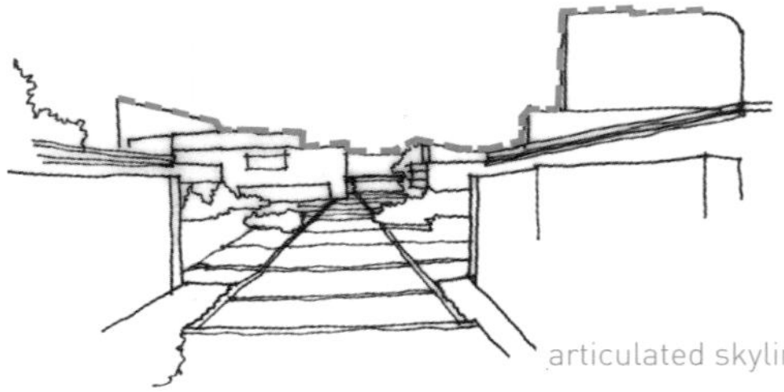

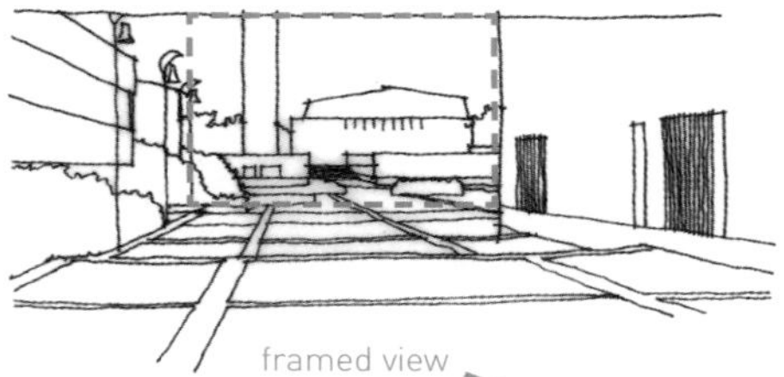

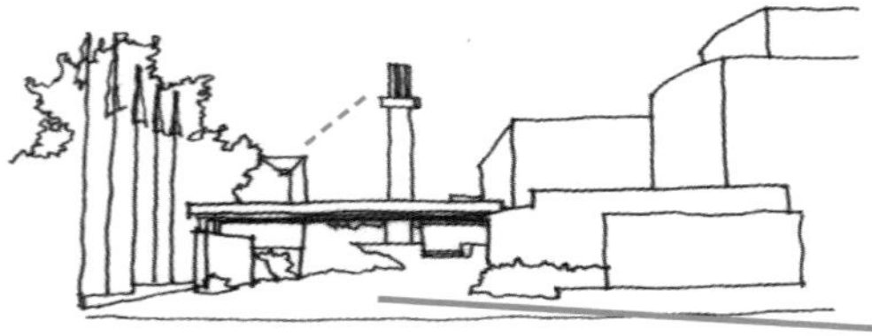

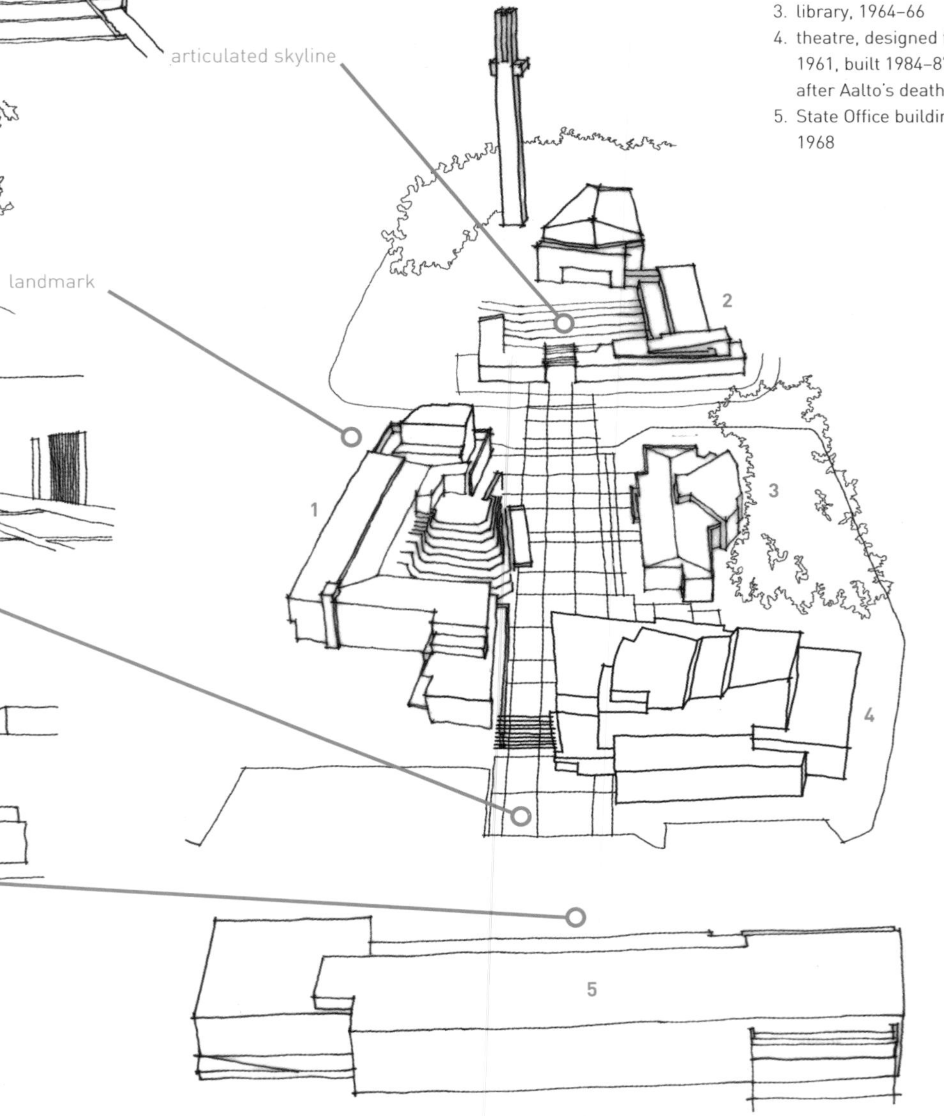

Key

1. town hall, designed from 1958, built 1961–65
2. Cross of the Plain church, designed 1951, built 1958–60
3. library, 1964–66
4. theatre, designed from 1961, built 1984–87 after Aalto's death
5. State Office building, 1968

articulated skyline

landmark

framed view

1

2

3

4

5

Looking along the pedestrian plaza, the roof of the council hall points up towards the church bell tower, symbolizing a link between civic and spiritual values.

Alvar Aalto's use of patterns
Aalto used a consistent set of design patterns in his work at all scales, from small products for the home to large city plans. All these patterns can be found in the town hall and in other parts of the civic centre.

Composite curves Controlled (not completely free-form) curves combine arcs of different radii, often with straight segments between them, as in this section through the hall ceiling and rooflight and side view of a door handle. The door handle was used on many Aalto buildings.

Divergence and fan shapes
Diverging lines and fan shapes animate compositions. The building edges diverge, and the grass steps follow this lead. The reflectors on the external lights combine a fan shape with composite curves.

Collage and overlay Different materials and finishes are used alongside one another or overlaid in a collage of colours and textures. The columns under the hall are white with rectangular grey stone panels superimposed on their surfaces. A balcony is faced in blue ceramic tiles and brought forward from the wall surface of white render and tiles. Strips of tiles in this wall continue over the front of a timber-framed window.

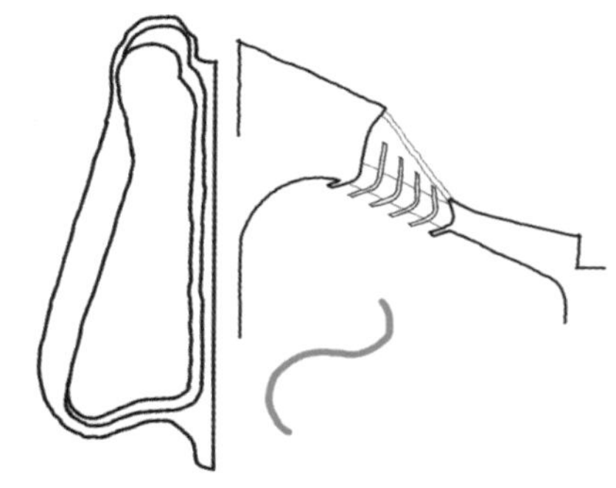

Offset lines and surfaces Lines and surfaces step backward and forward. The surfaces of the town hall exterior make a stepped skyline. A band of windows and doors is arranged with a stepped sill line.

Repetition and segmentation
Elements are repeated side by side, particularly linear elements. Planes are segmented into smaller parts with repetitive wood strips or tiles. The lamp over the doors at the top of the grass steps is repeated in a row. Windows are often covered by vertical timber slats.

Head and tail Compositions of form may have a dominant head and subsidiary tail. This is apparent in the building as a whole (in the relationship of the council chamber with the offices), and in the entrance foyer with its narrowing corridor. The lamp and reflector of the external lights can also be seen as head and tail.

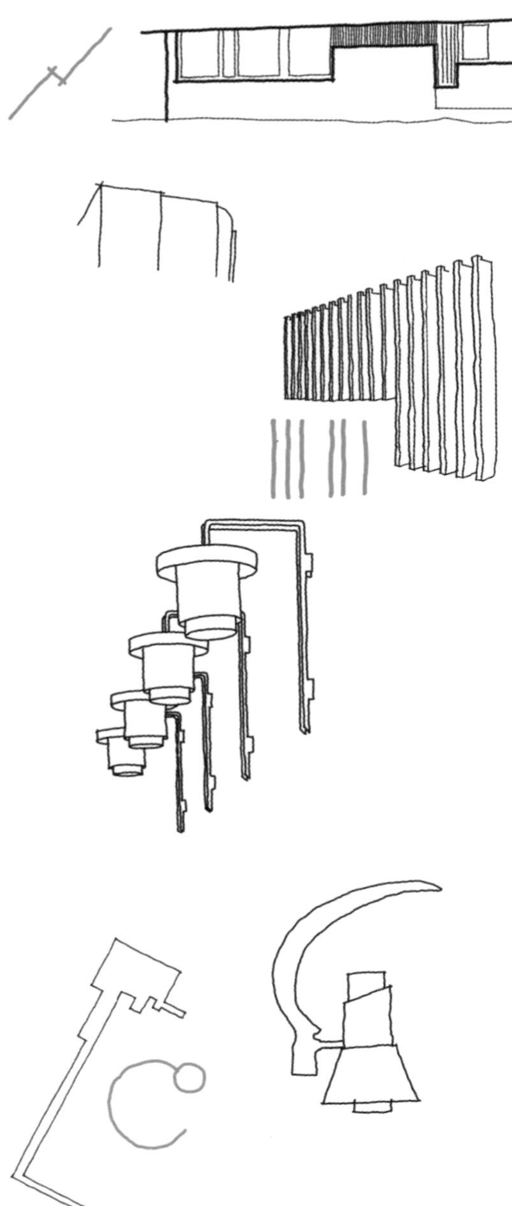

St Mary's Cathedral | 1961–64

Kenzo Tange

Tokyo, Japan

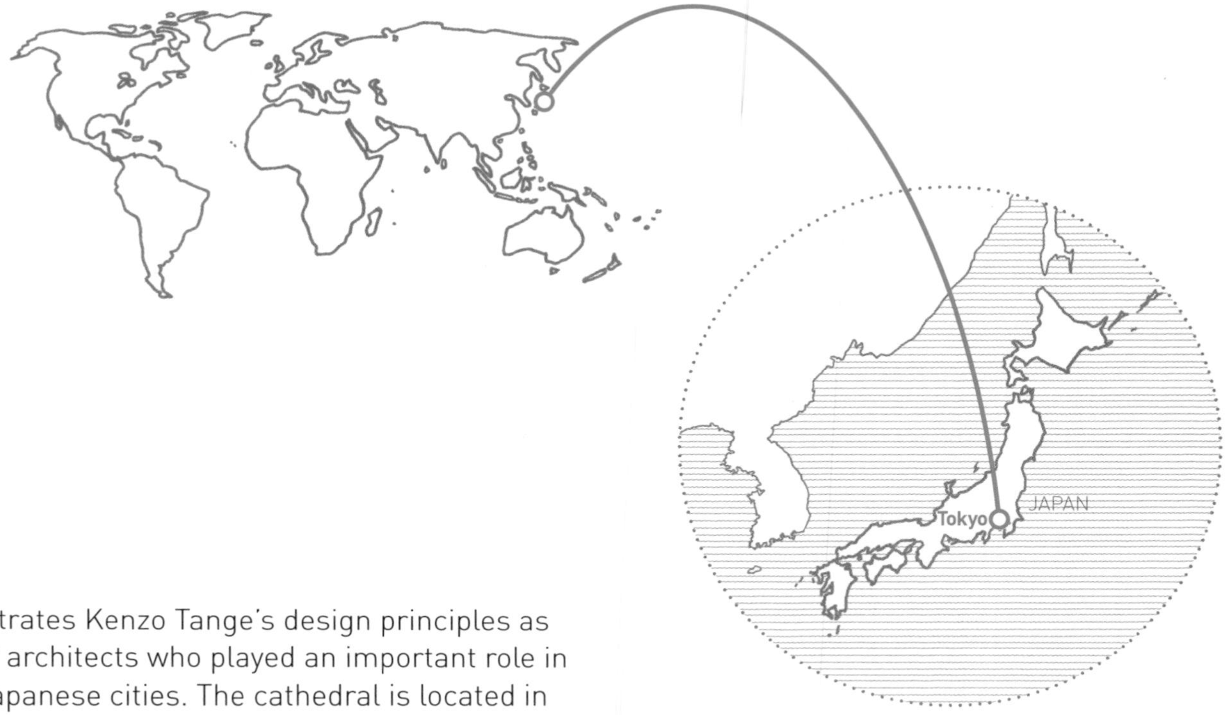

10

St Mary's Cathedral demonstrates Kenzo Tange's design principles as one of the first generation of architects who played an important role in the post-war rebuilding of Japanese cities. The cathedral is located in a busy urban district in Tokyo. Hidden between concrete buildings, it is surrounded by busy traffic and pedestrian over-crossings.

The old European Catholic Cathedral built in 1889 was destroyed in 1945. Tange won the architectural competition for its reconstruction in 1961 and the project was completed in 1964. Having worked with Le Corbusier, Tange was influenced by the Modernism, Structuralism and Metabolism movements. St Mary's Cathedral is an epitome of Modernist simplicity, honesty of materials and modern monumentality in harmonious dialogue with tradition.

Selen Morkoç, Halina Tam and Janine Fong

10

10 St Mary's Cathedral | 1961–64

Kenzo Tange

Tokyo, Japan

Context

The cathedral is located in the Bunkyo district of North Tokyo, accessed by a main road, Mejiro Dori.

The local urban context is a mixture of high-density residential, recreational spaces, government buildings, schools and libraries. Hidden between concrete buildings, St Mary's Cathedral is accessed by pedestrians via a ramped footbridge or a traffic-light crossing.

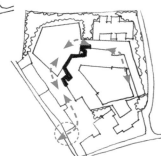

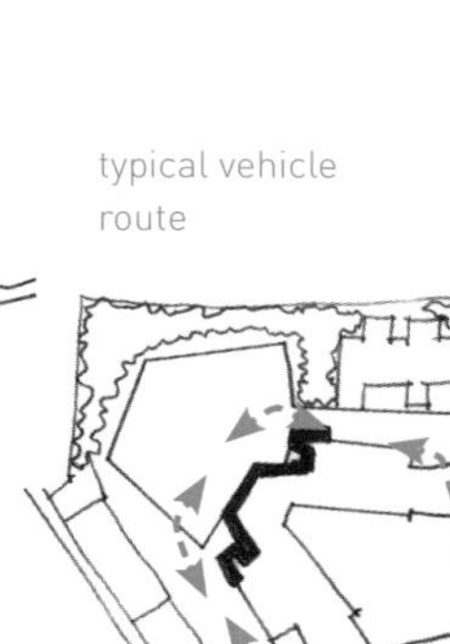

Both vehicles and pedestrians share the narrow access and exit route from Mejiro Dori.

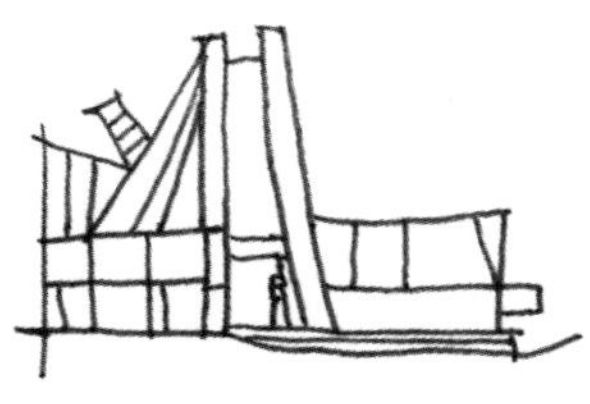

The cathedral exhibits unique and distinctive profiles from different angles.

The cathedral's profile points to the sky in spiritual symbolism. Contextually, it does not follow the design language of the streetscape, but its subtle grey materiality helps it blend into the busy suburban background.

The cathedral is distinguished from the surrounding blocks by its reflective cladding, as well as by its form and soaring height.

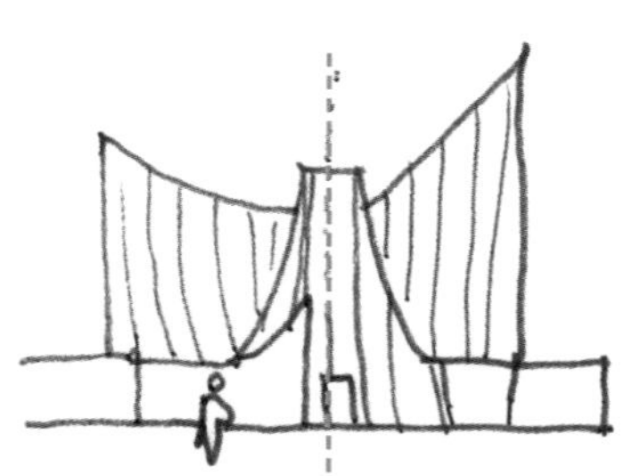

Structure and precedent

Tange followed many of Le Corbusier's design principles. The Philips Pavilion (1958) in Brussels, Belgium, designed by Le Corbusier, uses a cluster of nine hyperbolic paraboloids. Similarly, St Mary's Cathedral uses eight hyperbolic surfaces. Both the roof and the walls are formed by these unified concrete surfaces. The free-flowing and overarching form allows for large open interior spaces for gatherings.

A hyperbolic paraboloid is a saddle-shaped warped surface that can be constructed with two families of mutually skew straight lines.

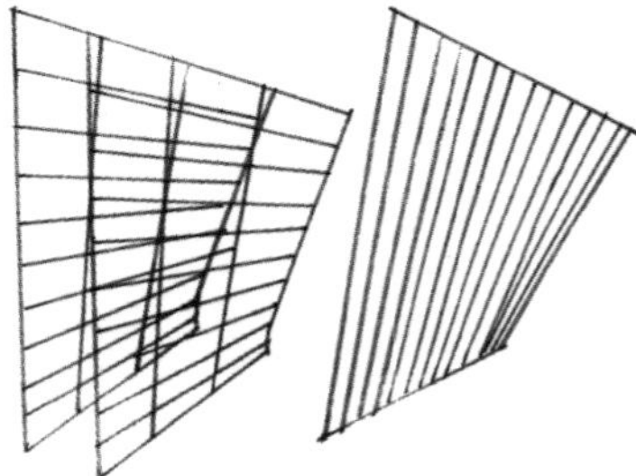

Sections of a hyperbolic paraboloid surface are the structural and formal basis of the cathedral building.

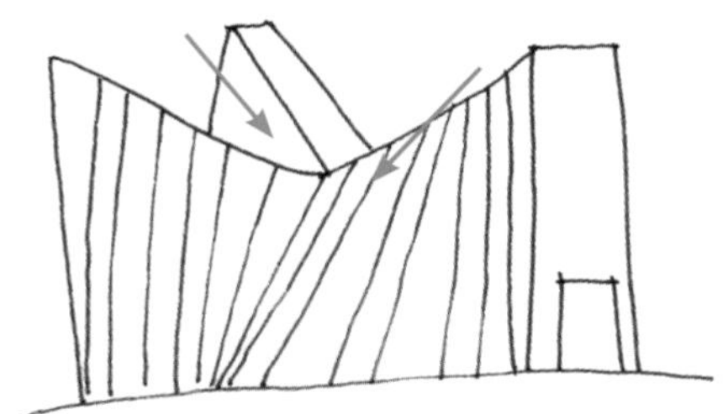

At St Mary's Cathedral, a structural cross cuts through hyperbolic surfaces.

The concrete core structure is clad in aluminium sheet metal.

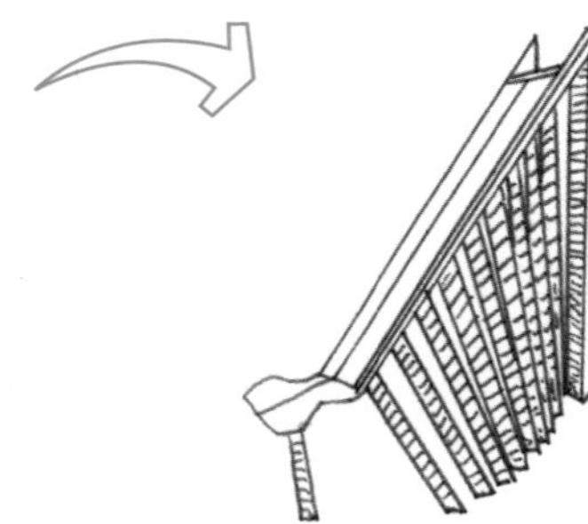

Skylights between the hyperbolic surfaces light the interior.

Symbolism

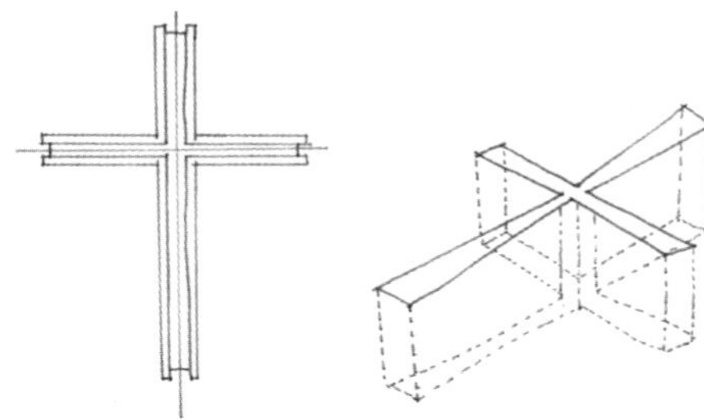

The traditional cross form as a symbol of the crucifixion of Christ is utilized to receive natural light both from the top and from the sides of the cathedral.

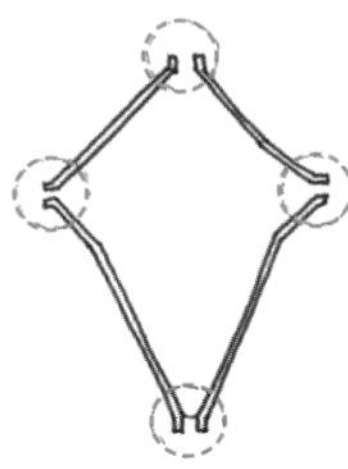

Vertical and horizontal gaps allow speckled light into the enclosed space. The soft interior light creates a spiritual atmosphere for connection with God.

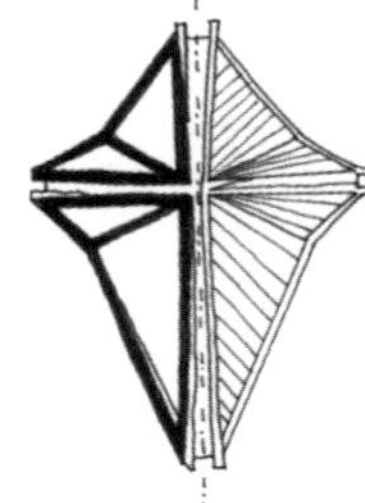

The roof shell is split into four symmetrical parts that form the perfect geometric form of the cross.

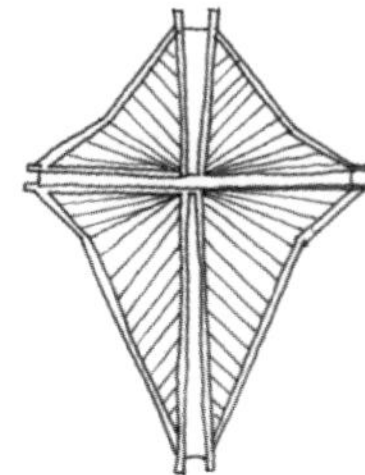

Both as a structural element and as a source of light, the cross form is integral to the design of the cathedral as its core element.

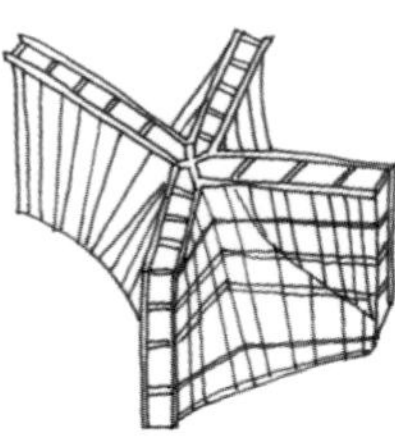

With the use of eight hyperbolic curves, the building envelope warps from the cross down to the diamond-shaped floor plan.

St Mary's Cathedral | 1961–64
Kenzo Tange
Tokyo, Japan

Form generation: through the cross

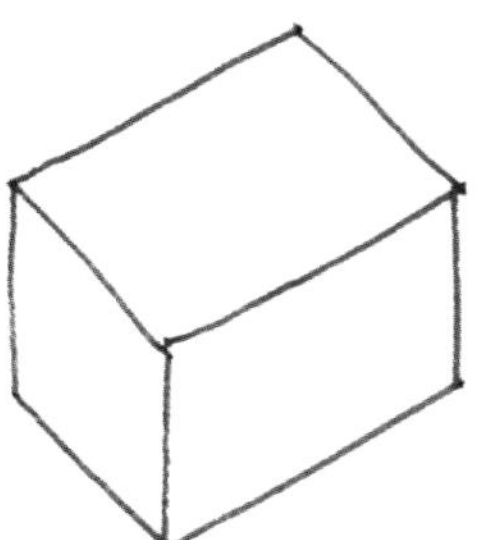
Solid object.

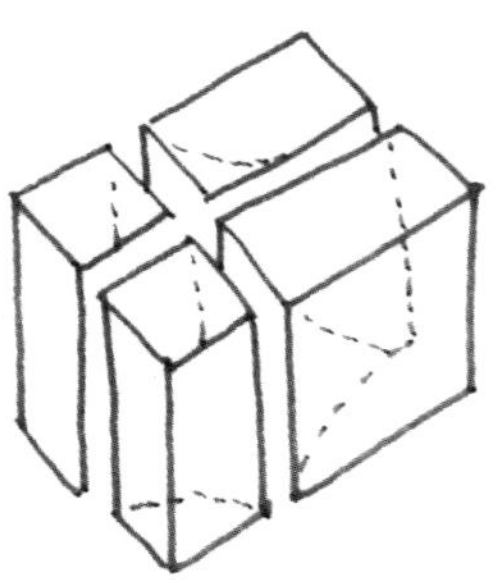
A void is extracted.

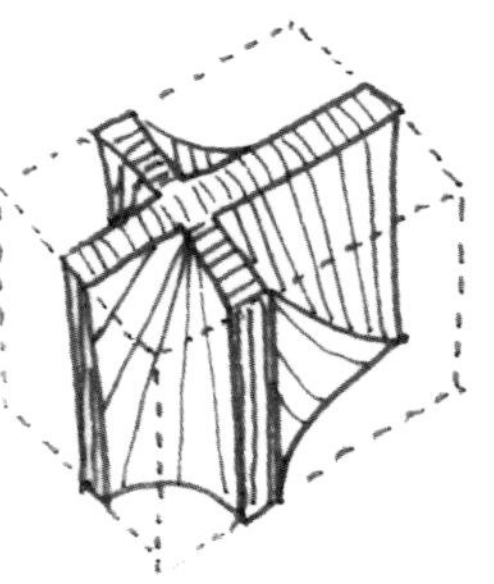
A cross is the formal reference for the void from the top.

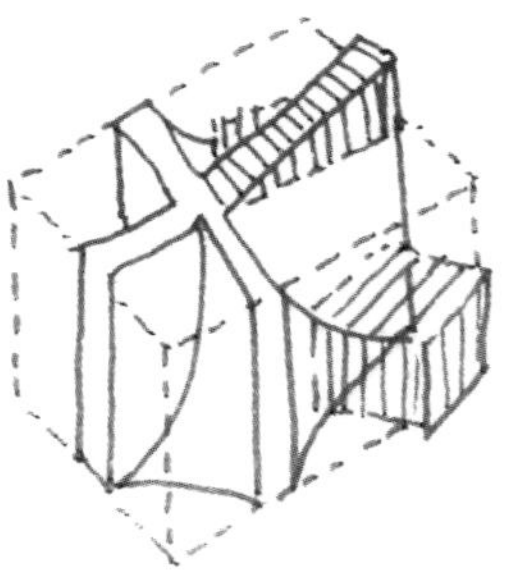
Additional volumes are secondary spaces.

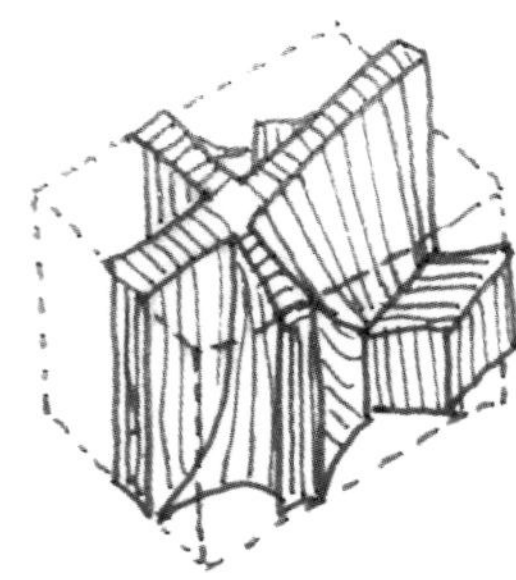
Overall form of the cathedral.

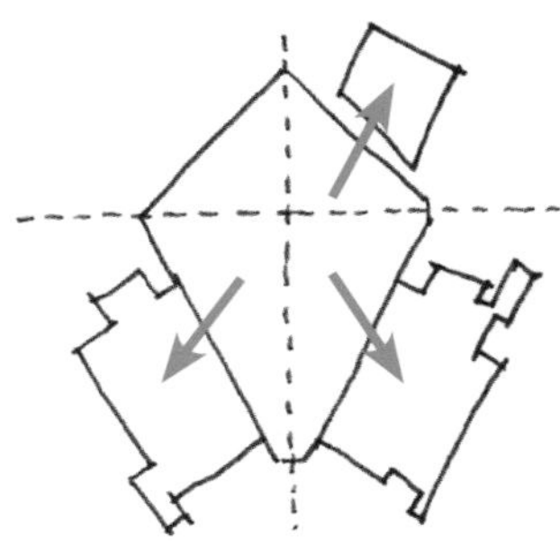
The plan reads as a diamond shape intersecting with secondary rectangular volumes.

Spatial arrangement

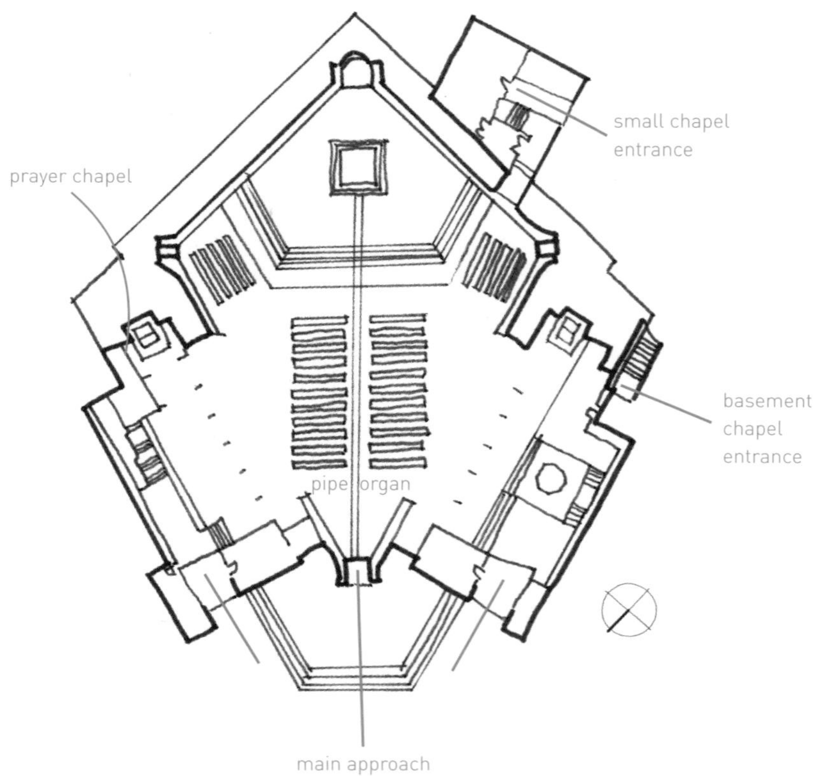

Controlled entrances: Tange designed many entry/exit points to the building. However, only the doors on each side of the main axial approach are open to the public for daily use. Other doors are available for emergency escape.

The open layout of the main level allows for multiple functions without compromising the rituals of a traditional cathedral.

The approach to the formal axial entrance is amplified by elevated steps and leads directly to the congregational space.

The platform in front of the entrances offers multiple views of the cathedral.

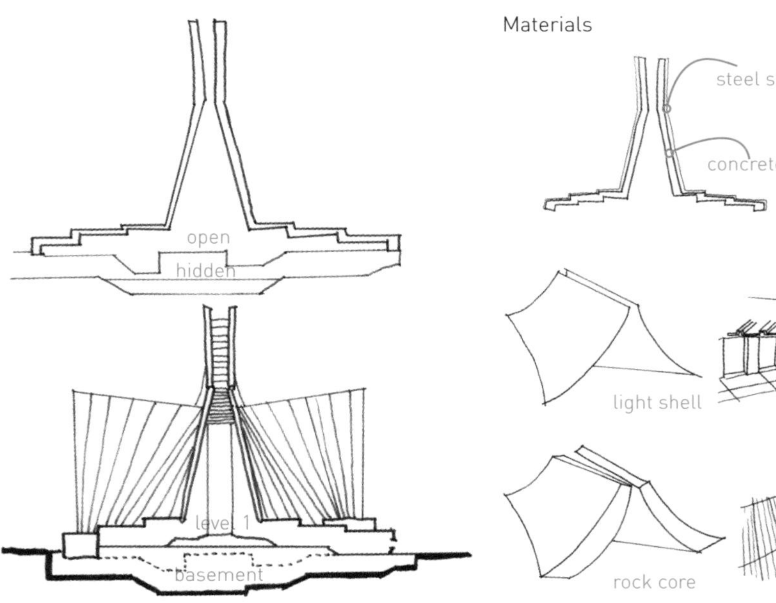

The basement is hidden and isolated from the rest of the building.

Materials

steel shell
concrete core
light shell
rock core

The double shell of the building makes different statements inside and outside. The light passes through the glazed gaps. It is a rather dark space, but the contrast of dark and bright areas enhances the symbolism of the cathedral.

Outside, the steel-aluminium shell is radiant and flexible. Its brightness symbolizes the light of religion.

Inside, the solidity and strength of concrete symbolizes timelessness.

The striped imprint of timber formwork on the concrete surfaces provides visual stability and continuity to the interior.

The concrete structure holds up the glass and transfers the load down to the ground.

The stainless-steel cladding of the outside emphasizes the dynamic form of the cathedral from outside.

The interior concrete walls create a dramatic effect in the cathedral.

The diffused light disseminating from behind the pipe organ increases the spiritual symbolism of the space below.

Human scale and monumentality

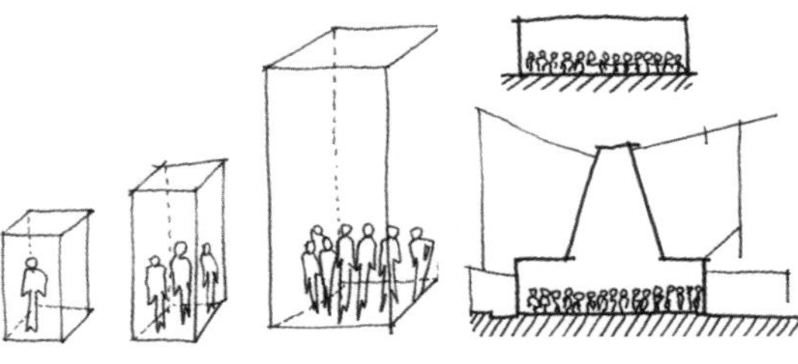

Tange uses a system in which he compares the proportion of people with the volume of the space. The height of the space increases as the number of people increases.

Comparing the sectional profile of the cathedral with a rectangular box of the same size, it can be seen how the additional space adds to the sense of monumentality and increases individual awareness during religious ritual in spite of the crowd.

Interior experience and light

Despite the soaring height of the interior, the ceremonial entry to the building is through a human-scale door.

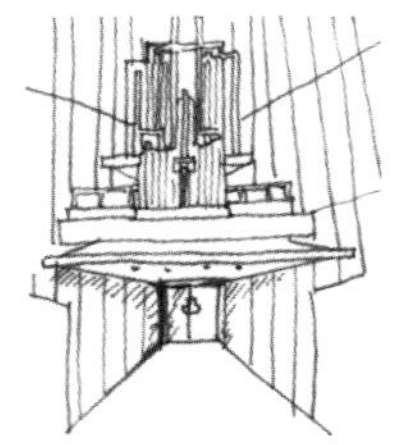

The door opens on to a low-ceilinged passage, which in turn gives on to the impressive height of the cathedral.

A view back towards the ceremonial entrance doors shows two higher levels.

The baptismal font is bathed in light from above.

To the right of the altar dais, a statue of the Pietà is displayed under natural light.

Hedmark Museum | 1967–79

Sverre Fehn

Hamar, Norway

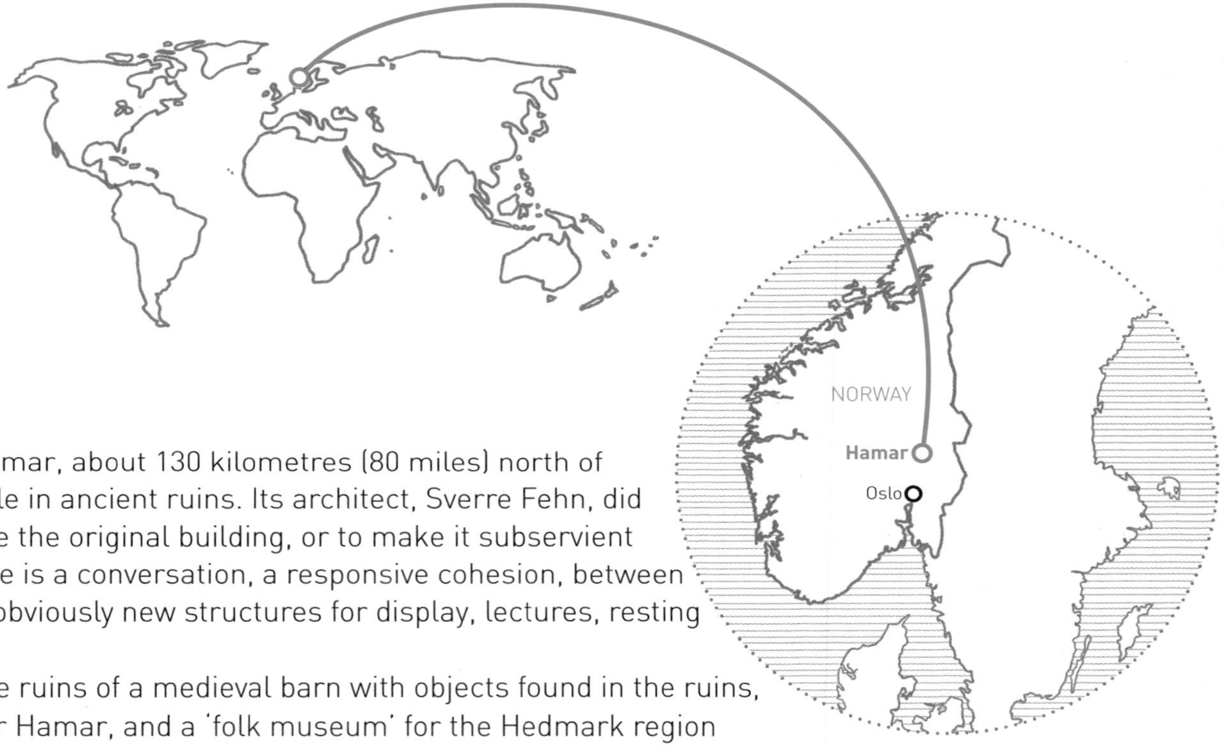

11

The Hedmark Museum in Hamar, about 130 kilometres (80 miles) north of Oslo, displays bold 1960s style in ancient ruins. Its architect, Sverre Fehn, did not aim to recreate or restore the original building, or to make it subservient to the additions. Instead there is a conversation, a responsive cohesion, between minimally altered ruins and obviously new structures for display, lectures, resting and protection.

The museum combines the ruins of a medieval barn with objects found in the ruins, Iron Age artefacts found near Hamar, and a 'folk museum' for the Hedmark region from the 1600s to the present time, including stories of trade and transport, hunting and fishing. The exhibition was designed by Fehn and is integrated with the building.

There are four principal elements: the stone ruins of a barn built in the 1800s and early 1900s using the ruins of a medieval bishop's palace as part of its walls; concrete platforms that thread through and above the ruins; timber and tile roof and upper walls to complete the enclosure of the ruins; and precisely engineered steel mounts for exhibits. The museum allows the historical remains – the record of the past – to speak for themselves. The new work is given purpose by the old, and the irregularity of the old is given structure by the order of the new.

Antony Radford

11

Hedmark Museum | 1967–79
Sverre Fehn
Hamar, Norway

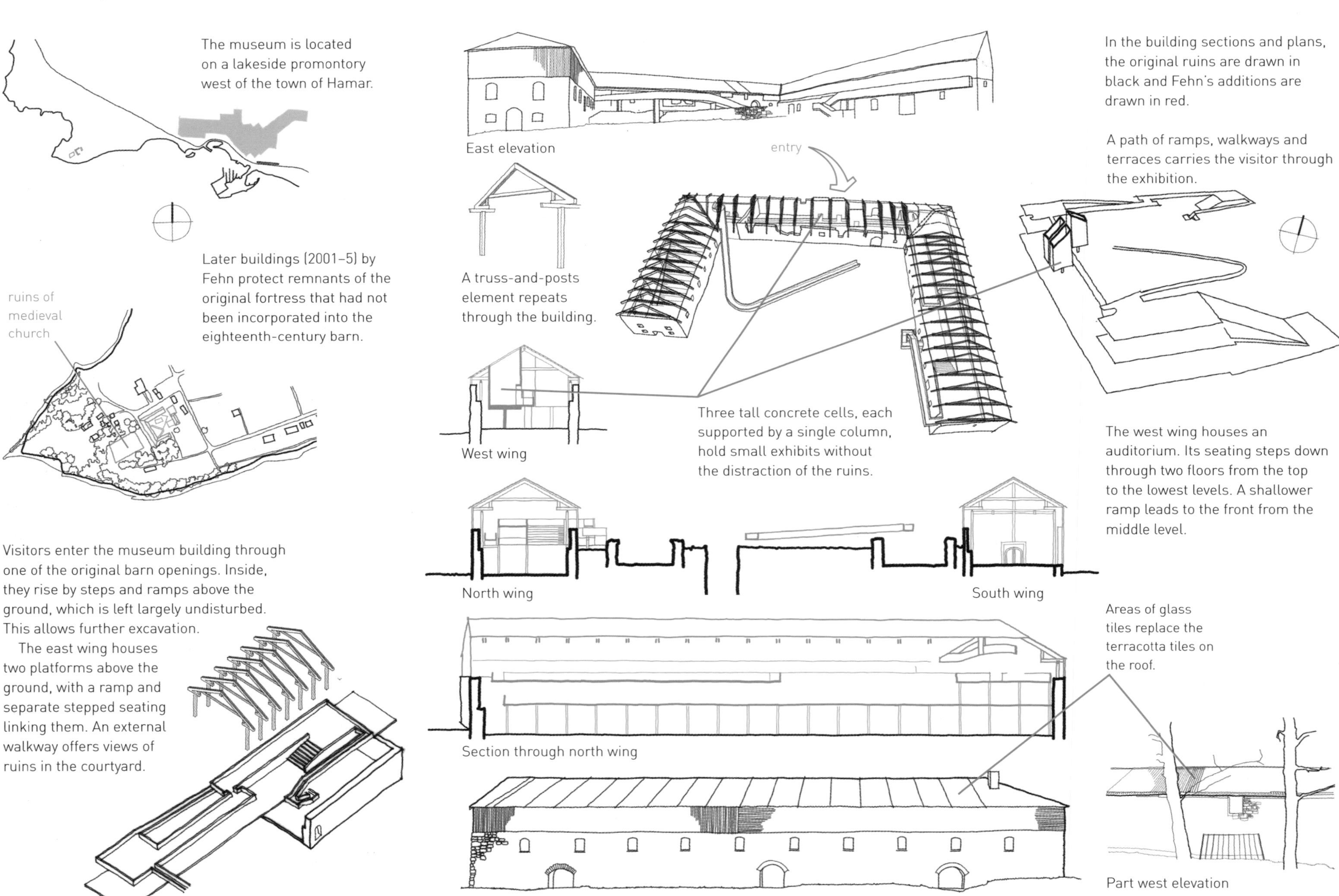

The museum is located on a lakeside promontory west of the town of Hamar.
Later buildings (2001–5) by Fehn protect remnants of the original fortress that had not been incorporated into the eighteenth-century barn.
ruins of medieval church
Visitors enter the museum building through one of the original barn openings. Inside, they rise by steps and ramps above the ground, which is left largely undisturbed. This allows further excavation.
The east wing houses two platforms above the ground, with a ramp and separate stepped seating linking them. An external walkway offers views of ruins in the courtyard.
East elevation
entry
A truss-and-posts element repeats through the building.
West wing
Three tall concrete cells, each supported by a single column, hold small exhibits without the distraction of the ruins.
North wing
South wing
Section through north wing
North elevation
In the building sections and plans, the original ruins are drawn in black and Fehn's additions are drawn in red.
A path of ramps, walkways and terraces carries the visitor through the exhibition.
The west wing houses an auditorium. Its seating steps down through two floors from the top to the lowest levels. A shallower ramp leads to the front from the middle level.
Areas of glass tiles replace the terracotta tiles on the roof.
Part west elevation

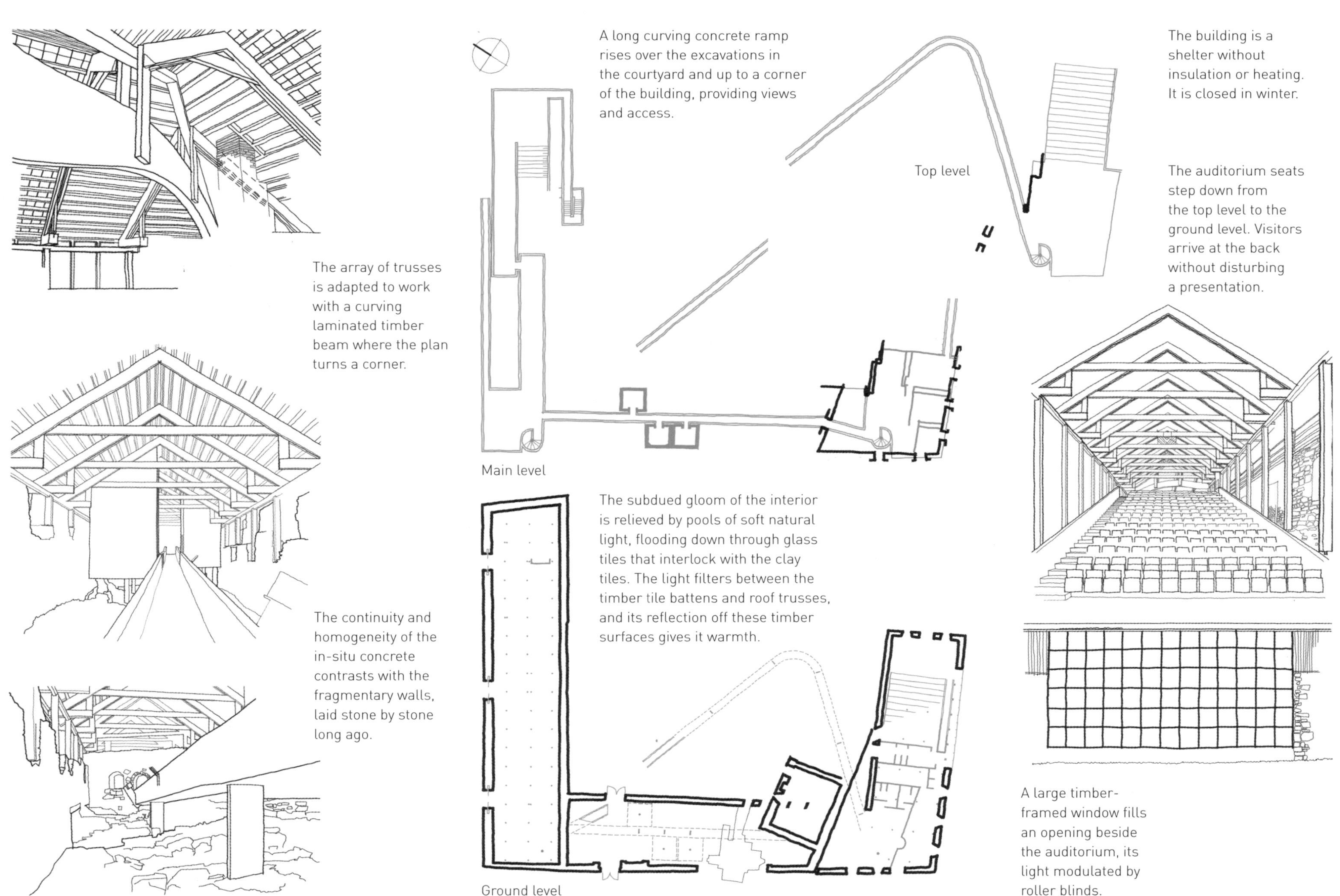

The array of trusses is adapted to work with a curving laminated timber beam where the plan turns a corner.

The continuity and homogeneity of the in-situ concrete contrasts with the fragmentary walls, laid stone by stone long ago.

A long curving concrete ramp rises over the excavations in the courtyard and up to a corner of the building, providing views and access.

The subdued gloom of the interior is relieved by pools of soft natural light, flooding down through glass tiles that interlock with the clay tiles. The light filters between the timber tile battens and roof trusses, and its reflection off these timber surfaces gives it warmth.

The building is a shelter without insulation or heating. It is closed in winter.

The auditorium seats step down from the top level to the ground level. Visitors arrive at the back without disturbing a presentation.

A large timber-framed window fills an opening beside the auditorium, its light modulated by roller blinds.

The language of the building elements

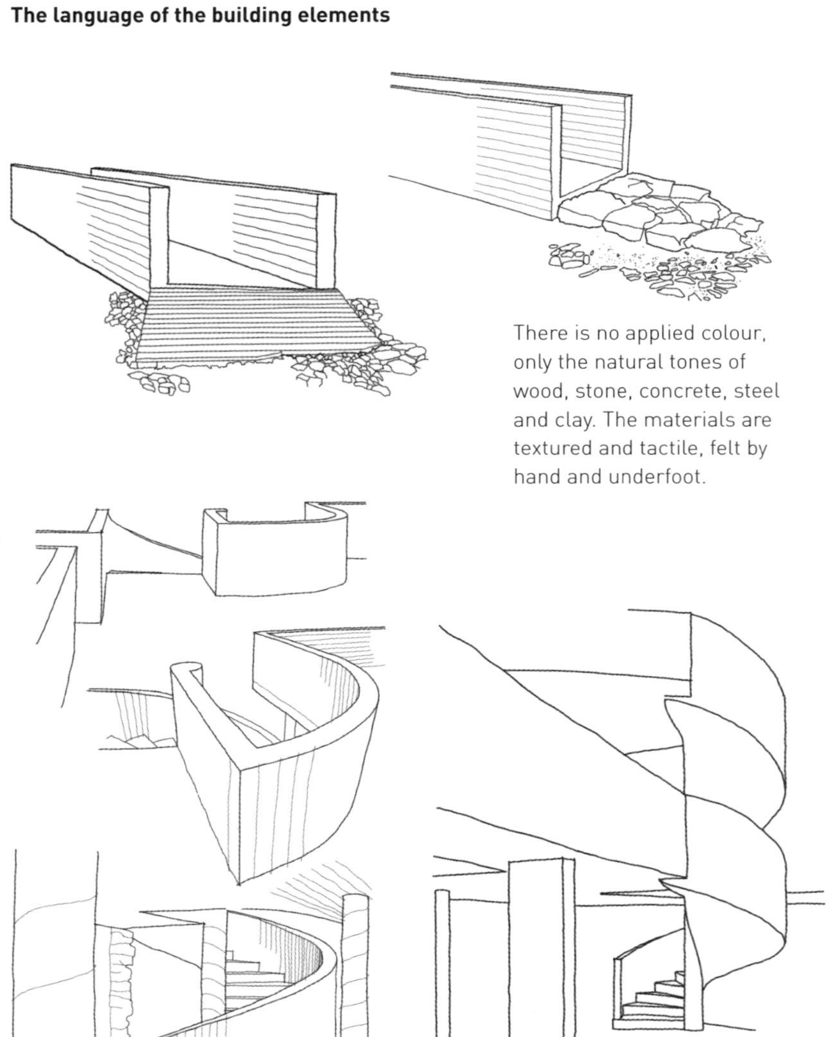

There is no applied colour, only the natural tones of wood, stone, concrete, steel and clay. The materials are textured and tactile, felt by hand and underfoot.

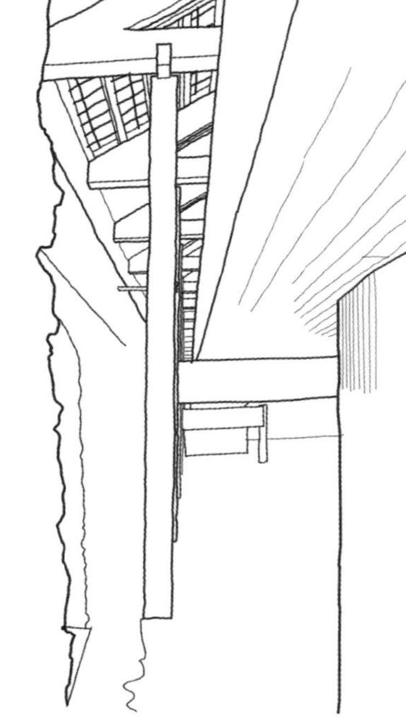

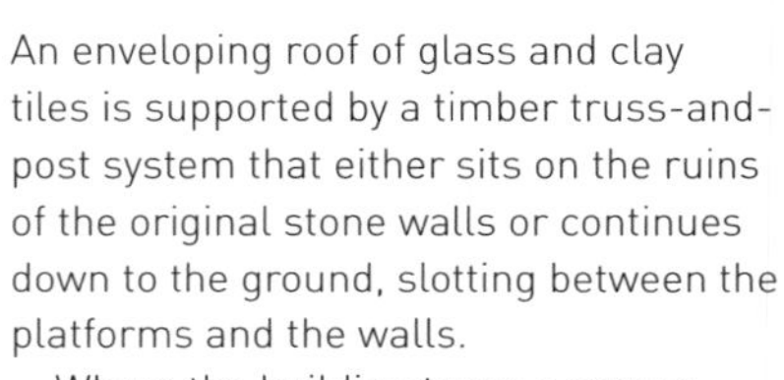

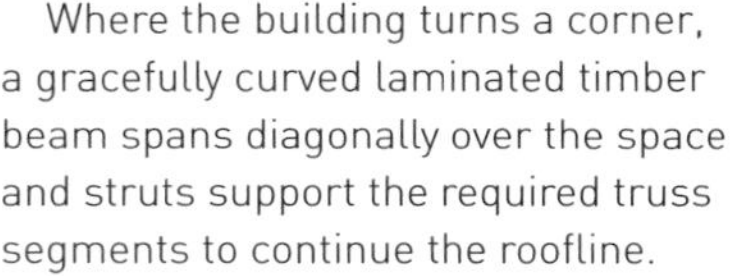

An enveloping roof of glass and clay tiles is supported by a timber truss-and-post system that either sits on the ruins of the original stone walls or continues down to the ground, slotting between the platforms and the walls.

Where the building turns a corner, a gracefully curved laminated timber beam spans diagonally over the space and struts support the required truss segments to continue the roofline.

Instead of 'making good' openings in the walls and replacing timber window and door frames, they are simply covered by unframed sheets of reinforced glass that span over the ragged-edged openings and are minimally bolted to the face of the surrounding external wall.

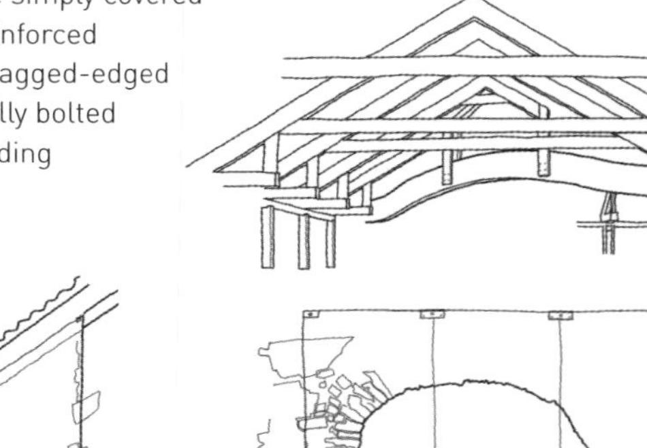

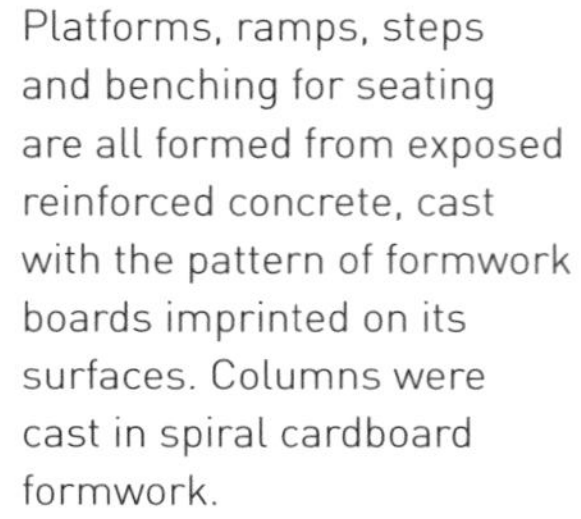

Platforms, ramps, steps and benching for seating are all formed from exposed reinforced concrete, cast with the pattern of formwork boards imprinted on its surfaces. Columns were cast in spiral cardboard formwork.

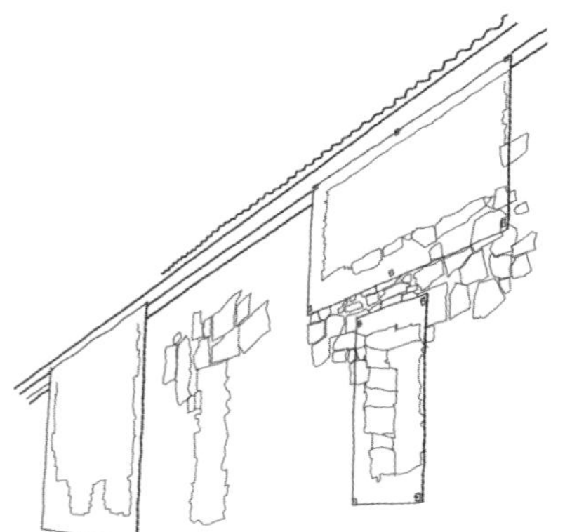

The language of the exhibit stands

Fehn's exhibit stands share a vocabulary of black steel rods, beams and plates, with glass covers and metal fixings.

Simple things such as household pots, farmers' tools, snow sleighs and clothing are treated with unfussy respect. Objects are kept in place without compromising their integrity or masking their surface qualities. Stands are used only when needed. Some exhibits (such as carriages) simply stand on the floor, and others (such as clothes and fishing nets) hang on the wall.

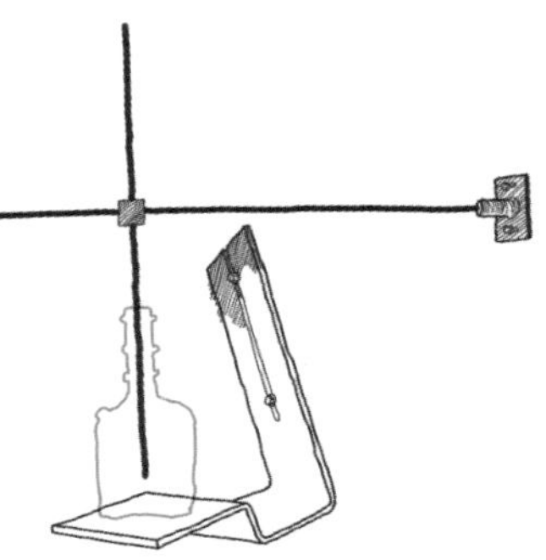

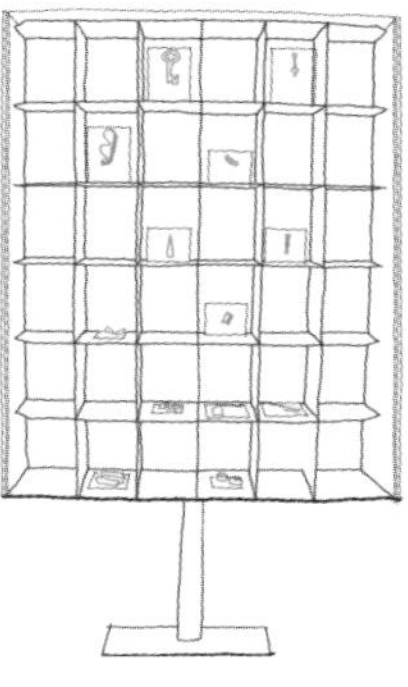

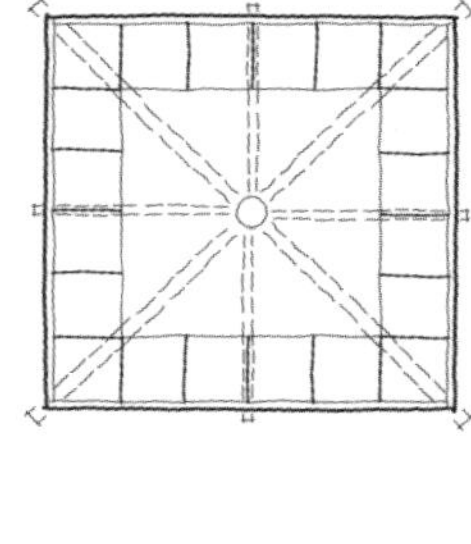

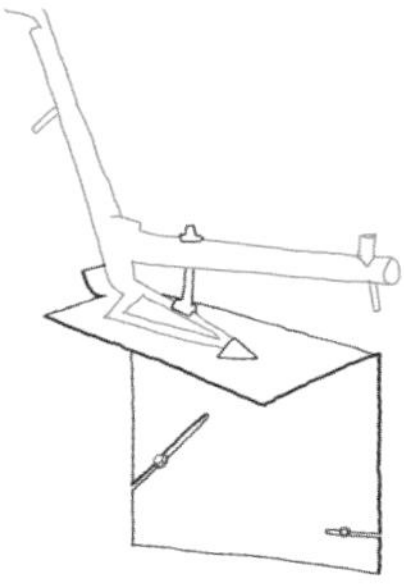

Steel plate is folded to suit the object and the way the stand is bolted to the building surface.

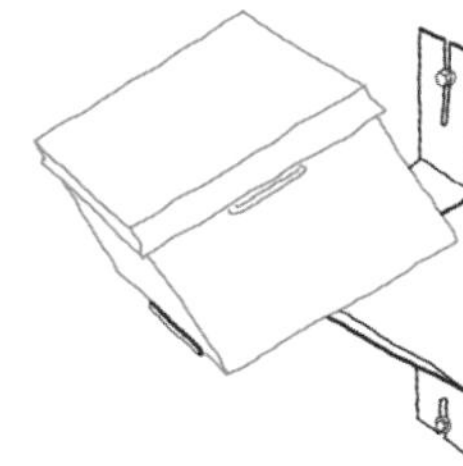

Crossed rods keep a bottle from falling. One rod threads through the bottle neck and the other is drilled into the supporting stone wall.

A backlit floor-standing case displays small objects.

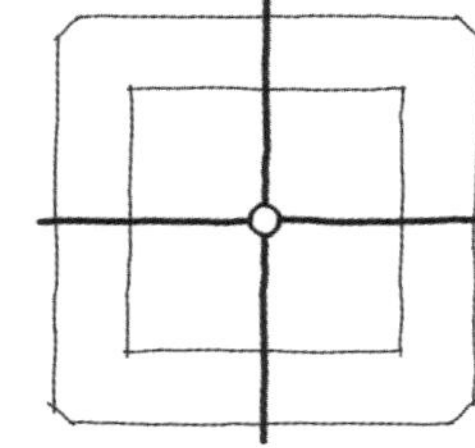

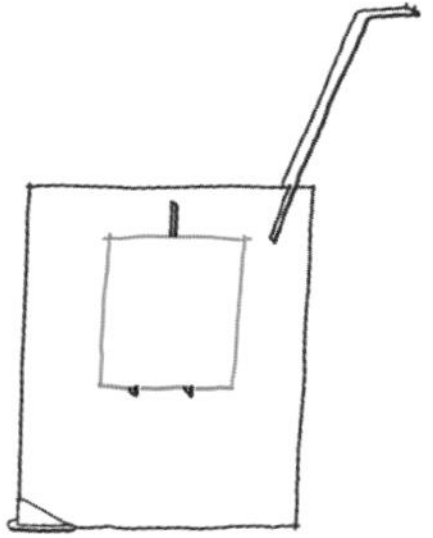

White screens are held on the floor by a metal shoe, and fixed at the opposite corner to a wall or ceiling.

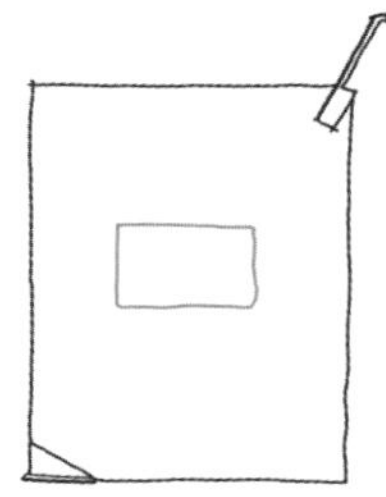

Wooden bench tops in the three enclosed display cells are hollowed for displays, with glass covers.

A still sits gently on a black steel frame.

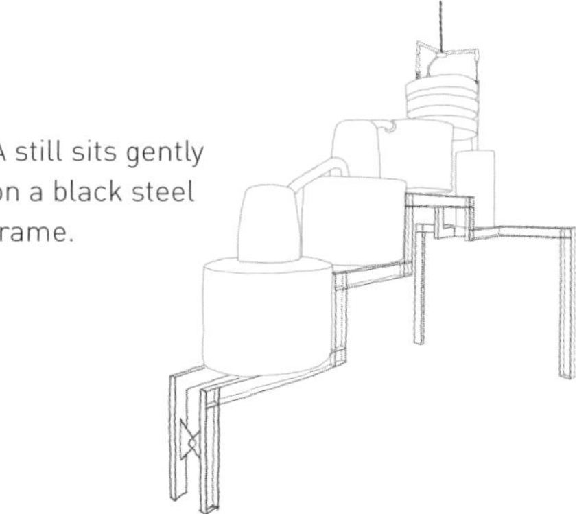

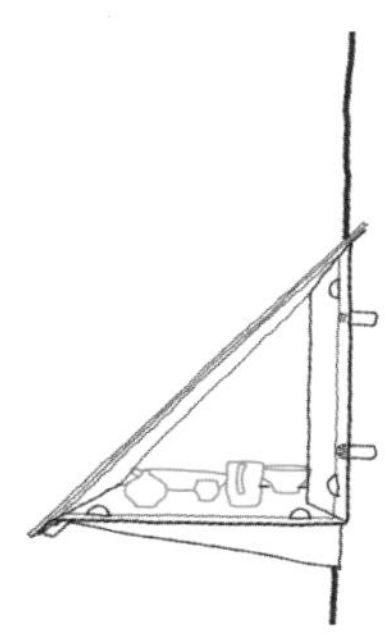

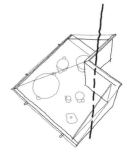

Triangular display cases are adapted to suit different kinds of wall surfaces and corners.

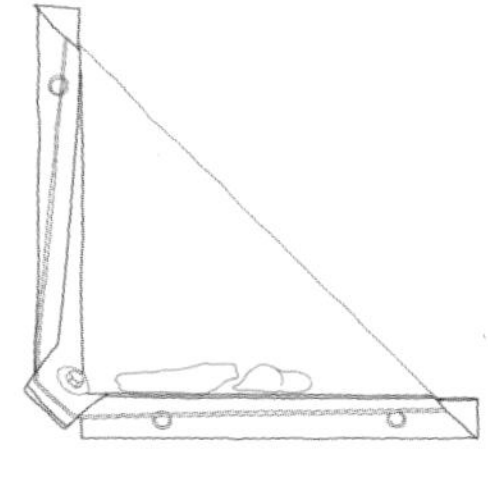

A farm tool rests on a folded steel plate.

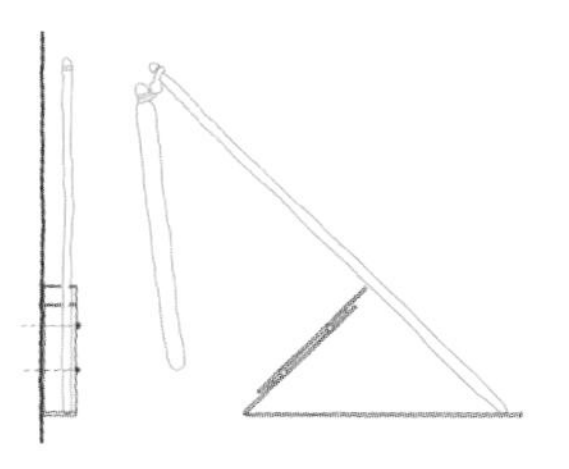

12

Indian Institute of Management | 1963–74

Louis Kahn

Ahmedabad, India

Ahmedadad

INDIA

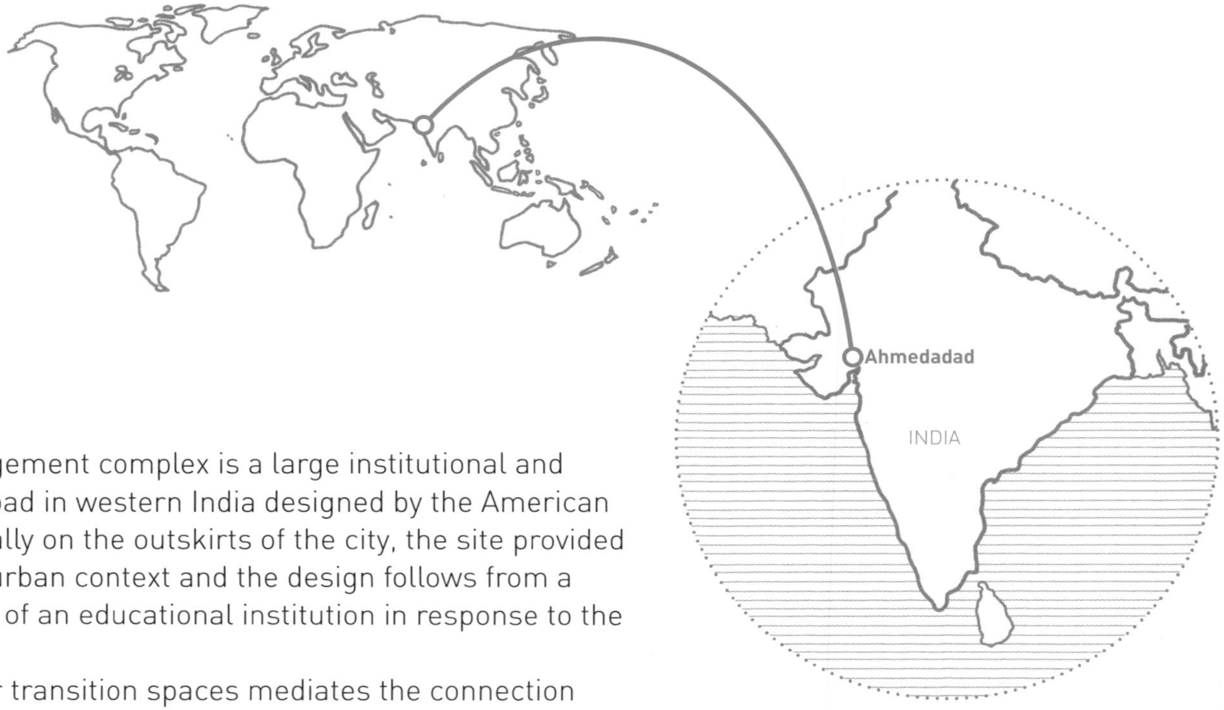

The Indian Institute of Management complex is a large institutional and housing campus in Ahmedabad in western India designed by the American architect Louis Kahn. Originally on the outskirts of the city, the site provided little in terms of immediate urban context and the design follows from a reconsideration of the needs of an educational institution in response to the act of learning.

A series of intermediate or transition spaces mediates the connection between different functional requirements and creates opportunities for social interaction. This connects the various functions of the complex into a cohesive whole. Kahn had developed a design language of monumental forms and large light-filled openings for another, unbuilt project, which he here adapted to the local cultural and building context. The result is a passionate essay engaging brick as a building material, helping to develop the potential of the material as well as the practices of the local construction industry. The design process included continuous consultation and collaboration between Kahn and local counterparts, a fine example of cross-cultural cohesion.

Amit Srivastava and Marguerite Therese Bartolo

Indian Institute of Management | 1963–74
Louis Kahn
Ahmedabad, India

Response to site – institution building
The campus for the Indian Institute of Management (IIM) is located along what at the time was the western fringe of the growing city of Ahmedabad, and formed part of the newly established university precinct. The site was relatively remote from the city centre and the design attempts to develop a self-contained institutional campus with school, student dormitories and staff housing. The various buildings of the campus thus act as a microcosm – a city within a city.

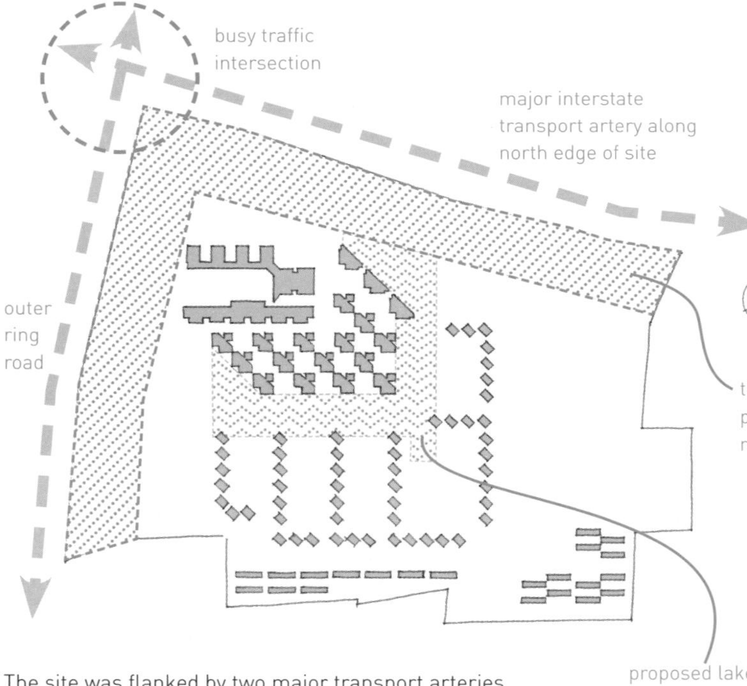

The site was flanked by two major transport arteries along the northern and western sides. In response, the major buildings of the campus are set back from the edges to allow institutional activities to continue unaffected by traffic noise. Dense plantations along these edges also help to isolate the campus and create the monastery-like environment that was wanted for educational activities. In the original scheme another layer of separation was proposed between the staff housing and the school buildings in the form of a lake, which would have given the residents more privacy.

The site was located on the outermost fringe of the new city.

The school, the dormitories and the staff housing relate to one another in a hierarchical organization.

school
student dormitories
staff residences

Spatial organization of different building types

The main school building is organized around a U-shaped court equal in size to the built mass.

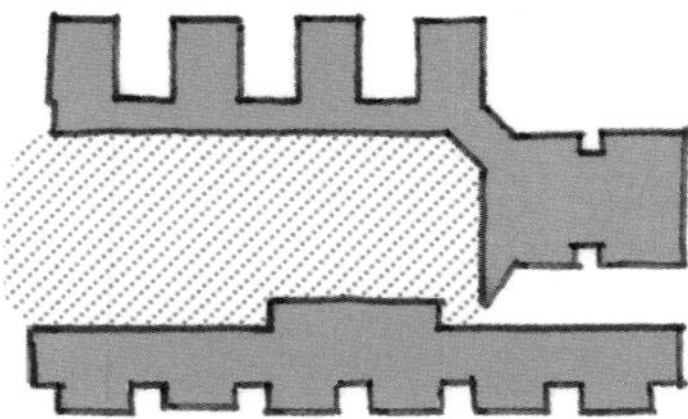

The student dormitories form a gridlike pattern, with alternating squares of built and open space.

The planning of the staff housing defines larger, U-shaped courts as shared space.

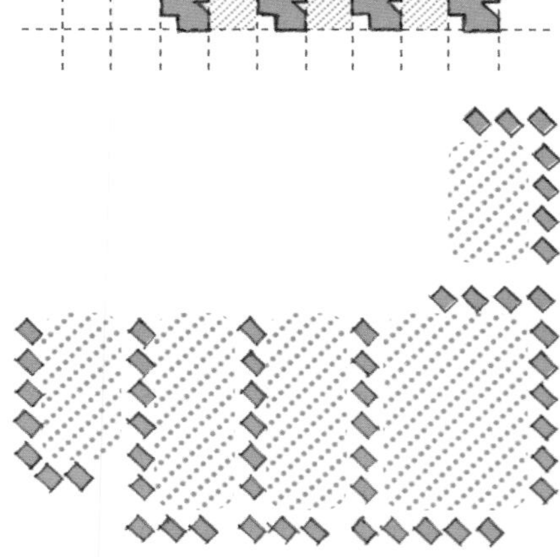

The three major building types relating to the school, the student dormitories and the staff housing are organized hierarchically based on the level of privacy required. The most public functions of the school are placed closest to the traffic junction, followed by the student dormitories and finally the staff houses, arranged concentrically. The hierarchy is also evident in section, where the school building occupies the highest point in the landscape, which slopes down towards the housing. Different relationships between the open and built spaces further define the characteristics of the three types.

Spaces for learning

The response to the programme is not only focused on providing for individual facilities but also considers the fundamental requirements of developing an institution for learning. The design takes the stance that learning takes place not only in classrooms but also in other places of social gathering, where chance encounters can lead to an exchange of ideas. The design thus provides a range of transitional spaces, within corridors or other communal areas, to allow for such encounters and promote learning. The relationship of these 'meeting places' with the formal requirements of the programme leads to a tripartite approach to planning, with the transitory meeting space acting as an overlap between two functional requirements.

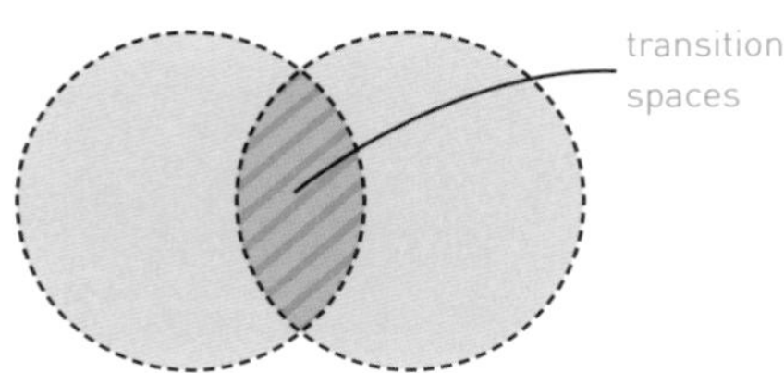

The concept of the meeting place was originally developed by Louis Kahn for his Salk Institute for Biological Studies project (1959–66), where he had proposed a separate facility based on these principles. As that facility was never built, IIM serves as the best exposition of these ideas.

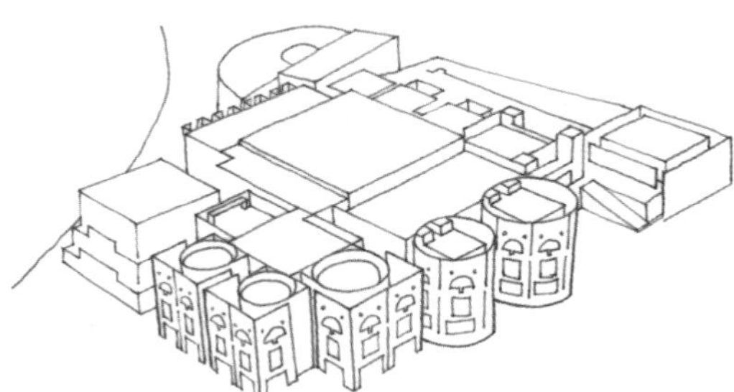

The Meeting House for the Salk Institute for Biological Studies (unbuilt)

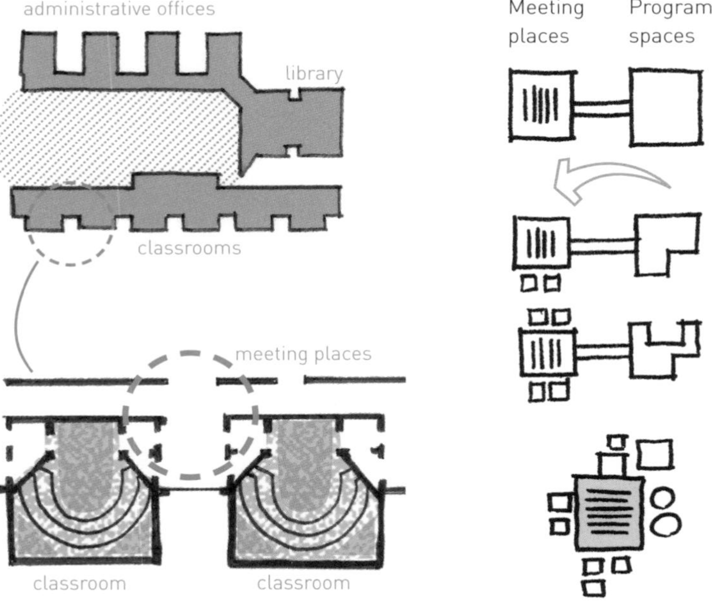

The main school building provides for a third space to mediate between two programmatic requirements, allowing for chance encounters.

The dormitories provide for opportunities of chance encounter through large undefined common areas separating private rooms and shared facilities.

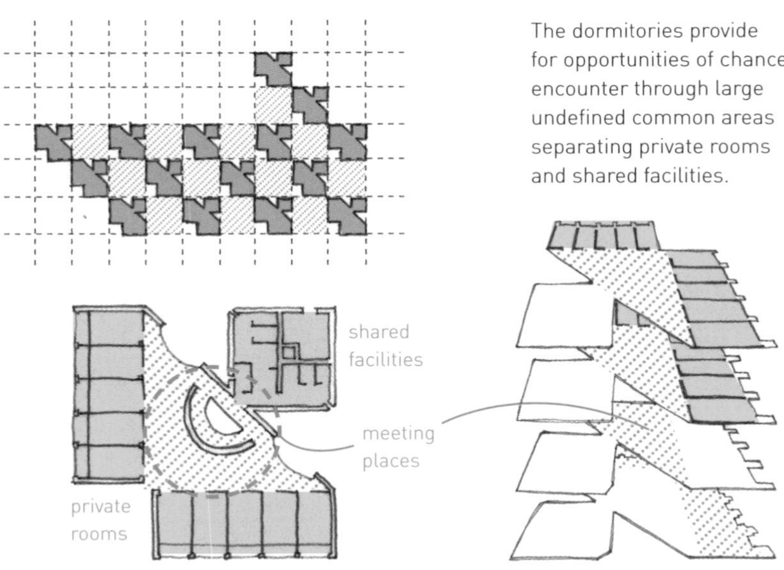

The large U-shaped court at the centre of the main school buildings binds the various institutional programmes together as an organizing centre. In the original design the court was conceived as having a dining facility enclosing it on the fourth side as well as other built structures in the middle, which would have activated it as a central sanctuary much like the traditional courtyards in South Asian buildings. As built, the large court is unshielded from the harsh Indian sun and unrelated functions on opposing sides do not encourage people to pass through it.

However, as people skirt around this large empty open space in the shadowed hallways that surround it, the contrast with the bright sunlit exterior reinforces the hallway as the place of sanctuary and makes it more successful as the intermediary space of encounters. The court itself becomes an 'empty centre' that may not serve as the intended place of activity and meetings but acts instead as a psychological pivot around which the various programmatic requirements of the school are organized.

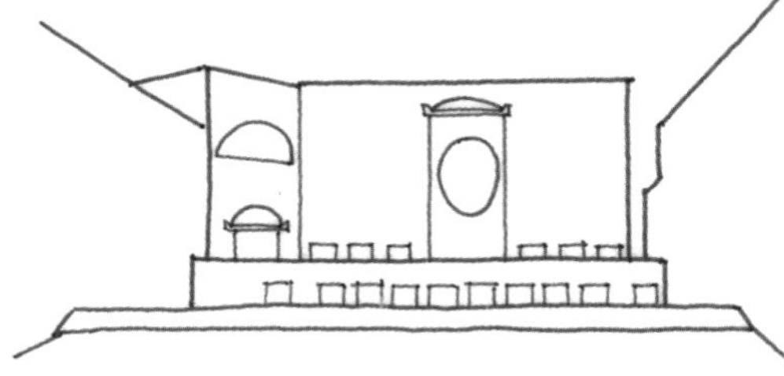

The central court space at the main school building

The student dormitories offer the best exposition of the concept of the meeting place. Each four-storey dormitory block has a conventional large common room on the ground floor where students can socialize and discuss ideas. On the upper floors, the private rooms of the students are separated from the common services block by a large space where chance encounters may take place. The character of this space, with its monumental openings, window perches and filtered sunlight, further encourages students to linger and engage in discussions.

Response to light and monumentality

Ahmedabad has a hot and arid climate with a harsh tropical sun, which causes problems of heat gain and glare. The design works to combat these issues while reducing dependence on mechanical cooling systems through the use of a unique architectural device – the 'glare wall'. The glare wall has a large opening and is separated from the internal glazed wall to allow light and heat to be filtered through this intermediate space before reaching the interior. The articulation of the glare wall also creates transitional places in which students can pause, and can enhance their experience of learning through chance encounters or silent meditation.

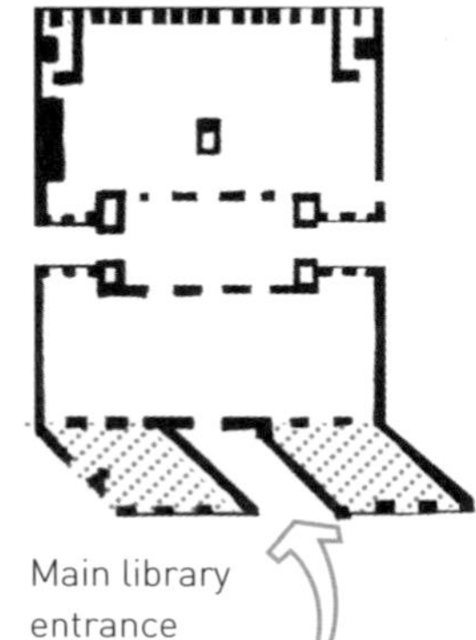

Main library entrance

The monumental five-storey-high main entrance to the library is slanted at an angle as it passes between two glare-wall systems. Looking up, the entrance is defined by the three large circular openings of the surrounding glare walls.

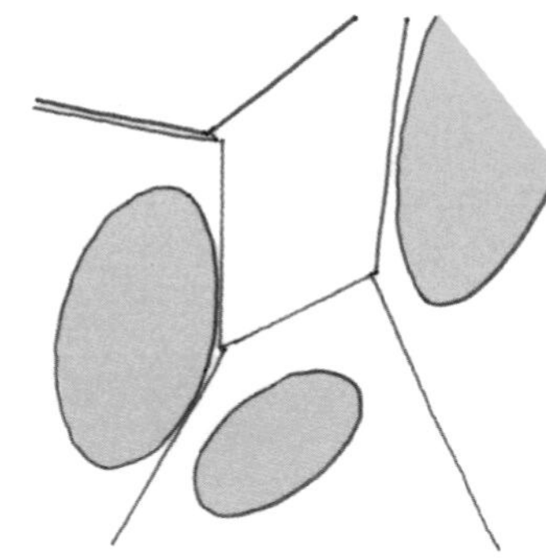

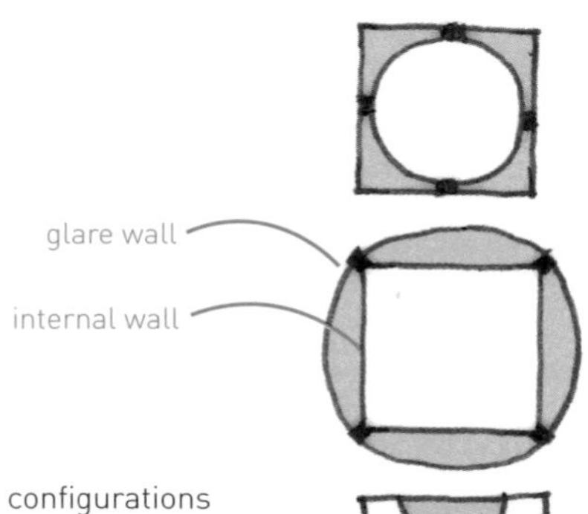

The various configurations of a double-walled system protect the interior spaces from glare and heat gain.

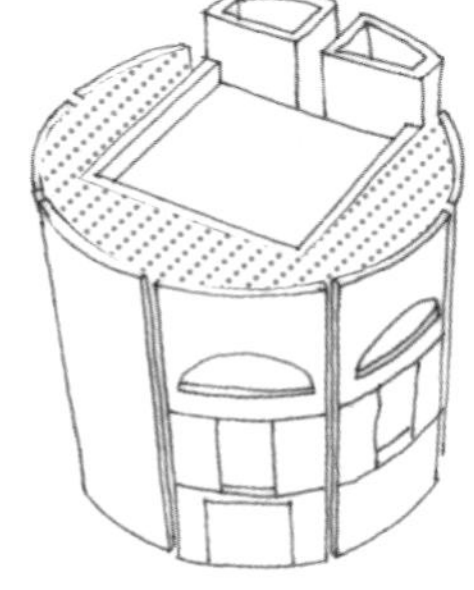

Meeting House, Salk Institute for Biological Studies (unbuilt)

The scale of these spaces and the monumental openings engender a sense of awe. The idea was originally conceived for the Meeting House at the Salk Institute for Biological Studies in California, but is more fully explored within the climatic and cultural context of India. A comparison of the form to the eyes of the local goddess Durga has been argued as a source for a strong religious or spiritual quality in these spaces.

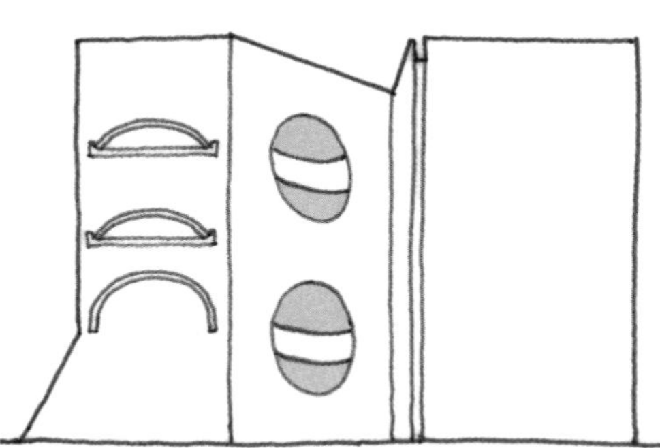

Student dormitories with external glare walls

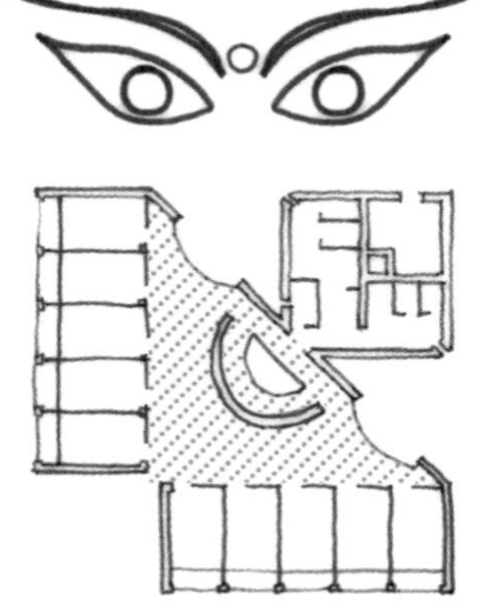

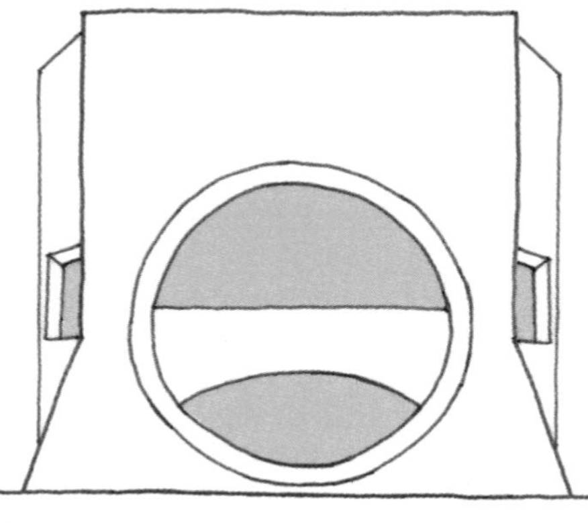

Monumental openings inspire a sense of awe.

Order, space and form

The design uses an interplay of primary geometric forms such as squares and circles to develop an order that defines the relationship of the various elements to one another and to the whole. This is evident in the relationship between open and built spaces, in the relationship of service areas to the usable areas, and even in the articulation of fenestration detail. For example, in the student dormitories an alternating series of squares is used for organizing the open and built spaces. While similar to the classical nine-square grid used by Kahn at the Trenton Bath House in New Jersey, USA (1955), this is a fuller exploration of the extended order of the grid, letting it operate in a non-rigid manner. Similar developments are visible in the approach to services.

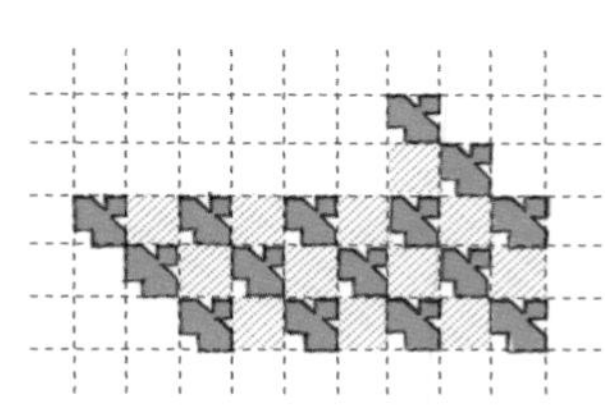

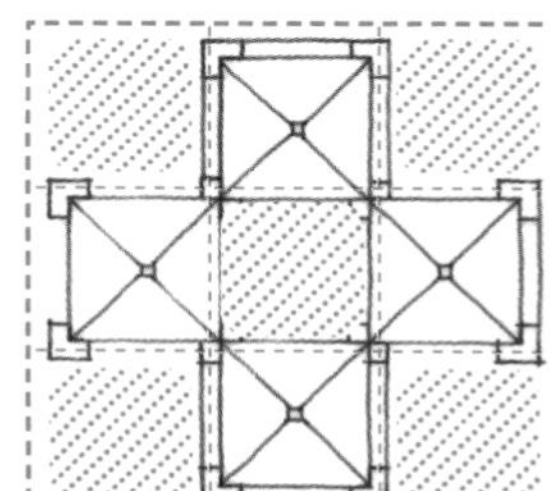

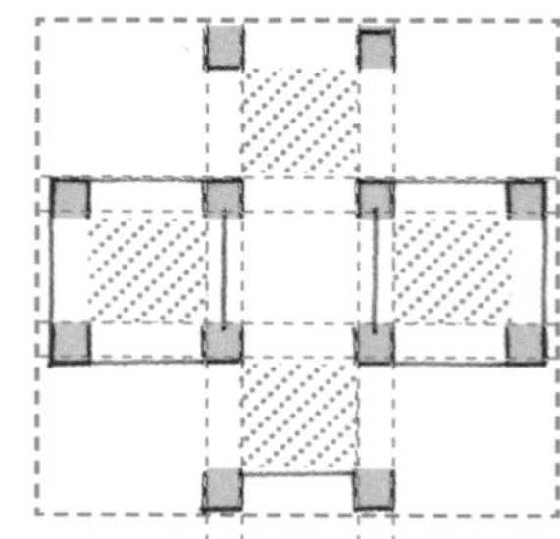

In the Trenton Bath House project Kahn used a system of squares to organize the relationship of the servant and served spaces, but these remain separated in an alternating plaid grid.

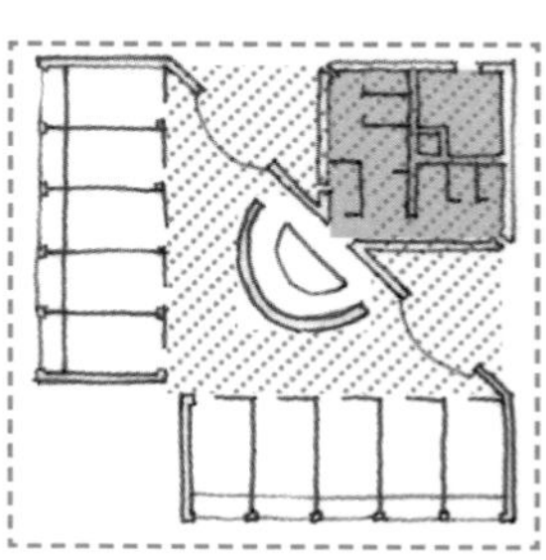

In the design of the student dormitories at the IIM the tripartite approach allows the servant and the served spaces to be mediated by a third transitional space, and these are all developed as a series of nested squares.

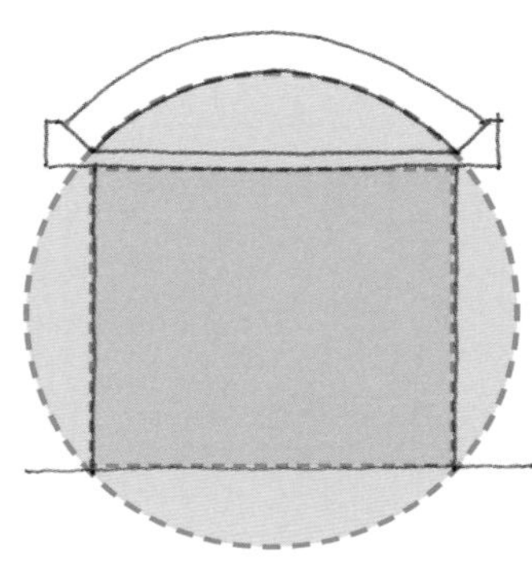

The use of primary forms is also evident in the design of the numerous types of fenestration. The glare-wall system allows for a monumental circle to be juxtaposed against a human-scale square. In other instances the persistence of the order allows the experience of these primary forms to be inferred through gestalt (an intuitive perception of the whole or complete composition).

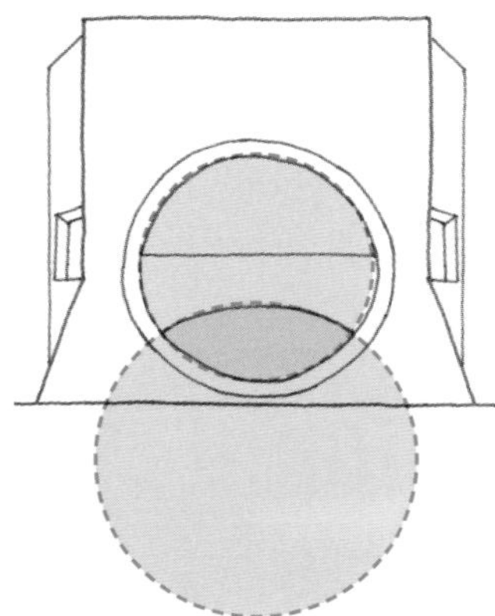
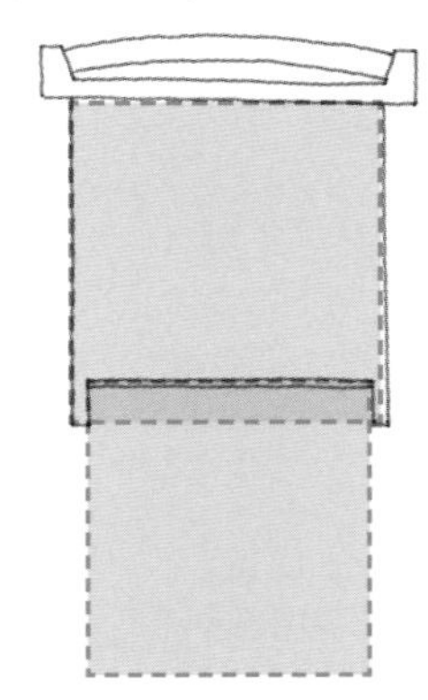

The repetitive experience of the order forms a gestalt and users are left to complete an unfinished series of forms in their mind, creating greater visual interest.

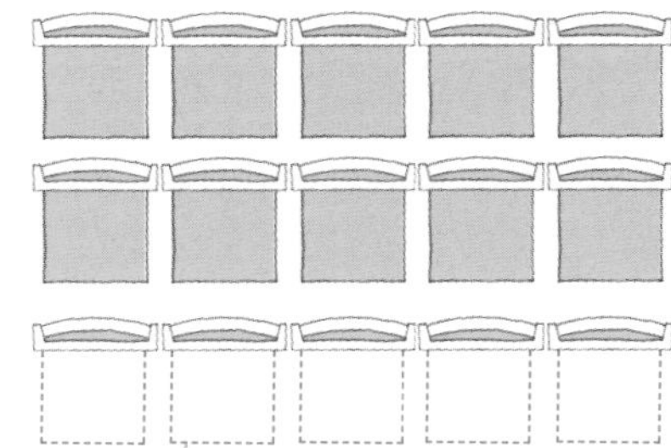

Response to material order

The design for IIM is conceived in the local material of brick. This goes beyond pragmatic concerns, as the entire design process is defined through the exploration of the potential of this one material. Where concrete is required to give openings a horizontal lintel, it is used in conjunction with brick arches, allowing the two materials to respond to each other and develop a composite tectonic order.

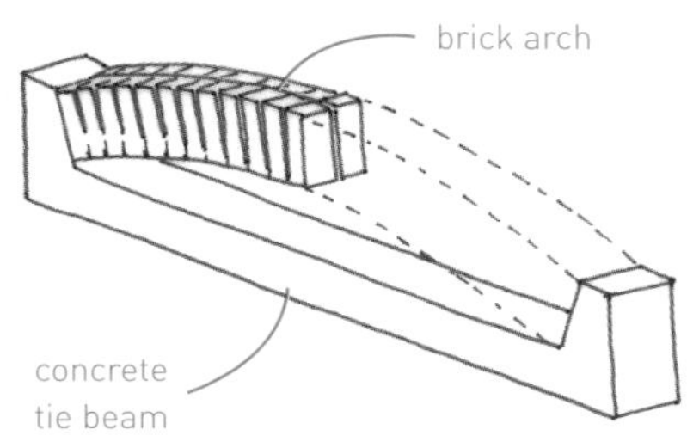

Brick arches in compression and concrete tie beams in tension work together to develop a composite order.

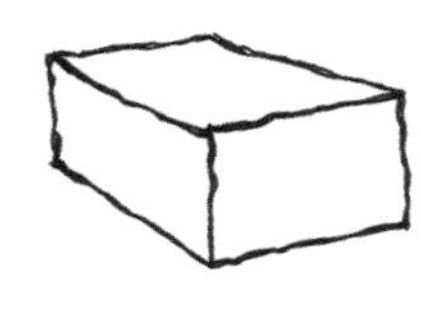
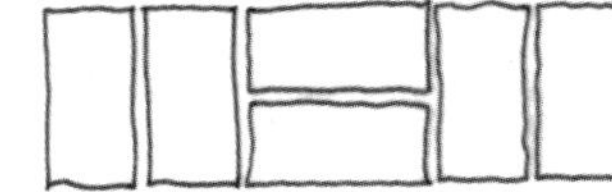
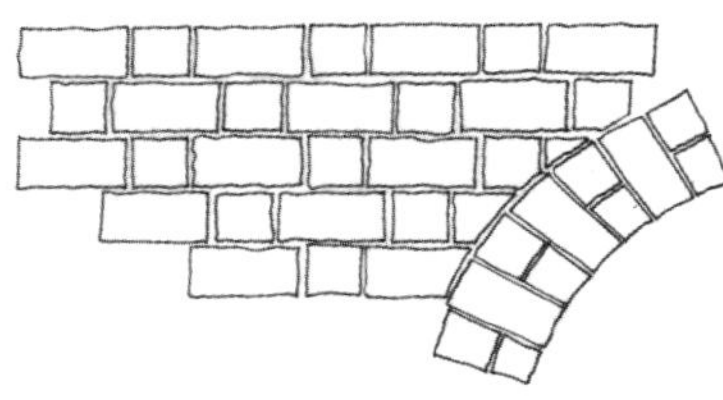

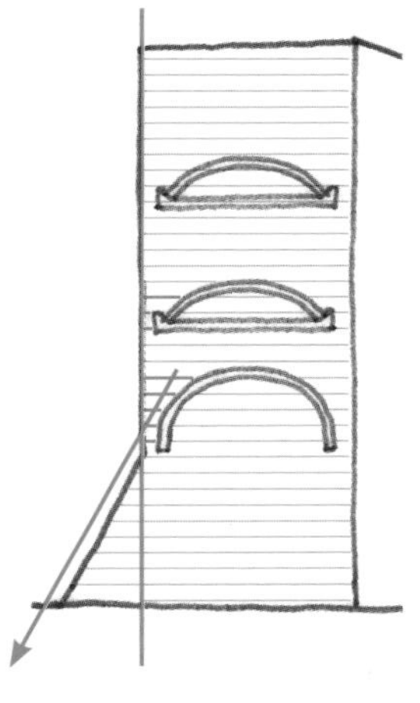
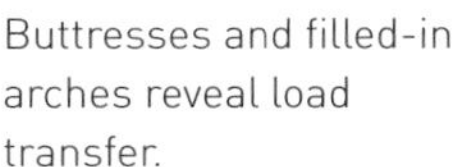

Buttresses and filled-in arches reveal load transfer.

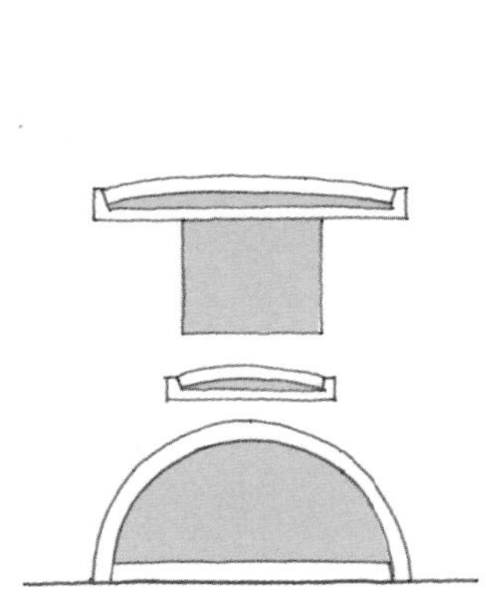

The composite order is used to create a variety of forms.

The unitary geometric form of the brick is explored through tectonic means to create myriad forms and openings that enliven the spaces. The tectonic forces of the brick construction are expressed in the overall form of the buildings, which use buttresses and filled-in arches to show the transfer of load in the masonry system.

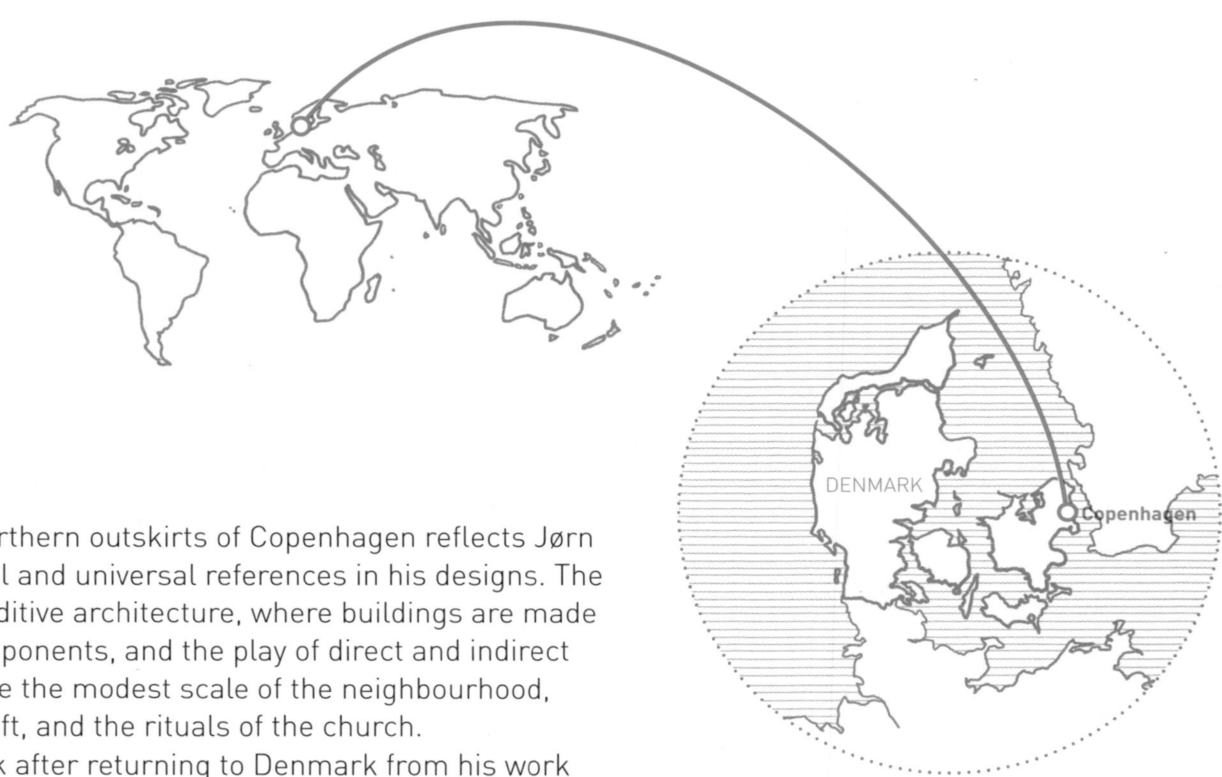

Bagsvaerd Church | 1974–76

Jørn Utzon

Bagsvaerd, Copenhagen, Denmark

Bagsvaerd Church on the northern outskirts of Copenhagen reflects Jørn Utzon's aim to reconcile local and universal references in his designs. The universal themes include additive architecture, where buildings are made up of clearly identifiable components, and the play of direct and indirect daylighting. Local themes are the modest scale of the neighbourhood, traditions of Danish woodcraft, and the rituals of the church.

This was Utzon's first work after returning to Denmark from his work on the Sydney Opera House in Australia. Two long corridors on the north and south sides of the building close spaces that seem to span between them. In contrast to the Sydney Opera House, the exterior is restrained and it is the cloudlike concrete ceiling of the sanctuary that is expressive, hidden from outside by tall flanking walls and planar roofs. Light from above illuminates the curving surfaces of this ceiling in subtle gradations of luminance as it swoops from high over the altar to low over the congregation. Pale beech-wood windows, doors and church furniture soften the white concrete ceilings and walls.

Selen Morkoç, Felicity Jones, Ying Sung Chia and Leona Greenslade

13

13 Bagsvaerd Church | 1974–76

Jørn Utzon

Bagsvaerd, Copenhagen, Denmark

Response to nature

The church is located in Bagsvaerd, a northern suburb of Copenhagen. It is a Lutheran church.

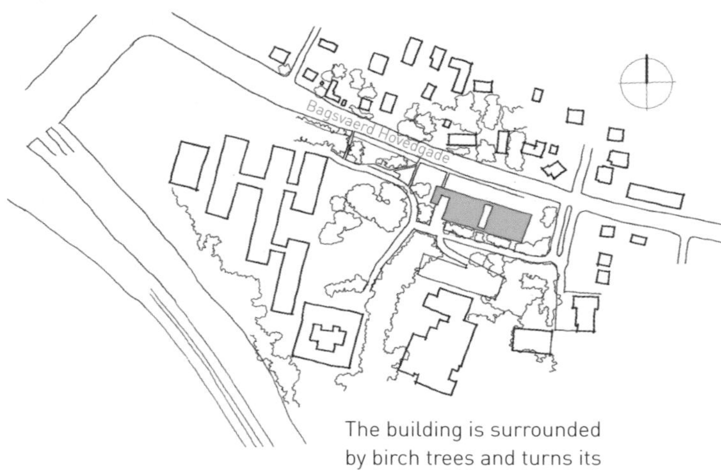

The building is surrounded by birch trees and turns its back to the road.

Landscape The hard exterior materials of white concrete panels and white-glazed tiles are softened by the birch trees that change colour according to the season. The trees diffuse the rectilinear form of the church in the landscape.

South elevation
Most of the openings face towards the sun.

North elevation
The façades are divided into regular segments by vertical lines. Strong horizontal lines divide two different materials. The windowless wall buffers the interior from the busy suburban road.

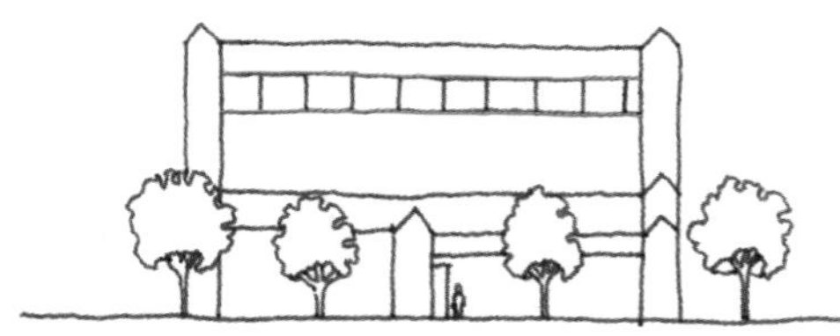

West elevation
The main window opening lighting the church ceiling faces east for morning sun.

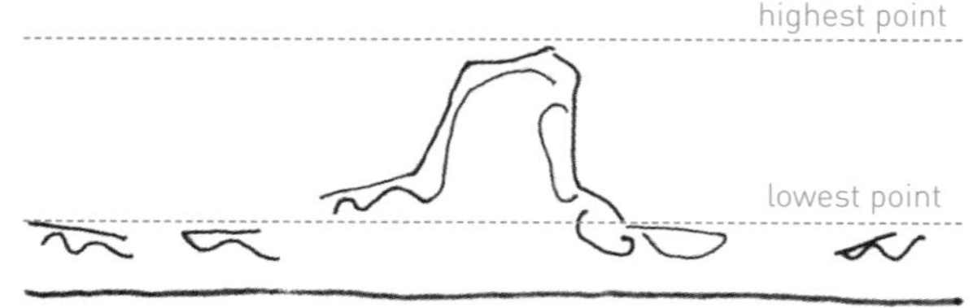

The curve rises from the lowest point above the back of the seating to its highest point above the altar.

Form generation: interior

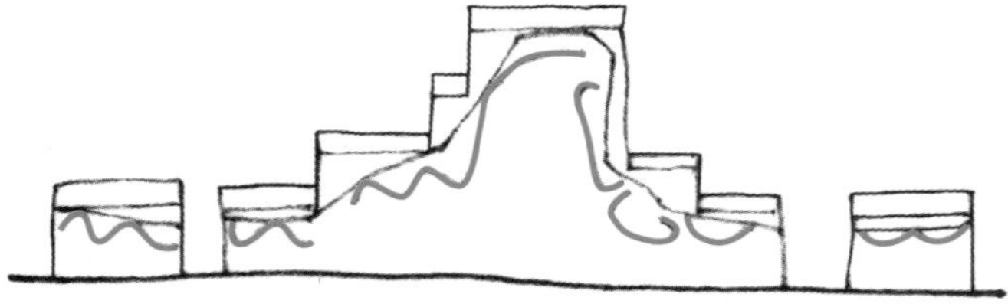

The interior form of the church has a different character from the exterior. The interior form is more complex, featuring a curving concrete ceiling that is covered and hidden by the flat structure above. The curving ceiling suggests clouds passing over water.

Form generation: exterior

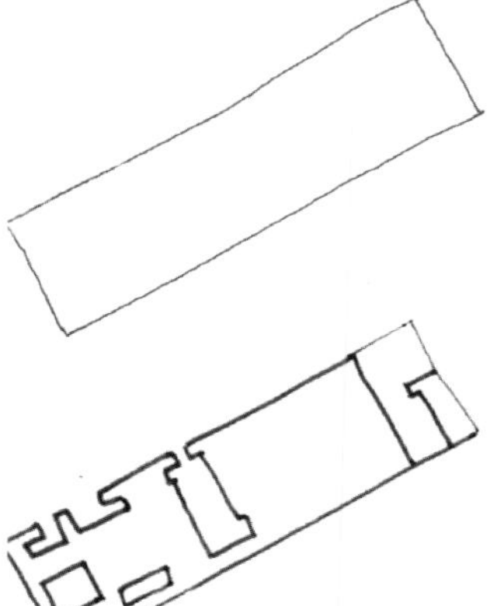

An unassuming simple rectangle is the basis of the church plan.

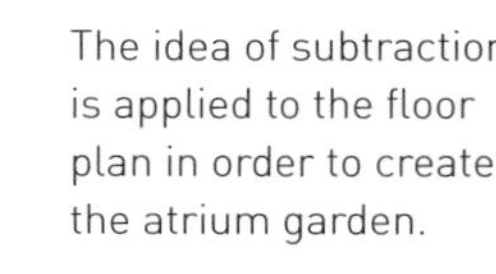

The idea of subtraction is applied to the floor plan in order to create the atrium garden.

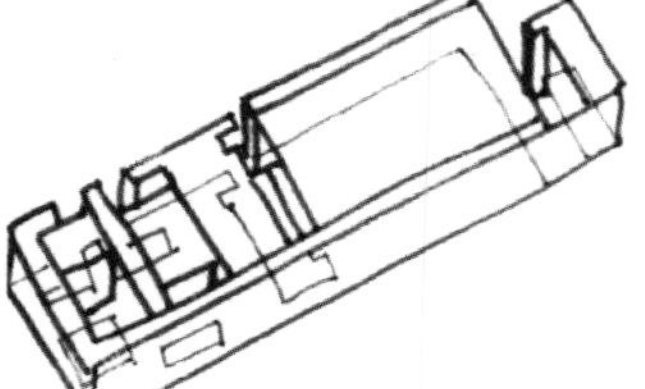

Extruding the 2D floor plan creates the basic form of the church.

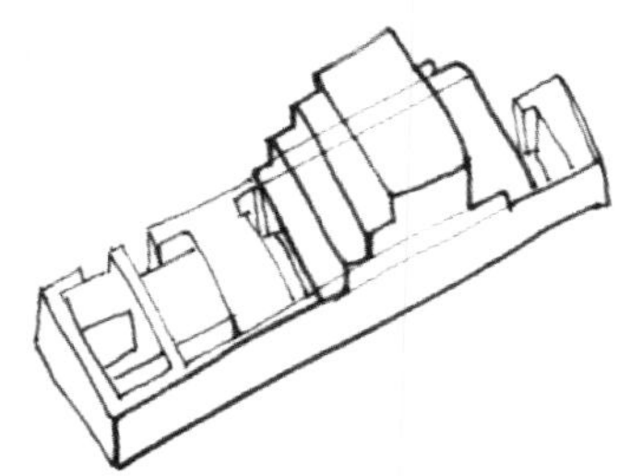

The form is extruded further above the main church space in order to give height and allow natural light to enter and be reflected off the curves of the ceiling.

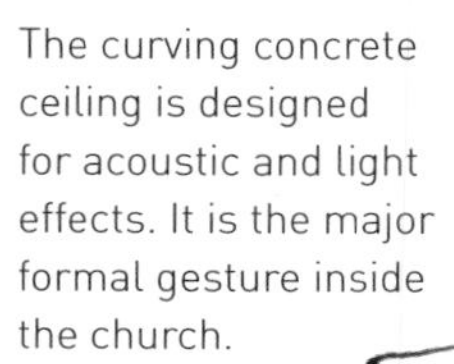

The curving concrete ceiling is designed for acoustic and light effects. It is the major formal gesture inside the church.

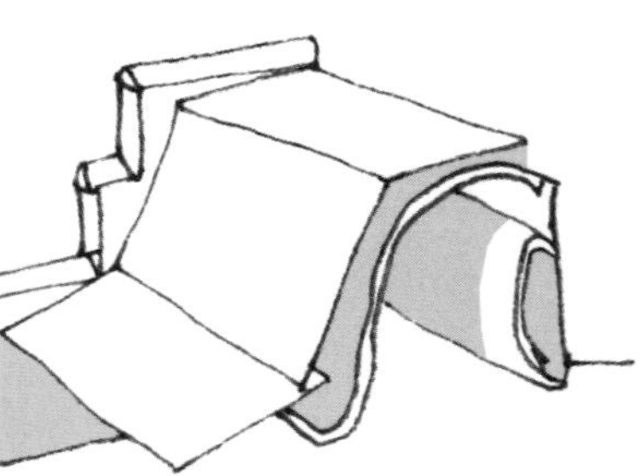

Universal language

Utzon's aim to follow universal design principles is evident in both the Sydney Opera House and Bagsvaerd Church, despite different scales and functions. Both projects have similar aesthetic qualities, such as white tiles that reflect changing light. Cohesiveness of form and vernacular symbolic references are other characteristics shared by the two projects.

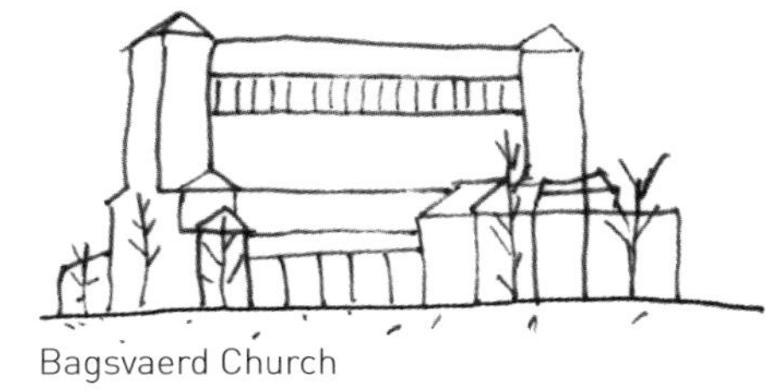

Bagsvaerd Church

Sydney Opera House, Australia (1957–73)

Acoustics

The organ plays an important role in the religious ceremony. The sound under the undulating ceiling evokes a sense of wonder through acoustics.

The organ

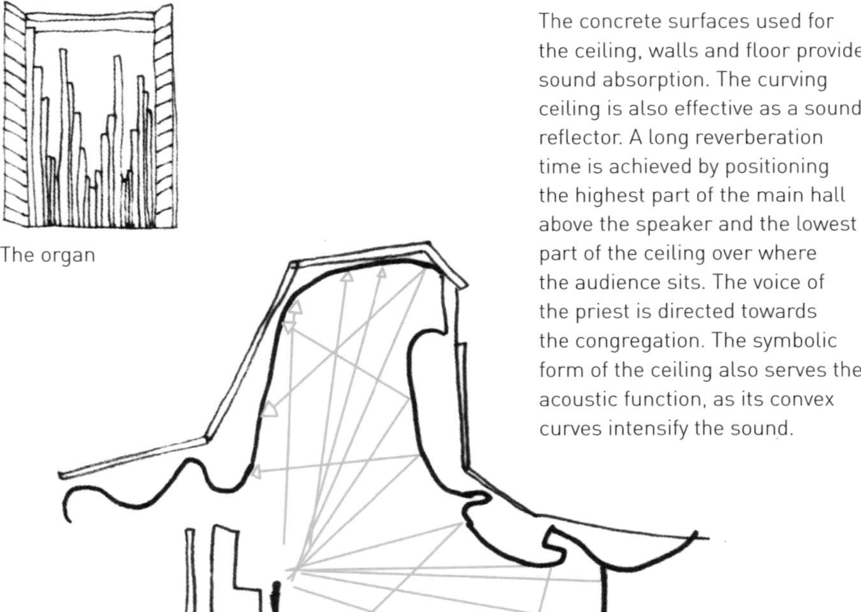

The concrete surfaces used for the ceiling, walls and floor provide sound absorption. The curving ceiling is also effective as a sound reflector. A long reverberation time is achieved by positioning the highest part of the main hall above the speaker and the lowest part of the ceiling over where the audience sits. The voice of the priest is directed towards the congregation. The symbolic form of the ceiling also serves the acoustic function, as its convex curves intensify the sound.

Lighting

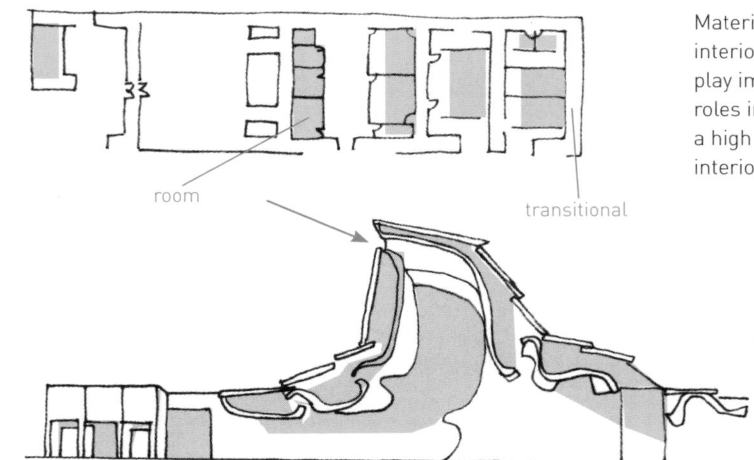

Materials and interior form both play important roles in achieving a high quality of interior lighting.

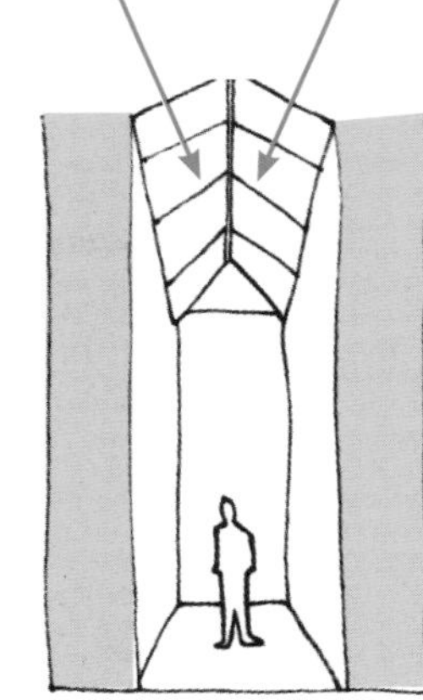

In the interior of the church, the hard reflective ceiling has a glowing surface quality reminiscent of a cloudy Nordic sky, and prompts spiritual reflection.

While the main space has indirect daylighting, in the side corridors skylights connect directly with the sky. They provide a bright, warm atmosphere inside the church. The admission of light from above suggests spiritual connections between heaven and earth.

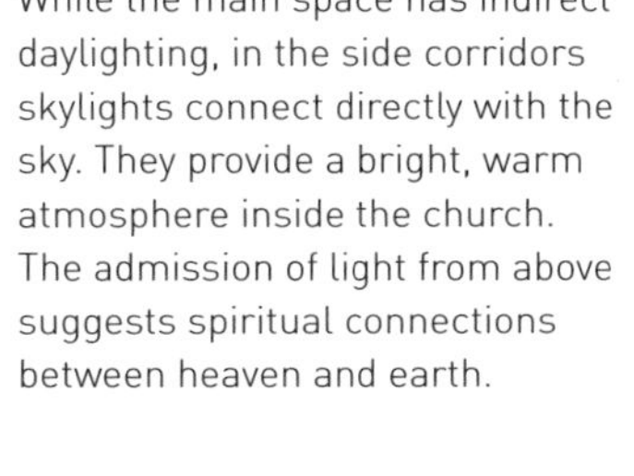

Bagsvaerd Church | 1974–76

Jørn Utzon

Bagsvaerd, Copenhagen, Denmark

Response to programme

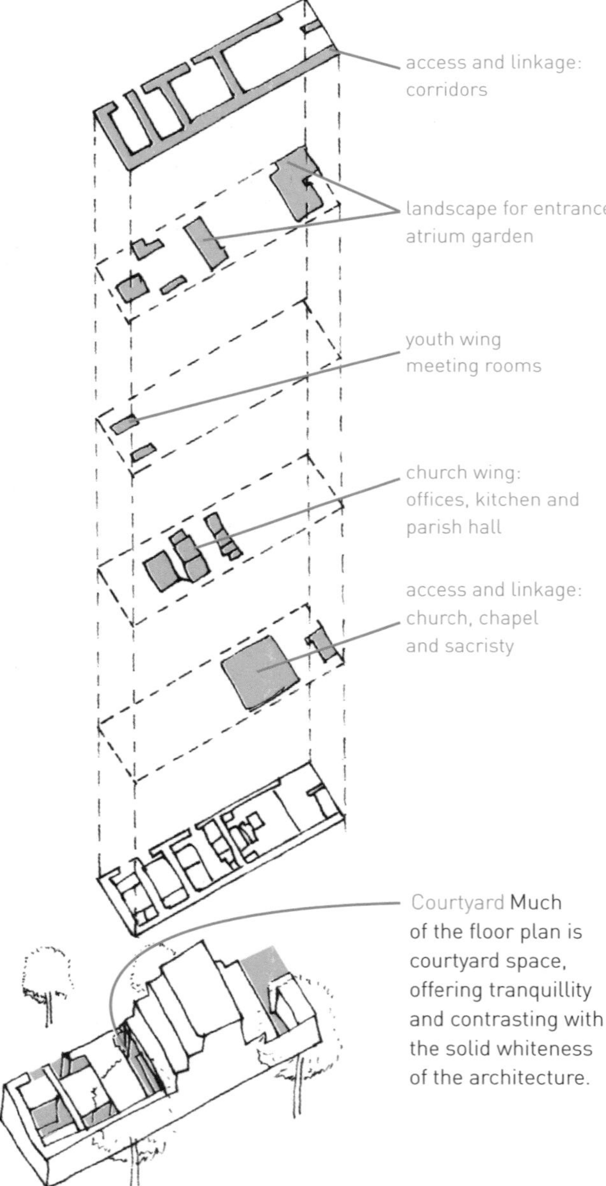

Courtyard Much of the floor plan is courtyard space, offering tranquillity and contrasting with the solid whiteness of the architecture.

Human experience

Contrasting forms and spaces containing references to vernacular and universal precedents enrich visual and auditory experiences.

The corridor pathways are narrow and tall. The glass ceiling helps to enlarge the space vertically while allowing natural light to flood in from above. The church hall has a strong aesthetic cohesion. The undulating ceiling form combined with the rationality of the linear floor grid results in a dramatic and uplifting experience of the space.

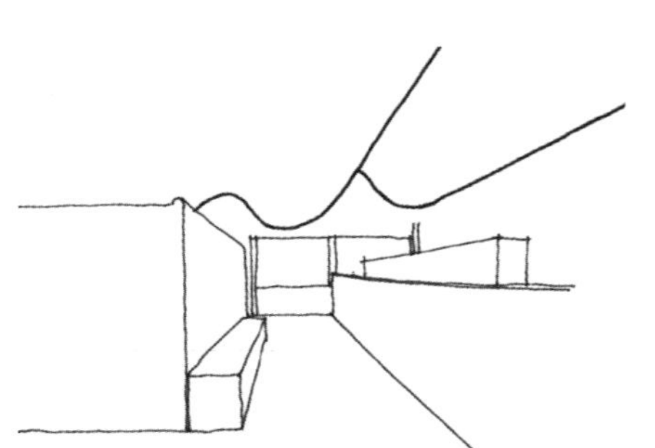

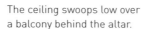

The ceiling swoops low over a balcony behind the altar.

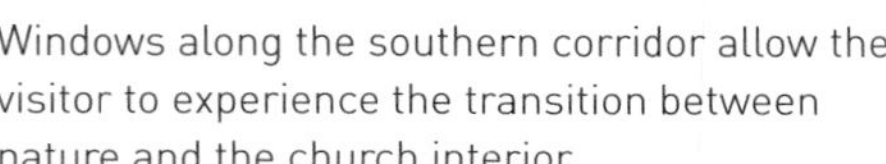

Windows along the southern corridor allow the visitor to experience the transition between nature and the church interior.

Balance between order and freedom
The free-form ceiling spans between two rigid structural linear arrangements.

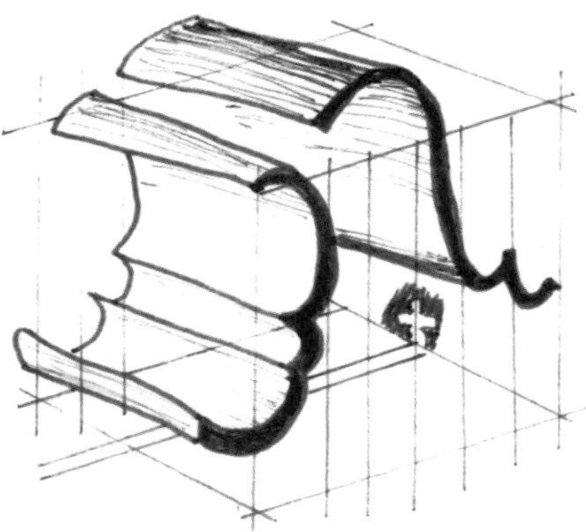

Materials
The exterior is constructed with an in-situ concrete frame, precast-concrete panels, and horizontal glazed ceramic tiles. The roof cladding is aluminium with glass skylights. Inside, a grey board-marked concrete frame and white concrete walls and ceiling are complemented by pale beech wood.

Axes The rectilinear plan and strong axes reference the layout of a Buddhist temple.

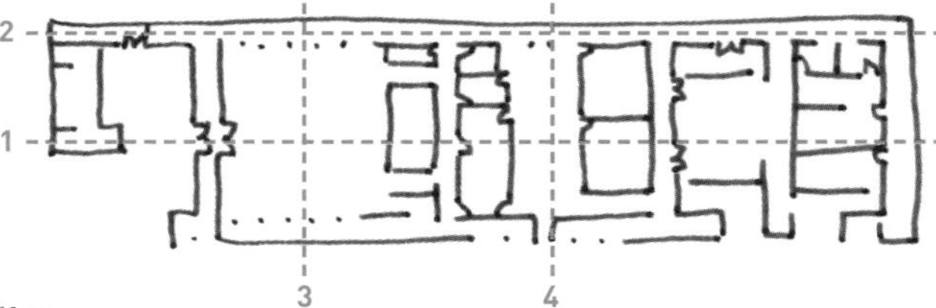

Key
1. main longitudinal axis
2. longitudinal corridors
3. main hall space with the roof
4. main courtyard space

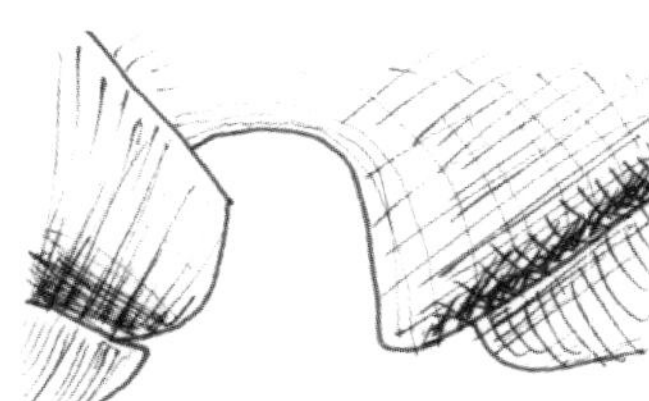

The white ceiling varies in tone from bright through soft shadow to dark, emphasizing its curves.

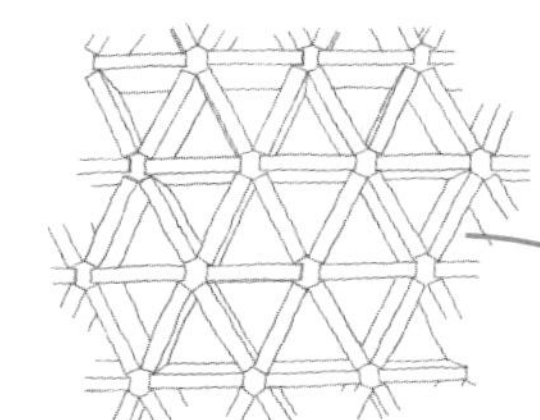

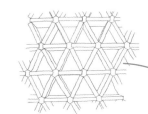

Reflective tiles composed of crushed marble give the building interior a pure, luminous quality. The altar screen is a trellis of white-glazed tiles.

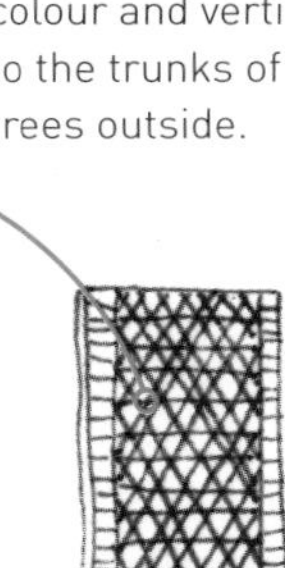

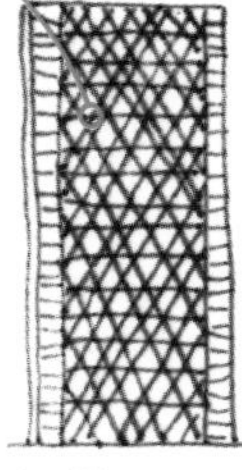

Colour Both the interior and the exterior of the church are predominantly white, consisting of precast-concrete panels and tiles. Rougher grey concrete columns along the corridors contrast with the whitewashed wall surfaces, and by colour and verticality refer to the trunks of the birch trees outside.

Textiles
Colourful textiles in the church were designed by Utzon's daughter, Lin Utzon. They embody religious symbolism while differentiating between the elements of interior space.

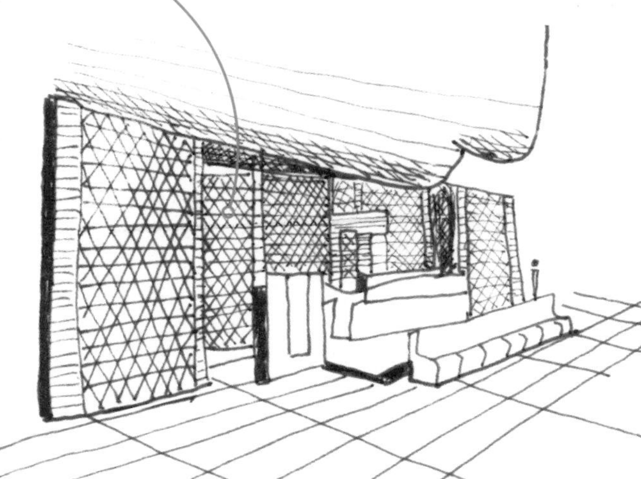

Bagsvaerd Church | 1974–76
Jørn Utzon
Bagsvaerd, Copenhagen, Denmark

Spaces

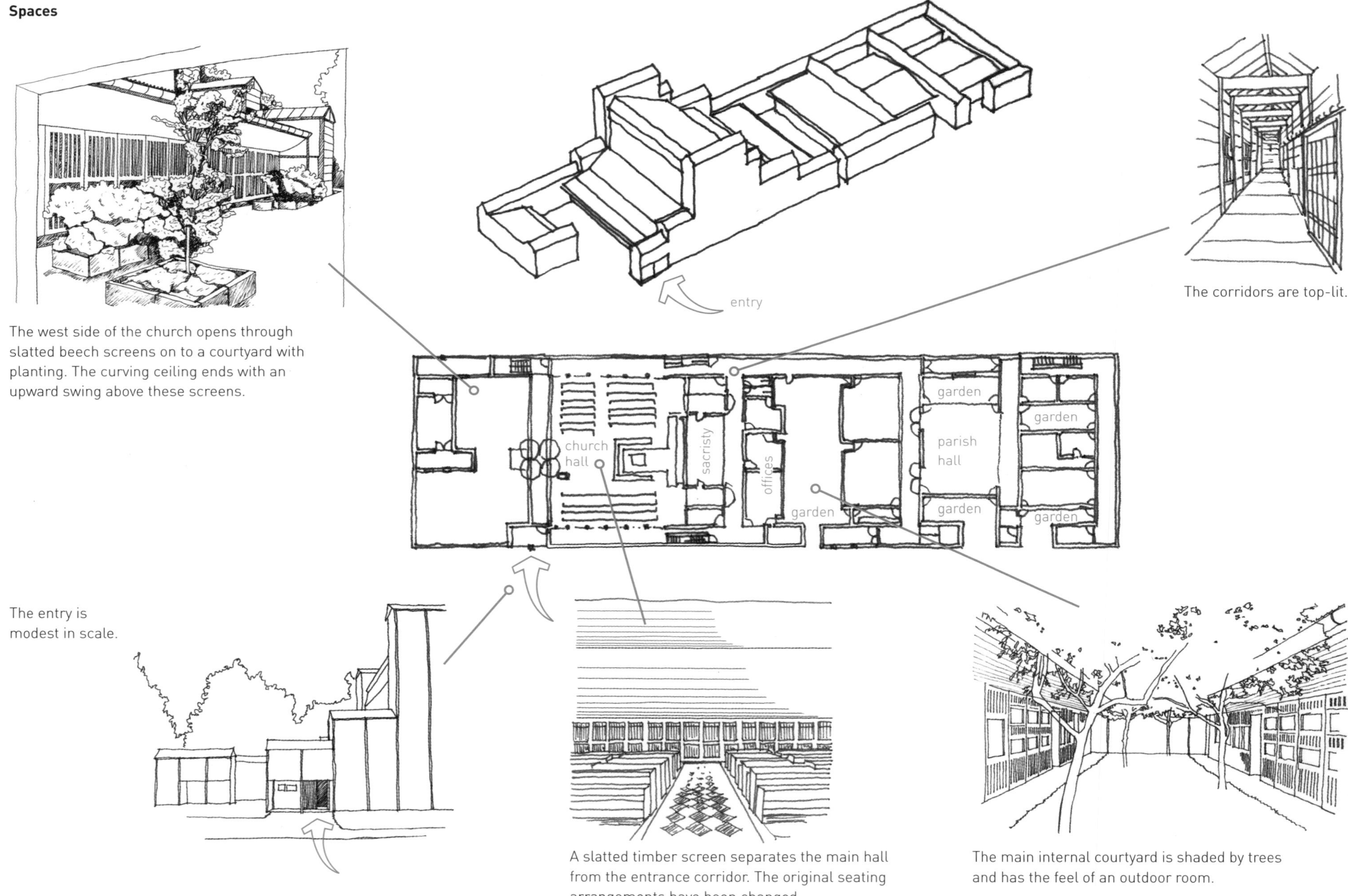

The west side of the church opens through slatted beech screens on to a courtyard with planting. The curving ceiling ends with an upward swing above these screens.

The corridors are top-lit.

The entry is modest in scale.

A slatted timber screen separates the main hall from the entrance corridor. The original seating arrangements have been changed.

The main internal courtyard is shaded by trees and has the feel of an outdoor room.

Continuity in details

The curvilinear form of the inside ceiling continues outside to make a canopy over doors and windows along the east side of the building.

Exterior

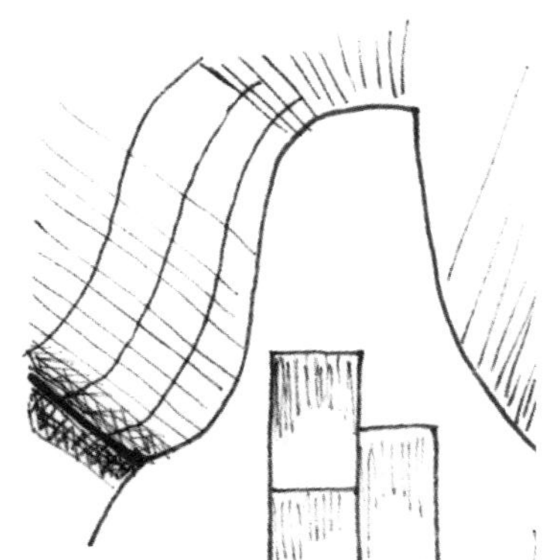

Interior

The side corridors of the building appear to be cut off at the west and east building ends. The altar, lectern and altar platform seem to be fine concrete extrusions that are similarly cut off.

The roof and ceiling of the main spaces appear to be extrusions flanked by the tall side corridors. The pews appear as comparable extrusions in beech wood flanked by tall side panels.

Local references

The influence of local vernacular cottages is evident in the simple façade and roof form of the church.

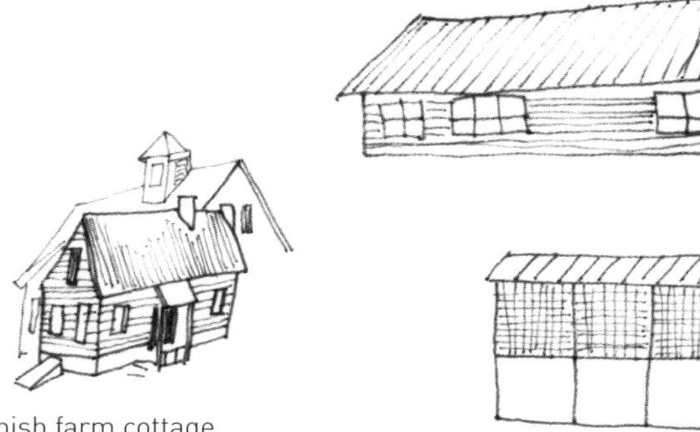

Danish farm cottage

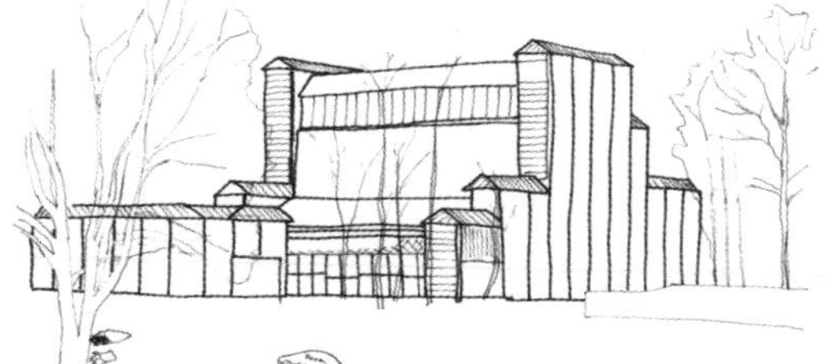

Exterior of Bagsvaerd Church

Furniture, such as the pews made of Swedish pine, has strong Scandinavian references.

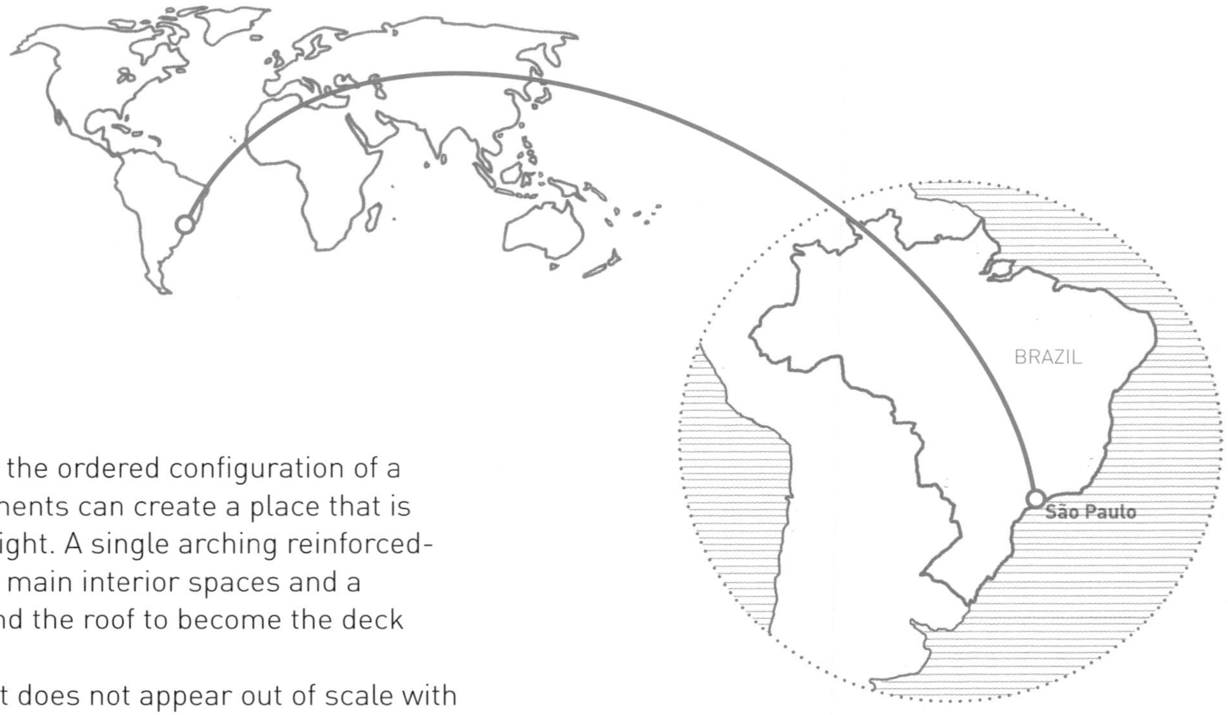

14

Milan House | 1972–75

Marcos Acayaba Arquitetos

Cidade Jardim, São Paulo, Brazil

The Milan House shows how the ordered configuration of a small number of design elements can create a place that is full of visual interest and delight. A single arching reinforced-concrete roof spans over the main interior spaces and a terrace, which extends beyond the roof to become the deck for a swimming pool.

This is a large house, but it does not appear out of scale with its neighbours in a green and prosperous area of São Paulo. Designed by Brazilian architect Marcos Acayaba, it has the feeling of a secluded resort in one of the southern hemisphere's biggest cities.

The house has a restrained palette of materials: concrete, tiles and glass. This is accompanied by a limited but important use of colour and of wood, leather and fabrics, which soften the effect. This economy of geometry and materiality contrasts with the lush vegetation around the house.

Amit Srivastava and Antony Radford

Milan House | 1972–75

Marcos Acayaba Arquitetos
Cidade Jardim, São Paulo, Brazil

Response to context

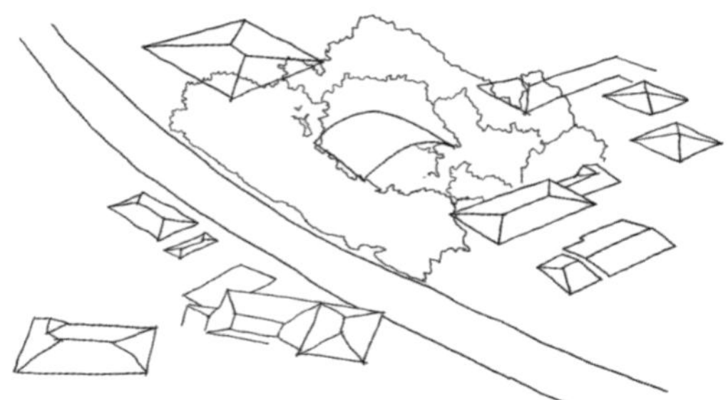

The Milan House is located in the Garden City (Cidade Jardim) area of São Paulo, a suburb with many trees and large blocks of land. The planting and distance between houses means that the outdoor living areas are secluded. Although the form of the house is very different from its brick-and-tile neighbours, it does not stand out because the height and scale are similar and the screen of trees masks the house from the street.

Response to climate

The Tropic of Capricorn passes through São Paulo. Because of its elevation, the city has a temperate climate without extremes of hot or cold weather. There is a high annual rainfall. The house responds to the climate with open terraces on both the north (sunny) and the south (more shaded) sides, and a large covered terrace between the living area and the pool.

The lines of thrust from the reinforced concrete arch are channelled to its four corners and into the ground. The arch shell is insulated with polyurethane.

Form and composition

The land is shaped to form three platforms.

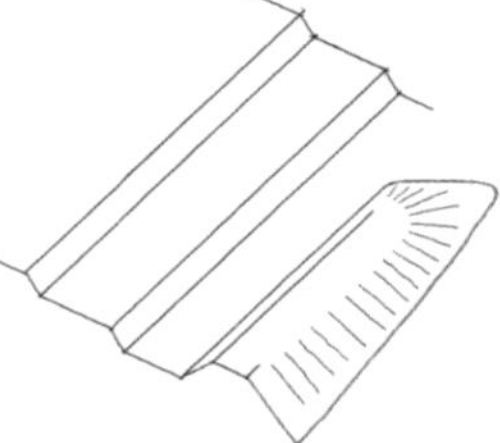

A pool is cut out of the largest platform.

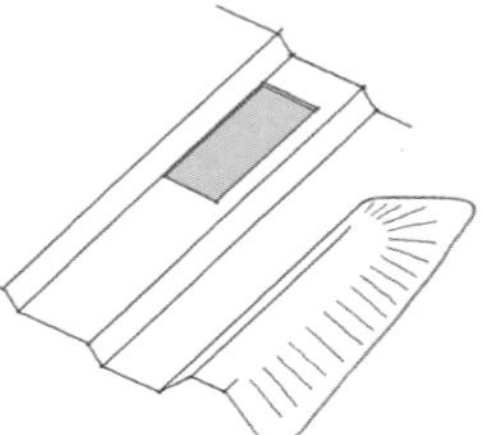

A fourth platform floats over the ground.

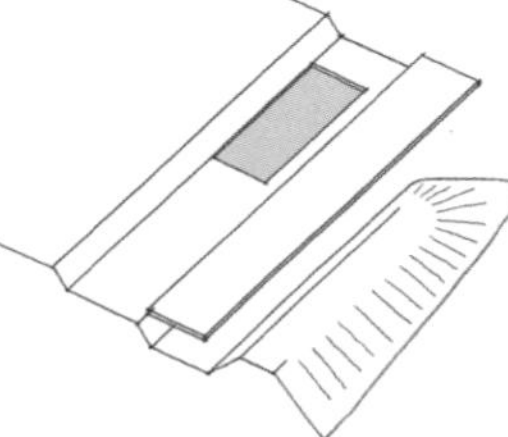

An arch spans over the platforms.

The sides of the arch are cut back to open side vistas.

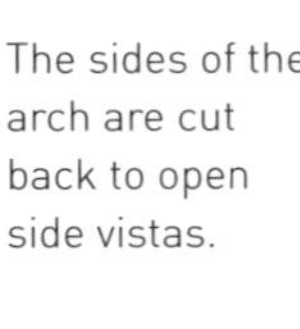

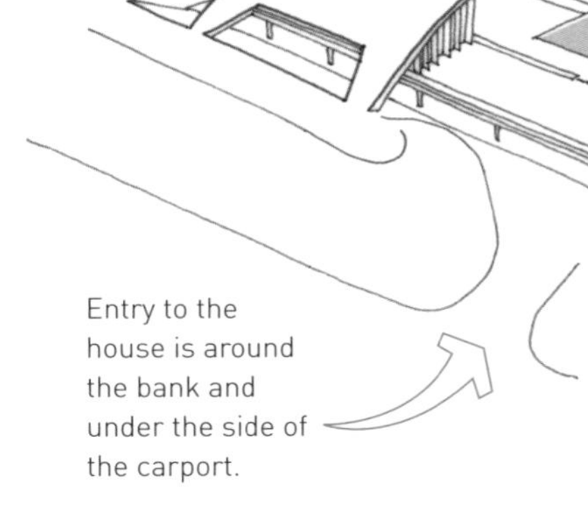

Entry to the house is around the bank and under the side of the carport.

The upper terrace is a flat slab of cross-ribbed reinforced concrete, so there are no visible beams disturbing its simplicity. Twelve cylindrical columns positioned on a regular grid support the slab.

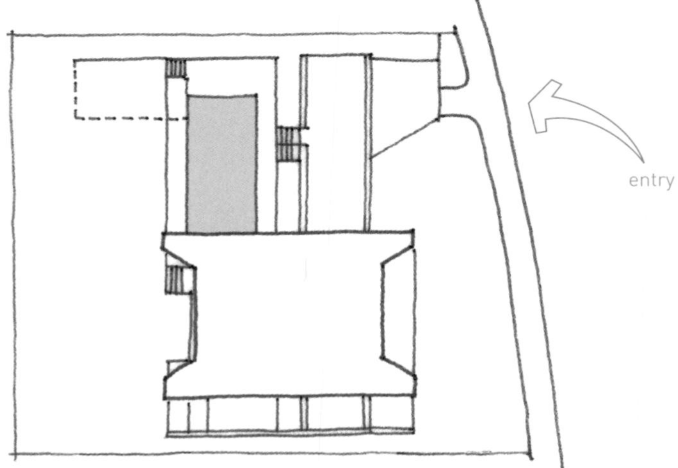

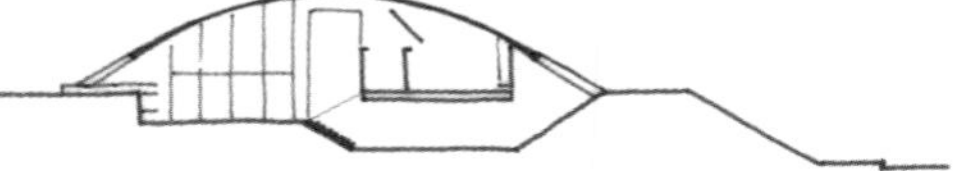

Glass fills the openings between the arch and the floor of the main living area.

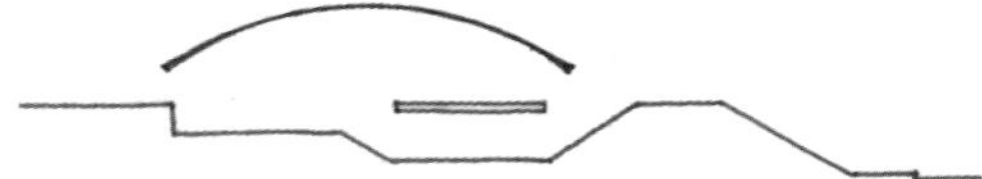

Simplified, the section is an elegant curve over a horizontal line over an undulating line.

Pivoted plywood panels cover openings between the bedroom and the more public spaces.

A unit of built-in furniture combines a sofa, fireplace and bookcase along the west wall of the living area. The chimney rises behind the fireplace, outside the room, and through the cut-out part of the roof arch.

Two concrete towers slot between the three levels of the house. They support the water tanks and contain bathrooms on the top and lowest floors.

The same polished red floor tiles continue from the interior of the living room out to the covered veranda and deck around the swimming pool, integrating the spaces.

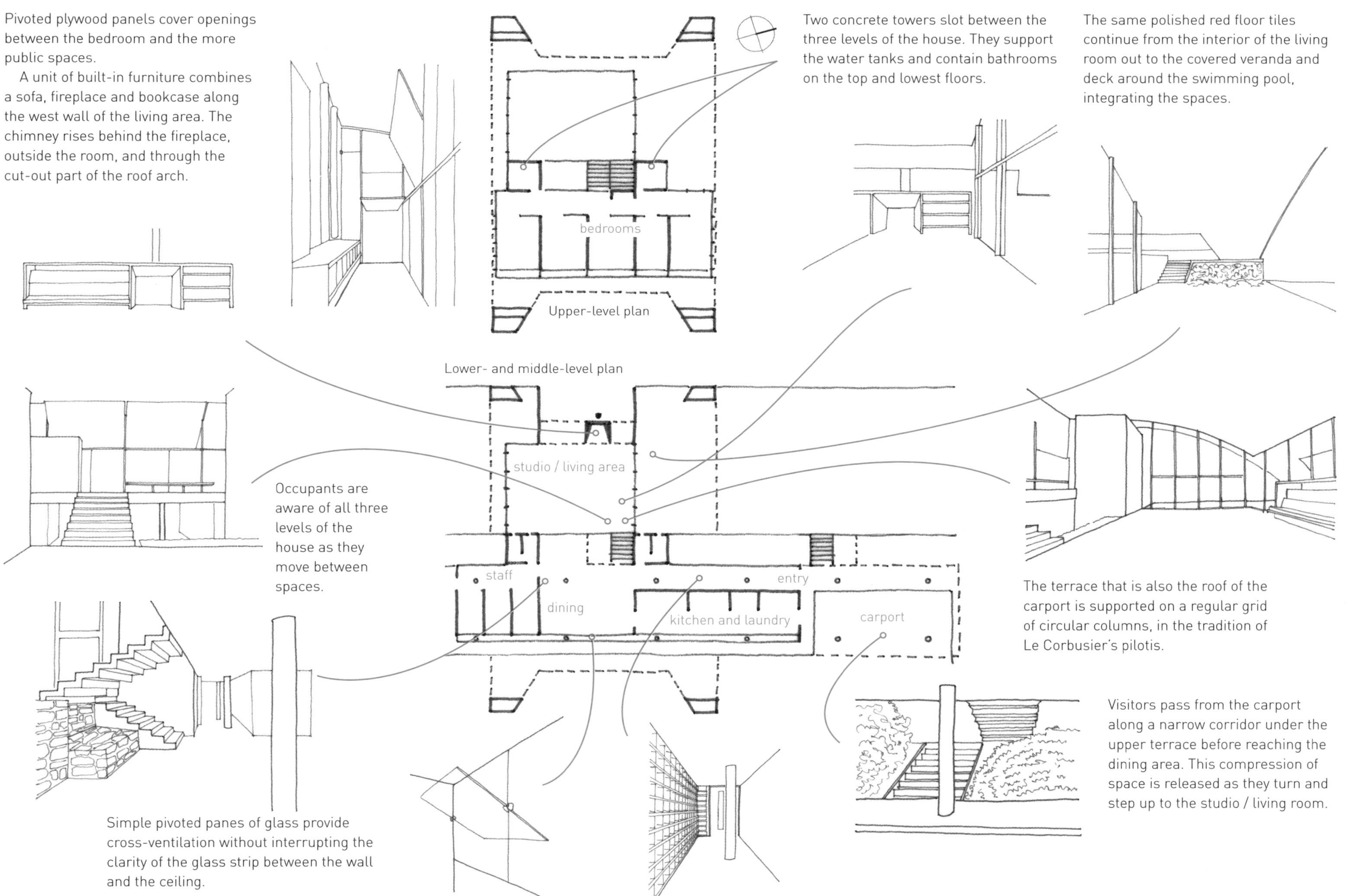

Occupants are aware of all three levels of the house as they move between spaces.

The terrace that is also the roof of the carport is supported on a regular grid of circular columns, in the tradition of Le Corbusier's pilotis.

Visitors pass from the carport along a narrow corridor under the upper terrace before reaching the dining area. This compression of space is released as they turn and step up to the studio / living room.

Simple pivoted panes of glass provide cross-ventilation without interrupting the clarity of the glass strip between the wall and the ceiling.

HSBC Office Building | 1979–86

Foster Associates

Hong Kong, China

15

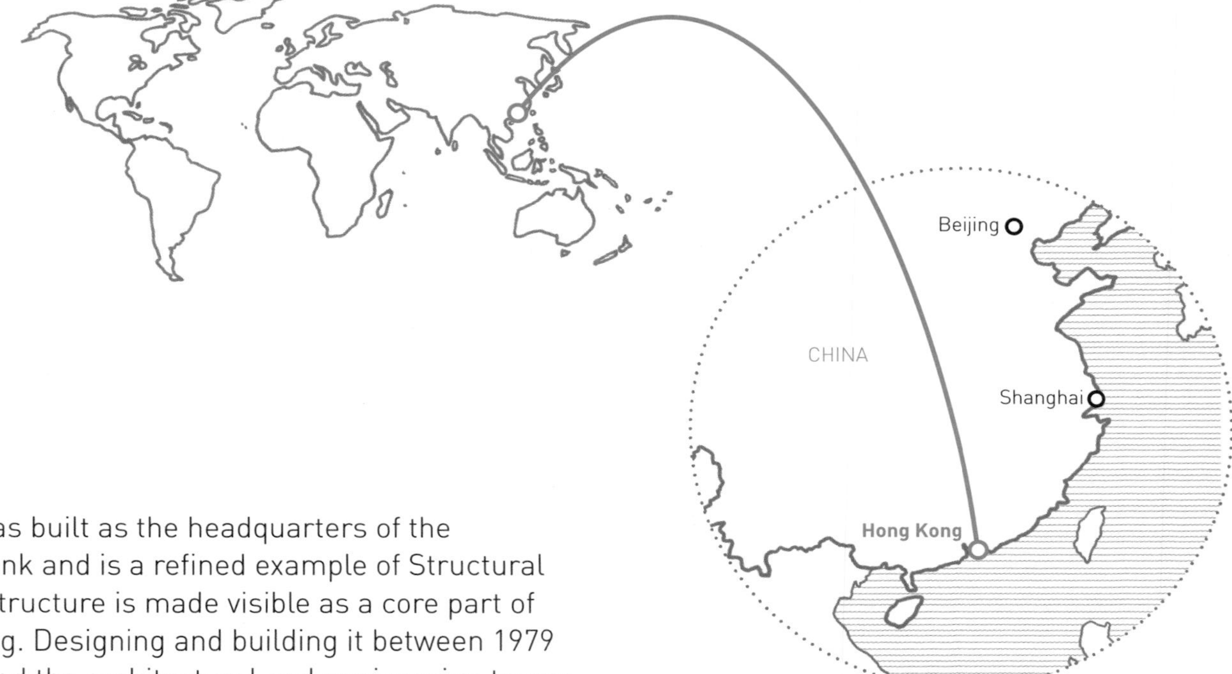

The HSBC office building was built as the headquarters of the Hongkong and Shanghai Bank and is a refined example of Structural Expressionism, where the structure is made visible as a core part of the aesthetics of the building. Designing and building it between 1979 and 1986, Norman Foster and the architectural and engineering teams adopted technologies from aviation, the offshore oil industry and other industrial fields. Many of the components were prefabricated and they were often imported, so the building has the character of a precise assembly of legible separate elements.

The aesthetic and technical aspects of architecture are integrated so that design responses for functional and symbolic objectives, structural integrity and climate work together as a cohesive whole. This outcome was achieved through the extensive exploration of options during the design process, from structural strategies to small details.

Antony Radford, Sindy Chung and Brendan Capper

HSBC

Response to site
Hong Kong has a long history as a trading and financial centre. The bank is located on Hong Kong Island looking north over the harbour towards Kowloon on the mainland. The Star Ferry across the harbour docks close to the site.

The site was once waterfront, but successive land reclamation projects have pushed the shore away. It is backed by the steep slopes of the Peak on Hong Kong Island. A strip of land between the site and the water has remained relatively open, so a harbour view is retained.

The contrast of robust structure with delicate transparency is a feature of Asian architecture.

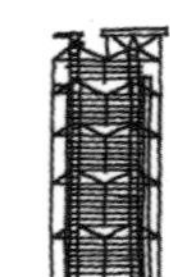

The building as an isolated object appears as a finely engineered metal and glass entity with themes of symmetry/asymmetry and robustness/fine detail; and rhythms of floor clusters, structural elements and module stacks.

The building had responsive cohesion with its setting at the time of its completion. Its scale is similar to its neighbours, and buildings have a consistent rectangular profile. The bank stood out because of the detail and interest of its façades, but it does not dominate its neighbours.

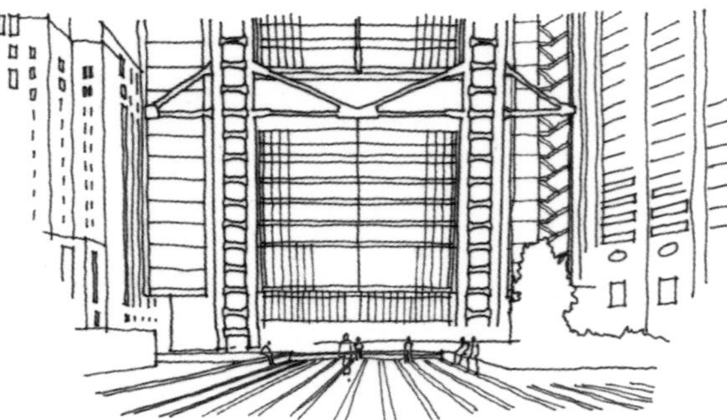

By 2012 larger buildings had been inserted nearby. The bank no longer had the same presence when seen from a distance, although its design remains strikingly different from its more conventional neighbours.

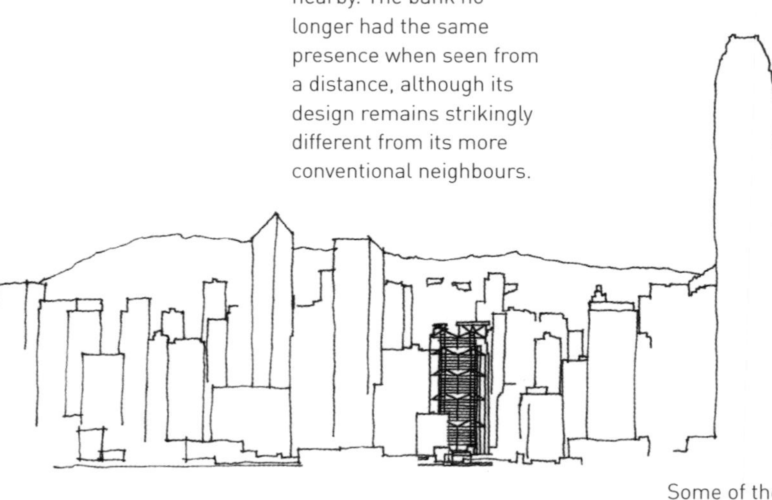

Some of these newer buildings compete for attention through size, darker skins, bigger signage and less subtle profiles.

The ground level of the building is open apart from service cores and escalators leading up the main banking hall.

Planning and use

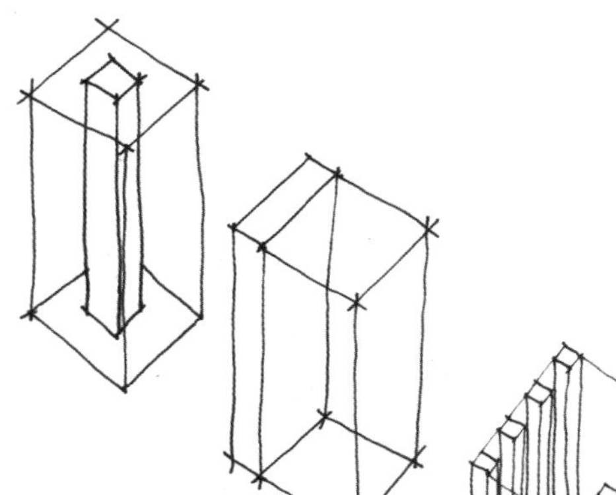

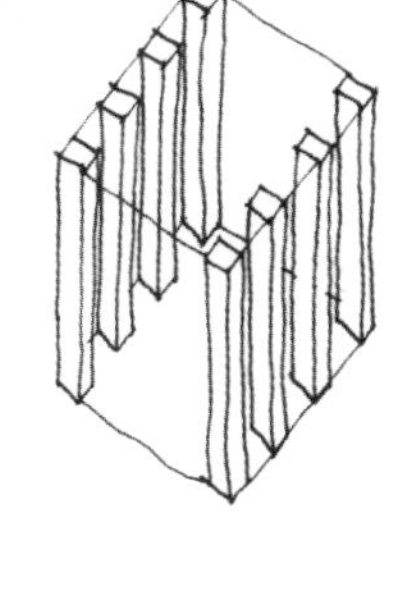

Most office towers built up to the 1980s had a central core of lifts and services. This suited a ring of individual offices that could have windows. With the trend to open-plan offices, the core shifted to one side of an unobstructed open space. The HSBC office building breaks the core into smaller components arranged along opposite sides, with windows between the components.

Between the cores, floors are set back on the west, north and south sides at upper levels to conform to zoning and light access regulations. The structure is designed to allow these setbacks to be filled in if future regulations allow, offering up to 30 per cent more floor space within the building footprint and overall height.

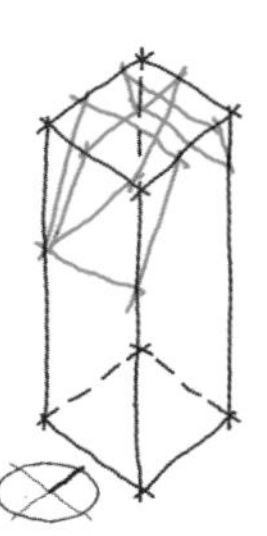

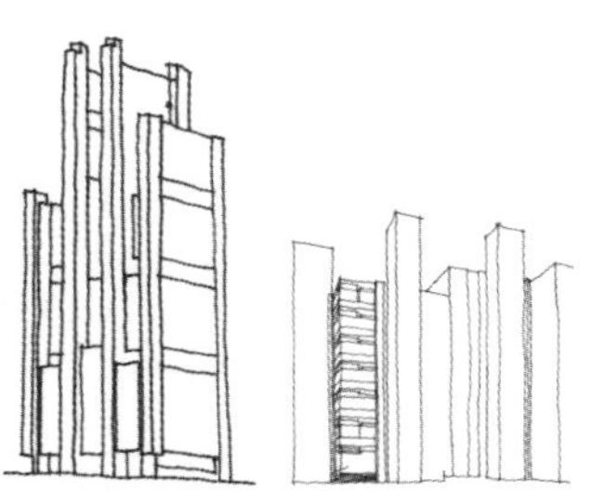

The clear distinction between 'served' and 'servant' spaces recalls Louis Khan's Richards Medical Research Laboratories, Philadelphia, USA (1957–62).

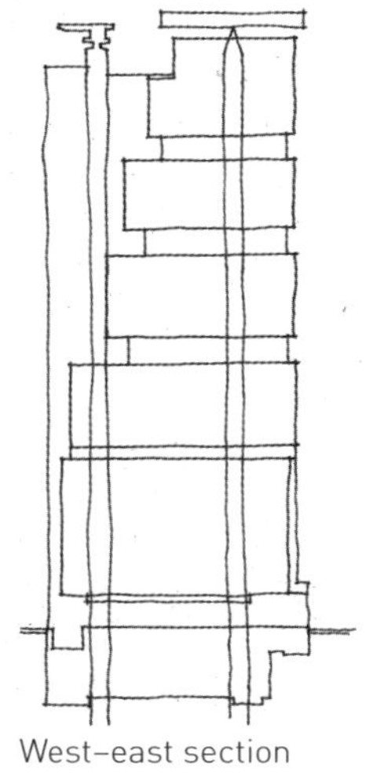

West–east section

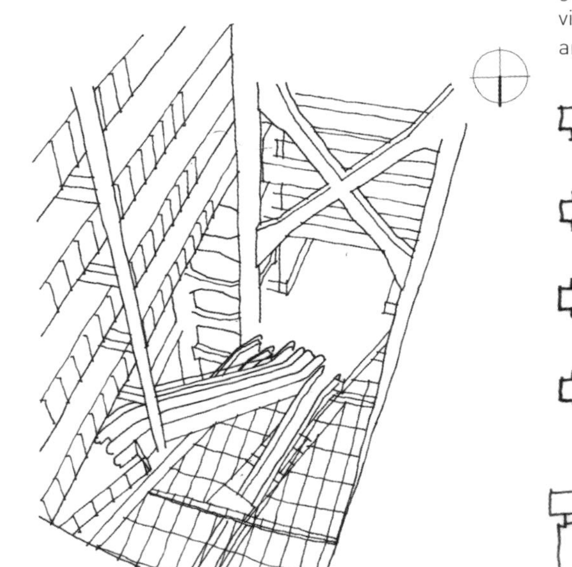

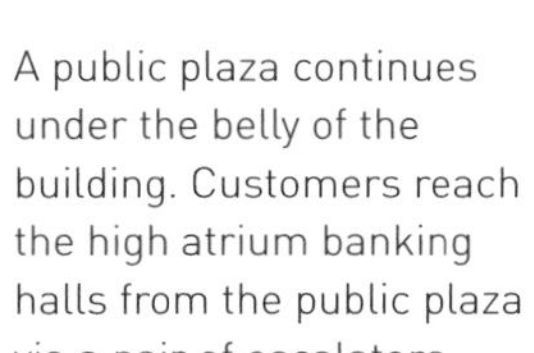

A public plaza continues under the belly of the building. Customers reach the high atrium banking halls from the public plaza via a pair of escalators.

With open-plan offices, everyone gets good space and access to the views over the harbour to the north and to the Peak in the south.

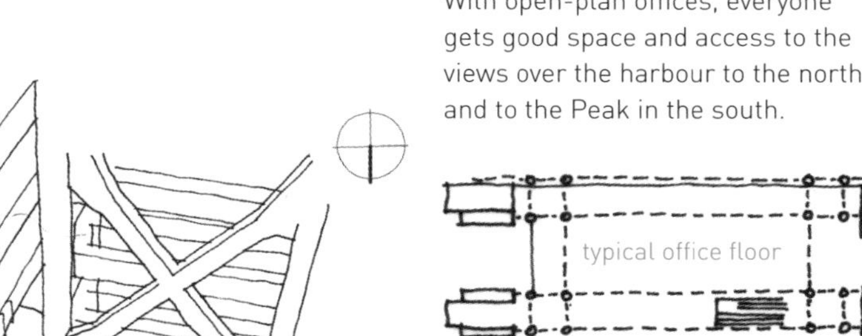

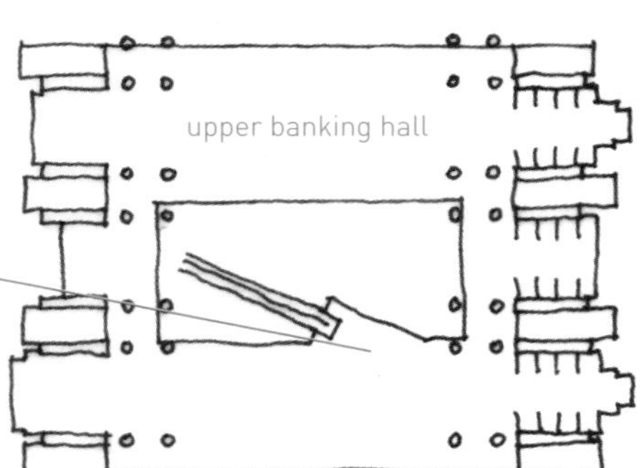

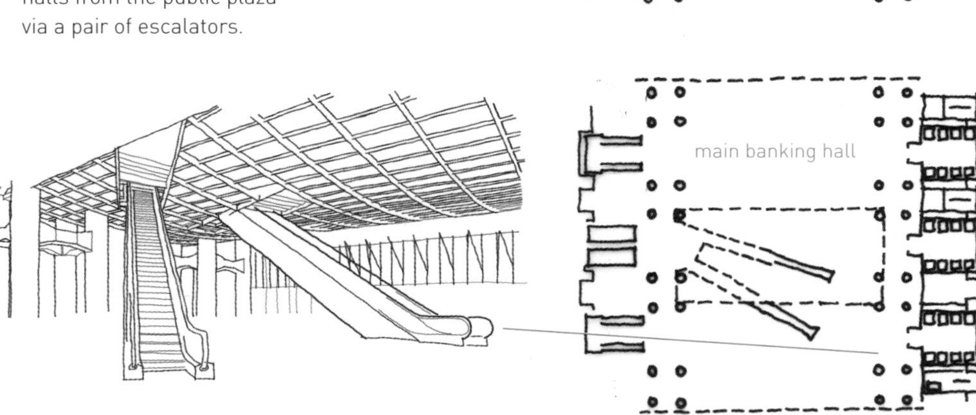

Spaces and services

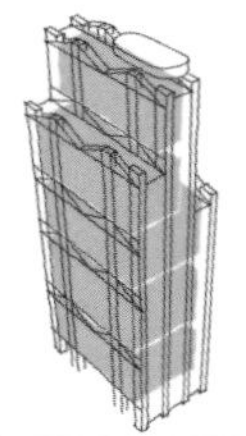

A series of five vertically stacked 'villages' breaks down the scale of a 'normal' high-rise building.

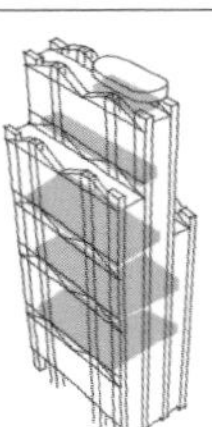

Between the 'villages' double-height spaces at the truss levels have setbacks offering broad verandas. In early design drawings, green plants and small trees are shown on these levels.

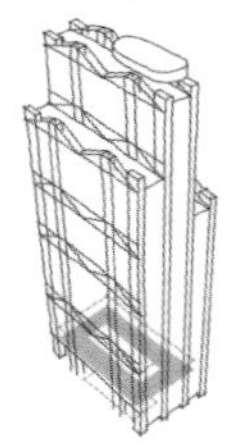

Three public banking halls – two on the lower floors of a large atrium above the plaza and one on the first basement level – are located closest to ground level.

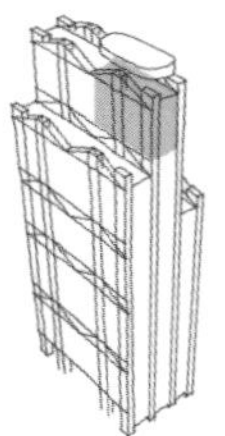

Senior executives occupy the highest 'village'. An apartment for the bank chairman was located at the top of the building.

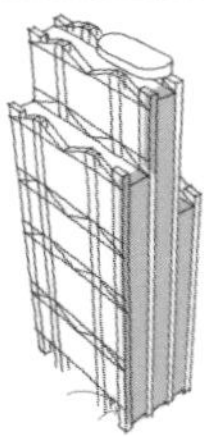

Three stacks of lifts are located along the east side of the building. These provide fast access to the double-height spaces that act as interchanges with local escalators.

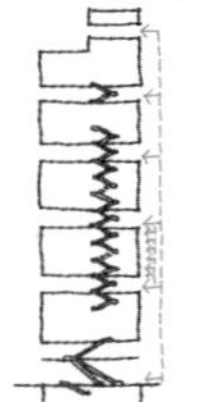

Public escalators from the plaza lead up to two floors of banking halls and down to one basement banking hall. Private high-speed lifts link double-height spaces that are interchanges with local escalators.

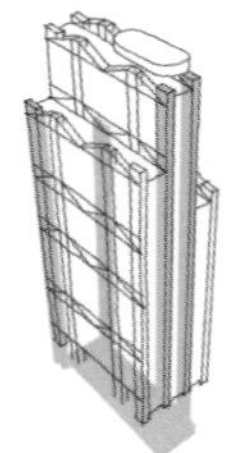

A basement plant room links via ducts to local air-conditioning units in the modules on each floor. Prefabricated lavatories are located in the stack of modules.

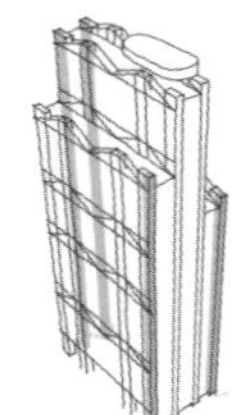

Four escape stairs with glass walls lead to ground level.

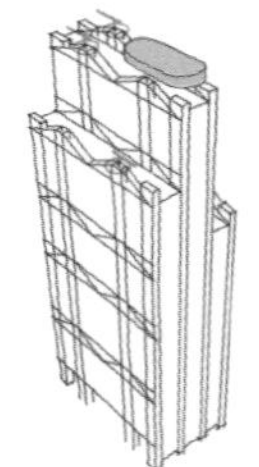

Two of the masts support a helipad that crowns the building. Permanent maintenance cranes at the top of the masts give an impression of an incomplete building still under construction.

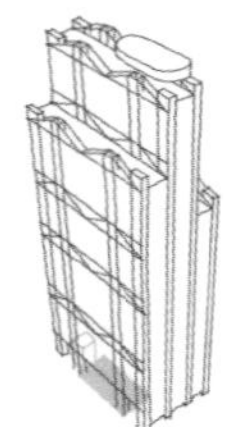

A vehicle lift takes small vehicles to a secure basement delivery area.

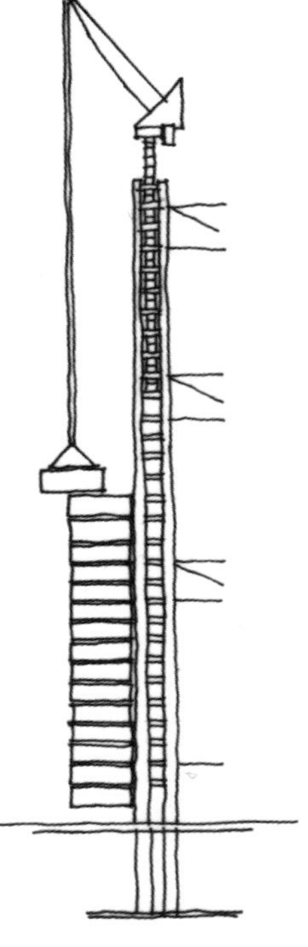

The modules
One hundred and thirty-nine prefabricated modules, about the size of shipping containers, contain the lavatories and air-handling plant for each floor, and other secondary plant such as generators and electrical substations. They were built and fully fitted out in Japan. They are linked by risers, also prefabricated, in two- or three-storey frames. They are sheathed in stainless steel.

The modules were hoisted into position using cranes on top of the building's masts.

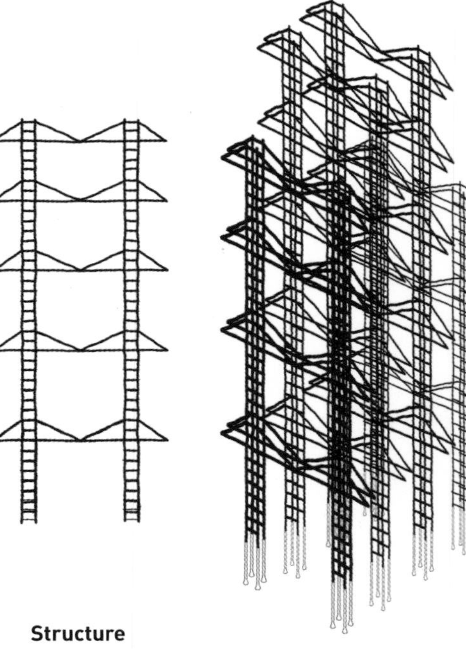

Structure
Eight masts support trusses like bridges at five levels. The floors are suspended from these trusses.

The masts are vertical Vierendeel structures, each with four sub-columns linked by rigid horizontal members at storey-height intervals. A Vierendeel truss has no diagonal bracing, relying on the stiffness of connections.

Steel structural members are wrapped in corrosion-resistant and fire-protection layers. A 5mm (0.2in.) skin of aluminium cladding follows the geometry of the underlying structure.

The glass underbelly is a suspended catenary structure hung from its edges – light and elegant.

Response to climate

The colonial buildings in Hong Kong provided shaded colonnades and overhangs. Few later commercial buildings do that. The HSBC building offers a shaded plaza at ground level and shaded verandas at upper levels.

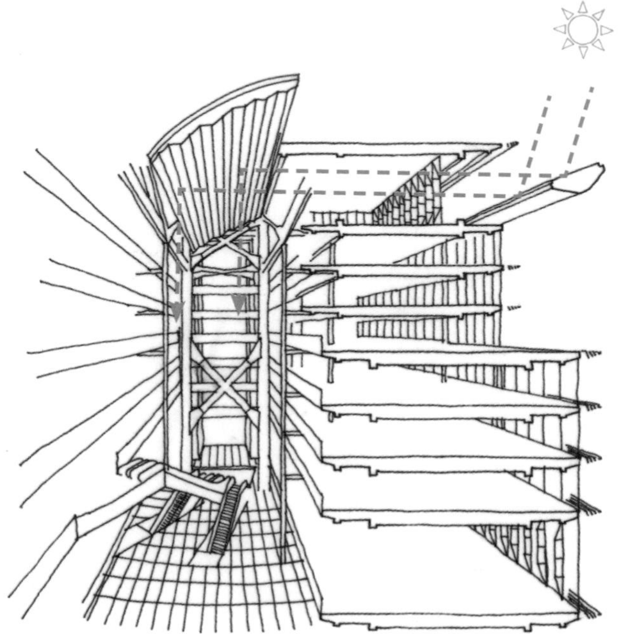

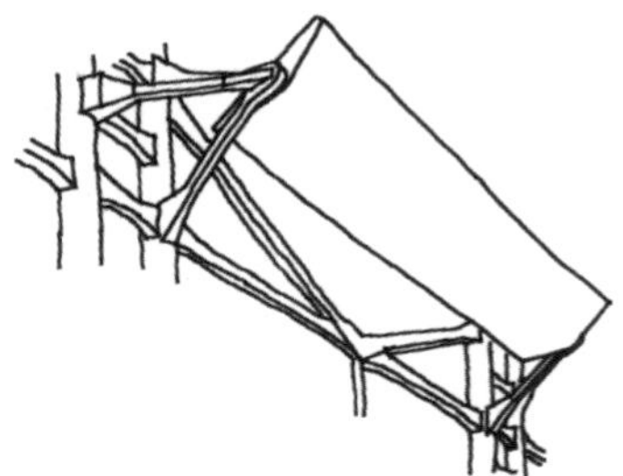

The outside part of the sun scoop is a bank of twenty racks of computer-controlled motorized mirrors that track the sun to keep constant the angle of reflected sunlight into the building.

The internal part of the sun scoop has rows of static mirrors at differing angles to spread the light. Between them artificial lights supplement the natural light, enhancing the apparent sun penetration.

Sea water from the harbour is piped in a deep tunnel through bedrock and used as a cooling medium for the air conditioning and to flush lavatories.

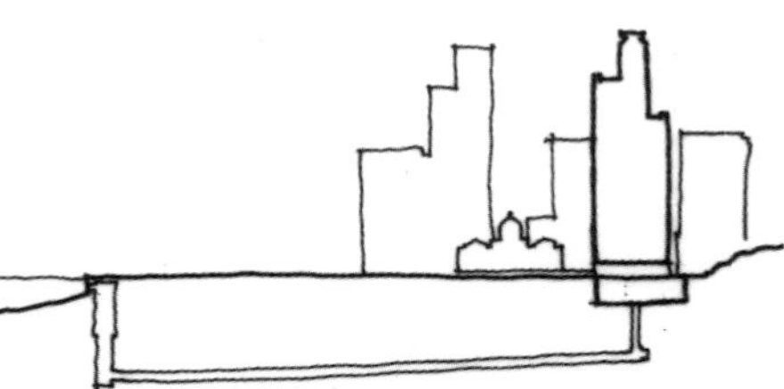

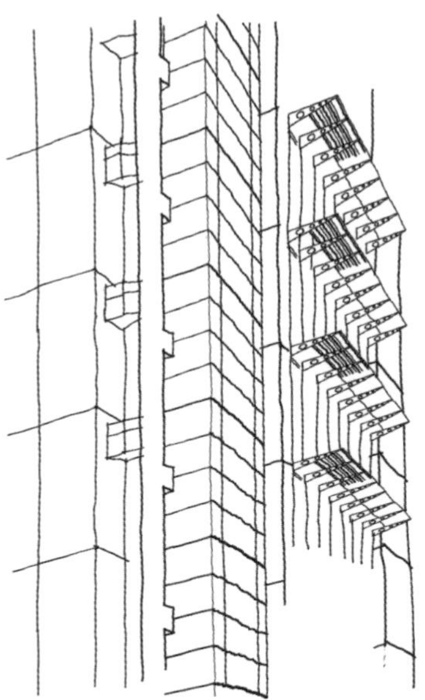

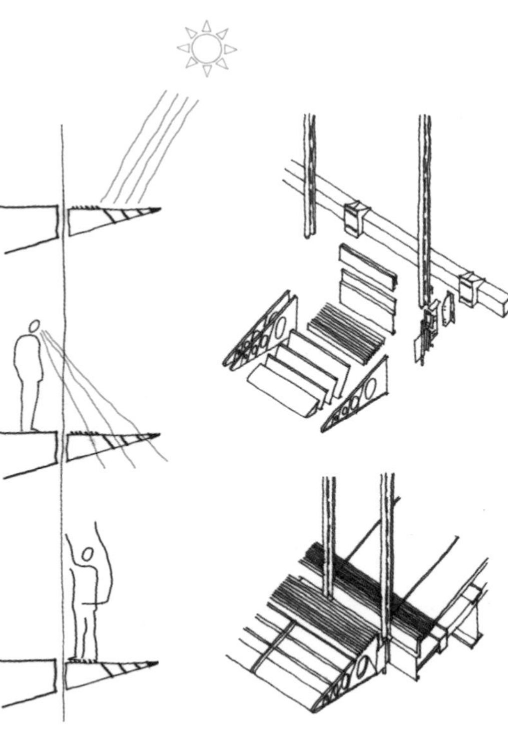

Horizontal sunshades have angled blades that block the subtropical sun while allowing a view down towards the street. A strip of closely spaced blades close to the window provides a walkway for window cleaning and maintenance.

Feng shui

The philosophical origins of feng shui stem from early Chinese beliefs in the unity of man and nature. In building it is concerned with beliefs about the way position, orientation and detailed design can affect the well-being of people and organizations. The bank's position – facing north towards water, backed by the Peak and cradled between two ridges – is good feng shui. A geomancer advised on design details, for example the positioning of the escalators to encourage entry towards the preferred north-west corner of the building.

Section from harbour to hill

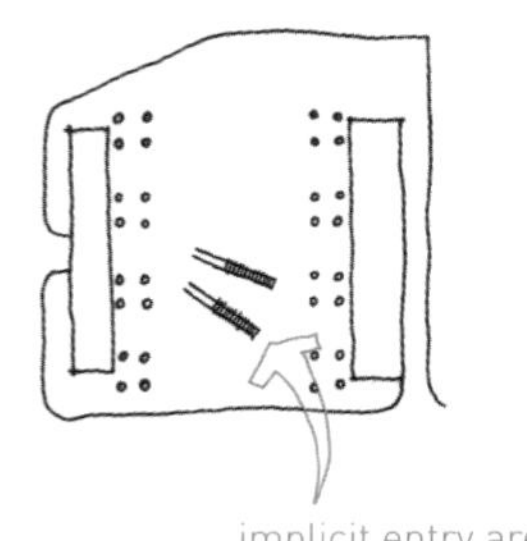

Neue Staatsgalerie | 1977–84

James Stirling, Michael Wilford & Associates

Stuttgart, Germany

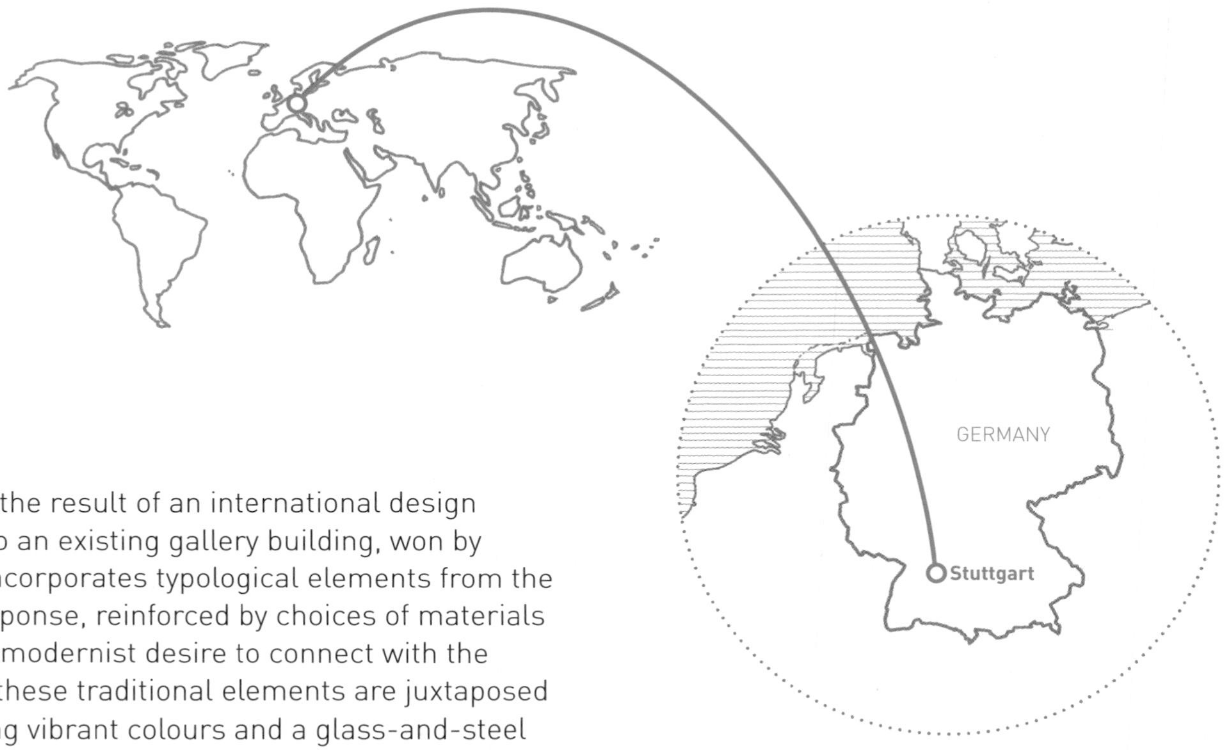

16

The Neue Staatsgalerie was the result of an international design competition for an addition to an existing gallery building, won by architect James Stirling. It incorporates typological elements from the old building as part of its response, reinforced by choices of materials and forms that reflect a Postmodernist desire to connect with the historical context. However, these traditional elements are juxtaposed against others that use strong vibrant colours and a glass-and-steel vocabulary to respond to contemporary idioms of architectural design. The overall design brings these heterogeneous elements from different architectural traditions together into a cohesive whole.

A series of open spaces separated by different-level accesses and ramps creates opportunities for public gathering at the front of the building, as well as offering pathways for people to cut through the complex and catch glimpses of the gallery's sculpture court. Through these strategies the design helps to integrate the institution with its surrounding urban context.

Amit Srivastava, Rimas Kaminskas and Lana Greer

GERMANY

Stuttgart

16

Neue Staatsgalerie | 1977–84

James Stirling, Michael Wilford & Associates

Stuttgart, Germany

Response to urban context

The New State Gallery is an extension to a pre-existing gallery structure and thus needed to respond to the existing building. The design does so by incorporating elements of the Neoclassical architecture present in the old building. Accordingly, the overall layout of the new building is based on a U-shaped plan that copies the traditional approach in the old building. It also incorporates the semicircular circulation pattern of the courtyard space enclosed within the old building's U shape, although this is differently interpreted to suit the specific urban context and increase the permeability of the site. The response to the civic context can also be seen in the decision to step back from the street edge and provide space for public interaction.

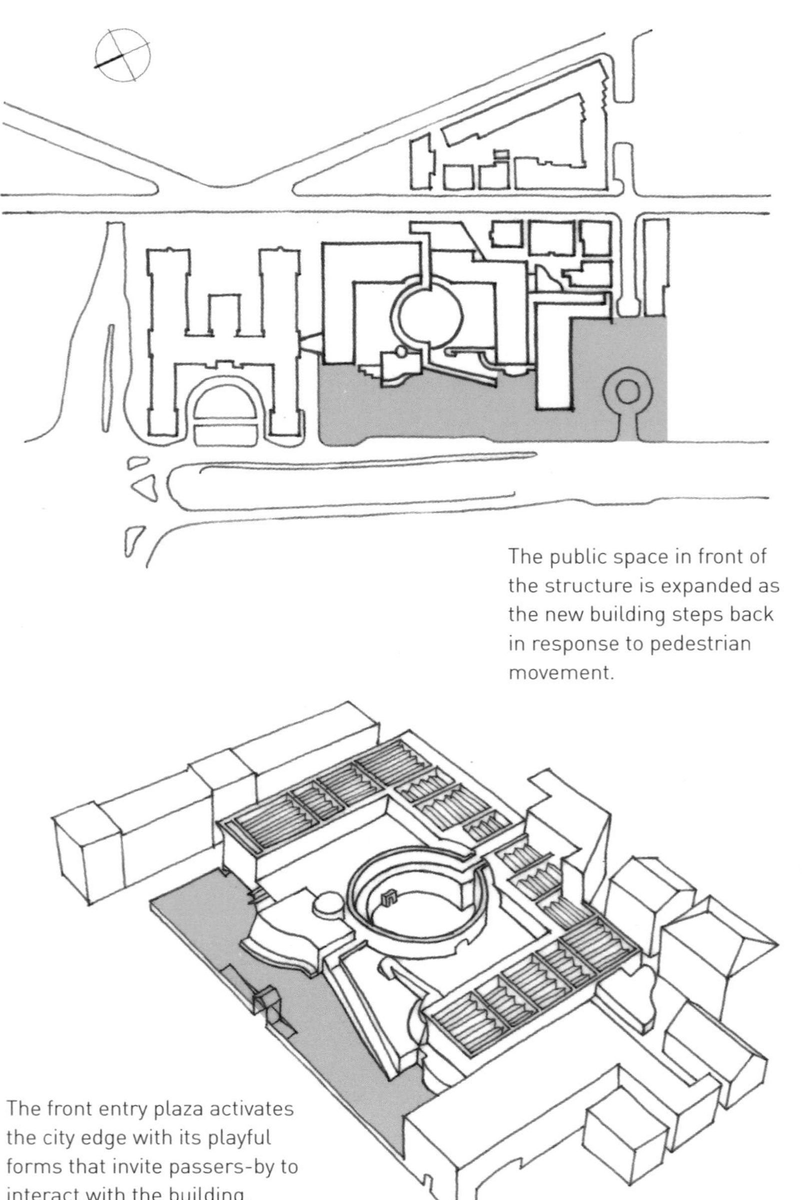

The public space in front of the structure is expanded as the new building steps back in response to pedestrian movement.

The front entry plaza activates the city edge with its playful forms that invite passers-by to interact with the building.

Response to typology and precedent

One of the most interesting design moves is the treatment of the courtyard that results from the adoption of the U-shaped plan. The resulting internal court space is resolved as two separate courts nestled into each other. While the upper court addresses the front street edge, the second, lower court addresses a separate pedestrian link that traverses the site. This link allows the civic space created in the front setback to be connected to the residential areas behind the building. Through this unique interpretation of the double-level court the design addresses both the front and rear streets and helps to bind the surrounding urban fabric into one experience.

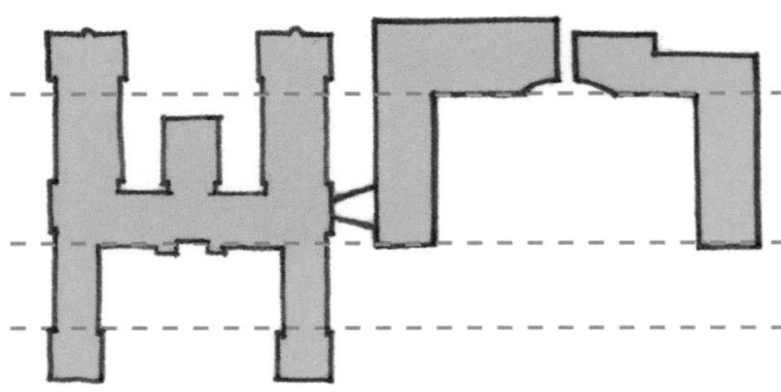

The new building replicates the U-shaped galleries of the old state gallery building.

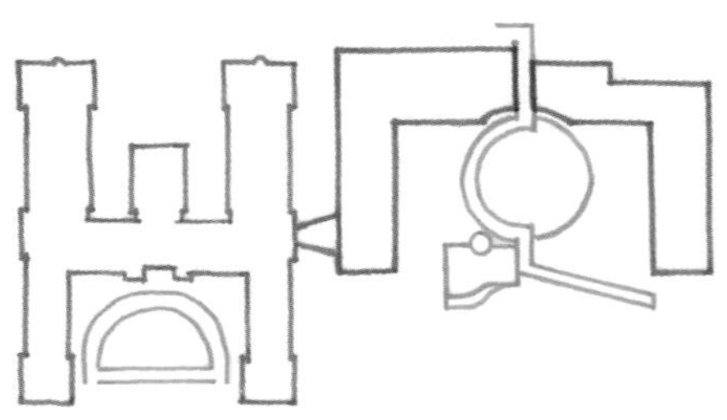

The new building incorporates the court but reinterprets it to increase permeability.

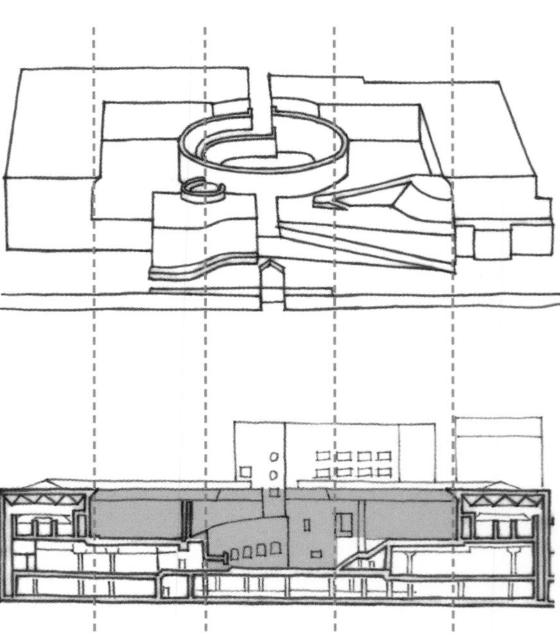

The upper and lower courts address two different vehicular and pedestrian streets.

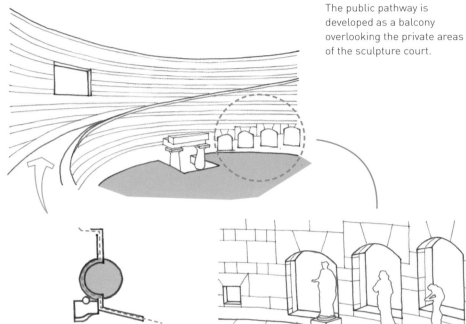

Courtyard as public and private

The decision to allow pedestrians to traverse the site presents new and interesting opportunities for the design of the courtyard. The courtyard needs to act as both a public thoroughfare and a private sculpture court for the museum display. A ramped pathway circuits around a circular court space, allowing pedestrians a glimpse of the sculpture court, while access to the court is reserved for museum patrons.

The public pathway is developed as a balcony overlooking the private areas of the sculpture court.

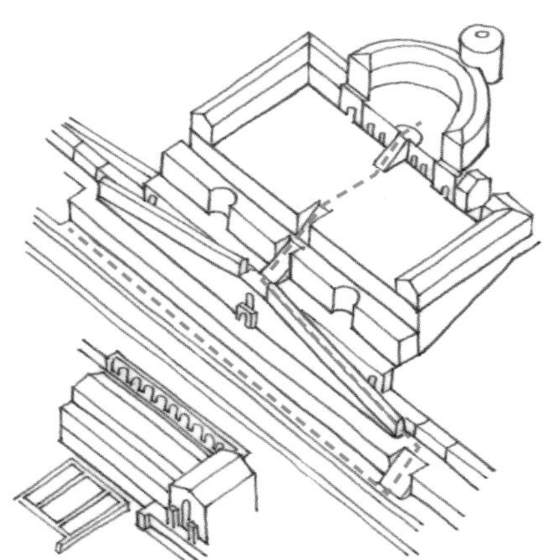

The design of the pedestrian link is based on the historical precedent of the Temple of Fortuna at Praeneste, near Rome (above). In the design of the Roman temple a series of ramps traces an indirect path ascending to the main temple. The design for the museum (below) similarly uses a series of ramps to develop a pedestrian path that cuts through the site and leads up to the street at the back. The ramps themselves define a journey and experience in which pedestrians must engage with the museum space on their way across.

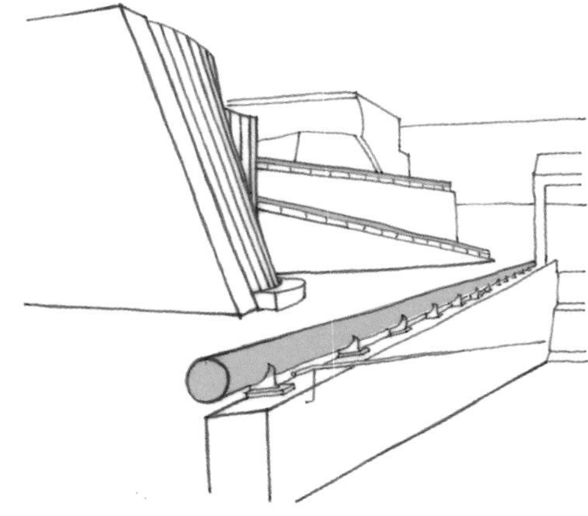

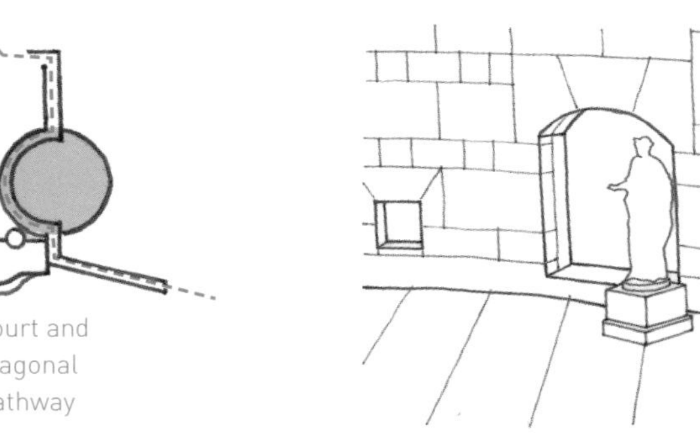

court and diagonal pathway

As the pedestrian ramp rises across the site, the central court is sunk to create a two-level courtyard. Here the museum patrons can enjoy physical access to the sculptures and artworks on display, while the pedestrian path acts like a balcony for passers-by to lean over and look at the sculptures. The path needs to be raised to allow access to the rear of a steeply sloping site, but this treatment of the court rethinks the path as a balcony and provides visual access that activates the path and invites more people to use it.

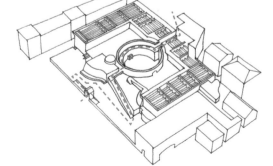

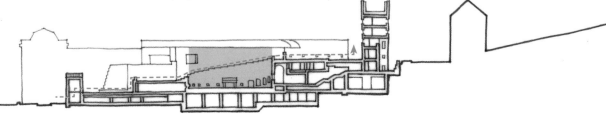

The old and the new

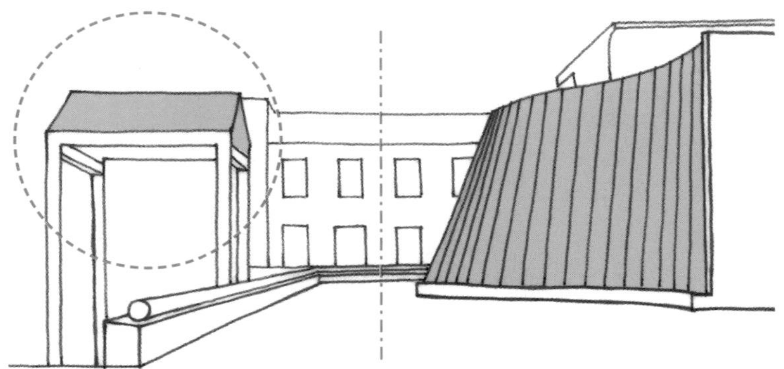

Elements derived from the form of the old museum, such as the gabled roof on the left, sit side-by-side with newer forms and materials.

As a Postmodernist structure, the building incorporates elements of both the old and the new into a single composition. It responds to the Neoclassical architecture of the old State Gallery and other neighbouring buildings through the use of Neoclassical elements such as gabled roofs, striated stone banding and arched openings. On the other hand, it also incorporates organic shapes and new materials to reflect the new. These organic forms, such as the entrance lobby structure with its curved glass-and-steel façade, are painted in bright industrial colours such as green and pink. The building design not only incorporates these contrasting forms and materials but also juxtaposes them in unexpected ways to highlight the contrast and create a dialogue between the forms.

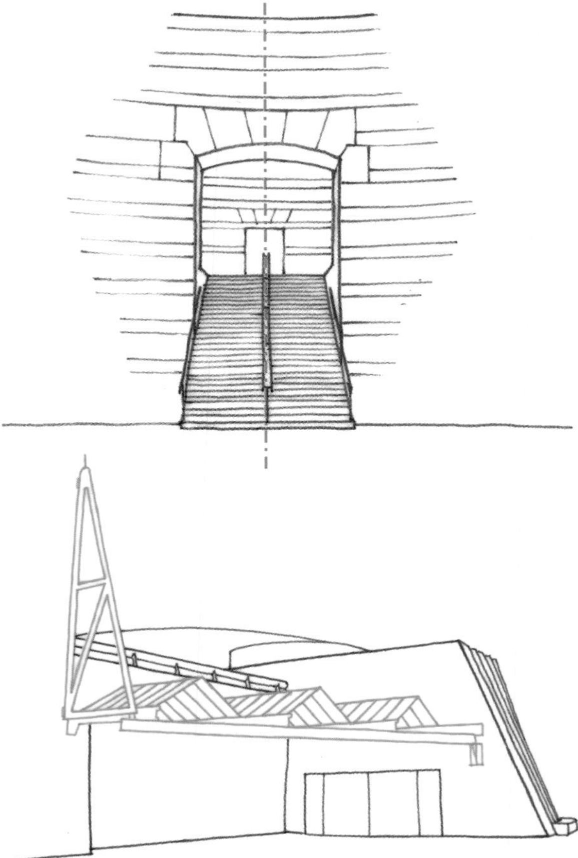

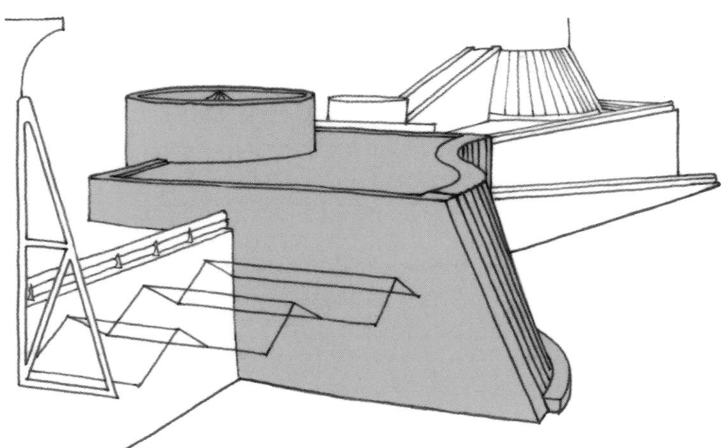

The curved forms of the entrance lobby, with its glass-and-steel façade and green colour, are in contrast with the muted stone renderings of the surrounding structures.

The State University of Music and Performing Arts (below), also designed by James Stirling and Michael Wilford, was finished in 1996 and completed the urban master plan for the area. It reflects the formal vocabulary of the Neue Staatsgalerie.

The language of contrast and balance is continued in the smallest of details. While some openings are treated as symmetrical gateways and developed in the style and materiality of the Neoclassical precedent (top), other elements are placed in asymmetrical balance with the built form. Here (above) the glass canopies, which might still reflect Neoclassical forms, are supported by brightly coloured steel pipes that stand in contrast with the natural stone of the walls in the background.

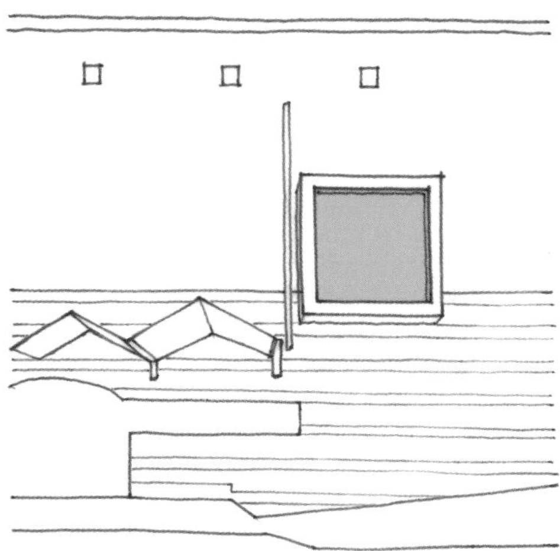

The contrasting details do not occur only as isolated instances, but are often juxtaposed in a single composition to highlight the playful nature of form-making. A slight asymmetry in an otherwise Neoclassical façade, or punctures in a stone wall with scattered stone pieces on the ground, create a series of playful experiences for the observer and reinforce the Postmodernist intentions of the designer.

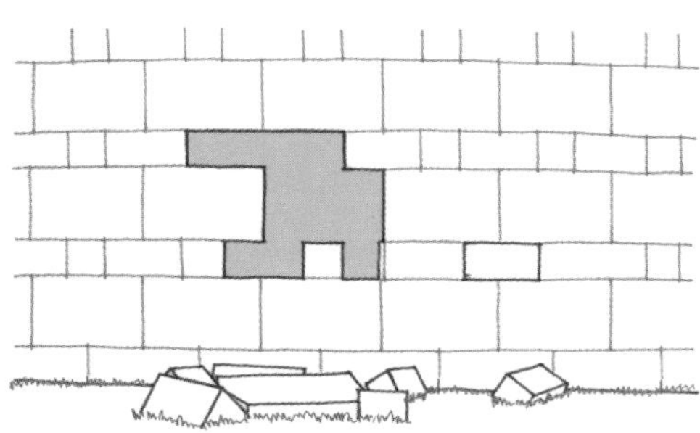

Response to user experience

The playful forms of the building also affect the experience of the interior space. The entrance hall with its distinctive curved wall allows for an unusual play of light and shadow. The glazed wall allows the room to be filled with light, and the bright green flooring reflects this to create an eerie experience. As the sun moves across the sky the mullions cast moving shadow patterns that make this otherwise empty interior space come alive.

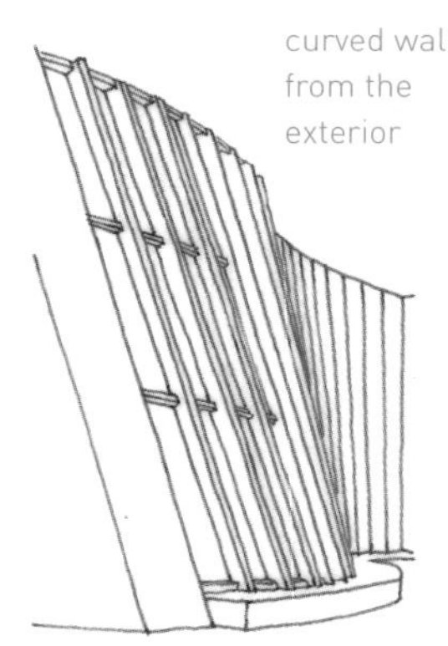

curved wall from the exterior

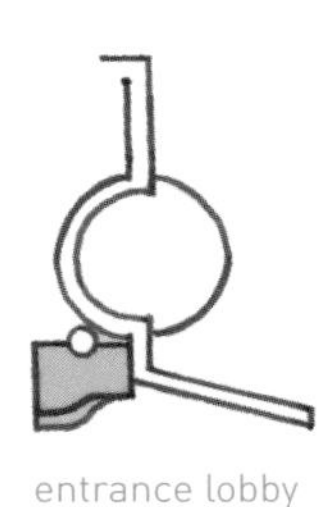

entrance lobby

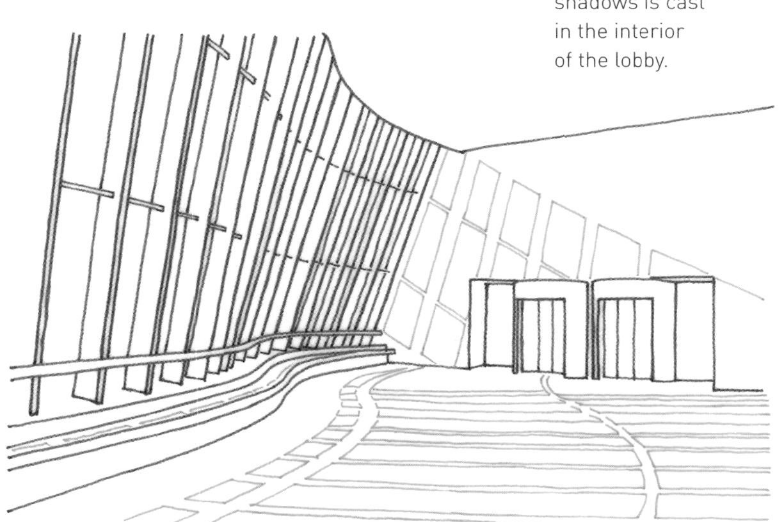

A pattern of shadows is cast in the interior of the lobby.

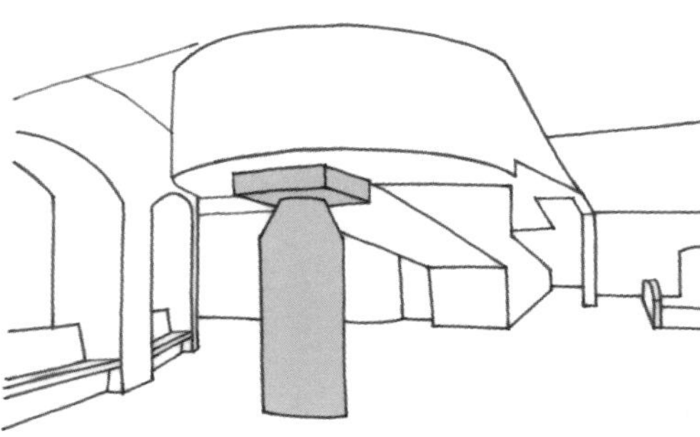

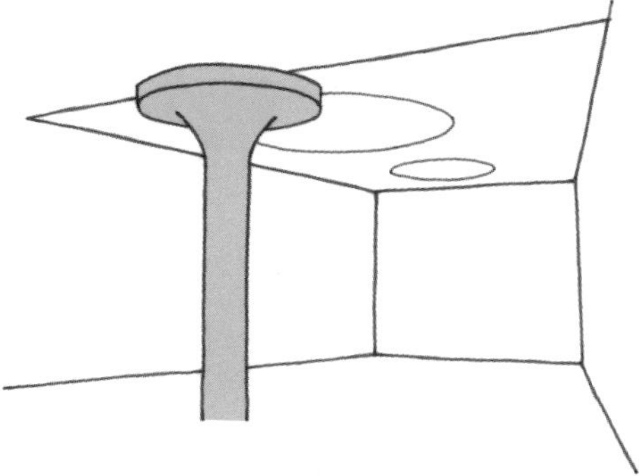

Various shaped columns act as sculptural pieces.

The large, light-filled interior spaces are ideal for the purposes of an art gallery. The interior wall surfaces are large and are painted white to allow for the various art pieces to be displayed easily and to be viewed without distraction. At the same time, certain architectural features are highlighted and exaggerated in scale to draw attention to the architectural object. Here the variously shaped columns act as sculptural pieces in themselves and make the architecture a part of the museum display.

House at Martha's Vineyard | 1984–88

Stephen Holl Architects

Martha's Vineyard, Massachusetts, USA

17

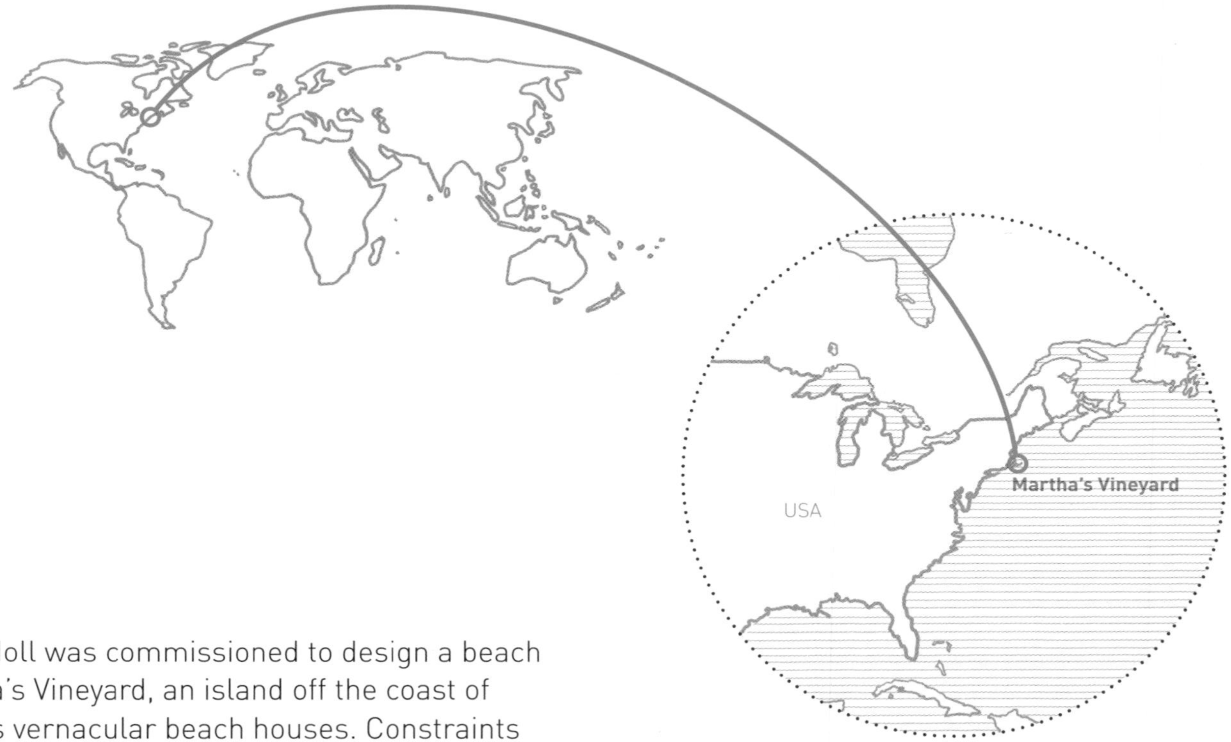

Martha's Vineyard

USA

American architect Steven Holl was commissioned to design a beach house for a couple in Martha's Vineyard, an island off the coast of Massachusetts known for its vernacular beach houses. Constraints included a narrow linear site and regional planning restrictions that allowed no more than a single storey along the beach line. The design responds to these parameters in a building that respects local houses in scale and material while standing out in its structure and form.

Overall, the design prioritizes human experience and transient moment over permanence. The transparency of the house and its response to the physical environment defy the boundaries between natural and artificial, inside and outside, light and dark, and the modern and the perennial.

Selen Morkoç and Victoria Kovalevski

17 House at Martha's Vineyard | 1984-88

Stephen Holl Architects

Martha's Vineyard, Massachusetts, USA

Site

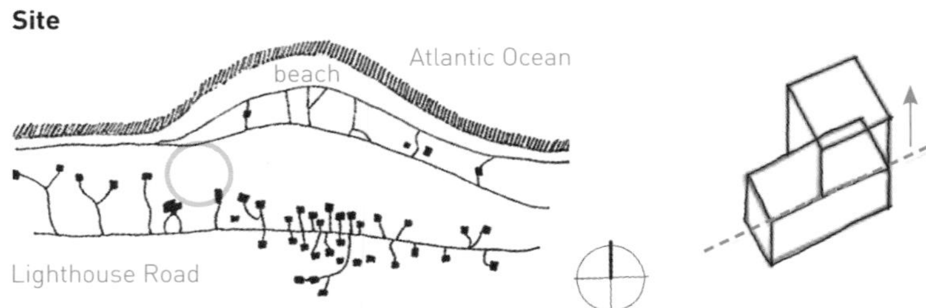

The site has a context of small-scale vernacular houses behind marshland. Planning restrictions dictated that the house must appear to have only one storey when viewed from the sea. The ocean view from nearby dwellings could not be blocked. These limitations led to a distinct narrow form for the house, which is in harmonious scale with neighbouring buildings.

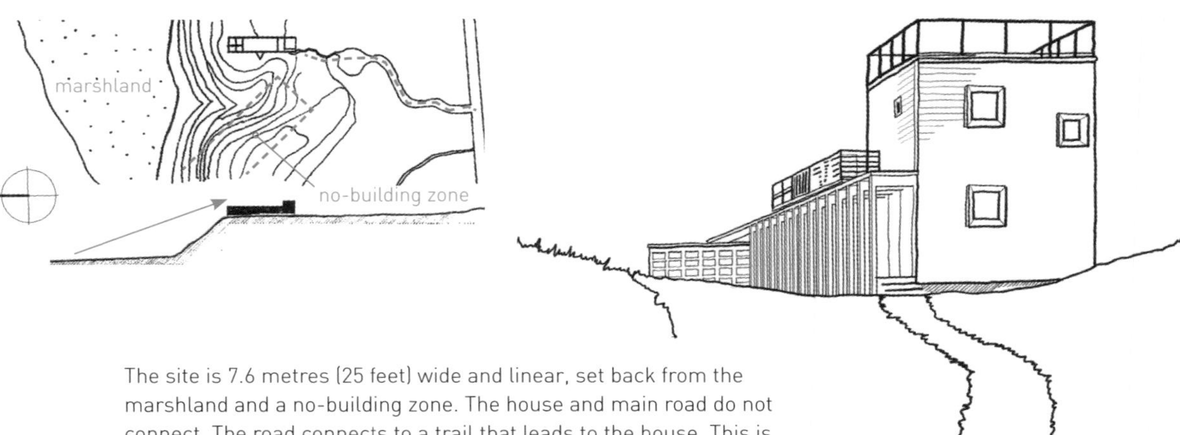

The site is 7.6 metres (25 feet) wide and linear, set back from the marshland and a no-building zone. The house and main road do not connect. The road connects to a trail that leads to the house. This is a pedestrian route aimed at conserving the vegetation around the site.

The second storey is restricted to the far end of the house from the beach.

Metaphor

Local native peoples and their life connected to the beach is a source of inspiration for the design, along with Herman Melville's novel *Moby-Dick* (1851). Locals would drag the skeletons of beached whales above the tide line and cover them with animal skins or bark in order to transform them into dwellings. The house is an inside-out frame of wooden construction, with its surrounding veranda resembling the dwelling built from a whale's skeleton. The roof and the walls are like a membrane unrolled over the frame, similar to the skins covering the whale skeleton.

Response to climate

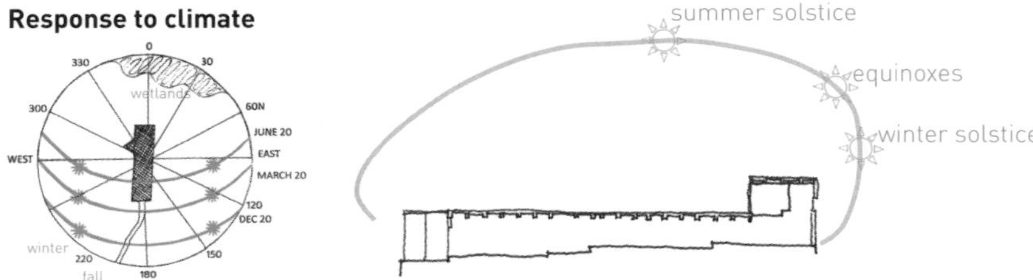

Average temperature varies between 2°C (35°F) in winter and 20°C (68°F) in summer. As a summer beach house in a temperate region, passive heating and cooling was not a major design concern. The view towards the sea takes preference over solar access to the living area. A skylight and multiple windows of various sizes allow a rich variety of natural light and sun penetration into the house.

Nature is a strong element in the design inspiration. The weathered greyness of the cladding, the spindly structure, the sparse interior and the exposure to the ocean's wind and sunlight promote a living style intimate with nature. The house is modern, with its shiplike form floating above the site overlooking the sea.

The use of timber frames on the west, east and north façades gives continuity. They mark a transition between closed, open and semi-open spaces while defying strict boundaries between the three.

Herman Melville's story *I and My Chimney* depicts an old man and his obsession with the huge old chimney at the centre of his house. The fireplace and chimney of this house is central in its location, solidity and size. On one side, the dining and living areas are visually connected. On the other side, the hearth continues as a step.

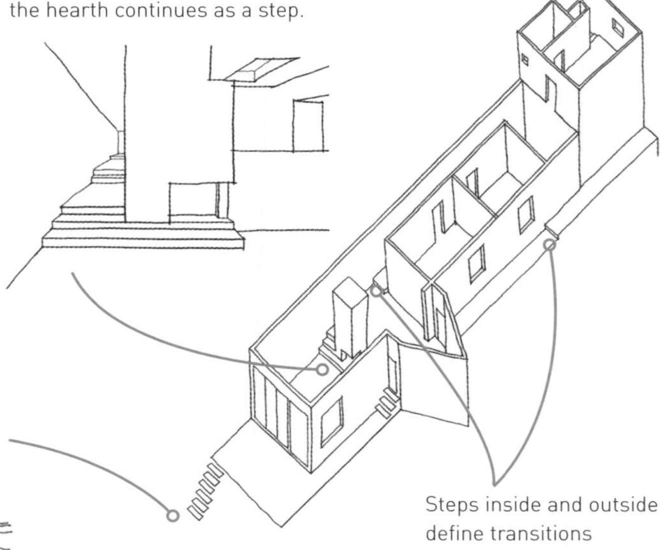

Steps inside and outside define transitions between spaces.

House at Martha's Vineyard | 1984–88

Stephen Holl Architects

Martha's Vineyard, Massachusetts, USA

17

Form generation

With the timber structural elements as a measure, the building is a combination of basic geometric forms along a longitudinal rectangular box, both horizontally and vertically.

The skeleton determines the volume where the skin is stretched. Repetition of timber columns provides a modular basis, and through this repetition diverse spaces are created, despite the limitations of the linear rectangular site.

The box on top of the building is balanced by subtracted volumes along the longitudinal side patio.

Two triangular volumes protrude outside the basic volume. One is the frame of a skylight suggesting a subtracted void. The other is a dining space added to the longer side of the rectangular volume.

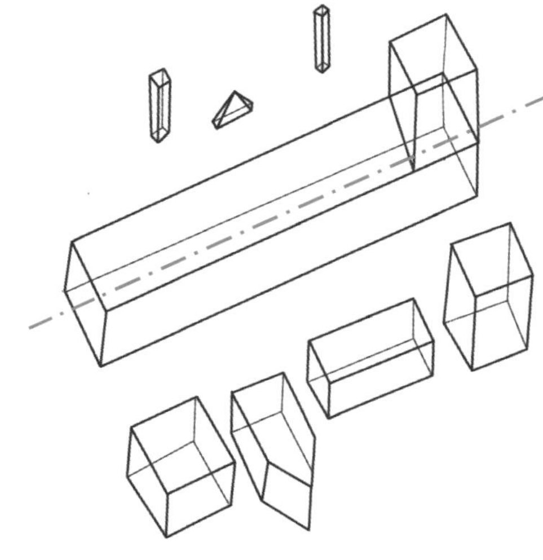

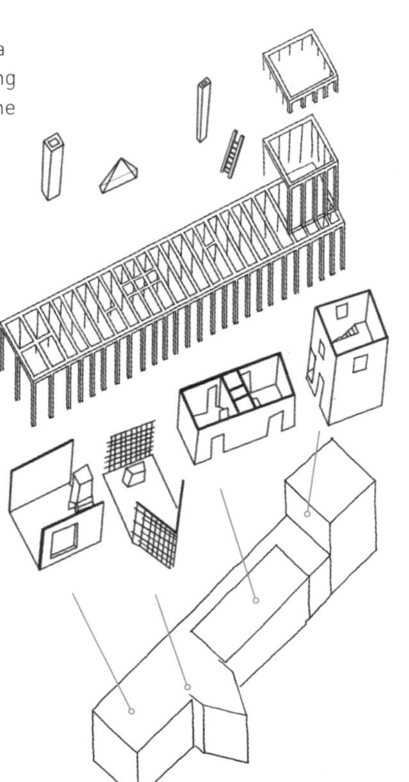

Form and construction

The house is supported on point foundations, typical for beach houses of the region in order to raise the house to maximize the views. They are used in this house in a modern way. The floor level varies along the longitudinal plan, following the ground slope. Despite this slope, the roof is a continuous flat plane, providing more height for the public rooms. A wide view is obtained from a rooftop deck.

Natural light

Pierced small openings along the dark hallway create bright spots. The dim hall opens up to the bright dining room. With its abundance of natural light, this is the focal point of the house. Light enters through several planes of the triangular window and the skylight.

The dining room's glass and wood mullion window is triangular in shape, allowing users a 180-degree view of the landscape.

Wooden frame details across the west elevation show variety in seeming repetition.

The exposed beams of the ceiling create a sense of depth and continuity across space.

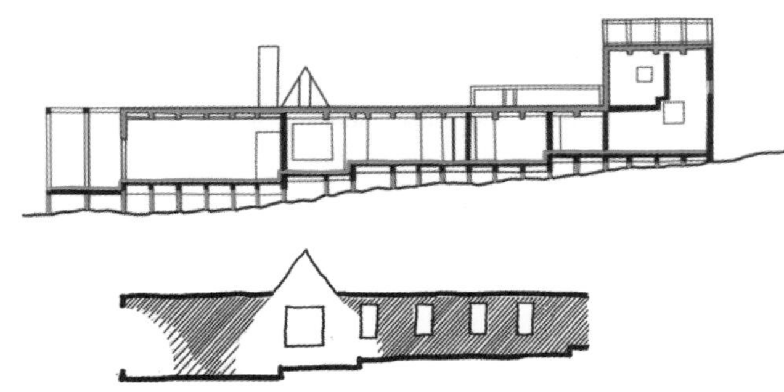

A view deck over the upper floor is reached by a ladder.

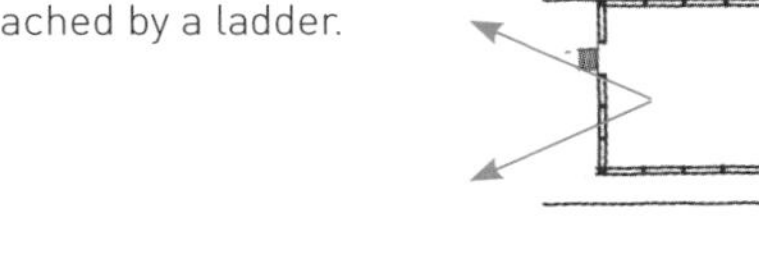

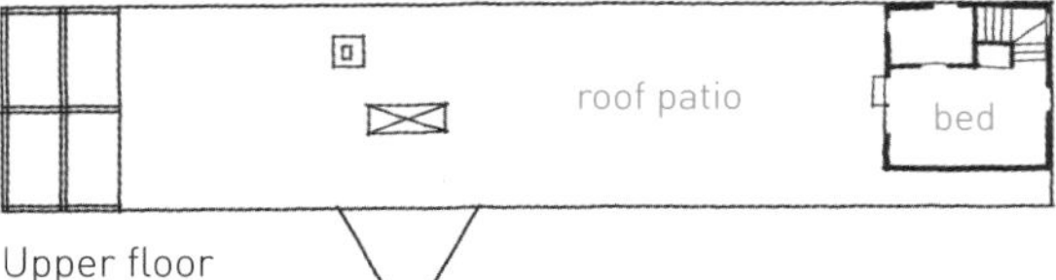

Upper floor

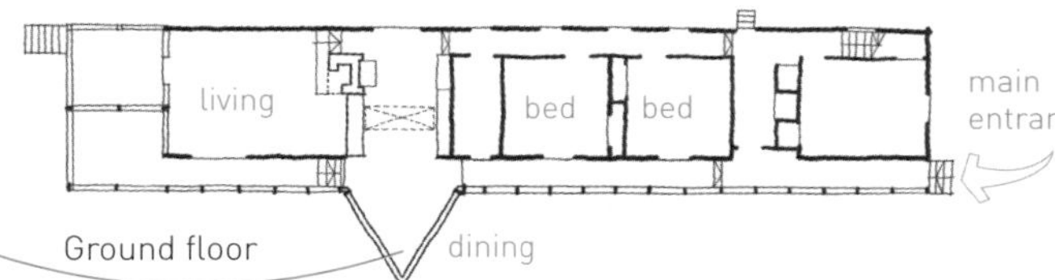

Ground floor

Shadows

Wooden frames with their diverse arrangements create a repertoire of shadows across the western façade, which enriches the human experience.

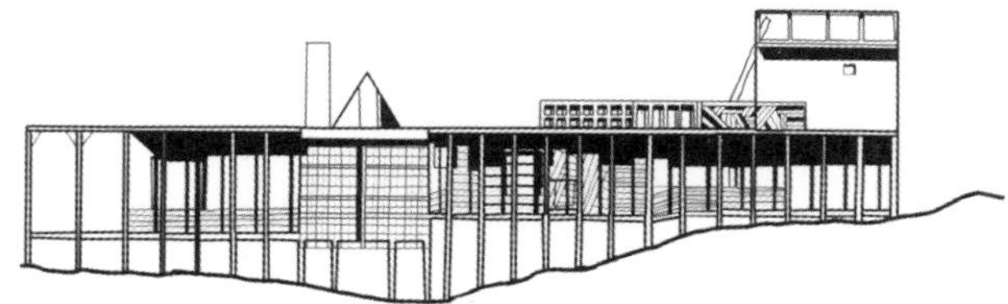

West elevation

18

Church on the Water | 1985–88

Tadao Ando Architect & Associates

Tomamu, Hokkaido, Japan

The Church on the Water was built to accommodate wedding ceremonies as part of the Alpha Resort Hotel in Tomamu, Japan. Its location and design are physically and visually distinct from the surrounding resort, reinforcing the difference between the sacred and the mundane.

Designed by Tadao Ando, the church brings drama to its response to the site and religious contexts. Boundaries such as inside/outside, sacred/mundane, darkness/light and traditional/modern are made apparent and then resolved in the design.

Selen Morkoç, Sze Nga Chan and Georgina Prenhall

18

Church on the Water | 1985–88
Tadao Ando Architect & Associates
Tomamu, Hokkaido, Japan

The context

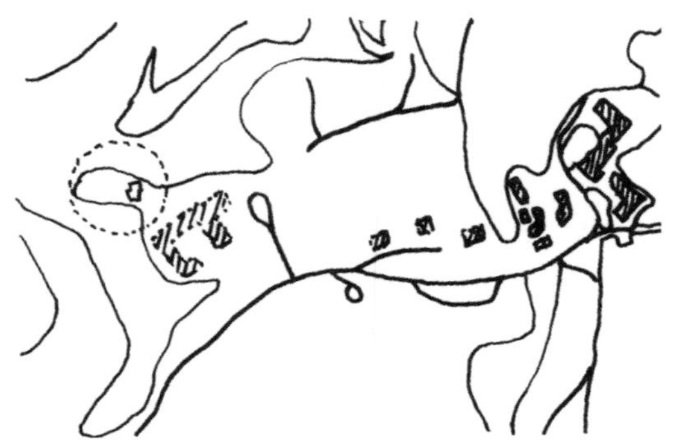

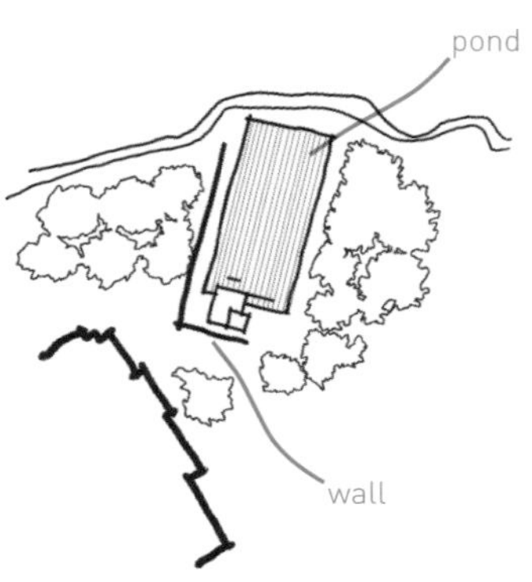

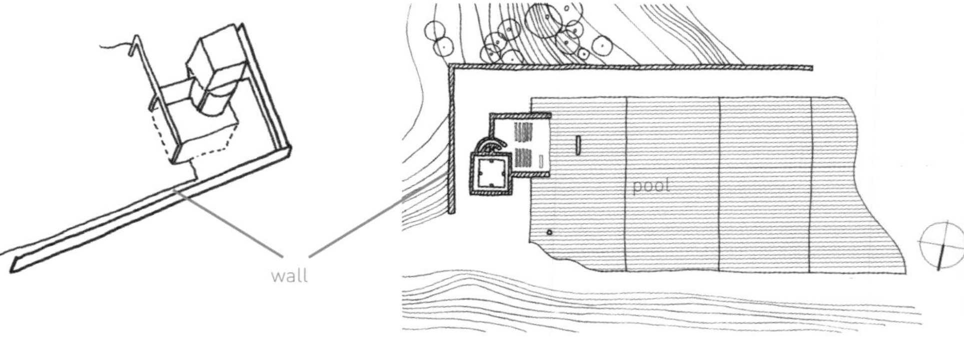

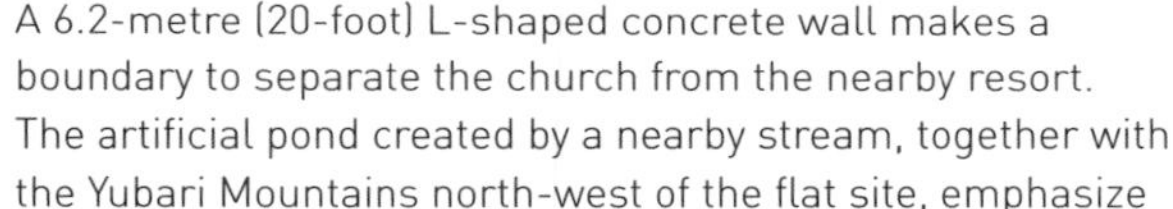

A 6.2-metre (20-foot) L-shaped concrete wall makes a boundary to separate the church from the nearby resort. The artificial pond created by a nearby stream, together with the Yubari Mountains north-west of the flat site, emphasize the connection of the church with nature. The wall wraps around the rear and side of the chapel. The chapel itself sits on the bank of the pond, with a small encroachment into the water.

The L-shaped wall acts like a punctuation mark that distinguishes the sacred inner space from the mundane aspects of the exterior. It bounds the chapel and the artificial pond on two sides.

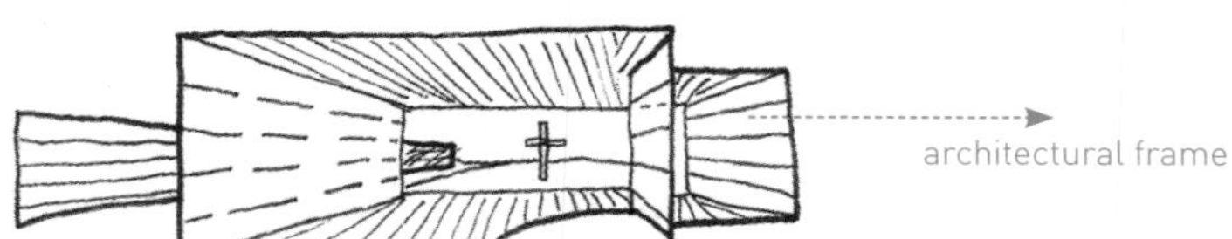

The cross in the water outside the building extends the symbolism beyond the architectural frame. A four-part glass wall slides away to leave no barrier between the interior and the water.

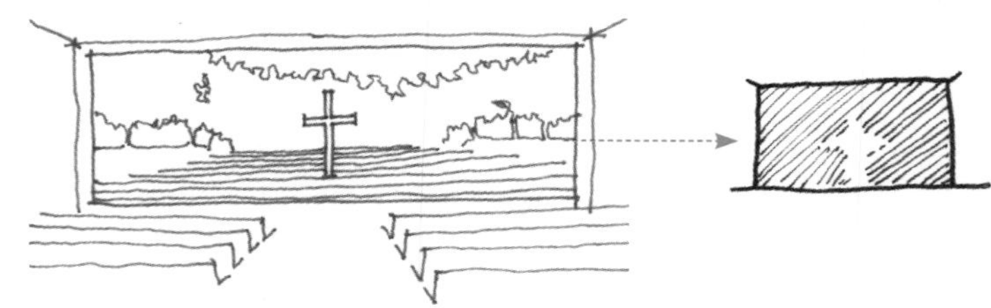

Seen from inside the chapel, the cross is framed within nature by walls. The changing seasons create different scenes.

The precedent
The Church on the Water is an engagement of modern architecture with traditional Japanese aesthetics.

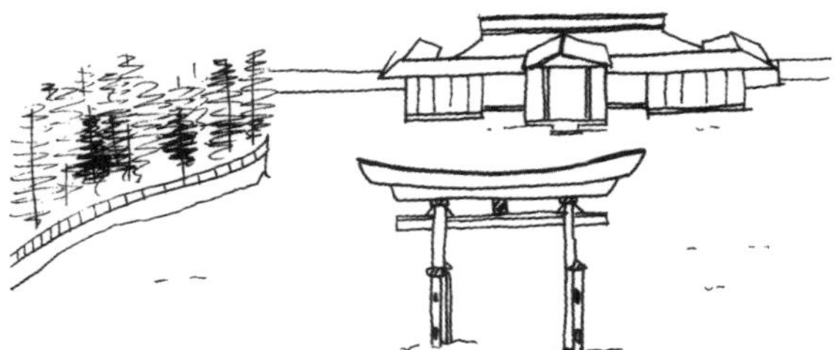

Torii gate, Itsukushima Shrine, Hiroshima, Japan

At the Itsukushima Shrine the *torii* gate is positioned in water far from the shore. Although distanced, it is situated on the central line of symmetry of the shrine as the central element in religious reflection.

Yoshikien Garden, Nara, Japan

Framing nature is another gesture Ando quotes from traditional Japanese architecture.

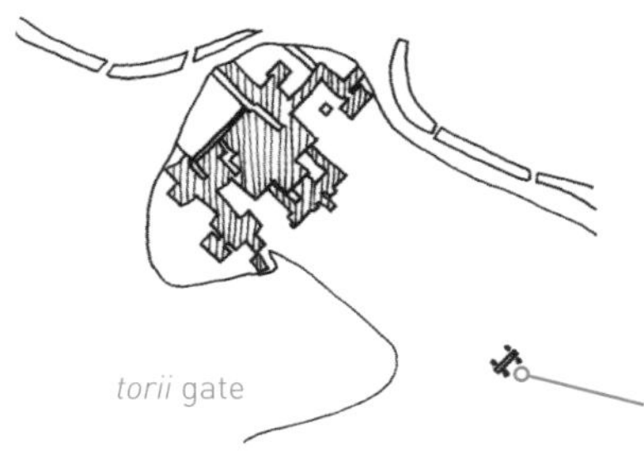

The relationship with water is an interpretation of traditional Japanese Zen Buddhist architecture, in which there is a dialogue between a building and surrounding nature through response and integration.

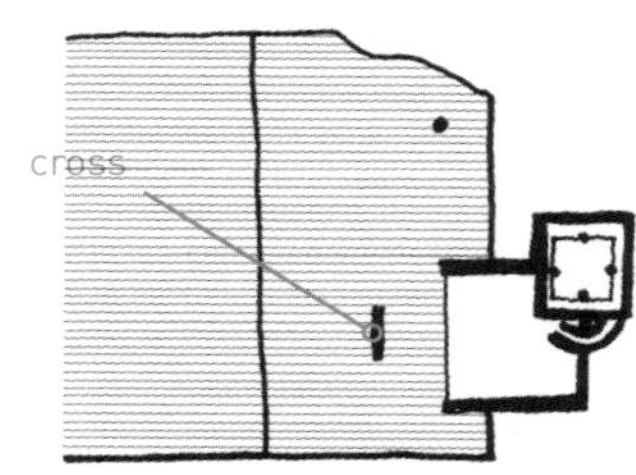

Similar to the layout of the *torii* gate, the main element of religious reflection (the cross) is positioned at a distance from the main chapel, on the water, along the central line of symmetry of the main structure.

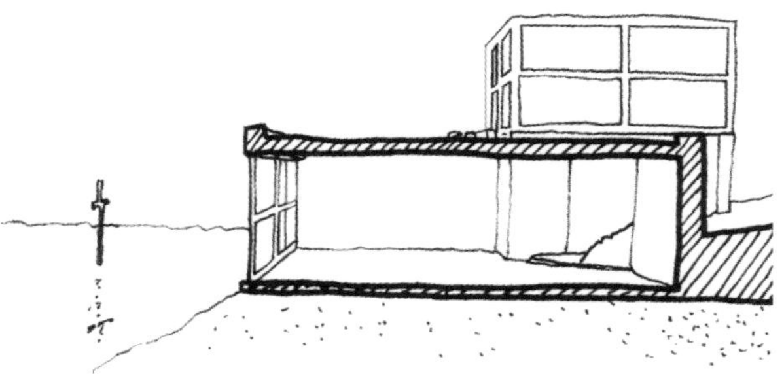

The main chapel 'frames' the landscape, prompting a relationship between the visitor and nature.

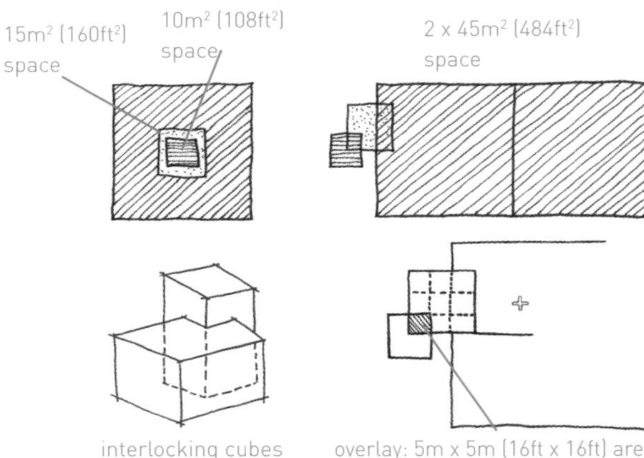

Building form and proportion

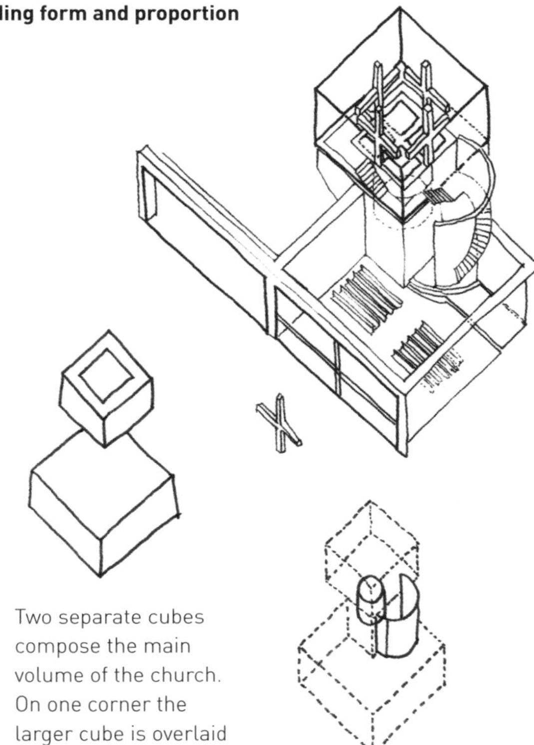

Two separate cubes compose the main volume of the church. On one corner the larger cube is overlaid by a smaller cube.

Spiral staircases fit between a cylindrical void and a curving wall to connect the spaces formed by the two cubes.

Space in the church is organized by strict proportioning of simple geometric relationships. The proportion of each space can be reduced to a simple ratio: 2:3:9.

Two interlocking cubic volumes share a corner area of 25m² (270ft²). The larger cube is aligned along the central line of the pond. The cross on the pond sits along the centre line of the cube.

Church on the Water | 1985–88

Tadao Ando Architect & Associates
Tomamu, Hokkaido, Japan

Space and levels
A path from the resort leads to an entrance flush with the wall. so the continuity of the surface is maintained.

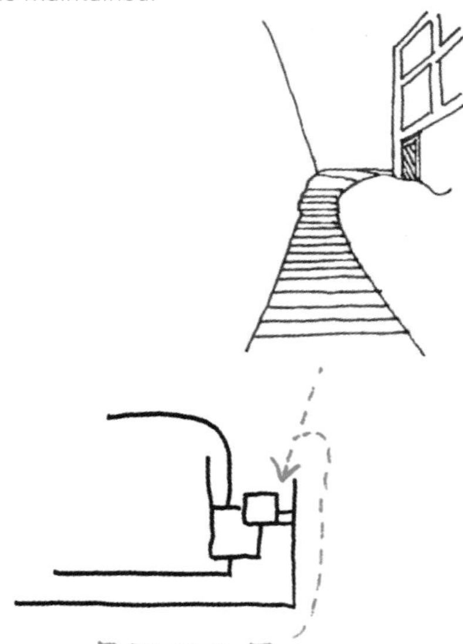

Inside, a corridor leads up steps to the top level, where four crosses are arranged in a square inside steel-framed glass walls. The route passes around the outside of these crosses. Steps then descend back to the level of the entrance but a wall prevents visitors returning to the outside. Instead, they turn right and descend a semicircular staircase to a lower level where there is a waiting room under the four crosses. They enter the back of the chapel faced with a view of the water and the solitary cross.

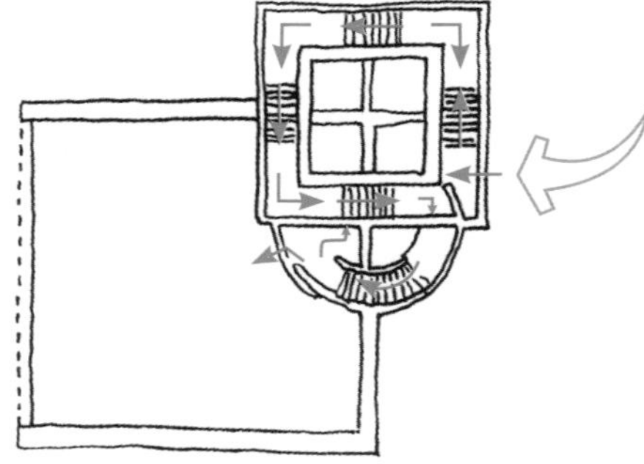

The circulation gives visitors multiple experiences of the created spaces and their connection with the landscape, enriching their preparation for the wedding or other ceremony in the chapel.

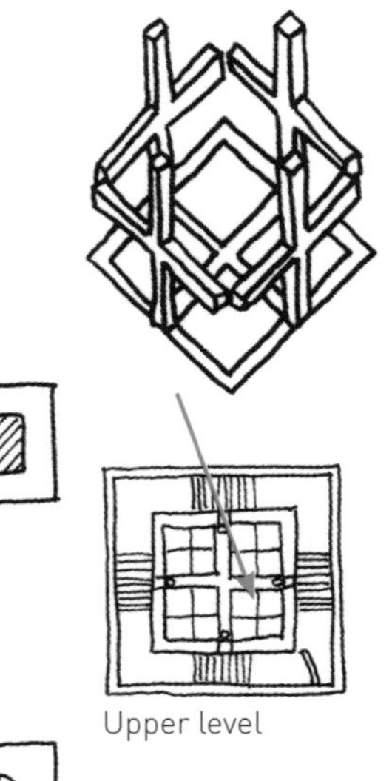

Upper level

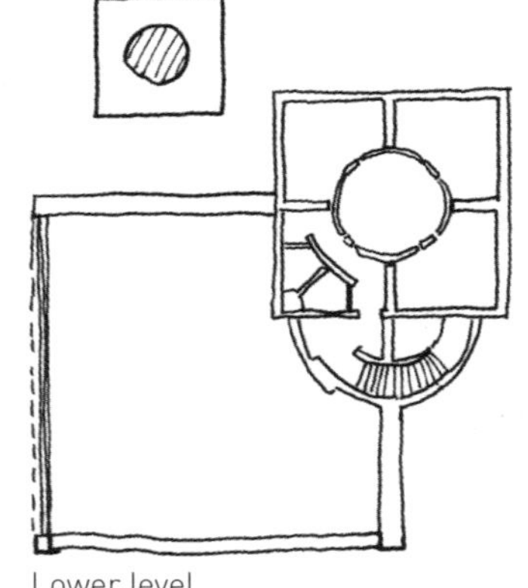

Lower level

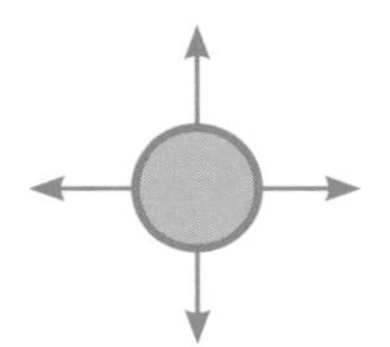

The four crosses indicate the four cardinal points, symbolizing the universe.

Space within a space
The space contains a smaller space within. The contained space slightly differs in form from the enveloping one; the formal contrast indicates a functional difference. The contained space reiterates the form of the enveloping space. Then, the contained space becomes a focus of attention.

Light
The contrast between light and darkness defines main points of interest in the building. Daylight comes from the glass box on the top level and from the open wall of the chapel. The cylindrical void acts like a light tube from the glass box into the waiting room. Reflected light brightens the semicircular stairway. The water surface bounces light into the chapel.

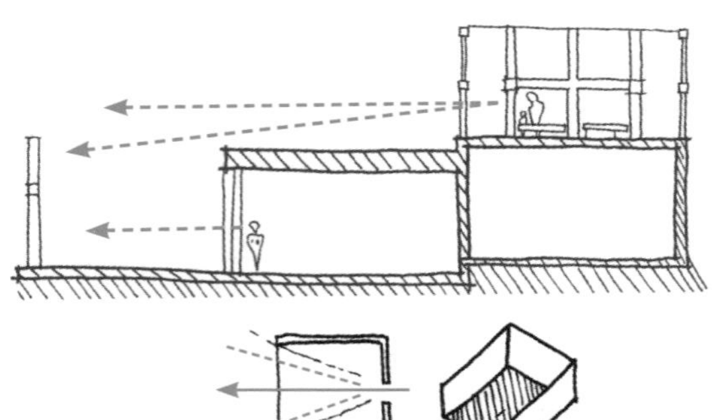

The cross in the water and its landscape setting is seen first as part of a wide vista from inside the glass box on the upper level. It is seen again as the focus of a carefully controlled view from inside the U-shaped enclosure of the chapel.

Experiential cohesion

The cross in the landscape is an anonymous yet strong pastoral symbol of spirituality.

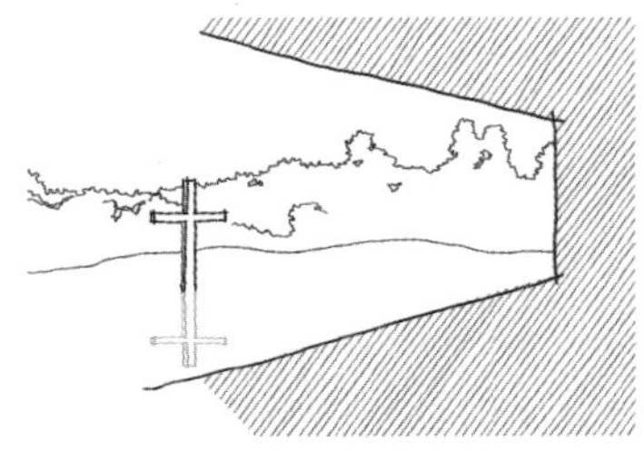
At the Church on the Water, the cross in water is framed within the landscape.

The strong geometrical form of the buildings stands in striking contrast with the amorphous forms of nature surrounding them.

The depth of visual engagement with the surroundings stretches to a distant view of the mountains and beech trees.

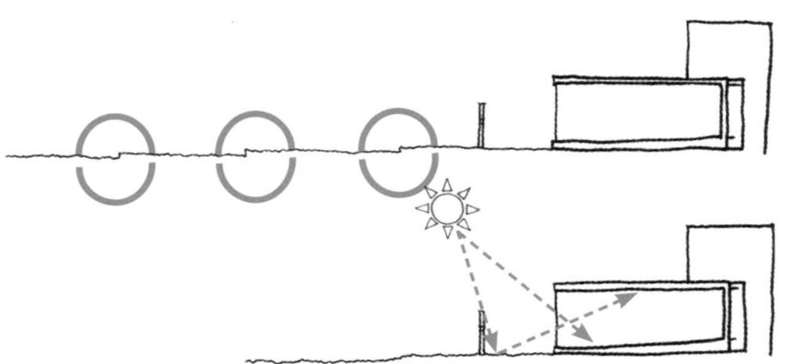
The pond has a tiered surface that creates soothing sounds as well as visual reflection and serves to enrich religious experience in both ways.

Natural light in the chapel is controlled, with the only glazed façade facing the pond. Reflected light from the water surface eliminates the need for additional lighting in the chapel space.

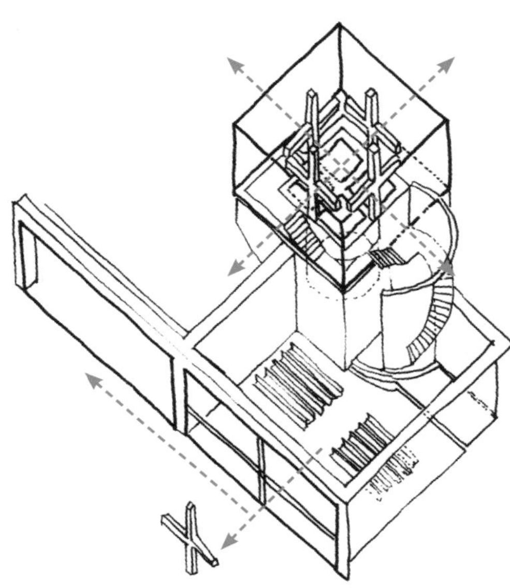
With the glass wall slid to one side, the chapel opens up to the cross and the landscape framing it. Inside/outside divisions are defied.

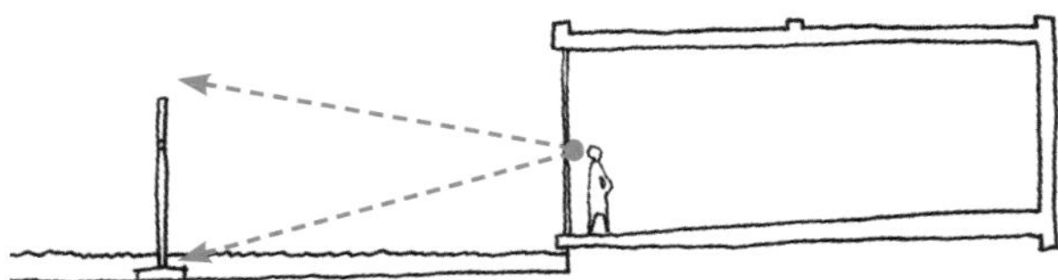
The contained space of the chapel extends into the landscape as the major object of the ritual (the cross) is embedded in the scene.

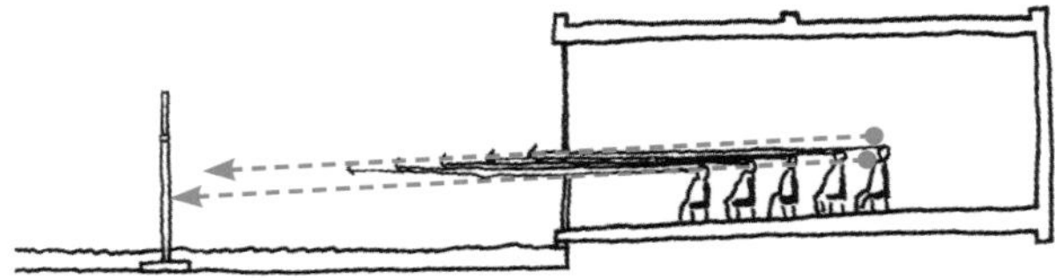
The slope of the chapel floor allows users to remain in direct visual contact with the cross and the landscape during religious rituals.

Response to the artificial

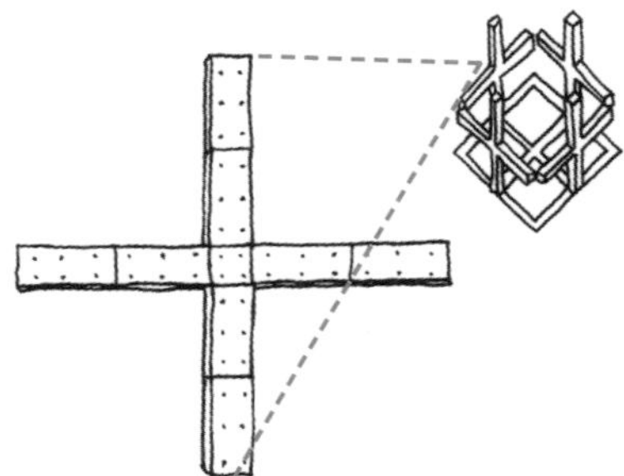

Concrete cross Located within the glass-walled box on the upper level of the chapel, its materiality and repetition in fourfold symmetry suggest community and strength.

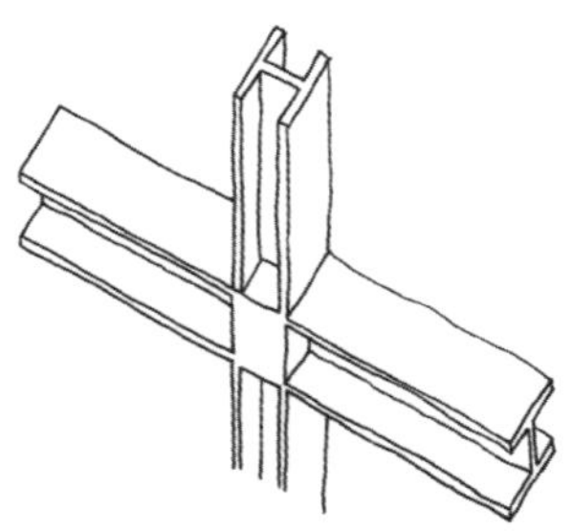

H-section steel cross Located in the water away from the chapel, its materiality and isolation suggest difference and spirituality.

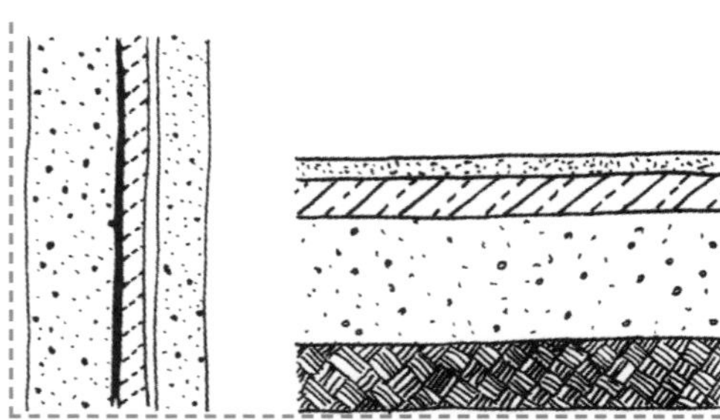

Walls and floors The granite floor seamlessly hides the underfloor heating. The thick double-layer concrete and granite insulated walls and floors ensure a comfortable internal temperature despite cold winters.

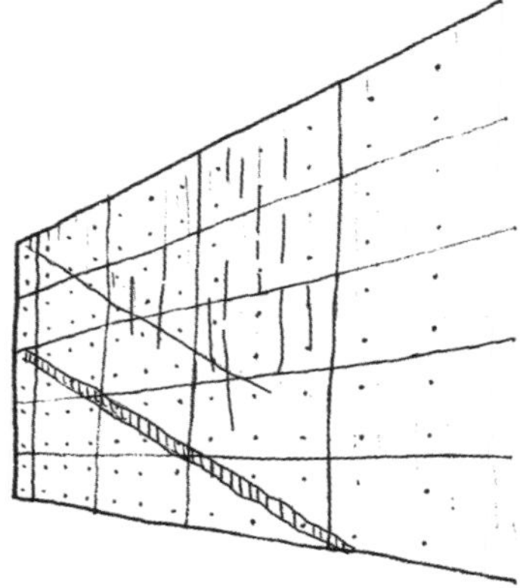

Concrete Concrete is the main material of the building. Its partly rough, partly reflective texture registers different qualities of light that enhance human experience.

Furniture The overall integrity of form continues in the specifically designed furniture.

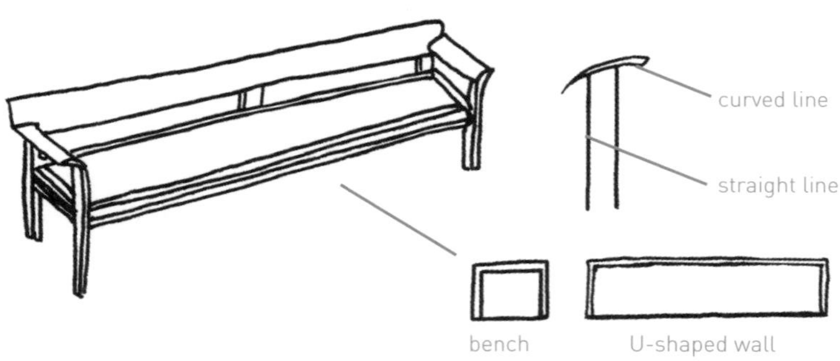

The benches, like the building elements, incorporate straight and curved lines. Their U-shaped form in plan repeats the form of the U-shaped wall of the chapel.

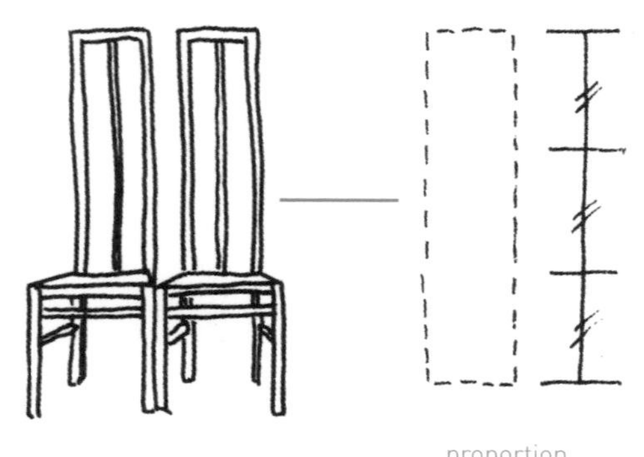

The height and width of the chairs are in 3:1 proportion.

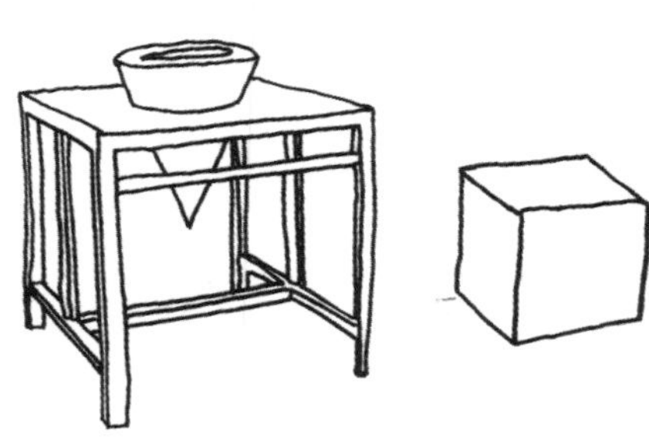

The wooden stand for flowers in the chapel has two interlocking forms: a cube and a cone.

Nature – sacred space trilogy

The Church on the Water is part of a design trilogy created by Ando through three sacred spaces, each highlighting a natural element. The other two represent the elements of wind and light.

The architectural trilogy indicates Ando's understanding of spirituality as a universal phenomenon in direct relationship with nature.

Water Temple for the Shingon Buddhist Sect, Awaji Island, Hyogo, Japan (1989–91)

Church of the Light, Ibaraki, Osaka, Japan (1987–99)

Lloyd's of London Office Building | 1978–86

Richard Rogers

London, England

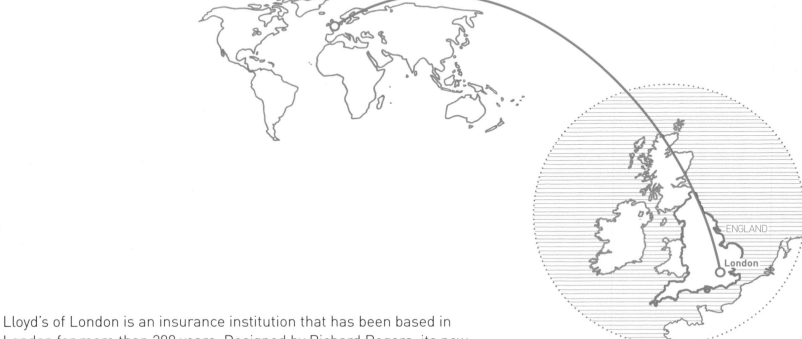

Lloyd's of London is an insurance institution that has been based in London for more than 200 years. Designed by Richard Rogers, its new office building reinterprets the tectonic and aesthetic qualities of the City of London's medieval architecture in the 'High-Tech' terms of modern construction and services. The result is a cohesive order that celebrates the values of traditional architecture without compromising its stance on the technological and industrial developments that are specific to its time. Lifts and services are on the edges of the building, leaving clear space inside. The Lloyd's building combines High-Tech's fascination with industrialized processes with a subtle response to the urban public realm.

Sean Kellet, Amit Srivastava and Saiful Azzam Abdul Ghapur

19

Lloyd's of London Office Building | 1978–86

Richard Rogers

London, England

Response to site context

The Lloyd's building is situated near Aldgate, the easternmost gateway of the medieval City of London, amid a dense urban fabric of narrow streets and alleyways. On the northern side the site opens on to the principal thoroughfare, Leadenhall Street, while on the south it is flanked by the Leadenhall Market complex. The site itself is an irregular wedge shape between existing buildings.

A central rectilinear office space is surrounded by six service towers in an overall amoebic plan that fills out the irregular shape of the site. The resulting interstitial spaces allow the interior to open up to the intense public life in the surrounding area.

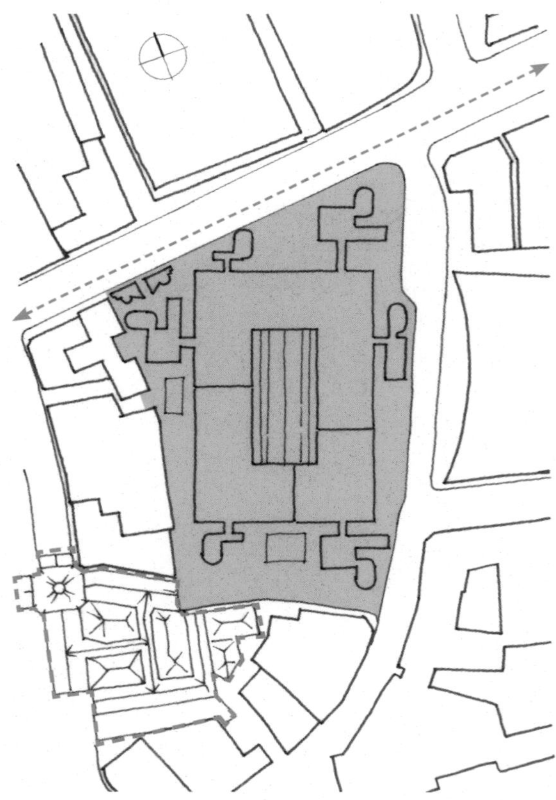

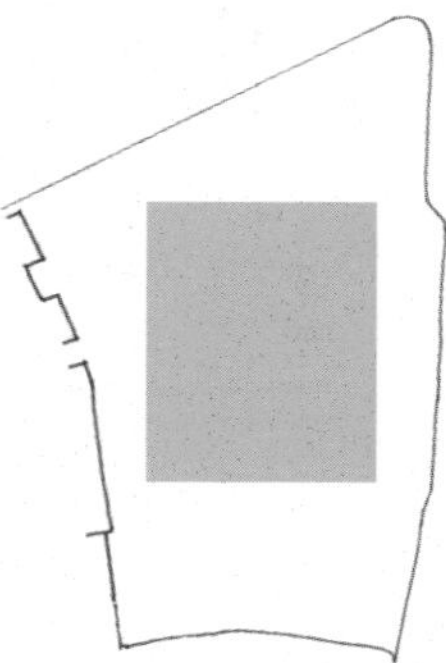

The design begins with a rectilinear space that serves the needs of the client.

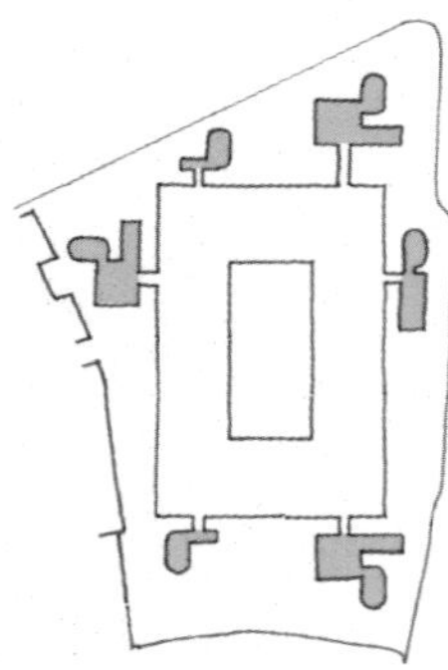

A series of supporting service structures is added in response to the irregular shape of the site, giving the building its distinctive plan form.

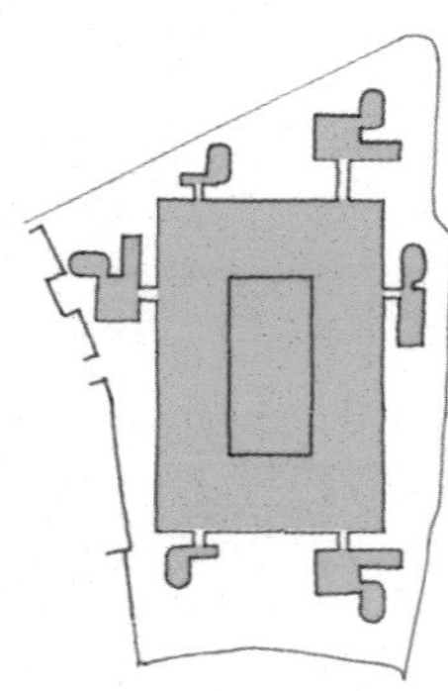

Response to surrounding context

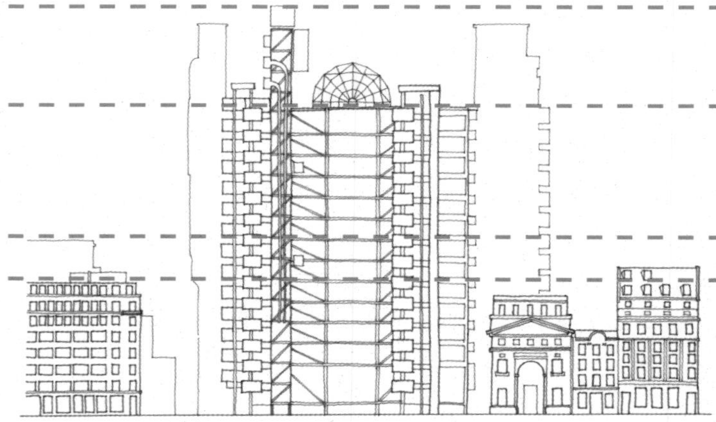

The Lloyd's building is not particularly high-rise, but sitting within its medieval architectural context it acquires a relative monumentality. This is most apparent on the northern side along Leadenhall Street, where the building's highly articulated façade helps to highlight the height difference with neighbouring buildings. The building steps down towards its southern end to respond to the low-rise pedestrian character of Leadenhall Market.

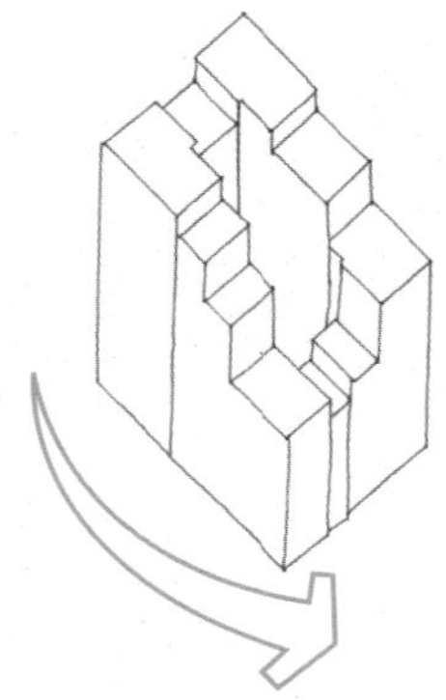

The building's scale is stepped down through a series of terraces to respond to the historic Leadenhall Market complex.

Response to architectural context

While at first glance the highly industrialized finishes and machine-like aesthetics of the Lloyd's building make it seem discohesive within the medieval architectural context that surrounds it, a closer look reveals a very deep and complex relationship with medieval architectural traditions.

The supporting service towers recall the projecting towers and battlements of medieval castles, which served to protect their central usable spaces and defined their external forms.

The response to the medieval architectural tradition is developed through an understanding of the relationships between various parts in defining the whole, and not through materiality or specific architectural elements.

The varied height of the service towers results in a highly articulated silhouette, a subtle yet rich response to the surrounding buildings.

The silhouette stands out in the wider London skyline as another layer in the varied architectural fabric that makes up the city.

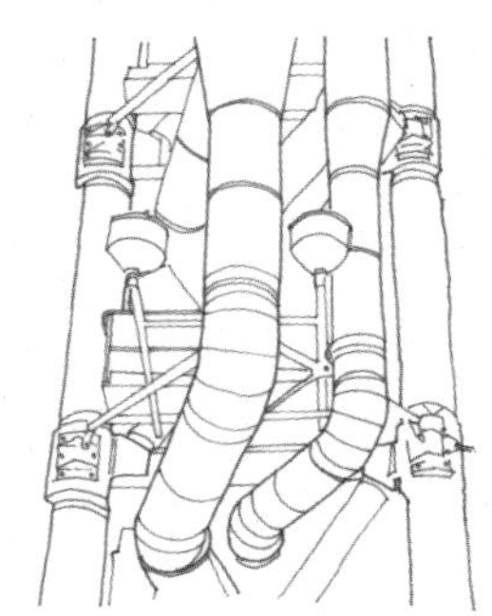

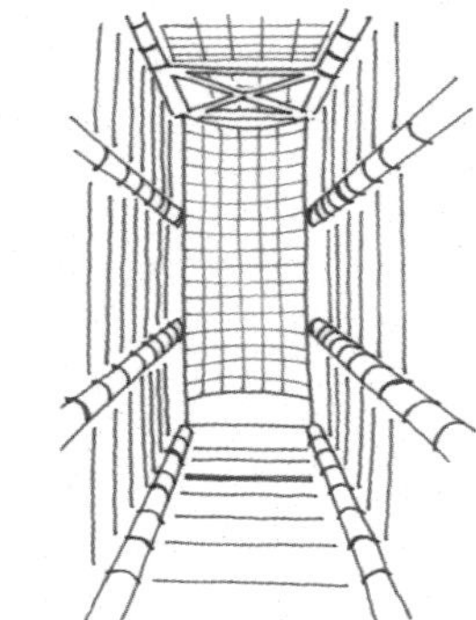

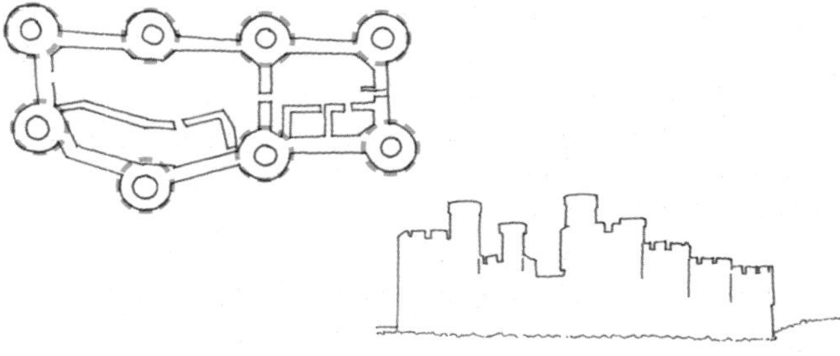

Conwy Castle, Wales (13th century)

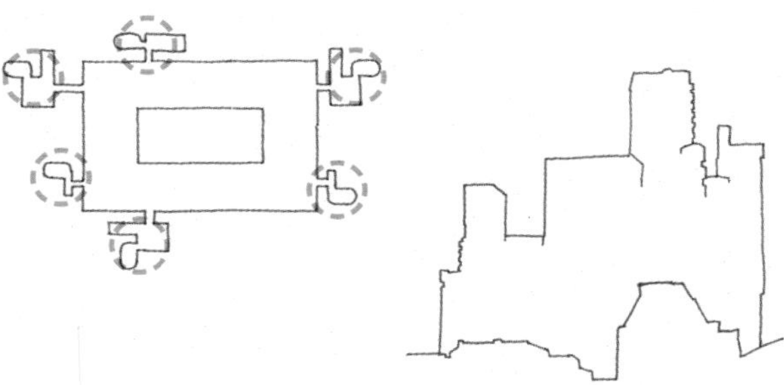

Lloyd's building with service towers (20th century)

The reference to medieval architectural traditions is carried forward through the adoption of Gothic-like detailing. The coexistence of varied parts in a complex whole is reinterpreted through the building's structure and such services as lighting and air conditioning. The results are orchestrated as architectural forms that have been developed in factories but retain a medieval sense of tectonic craft.

The light-bathed monumental interior of a Gothic cathedral is replicated in the central atrium, which cuts through all the floors and is capped by a glass vault.

The building is revealed slowly upon approach through the lanes. The ceremonial entrance is developed through an existing historical façade.

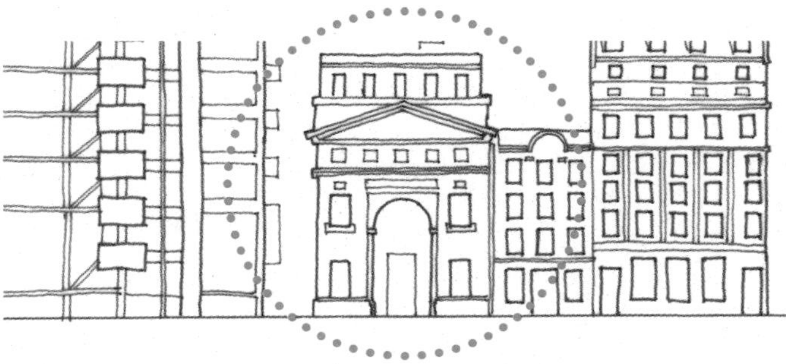

Lloyd's of London Office Building | 1978–86
Richard Rogers
London, England

Response to services and technology
The separation of the services from the central usable area allows for a greater net usable space in the middle and reduces circulation space. The lifespan of service elements is less than that of the central structure and their placement on the edges also aids future maintenance. This focus on the separation of the 'servant' and 'served' spaces was earlier theorized by Louis Kahn, who developed it through his design for the Richards Medical Research Laboratories project in Philadelphia (1957–62). The Lloyd's building applies the concept to prefabricated and plug-in systems.

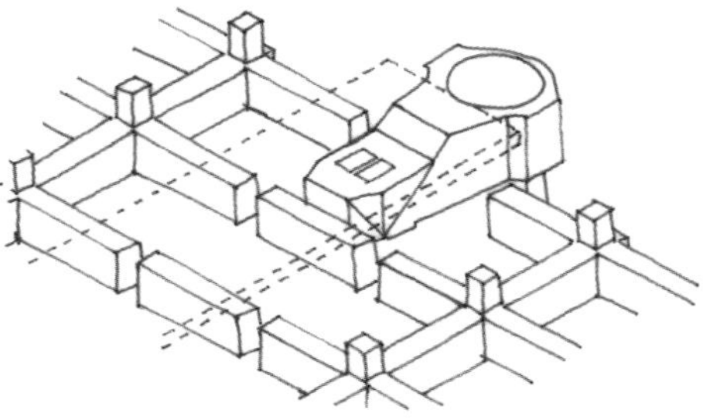

Prefabrication is also used for concrete structural elements that are assembled in a kit-of-parts construction.

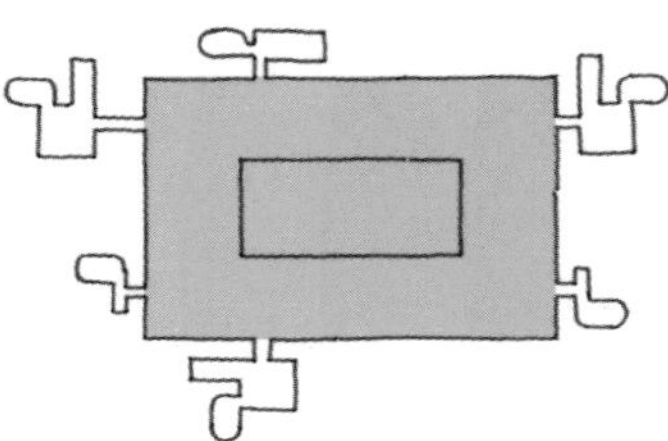

The central space is free of any barriers, allowing complete freedom of use.

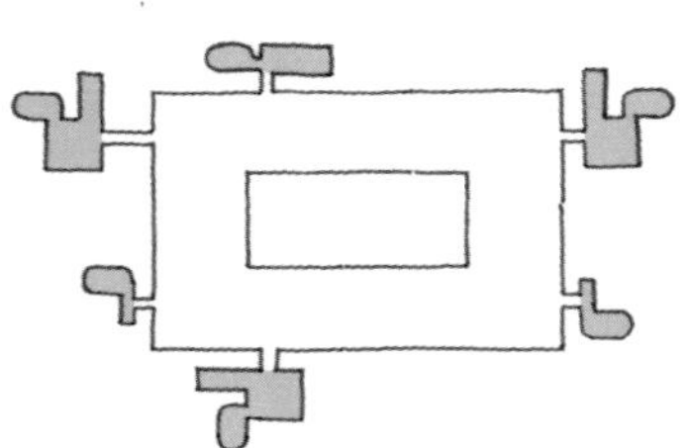

The 'servant' towers on the exterior serve the central usable, or 'served', space.

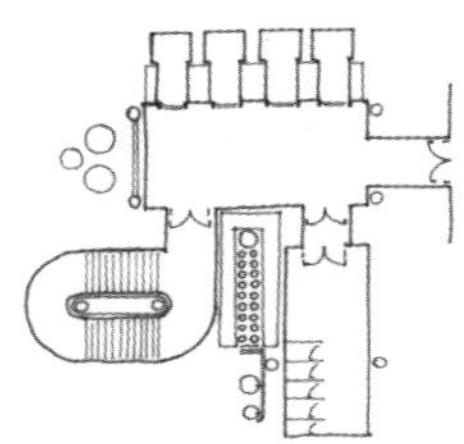

The simple brick 'servant' towers of the Richards Medical Research Laboratories are developed and articulated as a complete plug-in system of building services that rely on prefabricated elements to be added as required through a mounted crane system. The service towers can be replaced in response to the development of future technologies.

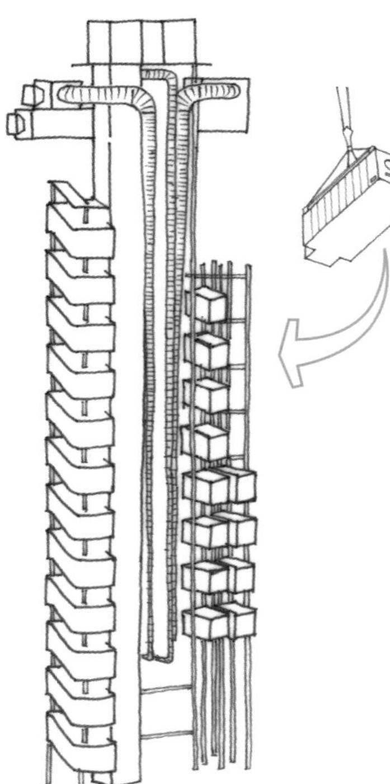

Developing a machine aesthetic
The technical developments of the service systems follow a 'machine aesthetic' that was originally developed in the visionary architecture of such movements as Futurism and Constructivism in the early 1900s.

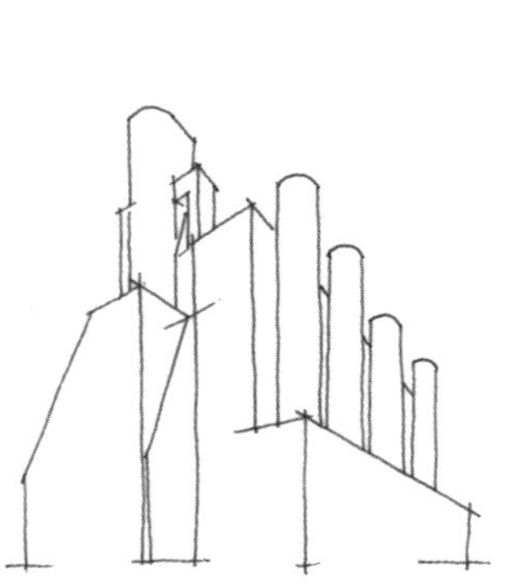

Futurism, Italy (1912). Sketch by Antonio Sant'Elia.

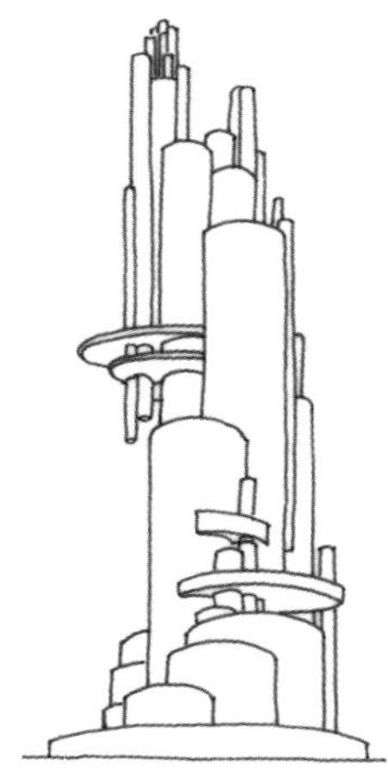

Constructivism, Russia (1925). Sketch by Iakov Chernikov.

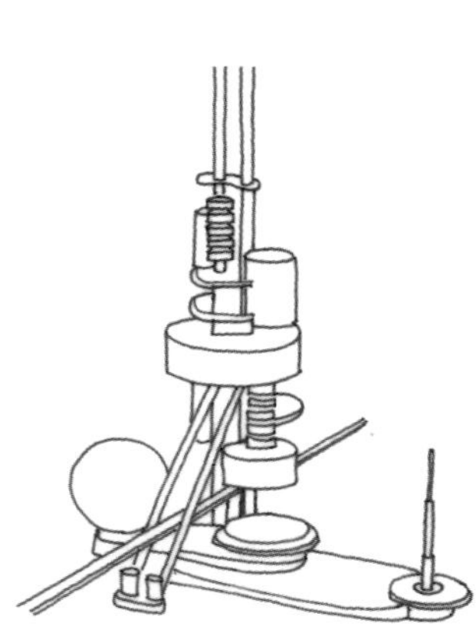

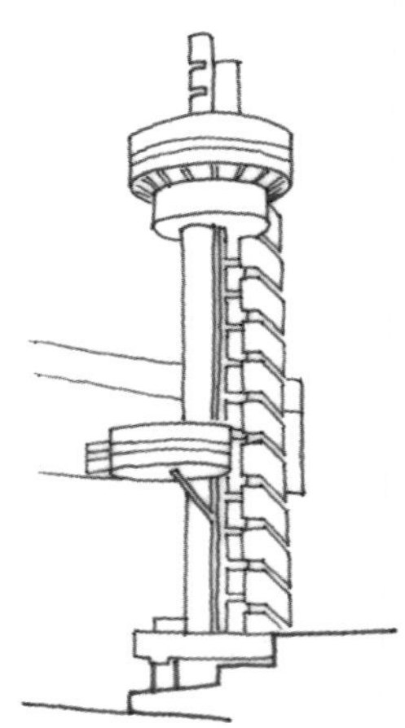

This aesthetic was developed by Richard Rogers in earlier unbuilt work in London during the 1980s: first in a development along the River Thames (above left) and then in his competition entry for an extension to the National Gallery (above right).

Response to the urban public realm

The service towers dissolve at ground level and the undercroft space becomes a public court. The opening of the ground plane to the public realm, coupled with the building's circulation pushed to the exterior, allows people to observe one another in action, turning the building and its surroundings into an urban theatre.

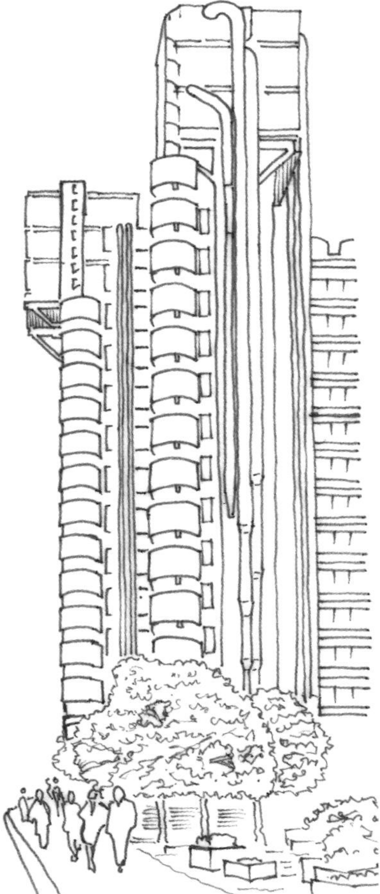

The rising tower is mediated at ground level to allow for urban life.

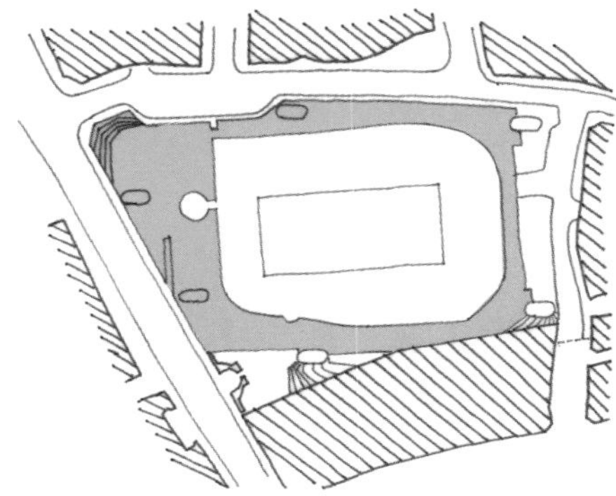

The lower ground level is dedicated to the urban realm and developed as a large public piazza.

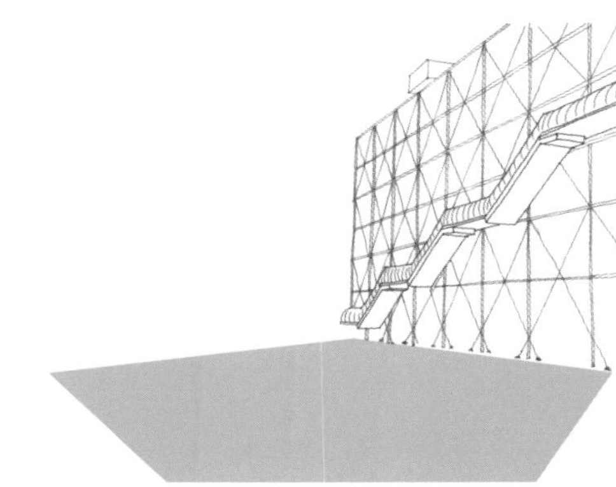

The Centre Pompidou, Paris (1971–77), by Renzo Piano and Richard Rogers, gave the city a large public square.

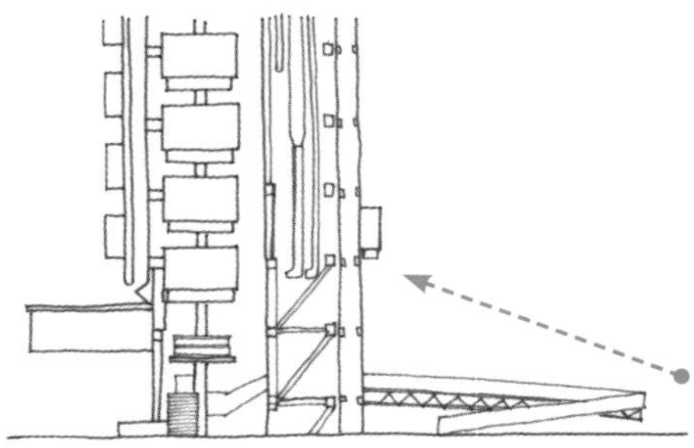

The layering of the building and the external glass lifts create visual interest from street level.

Internal space and user experience

The traditional structural grid system is modified to force the columns either outside the external edges or towards the central atrium. This ensures a clear 'doughnut' space free from any visual obstructions. This suits the operation of a trading floor.

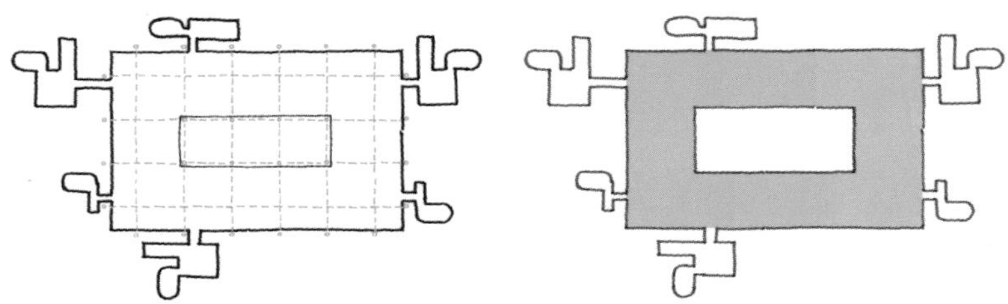

The doughnut-shaped space is repeated on all floors. They can be used as trading floors or subdivided into smaller offices. Allowing for all floors to be developed in this manner provides the required flexibility for future expansions, when increasing business might require more trading-floor space, or changing technology might make visual connection across the trading floor unnecessary.

The floors are further connected visually across various levels through the use of a central atrium that runs through the entire height of the building and is capped by a glass vault. The external glass faces are translucent, allowing the entire space to be bathed in a glow of natural light without creating glare or distracting shadows.

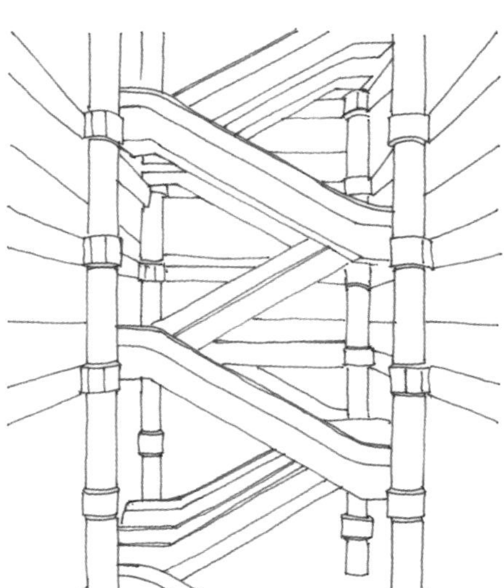

The escalators criss-cross up the atrium and draw the eye across the various levels.

Translucent rice-paper surfaces in traditional Japanese houses create a radiant effect.

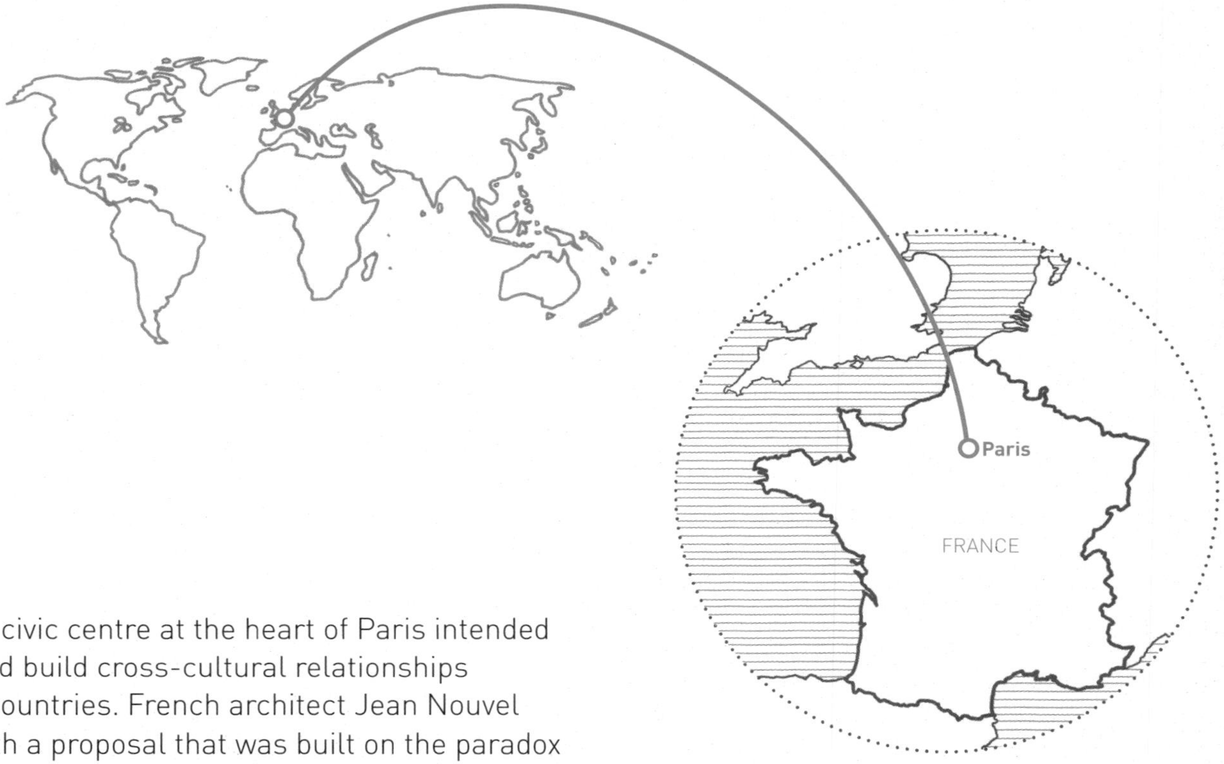

Paris

FRANCE

20 Arab World Institute | 1981–87

Jean Nouvel

Paris, France

The Arab World Institute is a civic centre at the heart of Paris intended to promote Arabic culture and build cross-cultural relationships between France and Arabic countries. French architect Jean Nouvel won a design competition with a proposal that was built on the paradox between modernity and tradition. Utilizing diverse precedents from traditional Arabic architecture, such as interiority and the manipulation of light, the building is a contemporary translation of these design elements into new technology, materials and structure.

The environmental response of the building is integral to its aesthetic and symbolic appeal. The south façade is a finely detailed metal interpretation of the Arabic device of a patterned screen to provide both privacy and shade. Its elements respond to the sun's movement and intensity, changing the pattern of light in the interior.

Selen Morkoç, Wei Fen Soh, Hilal al-Busaidi and Leona Greenslade

20

Arab World Institute | 1981–87
Jean Nouvel
Paris, France

Context

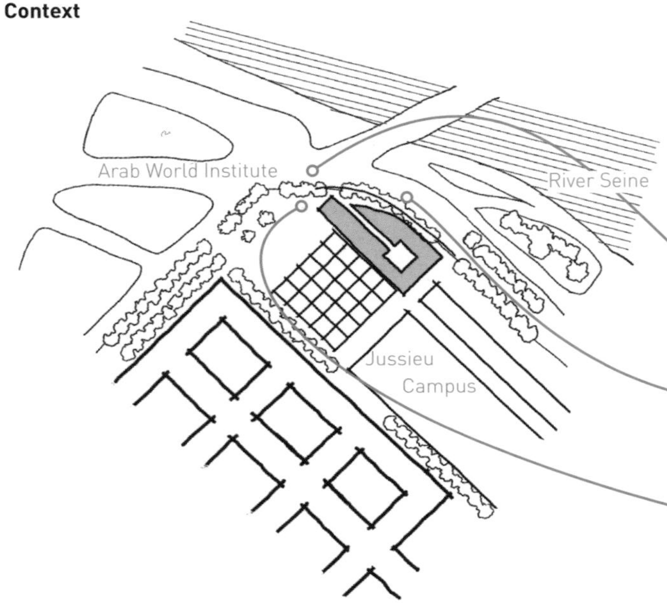

Arab World Institute
River Seine
Jussieu Campus

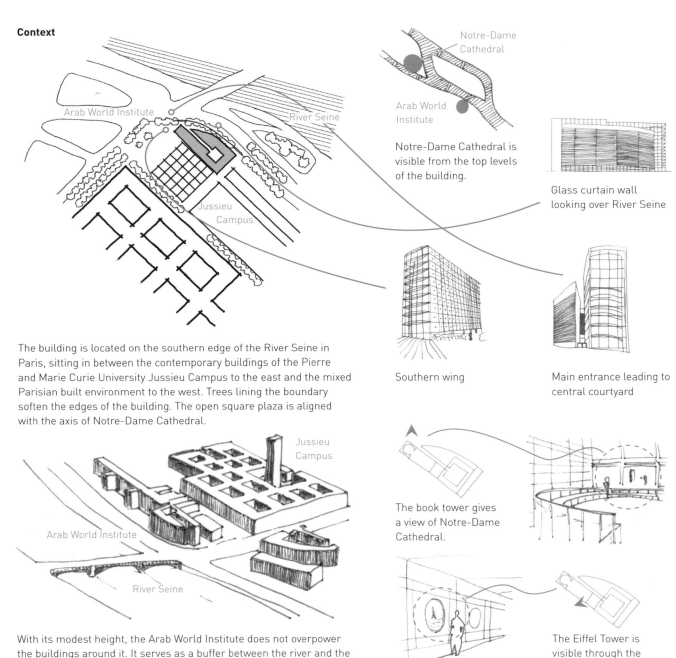

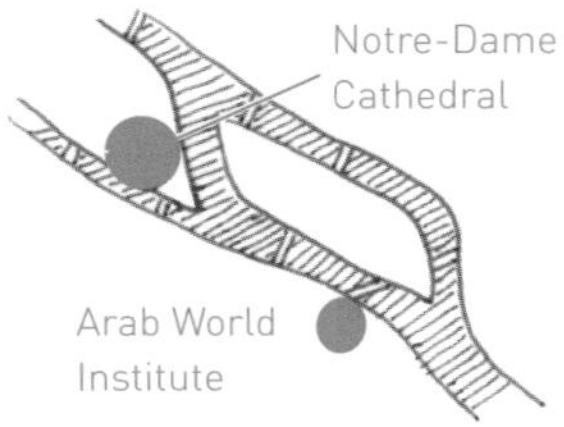

The building is located on the southern edge of the River Seine in Paris, sitting in between the contemporary buildings of the Pierre and Marie Curie University Jussieu Campus to the east and the mixed Parisian built environment to the west. Trees lining the boundary soften the edges of the building. The open square plaza is aligned with the axis of Notre-Dame Cathedral.

Jussieu Campus
Arab World Institute
River Seine

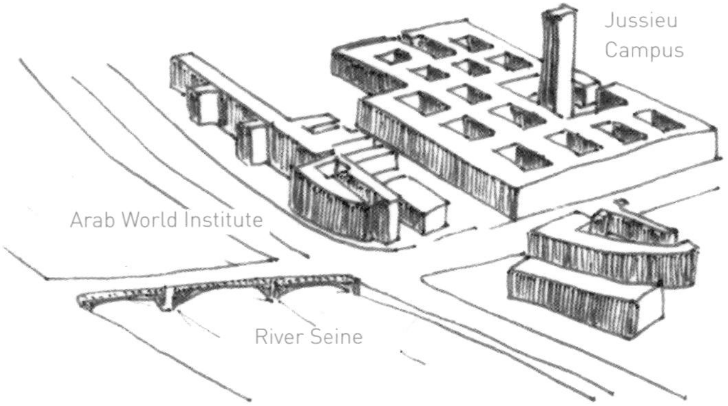

With its modest height, the Arab World Institute does not overpower the buildings around it. It serves as a buffer between the river and the Pierre and Marie Curie University campus.

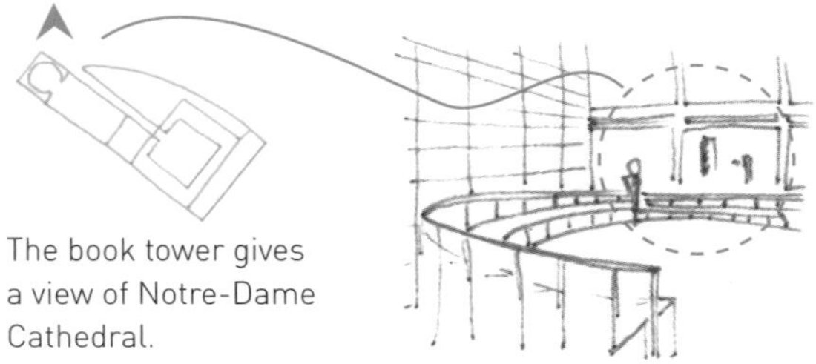

Notre-Dame Cathedral
Arab World Institute

Notre-Dame Cathedral is visible from the top levels of the building.

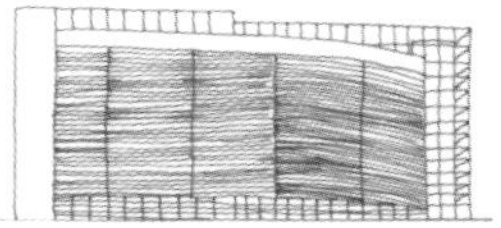

Glass curtain wall looking over River Seine

Southern wing

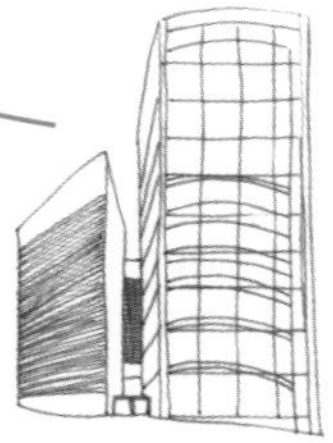

Main entrance leading to central courtyard

The book tower gives a view of Notre-Dame Cathedral.

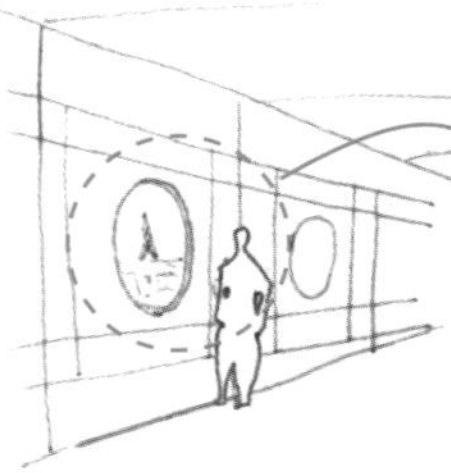

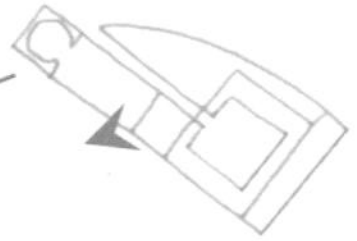

The Eiffel Tower is visible through the northern façade.

Views

The south façade is made of steel and glass, which reflects the views of the surroundings.

The steel-and-glass curved surface is hidden behind trees.

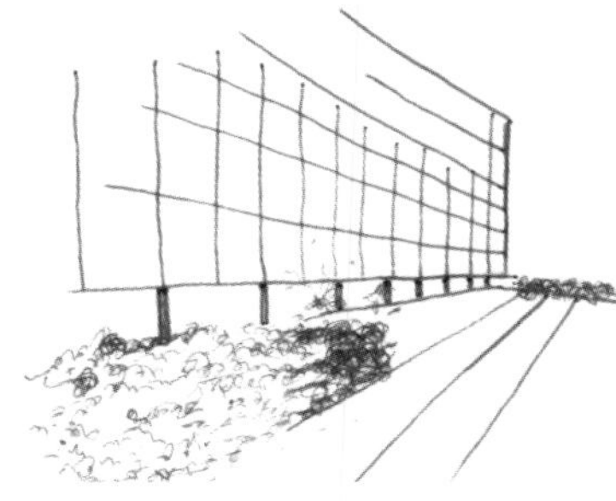

The longitudinal north façade is framed by planters, which serve as a connection between the built form and the surrounding landscape.

Climate Paris has a mild but wet climate. As a response, most spaces are internal with a small, very sheltered courtyard. The only exposed outdoor space is a terrace extension of the rooftop restaurant for use in good weather.

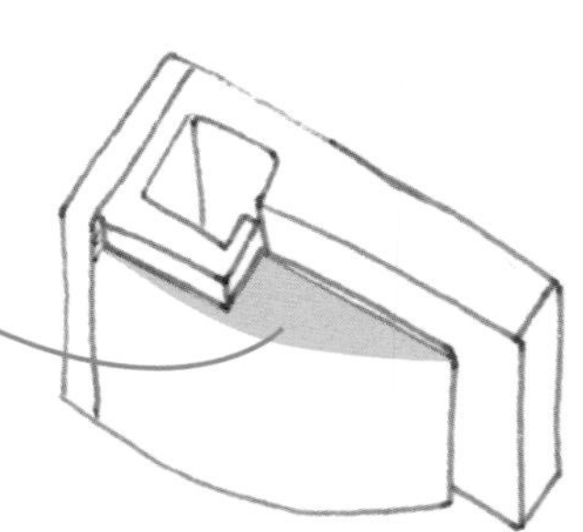

Arab World Institute | 1981–87

Jean Nouvel
Paris, France

20

Approach

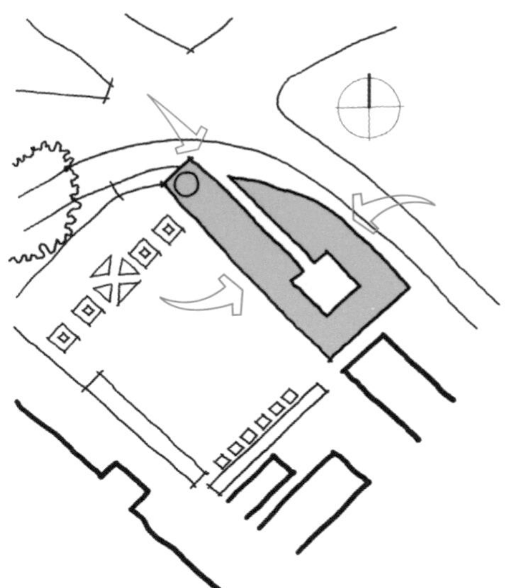

There are three entrances to the building: into the northern wing, into the southern wing, and between the wings through a slot.

Creating horizontal suspense

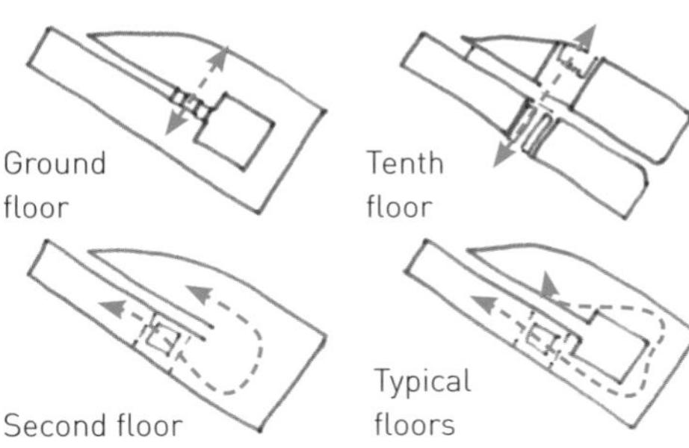

The only north–south connections are found on the ground floor and in a linking corridor on the tenth floor. This creates suspense through the layering of walls, whereby both sides can see through spaces but direct access is possible at only two levels.

Response to programme

Form generation

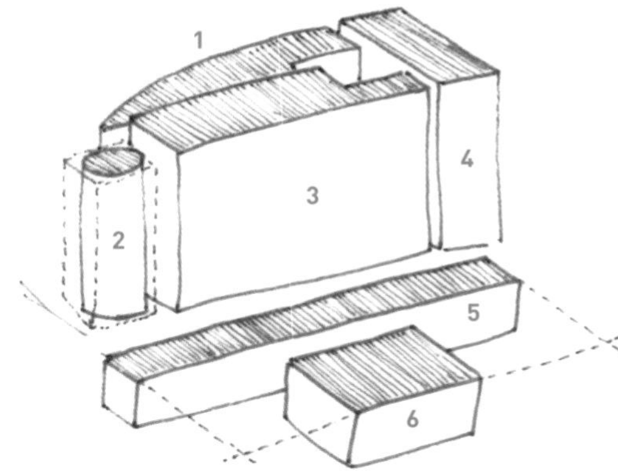

Key
1. museum
2. book tower
3. High Council hall
4. services
5. hypostyle hall
6. auditorium

The form organizes the space to suit functional requirements. The auditorium is located underground.

The large vertical elements are not only functional; they also allow a visual connection between levels and enhance the play of light inside.

Creating vertical suspense

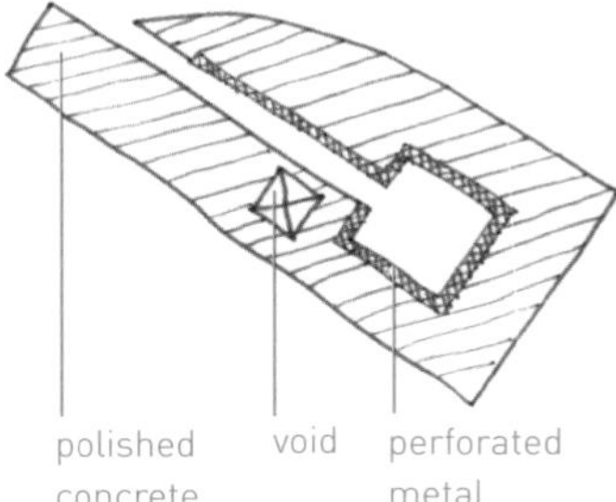

The perforated metal on the inner façades of the building creates semi-permeability, generating suspense across the levels with blurred views. The effect of differences in materials is also reflected in the filtering of light and shadow.

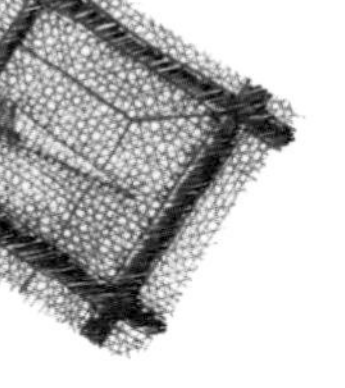

Through the metallic screens, the suspense is intensified when the view of the opposite space is ambiguous.

Looking up from a lower level, shadows and footprints can be seen indistinctly.

Dynamic spaces

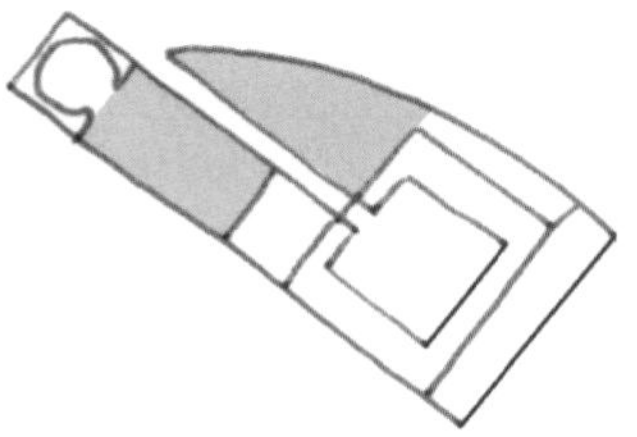

Flexible floor plans
Museum and exhibition spaces can be segmented with partition walls to create smaller spaces.

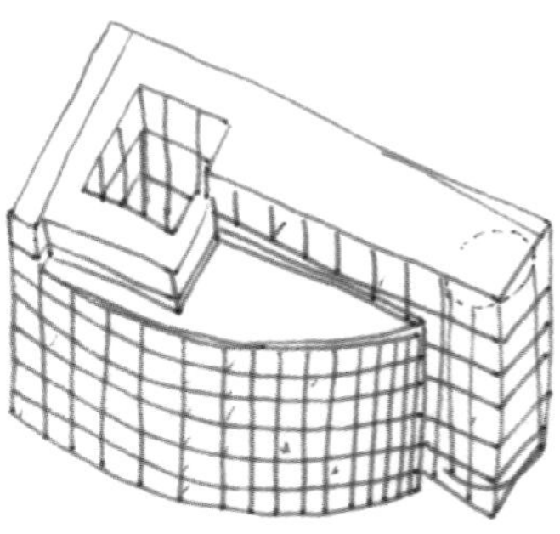

Transparency Despite several references from Arabic mosque typology, the Arab World Institute is not a place of worship, so has no need for privacy and enclosure. The envelope of the building of steel and glass reflects the notion of transparency.

Transparency blurs the boundaries between inside and outside, visually connecting the interiors with the surrounding views.

Light and function

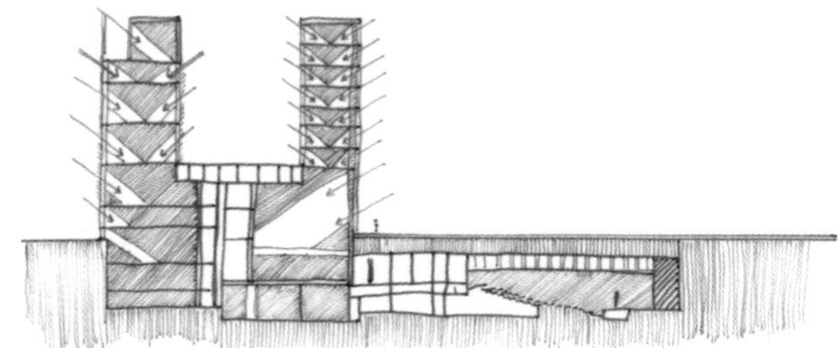

The exhibition spaces, library and restaurants are located on the higher levels to allow in natural light, whereas the auditorium, which does not need natural light, is located in the basement.

Arab World Institute | 1981–87

Jean Nouvel

Paris, France

A cohesive design language

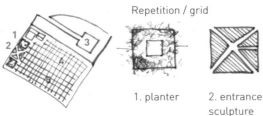

Repetition / grid

1. planter

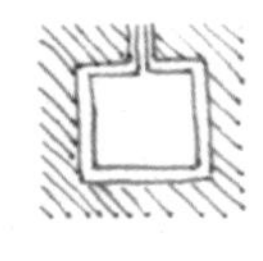

2. entrance sculpture

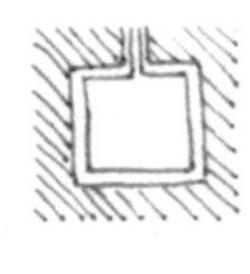
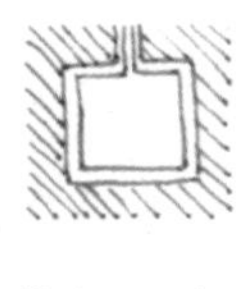

3. central courtyard

4. south elevation

5. plan of courtyard square

Framed views

1. south-west entrance
2. west entrance
3. north-east entrance

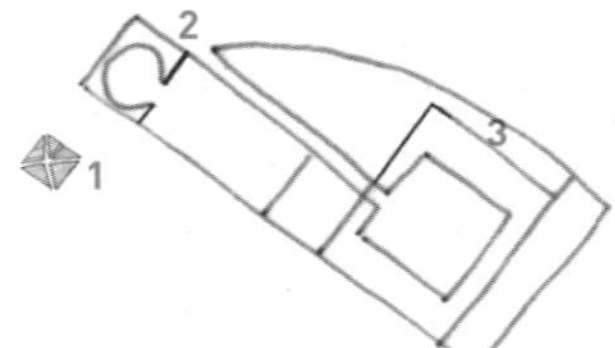

The main entrance inspires awe when visitors experience the narrow chasm between the extensive façades of the northern and southern wings.

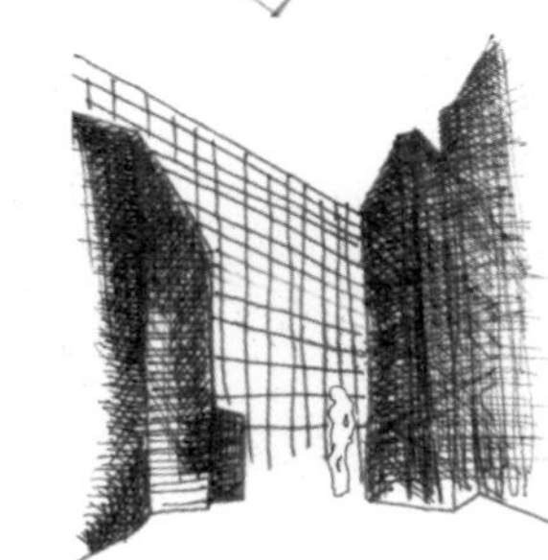

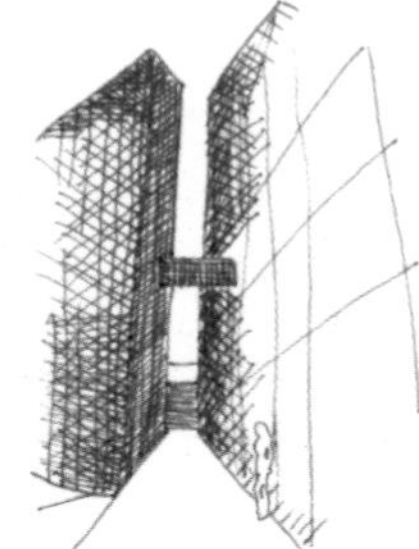

This narrow pathway leads to an inner courtyard, creating a spatial effect of confinement followed by spaciousness.

The inner courtyard receives ample natural light, creating a welcoming effect.

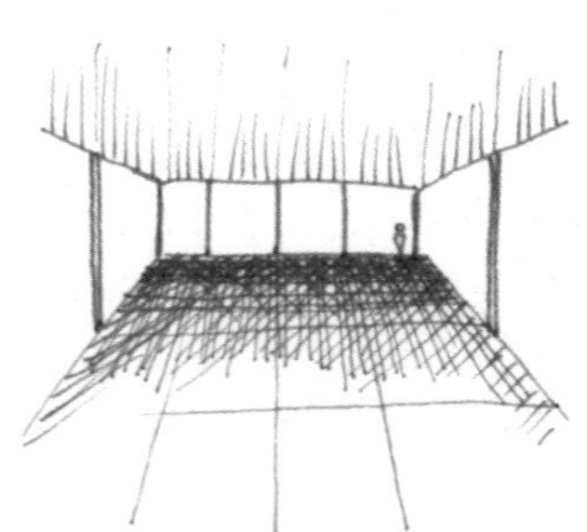

Contrast in design

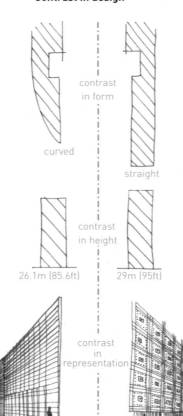

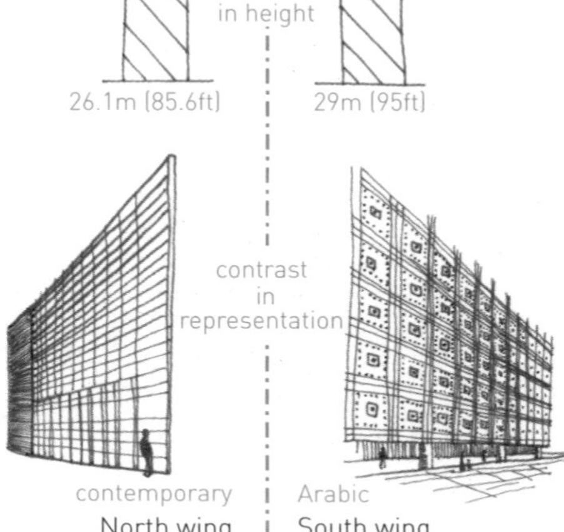

Natural light

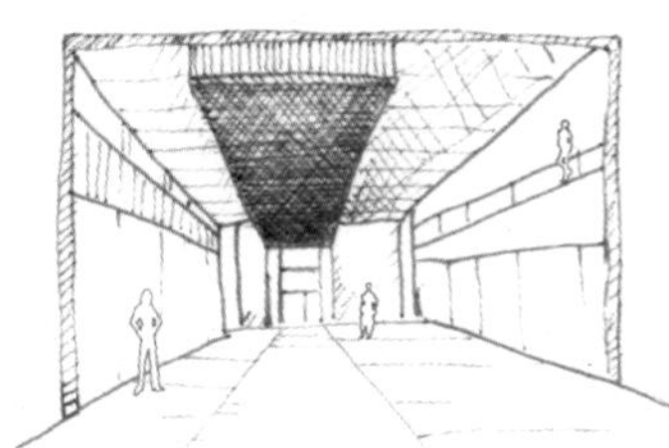

Suspended ceilings create an irregular space and reinforce a sense of depth by splitting an already long space into three narrower zones.

Alternating areas of glass and concrete in the façades create varying lighting effects in the interior.

The stairs act as a filter for light and cast shadows.

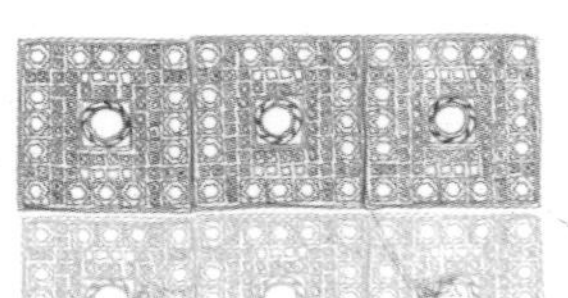

Light reflected off the polished concrete floor makes patterns that repeat those of the walls.

Climate

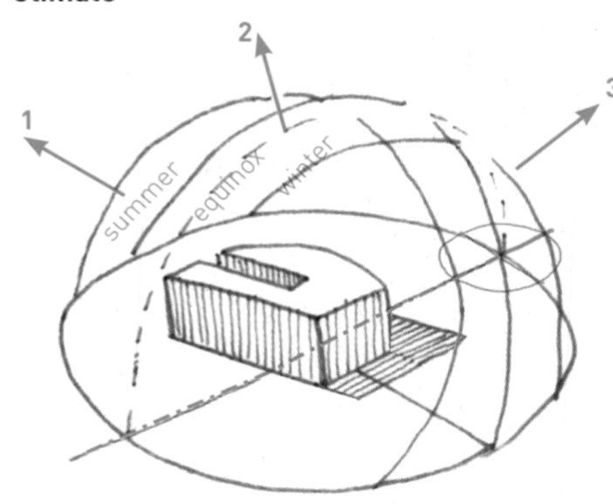

The straight southern wing gets the sun, whereas the curving north wing is located in the shadow of its southern neighbour.

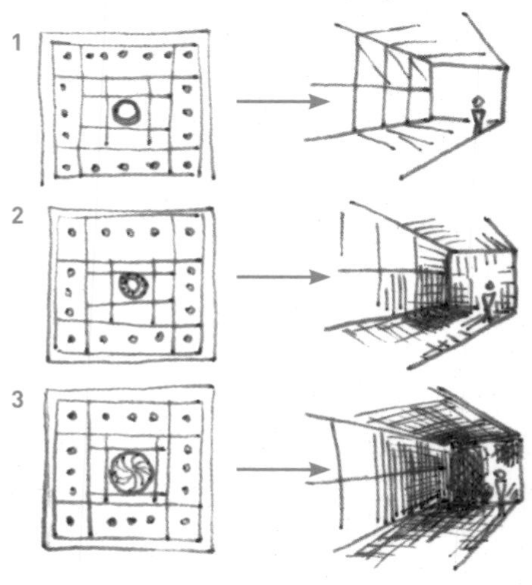

Artificial lighting

The spiral ramp of the book tower lights up at night and makes the building a highly visible attraction.

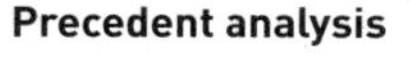

Precedent analysis
Mashrabiya screens

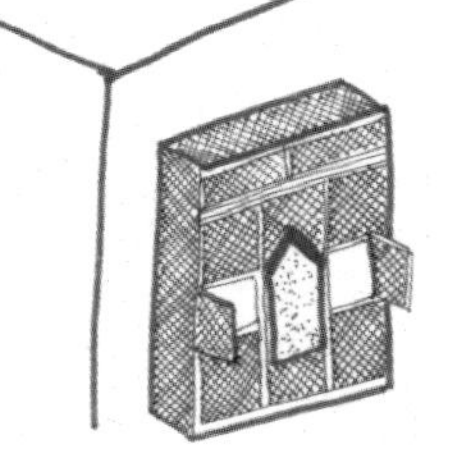

Mashrabiyas are screens used in traditional Arabic dwellings that filter light and enable a person to see out without being seen from outside.

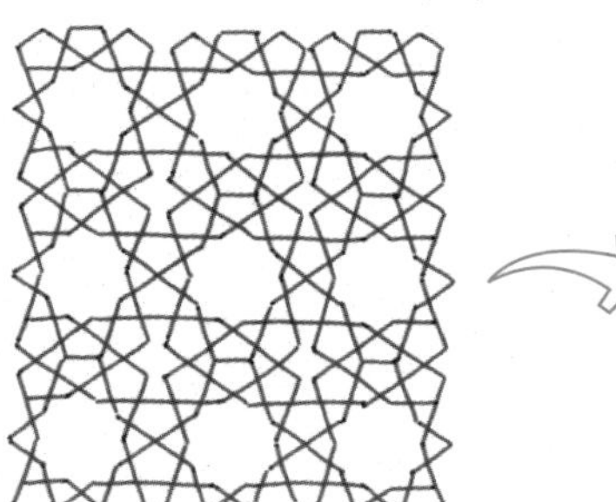

A traditional mashrabiya pattern

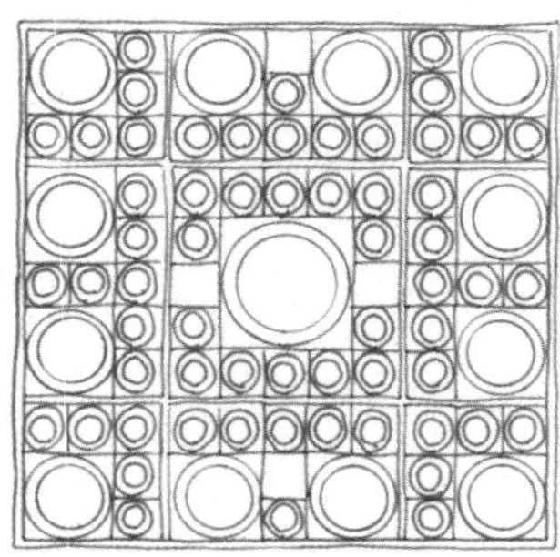

The geometry and the different sizes of apertures in a single square panel of the south façade of the Arab World Institute

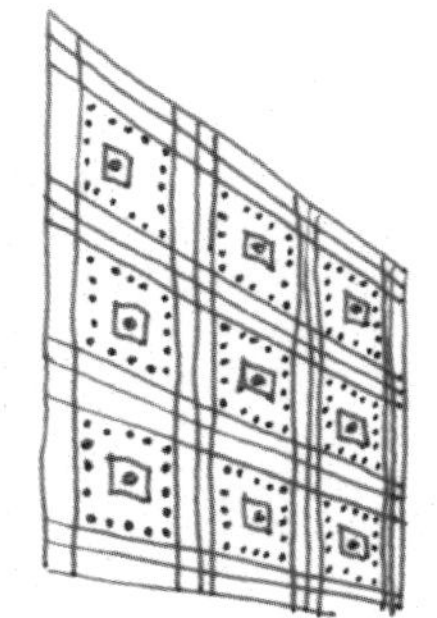

Aperture panels Square panels that include motor-controlled light-sensitive apertures are placed together to create a metaphorical Arabic mashrabiya.

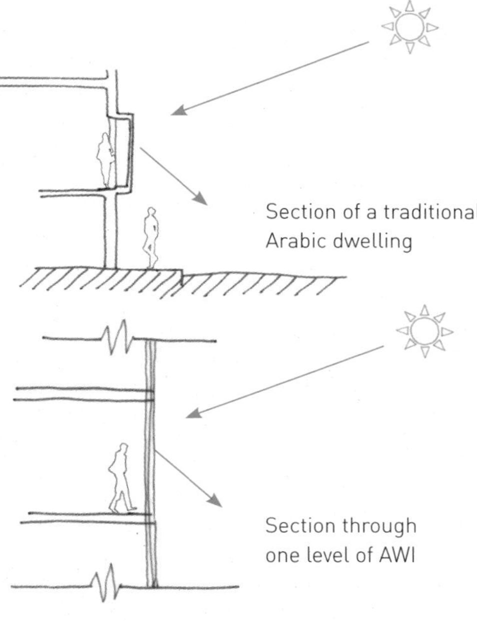

Section of a traditional Arabic dwelling

Section through one level of AWI

Courtyard

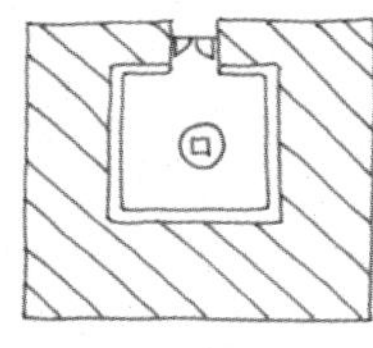

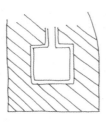

Arabic dwelling courtyard

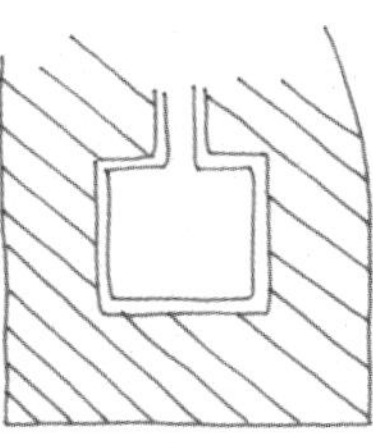

Central courtyard of Arab World Institute, used as a light well

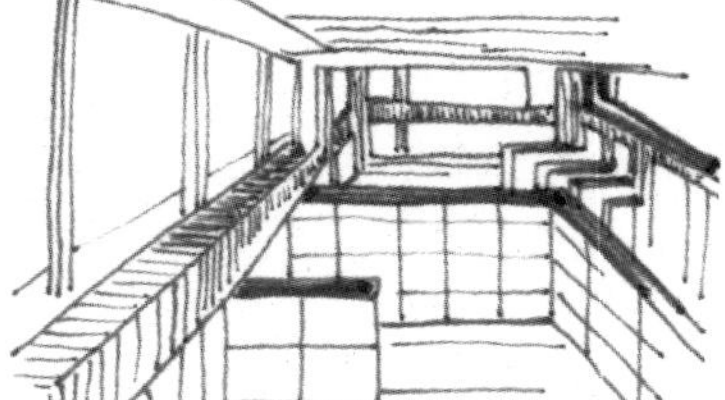

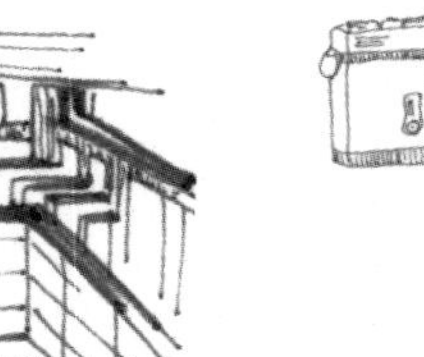

Aperture/shutter The high-technology photosensitive shutters, resembling a camera lens, are used to control the amount of light allowed into the building.

Public/private The transition between public and private spaces is gradual through the use of slopes and planters, defining a sense of separation and identity without the use of large fences and gates.

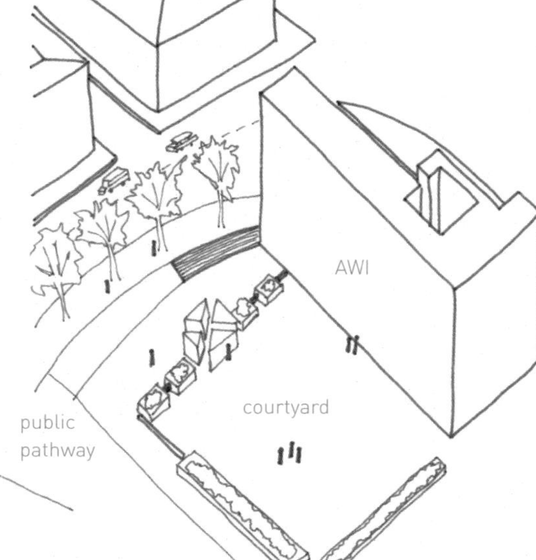

Minaret

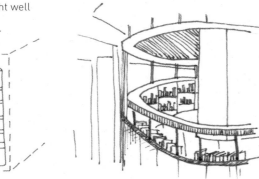

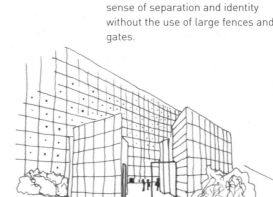

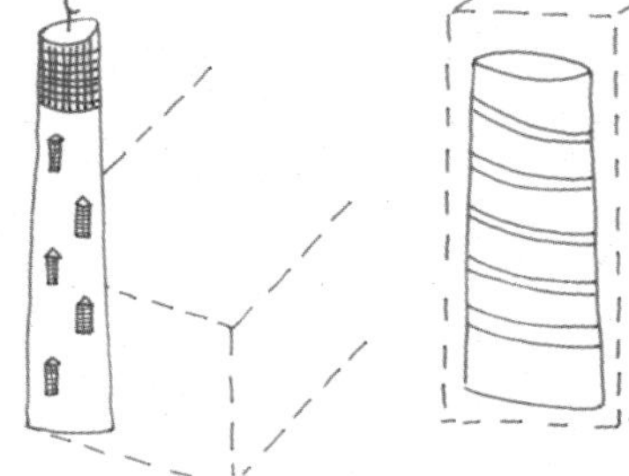

The cylinder containing the library bookshelves resembles a mosque minaret in form, but it is embedded in the rectangular envelope.

Next to the cylindrical book tower (above) is a double-height rectangular library (top).

Barcelona Museum of Contemporary Art | 1987–95

Richard Meier

Barcelona, Spain

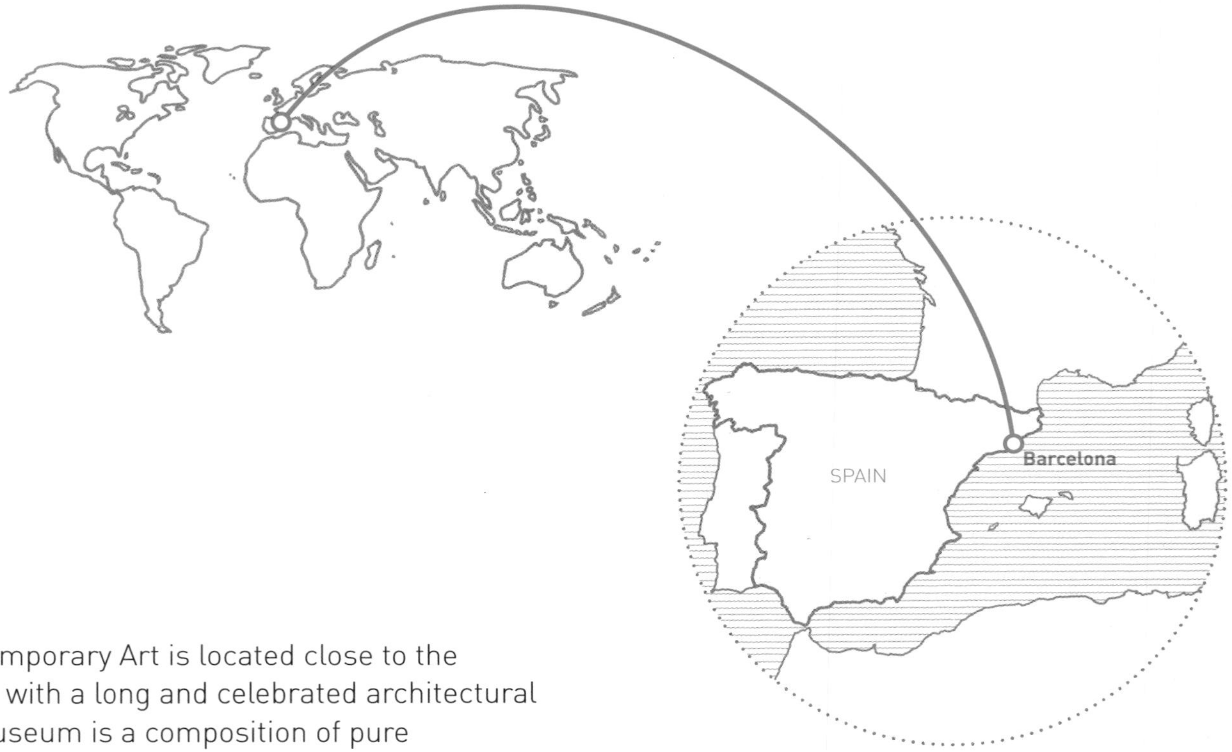

21

Barcelona Museum of Contemporary Art is located close to the centre of Barcelona. In a city with a long and celebrated architectural tradition, Richard Meier's museum is a composition of pure geometric forms in his characteristic white style.

The museum is an example of engaging the universal design principles of modern architecture with particularity of place and purpose through the sophisticated organization, contrast, layering, addition and subtraction of form. The result is a complex but legible whole in which the play of light and shadow is a major part of the aesthetic experience. While colour, materials and shapes are quite different from those of the building's older neighbours, its scale and detail respond to and enhance the urban scene.

Selen Morkoç, Hao Lv, John Pargeter and Leona Greenslade

21

Barcelona Museum of Contemporary Art | 1987–95

Richard Meier

Barcelona, Spain

Response to urban context

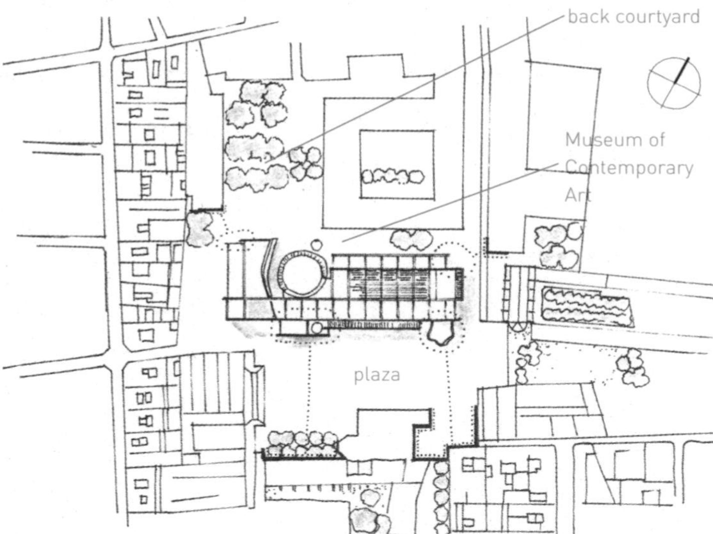

The museum is located next to Plaça dels Àngels, which is one of the most popular meeting points in Barcelona. Nearby buildings vary from large to small, but all have a similar height and are organized on a regular urban grid. Their materials are stone and brick.

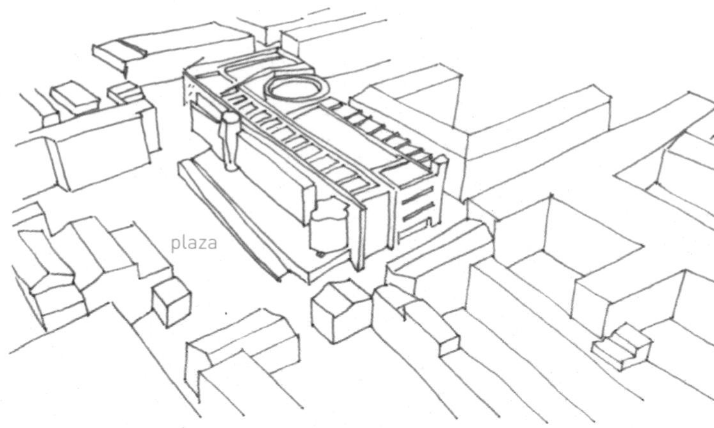

Architect Richard Meier's design strategy makes compositions of Modernist design elements, which are based on rectangles or other simple geometric forms, set in a grid and uniformly white in colour. This design language is adapted for the requirements of the given programme and site. The museum follows this pattern.

Existing site form and surroundings

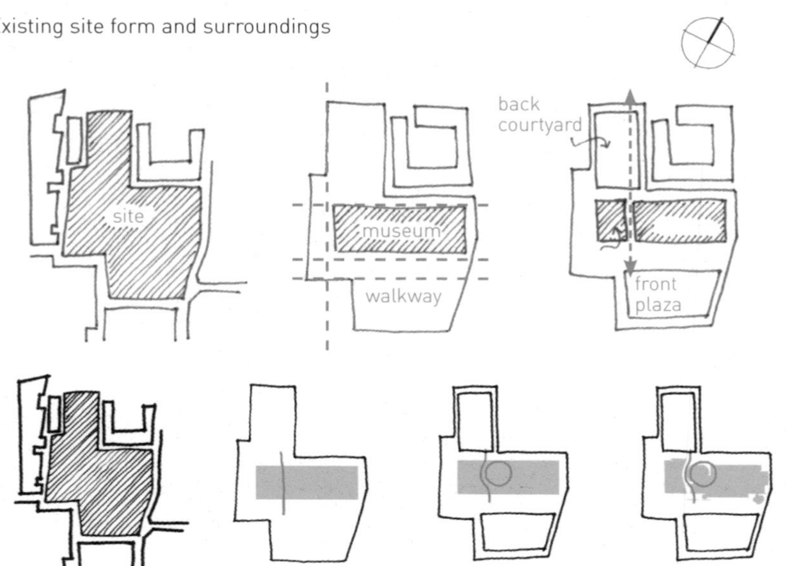

An implied axis links the plaza with the back courtyard. This divides the museum into service and exhibition areas. Cross axes order the major building elements.

The flow of movement from the front plaza through the gallery to the back courtyard is disturbed by a cylindrical element in the building composition. The resulting curved circulation space is the core of movement in the building.

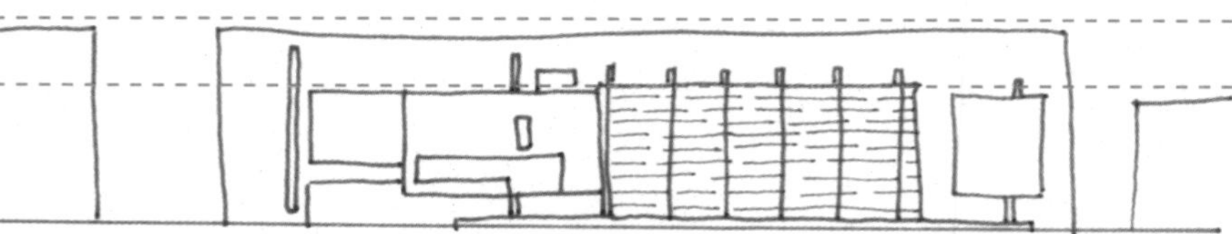

South elevation

The heights of the building and protruding elements on the main elevation respond to the heights of surrounding buildings.

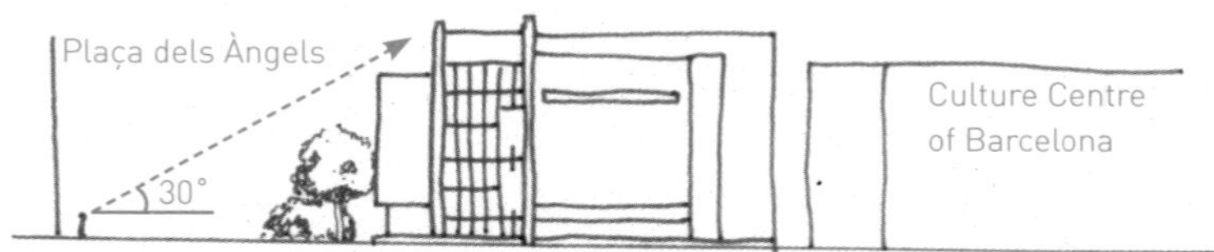

East elevation

The height and proportions of the south front of the museum respond to the scale and proportions of the Plaça des Àngels, so that visitors can view the whole façade easily.

Abstraction of elements

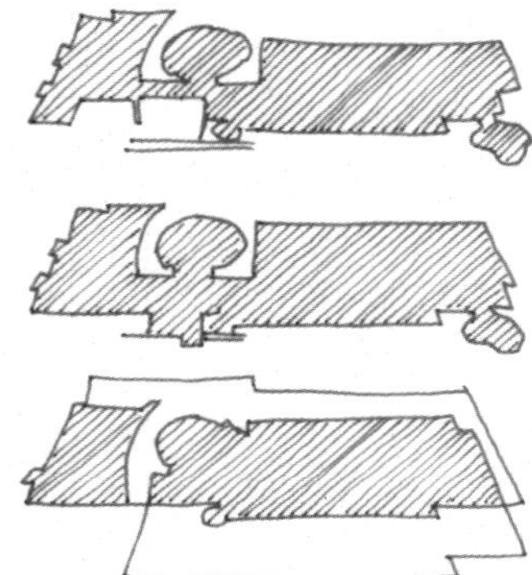

The varying floor plates suggest assemblies of eroded geometric shapes.

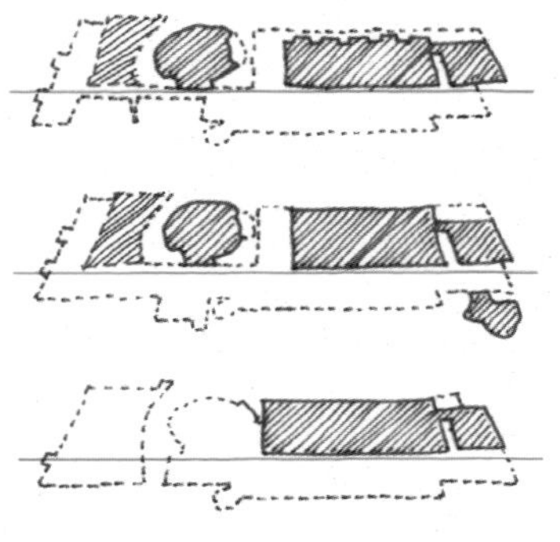

A variety of rectilinear and curvilinear galleries are arranged along an axis.

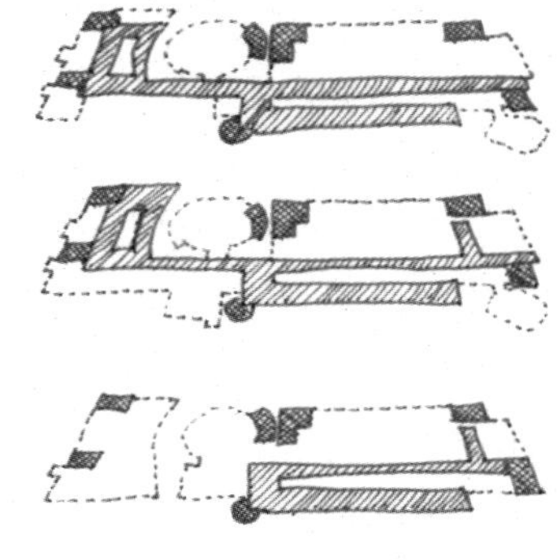

The main circulation elements are a ramp and a circular staircase, both on the south side of the building. Escape and service stairs are positioned on the corners of the building.

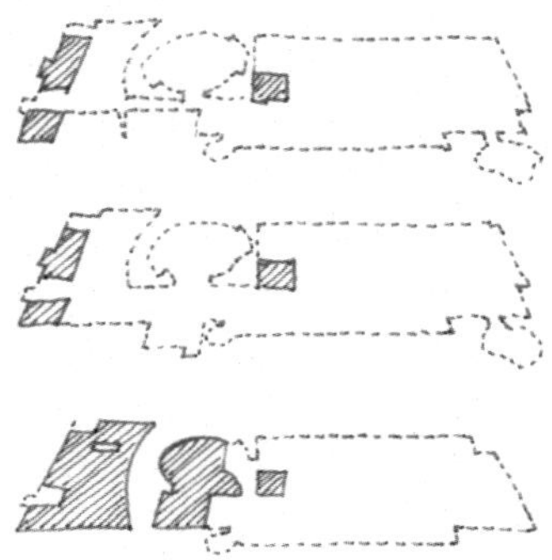

The main service spaces are located at the west end and clearly separated from the exhibition area.

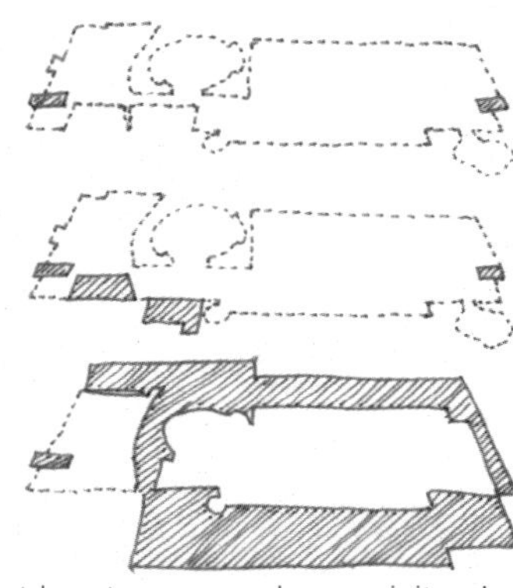

Outdoor terraces enhance visitors' experience of the surroundings.

The grid

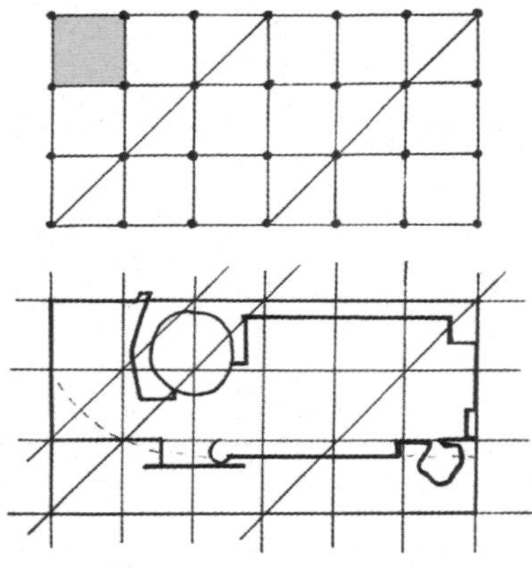

A grid that mimics Barcelona's urban grid system underlies the design composition.

Design elements, including the movement routes, are arranged on this underlying grid.

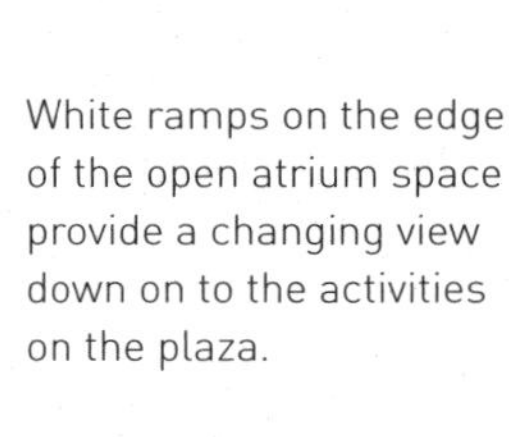

White ramps on the edge of the open atrium space provide a changing view down on to the activities on the plaza.

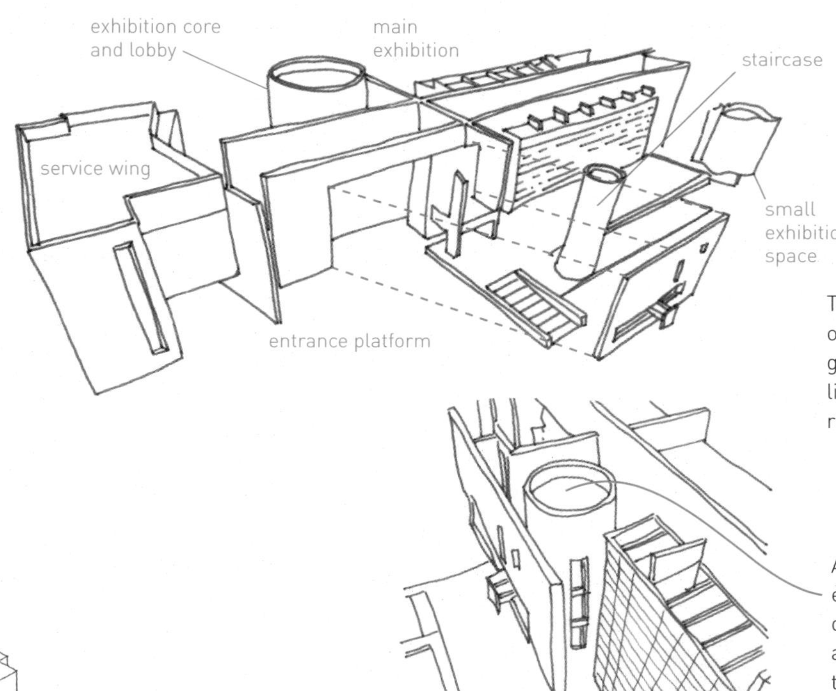

The building consists of a series of pure geometric forms that lie behind the overall rigorousness of form.

A circular staircase is enclosed in a concrete drum. Windows permit a constrained view along the side of the building, in contrast to the broad views from the ramp.

21 Barcelona Museum of Contemporary Art | 1987–95

Richard Meier

Barcelona, Spain

Form generation and light

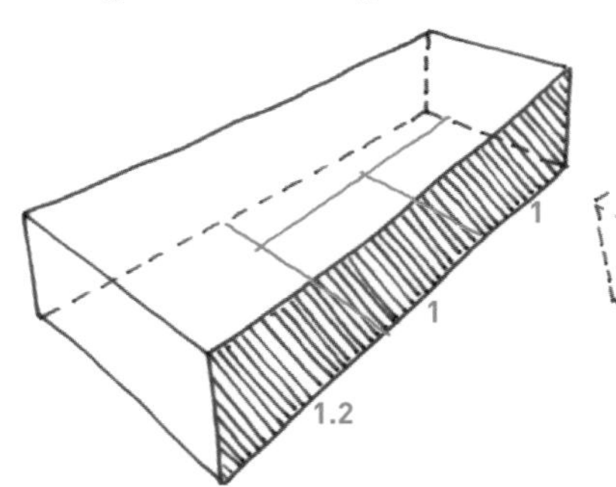

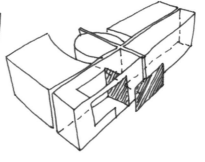

The basic form is a simple box. This is derived from three squares on plan, with side lengths in proportions 1:1:1.2.

The cuboid is cut by a cross of division along the edge of the large square.

A cylinder is inserted over the north–south arm of the cross. The side of the west wing is pushed back in response, making a curving void between the cylinder and the west wing.

A double-layer façade is formed on the south side by subtracting parts of its surface and adding new offset parallel surfaces.

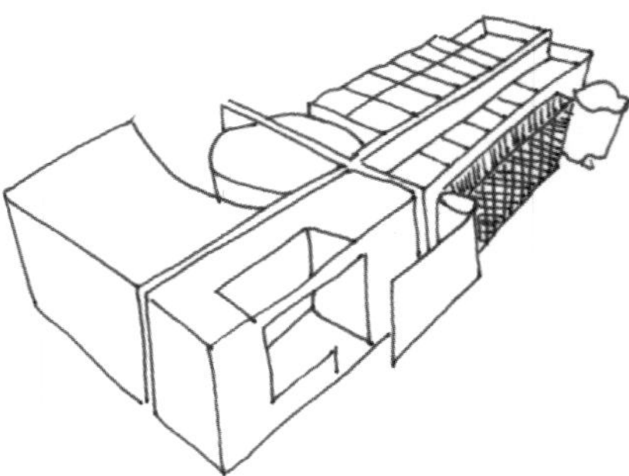

Natural light is provided via a curtain wall and skylights.

Exhibition space

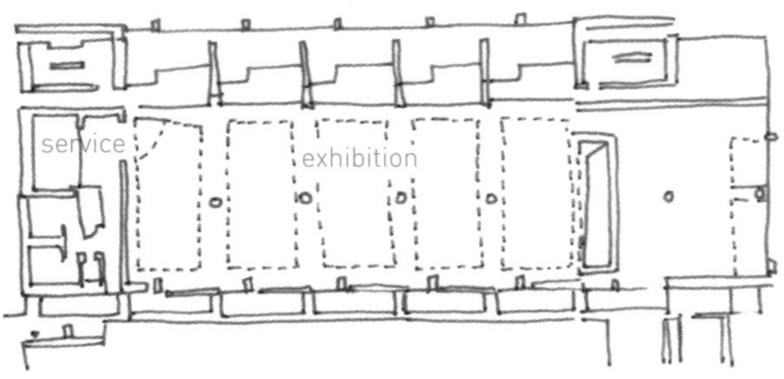

The major exhibition space is enhanced by skylights.

A triple-height ceiling in circulation spaces encourages movement between spaces and provides views to the plaza.

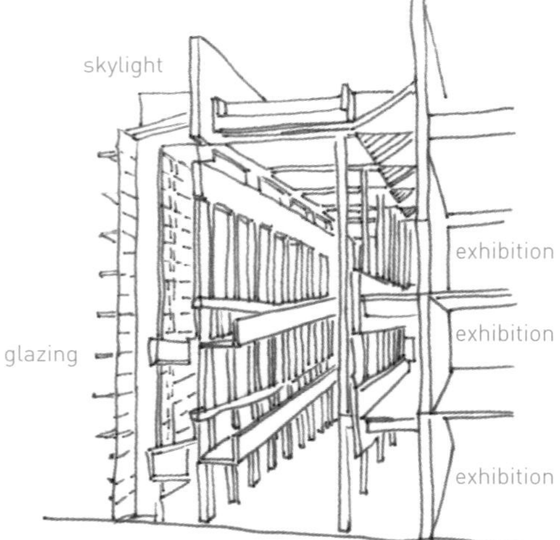

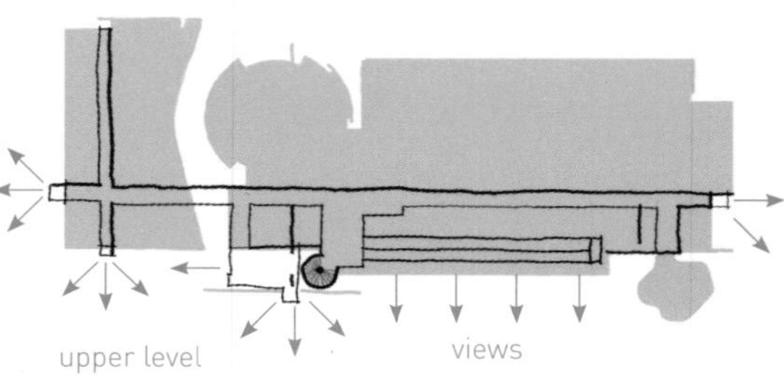

On the upper level there are balconies and windows from which to pause and gaze on the surroundings. The glass wall of the atrium allows visitors to watch activity in the plaza as they walk along the ramp.

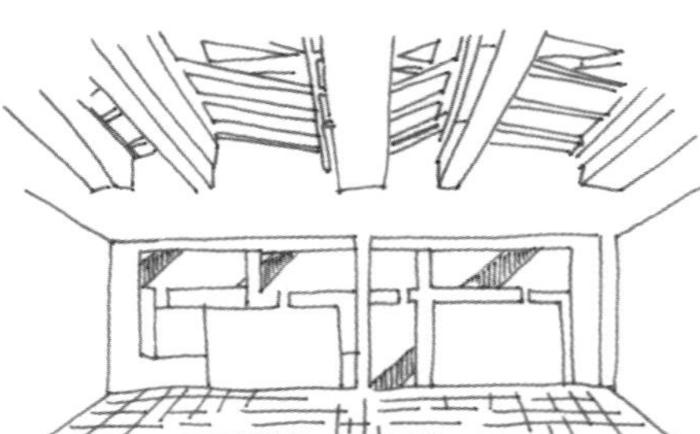

Light coming through the skylights casts strong shadows on white plaster walls. The varying shadow forms mark the passage of time.

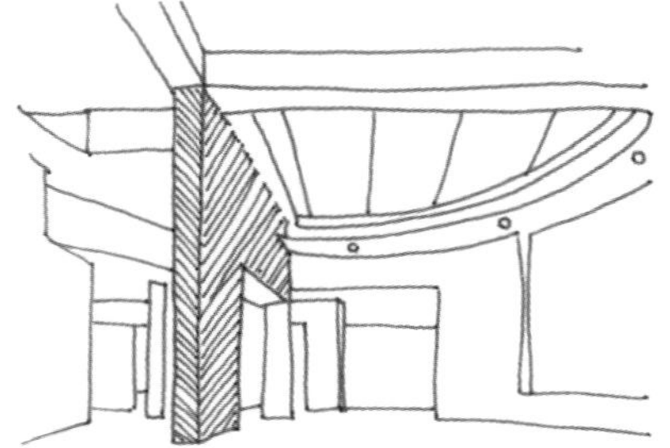

The dividing wall adds a geometric sense and a tectonic quality to the interior space.

The entrance to the museum and the circulation between galleries is carefully organized to make an engaging spatial and sensory experience for visitors as they move to and between galleries. Long internal views are coupled with balconies and terraces from which to gaze on the plaza below and the surrounding city. The whiteness of the building emphasizes colour in the clothes of visitors and in glimpses of the world outside as well as colour in exhibited artwork.

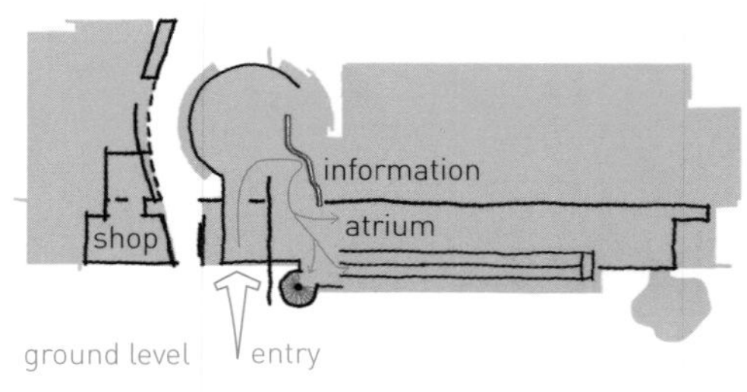

The main entry leads to a large foyer. The information desk is on the right. From here, visitors can move into the atrium to access the ground-level galleries or rest in comfortable seats, or go to the upper level via the ramp or stairs.

The large cylinder

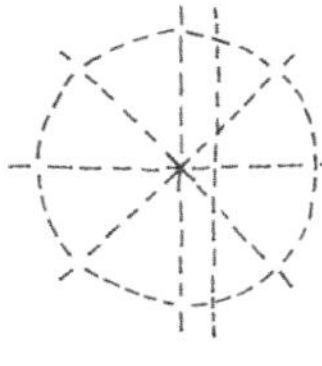

The basic element of the large cylinder is a simple circle with 45-degree segments. An off-centre line cuts across the circle.

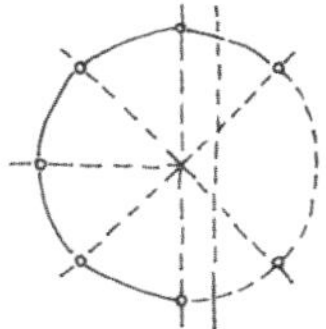

Columns are located regularly according to the geometric division.

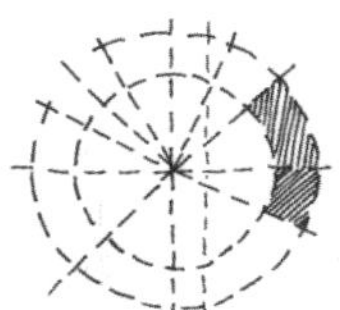

An inner circle is inserted into the cylinder and functional spaces such as the service staircase are formed through more detailed division.

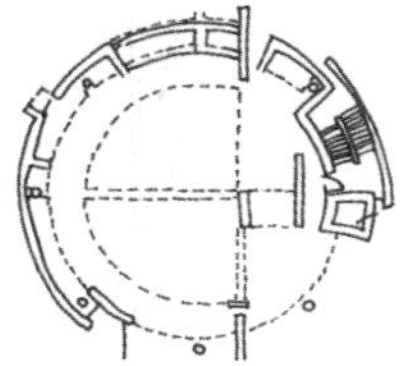

The inner and outer walls of the cylinder are defined using a notional third circle as a guide. A staircase located between two skins of a cylinder is typical of Meier buildings.

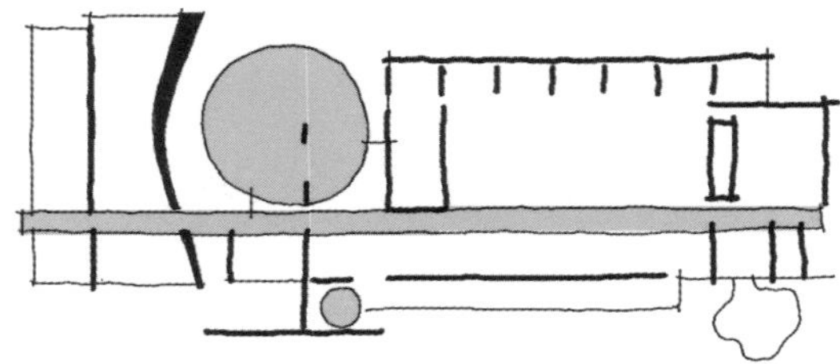

The large and small cylinders lie on each side of a narrow linear strip that extends from end to end of the building and acts as a circulation spine at the upper level.

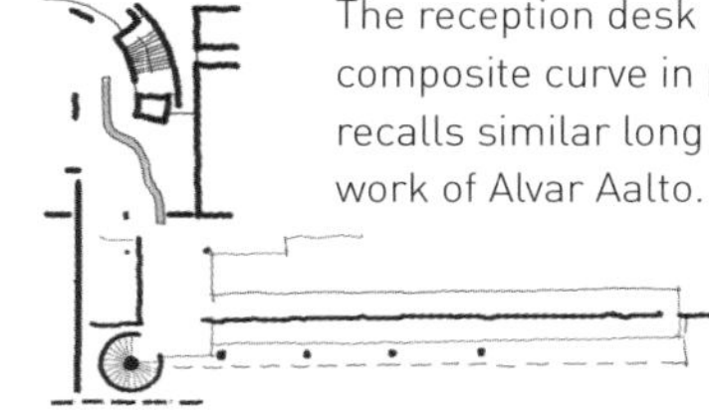

The reception desk is a snaking composite curve in plan that recalls similar long desks in the work of Alvar Aalto.

The smaller cylinder containing the circular stair is sandwiched between two parallel perforated walls. It is positioned as a hinge between the direction of the reception desk and the direction of the ramp.

Precedents

Meier's other works are designed according to similar geometrical combinations in the distinct style of the architect.

Grotta Residence, New Jersey, USA (1984)

Hypolux Bank, Luxembourg (1989)

Rachofsky House, Dallas, Texas, USA (1994)

United States Court House, Phoenix, Arizona, USA (1994)

Swissair North American Headquarters, Melville, New York, USA (1994)

Small gallery

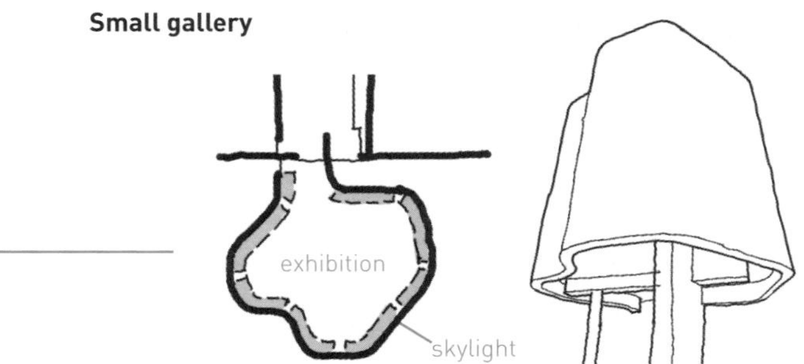

Breaking the pattern of simple geometric shapes, the small gallery on the south-east corner of the building has an irregular form. These playful free-form shapes have a responsive cohesion with the ordered body of the main building, recalling the work of Le Corbusier. The tonal variation on their surfaces varies as the sun moves across the sky.

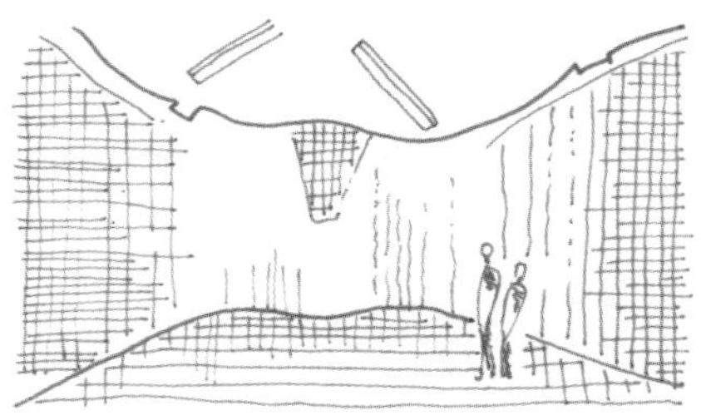

The shadows from the skylight enhance the dynamism of the small exhibition space.

Materials

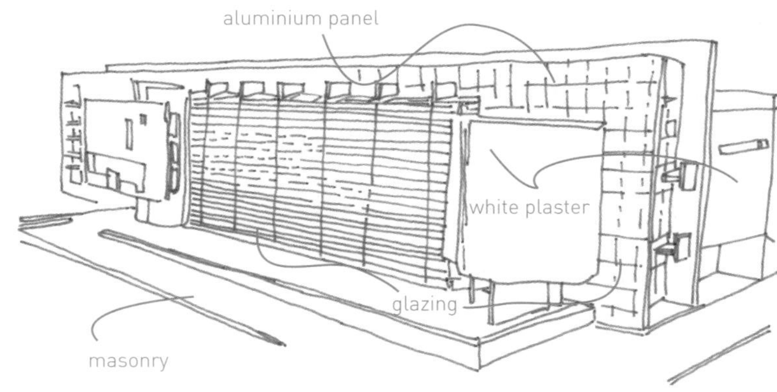

White is typical of Meier's architecture. The flat aluminium panel wall acts as a background to the glass and white forms that are layered in front. The use of three materials reflects a hierarchy of the exterior volumes.

22 Vitra Fire Station | 1990–93

Zaha Hadid Architects

Weil am Rhein, Germany

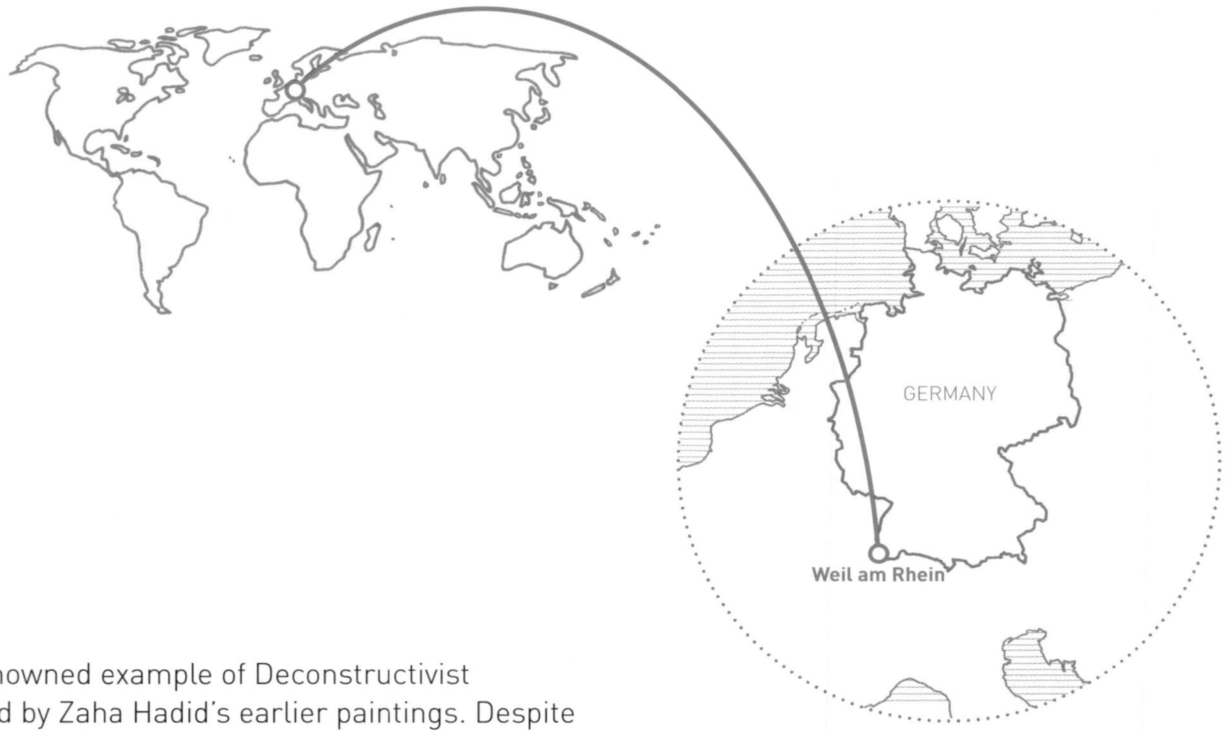

GERMANY

Weil am Rhein

The Vitra Fire Station is a renowned example of Deconstructivist architecture and was inspired by Zaha Hadid's earlier paintings. Despite its modest scale, it is a complex linear arrangement of tilting and bending concrete surfaces. The design references the patterns of the surrounding agricultural land and earlier buildings on the Vitra Design Campus. This is a site of factories, display and associated buildings designed by distinguished architects for Vitra, a furniture manufacturer.

The fire station was commissioned a decade after a major fire, and functionally and symbolically represents the prevention of future fires. This was Hadid's first built project and paved the way towards her international recognition.

Leo Cooper, Selen Morkoç and Philip Eaton

22

22

Vitra Fire Station | 1990–93

Zaha Hadid Architects
Weil am Rhein, Germany

The context

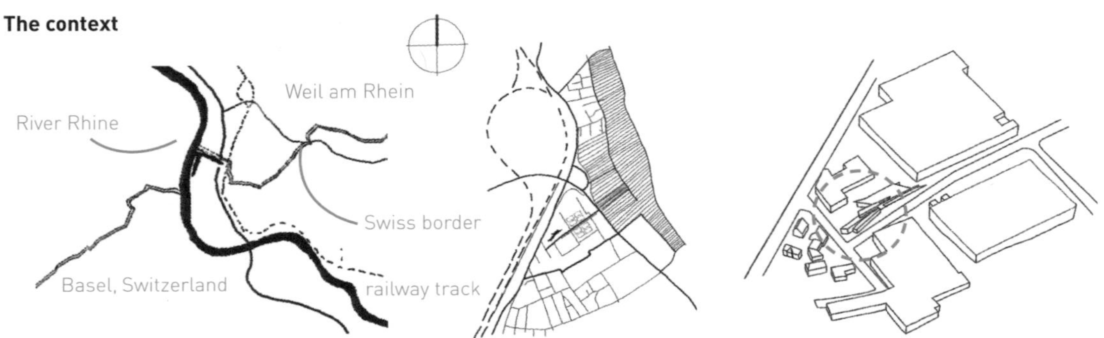

After a fire in 1981, a master plan for the Vitra Design Campus was designed by Nicholas Grimshaw. The Vitra Fire Station was an addition to this campus of factory and exhibition buildings, which now contains several examples of innovative architecture. The site is a meeting point of borders between countries, land and river. These seemingly arbitrary forces were taken into consideration in the design of the building.

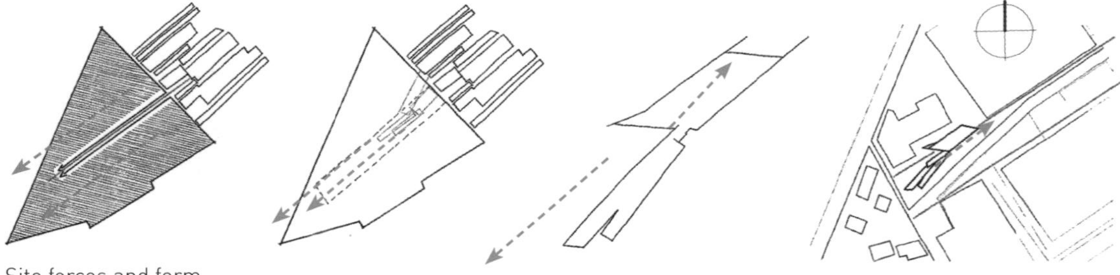

Site forces and form

The main street of the Vitra Campus aligns with fields and vineyards on the adjoining farmland. The building stretches along the connecting road.

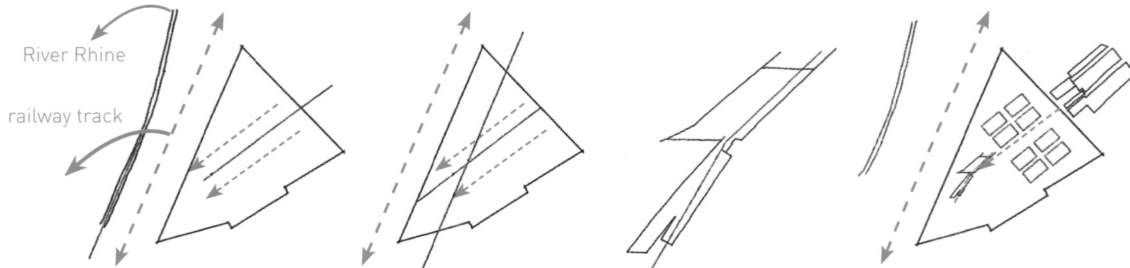

The lines of the river and railway track are offset to make the main axis of the building. The forms of the building collide at the point where this building axis intersects the site axis.

Disruption

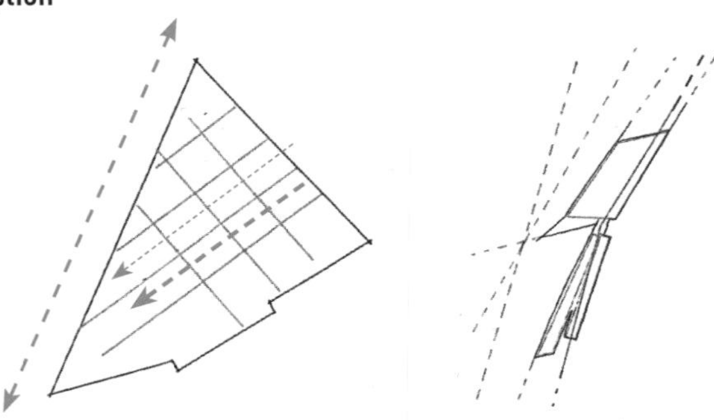

The building forms are in striking contrast to surrounding factory sheds. The site is divided into grid lines, which intersect with the line of the railway. The introduction of external forces such as the railway line and farm land justifies the logic of the site grids.

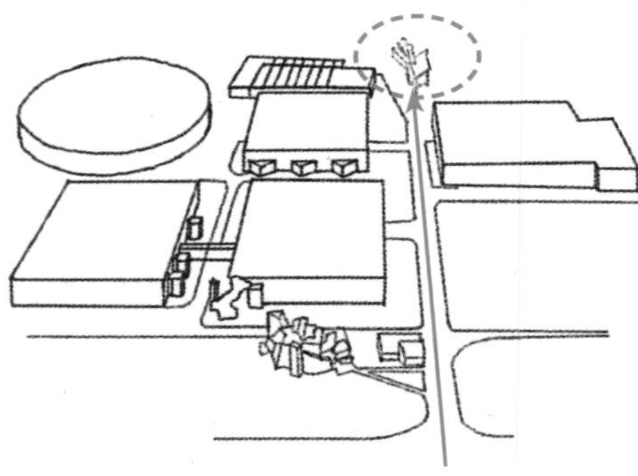

The fire station punctuates the end of the axial progression and marks the transition from agricultural space to built space.

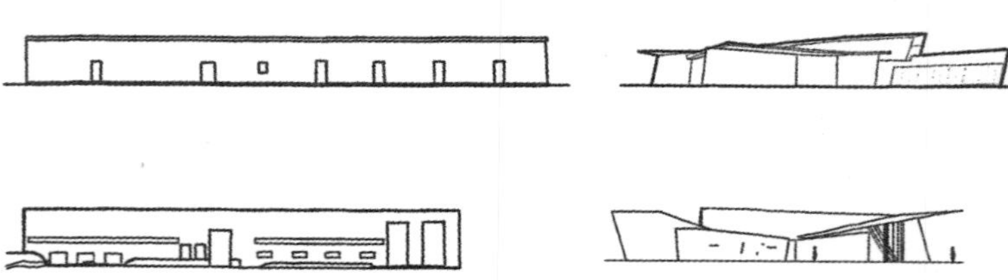

The design responds to the site forces by deconstructing the obvious site limitations. The small yet dynamic and intense form of the fire station is in striking contrast to the solidity of the factory masses.

Playful design vs functionalism

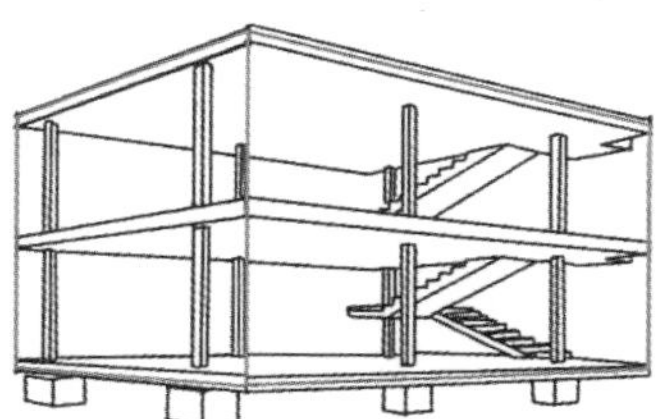

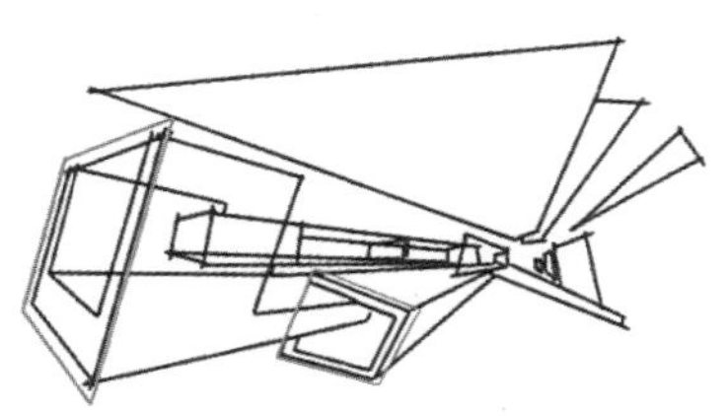

In contrast to the Modernist ideology of design as a product of function and rationality, Hadid's Suprematism (an art movement focusing on basic geometric forms) perceives design as a playful process of artistic creation shaped by the influences of technology, economy and culture. The 'pure box' of Modernism is deconstructed into shifting planes and dissolving angles while honesty to materials is maintained.

Hadid's conceptual paintings reveal her initial idea for form. Two key features are the free-flowing railway network and the geometric layout of farming properties.

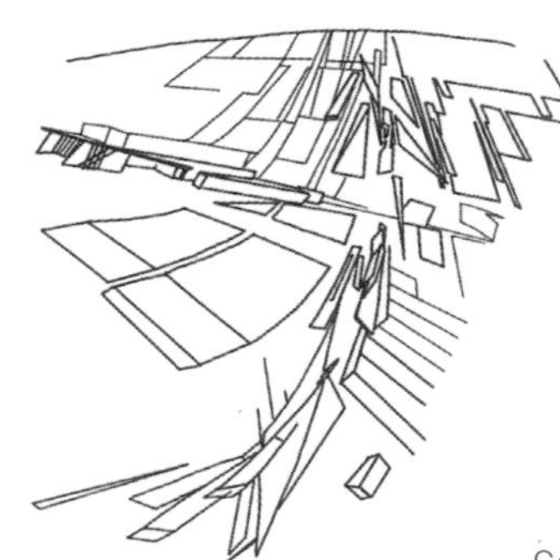

Response to programme

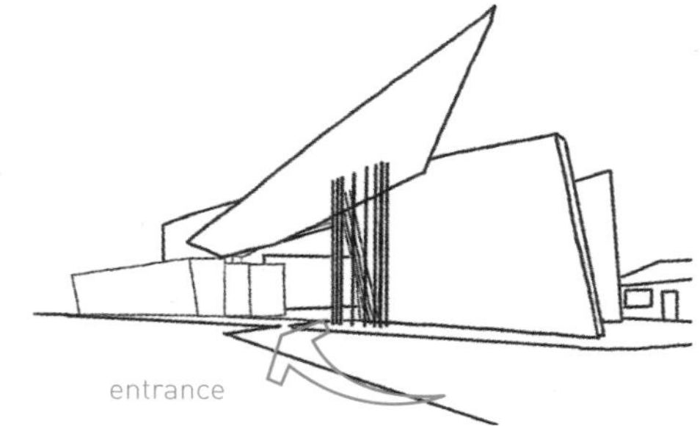

Three intersecting volumes constitute the design. There is hierarchy of spaces illustrated both in plans and in sections. The largest volume is the garage space of five parallel parking lanes. The second and third volumes are staff spaces.

Abstraction of site forces

The site forces determine the dynamic form of the building. Structural elements that hold dynamic planes in place horizontally and vertically are like snapshots of a moving composition.

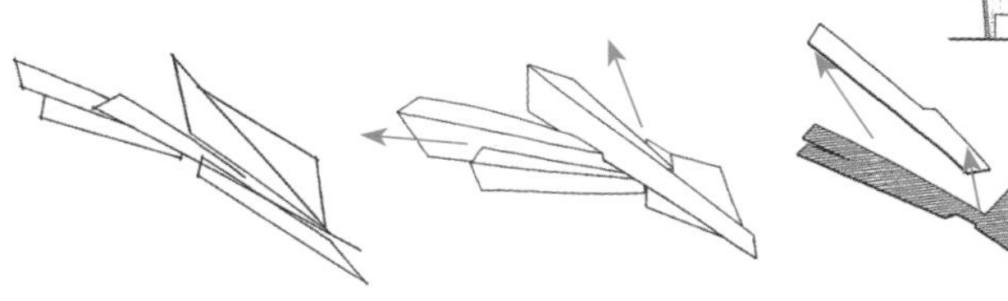

The sharp geometry of the living space represents the momentum of the nearby trains. The building contrasts with surrounding factory buildings but is in harmony with other unusual forms at the edges of the site, such as Frank Gehry's Vitra Design Museum (1988–2003).

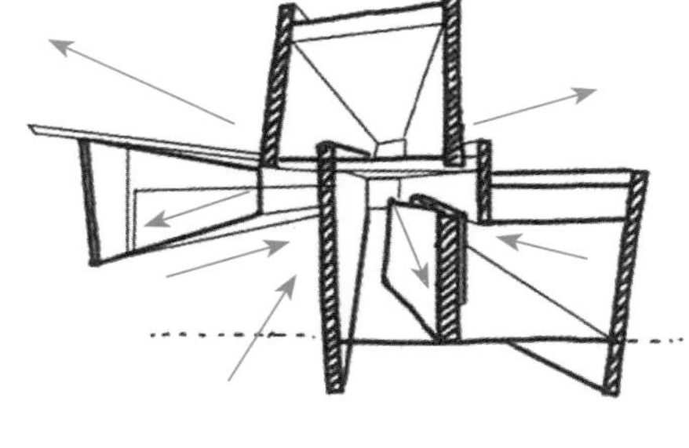

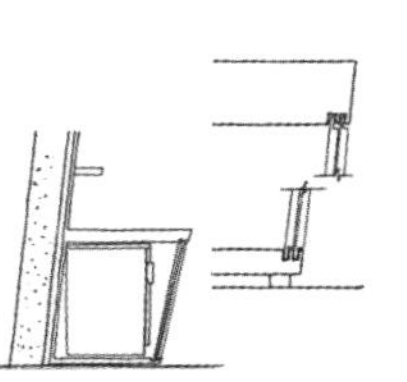

Construction details in such dynamic spaces maintain a sense of plastic refinement of form at a human scale.

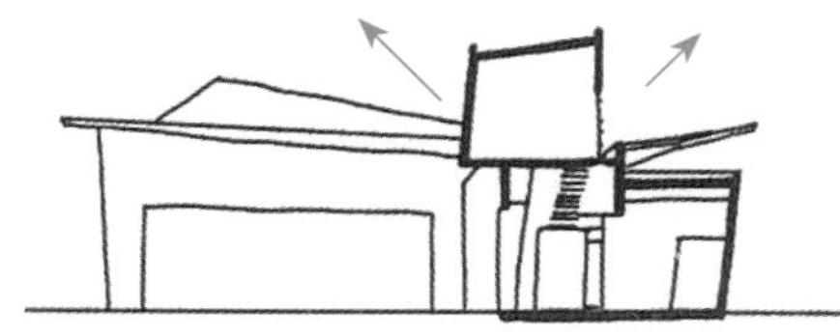

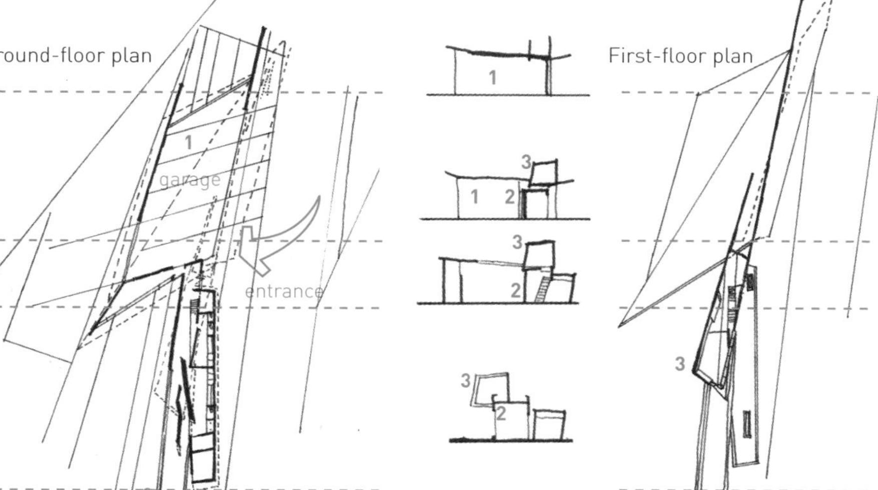

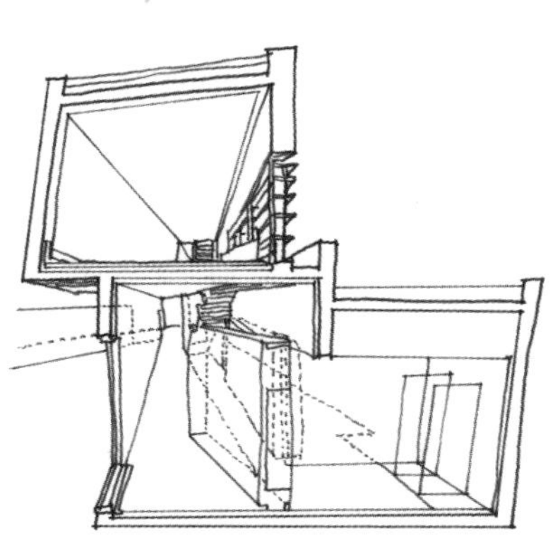

Angular planes are predominant. The walls puncture, tilt and break according to the programme.

22

Vitra Fire Station | 1990–93
Zaha Hadid Architects
Weil am Rhein, Germany

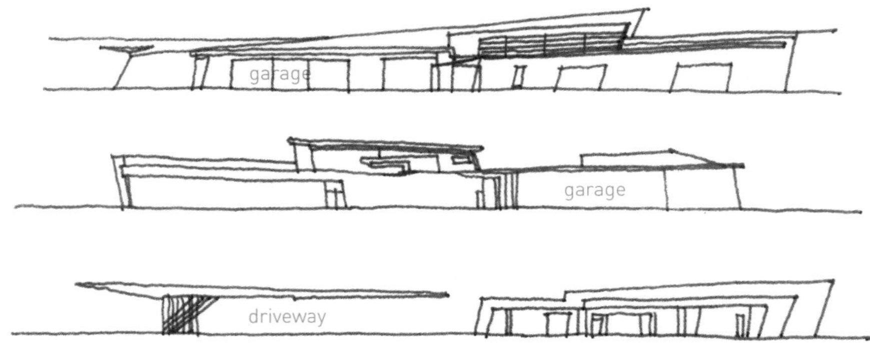

All the exterior walls of the building are solid reinforced concrete, cast in place and tilted in an outward direction. The dynamic geometry makes the building appear lighter, almost anti-gravitational. All walls are structural. They create free-flowing lines throughout the elevations.

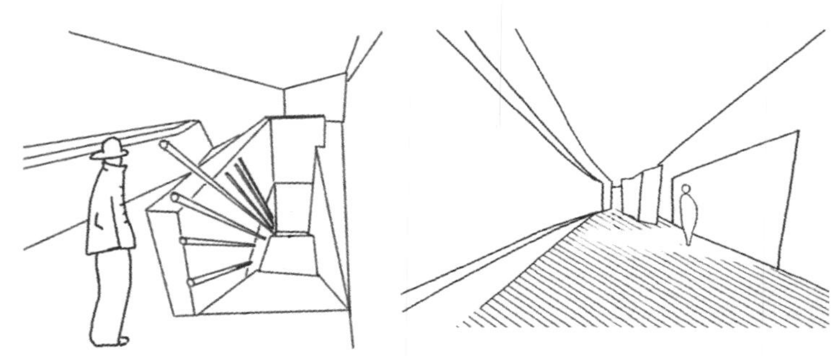

The flowing lines throughout the linear spaces of the building encourage human movement by defining direction through their repetition.

Public vs private

Public and private functions are separated in volumes that collide at the intersection of the axes.

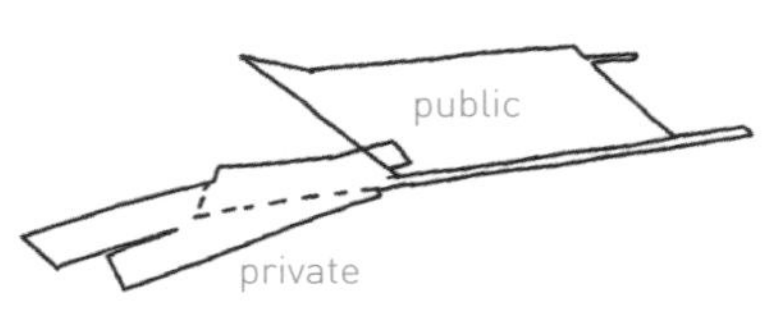

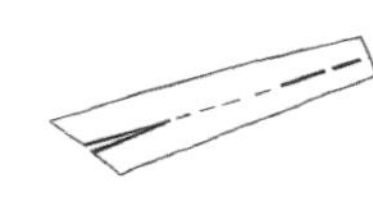

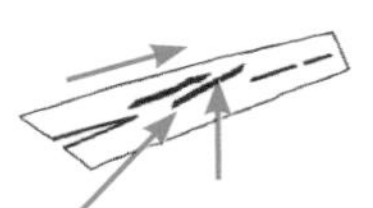

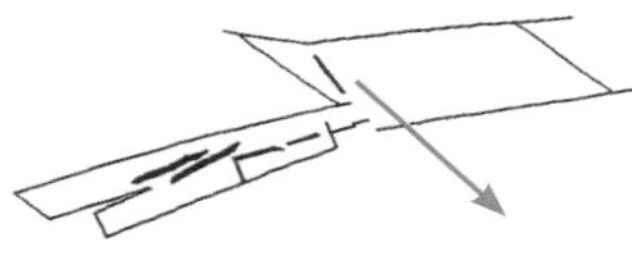

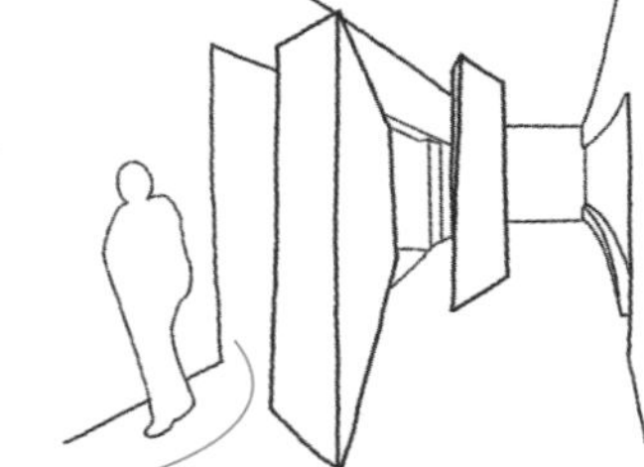

Apparently colliding spaces and competing corridors are expressed and resolved in the entrance area.

Asymmetrical balance

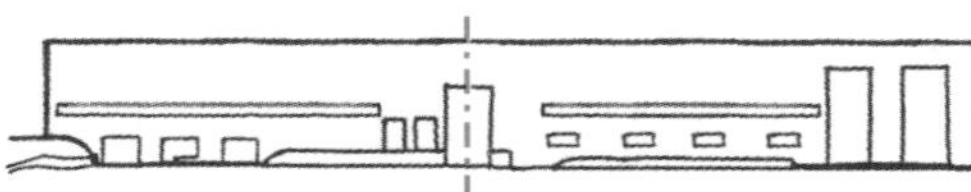

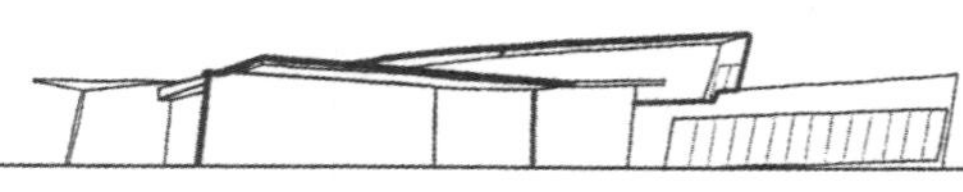

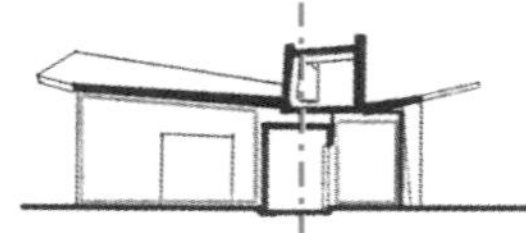

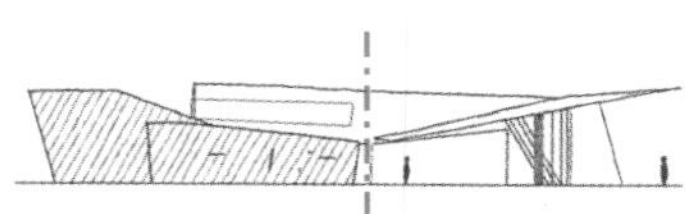

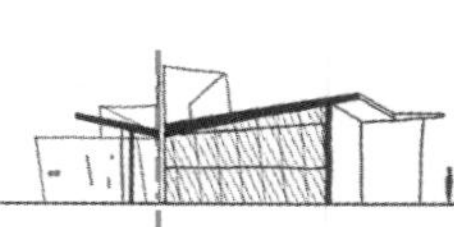

The traditional design tools of symmetry and balance are intentionally distorted in the design to unsettle the conventional form of a typical fire station. Although individual forms converge centrally towards the entrance point, dynamism is achieved through balanced asymmetry. Internally, the public area of fire trucks outweighs the private spaces of offices and recreation.

The heavy concrete wall without openings on one side contrasts strongly with the slender columns and thin-profiled roof.

Light and interior

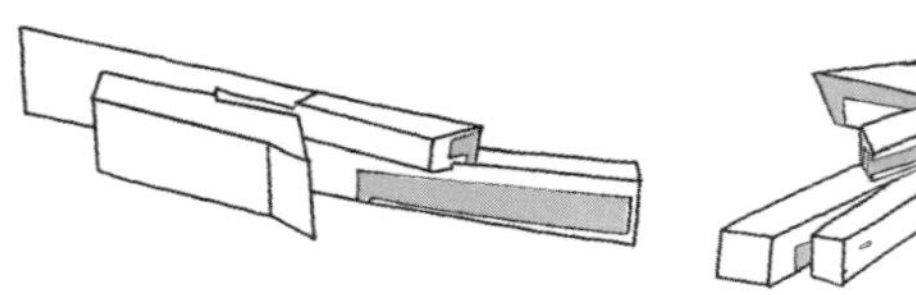

Strips of openings are cut into the walls and the roofs to let light in. The lines of light emphasize the programme, reflecting the function of the interior to the exterior. All lighting elements are integral parts of the design, based on lines rather than points, consistent with the overall formal dynamism.

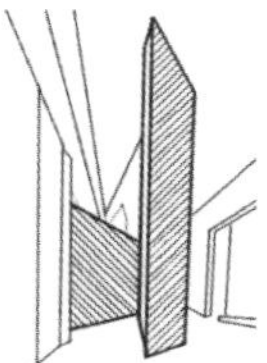

The stretching out of openings as horizontal beams of light emphasizes directionality and movement inside the building. Light successfully guides movement towards the exits. Roof openings letting daylight in and artificial fluorescent tubing at ground level attract attention to linearity.

Form and meaning

Dramatic visual impact
Extruded rectangles that create prowlike planes create a dramatic effect for the observer.

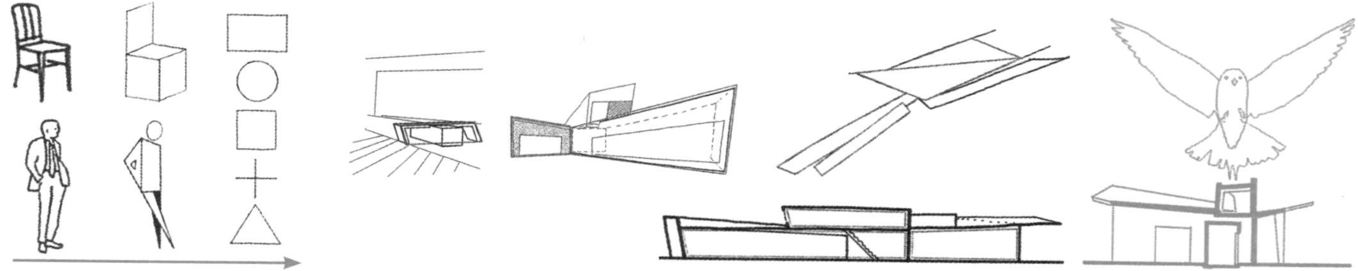

Hadid was influenced by Kazimir Malevich's early twentieth-century Suprematist art movement, which aimed to peel realism down to its purest form through geometrical abstraction. The result is a non-objective geometry of pure shapes.

Suprematist art was based on the premise of achieving pure artistic feeling through abstraction. Suprematist geometry is prevalent as the basic design language in both plans and sections as well as in overall 3D articulation. The collection of basic geometric elements in a dramatic assemblage results in a unique interconnection of spaces that has a strong impact on human experience.

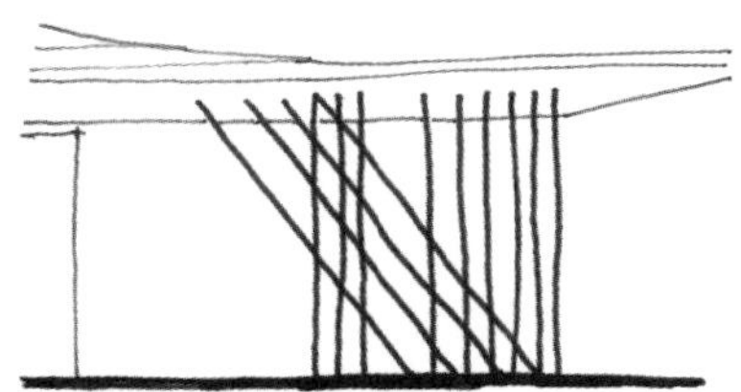

The repetitive array of Modernist columns evokes both similarity and difference through their variation in distances and angles.

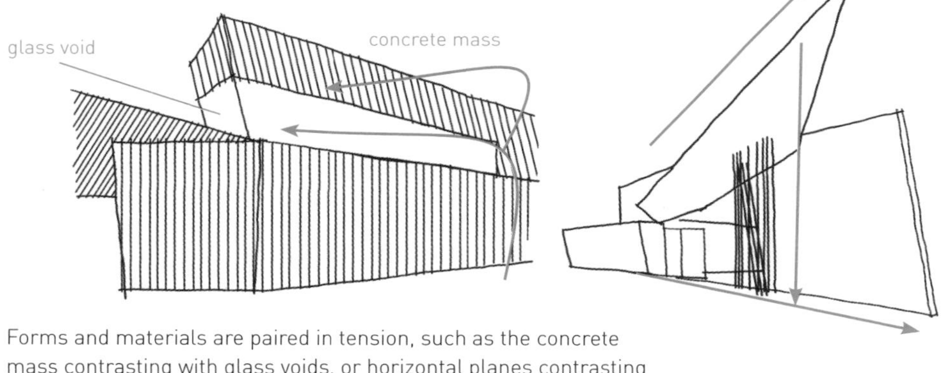

Forms and materials are paired in tension, such as the concrete mass contrasting with glass voids, or horizontal planes contrasting with vertical piloti marking the exit.

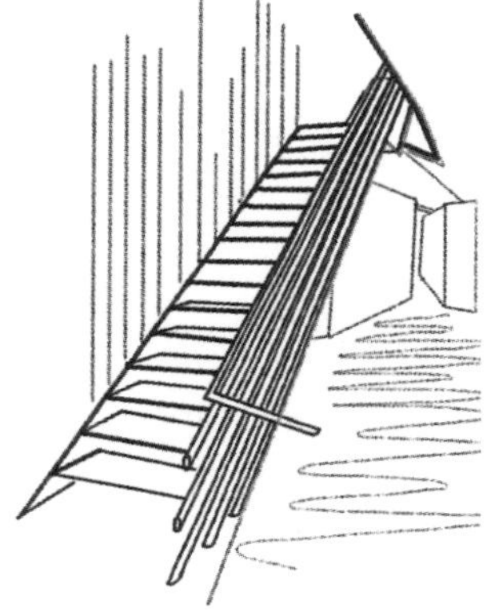

Planes are marked through movement horizontally and vertically. Repetition of lines is a common motif in design elements of different scale, such as the outside columns and the railings of the staircase.

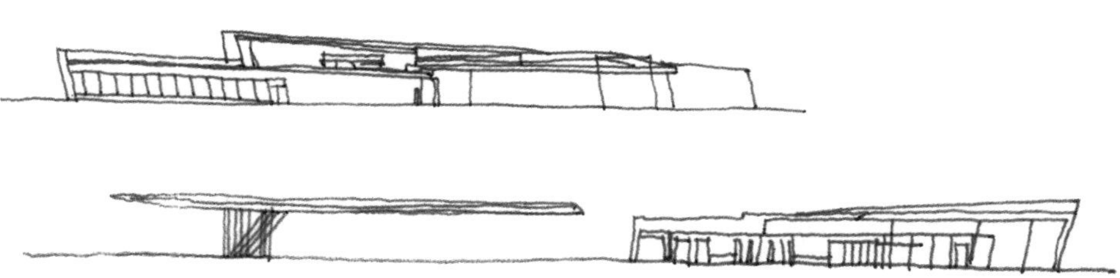

The solid mass of the building leaning in one direction is balanced by the floating canopy extending out above the sliding doors of the fire trucks' garage. The volume of the first floor is distinguished externally by a long, low opening with louvres set into it, almost as if the wall was sliced horizontally.

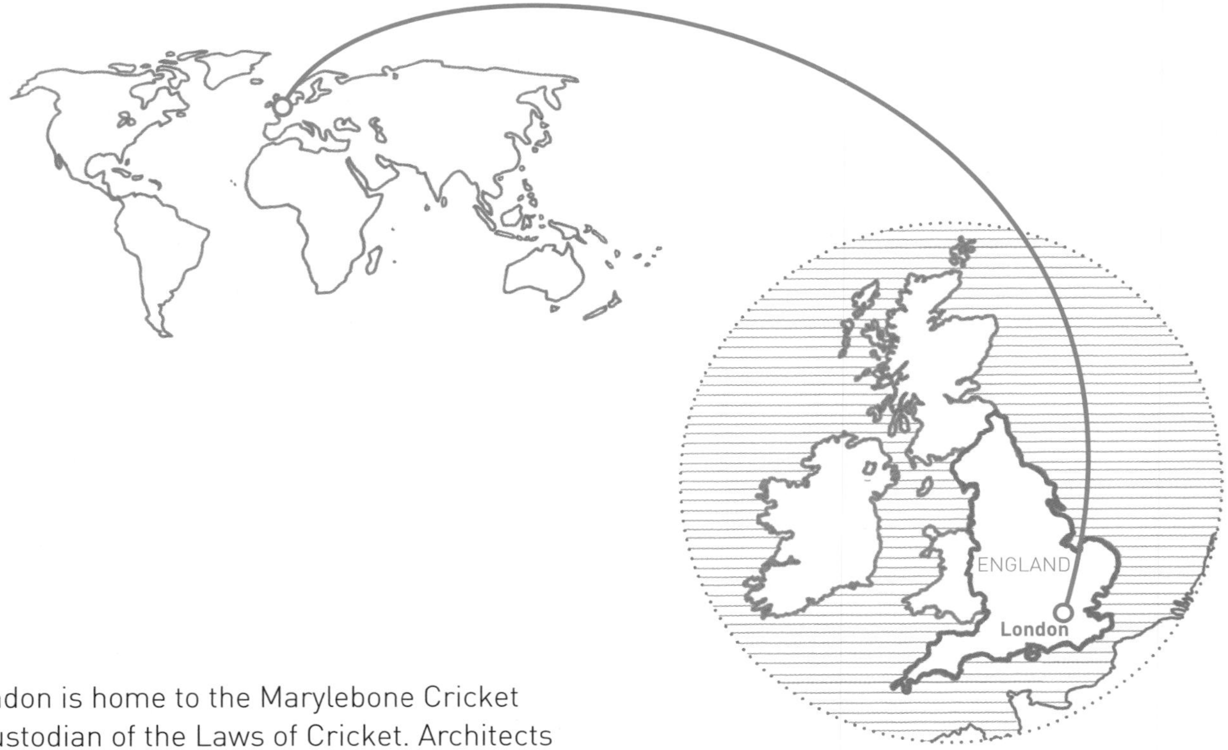

London
ENGLAND

23

Lord's Media Centre | 1994–99

Future Systems
London, England

Lord's Cricket Ground in London is home to the Marylebone Cricket Club, founded in 1787 and custodian of the Laws of Cricket. Architects Future Systems, led by Jan Kaplický and Amanda Levete, won a limited competition for a new media centre for broadcasters and writers. It was to be constructed over two closed seasons, the winters of 1997 and 1998, ready for the Cricket World Cup in 1999.

The building is significant in several ways: its prefabricated construction in aluminium, its integrity as a singular self-contained pod, its relationship to the terraces and stands of the cricket ground, and the clarity of its expression of function as a protected place from which to gaze at the pitch and players.

Danielle O'Dea, Antony Radford and Xuan Zhang

23

Lord's Media Centre | 1994–99
Future Systems
London, England

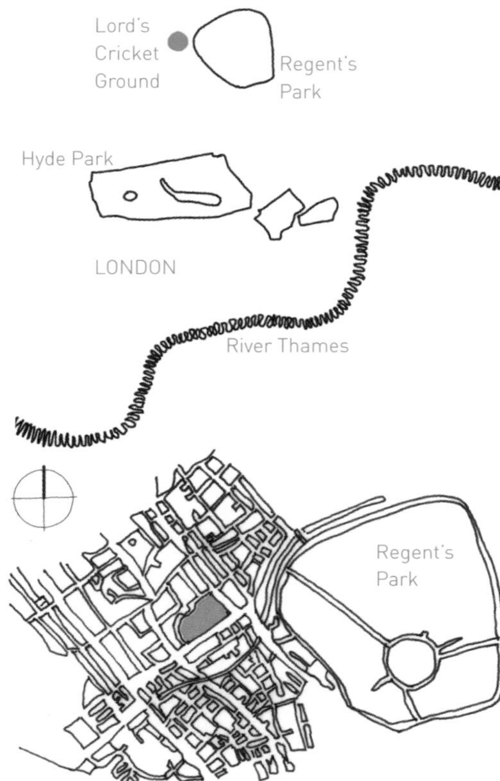

Lord's Cricket Ground is located in St John's Wood, surrounded by residential and commercial buildings, about 4 kilometres (2.5 miles) from central London. Several stands in the ground were remodelled in the late twentieth century, including the Mound Stand (Hopkins Architects, 1987), Edrich and Compton Stands (Hopkins Architects, 1991) and Grand Stand (Grimshaw Architects, 1998). The Media Centre is at one end of the ground, facing the heritage-listed Pavilion (Thomas Verity, 1889).

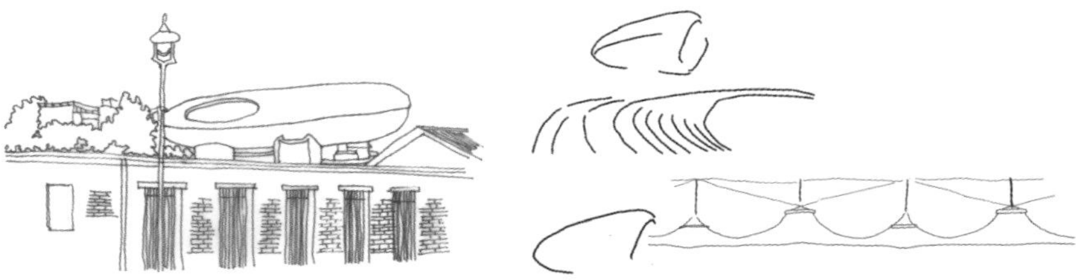

The Media Centre

The Media Centre was built without altering existing seating. Instead, it is inserted behind the terraces and looks over the top of them. It appears as a separate and distinct object in the landscape, which could be removed without trace. Its curves contrast with rectilinear walls but echo the sweeping terraces.

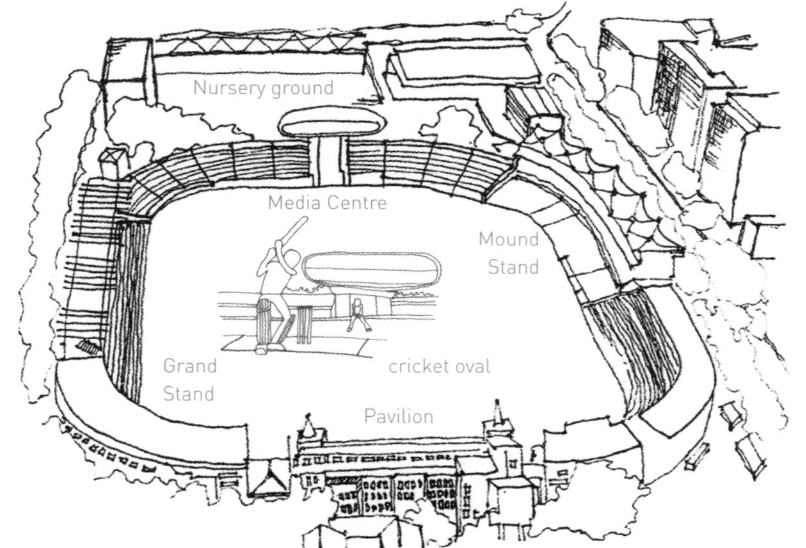

The ornate details of the Pavilion contrast with the curved, undecorated form of the Media Centre.

Contrast: the Mound Stand

The Mound Stand (below) was rebuilt in 1987, adding two additional terraces over the existing concrete terraces. As with the Media Centre, new and old are clearly differentiated, with a 'light' metal object above 'heavy' brick and concrete old work. There is a deep shadow gap between old and new.

The skyline of the Mound Stand is a series of concave curves, in contrast to the Media Centre's convex skyline.

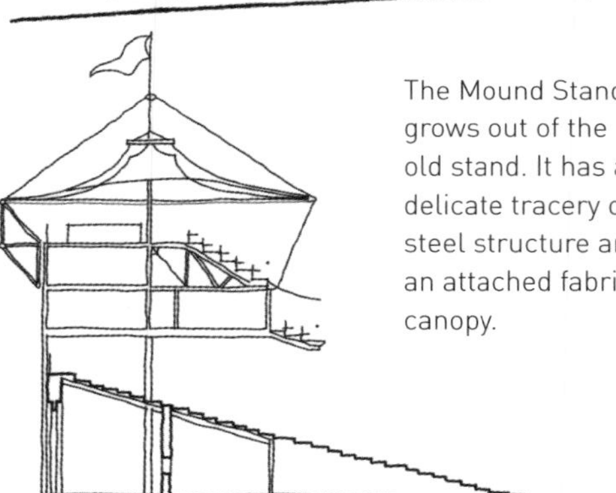

The Mound Stand grows out of the old stand. It has a delicate tracery of steel structure and an attached fabric canopy.

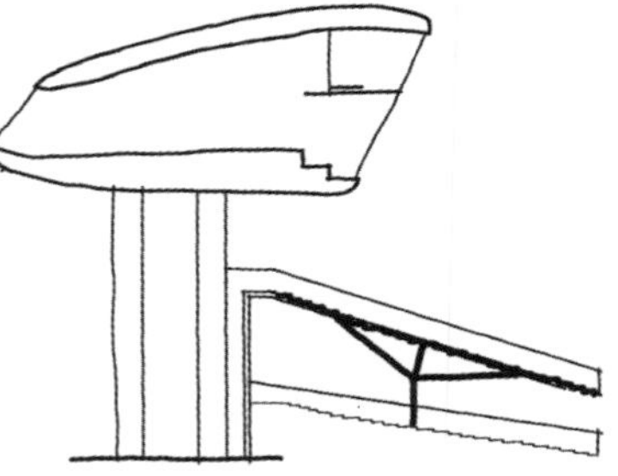

The Media Centre grows behind the old stand. It is a concentrated pod with its structure integrated with the skin.

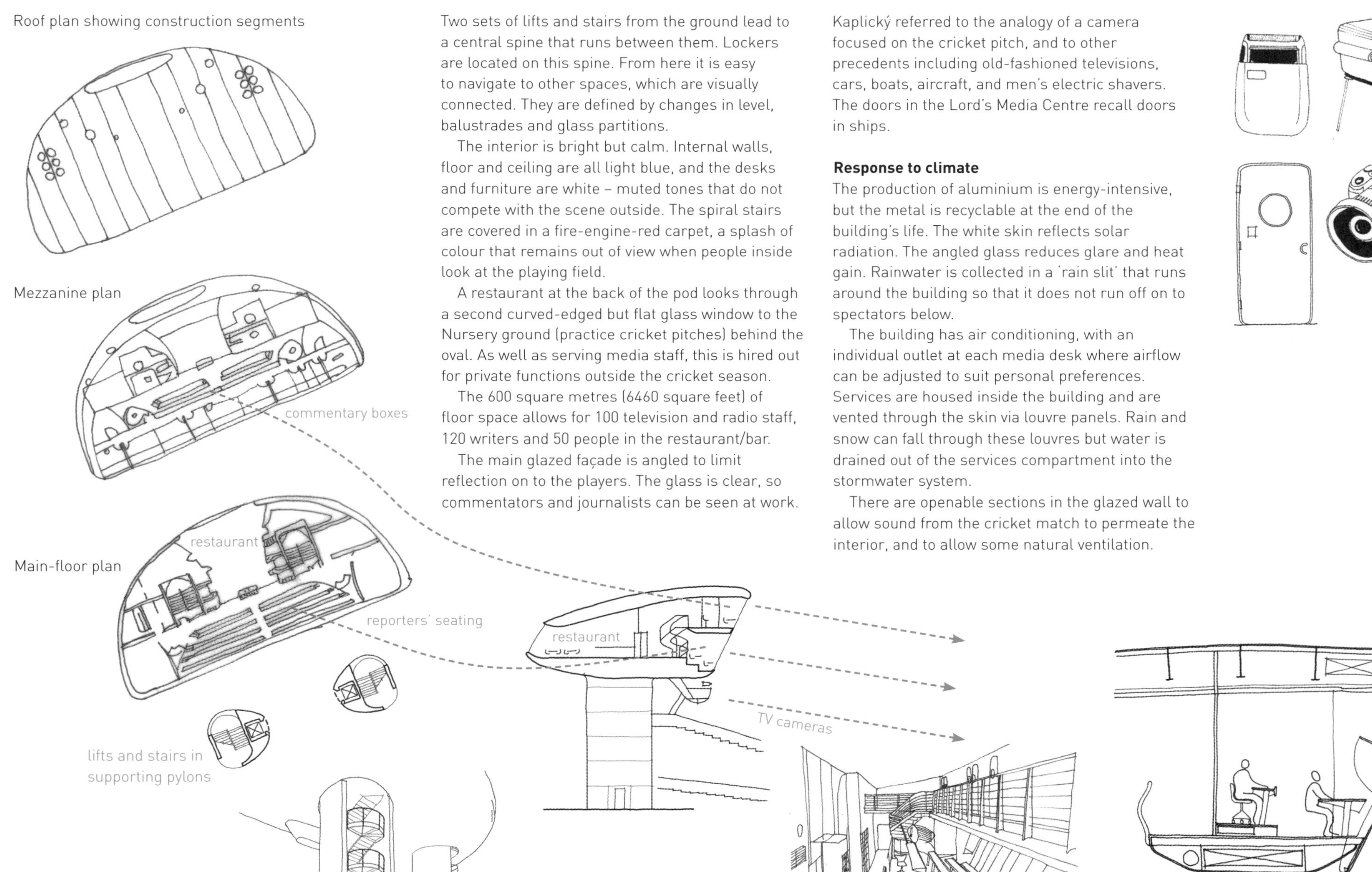

Two sets of lifts and stairs from the ground lead to a central spine that runs between them. Lockers are located on this spine. From here it is easy to navigate to other spaces, which are visually connected. They are defined by changes in level, balustrades and glass partitions.

The interior is bright but calm. Internal walls, floor and ceiling are all light blue, and the desks and furniture are white – muted tones that do not compete with the scene outside. The spiral stairs are covered in a fire-engine-red carpet, a splash of colour that remains out of view when people inside look at the playing field.

A restaurant at the back of the pod looks through a second curved-edged but flat glass window to the Nursery ground (practice cricket pitches) behind the oval. As well as serving media staff, this is hired out for private functions outside the cricket season.

The 600 square metres (6460 square feet) of floor space allows for 100 television and radio staff, 120 writers and 50 people in the restaurant/bar.

The main glazed façade is angled to limit reflection on to the players. The glass is clear, so commentators and journalists can be seen at work.

Kaplický referred to the analogy of a camera focused on the cricket pitch, and to other precedents including old-fashioned televisions, cars, boats, aircraft, and men's electric shavers. The doors in the Lord's Media Centre recall doors in ships.

Response to climate

The production of aluminium is energy-intensive, but the metal is recyclable at the end of the building's life. The white skin reflects solar radiation. The angled glass reduces glare and heat gain. Rainwater is collected in a 'rain slit' that runs around the building so that it does not run off on to spectators below.

The building has air conditioning, with an individual outlet at each media desk where airflow can be adjusted to suit personal preferences. Services are housed inside the building and are vented through the skin via louvre panels. Rain and snow can fall through these louvres but water is drained out of the services compartment into the stormwater system.

There are openable sections in the glazed wall to allow sound from the cricket match to permeate the interior, and to allow some natural ventilation.

Construction

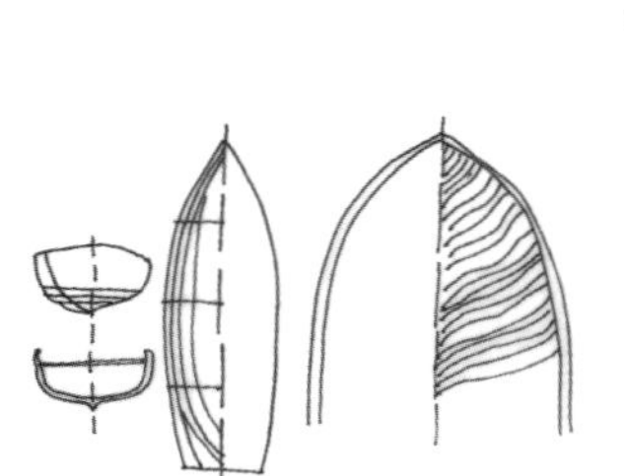

The construction split the skin into strips, as in the hull of a wooden boat.

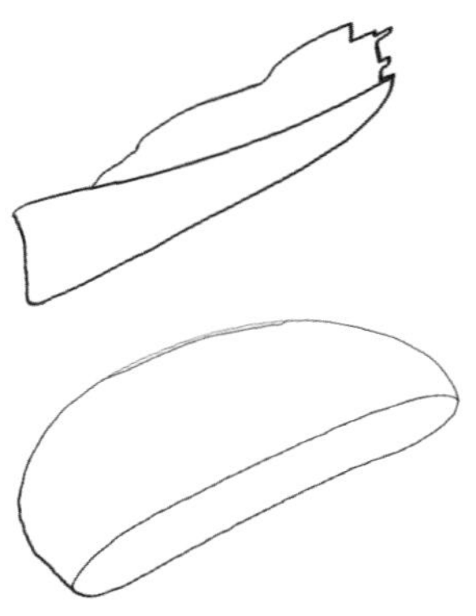

The building is about 40m (131ft) long, similar to a large cabin cruiser.

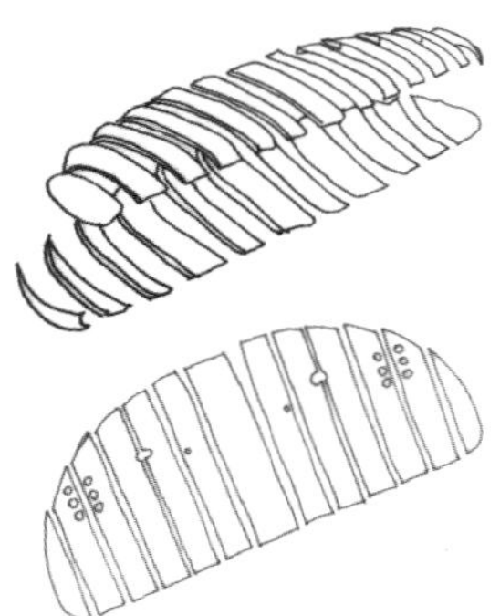

This kind of shell-and-ribs construction is common in the manufacture of aluminium boats, and the segments were fabricated in a shipyard. The whole pod was set up in a large shed.

Although large, the panels are comparatively light in weight because of their aluminium construction.

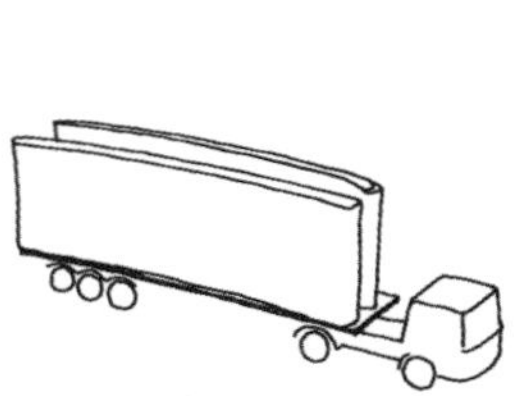

Completed strips of the top and bottom of the pod were transported to the site.

The sections were craned into place above the two previously constructed concrete legs.

The sections are welded together. There are no expansion joints, so minimizing thermal expansion by reflecting heat off the pod's white surface was important. The internal fit-out took place after the pod was assembled.

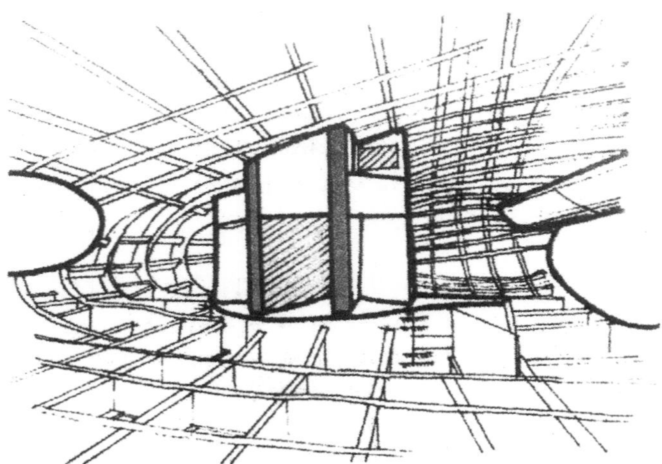

The structure is semi-monocoque, where the skin is an integral part of the structure rather than being attached to a separate structural framework. The skin is welded to the web of the structure's ribs and effectively replaces one flange of a conventional beam. The ribs continue across the roof, walls and floor.

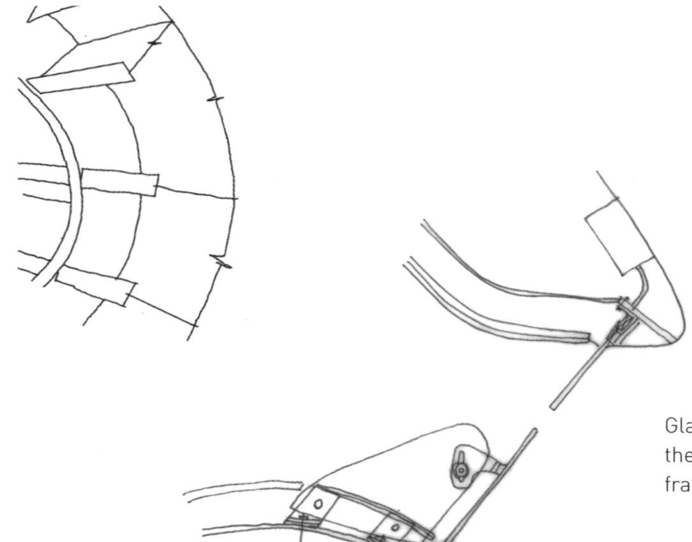

Glazing is mounted within the shell, so that edge frames are not visible.

Pods and blobs

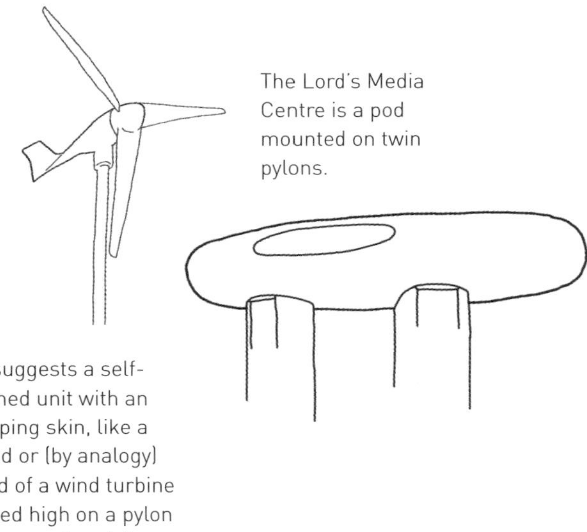

The Lord's Media Centre is a pod mounted on twin pylons.

'Pod' suggests a self-contained unit with an enveloping skin, like a pea pod or (by analogy) the pod of a wind turbine mounted high on a pylon to generate electricity.

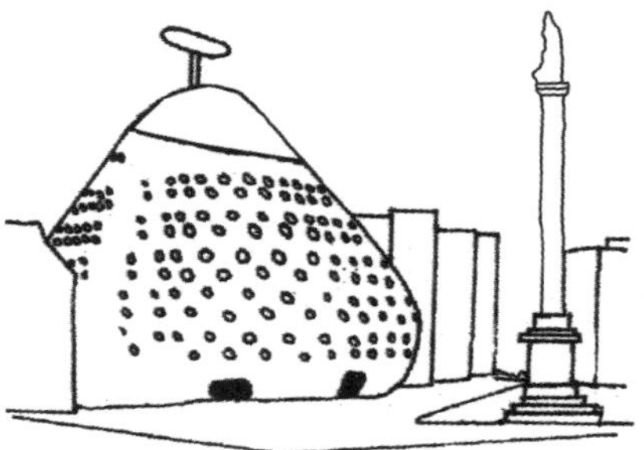

'Blob' suggests something more flexible. Future Systems called their competition design for an office building in central London (1985) a blob.

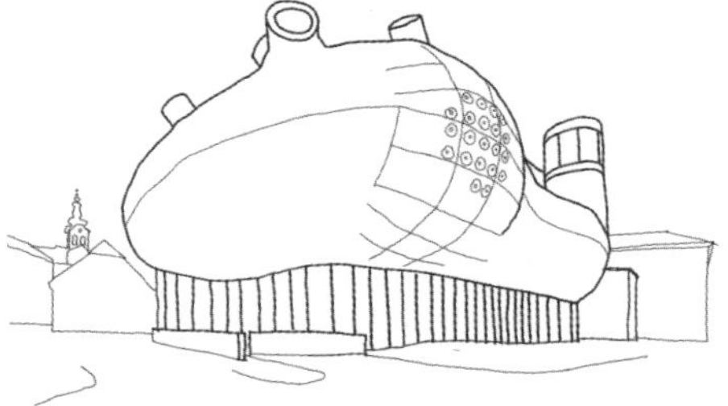

'Blob' architecture also describes the Kunsthaus Graz, in Graz, Austria, by Spacelab Cook-Fournier (2003). Like the Enzo Ferrari Museum, the blob adapts to existing adjacent buildings, but it does so by making the shape of the blob fit its context rather than apparently cutting away part of the blob.

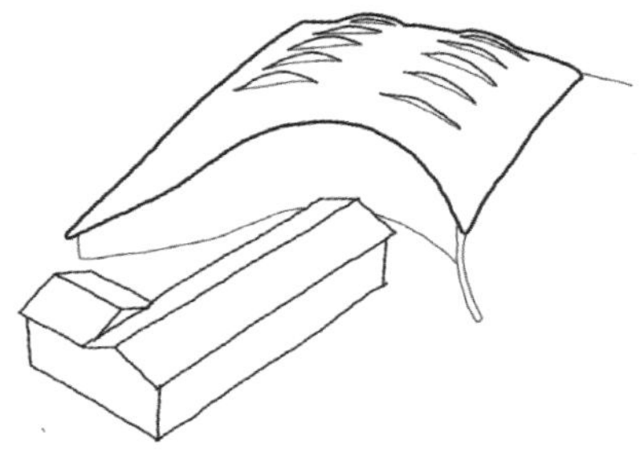

Future Systems' design for the Enzo Ferrari Museum in Modena, Italy (2009), is a blob-in-a-rectangle that appears to have been cut to fit next to an existing building.

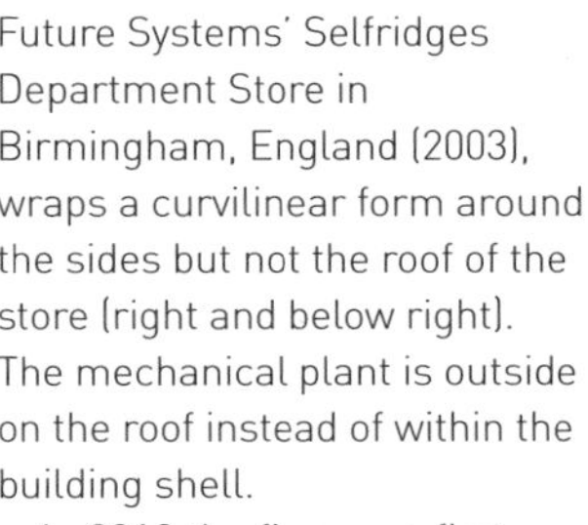

Future Systems' Selfridges Department Store in Birmingham, England (2003), wraps a curvilinear form around the sides but not the roof of the store (right and below right). The mechanical plant is outside on the roof instead of within the building shell.

In 2010 the firm won first prize in a competition for the National Library in Prague, Czech Republic (below), with a blob design that has a similar look-out window to that at the Lord's Media Centre.

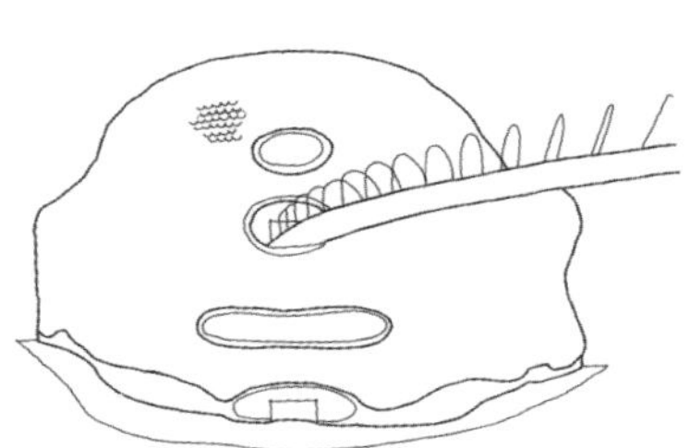

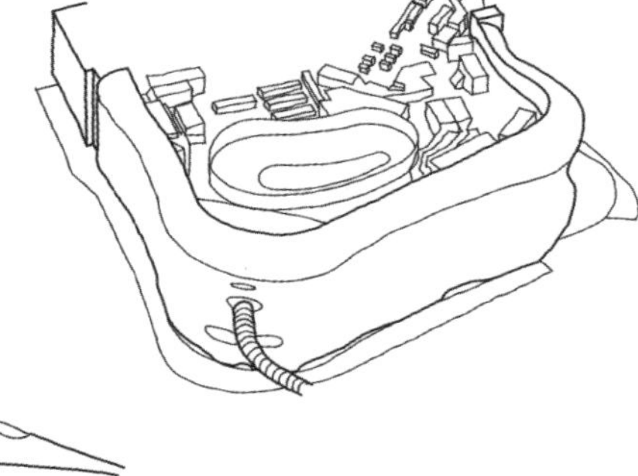

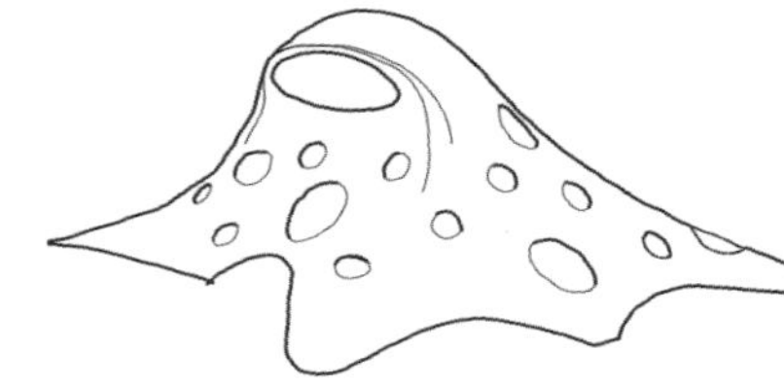

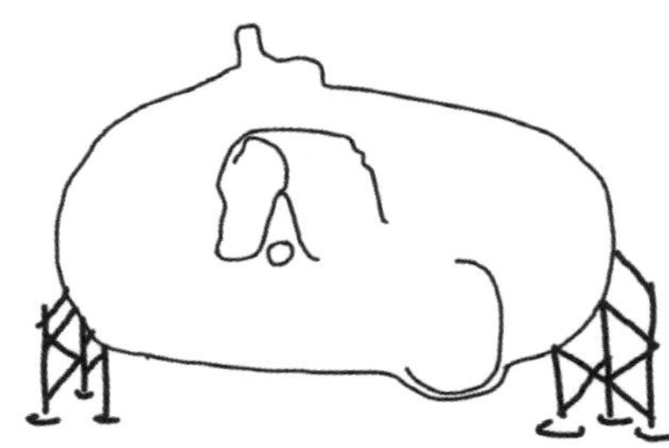

David Green used the term 'living pods' for his self-contained serviced units as a part of the Archigram movement in Britain in the 1960s.

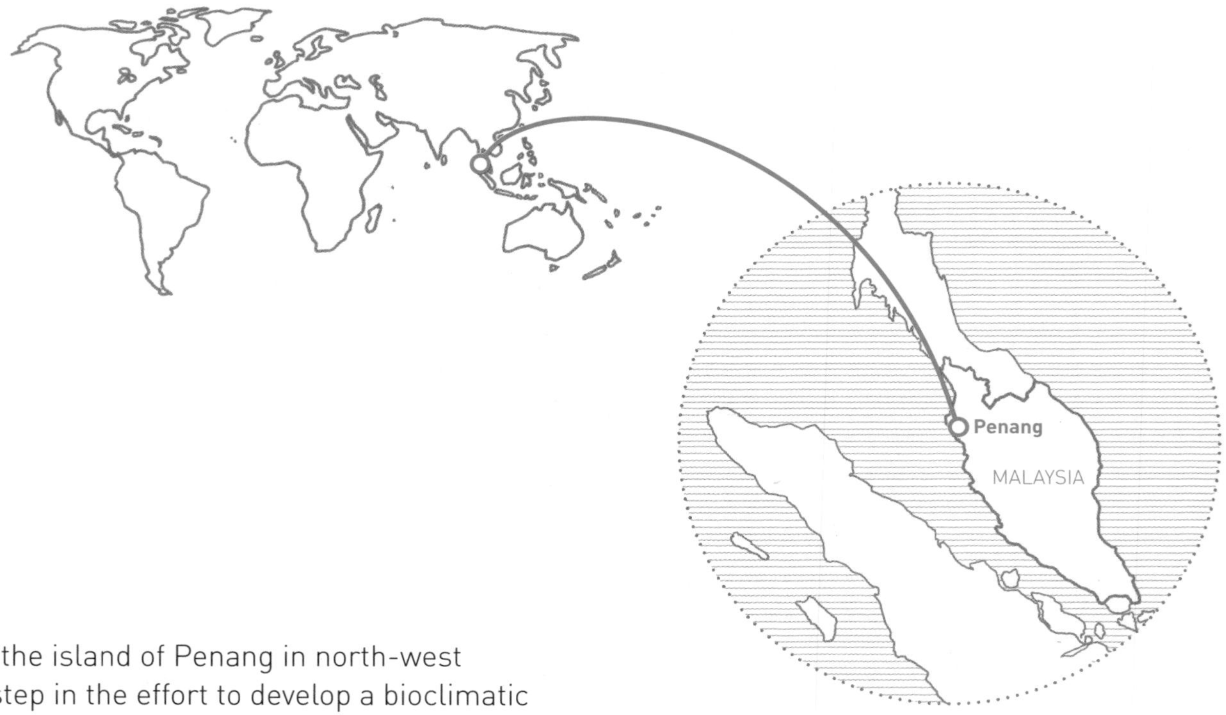

24

Menara UMNO | 1995–98

Kenneth Yeang, T. R. Hamzah & Yeang

Penang, Malaysia

Penang

MALAYSIA

Menara UMNO is located on the island of Penang in north-west Malaysia. It is an important step in the effort to develop a bioclimatic skyscraper for the tropics – a structure that combines the urban density of the high-rise building type with the climatic wisdom of traditional building types. The aim is to change the character of skyscrapers to make them more responsive to climate and to reduce energy use.

The architect Kenneth Yeang has designed several such buildings. This one is especially clear in the responsive cohesion between its features for catching the breezes, for shading and for functional operation. The building is naturally ventilated, which is rare for a tall office building.

Amit Srivastava, Kay Tryn Oh and Lana Greer

24

Menara UMNO | 1995–98

Kenneth Yeang, T. R. Hamzah & Yeang
Penang, Malaysia

Identity and context

Menara UMNO is located at the edge of the historic UNESCO World Heritage area of George Town (the capital of the state of Penang), which boasts a range of traditional Chinese shophouses. It is the headquarters building of the political party United Malays National Organisation (UMNO), and its height and iconic form helps to define its presence in the neighbourhood. As a tall building in an otherwise low-rise neighbourhood, it is not highly cohesive with its surroundings.

The identifiable profile of the building stands out against the sky as an identifiable landmark.

At twenty-one storeys the building towers over the surrounding low-rise district.

Response to urban context

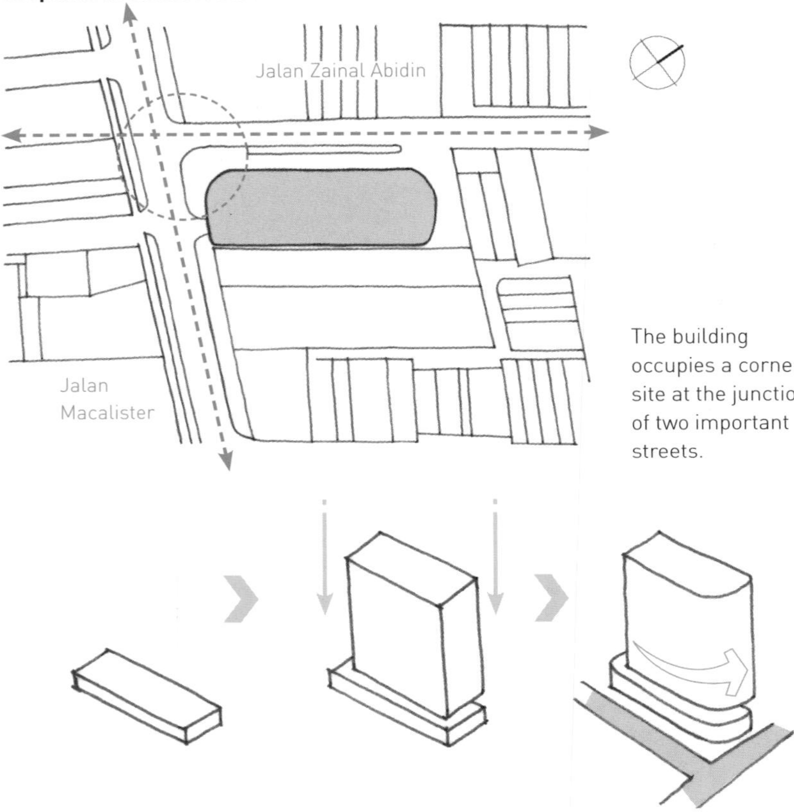

The building occupies a corner site at the junction of two important streets.

The simple additive form of a podium and a larger building block are both curved along the edge in response to the street junction.

The building form is developed as an aggregation of different functional requirements that are modified in relation to the building's immediate context.

Its mass is divided into a low-rise podium that responds to the neighbouring buildings and a larger office block that sits on top. This two-part division also allows for the separation of the noisy parking levels below from the office spaces above. Finally, the curved form responds to the building's location on a corner site, thereby allowing for a visual and physical transition between the two major streets.

Along the ground floor the building opens up to the street to allow for interaction with the public realm. The functions on the ground level are set back to allow space for pedestrians walking along Jalan Macalister (Macalister Street), and are positioned to give complete visual access to the entrance lobby from the corner.

The curved profile at the street junction acts as a welcoming gesture, and this visual openness towards the funnel-shaped entrance invites pedestrians into the building.

The separation of the vehicular access, which is towards the rear of the building along Jalan Zainal Abidin, helps this pedestrian-friendly context at the front entrance.

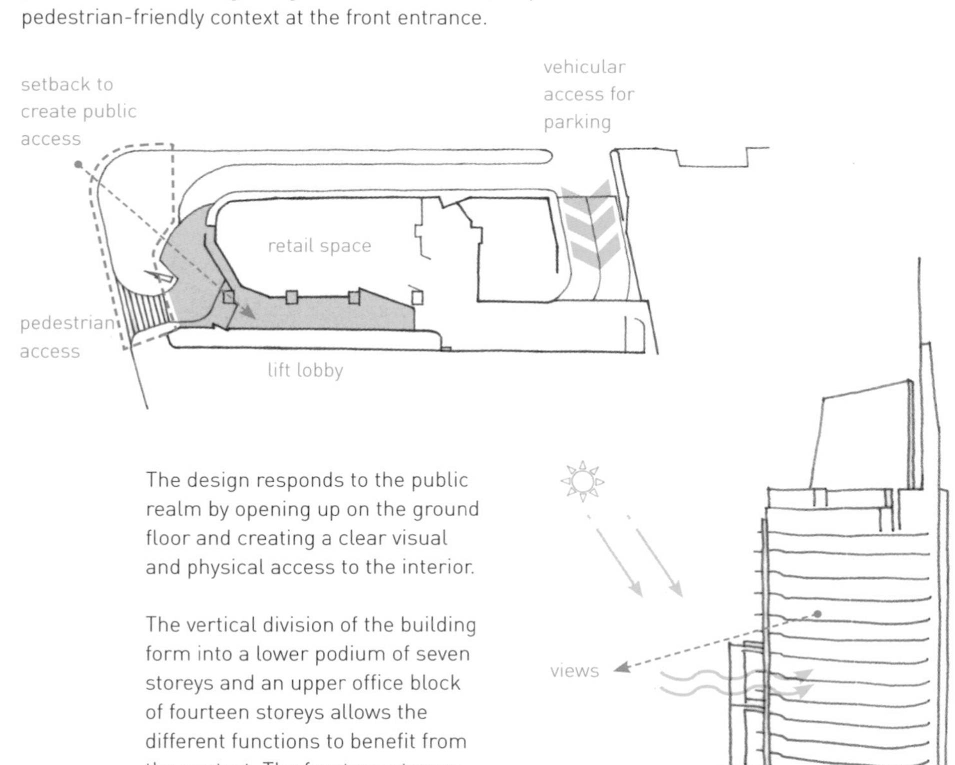

The design responds to the public realm by opening up on the ground floor and creating a clear visual and physical access to the interior.

The vertical division of the building form into a lower podium of seven storeys and an upper office block of fourteen storeys allows the different functions to benefit from the context. The fourteen storeys of office space stand clear of the surrounding structures and are exposed to ample sun and wind.

Response to programme

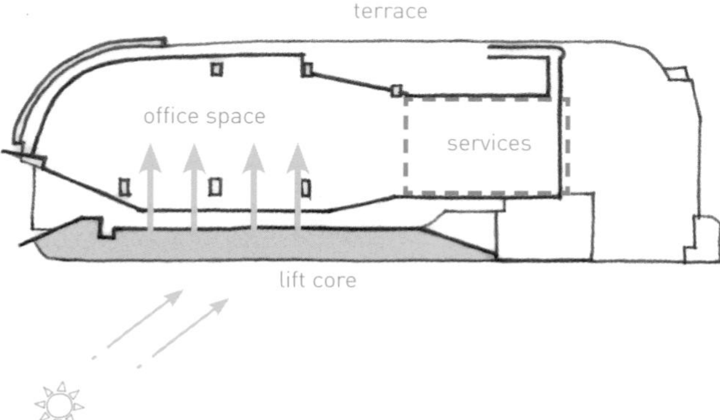

The building's users walk through an open, naturally lit and ventilated lobby to reach the office spaces from the lift core. The offices also have access to open terraces, allowing users an escape from the office environment and an opportunity to connect with the natural context.

Unlike the common configuration for office buildings, which relies on a centralized core, the circulation core for Menara UMNO is located along the south-eastern edge of the building. As well as providing less-obstructed office spaces, this allows for the lift shafts to increase the thermal mass along this façade and act as a solar buffer for the morning sun, reducing heat gain. The core is further separated from the office spaces through an open lobby, which helps to insulate the office spaces.

The south-eastern façade of the building with the service core behind does not need any fenestrations, and the entire façade is rendered as a solid wall outlining the profile of the building. This further serves as a billboard for the political party.

The lift core is employed as a solar buffer.

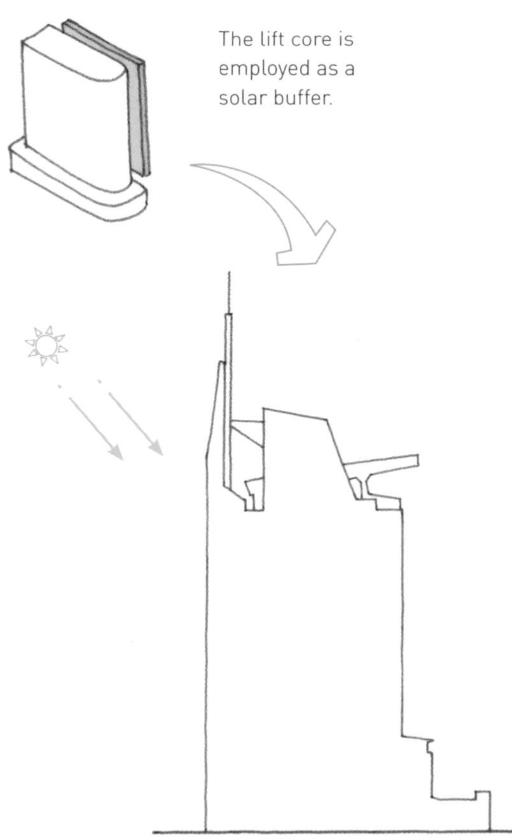

24

Menara UMNO | 1995–98

Kenneth Yeang, T. R. Hamzah & Yeang
Penang, Malaysia

Response to climate – bioclimatic skyscraper

Airflow in a traditional Chinese shophouse

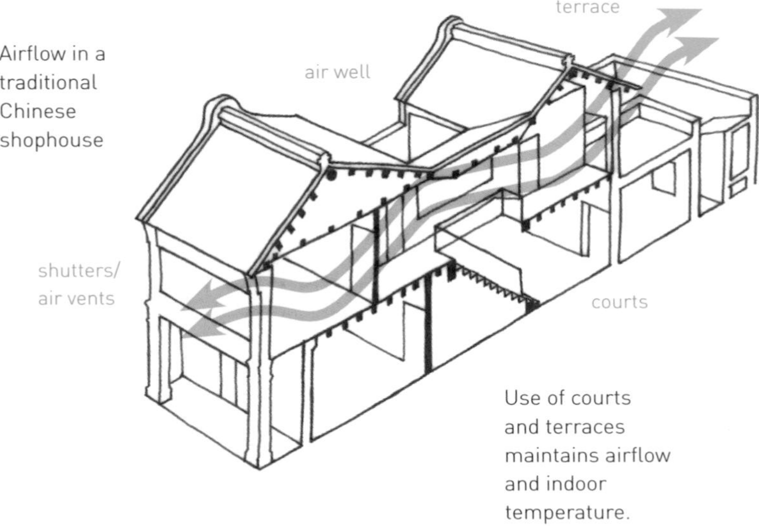

Use of courts and terraces maintains airflow and indoor temperature.

Adapting knowledge from traditional shophouses, the building incorporates terraces and 'sky courts'. The sky courts allow better cross-ventilation along the upper office levels. In a warm and humid tropical climate, natural ventilation reduces the need for air conditioning – the building was originally conceived to have none. The sky courts on the western façade also provide some much-needed sun shading.

The overall form resembling an aeroplane wing indicates a design intent based on airflow.

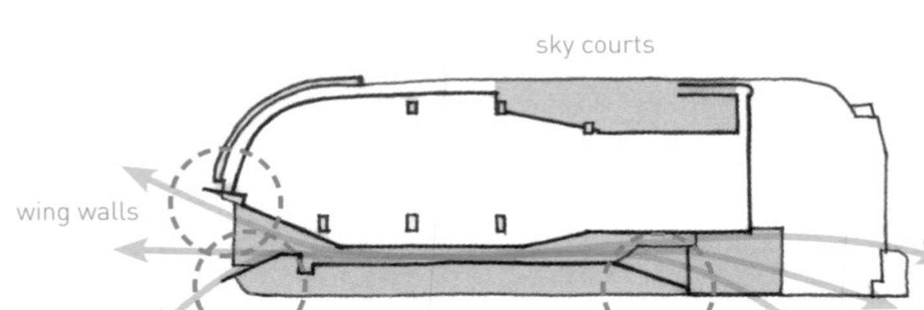

The external fin acts like a wing wall.

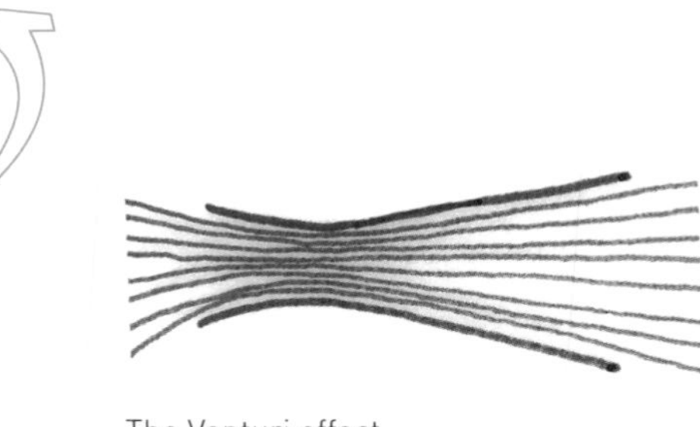

The Venturi effect increases airflow through a funnel.

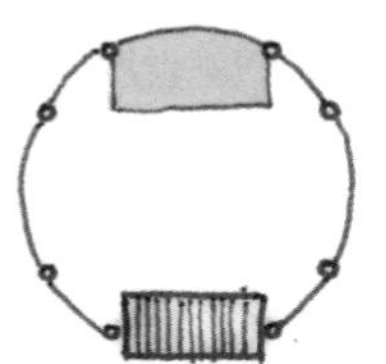

Menara Mesiniaga, Selangor, Malaysia, by Ken Yeang (1992)

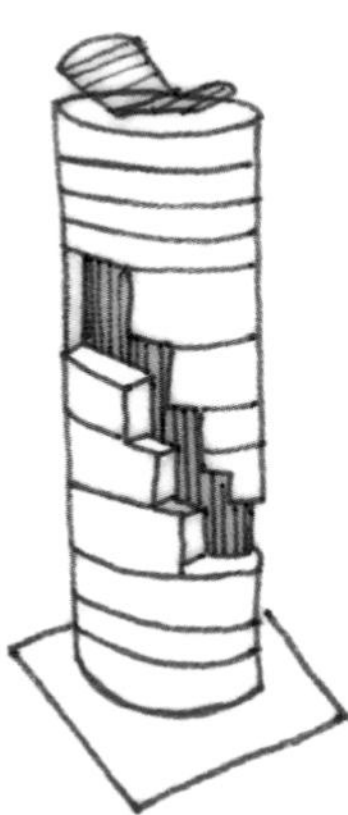

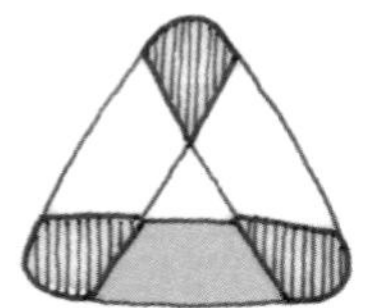

Commerzbank, Frankfurt, Germany, by Norman Foster (1997)

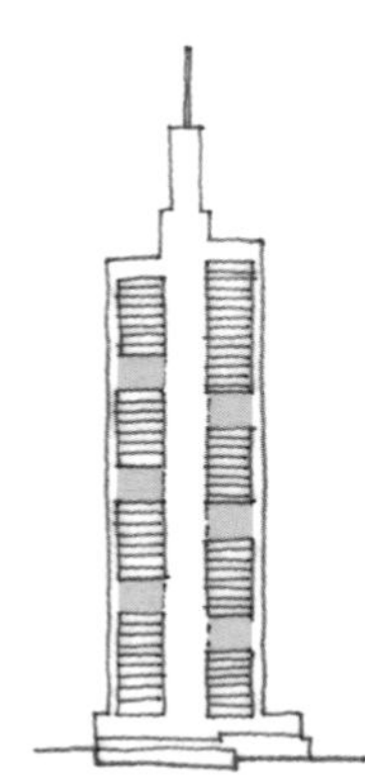

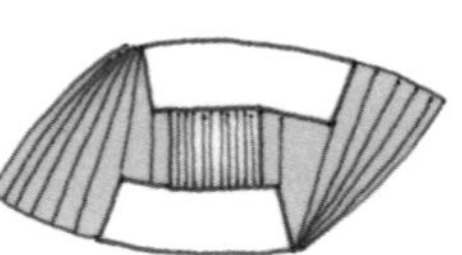

Menara Telekom, Kuala Lumpur, Malaysia, by Hijjas Kasturi (2001)

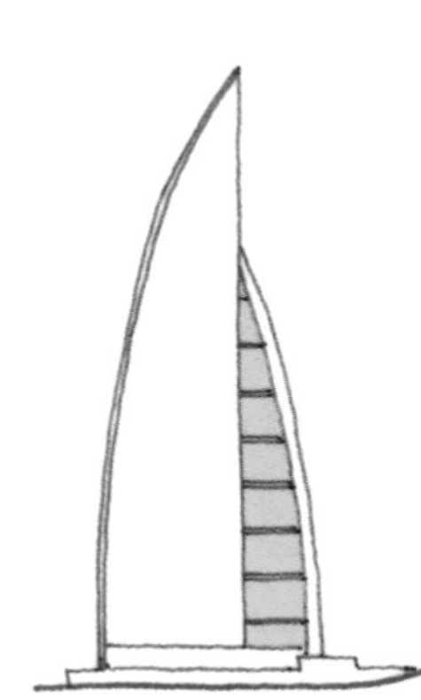

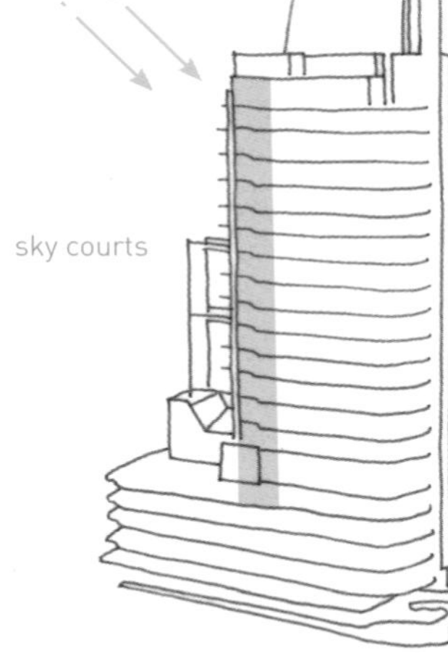

The design enhances the development of the bioclimatic skyscraper as a building type through the use of another feature: the wing wall. This is a fin-like projection located at an opening to capture the prevailing winds and enhance the natural ventilation through the building. While wing walls are used in low-rise buildings, Menara UMNO was the first high-rise to use this feature. The building is already oriented towards the prevailing wind direction from the north-east and south-west. The use of wing walls and the funnel-like shape of the central lobby creates a Venturi effect and increases the airflow within the building. This new system, along with the sky courts and openable windows, allows the interior temperatures to be moderated through passive means.

Response to climate – shading devices

The design of the structure follows the pattern of additive form generation to include a variety of design elements that act as shading devices and further enhance the performance of the building. A series of solar-shading panels runs along the north-western façade of the building as horizontal bands. These bands increase in depth as they move towards the western edge, allowing for better sun protection as well as aesthetic variations along the façade. The south-western corner, with the strongest afternoon sun, has a special curved buffer section that provides a deep cover and helps to stabilize indoor temperature.

The variable overlapping bandings that these devices create on the exterior of the building act as an expression of the climatic response of the design and make a pleasing aesthetic pattern.

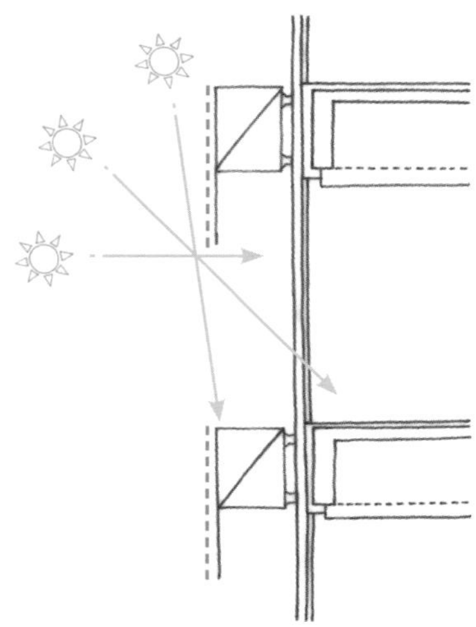

The horizontal shading devices protect the office interiors from the high summer sun but let in the low winter sun.

The south-west edge includes an additional shading panel for the afternoon sun.

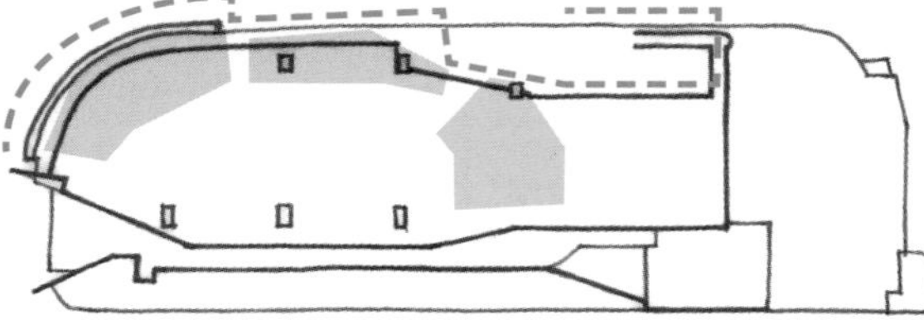

A series of bands extends along the western façade providing solar shading to the office spaces.

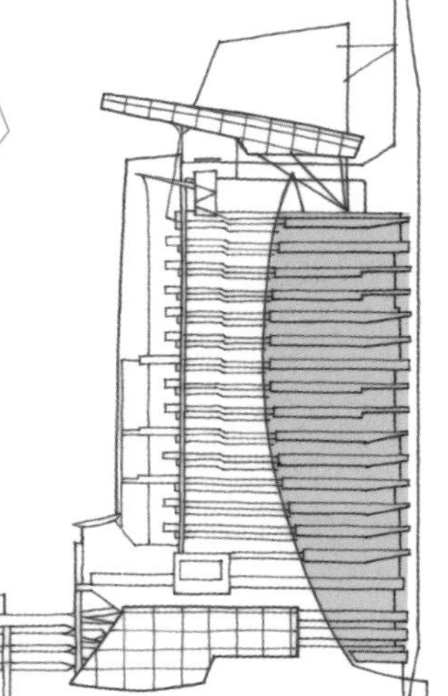

The external bandings act as a façade pattern.

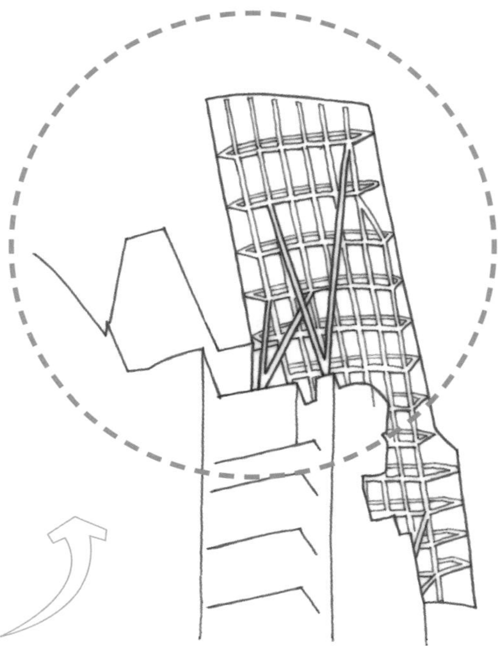

The large roof canopy provides extra solar shading for the entire structure.

In addition to the horizontal shading devices employed along the windows for the office areas, the entire building is covered with a massive canopy that provides shading to the roof and reduces heat gain. The treatment of this roof canopy also gives the design a distinctive roof profile and engages its fifth façade.

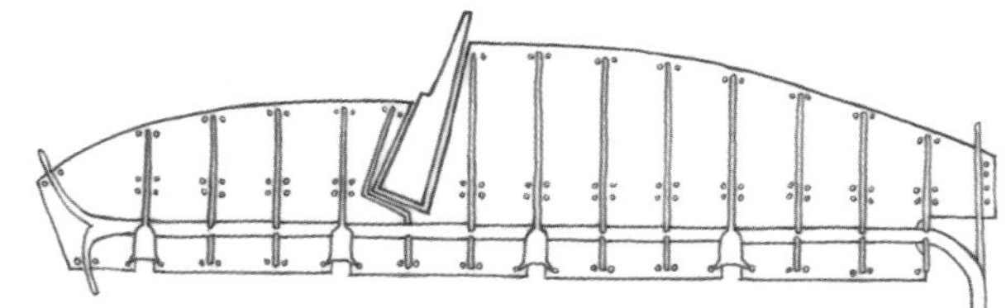

25

Dancing Building | 1992–96
Frank O. Gehry & Associates / Vlado Milunić
Prague, Czech Republic

In a dense heritage district of Prague, the 'Dancing Building' (also known as the 'Dancing House') is located on a busy corner among historically significant Baroque, Gothic and Art Nouveau buildings. Although controversially different, the building responds to its urban context in subtle ways to make a contemporary landmark that enhances the urban scene without dominating or detracting from its surroundings. Designed by American architect Frank O. Gehry in association with local architect Vlado Milunić, the building is a mark of globalization in the heart of Prague. It accommodates conventional café, retail and office functions.

In common with some of Gehry's other work, the façades distort the geometry of conventional buildings and in doing so encourage new interpretations of building elements.

Selen Morkoç, Gabriella Dias, Doug McCusker and Leona Greenslade

25

25 Dancing Building | 1992–96

Frank O. Gehry & Associates / Vlado Milunić

Prague, Czech Republic

Context

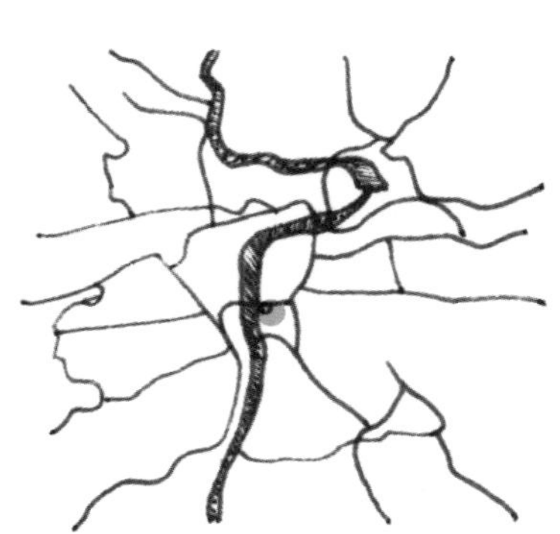

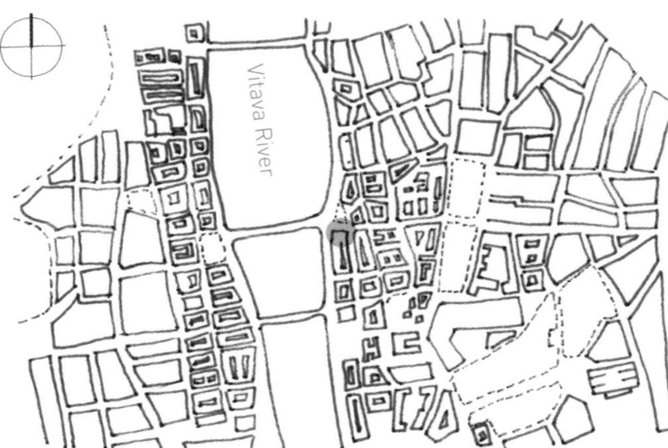

The Dancing Building is located on the banks of the Vitava River in the historical district of Prague. The surrounding environment, particularly the river and the urban texture, are formal references for the design. The wave pattern that dominates the plan and the façade treatment of the buildings are based on these references.

Although the design concept has no references to the past of the site, during the wartime bombing of Prague in 1945 the house that was then on the site was mostly destroyed and was left as a ruin until 1960.

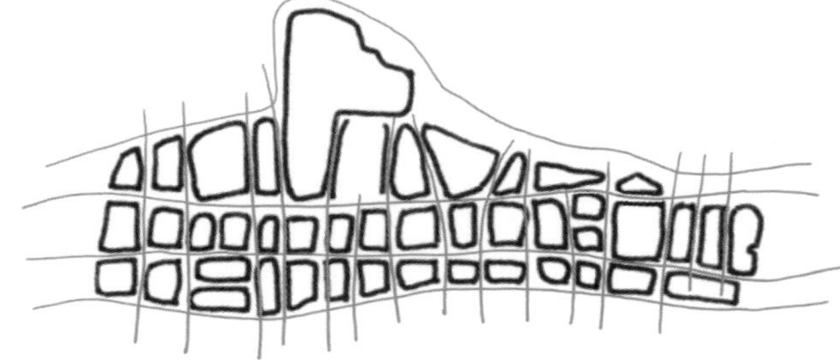

The urban fabric of Prague appears to be organized on a distorted grid, with wavy instead of straight street lines.

The 1945 bombing of the city abruptly fractured the stable order of the neighbouring buildings.

While the city of Prague has a dense urban texture, there is a local tendency to maintain public space with small park areas and inner courtyards between city blocks.

The Dancing Building is one of the three modern buildings allowed to be built within the historical district of Prague. It is surrounded by Neoclassical and Art Nouveau buildings.

The concept of the Dancing Building is based on a simple premise of two towers located on the prominent northern corner block facing the river. The playful form of the towers suggests a dancing couple. It has been likened particularly to famous American dancers Fred Astaire and Ginger Rogers, who starred in a series of Hollywood films from the 1930s.

Formal references

The basis of the design is the two towers leaning towards each other.

A wavy horizontality connects the two towers to each other and to the existing neighbouring buildings.

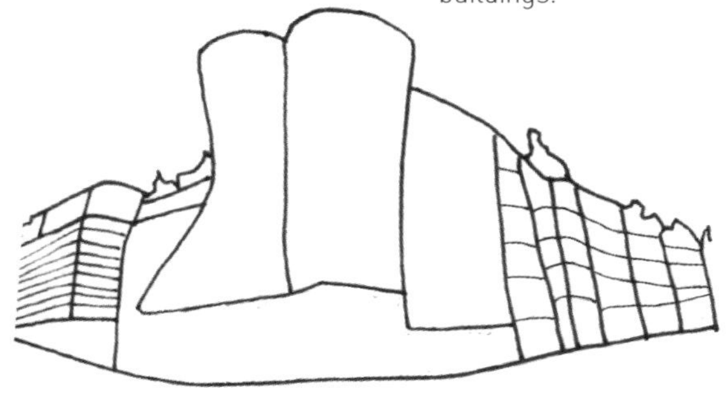

The first tower, with its convex-profile curve, has feminine qualities, in contrast with the other, which has a more stable conic form that narrows down towards the ground, manifesting masculine qualities. The prevailing wavy lines across the facades of both towers emphasize unity and continuity between the two buildings.

The two cylindrical forms protrude from the corner and form a canopy, which provides shelter to the pavement. The continuous outer skin of the glass tower drives the eye vertically.

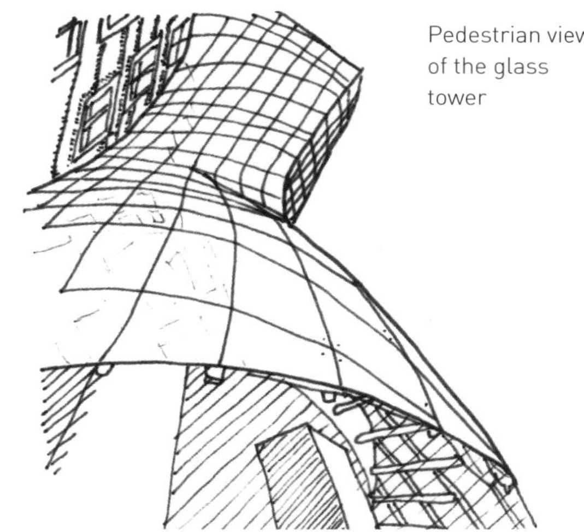

Pedestrian view of the glass tower

Despite its controversial form, the building melds into the surrounding buildings on both sides by following their height and window proportions.

The building is located in a busy district. It is seen from a variety of directions at many speeds, depending on the viewer's mode of transport on land or water.

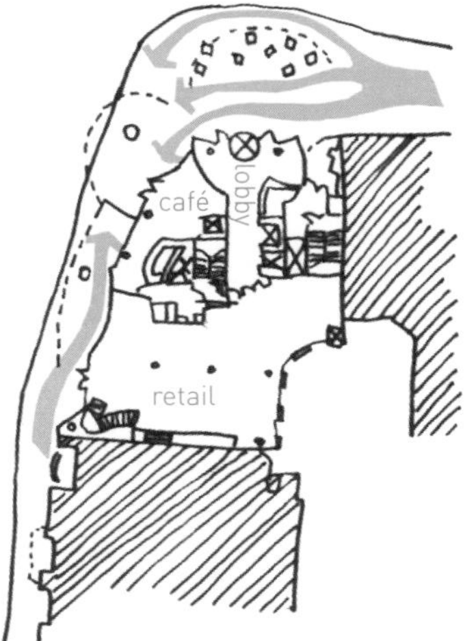

The overlap of the ground floor with public space changes pedestrian movement along the streets. The café provides a niche of social space within the building.

At ground level, the sculptural columns allow views towards the adjacent public square and down the river.

The columns break up the line of sight along the pavement and force pedestrians to experience the building as their line of movement changes.

Dancing Building | 1992–96

Frank O. Gehry & Associates / Vlado Milunić
Prague, Czech Republic

Interior elements

Space allocation

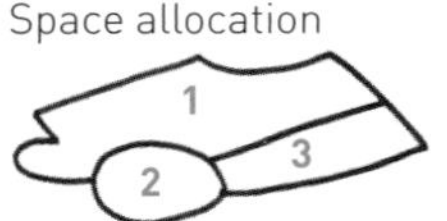

Level 8

Levels 2–7

Ground floor

Circulation / Private spaces

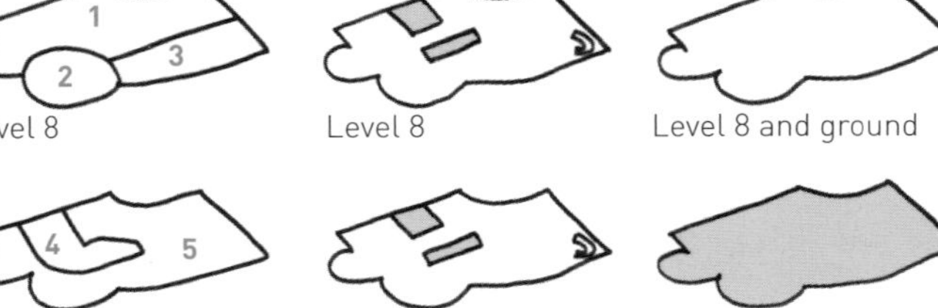

Level 8 / Level 8 and ground

Levels 2–7 and ground / Levels 2–7

key

1. restaurant and café
2. nest
3. balcony
4. access
5. commercial
6. lobby
7. café
8. retail

Columns

Level 8

Levels 2–7

Ground floor

Despite the building's dichotomous external form with two towers, the planning is conventional and treats the envelope as one space. The lobby, café and retail spaces are on the ground level, with offices above. A restaurant on the top floor and the 'nest' exploit the views. The vertical access core is centrally located.

Ground-floor plan

Office-level plan

The dichotomous outer look of the two towers is dissolved in the plan layout.

Form generation

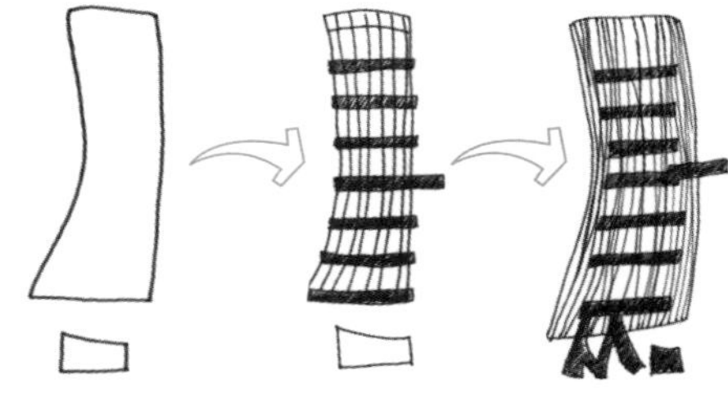

The two cylindrical volumes are generated through gestural twists and folding based on two metaphorical references: the feminine and the masculine. The 'feminine' tower has softer curves, further lightened by the use of a continuous glass surface. With its more stable and solid mass, the 'masculine' tower forms a bridge between the fluid materiality of the glass tower and the neighbouring buildings.

The windows in the concrete tower frame 'snapshot' views of historic Prague. The windows in the glass tower offer continuous panoramic views.

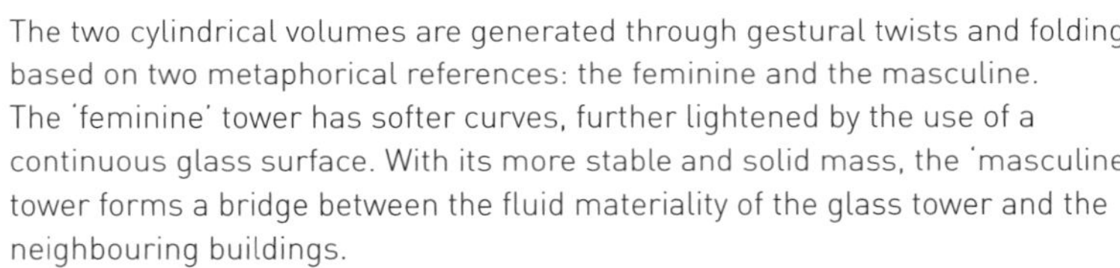

Section through the glass tower

The glass tower has a double skin. The exterior shingle-like glazing is the outer skin and the interior glazing seals the office spaces from the outside noise and pollution. The offices are mechanically ventilated.

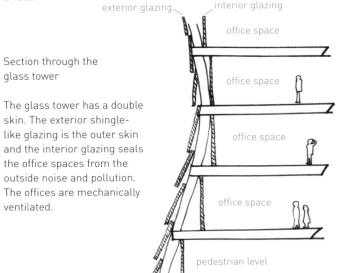

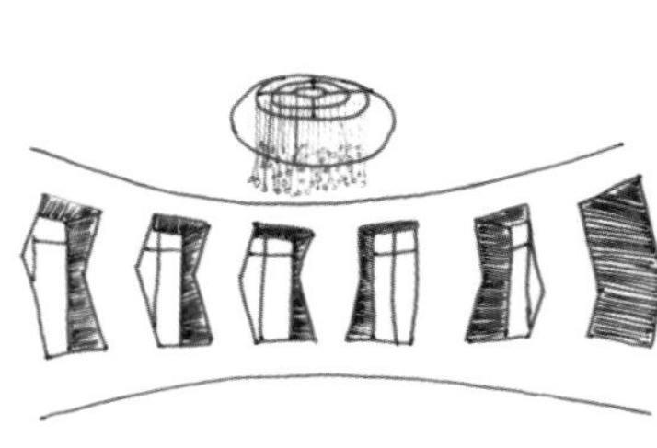

Inside the 'masculine' tower

The nest on top of the 'feminine' tower

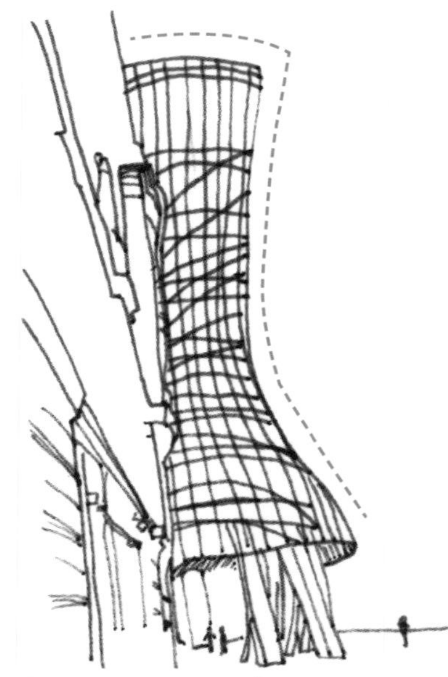

The projection of the 'feminine' glass tower provides the offices inside with views along the river and street. The narrowed waist reduces obstruction of the river view from adjacent buildings.

Response to context through the façade

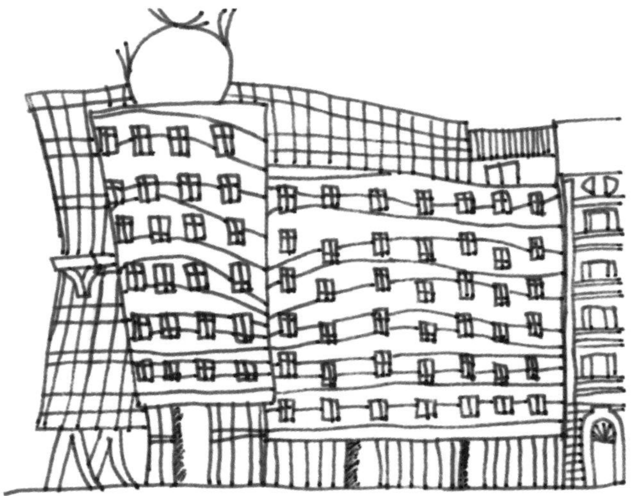

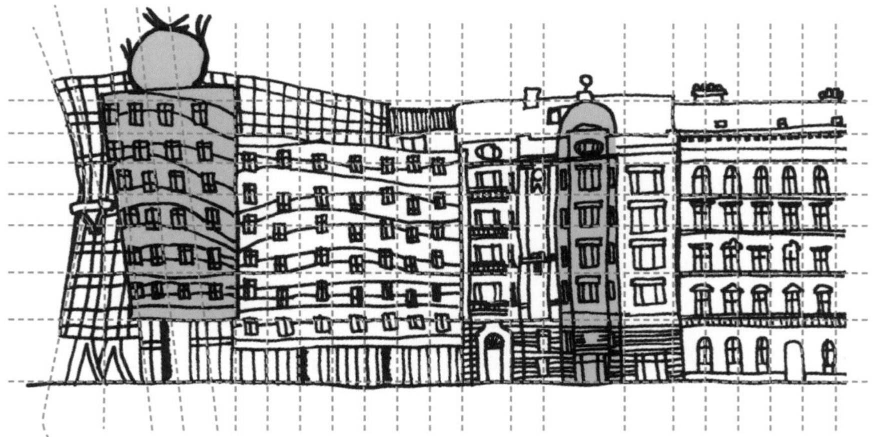

The façade is the core of the building's response to its urban context. The Dancing Building respects its neighbours by continuing their height and proportions despite its controversial contemporary form. The design of the façade follows common patterns in local buildings such as the separation of the ground-floor level, the expressed tower-like elements, the consistent setback of the general form and the alternating repetition of windows.

Details

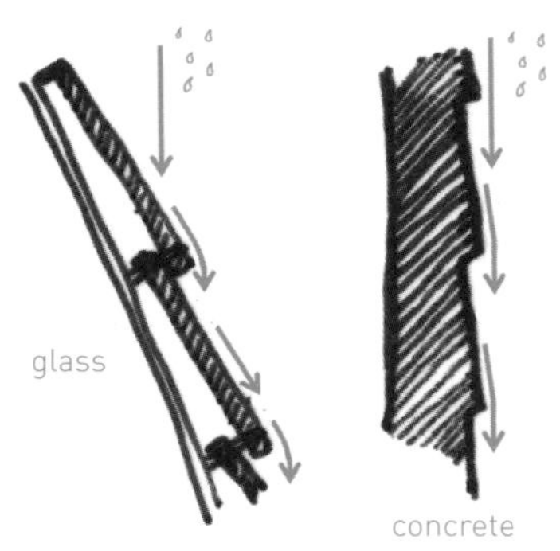

Both towers have shingle-like external skins, despite one being formed in glass and the other in concrete.

A diagrammatic plan shows how a simple recess is used to separate old and new buildings, making a strong shadow line on the façade.

Windows

Alternating windows

Wavy lines

Although windows are standard in size and shape, each protrudes differently from the wall to make a range of unique shadow patterns.

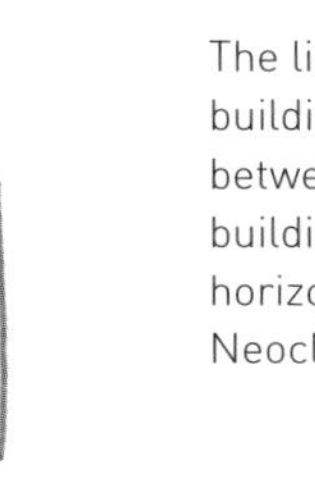

Dancing Building

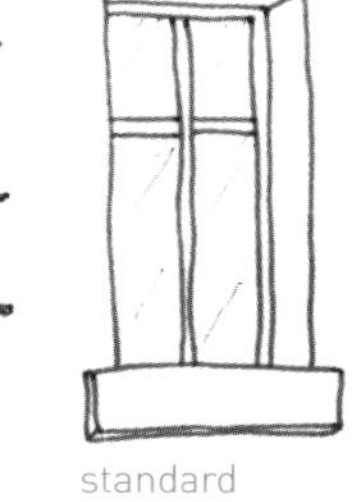

standard

Reversal gesture of the window frame

Instead of imitating the conventional local fenestration, the windows are extruded. The strong shadows they cast on to the façade intensify the wavy lines.

The lined façades of the new building soften the edges between the new and existing buildings by addressing the horizontal element of the Neoclassical cornices.

26

Eastgate | 1991–96
Pearce Partnership
Harare, Zimbabwe

Eastgate is a large mixed-use commercial building with a sense of African identity in a continent where most such buildings follow European and North American models. Its identity comes from its materials, colours and patterns, and the choice of construction techniques that allocated the budget to local manufacture and labour rather than imported products. The building houses a shopping mall, a food court, seven floors of offices and some parking.

Eastgate is also a demonstration of design in response to climate. Harare has hot days but relatively cool nights all year round. Exploiting cooling by air movement is a core aspect of the building, with its chimney-topped vertical shafts, raised floors and ducts. Along with air movement there is shade, planting, radiation to the cool night sky from a highly textured skin, and solar panels.

Antony Radford and Michael Pearce

26

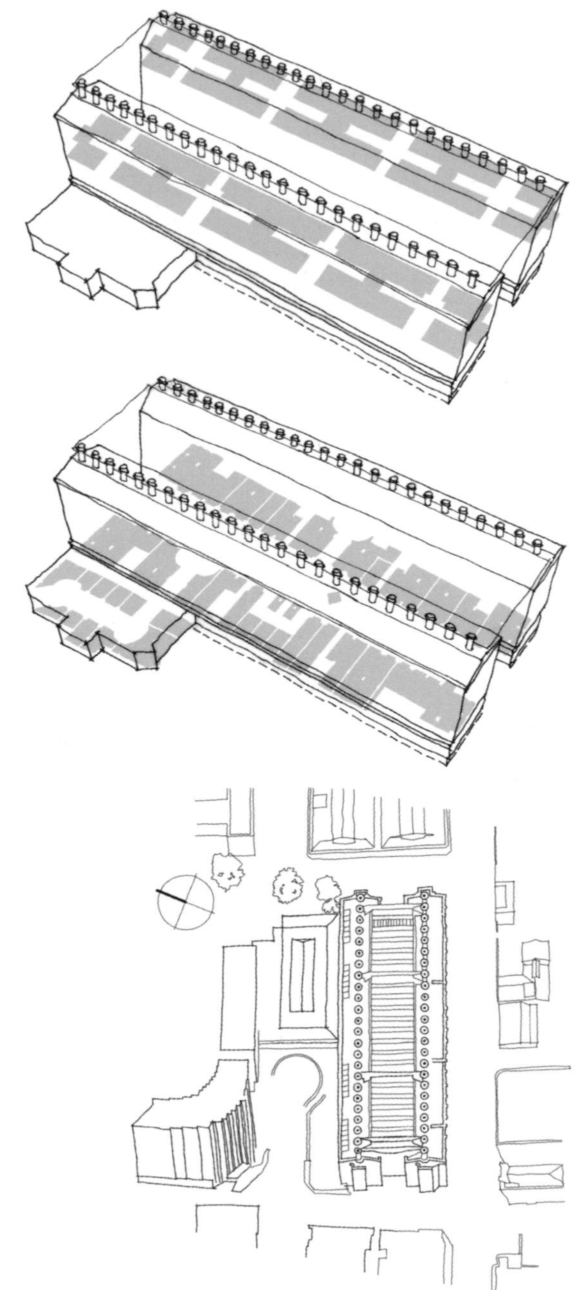

Context, planning and building form

Eastgate stands out in central Harare. Unlike other glass and concrete office buildings in the city, its texture, materials and green walls reflect its African origin.

Most of the building is linear and symmetrical. The ground level breaks out of this linear form to fill the site footprint.

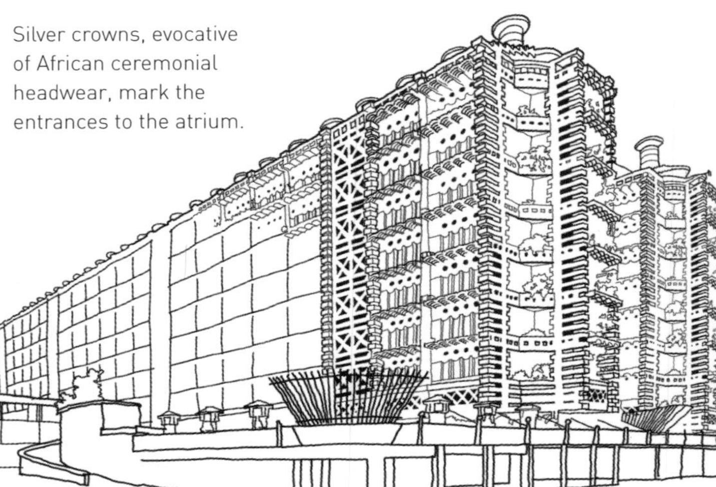

Silver crowns, evocative of African ceremonial headwear, mark the entrances to the atrium.

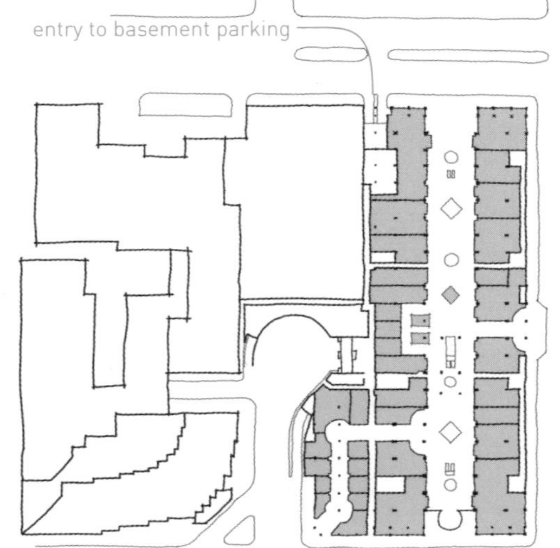

Ground-floor retail level

The two main blocks of Eastgate lie one each side of a street. This is protected from sun and rain by a roof, but is completely open at both ends.

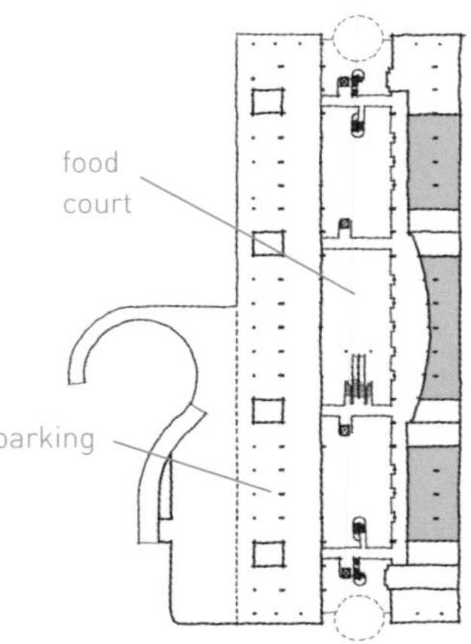

Upper-floor parking and food court

On one side the first floor (one level up from ground level) is occupied by a food court. On the other side it is used for parking. Additional parking is underground.

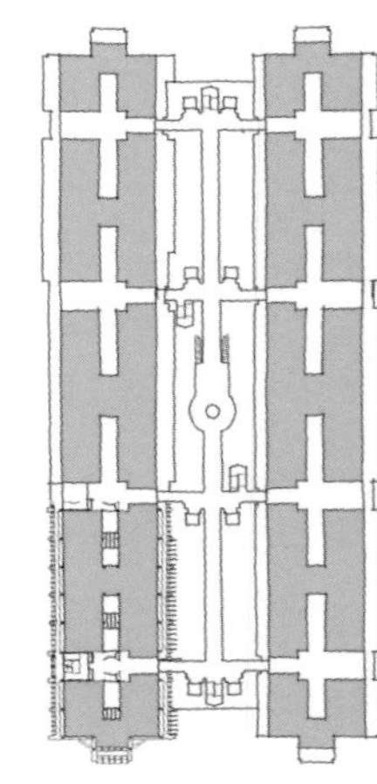

Six floors of offices

Biomimicry

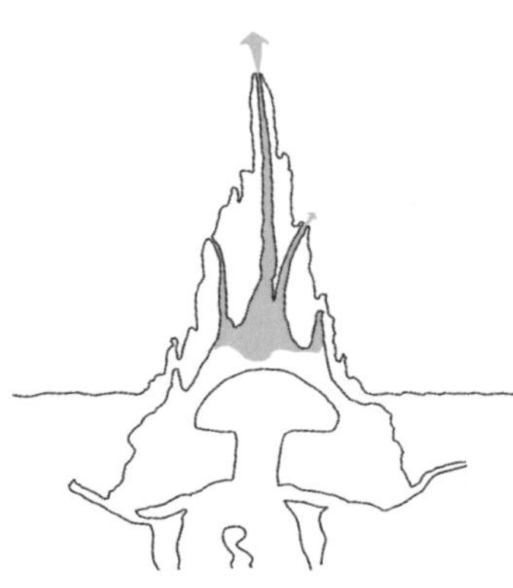

The precedent of a termite mound prompted holistic thinking in the design team. The temperature in a termite mound is stabilized by the earth's thermal mass and diurnal temperature change.

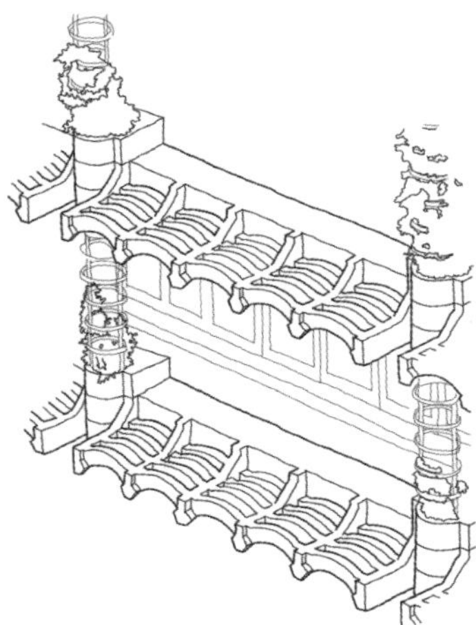

Office façades have deep precast-concrete overhangs and sunshades with planting trellises.

Design with climate

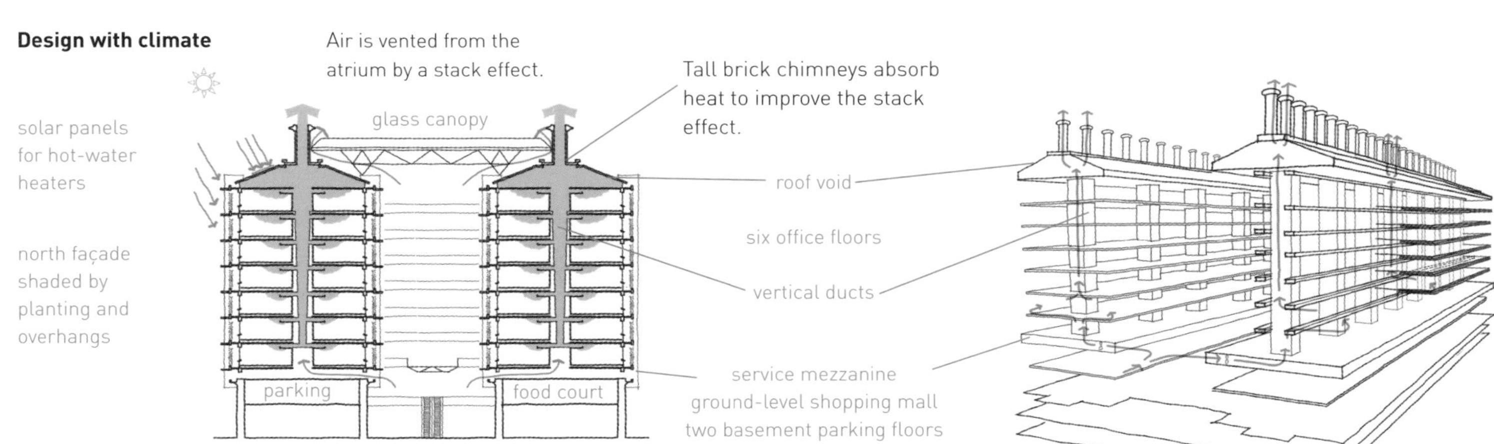

The building is mechanically ventilated combined with passive stacks to supplement fan power. The fans are in the service mezzanine floor. Use varies with the seasons.

During the day, air is taken from the shaded atrium and directed through large ducts in service cores to the offices and then up to the roof void and chimneys. There are about two air changes per hour. During the night, stack effect and fans draw cool night air into the atrium and up through the office floors to the roof void and chimneys. This airflow cools the floors and structure. Because the temperature difference is greater, so are stack-effect air-movement velocities: there are about ten air changes per hour. Air is also drawn from the atrium to ventilate the basement parking areas.

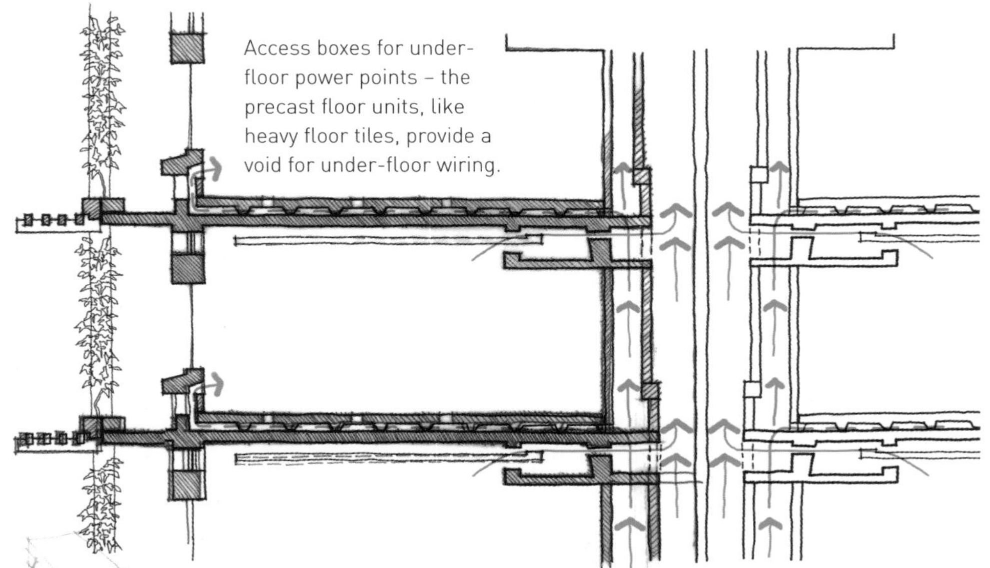

Access boxes for under-floor power points – the precast floor units, like heavy floor tiles, provide a void for under-floor wiring.

In the offices, air passes from the 'cold air' duct to the space under the precast-concrete floor units before entering the room below the perimeter windows. These precast floor units act as heat exchangers, cooled by night air and themselves cooling daytime air. Air is drawn from the room at the opposite corner by stack effect in the 'hot air' duct.

Fluorescent uplighters use the vaulted concrete ceiling as reflectors so that the slab above absorbs their radiant heat. Their ballasts are housed in the air extract duct so that their heat is drawn away from the room.

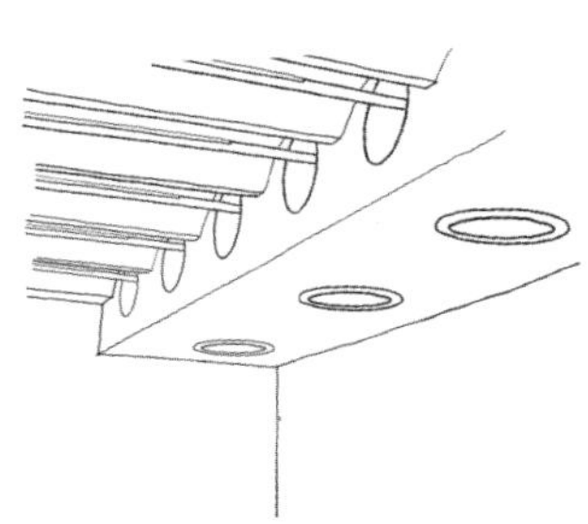

Precedents for surface patterns

The mass and texture point to local and global precedents: the massive walls of Great Zimbabwe, the rustications of French architect Ledoux's Saline Royale, the patterns of African craft, and the steel structures of the Zimabwe mining industry.

The main building material is concrete, but its brushed surface and an aggregate of granite sand and stones give it the character of natural granite. Other materials are steel, clay brick and glass.

Layering of stone blocks at Great Zimbabwe (1100–1500AD), a massive dry-stone structure and a product of a sophisticated African culture

A Shona stool, about 25cm (10in) high and carved by the local Shona people

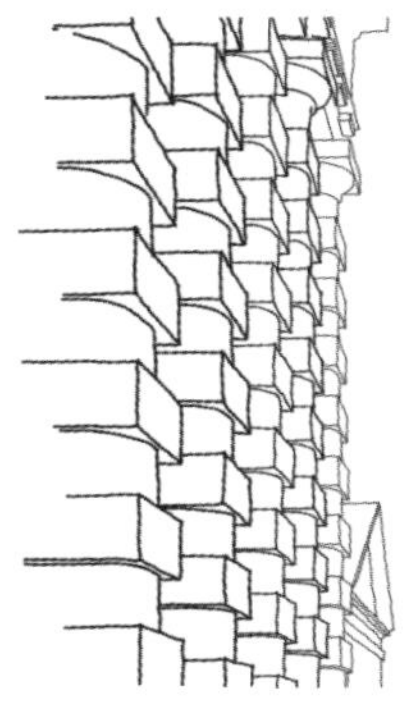

Rusticated wall of the Saline Royale (Royal Saltworks), Arc-et-Senans, France, designed by Claude-Nicolas Ledoux (1775–80)

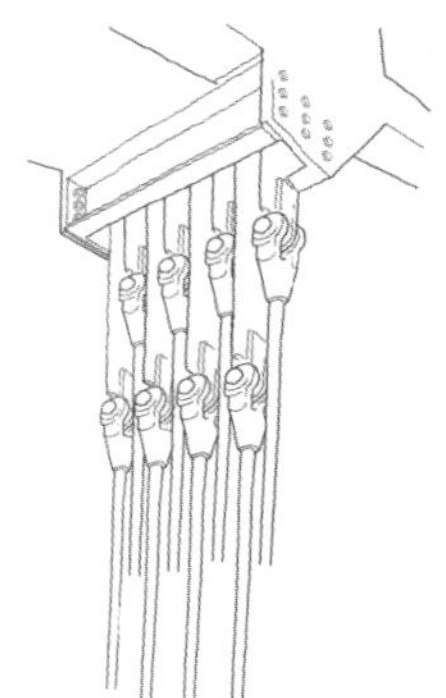

Industrial engineering: detail of steel cable connection to the trusses

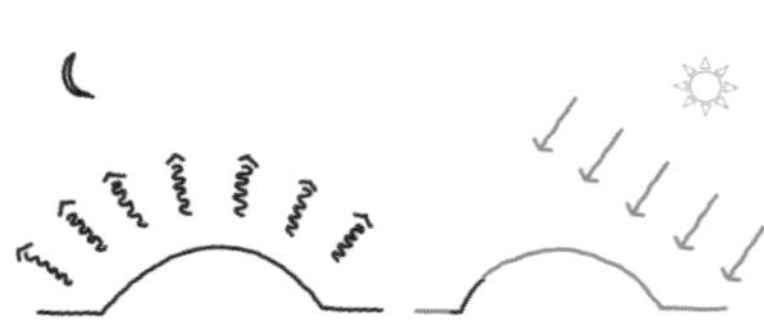

Prickly bodies absorb no more heat from solar radiation by day but emit more heat to the cool night sky from their greater surface area.

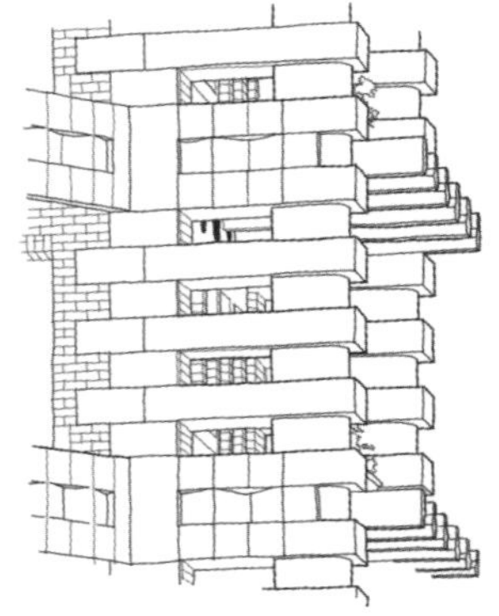

Layering of precast-concrete blocks in the 'prickly' wall surface at Eastgate

Geometric pattern of concrete screen over escape stairs at Eastgate

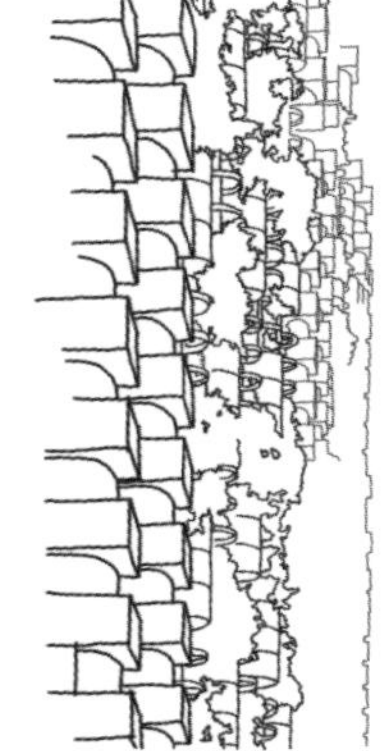

Rusticated wall of Eastgate, with planting

The street/mall

The mall is about 16 metres (53 feet) wide and 30 metres (98 feet) high, a busy place of many elements and textures, bright highlights and deep shade. The two building side walls are built in concrete with glass and brick infill. Between them, steel decks and lift assemblies are suspended from bold trusses like loads below huge gantry cranes in an industrial workshop. In contrast, mall shops have delicate fabric awnings and recessed doors as if they were a terrace of small units in a suburban street. A green tracery of plants climbs steel hoops up the side walls.

A glass canopy covers the mall in a sawtooth pattern typical of greenhouses and railway stations. Clay-tiled variations cover the big trusses over four lateral walkways and their associated lifts.

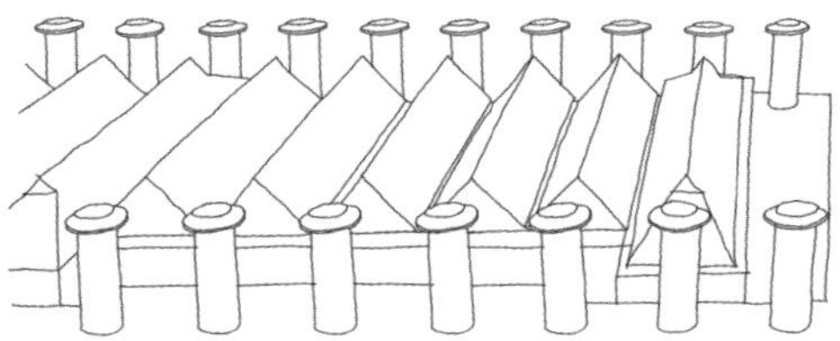

The mall roof between the chimneys

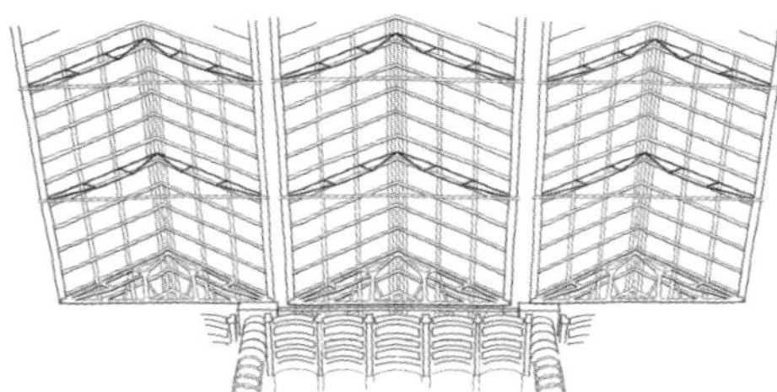

Looking up from the mall to the underside of the glass roof

Circulation

The vertical circulation uses escalators to the food-court level and lifts above this level. These lifts are suspended above the shopping mall, leaving the ground floor unobstructed. A skywalk links them. Open stairways supplement the lifts.

Scale contrast

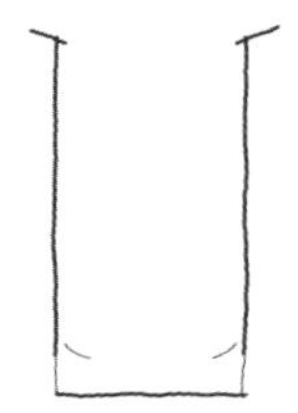

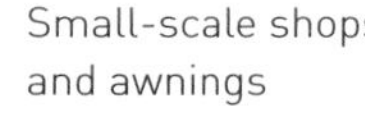

Small-scale shops and awnings

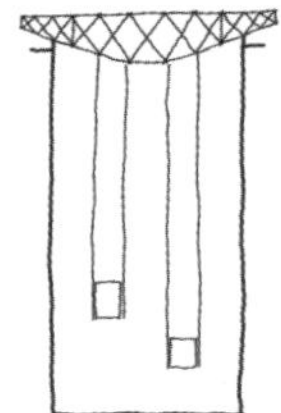

Large-scale engineering

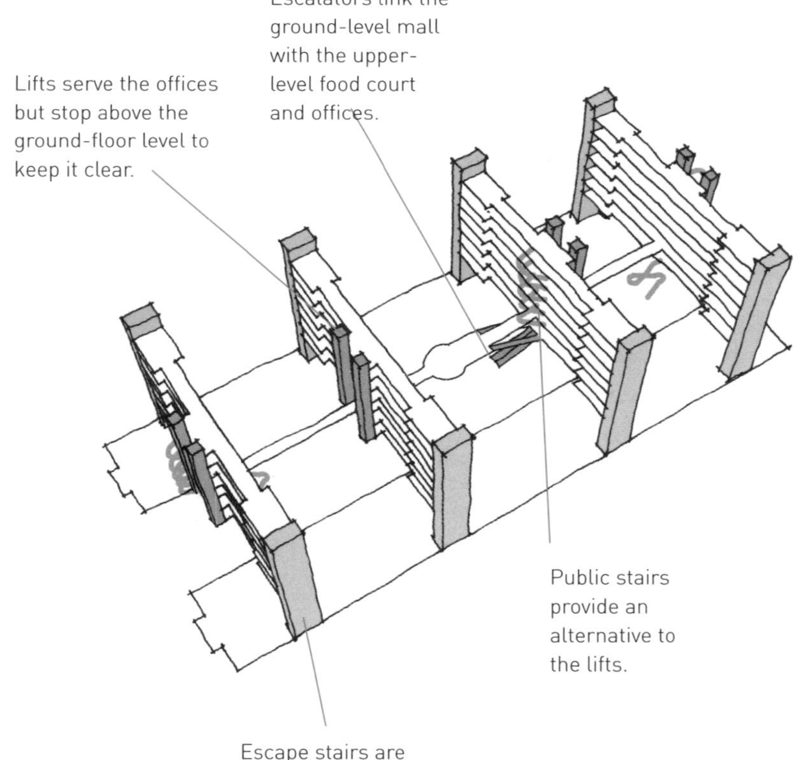
Lifts serve the offices but stop above the ground-floor level to keep it clear.
Escalators link the ground-level mall with the upper-level food court and offices.
Public stairs provide an alternative to the lifts.
Escape stairs are located on both long sides of the building.

Views up and down from the suspended walkways show the robust steel engineering between highly textured concrete and brick façades.

27 Thermal Baths in Vals | 1986–96

Peter Zumthor

Vals, Switzerland

Vals is a remote Alpine village in the canton of Graubünden in Switzerland. Swiss architect Peter Zumthor was commissioned to rehabilitate a 1960s hotel through the addition of thermal baths. Positioned on a steep slope and partly embedded in the mountain, the building uses local stone as a major tectonic and symbolic element of the design. The result is a modest response to local culture and environment with a sense of timelessness.

The interior suggests squared-off volumes carved like caves out of a solid mass, with carefully framed views along and across the valley. This is a building to experience in use, the spaces evoking feelings of rest and rejuvenation in bathers as they progress through the rituals of immersion in a sequence of hot and cold pools, steam rooms and relaxation areas. The sensory qualities of temperature, touch, smell, sight and sound are all engaged.

Selen Morkoç, Alix Dunbar and Huo Liu

Thermal Baths in Vals | 1986–96

Peter Zumthor

Vals, Switzerland

Response to context

There are many tunnels and galleries on the road between Vals and Ilanz, built into the slope to protect traffic from rock falls and avalanches. They set a precedent for the way in which the design of the Thermal Baths works with the mountain.

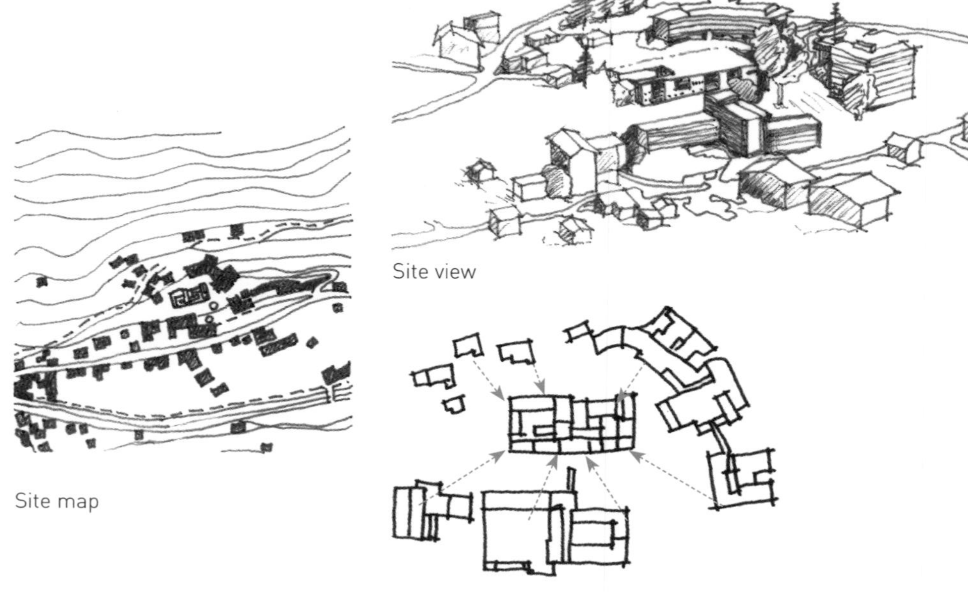

Site map

Site view

Partly submerged in the landscape, the building protrudes from the mountainside with dramatic elevations to the south, east and west. The hotel rooms behind the baths look over its grass roof.

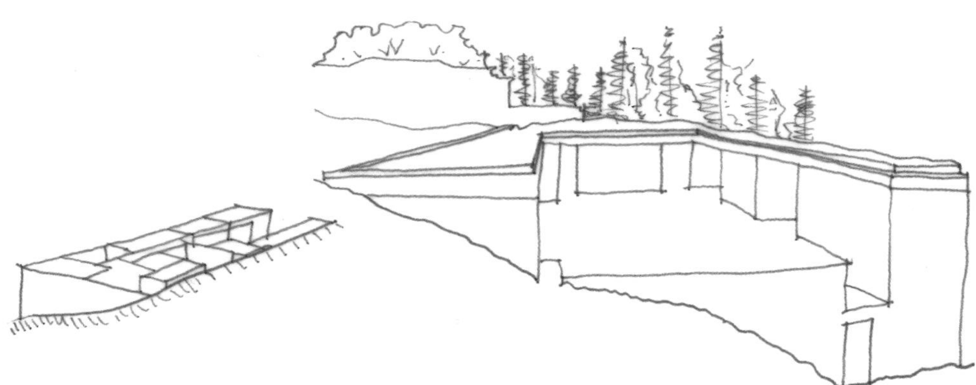

The Thermal Baths provide a gathering and attraction point for five surrounding hotel buildings dating from the 1960s. The only access from the main hotel building to the baths is through an underground corridor from the foyer.

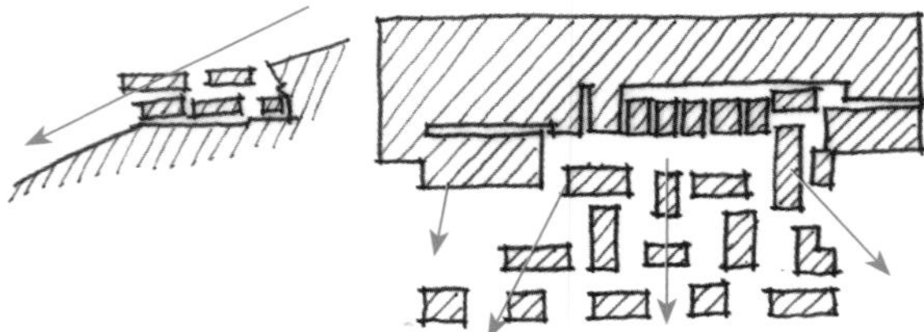

Embedded in the slope, the building in both plan and section resembles a giant rock coming apart from the hill. The design is influenced by the primordial stone on the site and features it both literally and metaphorically, along with the mountain and water.

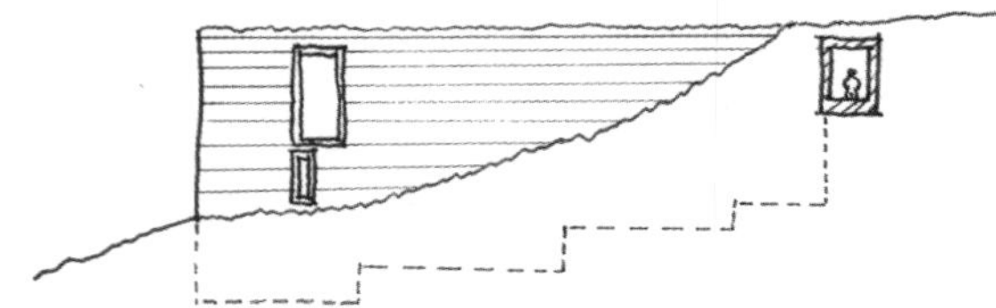

Site organization
Outdoor facilities are located in the south-west corner of the plan to utilize sunlight. They also capture dramatic views of the mountain and valley.

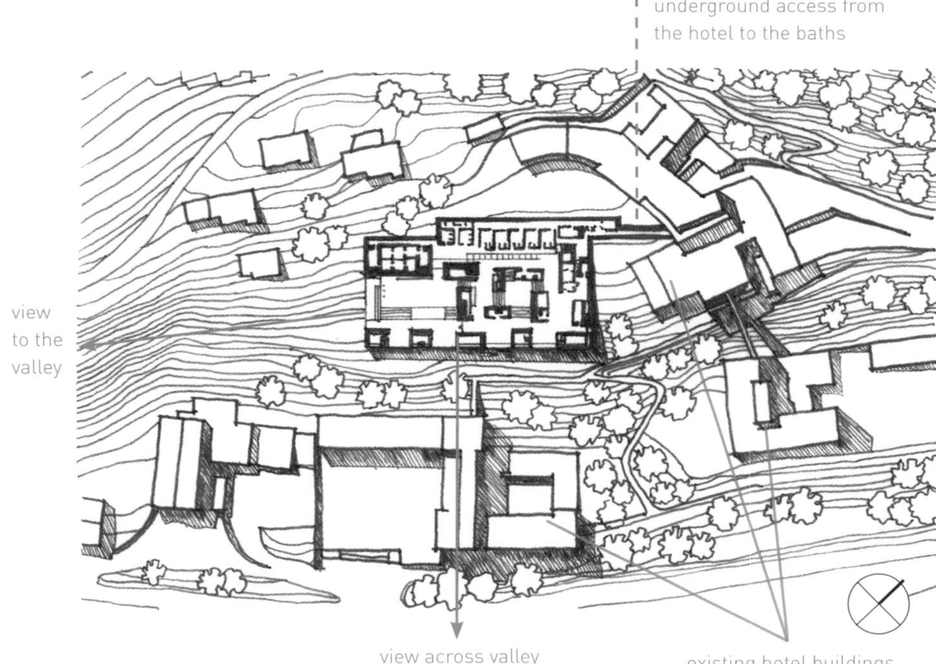

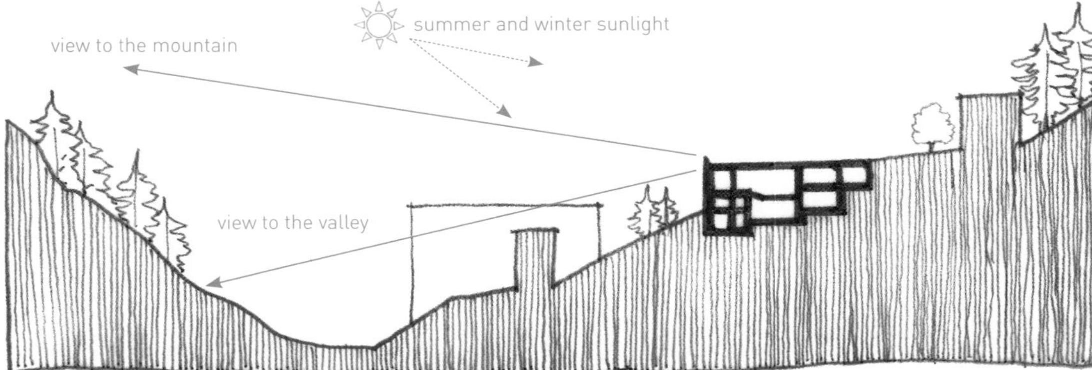

The geology of Vals is the major influence on the design concept. The Thermal Baths humbly respond to the existing buildings, topography and nature. The views of the mountains and the valley are not blocked for other buildings and they all receive sunlight in both summer and winter.

Form generation
The plan is organized as a series of cubic volumes scattered like stones in water. Their proximity and positioning determines the public and private spaces of the baths, ranging from showers, to sweating, drinking and resting spaces, to indoor and outdoor pools.

The pools, together with the open spaces surrounding them, serve as two nodes in the design. Steps allow users to immerse themselves peacefully in water of different temperatures, while also allowing more dynamic experiences of spaces, texture, temperature, sound and smell.

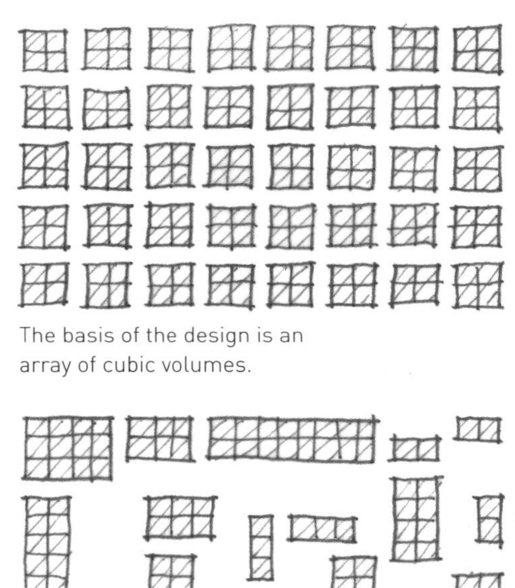

The basis of the design is an array of cubic volumes.

Components that have similar functions are grouped together.

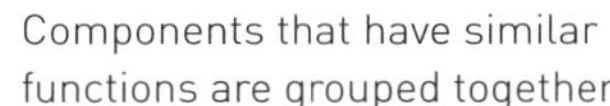

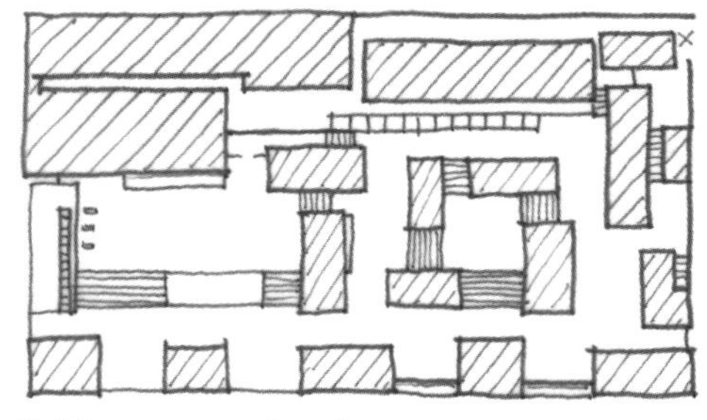

Public spaces and pools occupy the remaining area.

27 Thermal Baths in Vals | 1986–96

Peter Zumthor

Vals, Switzerland

The entrance to the baths is through a cave-like reception area and a dark and misty hallway. A raised platform connects the changing rooms to the main bath area. The spatial configuration is undirected, encouraging visitors to wander around the spaces.

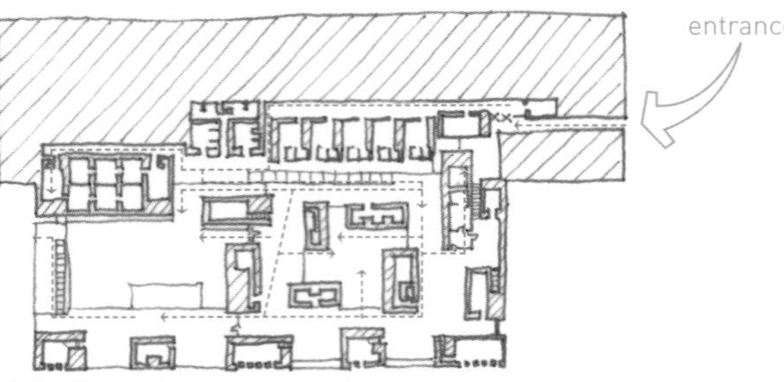

Main-floor plan, movements

Lower-level plan, therapy

Between the cubic volumes, there are larger, empty areas leading towards two large windows that frame the view of the mountains. Visitors are encouraged to wander around the space in between private and public spots. The lower level is the therapy level, containing smaller rooms for various types of massage and physiotherapy.

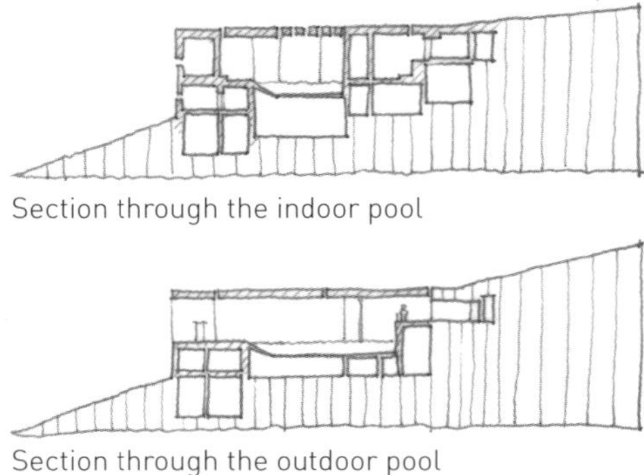

Section through the indoor pool

Section through the outdoor pool

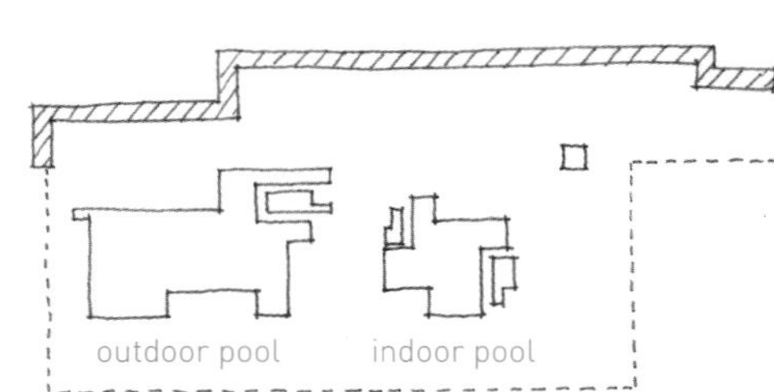

Water The major therapeutic element utilized indoors and outdoors is water. Hot- and cold-water pools sit in juxtaposition to one another, heightening the sensation of the bathing experience. Each body of water varies in temperature according to its use.

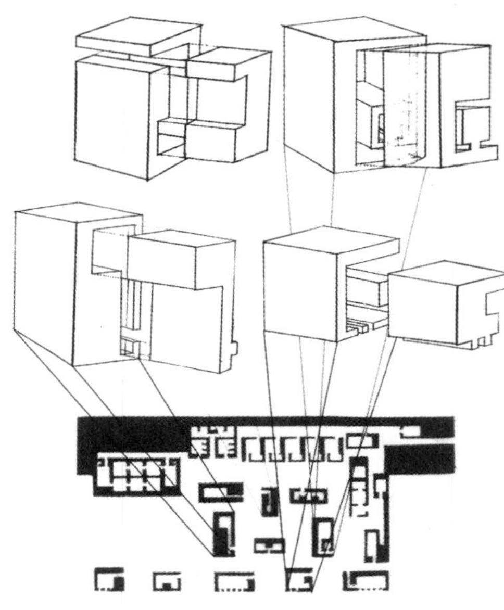

Mass and void The seemingly random spatial configuration of the cubic spaces allows people to make choices. The carved-out spaces all have unique forms determined by their functions. These units also shape the void around them through their mass and positioning.

Response to the natural

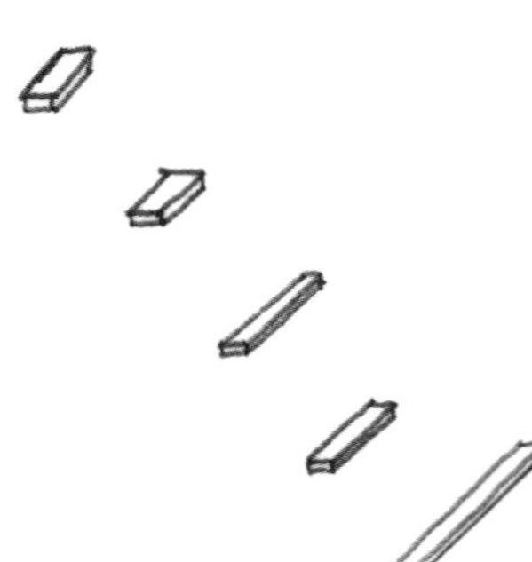

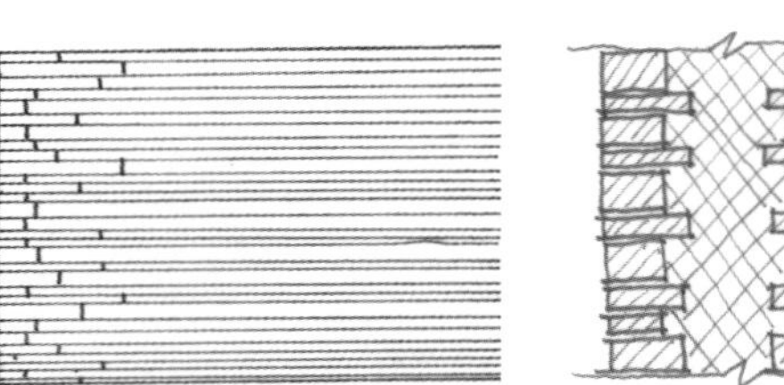

Locally sourced Valser quarzite stone is cut into three different thicknesses, giving a dramatic texture. The working of this stone requires centuries-old artisan skills.

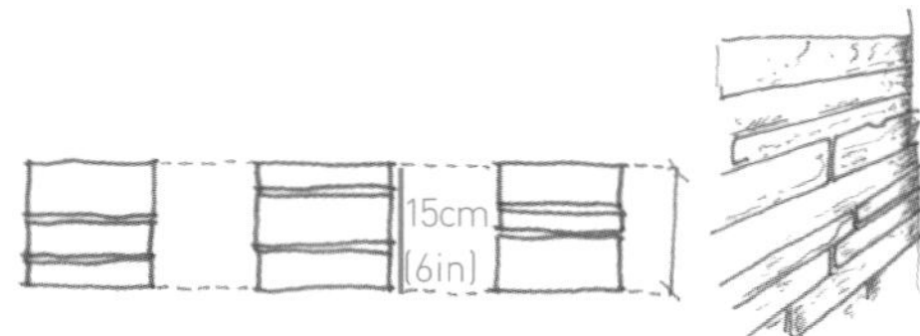

Exterior views

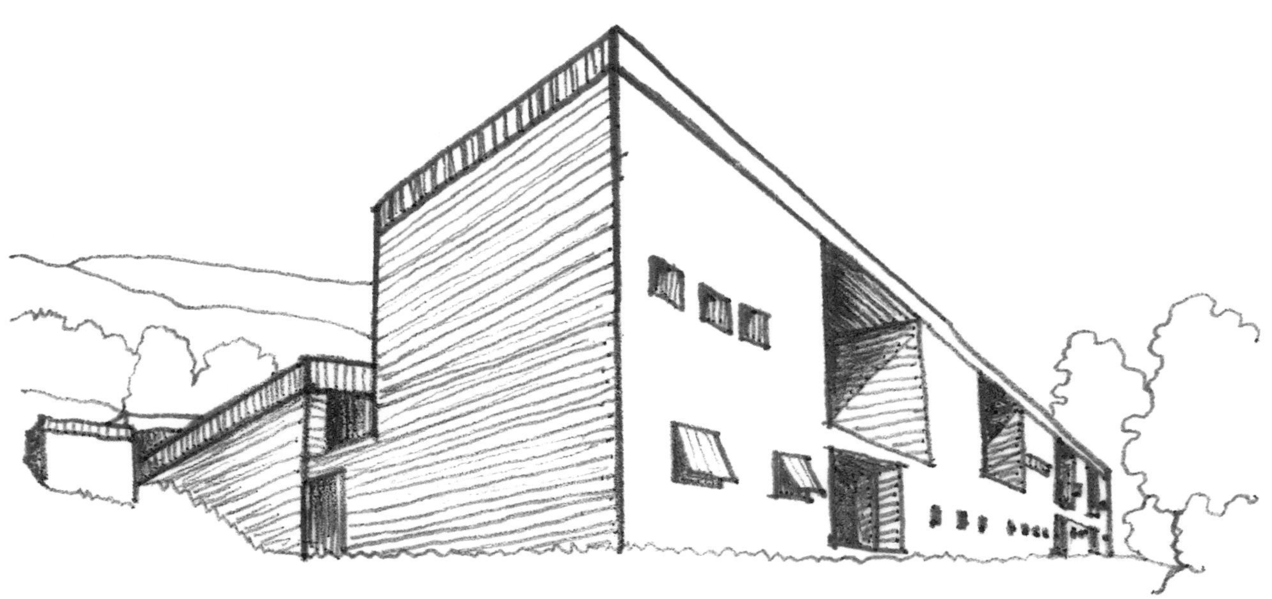

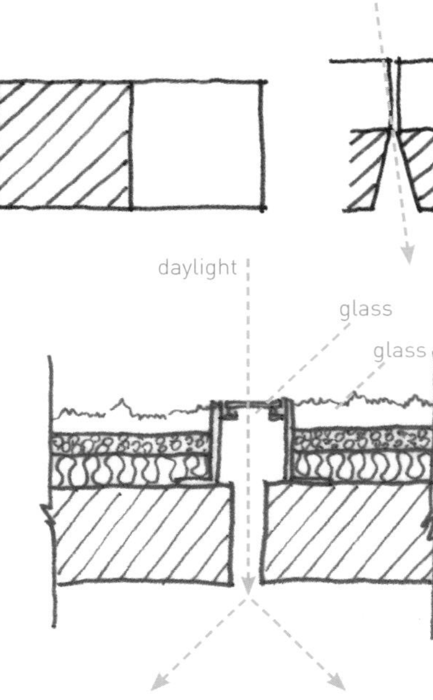

Light Light is utilized in the creation of tranquil, meditative and serene spaces. Shafts of light penetrate rooms from above, through the ceiling plane.

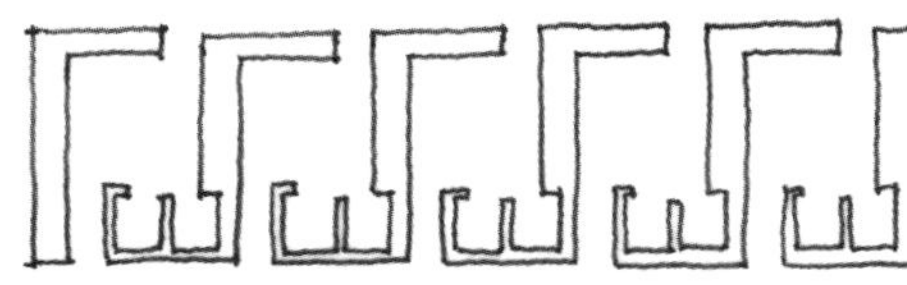

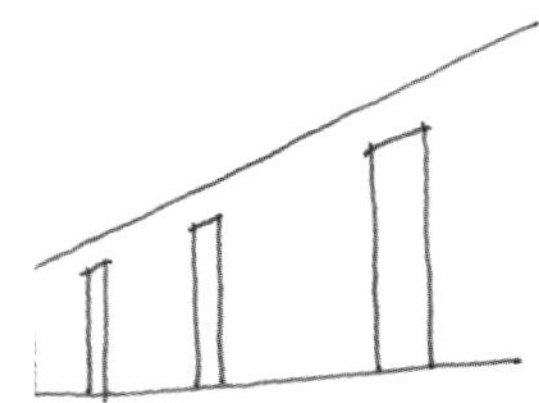

Changing rooms Private functions such as the changing rooms have intimate spaces with a quality of isolation. They contrast with the higher and larger public spaces.

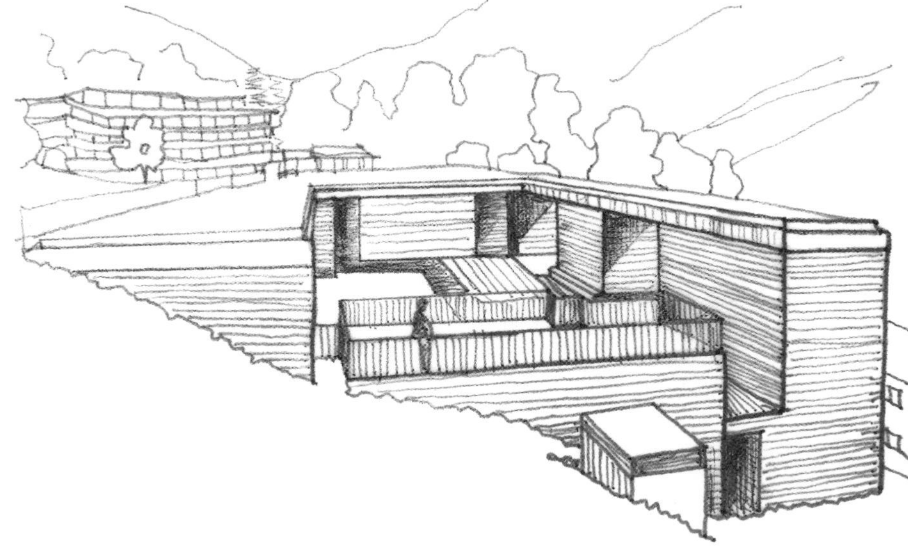

27 Thermal Baths in Vals | 1986–96

Peter Zumthor
Vals, Switzerland

Framed views: exterior experience

The view of the outdoor pool with its horizontal lines fits in harmoniously with the surrounding nature.

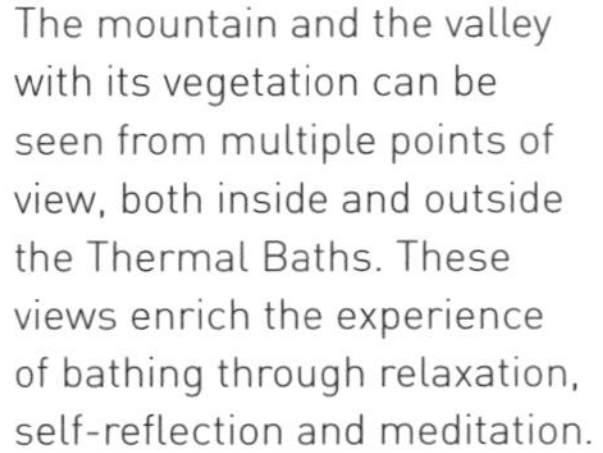

The mountain and the valley with its vegetation can be seen from multiple points of view, both inside and outside the Thermal Baths. These views enrich the experience of bathing through relaxation, self-reflection and meditation.

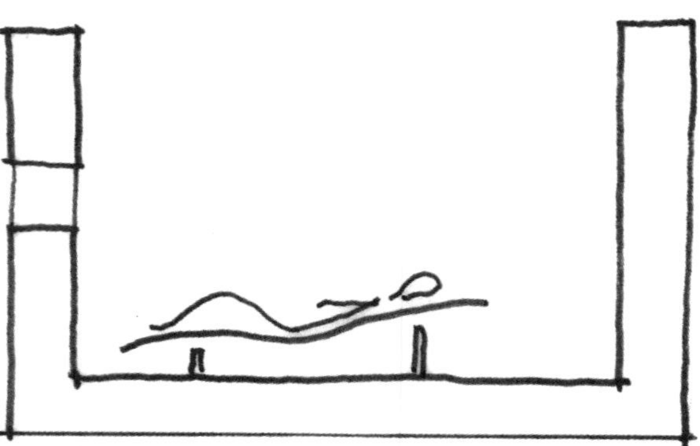

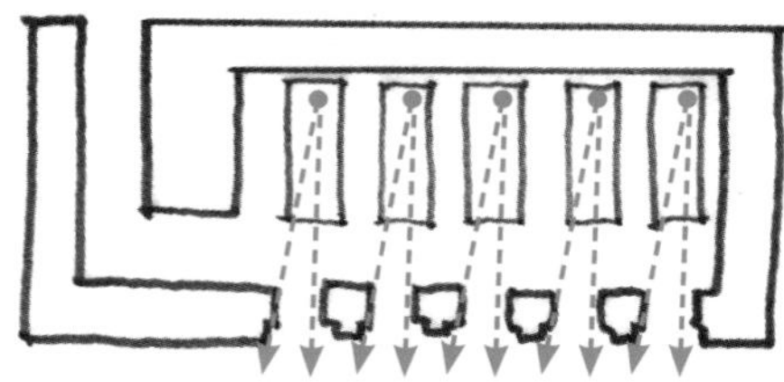

Views

In contrast to circulation, views to the outside are controlled through design in an attempt to guide visitors towards desired scenes.

Interior experience: isolation, revealing/concealing

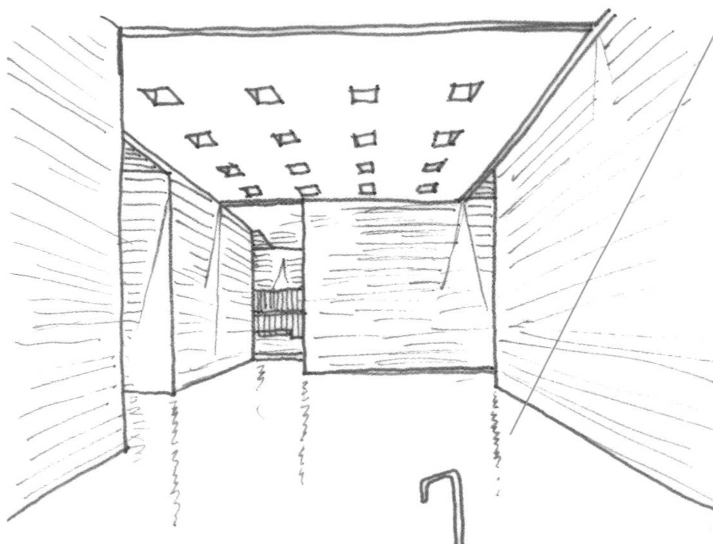

The interior space of the Thermal Baths is sensuous, quiet and primordial. With textured walls and water of different temperatures, it is a tactile environment for personal reflection. The indoor pool, surrounded by stone units, feels like a private space, despite its size that allows movement in many directions.

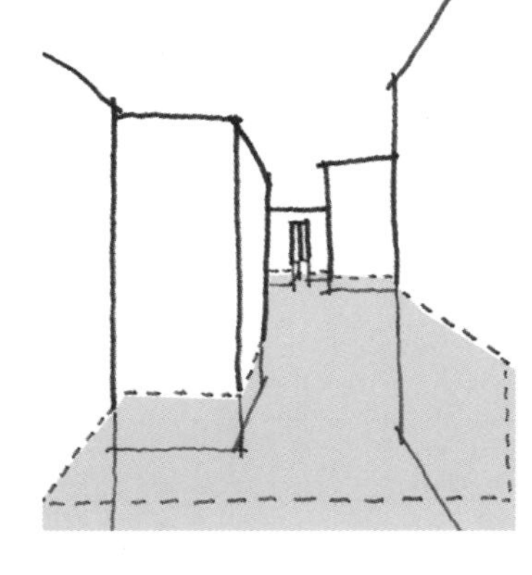

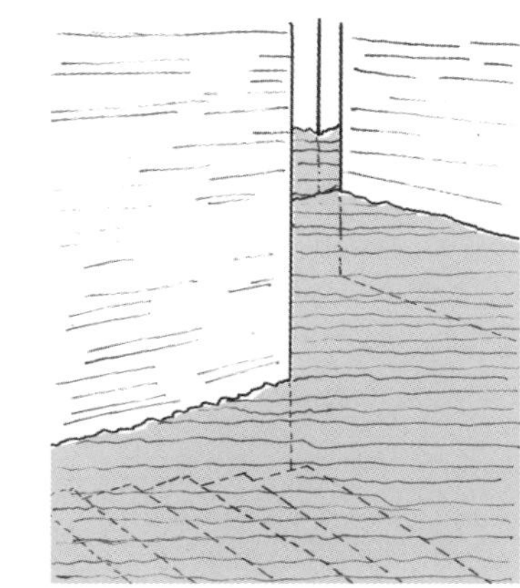

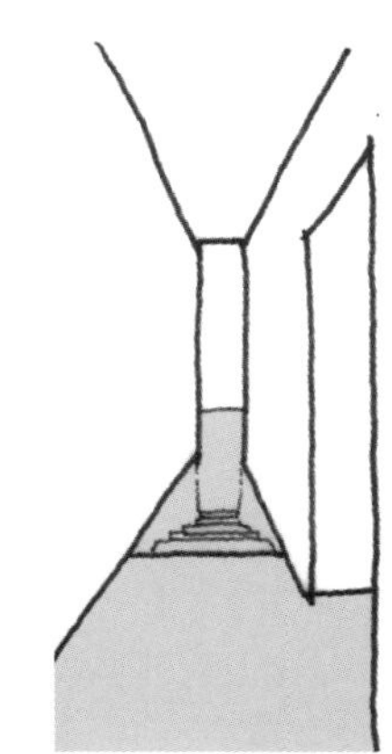

Levelling Multi-level floor plates add to a visitor's sense of bodily movement and exploration.

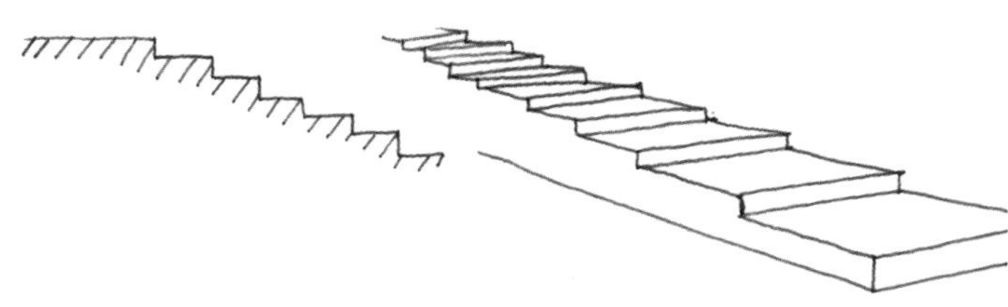

Isolation Isolated spaces create areas for self-reflection and segregation from public areas. This quality is amplified through narrow corridors and changes in ceiling heights.

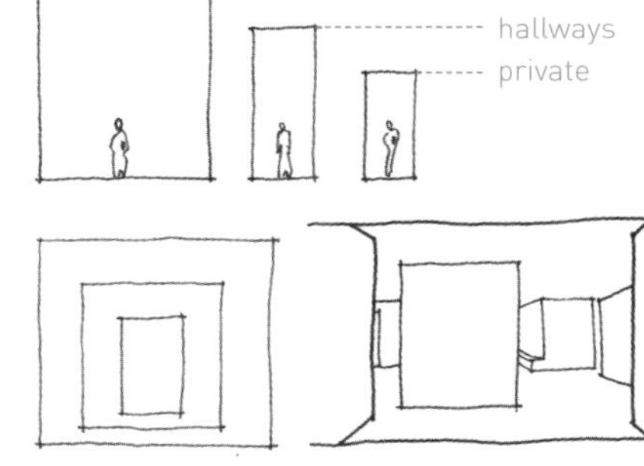

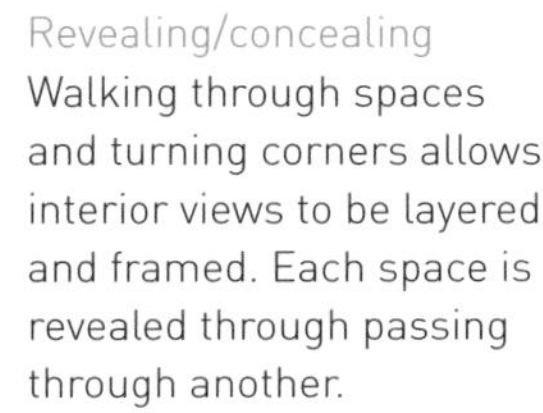

Steps The low steps that descend in long strides contribute to bathing as a process. Entering the water is a ritual.

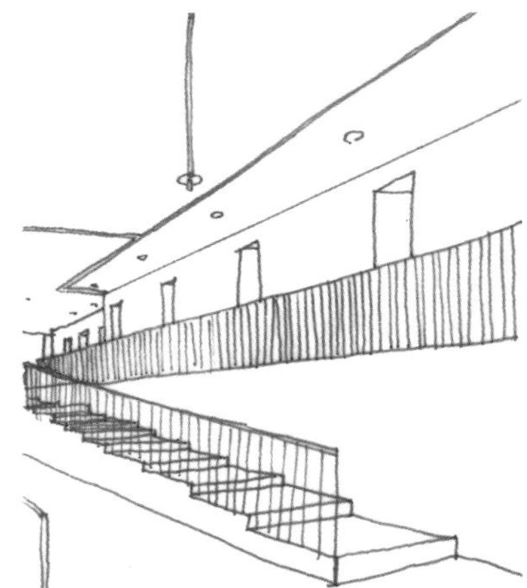

Revealing/concealing Walking through spaces and turning corners allows interior views to be layered and framed. Each space is revealed through passing through another.

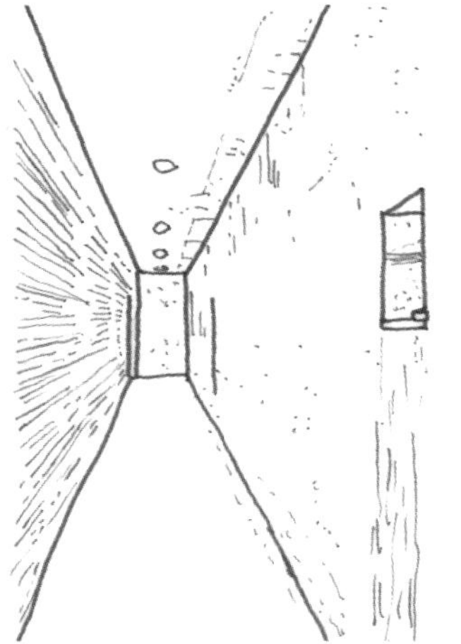

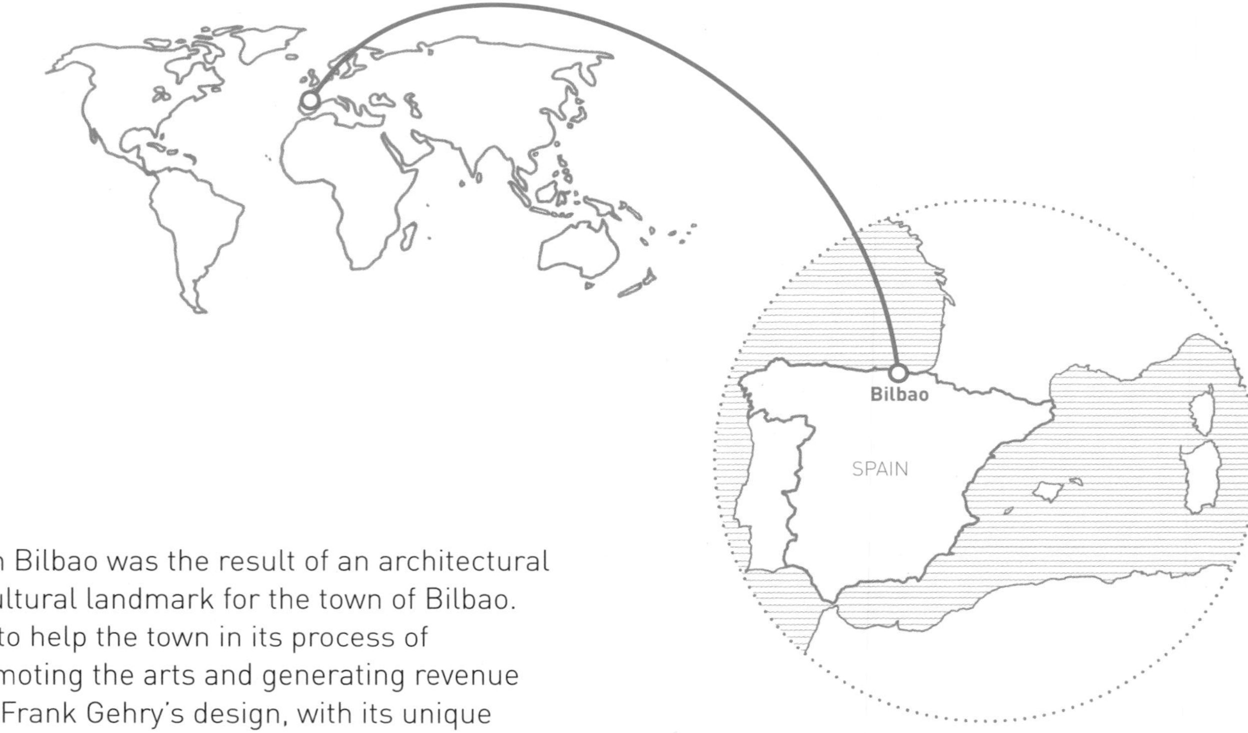

28

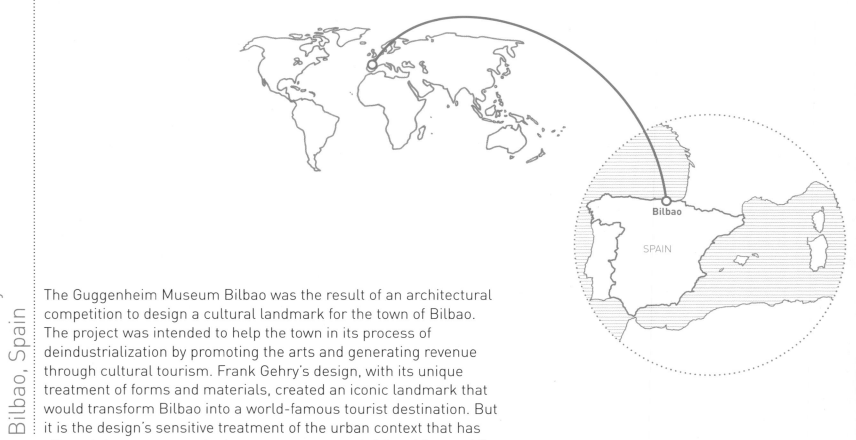

Guggenheim Museum Bilbao | 1991–97

Frank O. Gehry & Associates

Bilbao, Spain

The Guggenheim Museum Bilbao was the result of an architectural competition to design a cultural landmark for the town of Bilbao. The project was intended to help the town in its process of deindustrialization by promoting the arts and generating revenue through cultural tourism. Frank Gehry's design, with its unique treatment of forms and materials, created an iconic landmark that would transform Bilbao into a world-famous tourist destination. But it is the design's sensitive treatment of the urban context that has allowed the museum to become a monument of civic pride, providing the city with a sense of identity.

The design extends this interplay between the two roles of the building as a cultural artefact and as a functional object to other aspects of the built form, and various elements of the programme and the envelope are rethought and modified in response to one another.

Amit Srivastava, Brent Michael Eddy, Simon Ho and Lana Greer

28

28 Guggenheim Museum Bilbao | 1991–97

Frank O. Gehry & Associates
Bilbao, Spain

Response to urban context

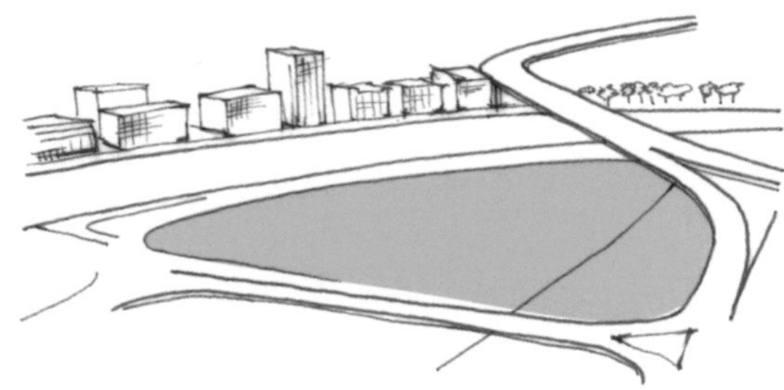

The triangular site is located on the city edge along the Nervión River, with La Salve Bridge city access cutting across one corner.

In response to the triangular nature of the site and the strong presence of a river and a bridge as edge conditions, the design is developed as three radiating arms that reach out towards various elements of the urban landscape and bring them together through a tall sculptural focal point. Views from important urban landmarks are maintained, while the sculptural forms of the building also respond to the immediate surroundings. The sculptural forms along the river edge extend under the bridge and rise up on the other side, including it into the folds of the building's design and forming a gateway into the city.

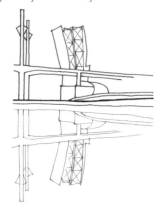

The sculptural tower along with La Salve Bridge forms a gateway to the city. The form itself takes cues from the river and resembles a sail captured in motion.

The design competition for the Guggenheim Museum Bilbao aimed from the start to make an iconic cultural landmark, not only to promote the arts and make the city a centre for cultural tourism, but also to create a monument of civic pride to bring together the disparate parts of the city and give them a sense of collective identity. The Bilbao project is thus deeply rooted in its urban context and serves as a centre that holds everything together.

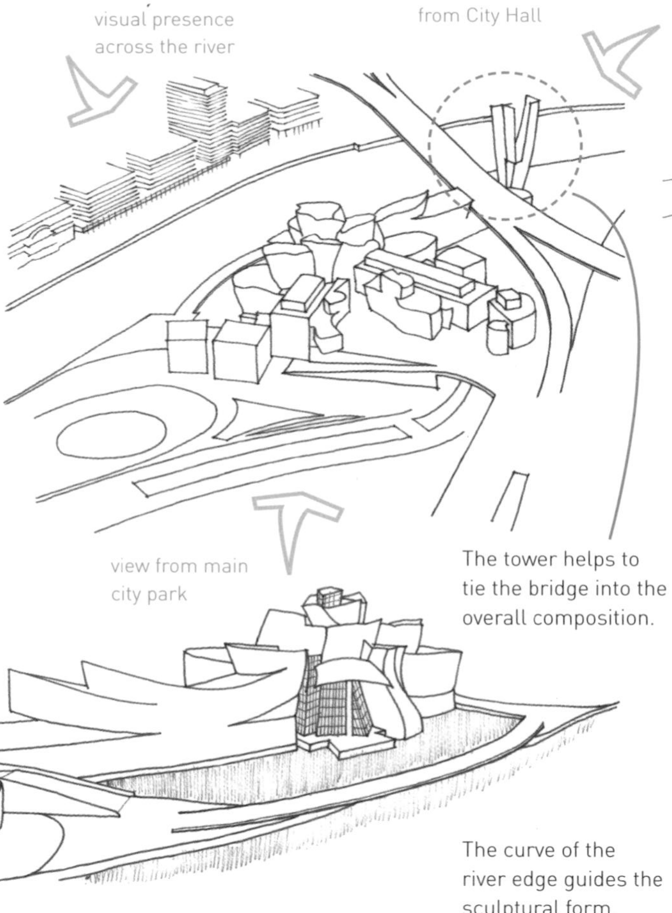

The tower helps to tie the bridge into the overall composition.

The curve of the river edge guides the sculptural form.

Along the river edge, the overall form is curved to align with the flow of water. A reflective metal cladding is used to build on the reflectiveness of the river surface, so that the entire design seems to rise out of the geography of the site.

The two orthogonal wings open up to embrace the connection towards the city and generate a large open public plaza.

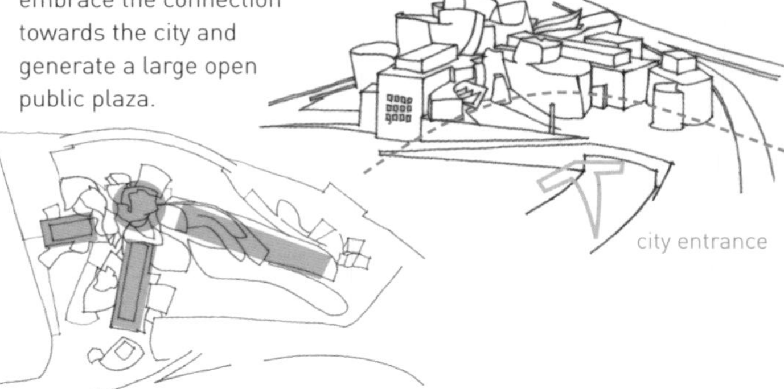

Two rectilinear blocks (facing the city) and a long sculptural gallery (along the river) radiate out from a towering central entrance hall.

On approach from the city, the sculptural metal forms floating above the stone buildings create a bold urban landmark.

To better integrate the design with the existing city fabric, the two wings facing the city are developed as rectilinear blocks and finished in stone to correspond to the surrounding buildings. The dialogue between the old and the new is maintained by increasing the height of the sculptural metallic forms on the river side such that they hover above the stone façade of the city wings and discreetly announce the arrival of the new. The function of sculptural elements such as the 60-metre (197-foot) high tower is to define an urban landmark.

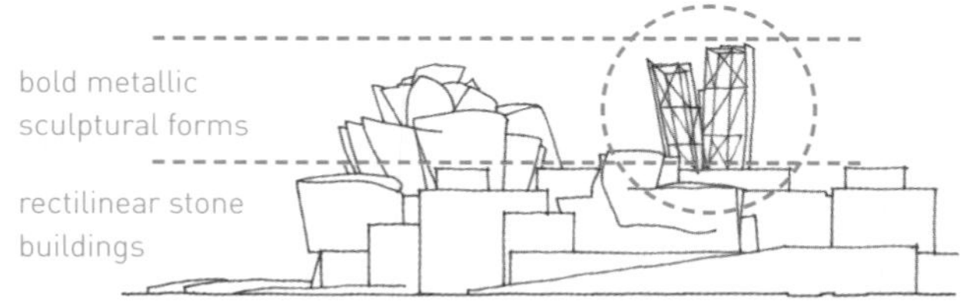

Wrapping the programme in plan

The overall design can be seen as responsive interplay between the programme and the envelope. The building is designed as an aggregation of simple plan forms serving separate programmatic requirements, brought together through a central shared space and wrapped in a single envelope.

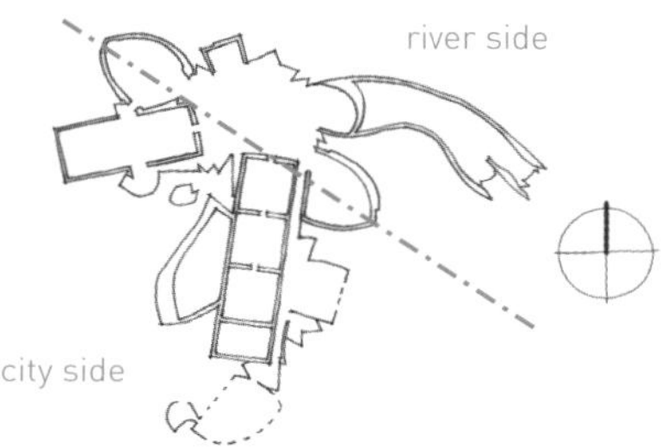

The two city-side galleries and the curved river-side gallery are distributed across a diagonal axis.

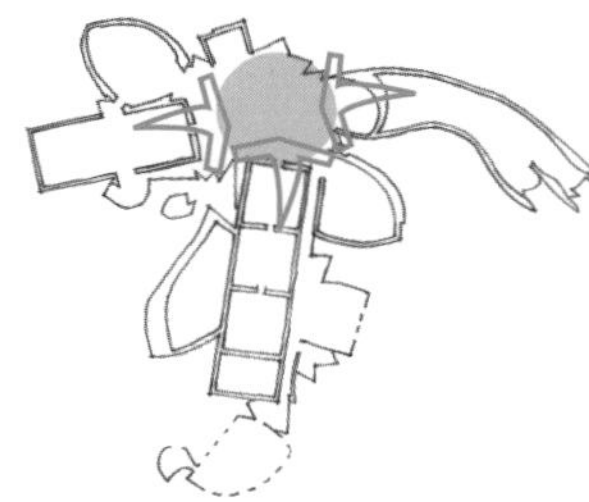

The three spaces are brought together through a depressed central atrium space that acts as a vortex.

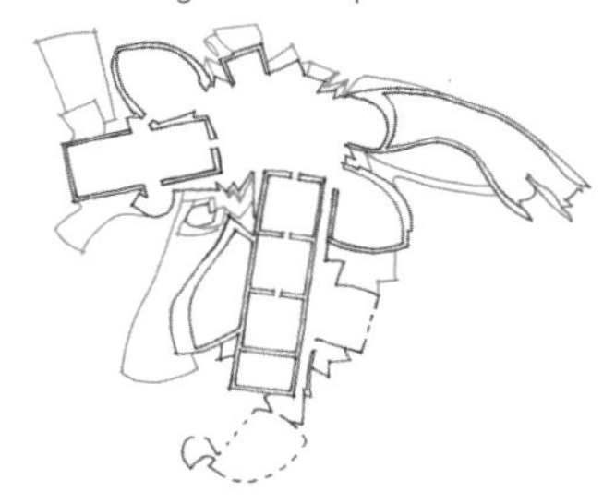

The disparate parts of the programme are then wrapped in a titanium skin to form a cohesive whole.

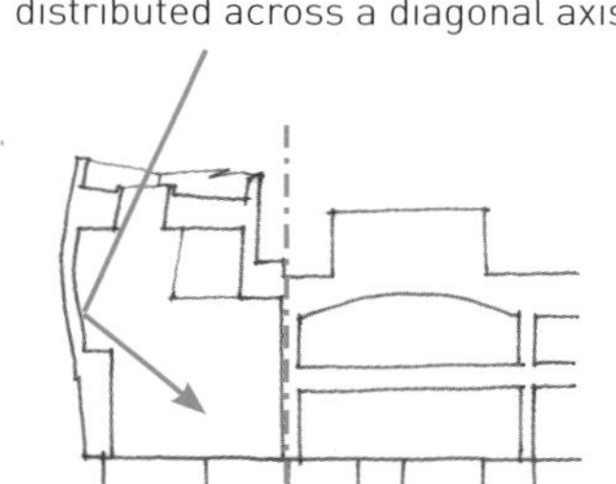

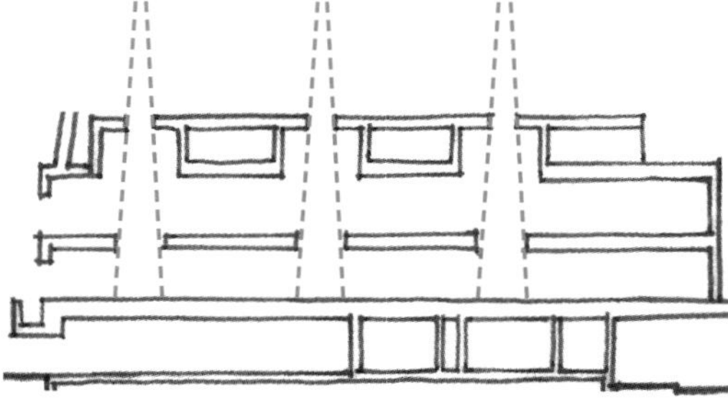

Skylights provide natural light, leaving the envelope to serve a different role as a wrapper.

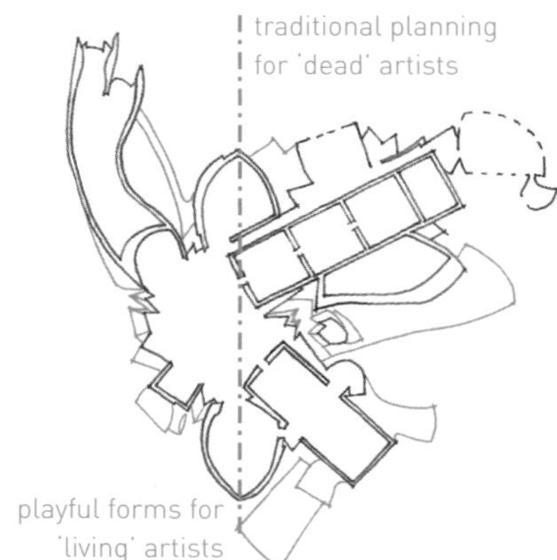

The planning allows for the coexistence of different kinds of spaces that serve different purposes. For instance, the simple orthogonal forms of the city-side galleries are based on traditional space-planning principles and are used to house the work of 'dead' artists, while the playful forms of the river-side gallery generate a lively dialogue with the artworks of living artists. Here the response to the building programme is not dictated by a preconceived notion of traditional building form. Both traditional and avant-garde plan forms are brought together to serve the programmatic requirements as a cohesive whole.

Roof as a sculptural umbrella

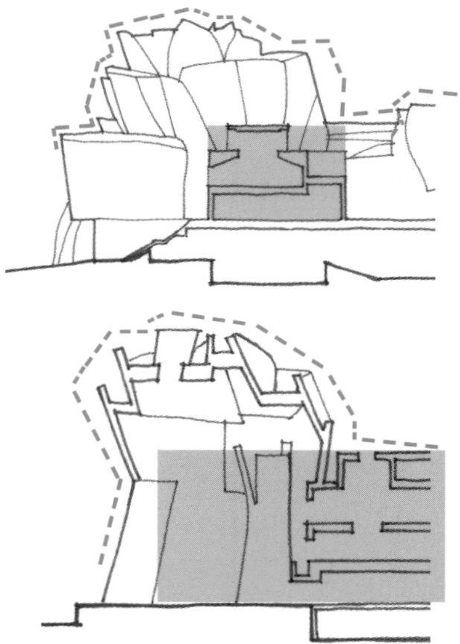

The two aspects of the programme and the envelope are shown in the treatment of the plan and the roof respectively. Here the plan and the roof enter into a dialogue as generators of overall form. Using the plan as a traditional form generator, the overall building section is first developed through a simple extrusion of the plan, defining the external walls. This simple extruded form is then eroded by the biomorphic forms of the sculptural roof as they extend downwards, to generate interesting internal volumes.

The biomorphic forms of the curved roof are seemingly draped over the orthogonal extrusions of the plan, and the overall form is developed as a responsive interplay between these two elements. On the exterior this dialogue is expressed through an interplay of materials where the metal roof floats above the stone base like a sculptural umbrella.

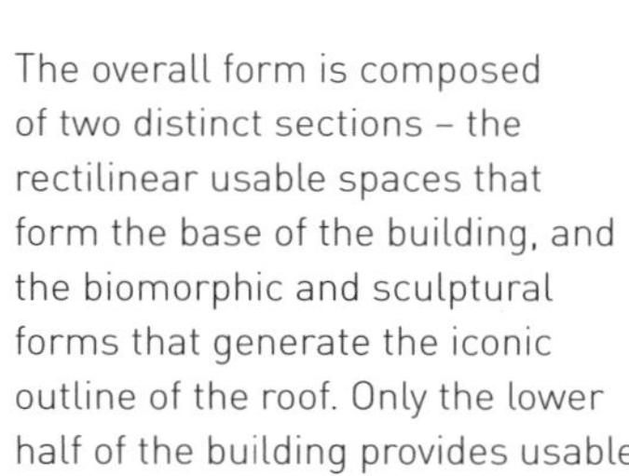

The overall form is composed of two distinct sections – the rectilinear usable spaces that form the base of the building, and the biomorphic and sculptural forms that generate the iconic outline of the roof. Only the lower half of the building provides usable floor space.

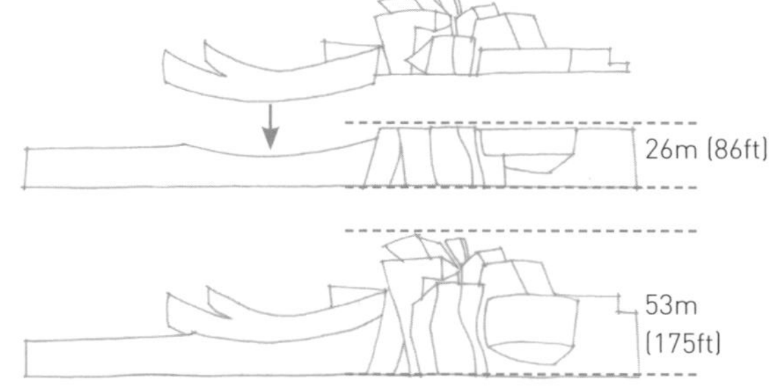

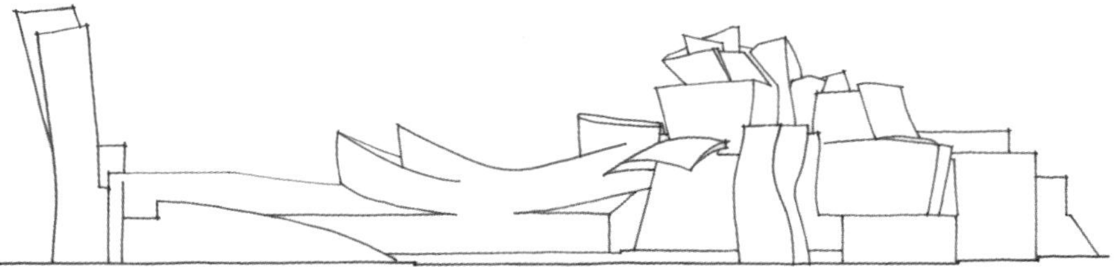

The composition, where the biomorphic metal umbrella roof drapes over an orthogonal and functional base, allows for an iconic and sculptural urban landmark to emerge out of a simple aggregative plan addressing the programme's requirements.

28

Guggenheim Museum Bilbao | 1991–97

Frank O. Gehry & Associates

Bilbao, Spain

Memory, analogy and form

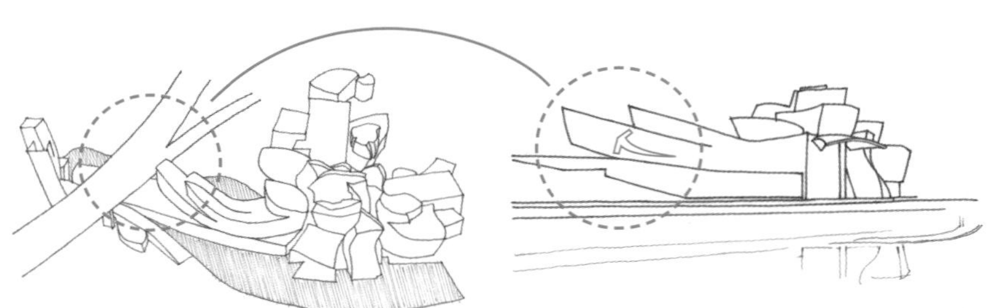

The curved plan form along the river edge is further developed to generate an analogical connection to the city's past. Here the upper levels of the gallery are slightly lifted towards the sky to give it the appearance of a ship's hull. This nautical imagery is appropriate given the city's history as an industrialized maritime centre whose early fortunes were derived from its nineteenth-century shipbuilding industries.

Framing views and access

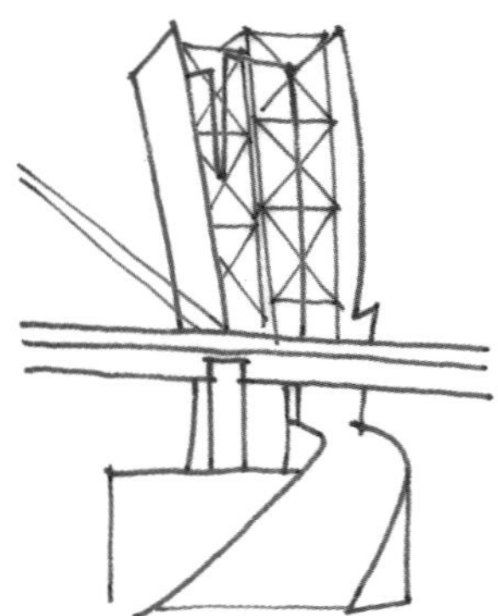

The ramp helps to build the monumental quality of the tower, while the footbridge along the river edge provides a vantage point to step away from the building and view the shiplike forms of the gallery.

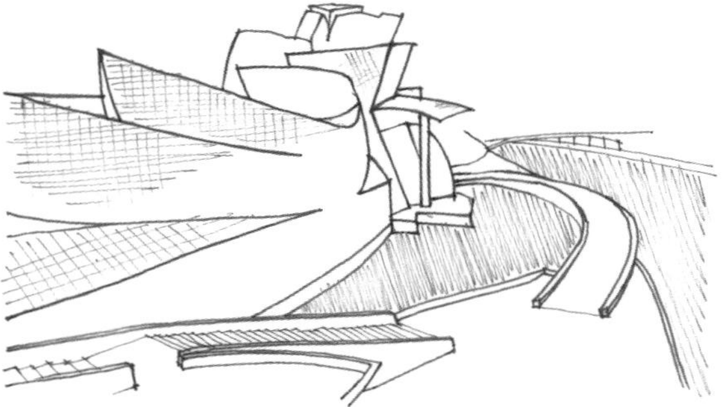

Large plazas offer the requisite space to observe the formal composition.

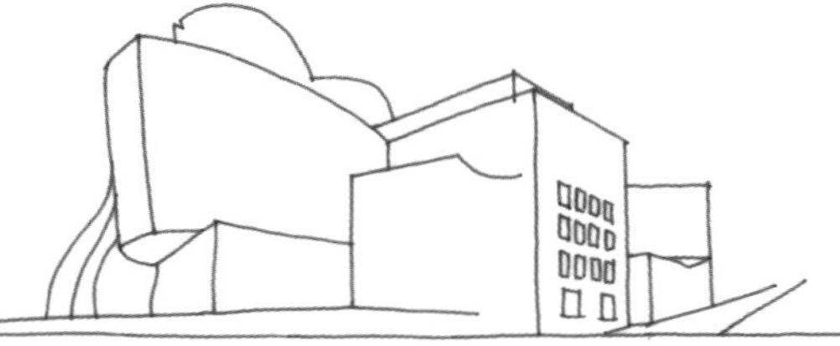

The analogical and compositional aspects of the overall form are supported through a careful orchestration of approaches that frame the views and experiences for the observer. Along the river edge, a pedestrian footbridge takes people away from the building and aligns them with a vantage point perfect for experiencing the shiplike form of the building. Another ramp leads up towards the soaring sail-like forms of the tower. Towards the city, the large urban plaza provides the foreground space needed to appreciate the overall composition of the rectilinear stone and the curved titanium forms.

Form and effect

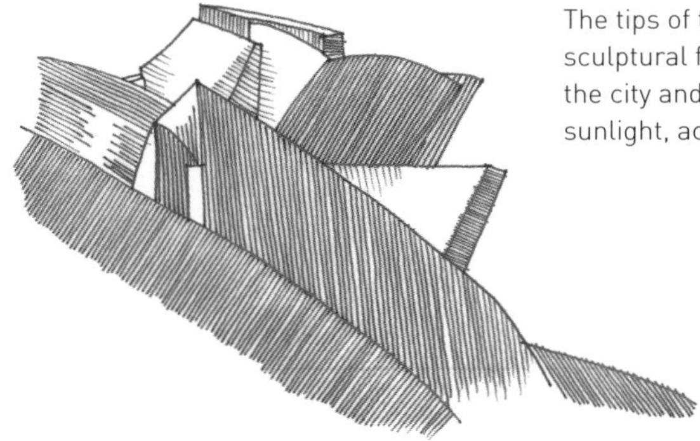

The tips of the dynamic and sculptural form rise above the city and shimmer in the sunlight, acting as a beacon.

The form of a fish serves as an analogy dynamism and energy

To serve its complex role as a vibrant landmark the building resorts to a dynamic formal composition. Gehry uses the analogy of a fish, whose contorting forms are abstracted and captured in the elevation. The analogy builds on the nautical theme of the ship and the dynamism of the river, but also works to enhance the effect of the metal skin. The contorted forms draped with the metal skin are in a state of perpetual change as they respond to the movement of the observer and of the sun across the sky.

Abstraction creates dynamic building form.

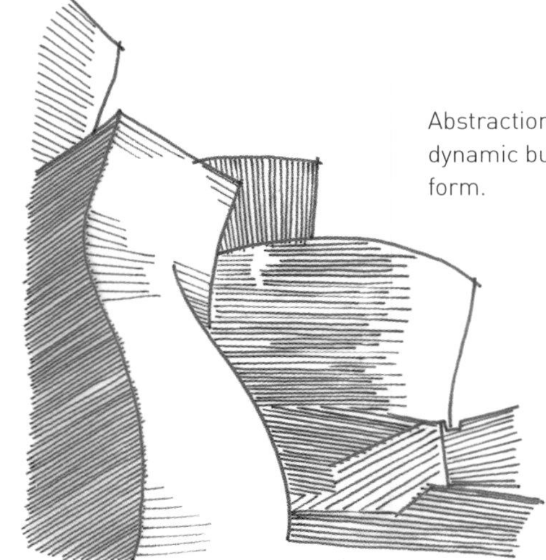

The contorted form and the metal skin create a dynamic composition that responds to light and movement.

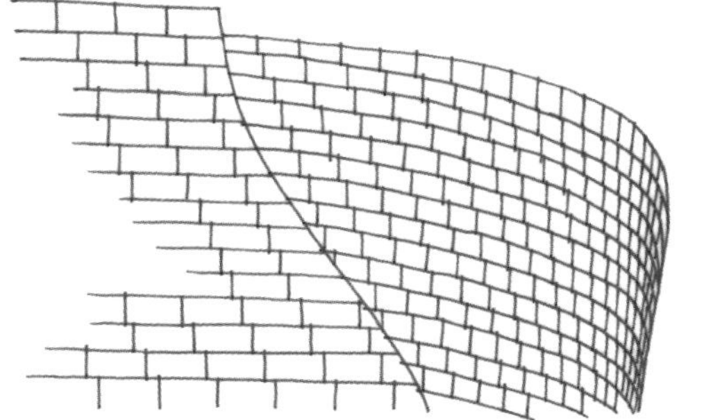

The texture generated by the overlapping titanium panels further mimics the scales of a fish and extends the analogy. The shallow dent created by the fixing clip for each of the panels enhances the shimmering effect as the surface appears to ripple in the sunlight. The textural play of the titanium against glass and stone enlivens the entire built mass.

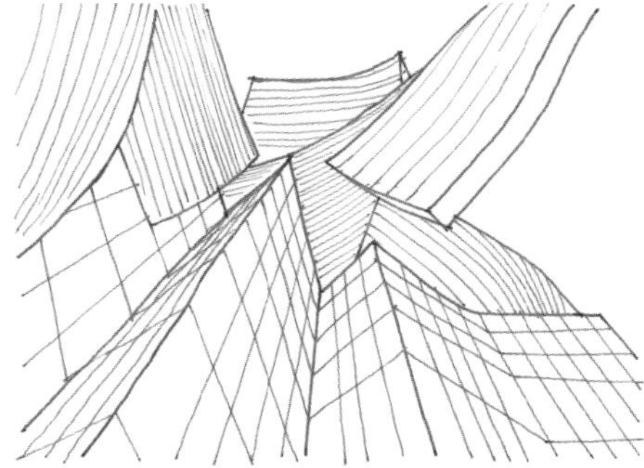

The curved lines of the titanium roof float above the glass curtain wall.

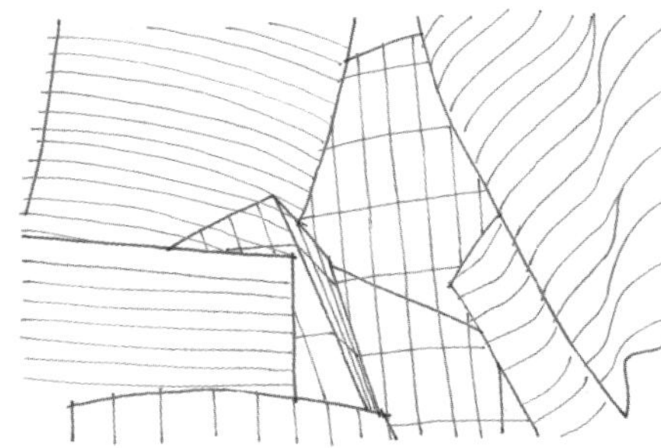

The warped and straight lines of titanium, glass and stone meet to create a dynamic composition.

Visitor experience

As a visitor approaches the building, the patterns of the overall form give way to other details that correspond to the human scale. This is clearly evident in the treatment of the entrances. While on the river side a large canopy supported by a monumental pillar announces the presence of the central entrance lobby, on the city side the entrance is hidden and a visitor is forced to descend below the plaza level. Here Gehry employs a well-established architectural technique whereby a visitor is taken through a compressed space before being released into an awe-inspiring monumental interior. Accordingly, the visitor arrives at the base of the central atrium, whose monumental character is enhanced by the basement-level entry. The more than 50-metre (165-foot) high space is also a reference to the grand central volume of the Guggenheim Museum in New York, designed by Frank Lloyd Wright in the 1950s.

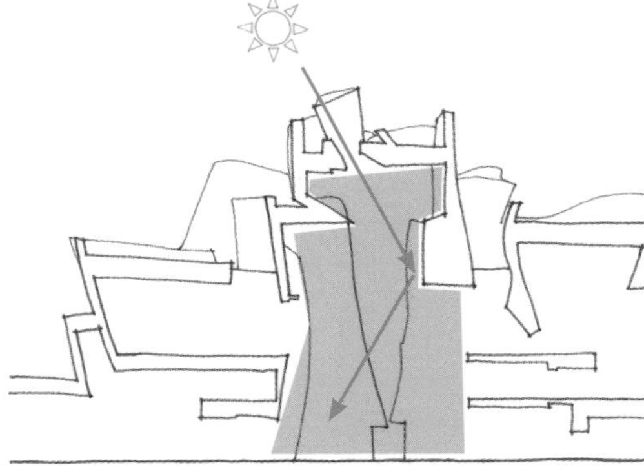

The lobby carries the textural details of the titanium, stone and glass into the interior.

The lobby area brings the textural interplay into the interior, binding the overall visitor experience. While these textures are muted in the display spaces, the gallery for the 'living' artists follows the lead of the Guggenheim Museum in New York as a formal experiment in new interactions between architecture and artistic display.

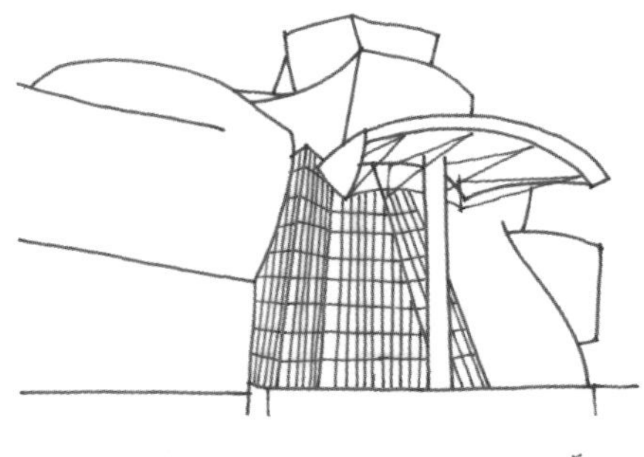

Towards the river, a large canopy marks the presence of the central entrance lobby.

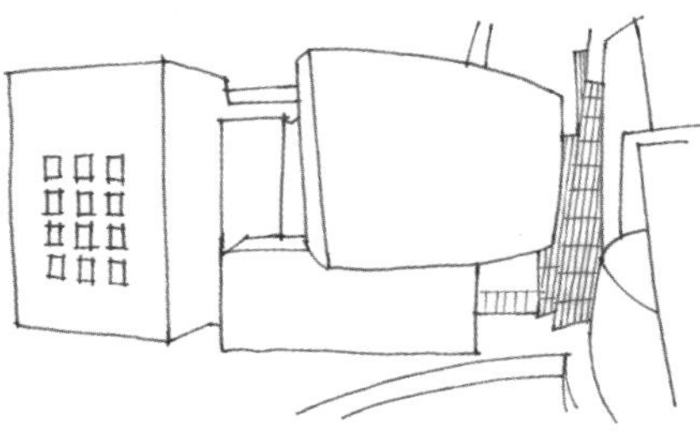

Towards the city, the entrance is obscured and the visitor is obliged to descend below the plaza level.

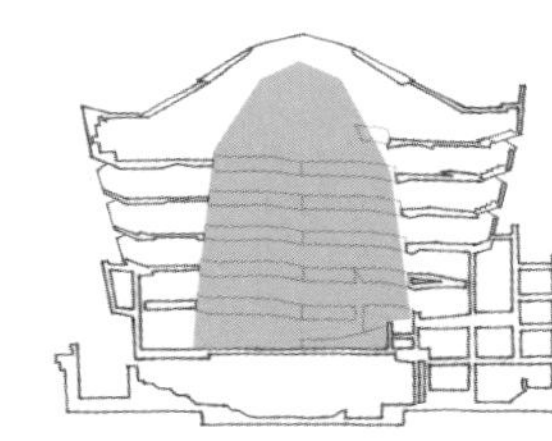

Visitors are released into a vast interior space (above left) reminiscent of the Guggenheim Museum in New York (above).

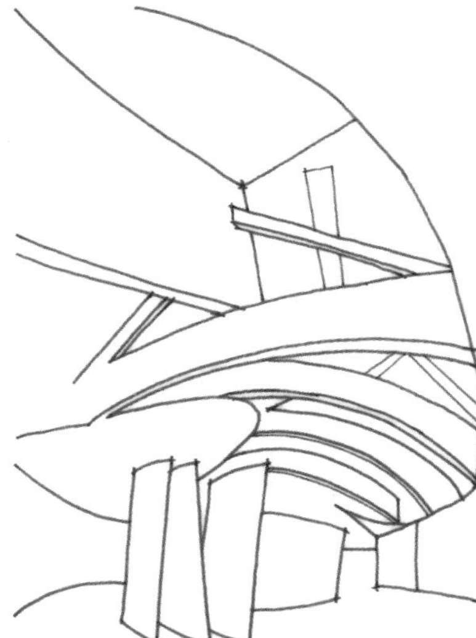

The gallery of the 'living' artists echoes the ideals of Wright's Guggenheim by creating a space that is in dialogue with the art.

ESO Hotel | 1998–2002

Auer+Weber

Cerro Paranal, Chile

29

Cerro Paranal

CHILE

The ESO Hotel is a residential facility for employees and guests of the European Southern Observatory (ESO) stationed at a remote astronomical observatory on the top of Cerro Paranal, a 2635-metre (8645-foot) high mountain in northern Chile. The main objectives of the design were to cope with a harsh arid climate, to have a low impact on the natural landscape, to counter the effects of seismic activity, and most importantly to avoid any light pollution at night that would have an impact on the work of the observatory.

The design by German architects Auer+Weber adopts strong geometric shapes – rectangles and a circle – that contrast with the curves of the local topography, and beds the building low across a natural valley in a straight line from side to side. The effect is to draw attention to a strange, bare landscape by the insertion of a building with strong forms that match the landscape's scale and strength.

Katherine Snell, Michael Kin Pong Ng and Amit Srivastava

ESO Hotel | 1998–2002

Auer+Weber

Cerro Paranal, Chile

Response to natural landscape

As a residential facility for employees and guests of the European Southern Observatory (ESO), the ESO Hotel is not open to the general public. Accordingly, the design of the building takes an approach to the site that aims to create a somewhat hidden sanctuary nestled within the folds of the undulating landscape.

The entire facility is designed to sit within a natural valley with only the central dome rising above the horizon. This approach ensures minimal visual impact on the context, and also that the built block does not interrupt the breathtaking views of the landscape. While the siting of the building ensures a nonobtrusive response to the context, the use of a strict rectilinear profile creates enough contrast against the undulating forms of the hills for visual interest and to demarcate the presence of civilization within the surrounding wilderness.

view towards
Pacific Ocean

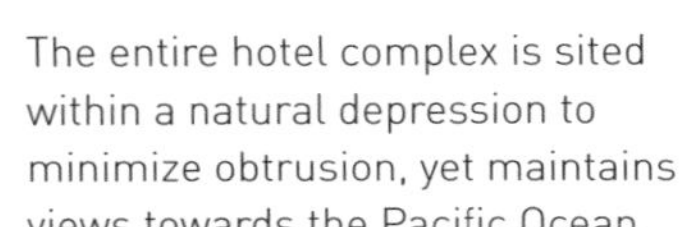

The entire hotel complex is sited within a natural depression to minimize obtrusion, yet maintains views towards the Pacific Ocean.

Response to the observatory complex

The ESO complex is home to some of the largest earth-based telescopes, and the design intervention for the hotel takes this central operative task of the observatory into account. The design ensures that any light source within the hotel complex does not interfere with the operations of the telescopes. The siting of the hotel in an existing depression itself reduces the surfaces through which light can escape, but the central dome structure with its skylight can still emit some residual light. This is countered through the inclusion of a special shading feature that allows for a mechanical cover to be deployed within the dome to create a blackout when required at night.

The dome is the only part of the hotel visible above the horizon. The entrance is down a ramp from the north-east.

The natural depression is used to define the building's sectional profile, with only the dome extending above a common roofline.

The uncompromising straight line of the building profile offers contrast with the curved profiles of the hills, while the use of iron-oxide-coloured concrete helps the building to blend into the landscape.

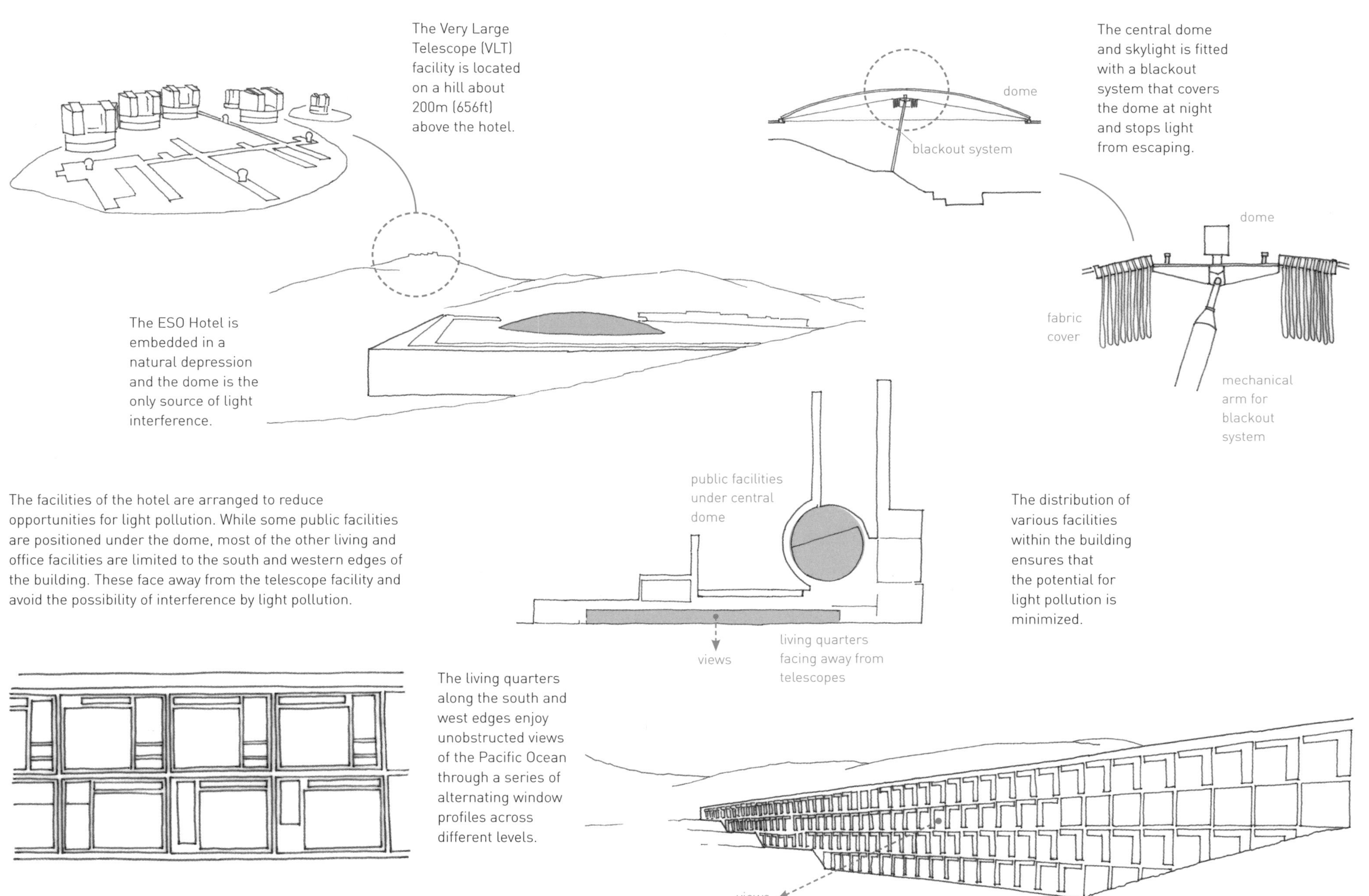

The Very Large Telescope (VLT) facility is located on a hill about 200m (656ft) above the hotel.
The central dome and skylight is fitted with a blackout system that covers the dome at night and stops light from escaping.
dome
blackout system
dome
fabric cover
mechanical arm for blackout system
The ESO Hotel is embedded in a natural depression and the dome is the only source of light interference.
public facilities under central dome
views
living quarters facing away from telescopes
The distribution of various facilities within the building ensures that the potential for light pollution is minimized.
The living quarters along the south and west edges enjoy unobstructed views of the Pacific Ocean through a series of alternating window profiles across different levels.
views

The facilities of the hotel are arranged to reduce opportunities for light pollution. While some public facilities are positioned under the dome, most of the other living and office facilities are limited to the south and western edges of the building. These face away from the telescope facility and avoid the possibility of interference by light pollution.

Response to a harsh arid climate

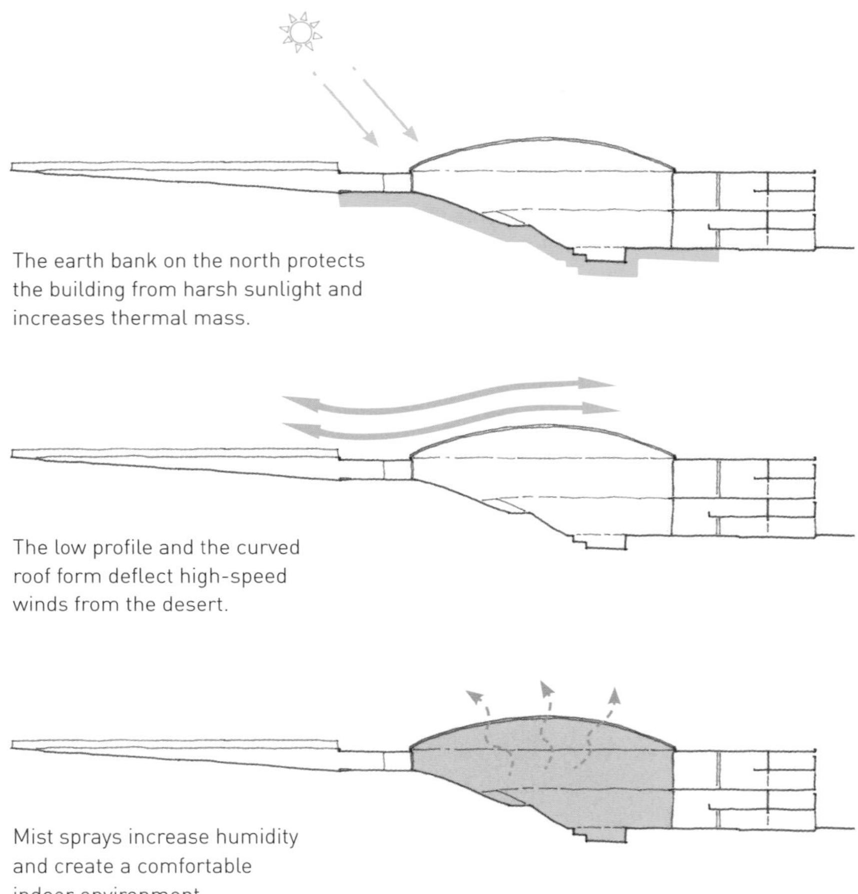

The earth bank on the north protects the building from harsh sunlight and increases thermal mass.

The low profile and the curved roof form deflect high-speed winds from the desert.

Mist sprays increase humidity and create a comfortable indoor environment.

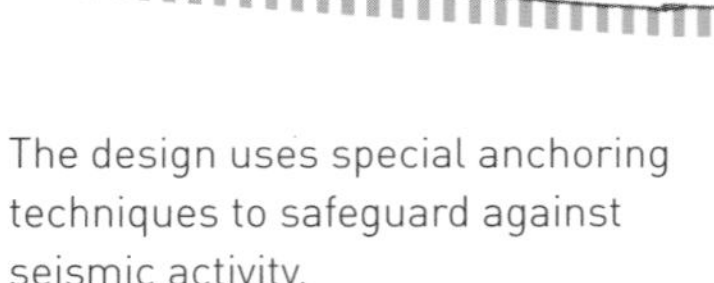

The design uses special anchoring techniques to safeguard against seismic activity.

The ESO complex is located in the arid environment of northern Chile near the Atacama Desert. The desert is prone to intense sunlight, but the siting of the hotel structure within the depression in the earth reduces exposure. The thermal mass of the surrounding earth further moderates heat gain. . The main exposed face of the building is on the south side and, being in the southern hemisphere, receives little sunlight.

The site is also exposed to high-speed winds travelling from the Andes ranges in the east to the Pacific Ocean in the west. Coming from the direction of the desert, these winds can reach high temperatures and need to be avoided. The low profile of the structure along with a curved dome helps to deflect the airflow and protect the interiors.

The arid climate is also a challenge, with low rainfall and a relative humidity as low at 5–10 per cent. In response the hotel features a sealed central dome area where mist sprays help to increase the humidity and make a comfortable environment. This controlled interior also helps to protect against the extreme temperature changes of the desert climate.

As the region is prone to seismic activity, the design incorporates a technique by which concrete blocks are anchored to the ground with fibreglass mats to absorb any movement. Also, the complex is conceived as a series of smaller buildings rather than one large structure, so as to reduce the impact of earthquakes.

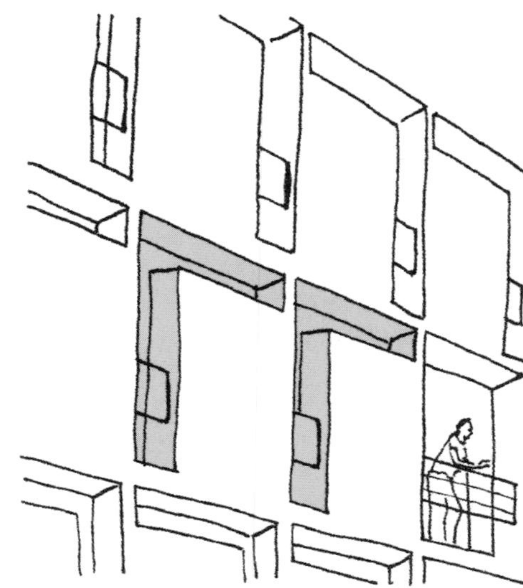

The small windows along the south and west façades protect against heat gain and provide glimpses of the harsh desert environment outside.

ESO Hotel | 1998–2002
Auer+Weber
Cerro Paranal, Chile

29

Response to users – an oasis in the desert

The entire design of the hotel is structured around a central retreat space that allows the scientists and other staff working at the observatory an opportunity to relax. The various programmatic requirements for individual residential facilities, offices and communal areas such as the dining room are all organized around this shared retreat facility. The spatial organization of functions means that this retreat space can be accessed from any part of the hotel, and serves as the heart of the composition. To add to the sense of arrival and enhance the experience of escape, the access to this large double-storey area with its spacious sky-lit dome is organized through a series of narrow, dimly lit, rectilinear pathways that connect it to various other facilities.

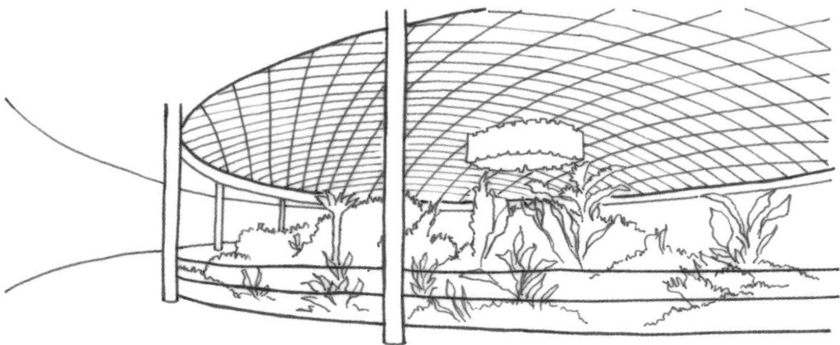

The double-height domed space in the centre helps to tie the entire complex together.

Since most of the staff working at the observatory are not from the local area, the hotel endeavours to provide them with an opportunity to escape the experience of being in a harsh desert climate. This central retreat space, thus, not only offers an escape from the technologically oriented work environment of the observatory, but also provides a tropical oasis in which to escape the experience of the desert. The oasis is complete with a range of tropical plants and a swimming pool, allowing visitors to spend their time away from work in a safe and comfortable environment that aids their rest. The semitransparent dome acts like a greenhouse and the plants and pool help to increase the humidity of the interior. In addition, mechanical misters spray water and add to the tropical feel of this oasis. The raw treatment of the materials in the interior helps to maintain an earthy feel and enhances the overall experience of this retreat space.

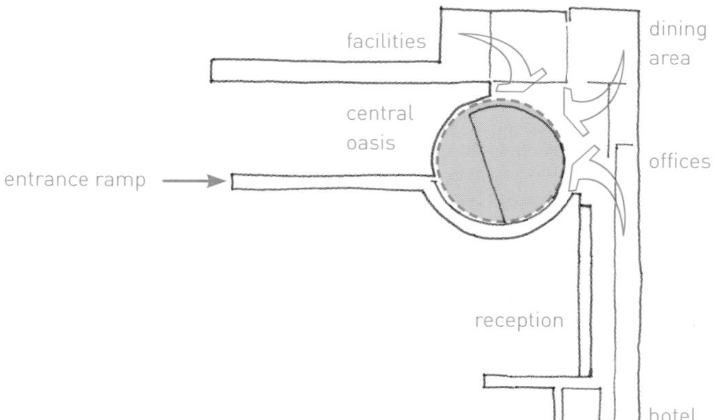

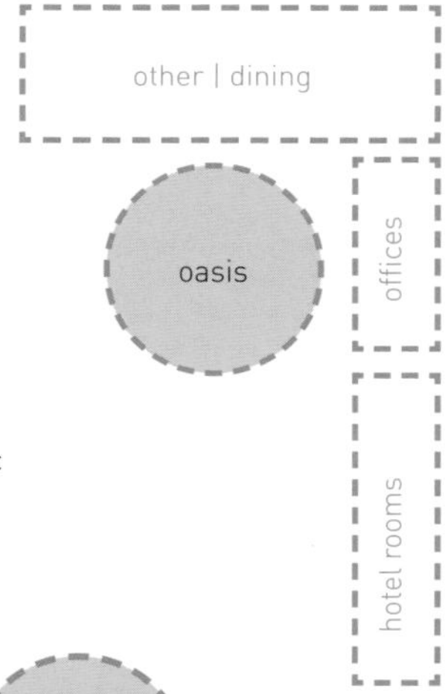

facilities
dining area
central oasis
entrance ramp
offices
reception
hotel rooms

other | dining
oasis
offices
hotel rooms

Spatial organization of functions

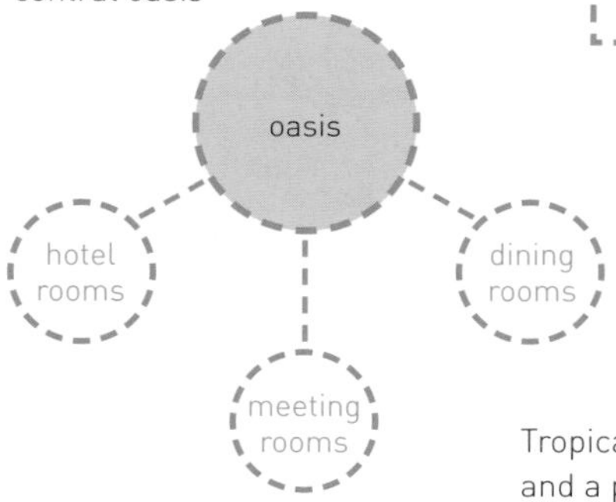

Programmatic diagram structured around a central oasis

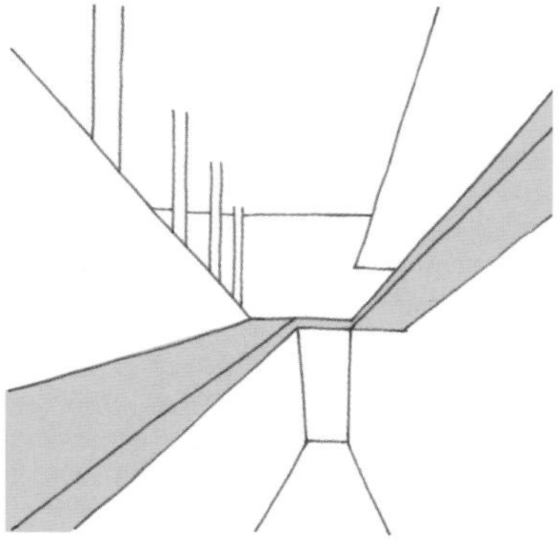

oasis
hotel rooms
dining rooms
meeting rooms

Thin dimly lit pathways connect different levels to the large interior of the central oasis space and help to create a sense of arrival.

Tropical plants and a pool help to create an oasis in the desert.

Arthur and Yvonne Boyd Education Centre | 1996–99

Murcutt Lewin Lark

Riversdale, New South Wales, Australia

Australian painter Arthur Boyd and his wife, Yvonne, donated their property in the Australian countryside south of Sydney to the nation as a centre for all the arts. The Arthur and Yvonne Boyd Education Centre (AYBEC) is a place for primary and secondary school children to 'camp', to enjoy this place of native plants and animals, sandstone and river, and to engage with the arts. The architects were Glenn Murcutt, Wendy Lewin and Reg Lark.

The building is crafted with an elegant order and clarity in both whole and details. Internally, cohesion follows from rational planning and consistency in the way materials are used and in how details respond to their contexts. Externally, the building relates to its beautiful natural setting by contrast. It appears to have arrived without change or impact on the site, its linear order contrasting with the organic forms of nature.

Antony Radford, Verdy Kwee and Samuel Murphy.

30

30

Arthur and Yvonne Boyd Education Centre | 1996–99

Murcutt Lewin Lark

Riversdale, NSW, Australia

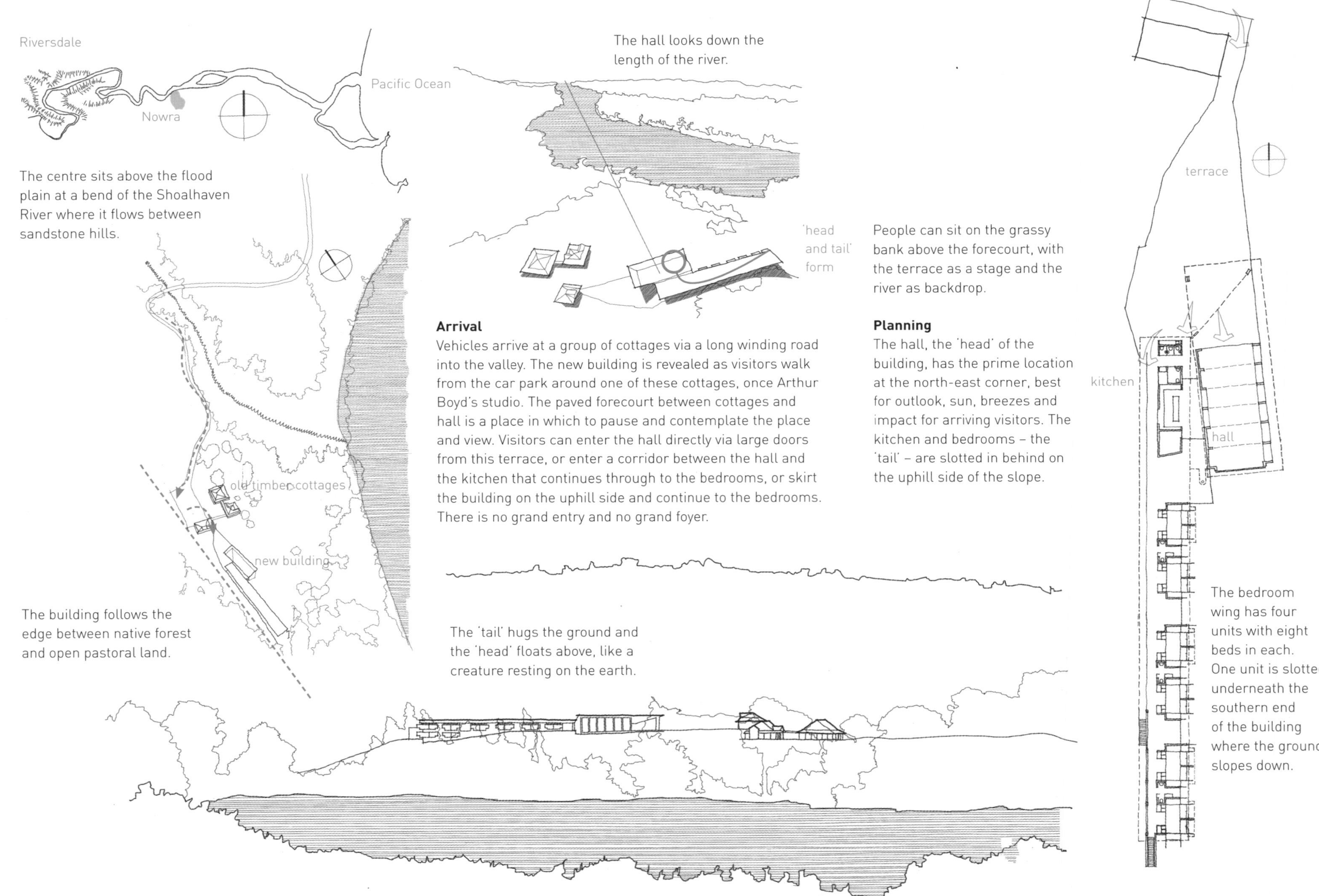

The centre sits above the flood plain at a bend of the Shoalhaven River where it flows between sandstone hills.

The building follows the edge between native forest and open pastoral land.

The hall looks down the length of the river.

Arrival

Vehicles arrive at a group of cottages via a long winding road into the valley. The new building is revealed as visitors walk from the car park around one of these cottages, once Arthur Boyd's studio. The paved forecourt between cottages and hall is a place in which to pause and contemplate the place and view. Visitors can enter the hall directly via large doors from this terrace, or enter a corridor between the hall and the kitchen that continues through to the bedrooms, or skirt the building on the uphill side and continue to the bedrooms. There is no grand entry and no grand foyer.

People can sit on the grassy bank above the forecourt, with the terrace as a stage and the river as backdrop.

Planning

The hall, the 'head' of the building, has the prime location at the north-east corner, best for outlook, sun, breezes and impact for arriving visitors. The kitchen and bedrooms – the 'tail' – are slotted in behind on the uphill side of the slope.

The 'tail' hugs the ground and the 'head' floats above, like a creature resting on the earth.

The bedroom wing has four units with eight beds in each. One unit is slotted underneath the southern end of the building where the ground slopes down.

The hall

The hall is used as a workplace and studio, as a dining room for up to eighty, and occasionally as a theatre or concert hall for more people. The sloping ceiling above the forecourt funnels north and north-east breezes to the main entry doors and into the widening volume of the corridor between the hall and kitchen, boosting natural ventilation where the building is deep and cross-ventilation hard to achieve.

Rainwater is collected from the hall and kitchen roofs and stored in a basement tank. The gutter projects beyond the building footprint to end in large funnels and downpipes. One is a sentry beside the veranda, the other marks the hinge where the head (hall) is angled to the tail (bedrooms). The formal qualities of the building's design are symbiotic with its functional operation.

A shade like an eyebrow wraps around the north and east edges of the roof.

Among hard surfaces, the leather binding on door handles is soft to the touch.

A downpipe appears to be a hinge point between the hall block and the bedroom/service block.

Vents are located in the corners at both ends of the hall.

Hatch to serve outside.

The columns and transoms of the hall place a grid over the landscape view.

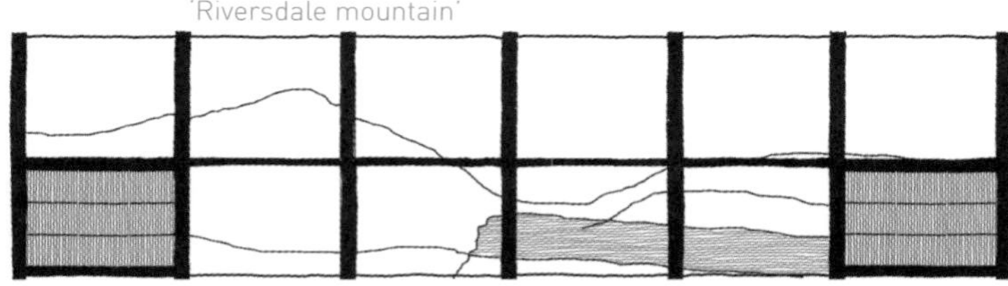
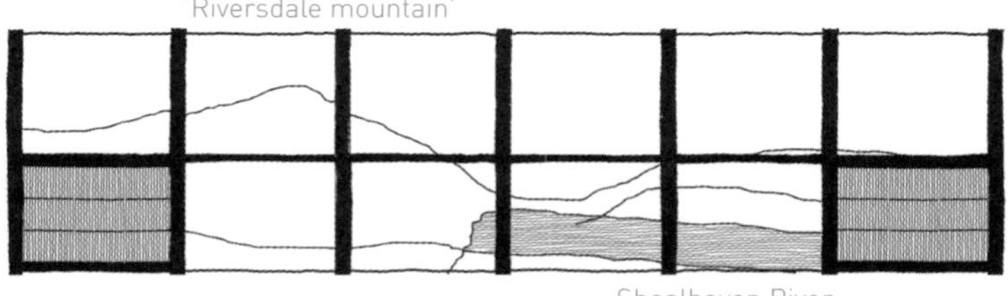

From outside: with screens and doors open the whole interior volume is apparent.

From inside: both light and the view are filtered by slatted timber screens. The slats are for acoustic reasons and can easily be removed for cleaning.

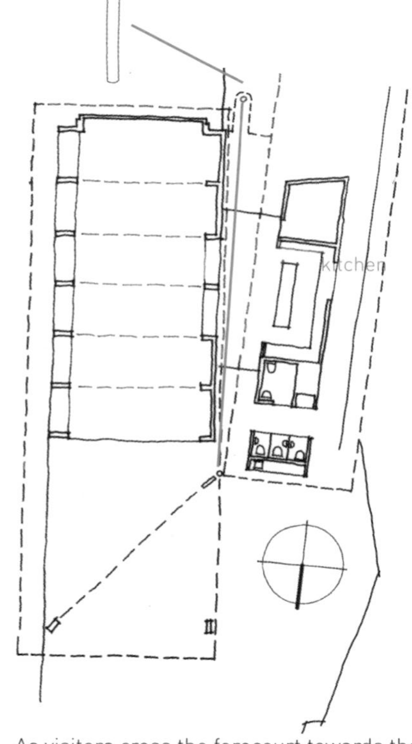

As visitors cross the forecourt towards the building they see on the left the dignified entry to the main hall, on the right a sink and draining board. The contrast is surprising and beautiful.

Concrete columns stop short of the ceiling, with a steel blade connecting to the roof structure.

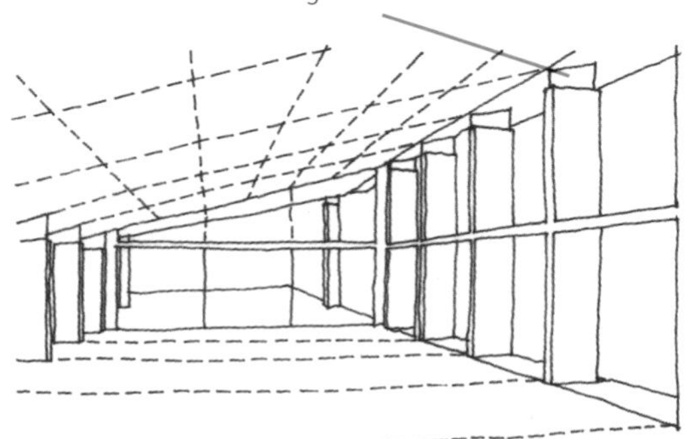

The structural grid is evident in the columns, door mullions, floor pattern and ceiling panels.

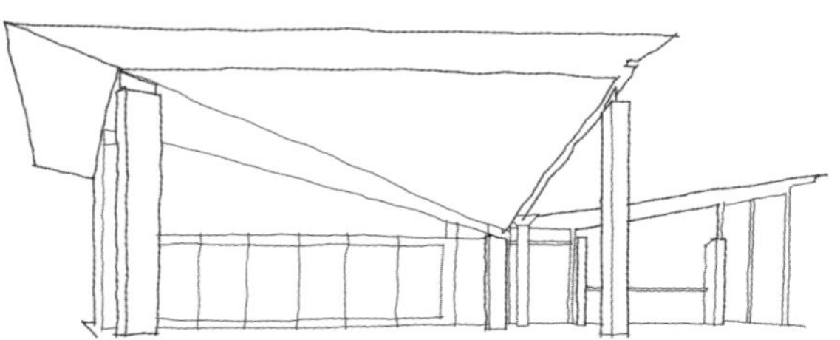

In memory and in photographs the hall and its forecourt suggest grand temples and plazas, while in their presence they evoke as much a tent and its extended awning.

Arthur and Yvonne Boyd Education Centre | 1996–99
Murcutt Lewin Lark
Riversdale, NSW, Australia

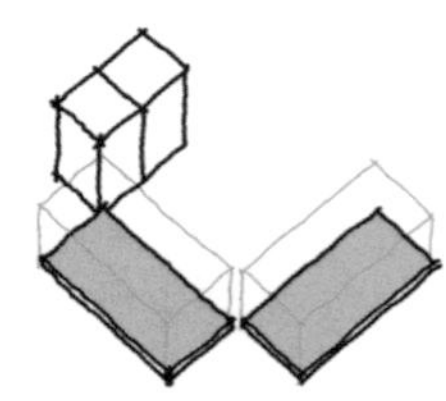

Additive elements

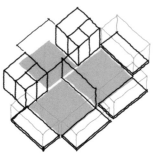

The basic unit is a set of two beds with wardrobes. The beds are arranged at right angles, so sitting on them is good for conversation. The arrangement is reflected with a sliding visual privacy screen to subdivide the bigger room. Cupboards for staff back on to the wardrobes. Each bed has a lower ceiling and its own window, and feels like a semi-separate space, which extends beyond the skin of the building between large vertical sunscreens. These break the morning sun and frame the view. The room divider slides between two of these fins when not needed. Lavatory, washbasin and shower room slot between pairs of rooms. These are in separate spaces so they can all be used at the same time.

At the end of the access walkway, a flight of steps between tall concrete side walls leads back to ground level. Like the tree canopies, the roof feathers to a thin edge.

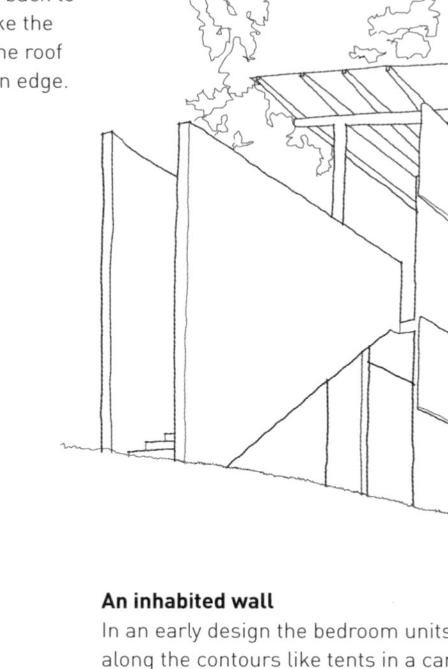

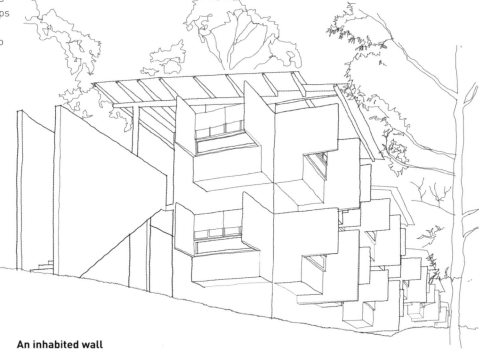

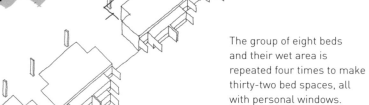

The group of eight beds and their wet area is repeated four times to make thirty-two bed spaces, all with personal windows.

An inhabited wall

In an early design the bedroom units were distributed along the contours like tents in a campsite. In the final design they are side by side like the inhabited wall of an ancient fortified town. Where the ground slopes down, extra units are tucked underneath. Between each pair of four-bed rooms is slotted a lavatory with handbasin, washbasin and shower room, making a group of eight beds with its own wet area. Each group is kept apart for identity, and there are views between them from the access walkway.

Bedrooms as cabinet-tents

Fingers of wood make low ceilings over the bedroom entrances, so that the rooms themselves seem tall between the bed bays. The thinness and apparent delicacy of these fingers suggest the delicacy of the eucalypt trees above the building. Sliding away the partition and opening shutters changes the character of the space. Without blinds or curtains (morning sun wakes sleepers) the view is ever-present.

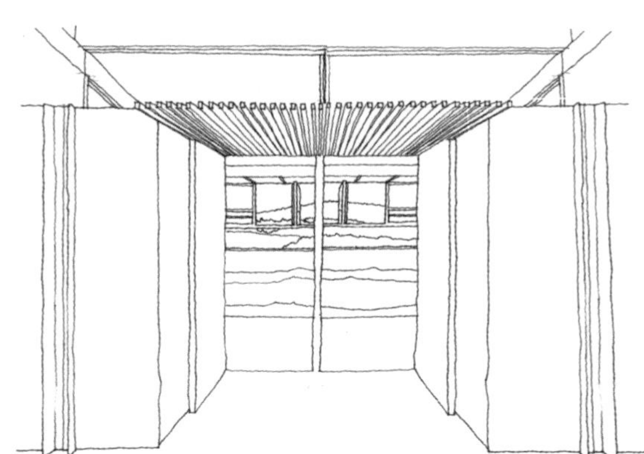

The structure of the sloping roof is exposed except inside the bedrooms, where plywood ceilings cover insulation.

Within a bedroom, zones of space are defined for each bed bay.

Beds have their own window and framed view.

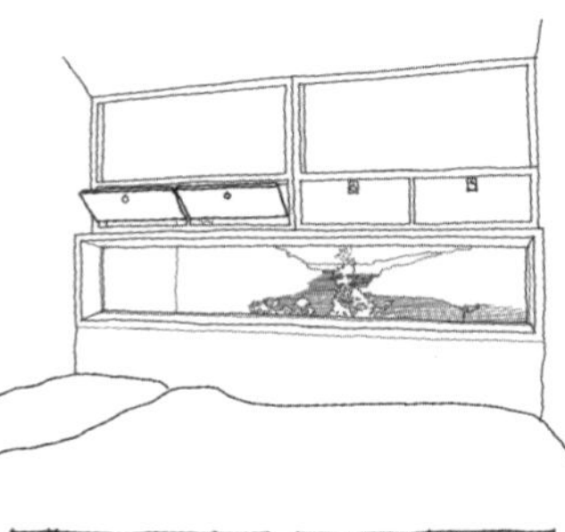

Windows can be opened in many ways to vary ventilation and light. Each way of opening frames the view differently and makes a pattern of light and shade.

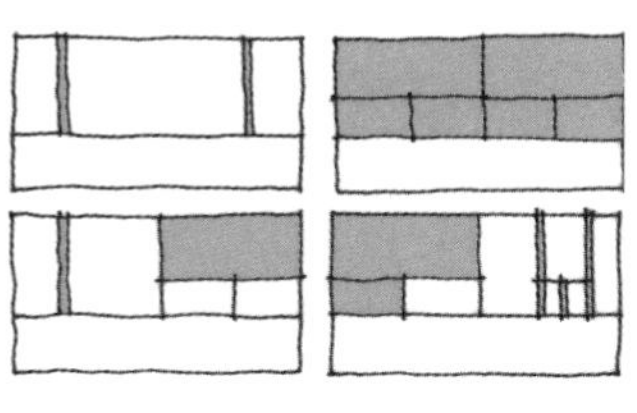

Fixed glass above the bed bays and over the doors and cupboards seals the room while letting the roof appear to float above the space.

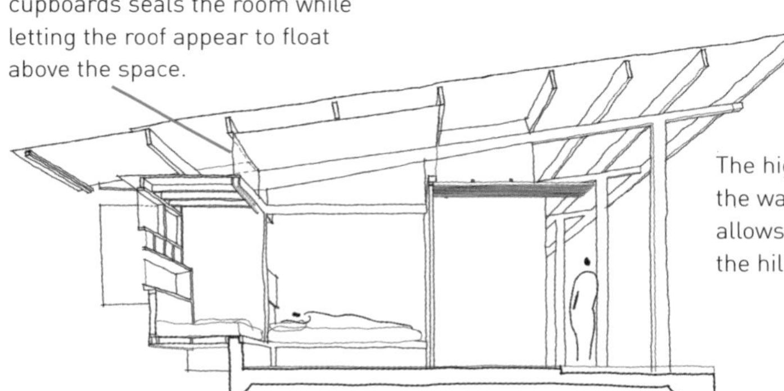

The high roof on the walkway side allows a view up the hill slope.

The outer bed bays hang beyond the concrete east wall of the bedroom wing.

The big blades of the roof capture the north-east breezes, break the early morning sun and bounce light back into the bedrooms later in the morning. Bedroom ceilings are insulated. There is no built-in heating or air conditioning. It can be cool in winter – as it would be in a tent.

The shower is essentially outdoors under a veranda (there is no glass), but timber Venetian blinds can be adjusted to personal choices between privacy and views.

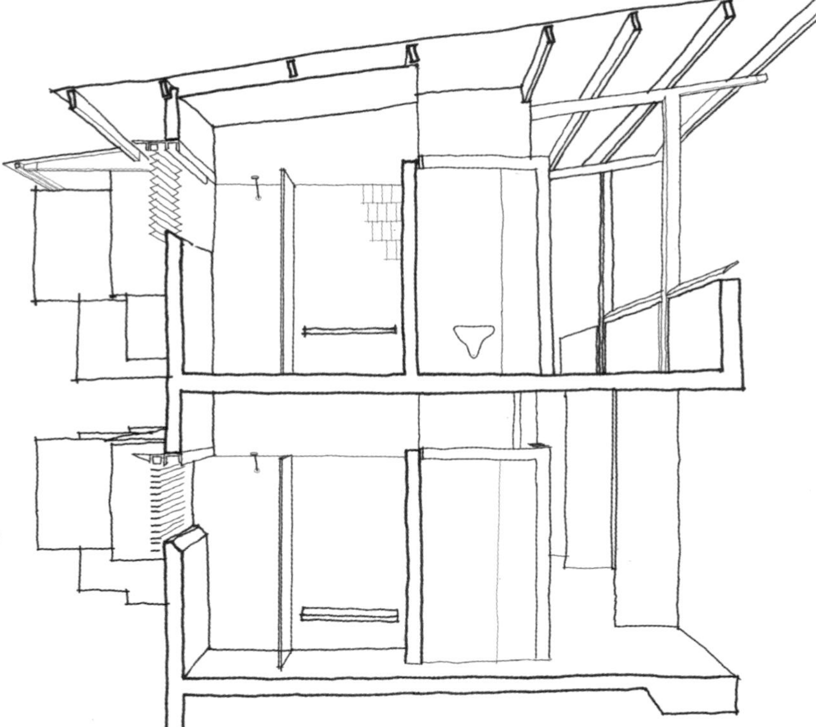

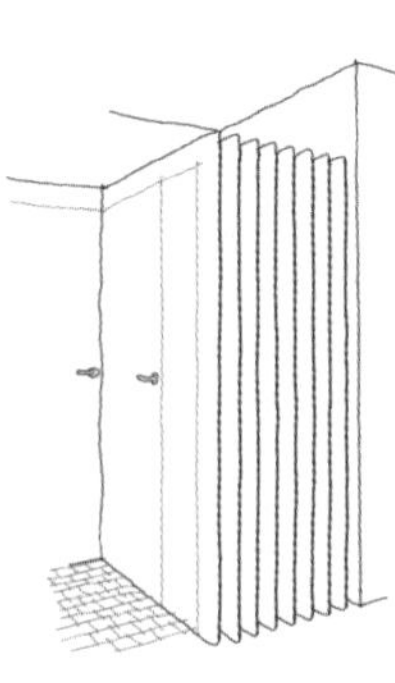

The walls of the lavatory stop short of the roof. A ceiling over the lavatory is partially open for ventilation. On the walkway side the partiton is obscured glass between timber strips, so the space is both well ventilated and light.

Arthur and Yvonne Boyd Education Centre | 1996–99
Murcutt Lewin Lark
Riversdale, NSW, Australia

Building forms (not to scale)
All are located in New South Wales, Australia.

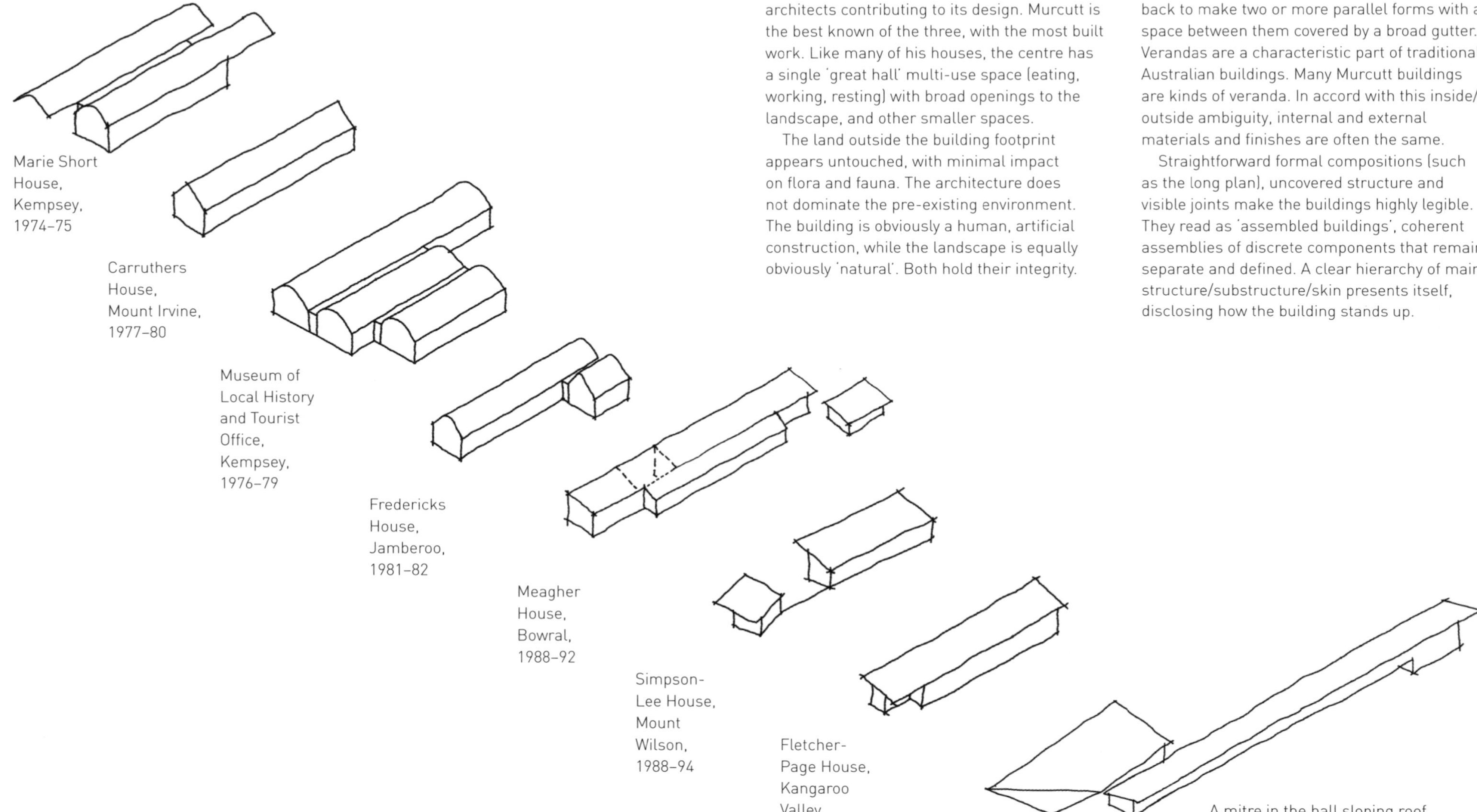

Murcutt emphasizes that the Arthur and Yvonne Boyd Education Centre is the product of his collaboration with Lewin and Lark, with all three architects contributing to its design. Murcutt is the best known of the three, with the most built work. Like many of his houses, the centre has a single 'great hall' multi-use space (eating, working, resting) with broad openings to the landscape, and other smaller spaces.

The land outside the building footprint appears untouched, with minimal impact on flora and fauna. The architecture does not dominate the pre-existing environment. The building is obviously a human, artificial construction, while the landscape is equally obviously 'natural'. Both hold their integrity.

Many of Murcutt's buildings have linear, single-room-deep planning. Where the plan becomes impossibly long, it is simply doubled back to make two or more parallel forms with a space between them covered by a broad gutter. Verandas are a characteristic part of traditional Australian buildings. Many Murcutt buildings are kinds of veranda. In accord with this inside/outside ambiguity, internal and external materials and finishes are often the same.

Straightforward formal compositions (such as the long plan), uncovered structure and visible joints make the buildings highly legible. They read as 'assembled buildings', coherent assemblies of discrete components that remain separate and defined. A clear hierarchy of main structure/substructure/skin presents itself, disclosing how the building stands up.

'Touch the earth lightly'

Murcutt quotes the Australian Aboriginal advice to 'touch the earth lightly'. This is a desire for minimal environmental damage from human activities, a kind of responsive cohesion with the world. It is not a statement about style. While many of Murcutt's early houses are raised off the ground with framed timber floors (a literal expression of 'touch the earth lightly'), others sit on the ground on concrete slabs, or even cut into the ground with a basement. In his more recent projects he uses raised floors in warmer climates and contact with the ground in cooler ones, combined with more thermal mass in the construction. The Arthur and Yvonne Boyd Education Centre has this thermal mass. In all of these cases the ground form up to the edge of the building footprint appears unaltered.

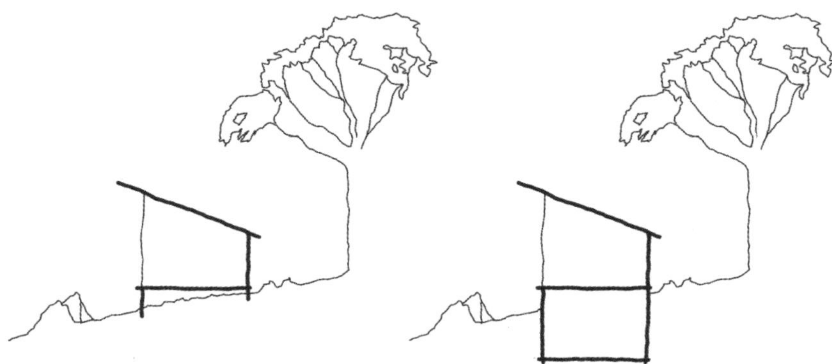

The design language is closely allied with the palette of materials and construction techniques. Connections and details are simplified to achieve a legible minimalism. The distinction between elements is accentuated, including the contrast between heavyweight (homogeneous, solid, apparently strong) and lightweight (thin, feathered, apparently fragile). At openings, several layers with different functions such as slats, insect screens and glass often modulate the edge between inside and outside.

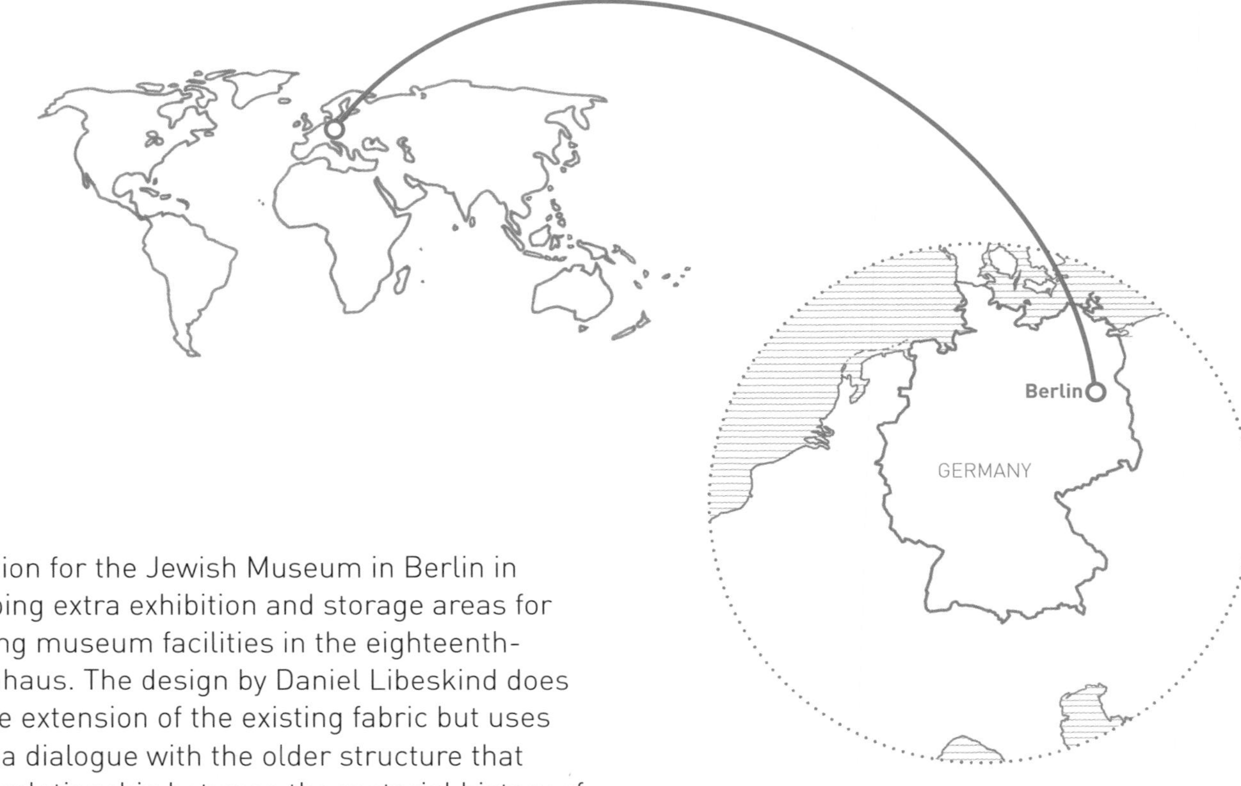

31 Jewish Museum Berlin | 1988–99

Daniel Libeskind

Berlin, Germany

The architectural competition for the Jewish Museum in Berlin in 1988 was aimed at developing extra exhibition and storage areas for the expansion of the existing museum facilities in the eighteenth-century Baroque Kollegienhaus. The design by Daniel Libeskind does not interpret this as a mere extension of the existing fabric but uses the opportunity to develop a dialogue with the older structure that highlights the paradoxical relationship between the material history of the city of Berlin and its invisible Jewish past. The design uses a system of indexical signs – whereby the relationship with the past is explored through a language of physical imprints that point to events and experiences – to make this act of erasure present once again.

Other aspects of materiality and light are employed to elicit an emotional response in visitors that might assist them to identify with the pain and suffering of the Jewish people, thereby generating a more cohesive overall experience.

Amit Srivastava, Rowan Barbary, Ben McPherson, Manalle Abiad and Alix Dunbar

31

Jewish Museum Berlin | 1988–99

Daniel Libeskind
Berlin, Germany

Response to urban context

The new building for the Jewish Museum is an addition to the original museum facilities in the Kollegienhaus, an eigheenth-century Baroque building. The addition is a response to the immediate and extended historical fabric. The forms and materiality of the new structure are in obvious contrast to the historical forms of the existing museum and at first appear discohesive. However, instead of attempting a simpler visual harmony, the design explores a different, more paradoxical relationship with the past, where the present has a distinct identity yet is deeply dependent on the past.

The rectilinear forms and oblique cuts are in sharp contrast to the Kollegienhaus building.

This paradoxical relationship with the past is first explored through an obscure but essential physical connection between the old and the new. The treatment of the street façade for the Jewish Museum clearly identifies it as a separate structure from the Kollegienhaus, but there is no visible entrance to this formidable fortress-like building. The visitor is forced to gain access to the building through the old Kollegienhaus structure, where the access to the 'new' is literally embedded in the depths of the 'old', in the form of a basement stair access. The relationship with the 'old' is further reinforced by letting this access stairwell cut through all floors of the existing structure.

The addition acquires its full meaning in dialogue with its older counterpart. The complex plan of the new building is seen as an 'expectant' form that coexists with the 'common' form of the city grid captured in the old building, to reveal the 'invisible matrix' of the city.

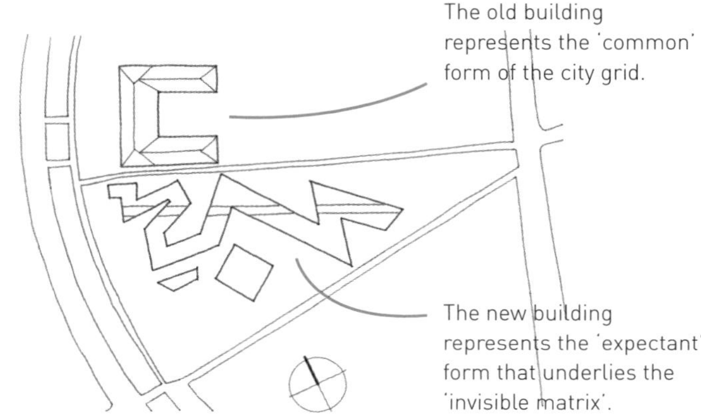

The old building represents the 'common' form of the city grid.

The new building represents the 'expectant' form that underlies the 'invisible matrix'.

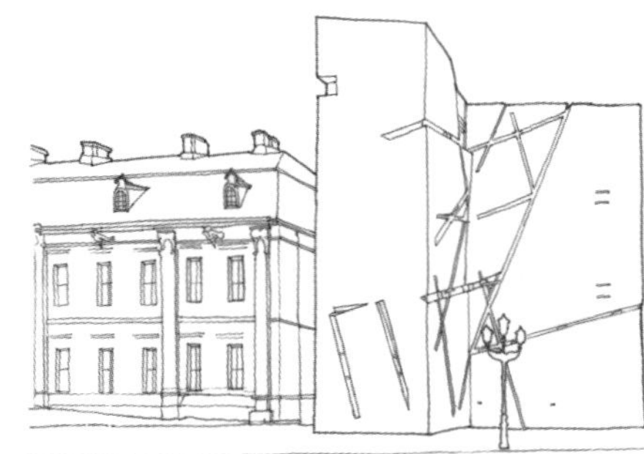

The fortress-like structure makes its presence felt in contrast to the Kollegienhaus, but the visitor must gain access through this historical structure, reinforcing the building's connection to the 'old' and the city's past.

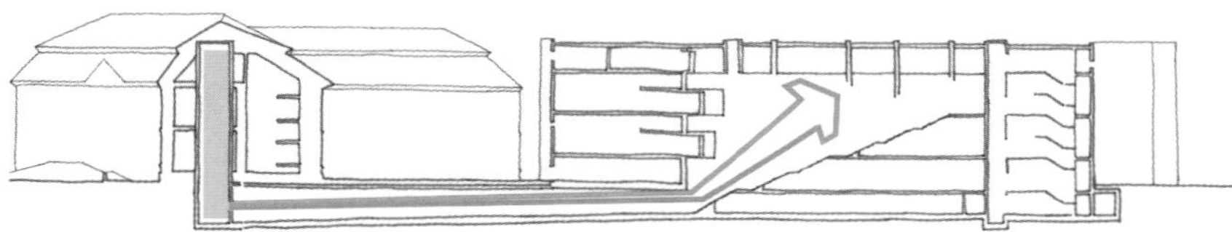

The visitor must descend into the basement of the 'old' structure and slowly rise via a subterranean ramp and stairs to reach the new exhibition spaces.

Response to Jewish history

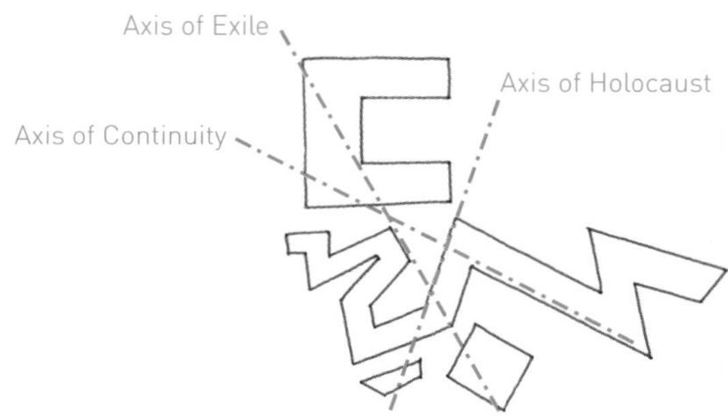

The conceptual relationship with the invisible Jewish past is explored by introducing the idea of three axes – of Continuity, Holocaust and Exile – which recreate the Jewish experience in Germany. The three linear axes lead to the three major design elements: the exhibition space, the Holocaust Tower and the Garden of Exile respectively.

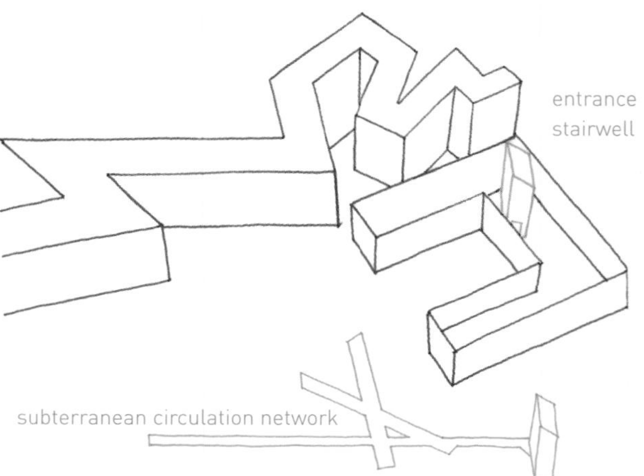

The two separate concepts of the physical connection with the old building and the three axes referring to the Jewish past of Berlin are brought together in the organization of the entrance and the circulation path within the building. Together these form the subterranean circulation network that connects the various elements of the design.

The expression of the Jewish past in the built form of this structure has been argued in many ways. On the one hand the formal qualities of the zigzag plan form are used to argue for a literal dismantling of the symbolic marker of Judaism – the Star of David – as a technique for developing the overall form of the building.

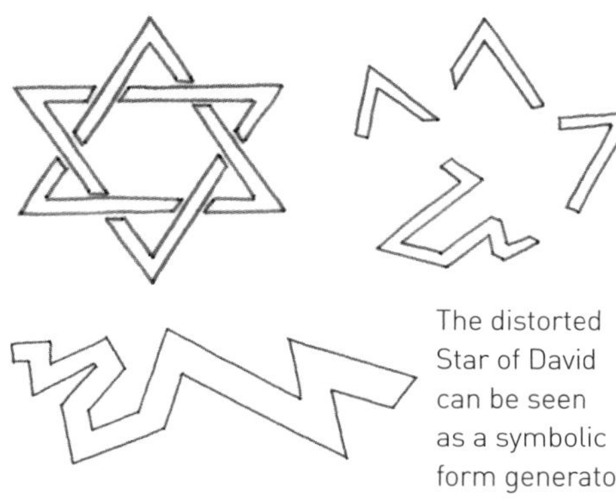

The distorted Star of David can be seen as a symbolic form generator.

Other comparisons relate it to the expression of a tortured landscape, as attempted earlier by Michael Heizer in his 1968 project 'Rift' in Nevada, USA (below). This was one of the massive earthworks land art projects of the 1960s.

Mapping intertwined histories

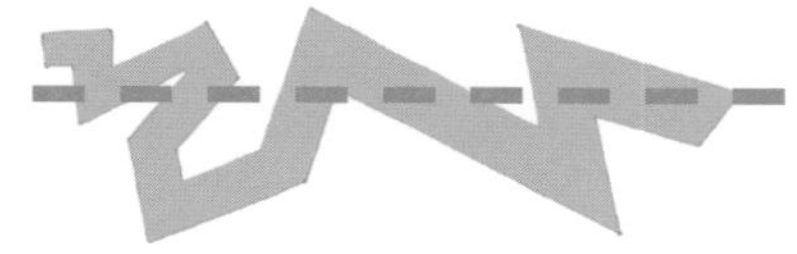

A continuous but tortured history of Berlin intertwines with a straight but ruptured history of the Jewish experience.

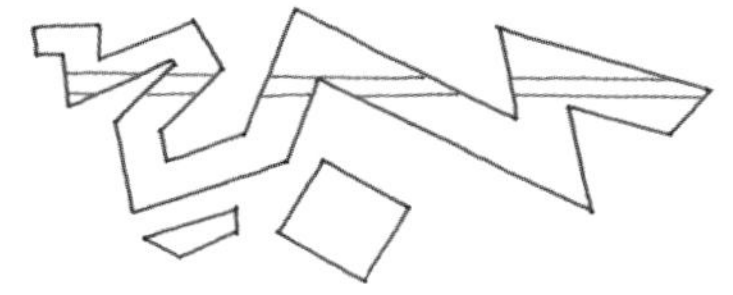

The two lines of history are embraced through an uncompromising integration of the voids into the built form.

While references to Jewish symbolism or iconic artistic expressions of torture are easier to relate to, the design also explores a more philosophical understanding of the nature of history and our relationship with the past. The absent history of the Jewish experience in Berlin is seen as intertwining with the material history of Berlin itself, and the design attempts to make this absence felt through exposing the traces of one on the other. The resulting diagram is a cohesive picture of Berlin's history where the absence accounts for the presence of another parallel timeline.

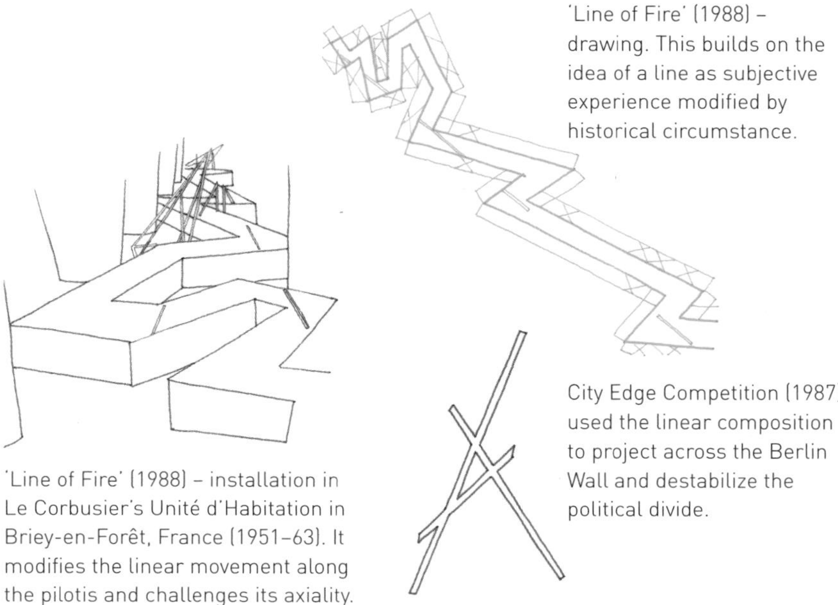

'Line of Fire' (1988) – drawing. This builds on the idea of a line as subjective experience modified by historical circumstance.

'Line of Fire' (1988) – installation in Le Corbusier's Unité d'Habitation in Briey-en-Forêt, France (1951–63). It modifies the linear movement along the pilotis and challenges its axiality.

City Edge Competition (1987) used the linear composition to project across the Berlin Wall and destabilize the political divide.

The use of lines to diagram the nature of time, as seemingly modified by historical circumstance, was previously explored by Libeskind in his 'Micromegas' drawings (1979) and in several subsequent works. Here the drawing did not serve as a 'sign' – a material representation of something else – but as a 'trace' of an event or experience.

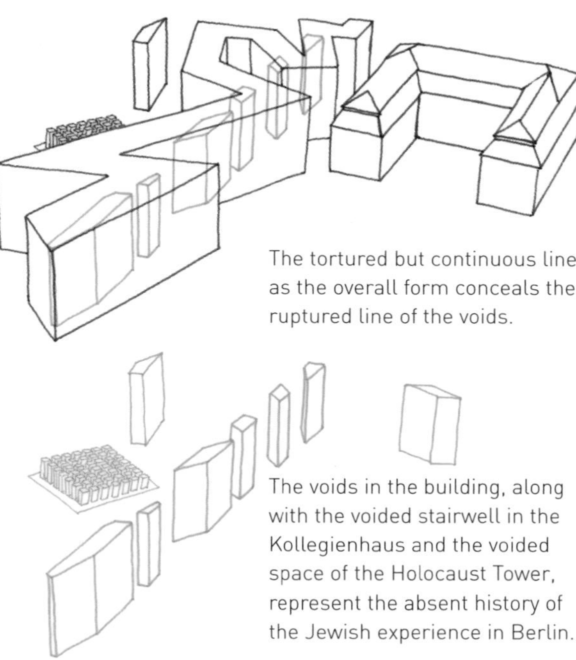

The tortured but continuous line as the overall form conceals the ruptured line of the voids.

The voids in the building, along with the voided stairwell in the Kollegienhaus and the voided space of the Holocaust Tower, represent the absent history of the Jewish experience in Berlin.

In the built form the diagram is developed through the two spatial elements of habitable space and uninhabitable void. While the habitable space maintains the continuity of the material presence of Berlin, the uninhabitable voids mark the seemingly absent yet undeniable existence of the Jewish past. This absence of Jews from Berlin is overlaid on the three axes that separately define a specifically Jewish experience.

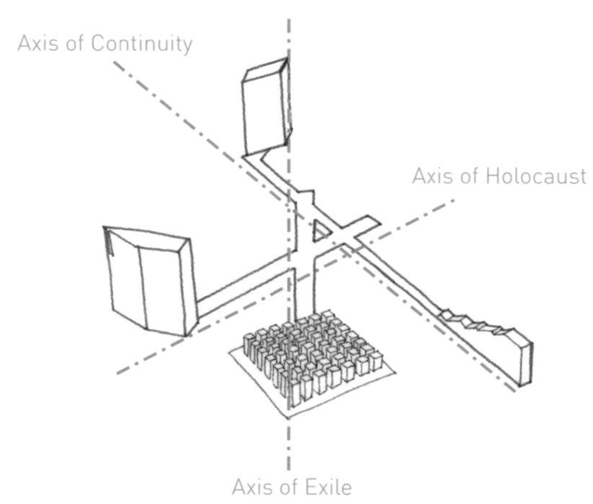

31 Jewish Museum Berlin | 1988–99

Daniel Libeskind
Berlin, Germany

User experience

The diagrammatic explorations of Jewish suffering and its historical relationship with Berlin are further made evident through the built fabric as a series of experiences that continuously challenge and provoke the viewer. An emotional response is incited through a series of architectural manipulations including movement, materiality and light, as well as subtle modulations of the ground plane.

The experiential journey begins with the entry point in the Kollegienhaus, where visitors must descend into a dimly lit subterranean passage and make their way into the labyrinthine interior of the new building. The rest of the journey is structured around the three main elements of the design, namely the exhibition space, the Holocaust Tower and the Garden of Exile. Each of these forms the terminal point of one of the three axes of the subterranean network.

The dark void of the entrance staircase in the Kollegienhaus marks the beginning of the subterranean journey.

A seemingly never-ending flight of stairs with no sense of destination or arrival extends the Axis of Continuity.

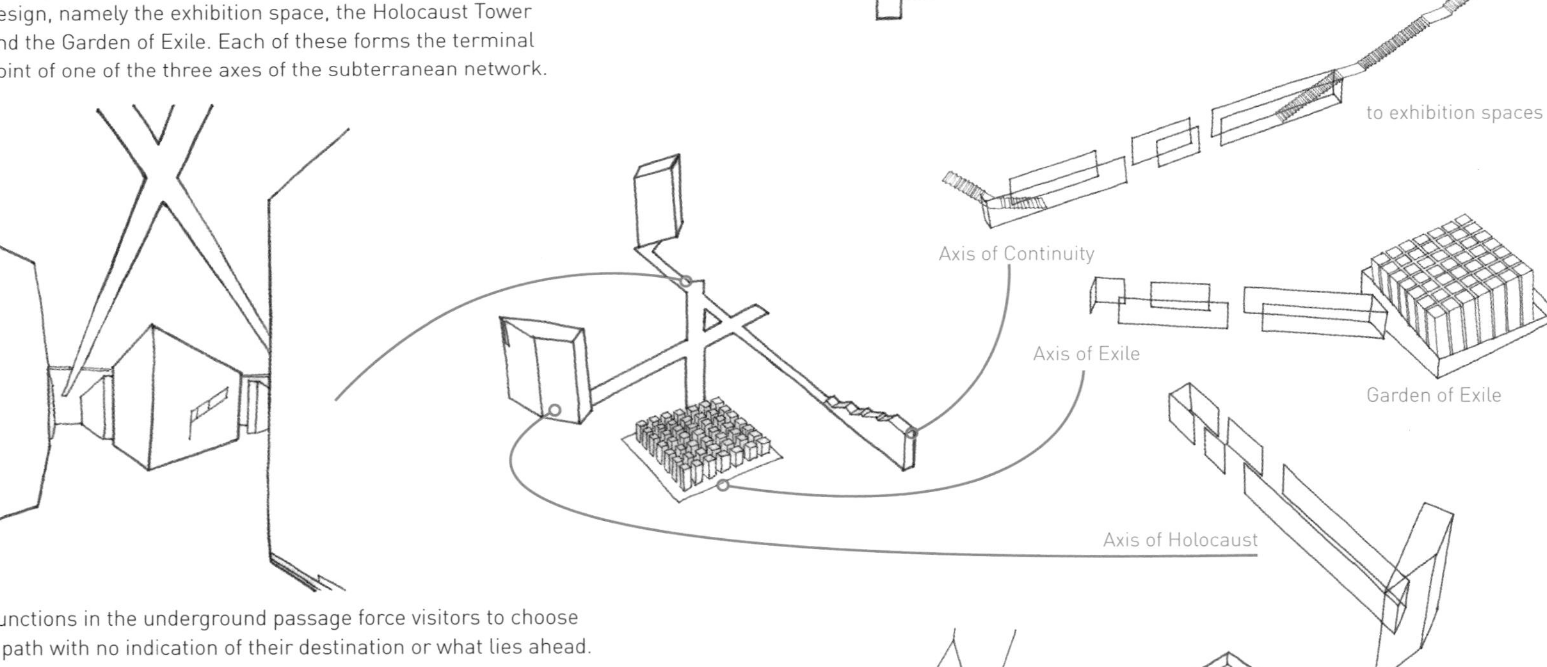

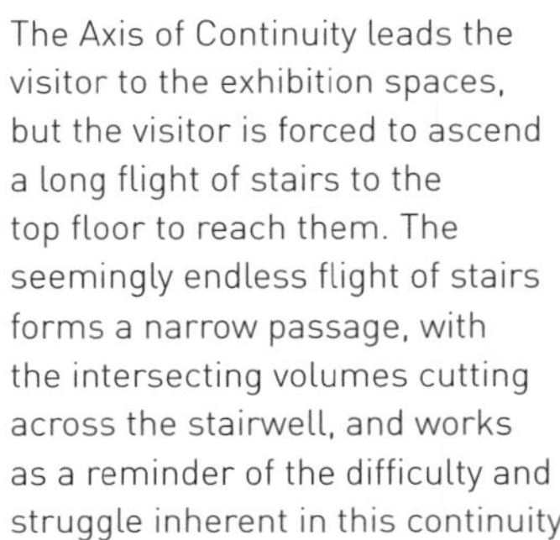

The Axis of Continuity leads the visitor to the exhibition spaces, but the visitor is forced to ascend a long flight of stairs to the top floor to reach them. The seemingly endless flight of stairs forms a narrow passage, with the intersecting volumes cutting across the stairwell, and works as a reminder of the difficulty and struggle inherent in this continuity.

Junctions in the underground passage force visitors to choose a path with no indication of their destination or what lies ahead.

The design wields the power of materiality and light to extract an emotional response from visitors that might assist them to identify with the pain and suffering of the Jewish people to which the museum is a monument. This is most strongly experienced in the Holocaust Tower, where a sliver of light penetrates the cold, dark, concrete interior and signals the possibility of an escape from the tortured existence into the afterlife.

The small slit on top of the vertical volume serves as a highly evocative light source.

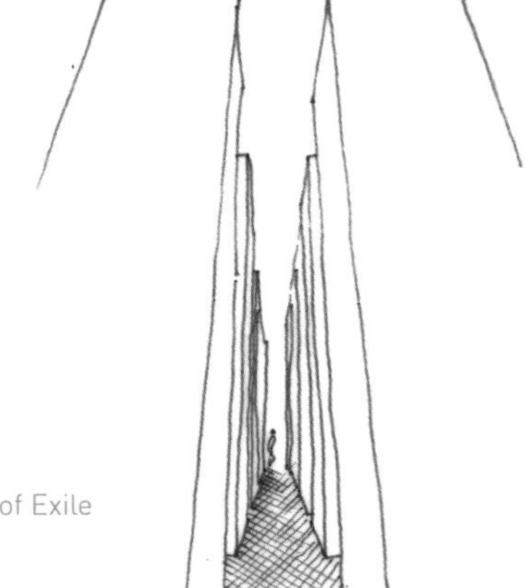

Garden of Exile

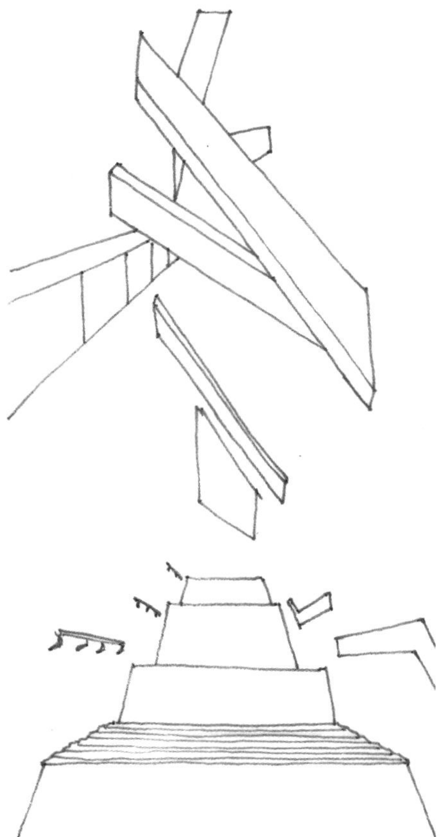

The Garden of Exile is another confronting experience, in which the visitor is led into an outdoor space and obliged to navigate around the bases of forty-nine concrete tree-planters on a sloping ground plane. The expectation of escape into free air with trees is thwarted by the experience of the constricted and disorienting space, which does not have an exit and forces the visitor to return to the main building. The garden serves to remind visitors of the feeling of imprisonment inherent in exile, where the notion of escape is an illusion and the person is imprisoned by being separated from the history and reality of that which defines their place and existence.

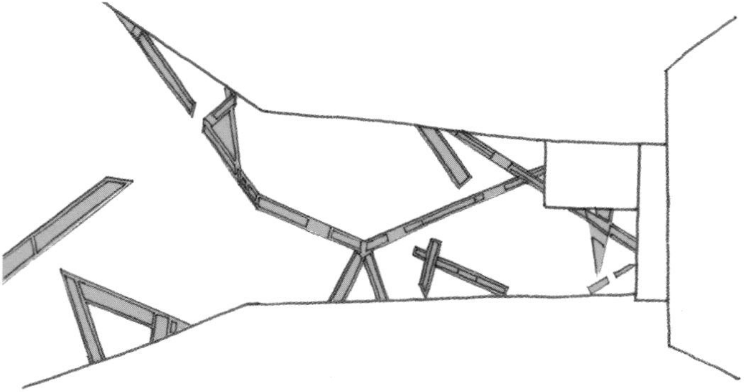

The internal exhibition spaces are lit by a series of slits in the wall, which continue the formal vocabulary of 'cuts' applied on the exterior façade into the interior space.

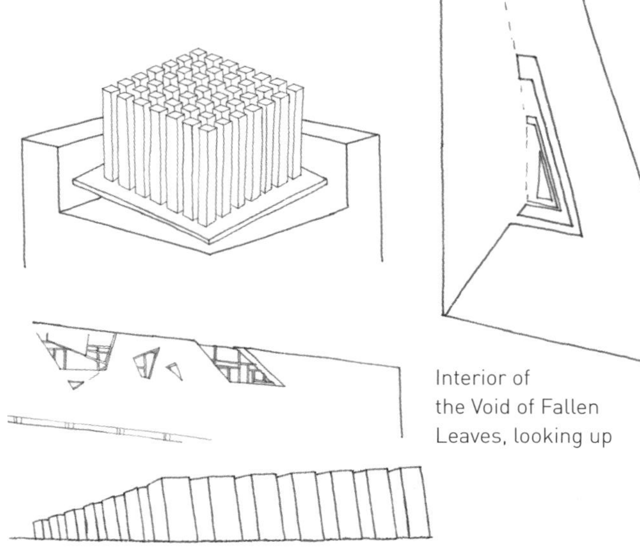

Interior of the Void of Fallen Leaves, looking up

Navigating through the Garden of Exile with its two-storey-high concrete tree-planters and its sloping ground plane is a powerful, disorienting experience.

The internal void spaces also use the power of sound to create a similarly uncomfortable experience. The Void of Fallen Leaves echoes the sounds of visitors walking on metal discs, which is meant to recreate the feel of tortured human cries.

Façade as indexical map

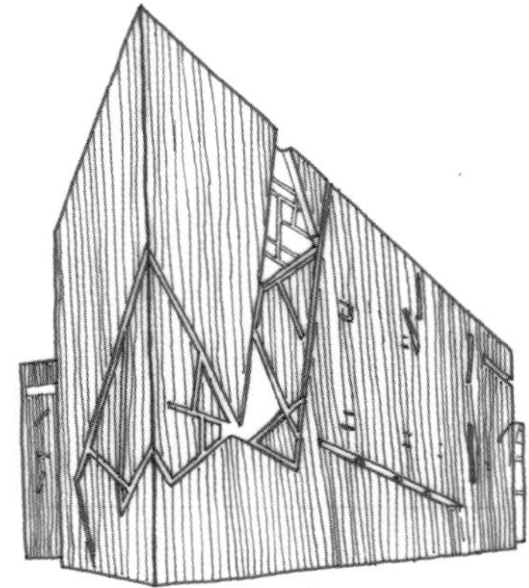

The cuts in the building skin act as an indexical marker of Berlin's Jewish and German heritage.

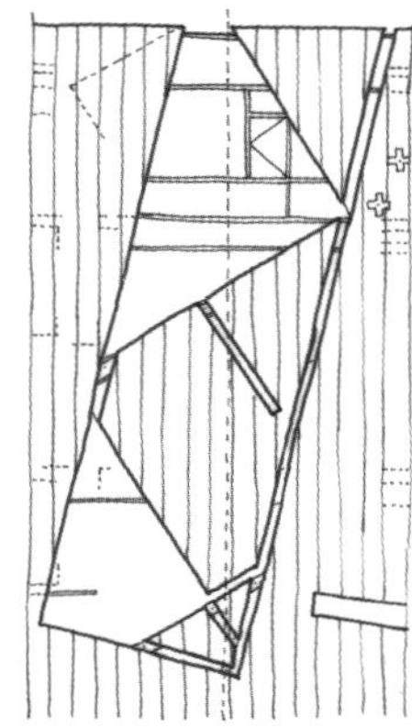

The voids are cast into the concrete skin, and the exterior is clad with zinc.

The external skin of the building continues with the mapping exercise and serves to connect the built form to Berlin's Jewish and German heritage. The façade is developed as a network of lines connecting the addresses of influential Jewish and German figures. Following on from Libeskind's experiments with lines as indexical markers of time and space, the 'trace' of these lines is recorded as cuts into the building skin. These cuts are cast as voids in the reinforced-concrete skin and the window is transformed from a functional source of light to an indexical marker of historical circumstance. This connection to the glorious past of Berlin is also carried forward in the choice of zinc cladding, which was the building material of the past. It is expected that with weathering over time the zinc will transform its material properties and add to the narrative potential of the built form.

The exposed concrete forms of the Holocaust Tower and the Garden of Exile contrast with the zinc-clad backdrop.

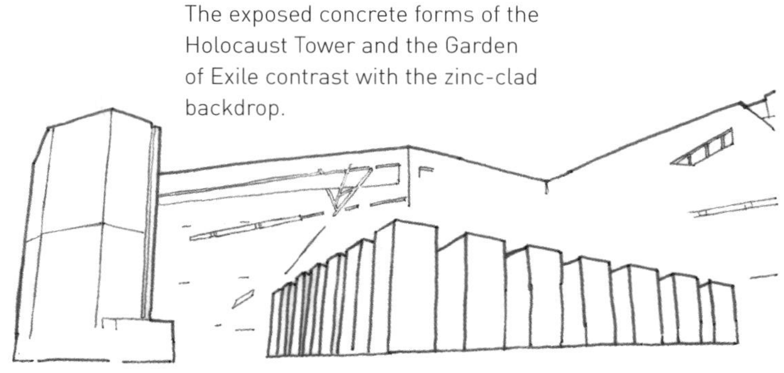

32

Quadracci Pavilion | 1994–2001
Santiago Calatrava
Milwaukee, Wisconsin, USA

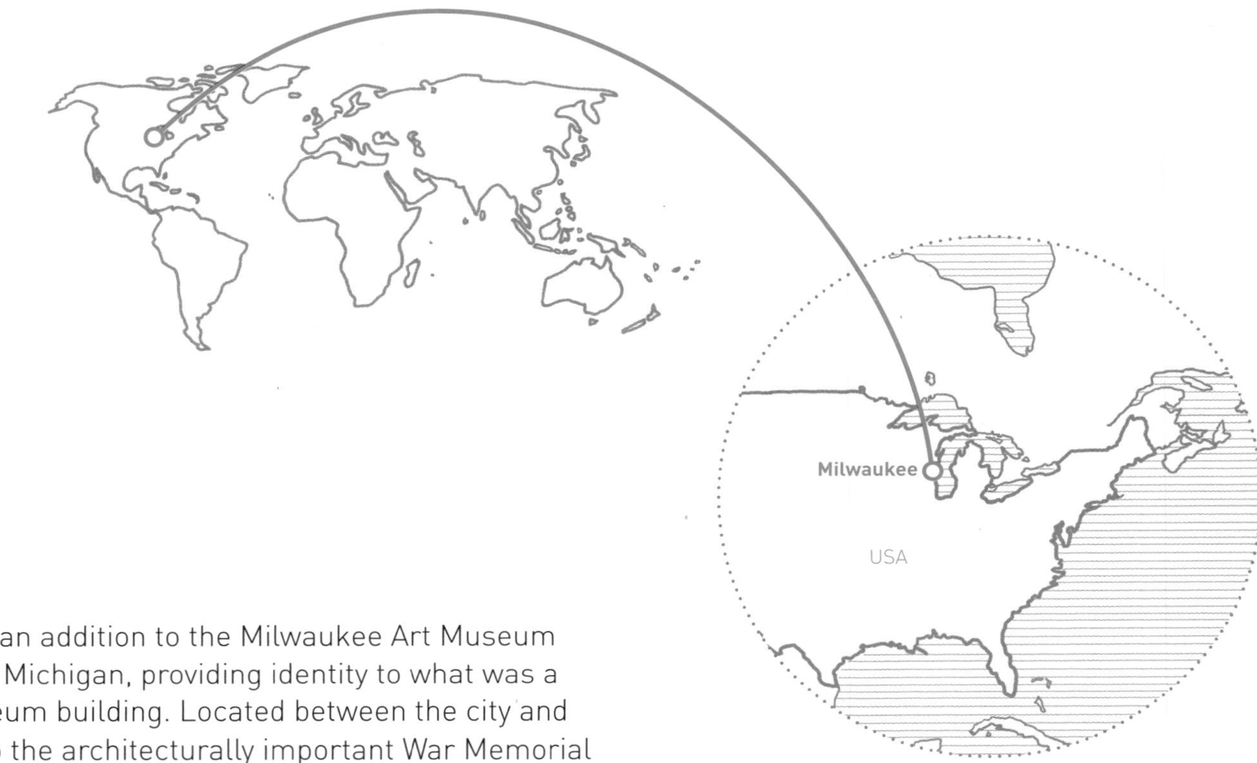

The Quadracci Pavilion is an addition to the Milwaukee Art Museum on the west coast of Lake Michigan, providing identity to what was a large but restrained museum building. Located between the city and the lakeshore, and next to the architecturally important War Memorial Center by Eero Saarinen (1957), the pavilion responds to its physical and climatic contexts with a highly sculptural form.

The pavilion was Spanish architect-engineer Santiago Calatrava's first building in the United States and shows his ability to use innovative engineering in the making of expressive buildings. He melds insights from nature with architectural precedents. A huge adjustable brise-soleil (sun breaker) opens and closes in response to sun and wind, its winglike structure suggesting flight and adding to the visual tension of the composition.

Selen Morkoç, Paul Anson Kassebaum and Xi Li

32

32 Quadracci Pavilion | 1994–2001

Santiago Calatrava
Milwaukee, Wisconsin, USA

Context

Key

1. Quadracci Pavilion
2. War Memorial Center
3. Milwaukee Art Museum
4. Reiman Pedestrian Bridge

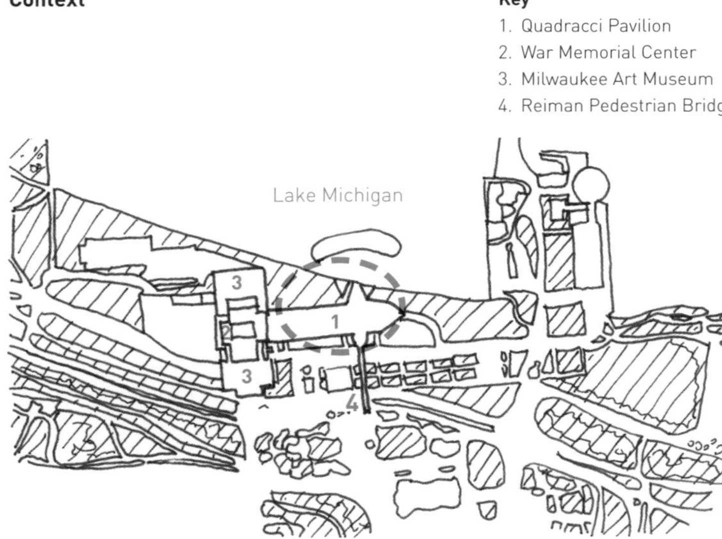

Site plan

The Quadracci Pavilion is one section of the Milwaukee Art Museum, located on the west coast of Lake Michigan. The Pavilion responds to its context in many ways, including responses to sailboats on the lake, the weather, birds in flight, the topography, and an existing war memorial designed by Eero Saarinen.

The concrete mass of War Memorial Center sits adjacent to the site, and retaining its views of the lake and surrounding parks was an important design objective.

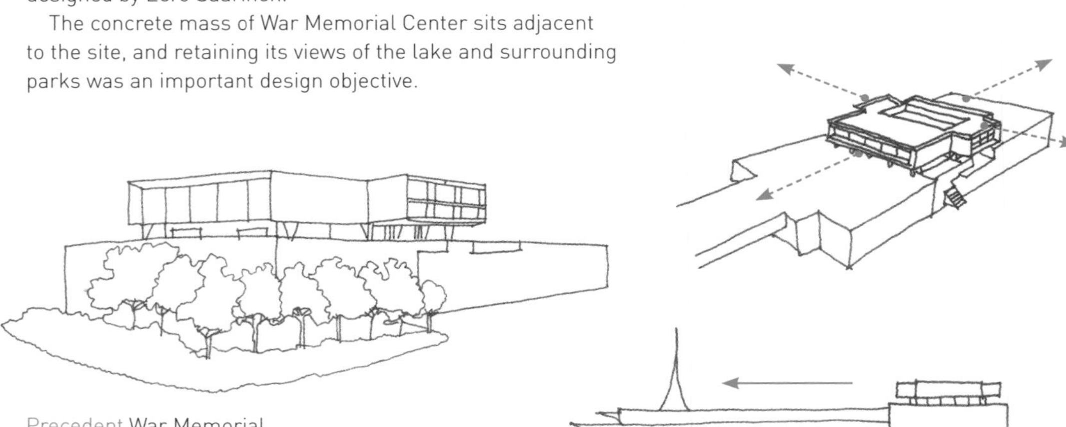

Precedent War Memorial Center, Eero Saarinen (1957)

The pavilion is located at the end of East Michigan Street, surrounded by high-rise business buildings, in striking contrast with its form. It is connected by a thin footbridge (also designed by Calatrava) over North Lincoln Memorial Drive joining the city to the shoreline. From the lake, the pavilion stands out from its neighbours with its dynamic triangular form and bright white wings of the brise-soleil (sun breaker).

The major window openings of the pavilion face south and east for solar access and natural light. Glare and reflection on the artworks inside are avoided by shielding direct sunlight.

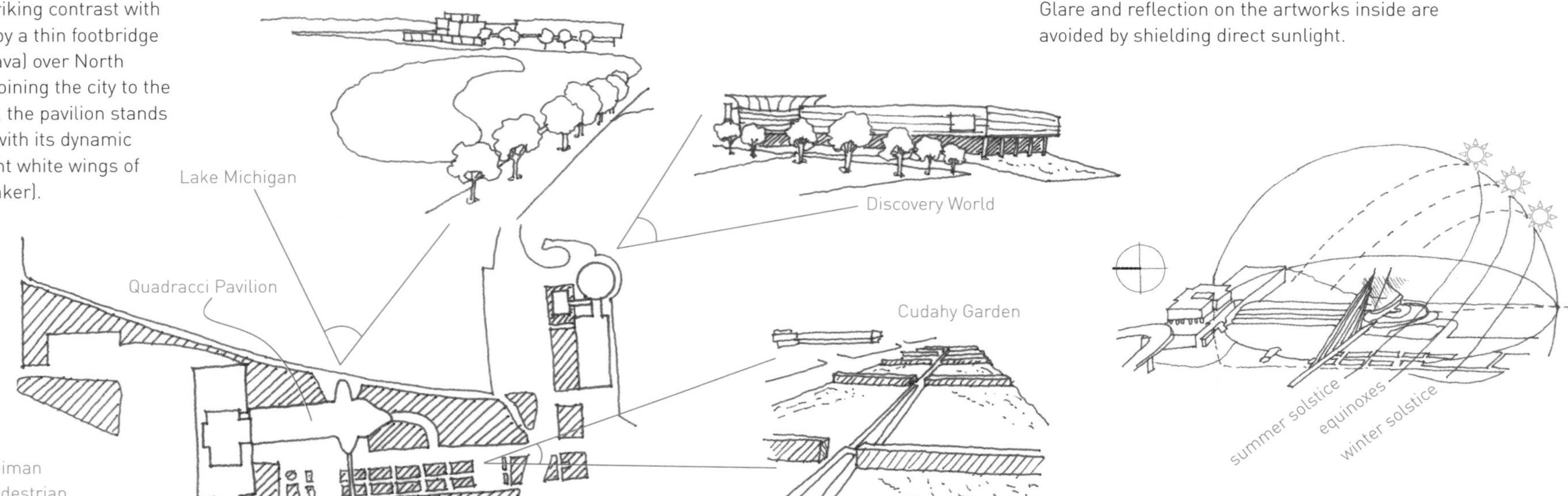

Organic precedents

The human body was an inspiration for the internal-forces study of the cable system for Calatrava's Reiman Pedestrian Bridge.

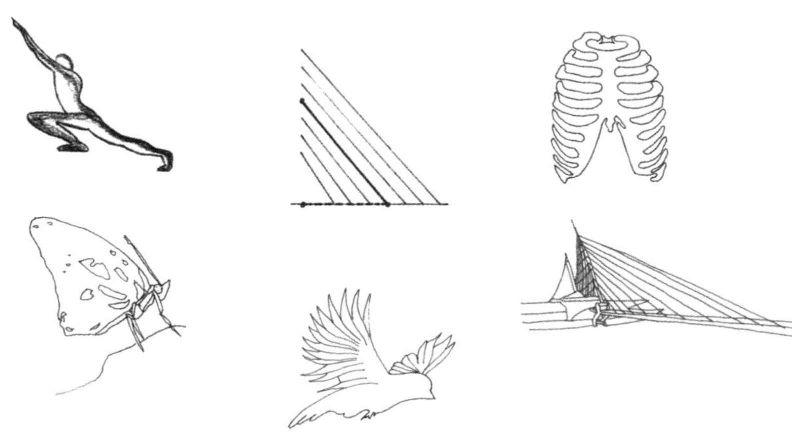

The wings of animals and their dynamic function inspired Calatrava's concept for the brise-soleil.

Brise-soleil

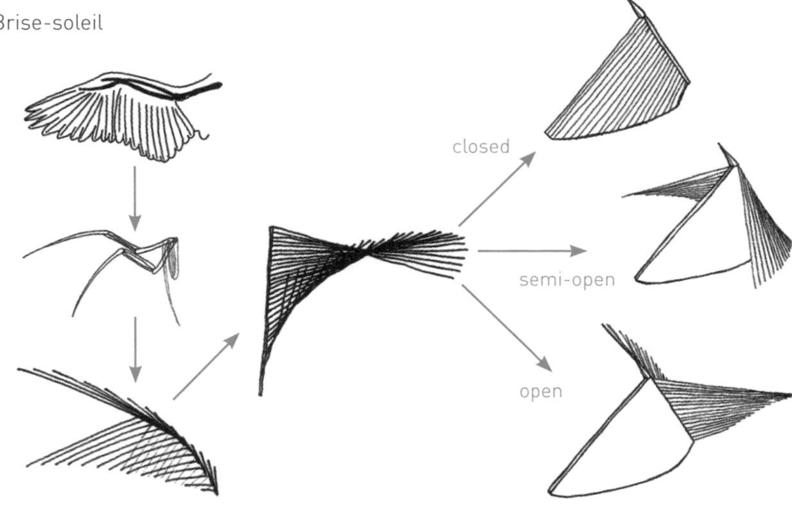

Nature is a source of design inspiration for Calatrava. Wings are one of the recurring themes in his work. The museum's signature brise-soleil forms a kinetic sunscreen, serving as both a symbolic and a functional element that controls the level of light while giving the pavilion its distinctive look. The brise-soleil is adjusted according to weather conditions and special events.

Architectural precedents

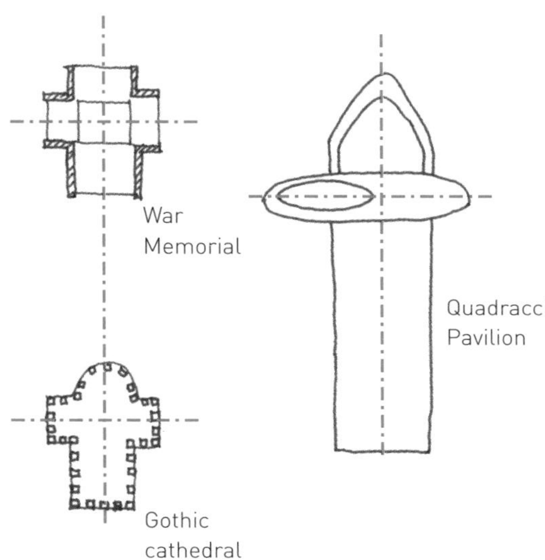

The Quadracci Pavilion can be interpreted as a Postmodern reinterpretation of a Gothic cathedral. The plan layout is symmetrical, with a structure evoking flying buttresses and ribbed vaults. These structural elements create shadow patterns and enhance the visual experience inside.

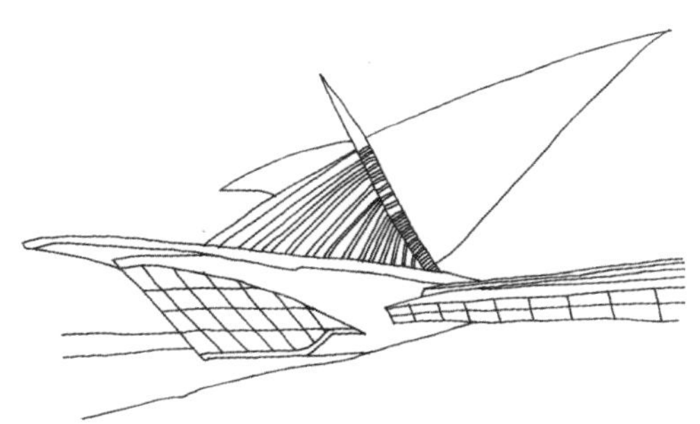

Symmetry and axial plan

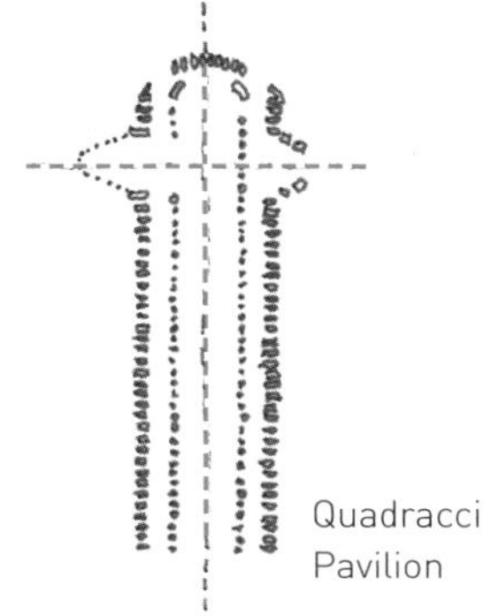

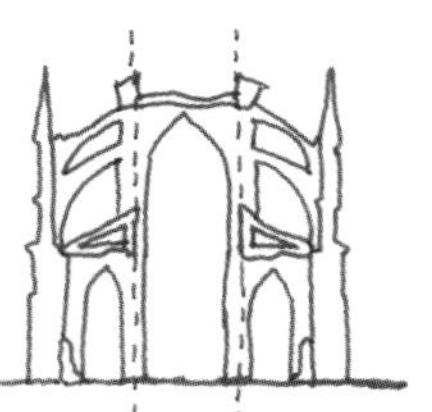

Section of the nave of a Gothic cathedral

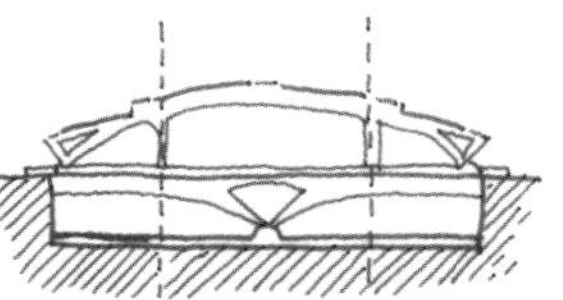

Section showing the exhibition space and underground parking

Classical dome structure

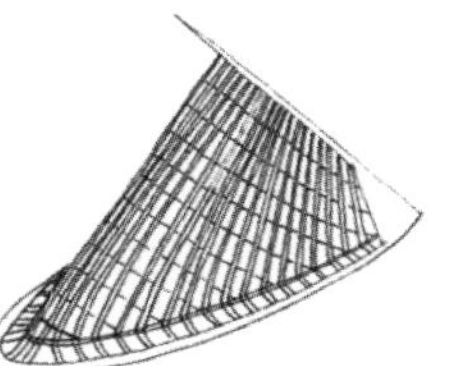

Steel and glazing structure of Windhover Hall (main volume of pavilion)

Interior view of the apse of a Gothic cathedral, looking up

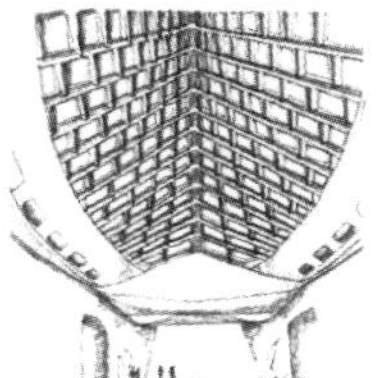

Interior view of Windhover Hall

Structural cohesion

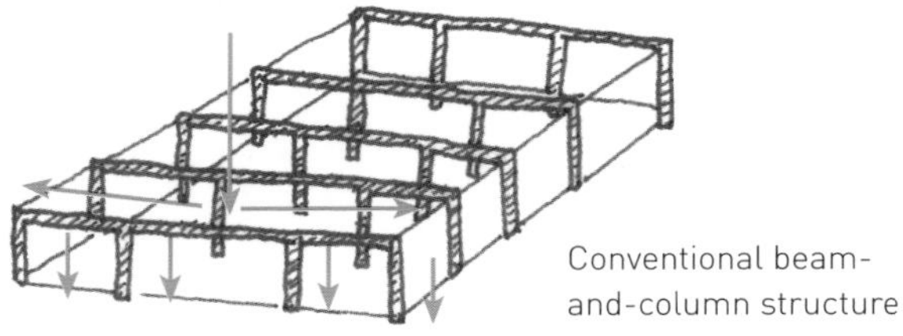

Conventional beam-and-column structure

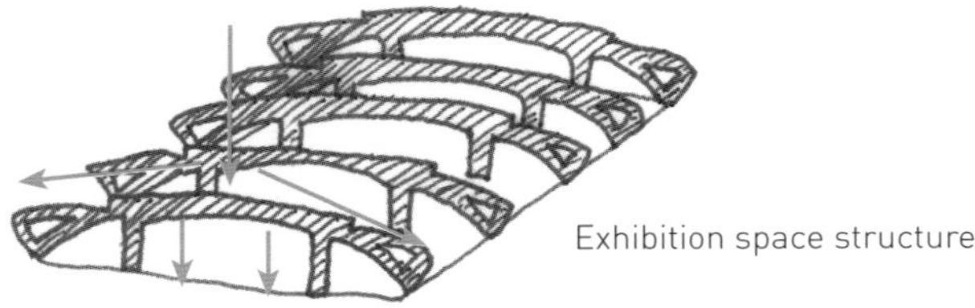

Exhibition space structure

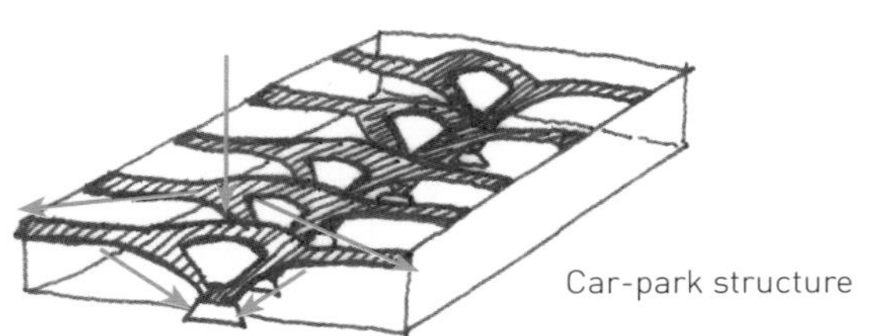

Car-park structure

Instead of detouring forces around right angles, beams flow into arched columns that directly transmit forces to the earth in the shortest possible way, with fewer columns.

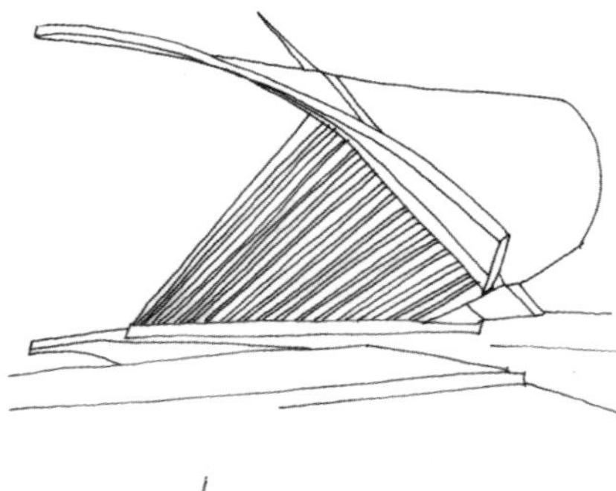

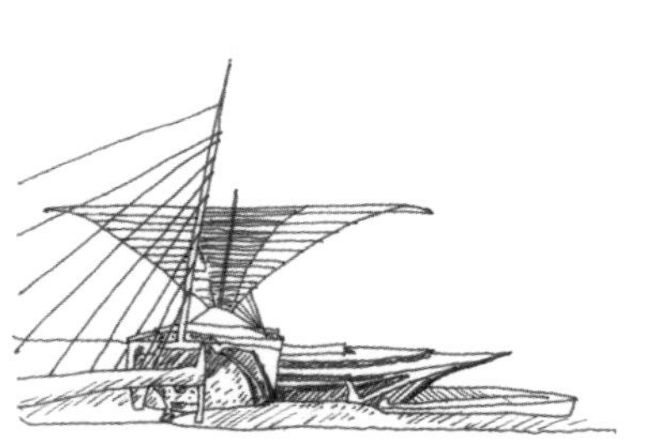

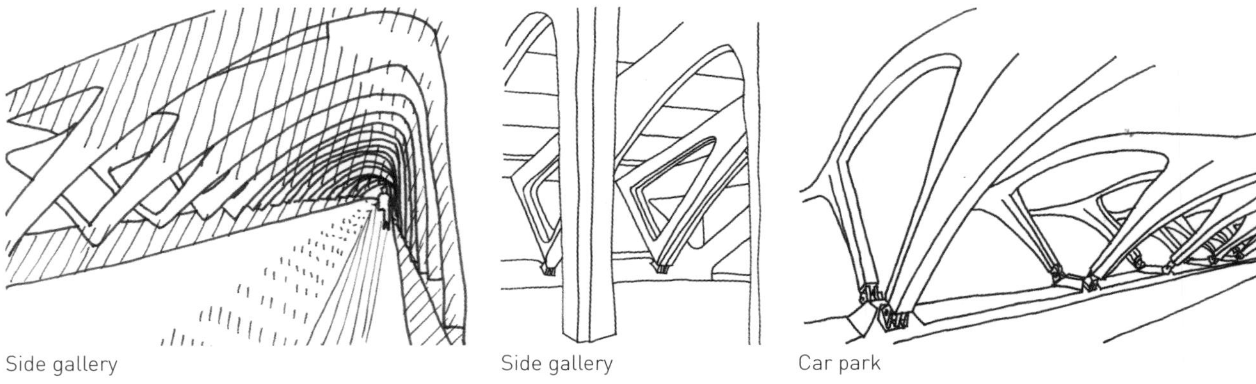

Side gallery   Side gallery   Car park

The gallery spaces on the east and west sides are supported by a series of precast-concrete elements. Apart from being structural, they have a visual impact, dividing the space between supports. The car-park area has similar columns defining smaller volumes within the large space.

Structural details

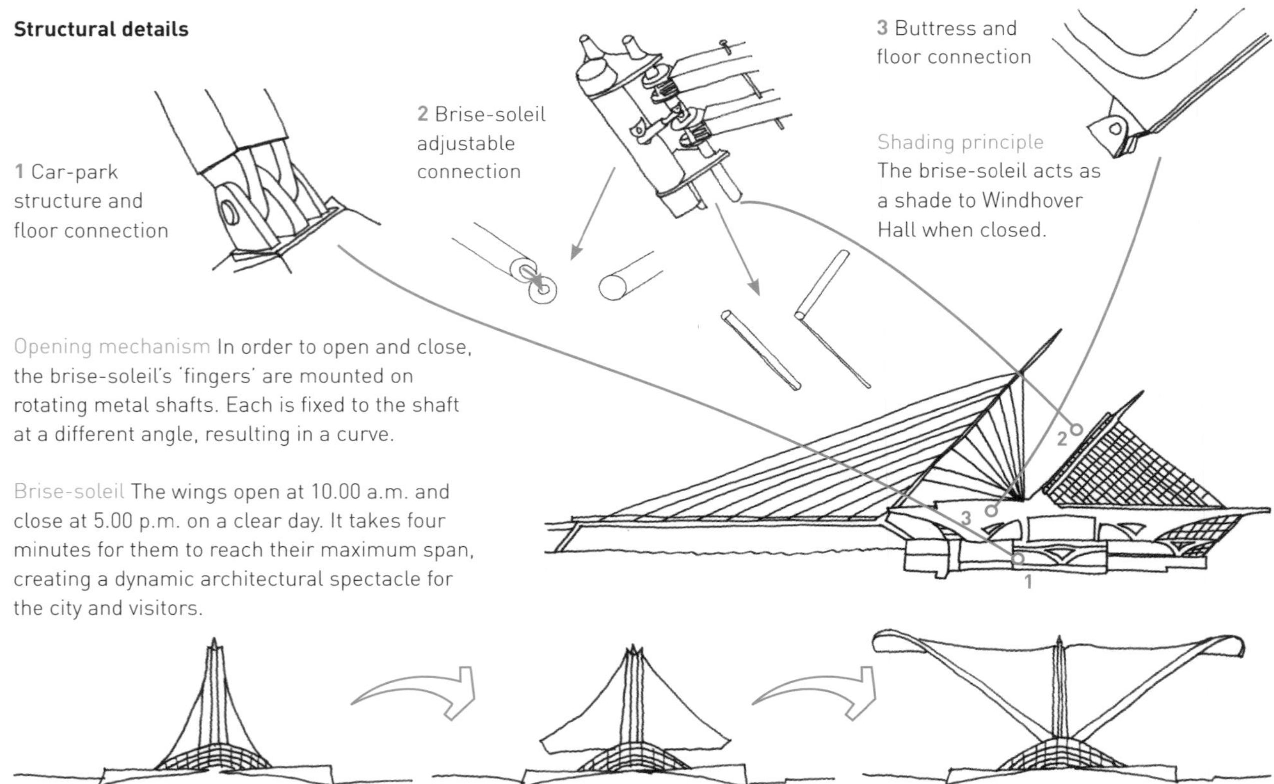

1 Car-park structure and floor connection

2 Brise-soleil adjustable connection

3 Buttress and floor connection

Shading principle The brise-soleil acts as a shade to Windhover Hall when closed.

Opening mechanism In order to open and close, the brise-soleil's 'fingers' are mounted on rotating metal shafts. Each is fixed to the shaft at a different angle, resulting in a curve.

Brise-soleil The wings open at 10.00 a.m. and close at 5.00 p.m. on a clear day. It takes four minutes for them to reach their maximum span, creating a dynamic architectural spectacle for the city and visitors.

Design precedents
Quadracci Pavilion shares similarities with Calatrava's other works. The footbridge uses the idea of counterbalance similar to his Alamillo Bridge in Seville, Spain (1992), while the glass façades are reminiscent of his railway terminal attached to Lyon-Saint Exupéry Airport, France (1994).

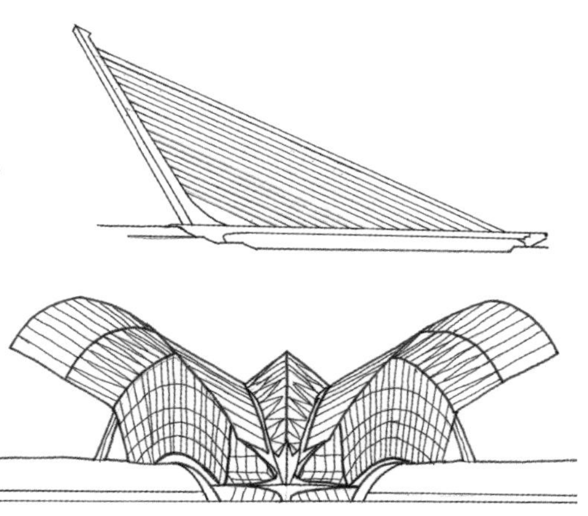

Plan layout

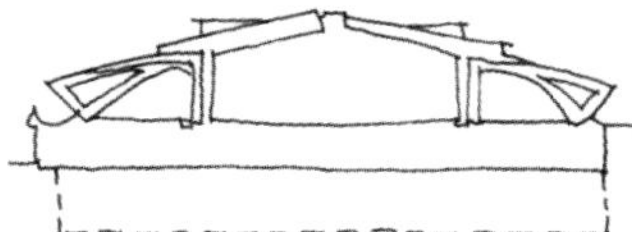

1 The galleries have a line of symmetry along their north–south axis. Side galleries capture views of Lake Michigan that encourage people to linger.

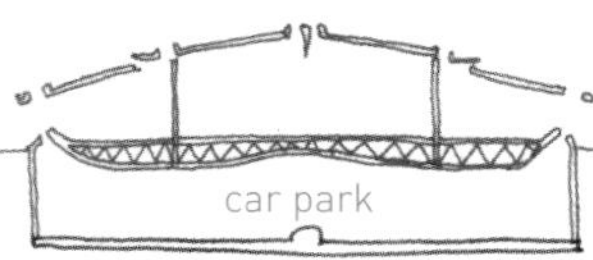

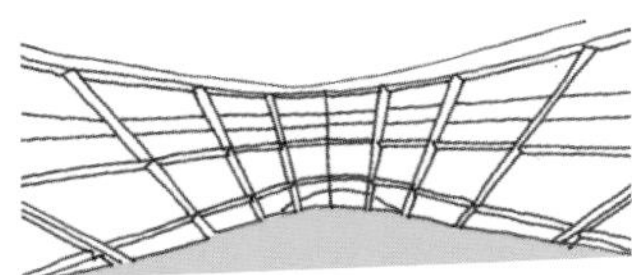

2 Windhover Hall is the main volume of the pavilion. It has a very high ceiling and is filled with light when the brise-soleil is open. It addresses the garden space to the south of the pavilion with an outdoor terrace that covers the car park entrance.

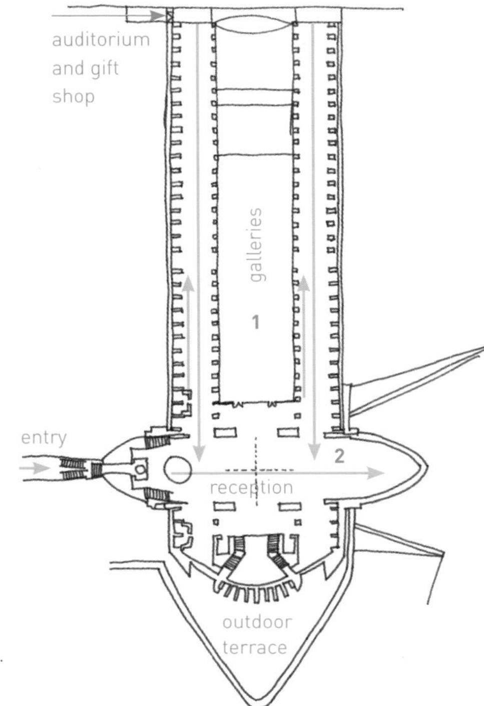

Approach
With its triangular form and the bright white wings of the brise-soleil, the pavilion is a landmark and a visual link between the urban context and the shoreline.

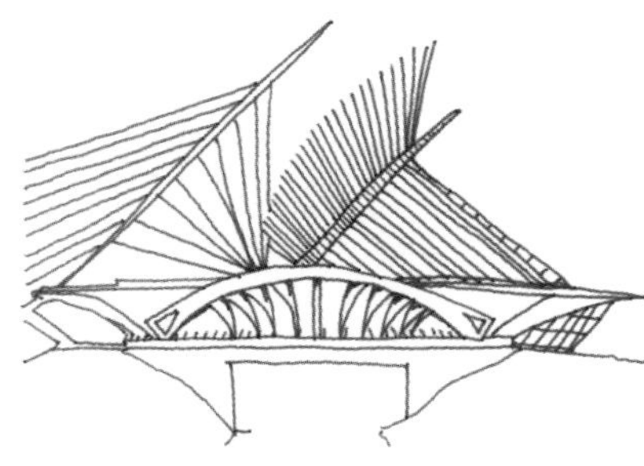

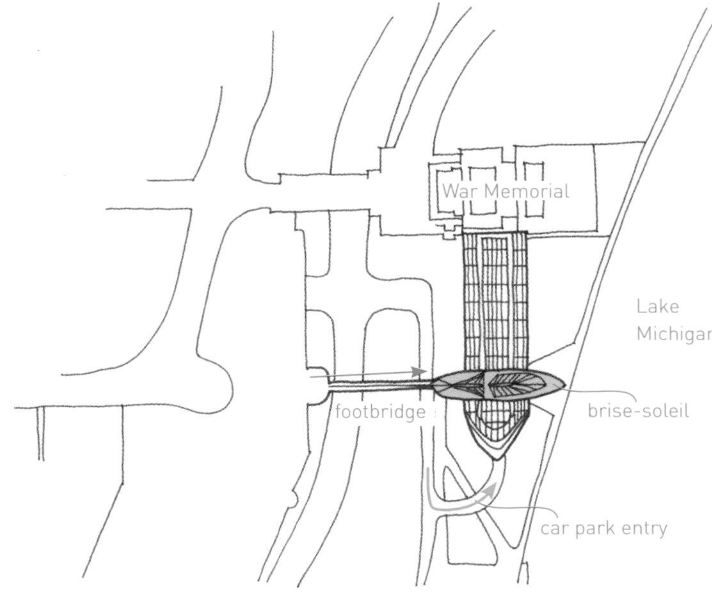

Repetition When one looks along the gallery, the exposed supporting structure gives the sense of a vast space that is divided, despite there being no solid walls between spaces.

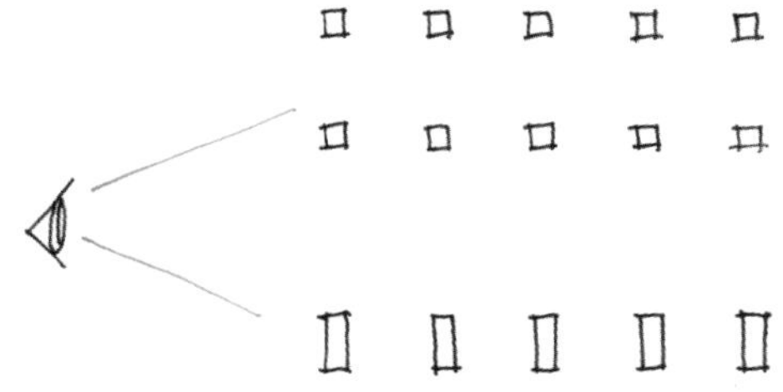

Framed views Glazed horizontal openings, extending longitudinally, visually link the two sides of the pavilion while framing views between their divisions that emphasize the repetition of structural elements.

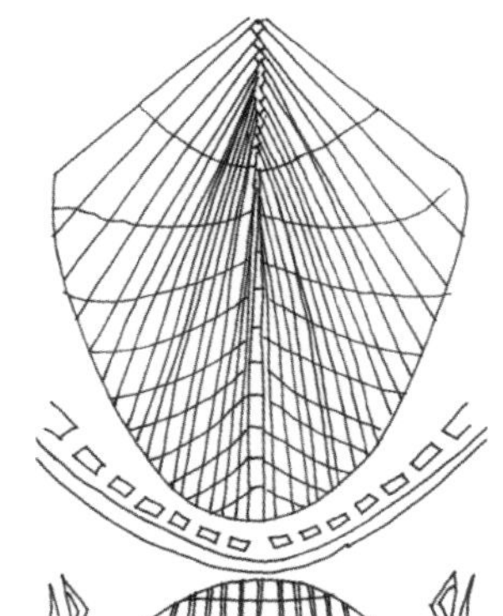

32 **Quadracci Pavilion** | **1994–2001**

Santiago Calatrava
Milwaukee, Wisconsin, USA

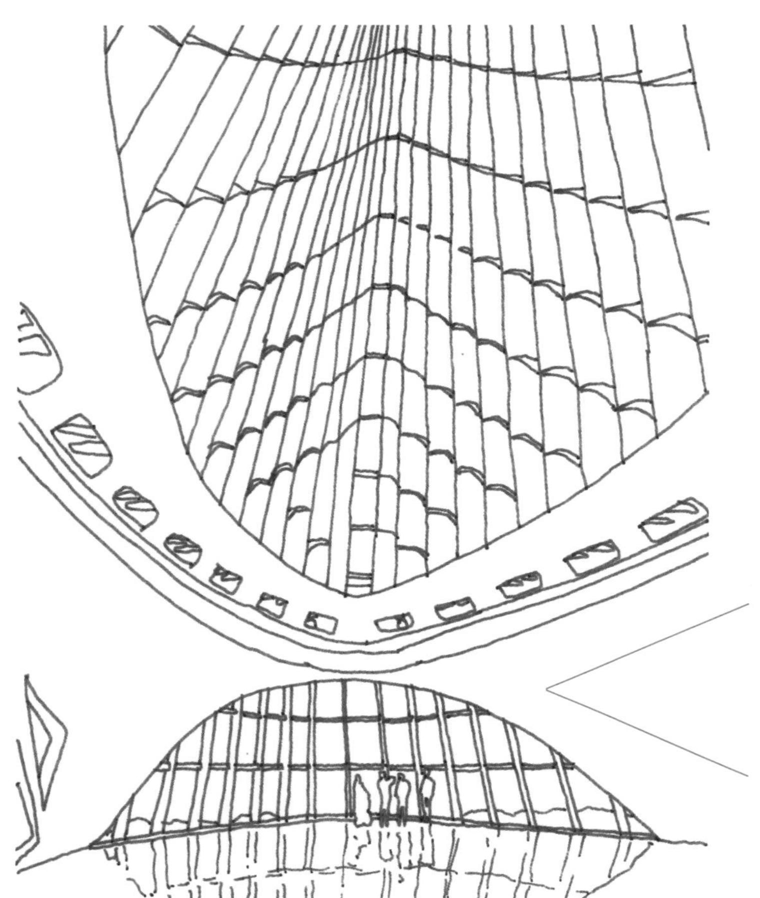

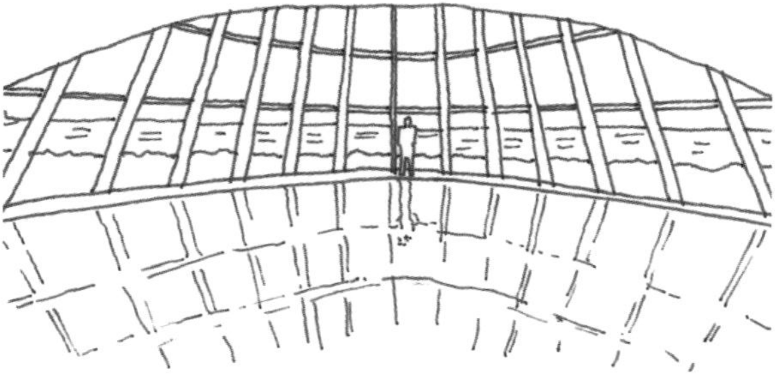

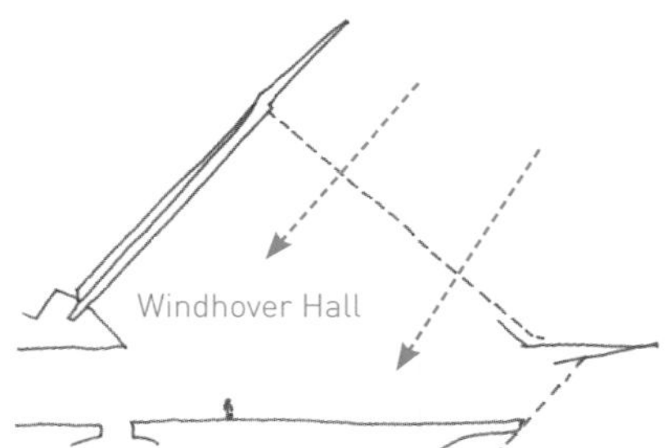

Light With its large-windowed façades, when the brise-soleil is open the hall's light-filled expanse inspires a sense of wonder in the visitor.

Spatiality The height and scale of the hall appearing vast, the pavilion has a feeling of grandeur similar to that of a cathedral.

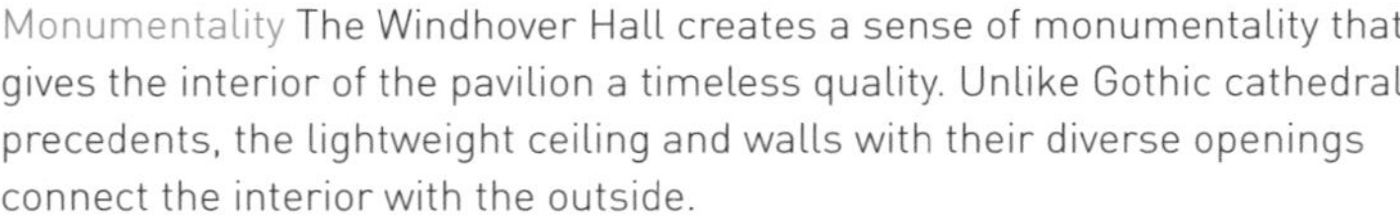

Monumentality The Windhover Hall creates a sense of monumentality that gives the interior of the pavilion a timeless quality. Unlike Gothic cathedral precedents, the lightweight ceiling and walls with their diverse openings connect the interior with the outside.

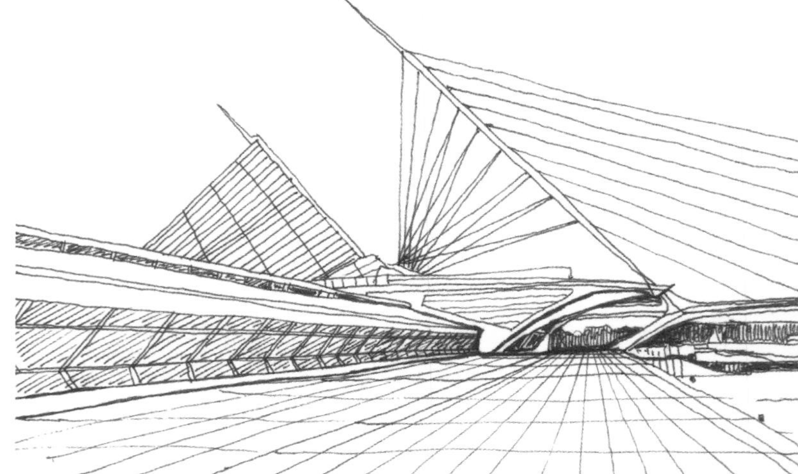

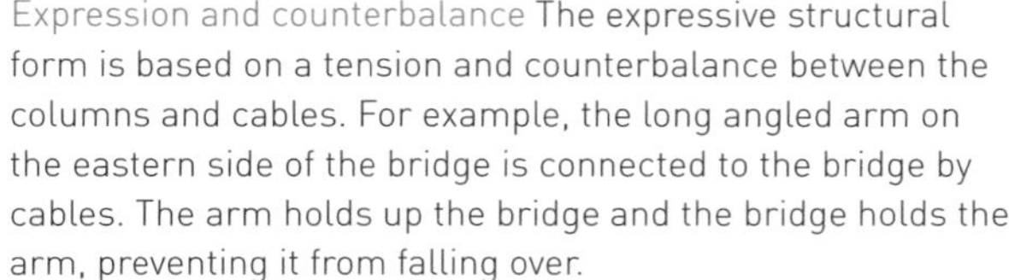

Expression and counterbalance The expressive structural form is based on a tension and counterbalance between the columns and cables. For example, the long angled arm on the eastern side of the bridge is connected to the bridge by cables. The arm holds up the bridge and the bridge holds the arm, preventing it from falling over.

Mass and light The structure and the interior are linked by mass and light, thus enhancing the experiential quality of the exhibition space. Inside, changes of light and shadow throughout the day remind visitors of the flow of time. Outside, the sculpturesque form is an urban landmark that invites viewing from multiple angles and perspectives.

33

B2 House | 1999–2001
Han Tümertekin
Büyükhüsun, Ayvacık, Turkey

Located near the south-east boundary of the village of Büyükhüsun near Ayvacık in western Turkey, B2 House was designed by Turkish architect Han Tümertekin as a weekend escape for two brothers living two hours' drive away in Istanbul.

The house can be interpreted as critical regionalist in its engagement of the modern with the local context. In its form, scale and organization of space, it is functional and minimalist. While it takes typical vernacular houses from the region as precedents and references them in its choice of materials, it makes a modern statement with its form, texture and siting. B2 House crowns a hill near the village and the three-quarter view from the village gives the impression of a monument in the landscape in striking contrast with its humble scale.

Matthew Rundell, Selen Morkoç and Alan L. Cooper

33

B2 House | **1999–2001**
Han Tümertekin
Büyükhüsun, Ayvacık, Turkey

B2 House is a stone, concrete and timber weekend getaway located on the outskirts of Ayvacık village. The house adopts local domestic planning and construction techniques in response to the surrounding social and physical environment.

Ayvacık village

Site view
Although modern in its form, the house fits harmoniously in the local environment with its scale and materials.

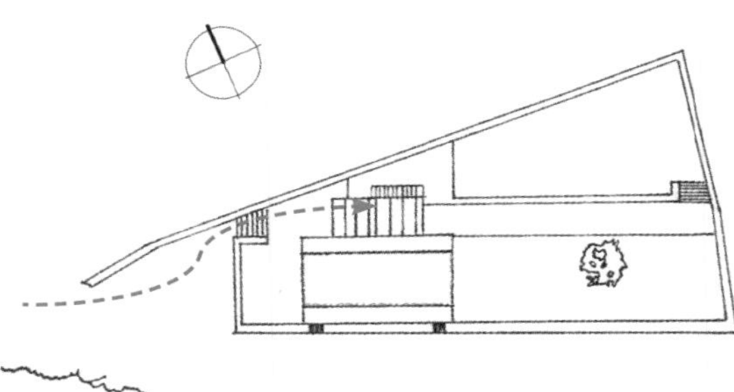

Site plan
B2 House is oriented towards the south to respond to the sun, views and topography.

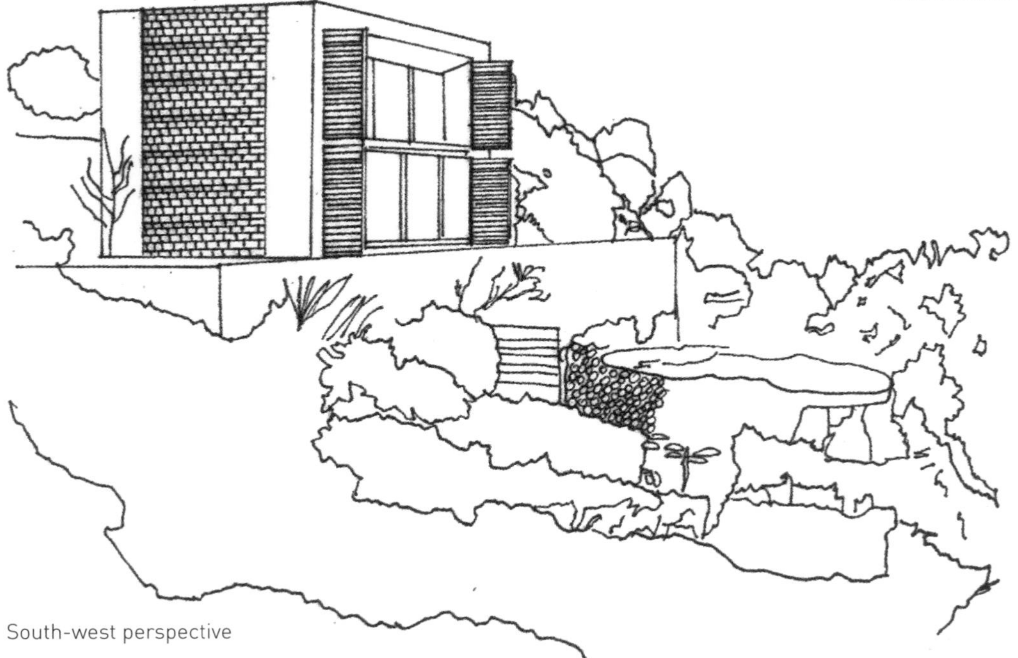

South-west perspective

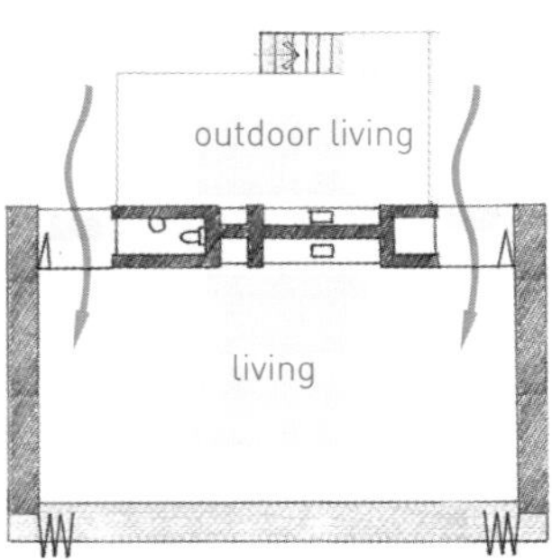

Ground-floor plan

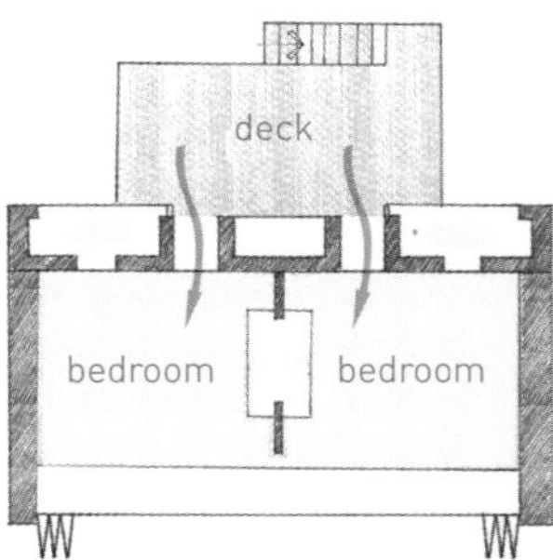

First-floor plan

The plan scheme is minimalist in providing for basic living functions for the owners of the house.

Exterior form development

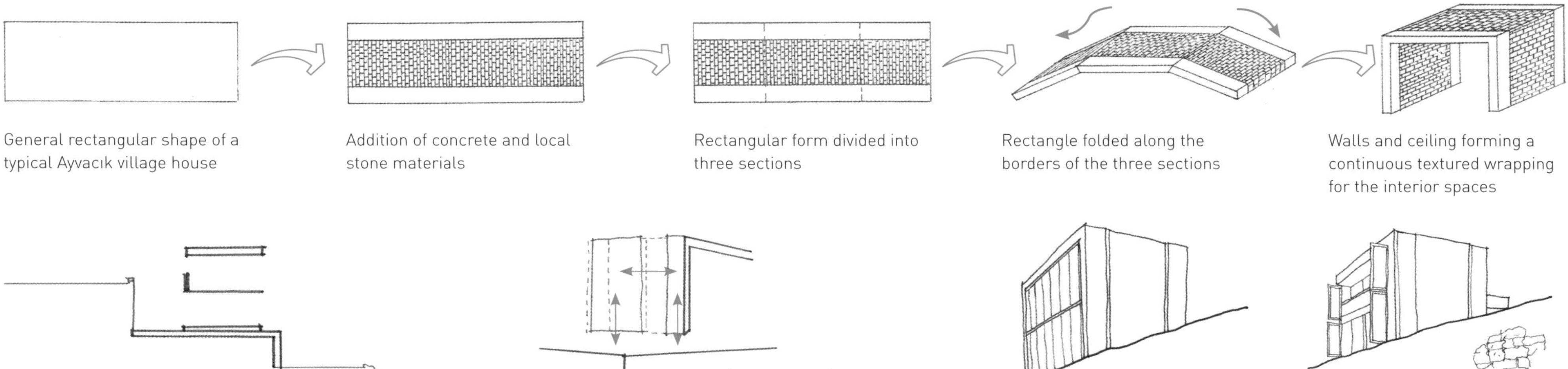

General rectangular shape of a typical Ayvacık village house

Addition of concrete and local stone materials

Rectangular form divided into three sections

Rectangle folded along the borders of the three sections

Walls and ceiling forming a continuous textured wrapping for the interior spaces

Structural vertical and horizontal lines are repeated through the site and the building, creating an unspecialized space providing access to rooms.

The tripartite composition that makes up the main structure of the house gives clues about the organization of the interior space. All materials are exposed, with man-made materials offset against natural ones.

The north and south façades are framed by the offsetting of man-made elements and natural materials. On the south façade (above right), aluminium-framed reed shade screens contrast with monolithic cast-concrete walls. The inner spaces open up wholly to the landscape.

Environment and the house

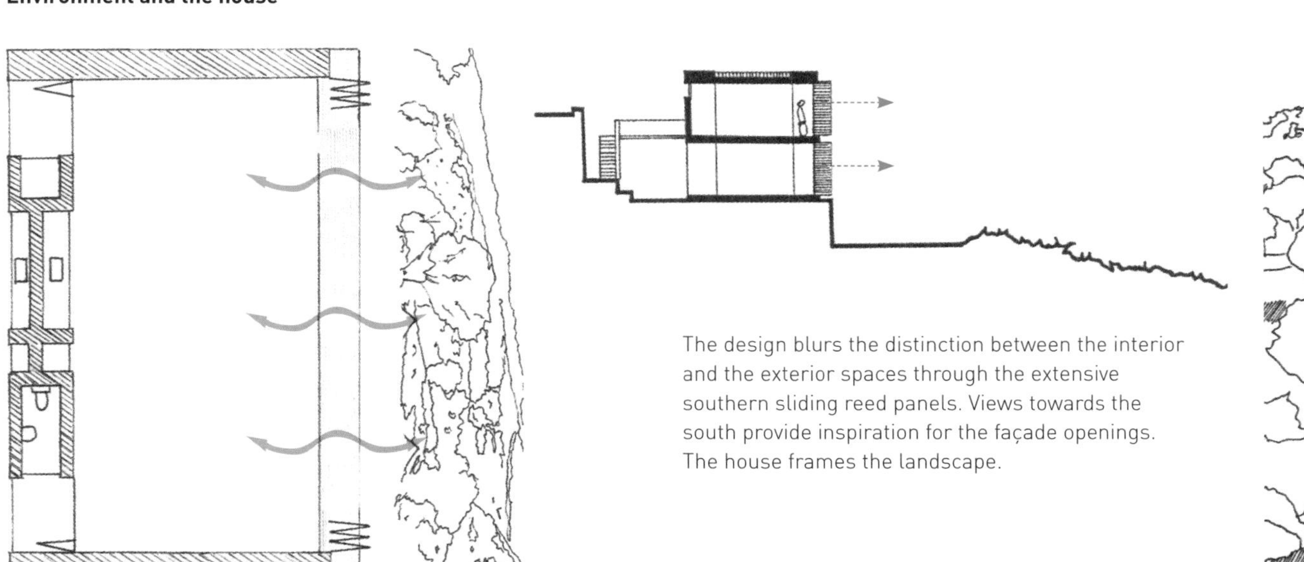

The design blurs the distinction between the interior and the exterior spaces through the extensive southern sliding reed panels. Views towards the south provide inspiration for the façade openings. The house frames the landscape.

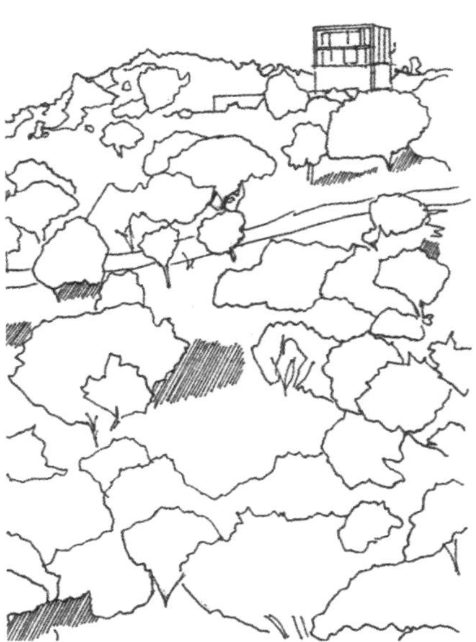

Set in the sloping landscape, from the nearby village the building looks like a monument placed on a pedestal. Its positioning emphasizes the house and its platform, forming a contrast with its humble scale. In this way, the house is distinguished from the vernacular by its monumentality.

33

B2 House | **1999–2001**
Han Tümertekin
Büyükhüsun, Ayvacık, Turkey

Response to environment

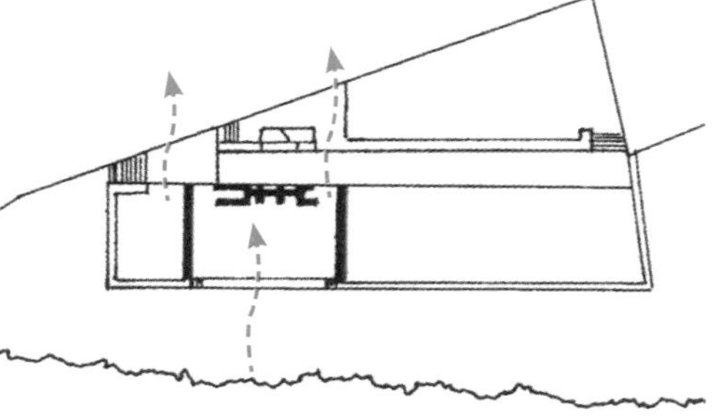

Wind protection Harsh prevailing north-westerly winds are blocked by the windowless side walls of the house.

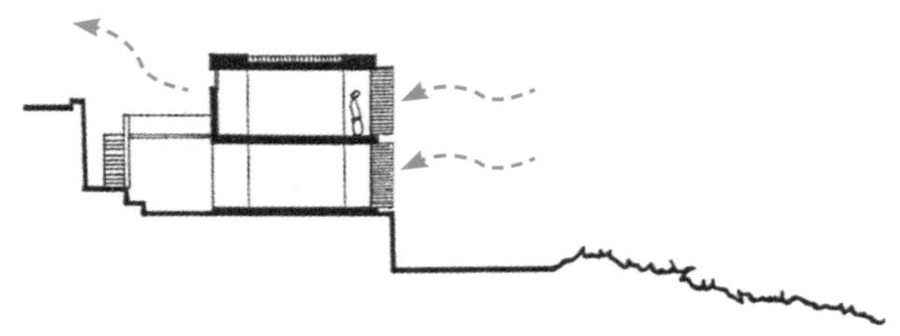

Ventilation Openings on northern and southern façades allow effective cross-ventilation.

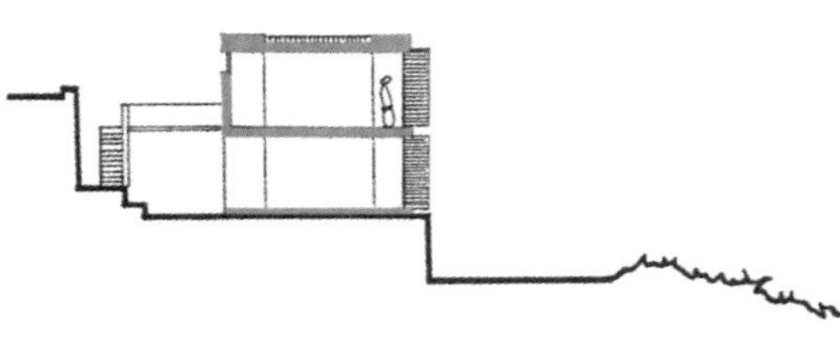

Thermal mass Materials of concrete and stone provide thermal mass for natural heating in winter.

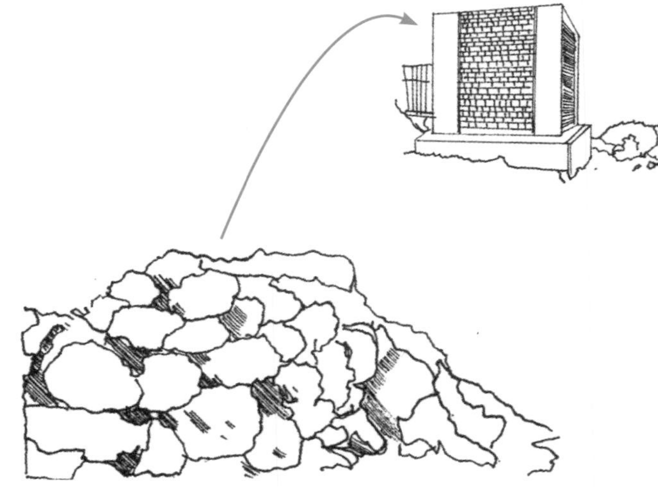

Continuity B2 House establishes a dialogue with its surroundings through use of materials.

Culture and design

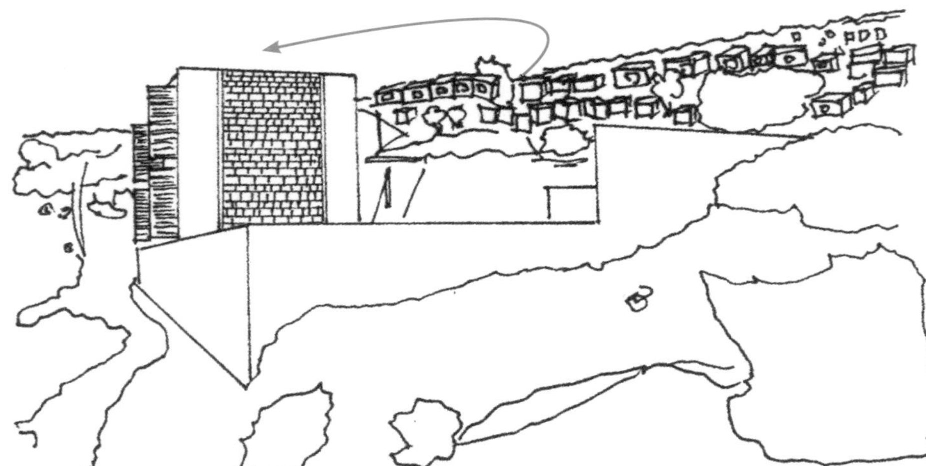

Integrity Local materials, including stone, concrete, timber and reeds, provide a rich contrast in texture. Materials are clearly expressed in their structure and construction processes.

Integration A mixture of Mediterranean construction techniques has been implemented through scale, colours and textures.

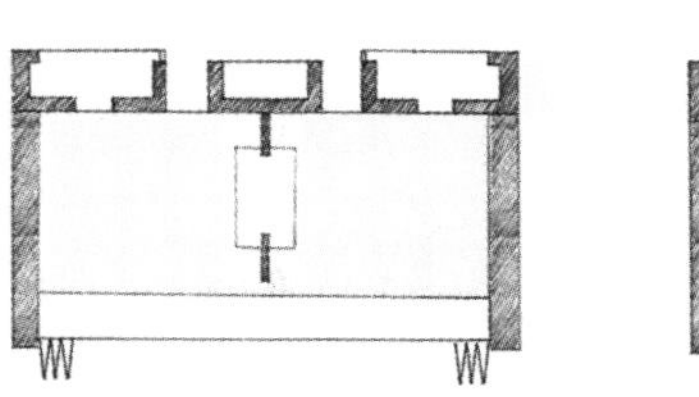

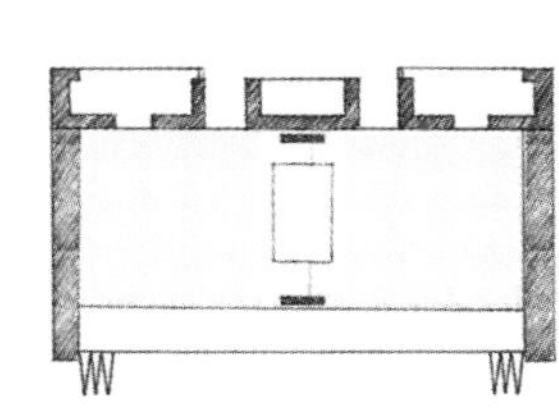

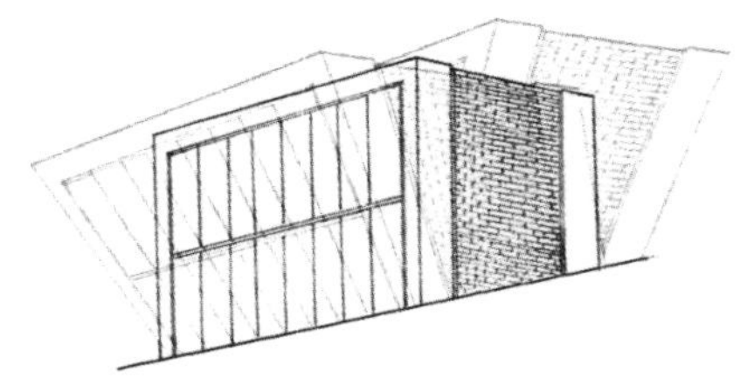

Flexible spaces The dividing walls of the upstairs bedrooms can be altered to unify the space when required. Two isolated spaces can become a single collective space.

Durability Rigid monolithic walls are able to resist seismic forces in a region with a high frequency of earthquakes.

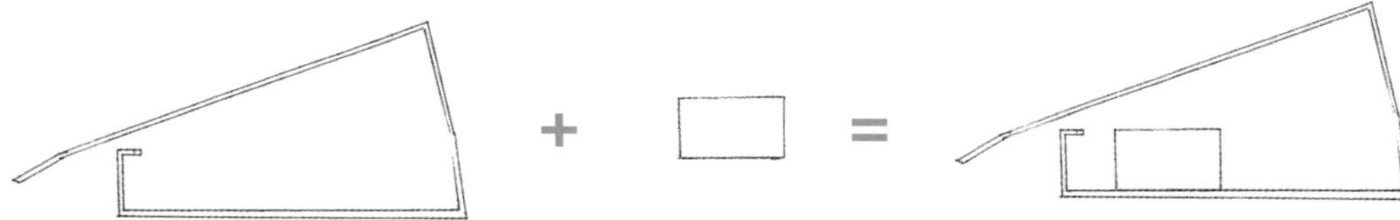

Minimalism The triangular box-shaped site responds to constrictions of the landscape. The house repeats the form of a generic Ayvacık village house. The minimalist site plan combines two design intentions.

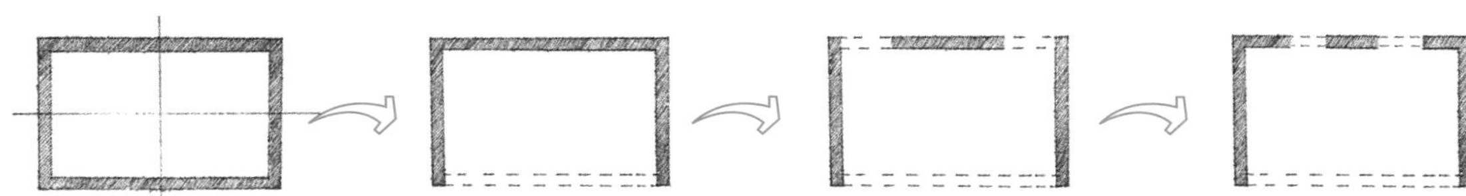

Order and unity From the generic symmetrical rectangular mass of a typical Ayvacık house, the southern façade is removed to respond to the environmental context. Partial removal of the northern façade provides access and ventilation on both the ground floor and the first floor.

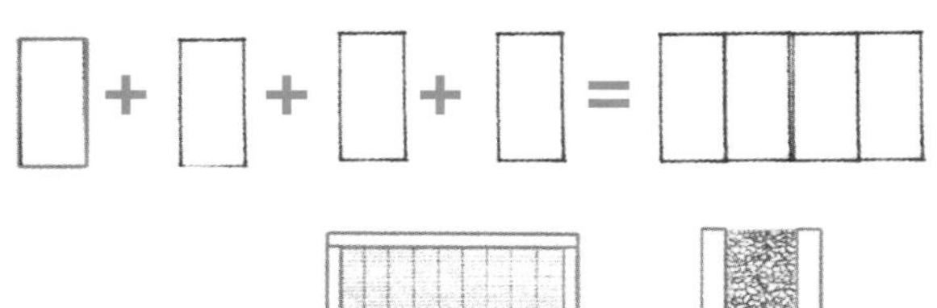

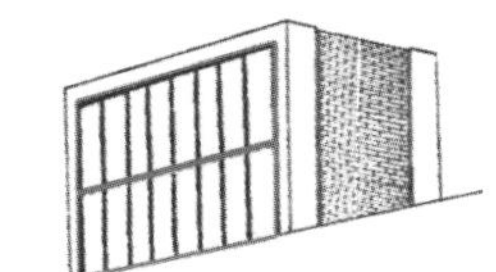

Elements in the house are typically made up from the addition of smaller elements.

Formal repetition defining boundary Similar rectangular forms are used to express boundaries between different materials.

Typical Ayvacık house

B2 House

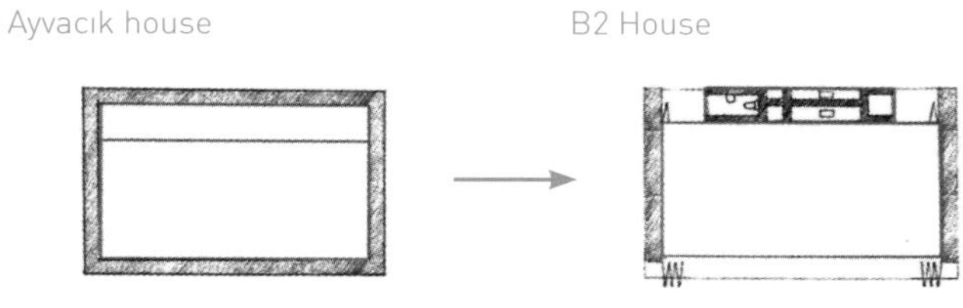

Living spaces are on the ground floor.

Bedrooms are on the upper floor.

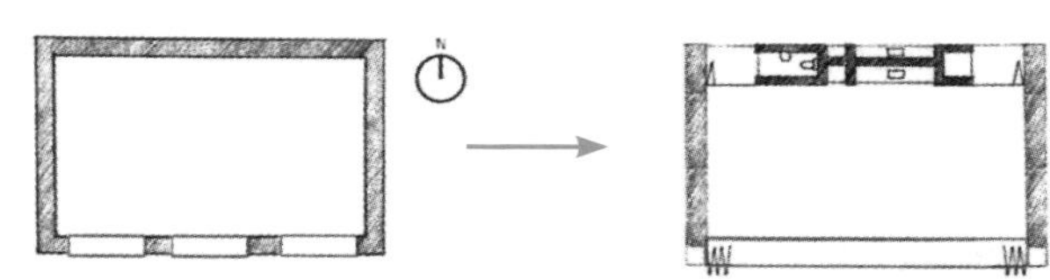

Windows are on the southern façade, isolated from north-westerly winds.

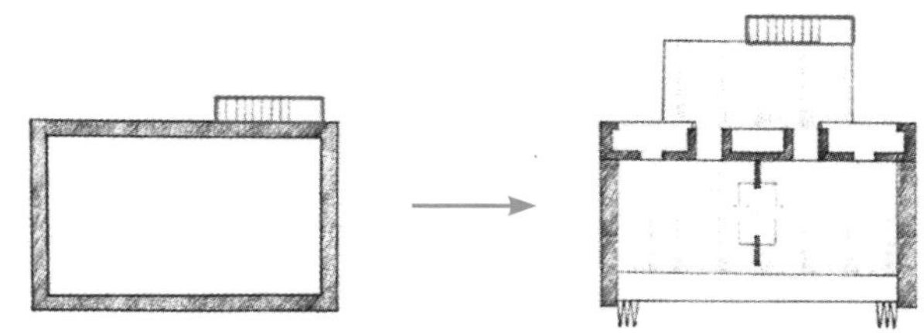

Stairs are located externally to allow maximum use of inner spaces.

33

B2 House | **1999–2001**
Han Tümertekin
Büyükhüsun, Ayvacık, Turkey

Use

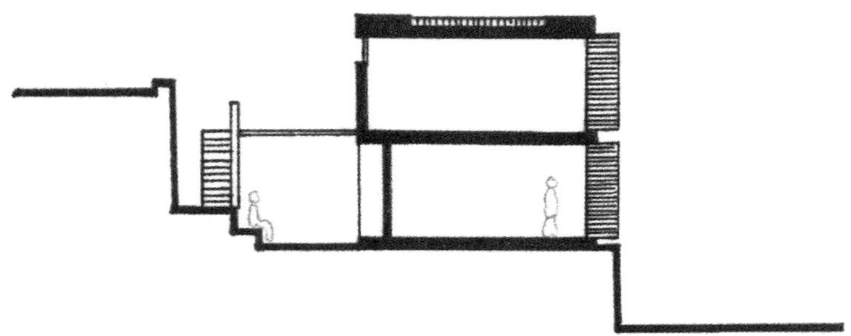

The ground-floor terrace provides a sheltered outdoor space in which utilities serving exterior and interior spaces are located. The blurring of boundaries between the exterior and the interior is maintained.

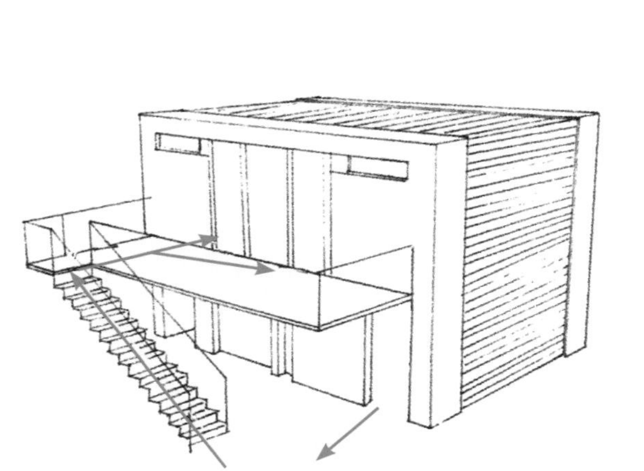

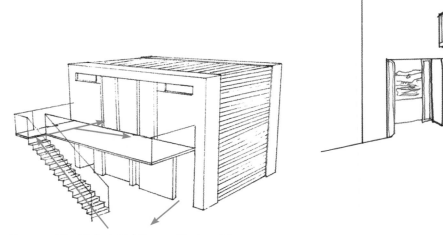

Movement (inside/outside) The positioning of the stairs outside suits the way the house is used.

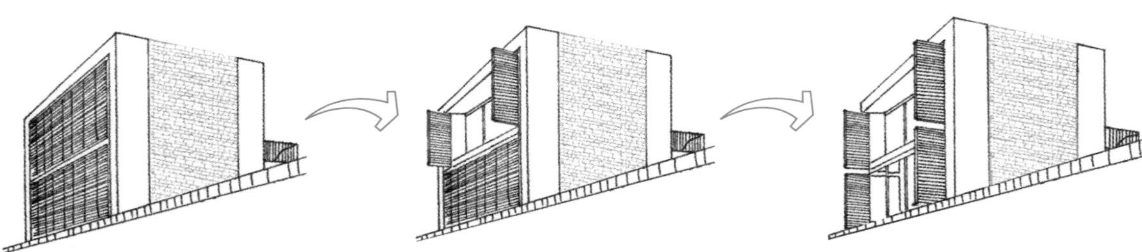

Functional box The house, with the bi-fold aluminium-framed reed sliding doors, responds to its environment with different degrees of disclosure according to need.

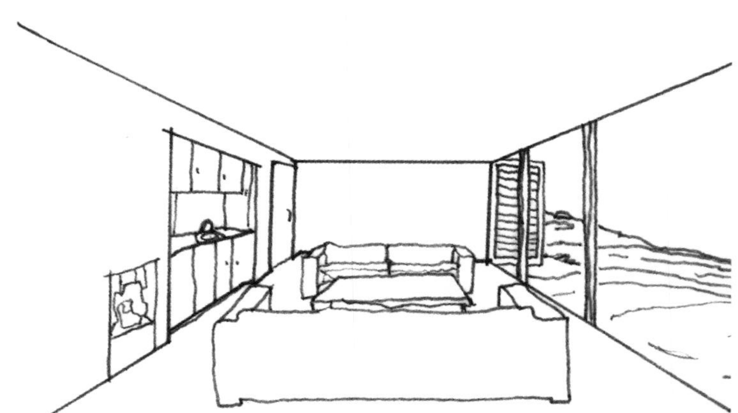

Precedent and responsive cohesion

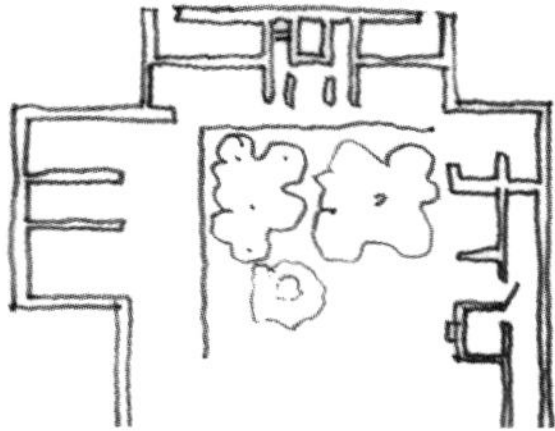

Plan of an Ayvacık house

In B2 House the location of rooms, utilities, windows and stairs, along with scale, form and materiality, all take note of the local vernacular.

Similarity of design intentions can be traced back to Tümertekin's earlier and later projects. The Cital Residence uses similar materials, construction techniques, forms, size and colours to those of B2 House. Later projects such as the Optimum Housing can be seen as the architect taking his design intentions and use of materials a step further, although each project also uniquely responds to its own context.

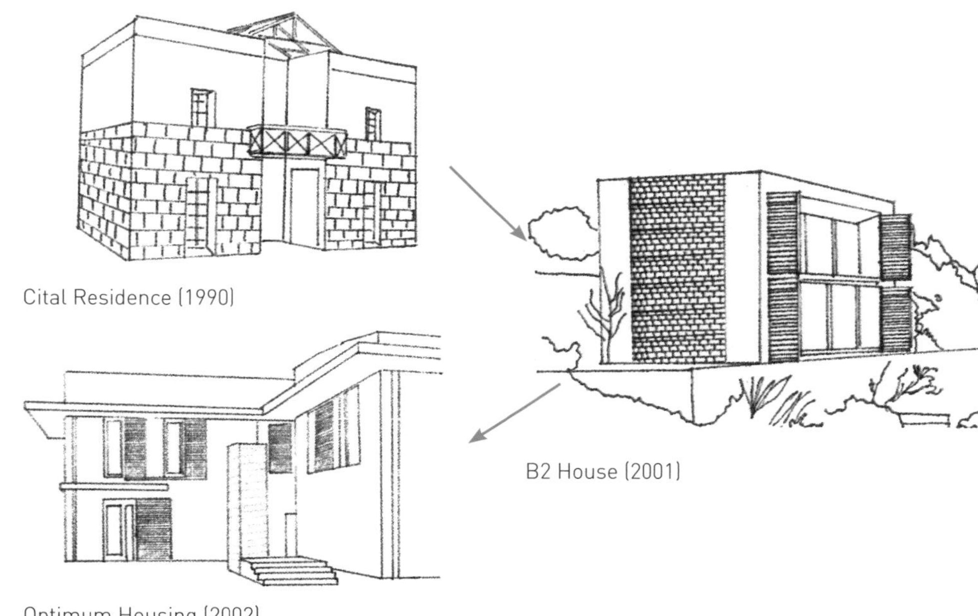

Cital Residence (1990)

B2 House (2001)

Optimum Housing (2002)

34

CaixaForum | 2001–3
Herzog & de Meuron
Madrid, Spain

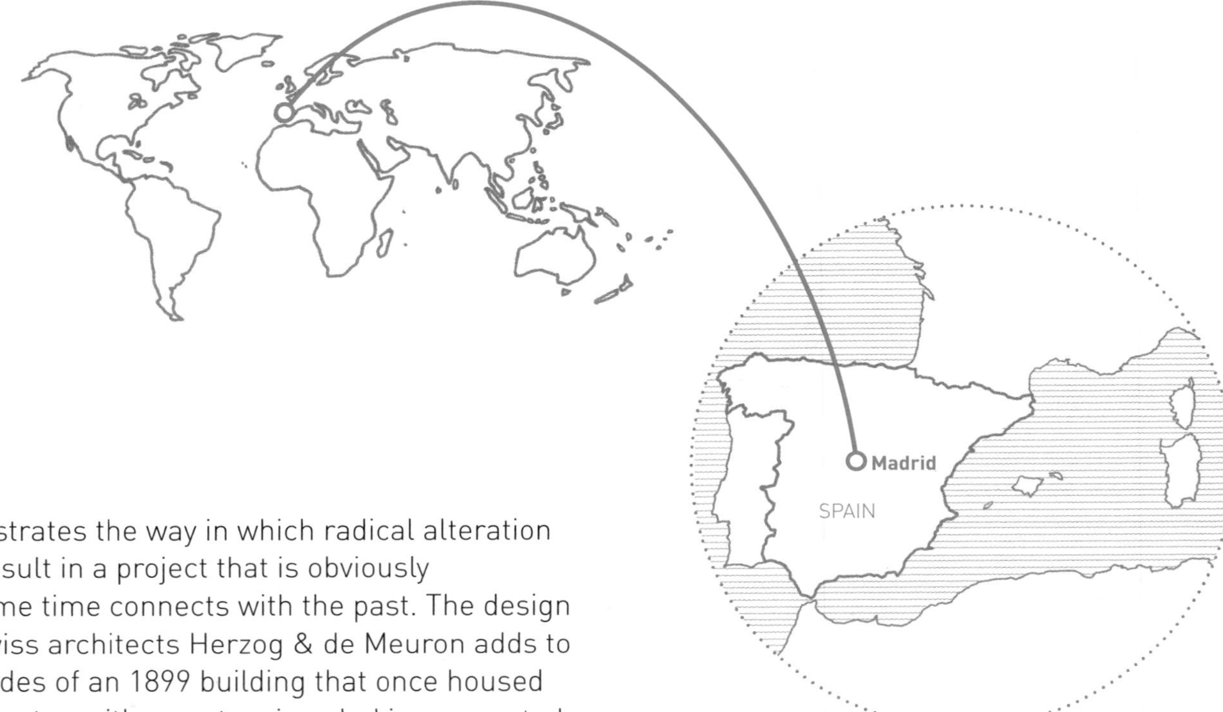

CaixaForum Madrid demonstrates the way in which radical alteration instead of demolition can result in a project that is obviously contemporary but at the same time connects with the past. The design of this cultural centre by Swiss architects Herzog & de Meuron adds to and subtracts from the façades of an 1899 building that once housed a power station. It adds to the top with an extension clad in pre-rusted steel that follows the profile of the walls, and subtracts from the bottom by cutting away the ground level. The mass of the building appears to float over the ground in defiance of gravity. The result is a building that sits comfortably in its urban context and makes its presence felt by subtlety rather than grandeur or confrontation.

A green-wall 'living painting', designed by French botanist Patrick Blanc, is a foil to the hard façade of the gallery. Both are obviously human creations: one composed with living plants, the other with bricks and steel.

Sarah Sulaiman, Allyce McVicar and Antony Radford

34

34

CaixaForum | 2001–3
Herzog & de Meuron
Madrid, Spain

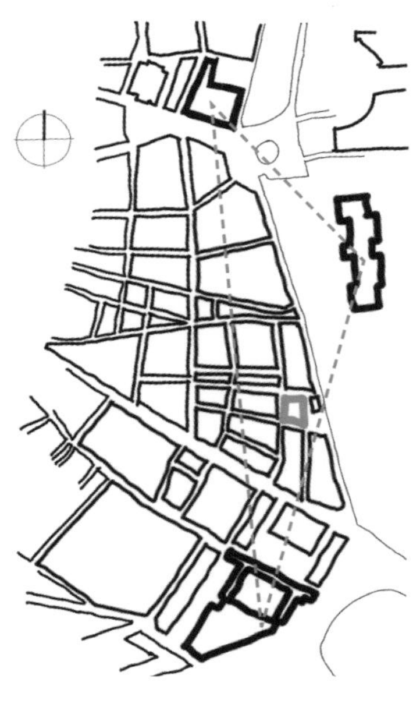

The CaixaForum is situated in the heart of Madrid's cultural district, the 'golden triangle of art' with its corners formed by the Museo del Prado, the Museo Reina Sofía and the Museo Thyssen-Bornemisza. It can be approached through narrow streets or from the broad Paseo del Prado that borders the city's botanical gardens.

Urban context

The 1899 building was lower than most of its neighbours, so the additional height of the upper floors brings it into scale. The deep cuts into the upper levels create a broken skyline that responds to the Madrid skyline. Retaining the pattern of windows in the old façade reflects the pattern of window openings on neighbouring buildings.

A green wall that flanks a new plaza created in front of the building responds to the botanical gardens, as if plants had migrated over the road and colonized the wall. It gives the plaza two green edges and provides identity on the Paseo del Prado.

The narrow footpaths of the bounding streets expand into the building's undercroft.

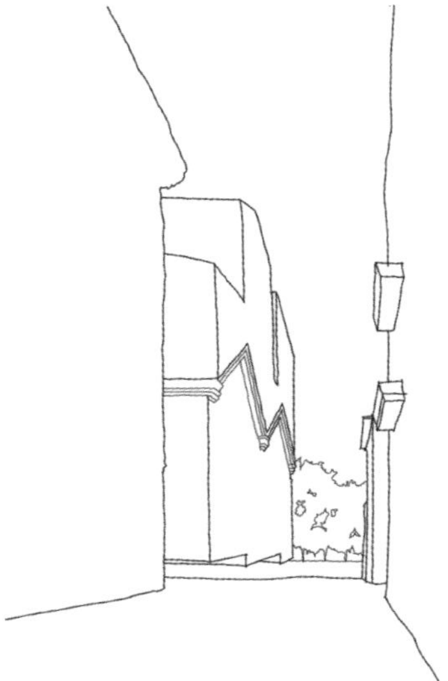

The view along the south side of CaixaForum looks towards the botanical gardens.

Paseo del Prado
green wall
green edge of botanical gardens

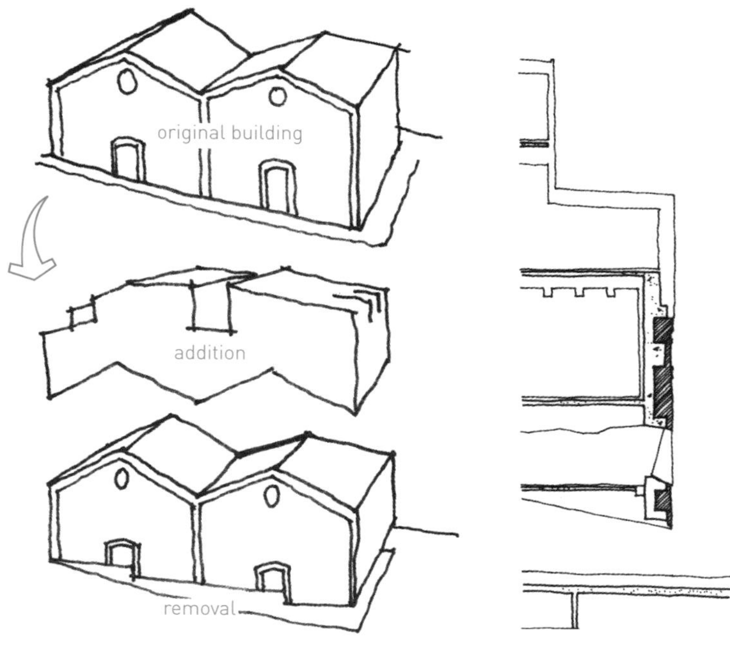

Old and new
The architects do not treat old buildings with a museum-like desire to preserve. Instead, they simply remove what is not needed, clean up what remains and incorporate the old in the new.

Only the brick skin of the 1899 structure is retained, with a new building built inside that skin and extending above. There is no sense of entering an old building; entry stairs and foyer are glossy and modern. Walls inside are concrete and floors are white terrazzo.

Where the concrete building rises beyond the brick skin it is wrapped in pre-rusted steel. This is a material that seems to begin life with patina of age. Its colours and tonal variation work well with the weathered brick walls.

Response to climate
In the harsh heat of the Madrid summer sun (the main tourist season) the deep shade of the undercroft is welcome. Upper-level windows are shaded. The thick walls of the building and its underground component provide thermal mass and more stable internal conditions. The new green wall provides the neighbouring building with insulation and acts as a natural cooling system in summer, though these benefits come at the cost of continuing maintenance.

Old windows that are not needed are bricked up. Where windows are needed they punch through the retained brick façade or are veiled behind perforations in the pre-rusted steel skin.

Adding and cutting
Herzog & de Meuron have adopted the strategy of adding to and surgically cutting away from an existing building in other projects.

In their conversion of a grand power station in London, England, into the Tate Modern gallery (1995–2000) they cut away a lower corner of its massive walls, leaving an improbable heavy mass above space and glass. To make a broad opening into what was the turbine hall they lowered its floor to the original basement level and burrowed under the walls. On top of the building, smooth rectangular boxes extend the volume.

For the Museum of Cultures in Basel, Switzerland (2001–11), they burrowed below the existing walls to make a wide opening that did not disturb the existing façade. On top are new levels in an attic volume that echoes the steeply pitched roofs of its neighbours but with a perforated, highly textured skin.

The Elbe Philharmonic Hall that at the time of writing was under construction in Hamburg, Germany (2003–16), has a wide opening cut through the walls of an old warehouse at ground level and a large glazed addition on top. The delicacy and the playful roofline of this addition contrast with the sombre brick mass of the original building. Unlike at the Caixa building, there is a recess around the top of the old walls that creates a shadow gap and separates new from old.

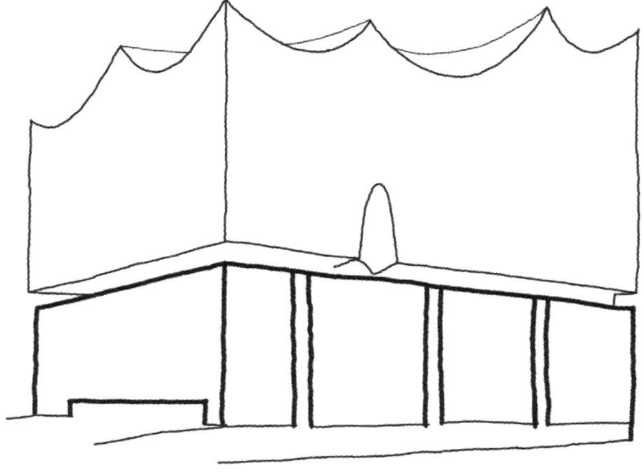

Planning

Top level:
small spaces
for restaurant
and offices

Gallery levels:
large, flexible
neutral spaces

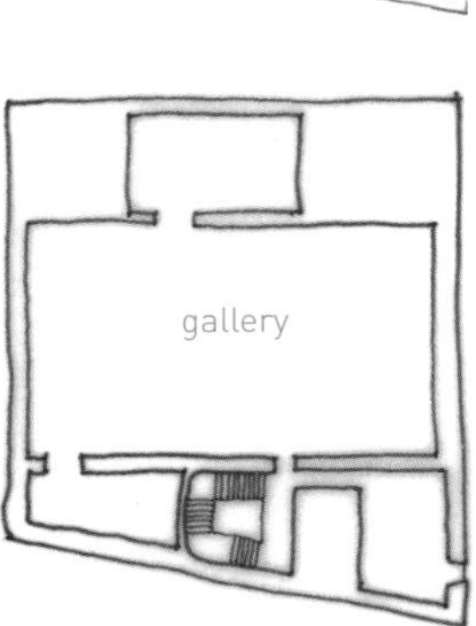

Foyer level:
dynamic space
with bright
lights and shiny
surfaces

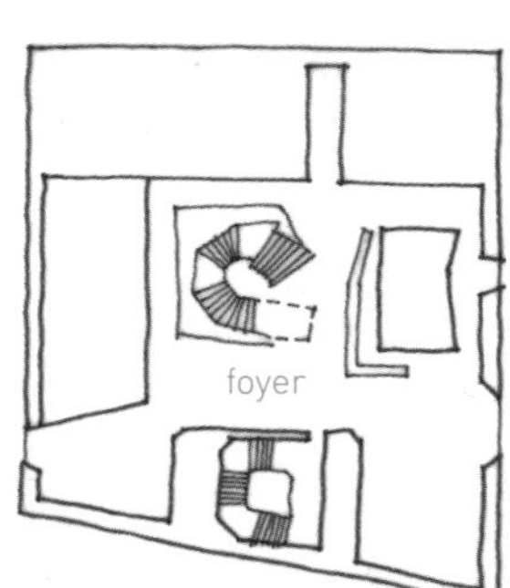

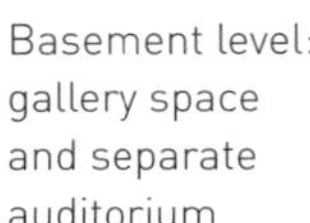

Basement level:
gallery space
and separate
auditorium

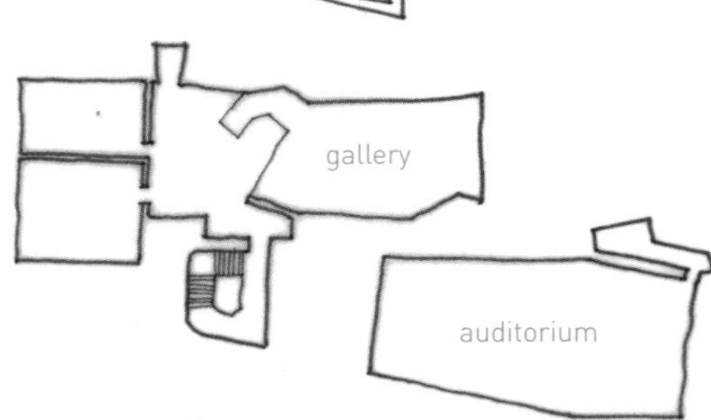

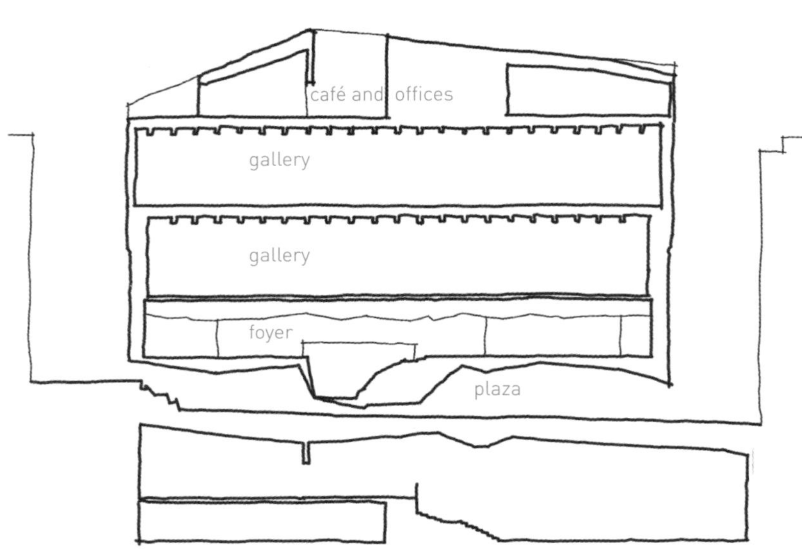

The plaza flows under the belly of the building, where old brick walls have been cut away.

Plaza level: triangulated pavement and ceilings

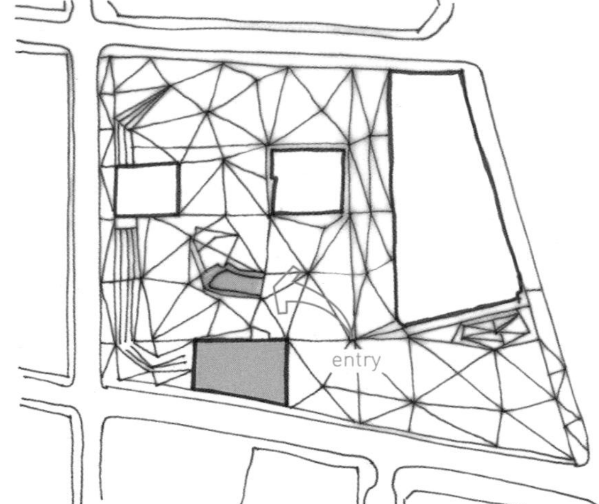

Fragments are apparently cut away from the top of the addition.

The top-lit stair shaft acts as a pin through all the levels of the building.

New walls of pre-rusted steel and old walls of brick are skins around all-new interiors.

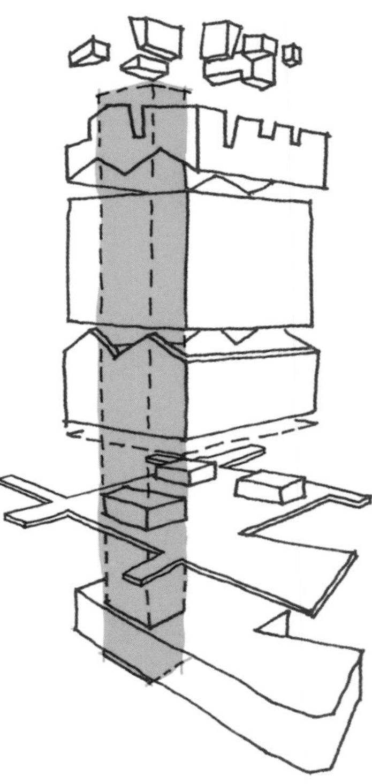

At the south side of the foyer a bright top-lit atrium stair leads to the upper levels, providing a starting point to navigate the galleries, together with access to the top-level café. Lifts and escape stairs augment this main circulation route.

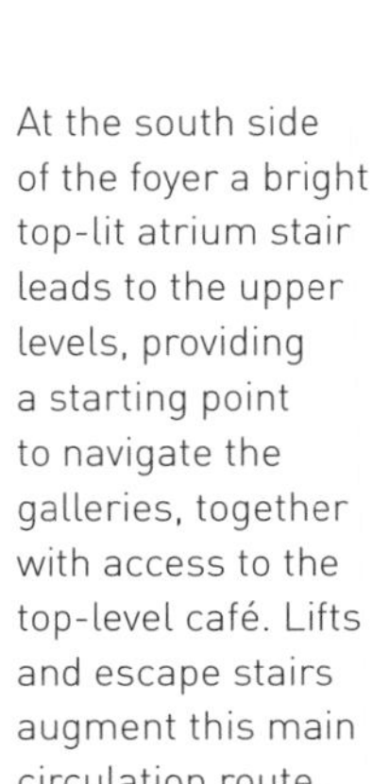

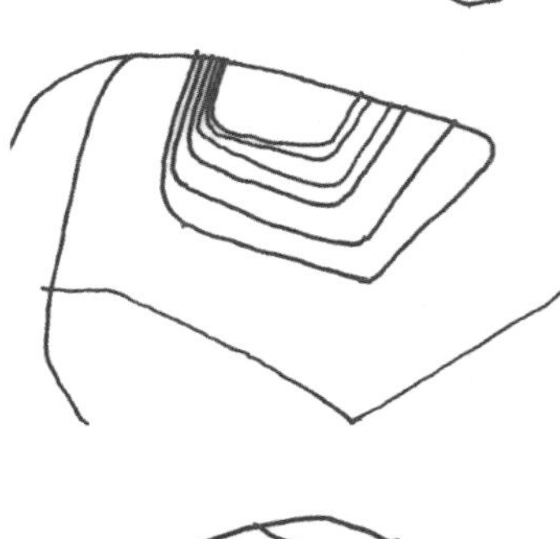

Below the foyer, the same atrium stairs lead down to an underground theatre and more galleries.

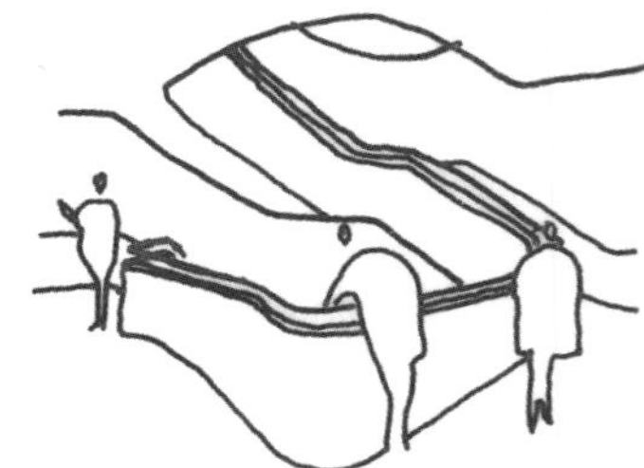

Entry

The lit text 'CaixaForum' signals the entrance in the low light of the undercroft.

Near the centre of the undercroft are the entry stairs.

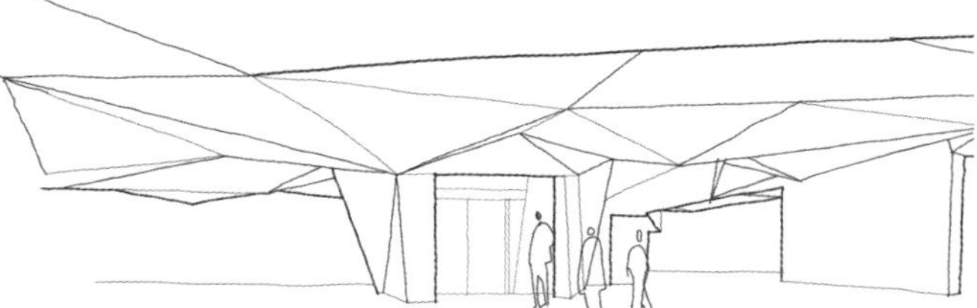

A broad open stairway leads up to the foyer, the sides triangulated and splayed outwards. The foyer has an open ceiling with exposed services. Tubular lights hang from the structure.

A large window offers a view of the plaza and the botanical gardens.

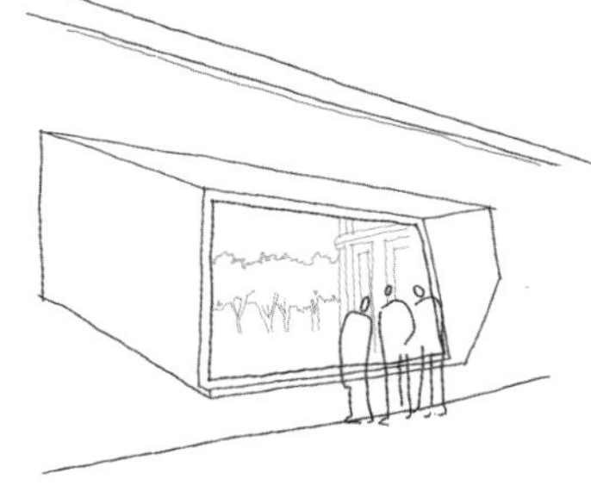

The galleries are lit with artificial light and provide flexible space that can be partitioned to suit exhibitions.

A perforated skin

Parts of the Corten steel skin are perforated with a repetitive pattern of cut holes that recalls the traditional Spanish lace of the region. Offices and the café windows look through this screen to the view, as if through a dense veil. This device distances the viewer from the external scene. It also simplifies the exterior, strengthening the building's identity.

There is no shadow gap between the sheet steel and the brick walls – the sheet steel appears to be fitted perfectly to the top of the original walls.

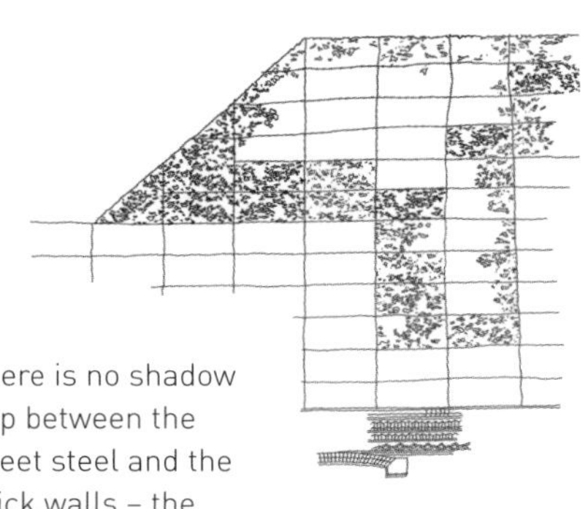

The decorated brick cornices of the original walls contrast with the 'cut-off' top of the new steel addition.

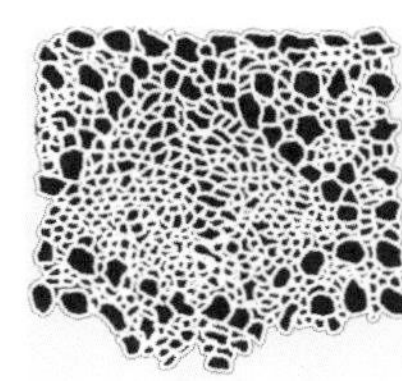

Spanish lace

Detail of perforated panel

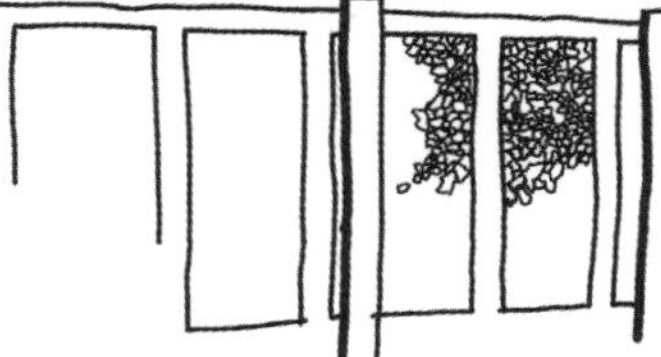

Views from windows in the top-floor café are partially blocked by the perforated steel screen.

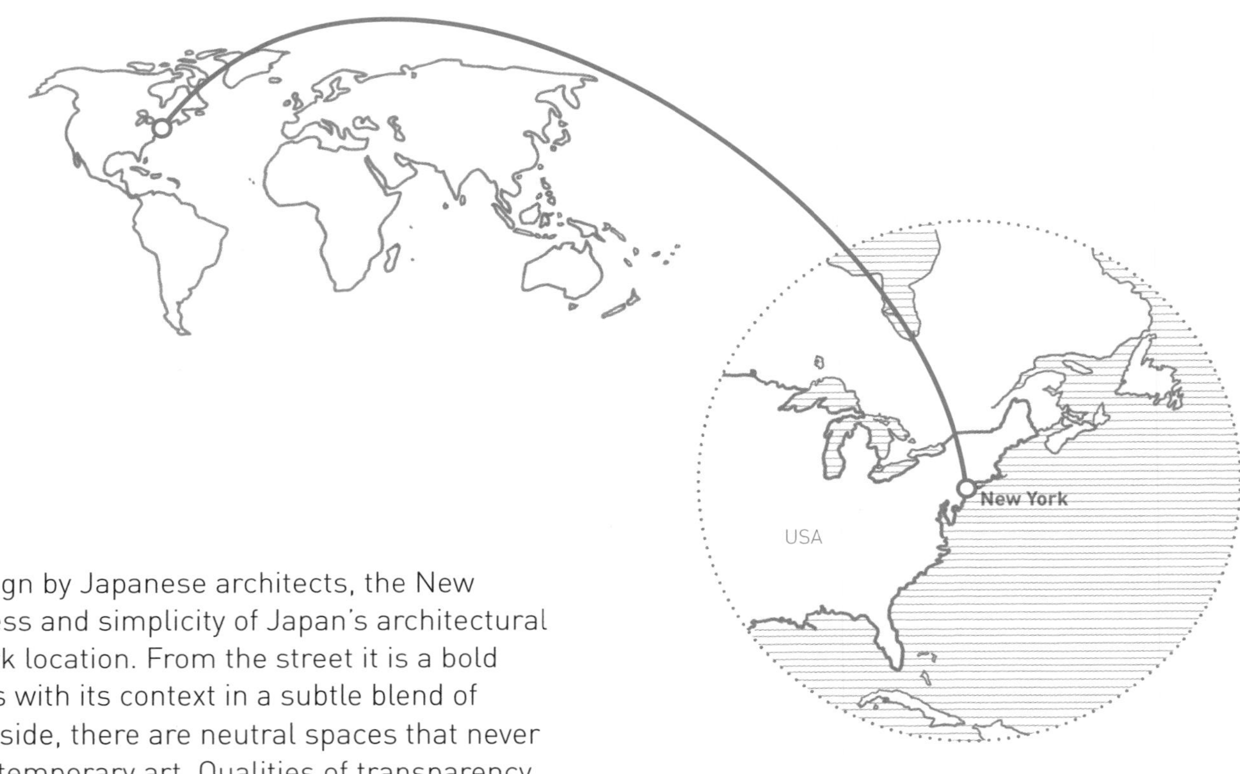

New Museum | 2001–7

SANAA (Kazuyo Sejima and Ryue Nishizawa)

New York, USA

A competition-winning design by Japanese architects, the New Museum adapts the lightness and simplicity of Japan's architectural tradition to a gritty New York location. From the street it is a bold stack of boxes that engages with its context in a subtle blend of sensitivity and assertion. Inside, there are neutral spaces that never dominate the exhibited contemporary art. Qualities of transparency, lightness and reflection suggest the ephemerality of virtual worlds in digital architecture. Clarity in planning organization and pragmatic functionality make it work in the physical world. The building demonstrates that good architecture can be achieved on a tight site with a limited budget.

SANAA is a joint office of architects Kazuyo Sejima and Ryue Nishizawa. Both still operate individual offices, with SANAA focusing on large and international projects.

Daniel Turner, Antony Radford and Sonya Otto

35

35 New Museum | 2001–7

SANAA (Kazuyo Sejima and Ryue Nishizawa)
New York, USA

Response to site

The building is a stack of differently sized boxes that are offset from one another. The surrounding streets contain narrow early twentieth-century masonry buildings, taller than they are wide, of differing heights. The museum keeps this traditional scale but turns the division on its side, so that horizontal layers and not vertical slices are emphasized.

The bottom section references the typical setback upper floors seen in New York. Its setbacks respond to the buildings next door, low on the west side and higher on the east side. The cantilevered projection of the upper section is strikingly different, with no precedent in the traditional built form. A long rectilinear window on the fifth floor partially separates these upper levels, allowing them to 'float' above the skyline.

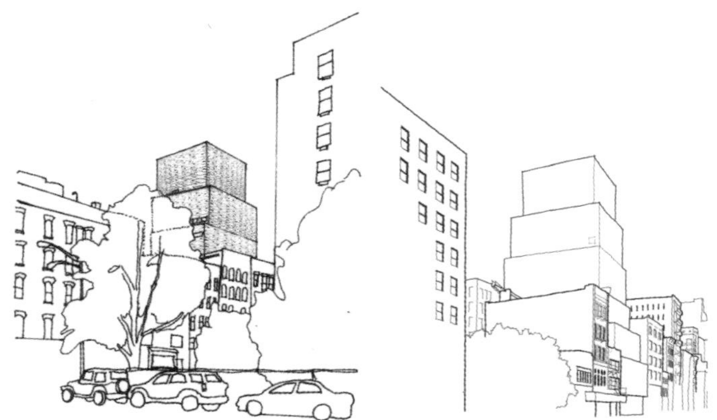

The building symbolizes confidence and culture, and attracts tourism to the area. It is larger and brighter than its neighbours, acting as a beacon.

It functions as an exhibit on the street, a bold, blocky expression of contemporary design and values. Its sleek precision contrasts with its much rougher neighbours, many of them well past their youthful prime. Inside, the museum has an aesthetic of robust semi-industrial simplicity.

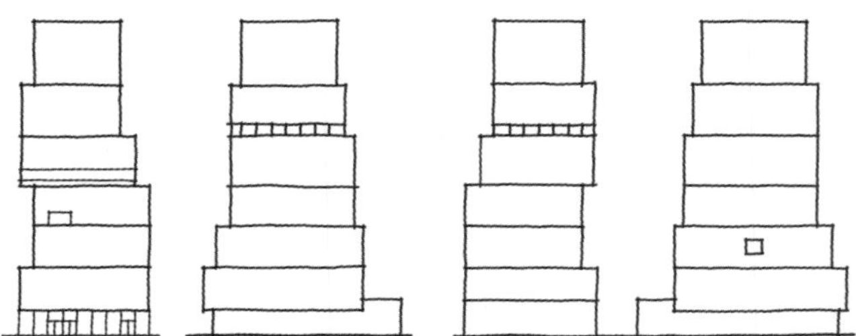

The elevations do not display the division into storeys. While the building has nine levels above ground, including the rooftop enclosure, from the outside only up to seven levels seem to be present, depending on the elevation.

The shifting of the boxes allows skylights and terraces while keeping within the zoned building envelope.

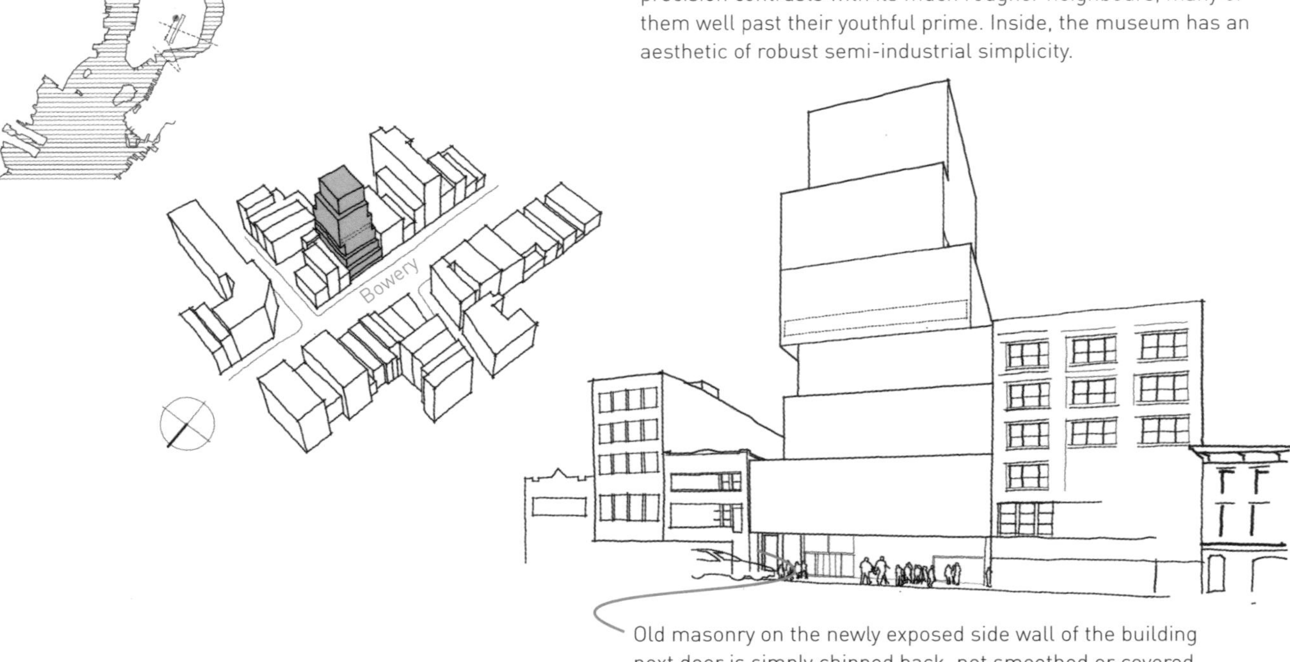

Old masonry on the newly exposed side wall of the building next door is simply chipped back, not smoothed or covered.

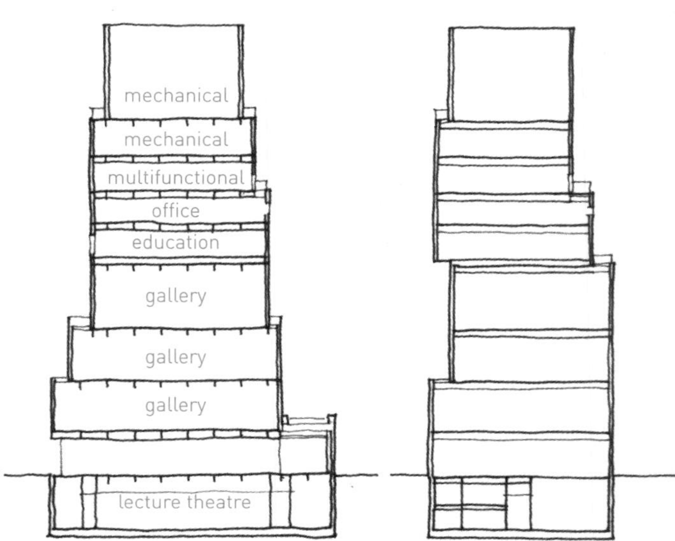

Key
1. stairs between upper levels
2. lifts
3. stairs to upper floors and basement
4. down stairs to basement
5. shop
6. entry
7. reception desk
8. escape to street
9. loading dock

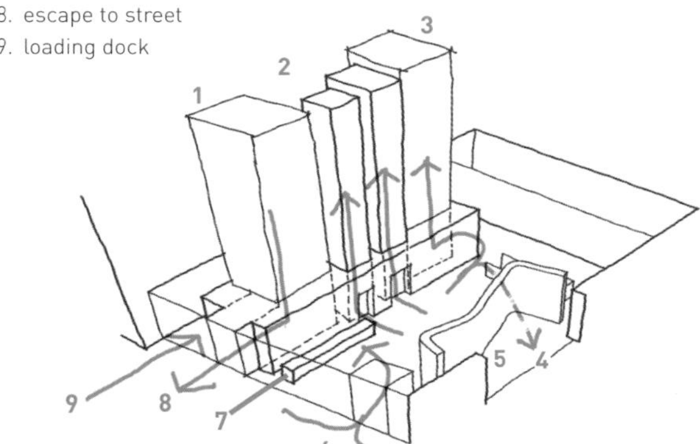

Entry and planning

A floor-to-ceiling street window invites visitors with a view of the activity inside. Once inside, they find a long metallic reception desk on one side (open and obvious) and a curving mesh room divider on the other (intriguing and teasing). This turns out to be the back of shelves in the gallery shop, exposing yet shielding the colourful displayed objects so that they draw the viewer to inspect more closely. A small café is at the back, together with a glass wall into a top-lit gallery that lets natural light into the back of the building.

The spreading natural light makes the whole ground floor a transition between outdoors and the enclosed galleries above, where blank walls are needed for display. These upper galleries are uncluttered and neutral, their character determined by the artwork of the temporary exhibitions they house.

The building's structure and guts are exposed: beams, ducts, lights, sprinklers, fireproofing.

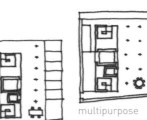

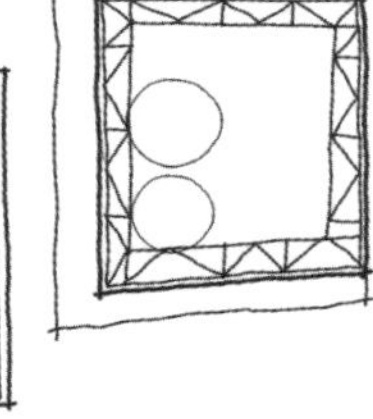

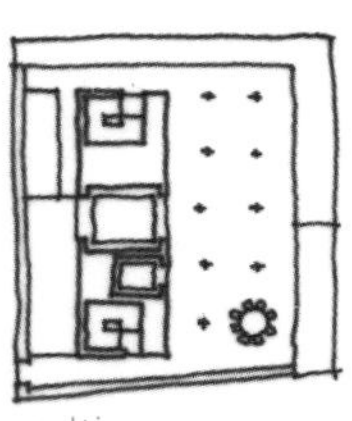

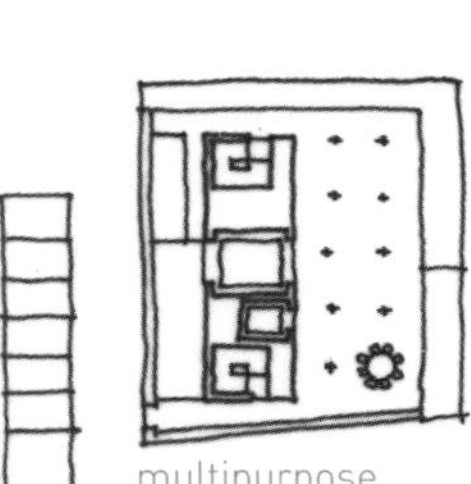

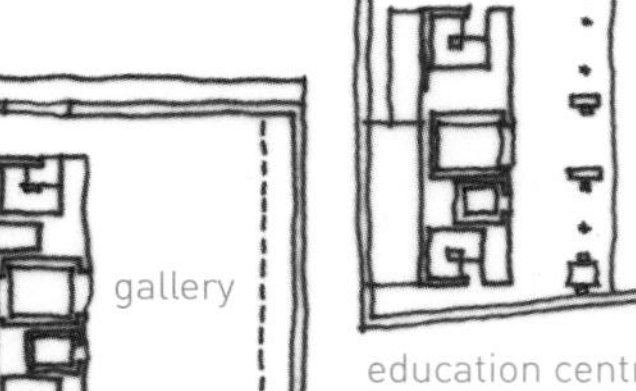

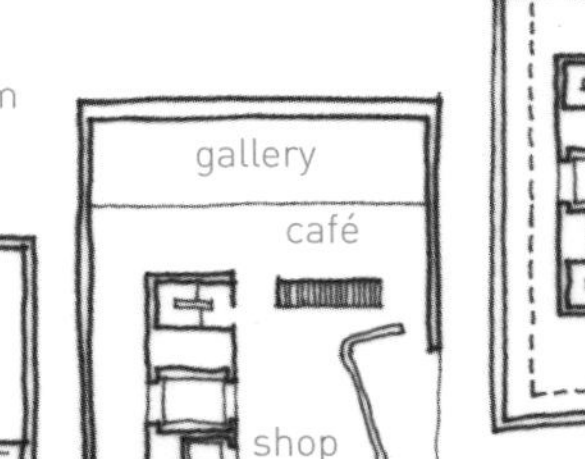

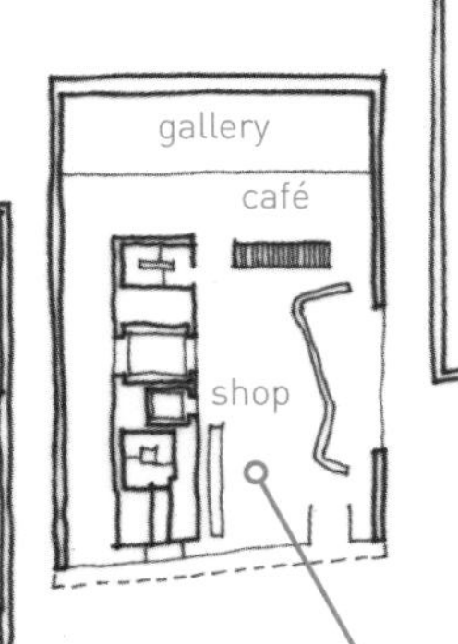

A vertical service core of stairs, lifts and ducts penetrates the boxes like the post of a child's toy.

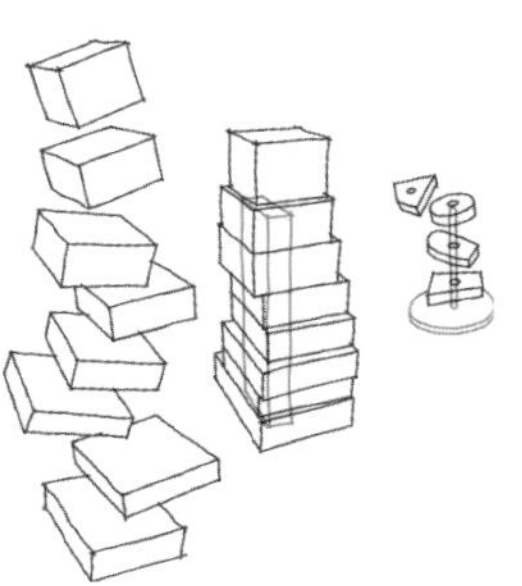

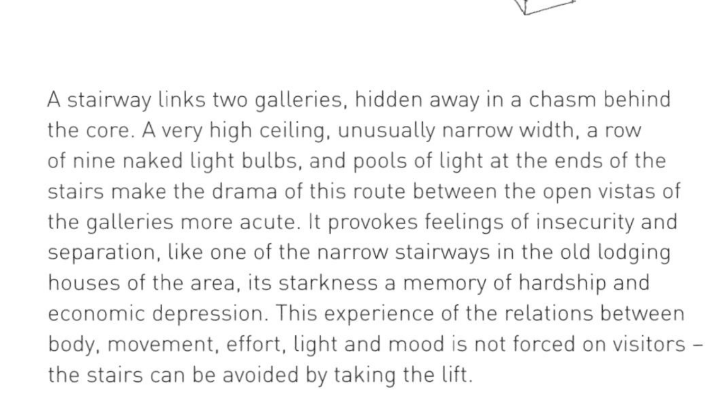

A stairway links two galleries, hidden away in a chasm behind the core. A very high ceiling, unusually narrow width, a row of nine naked light bulbs, and pools of light at the ends of the stairs make the drama of this route between the open vistas of the galleries more acute. It provokes feelings of insecurity and separation, like one of the narrow stairways in the old lodging houses of the area, its starkness a memory of hardship and economic depression. This experience of the relations between body, movement, effort, light and mood is not forced on visitors – the stairs can be avoided by taking the lift.

35

New Museum | 2001–7

SANAA (Kazuyo Sejima and Ryue Nishizawa)

New York, USA

Transparency and reflection

Mesh screens, glass balustrades, polished floors, bright white walls and shiny metallic benches are all found in the design. Transparency creates intrigue and interest, whether it is the desirable objects behind the screen on the shop shelves or the southern city skyline behind the screen over the window strip on level 4. Reflection creates ambiguity, as in an unexpected reflection of the city in an unscreened terrace window.

Lightness, thinness, transparency and reflection are all typical characteristics of computer-generated virtual worlds.

The edges of the building are precise, but there are connections across these edges, between rooms and between interior and exterior, that blur those edges and what can be seen across the edges.

Materiality

The façades are wrapped in anodized expanded aluminium mesh, reflecting sunlight and the changing sky and often seeming to fade and dematerialize. At night, light filtering through windows and skylights turns the building into a glowing beacon, like a giant origami lampshade.

Most interior walls are white, with polished grey concrete floors and ceilings, where substructure, exposed services and fluorescent tubes are ranged in parallel lines across the building's width. Coherence is achieved through these consistent materials and rectilinear forms. The quiet tones promote a mood of contemplation. This seemingly uniform interior is disrupted by dashes of bright colour: the lifts are lime green and the basement washrooms have bright cherry-blossom tiles.

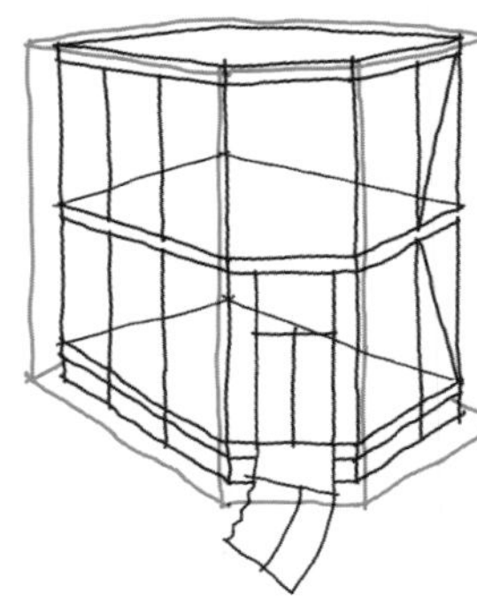

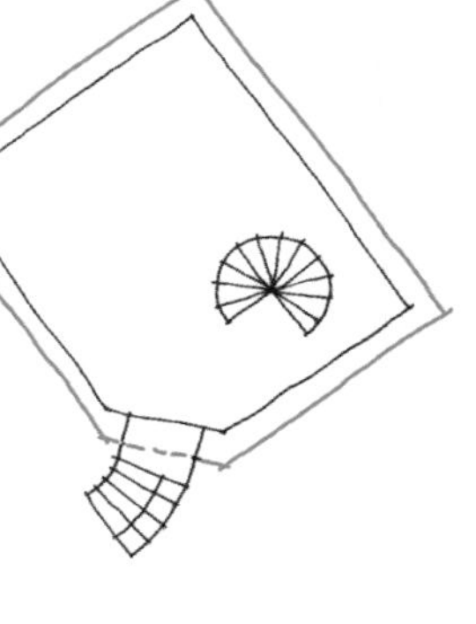

Canna Store, Tokyo, Japan (2009). A screen around the building

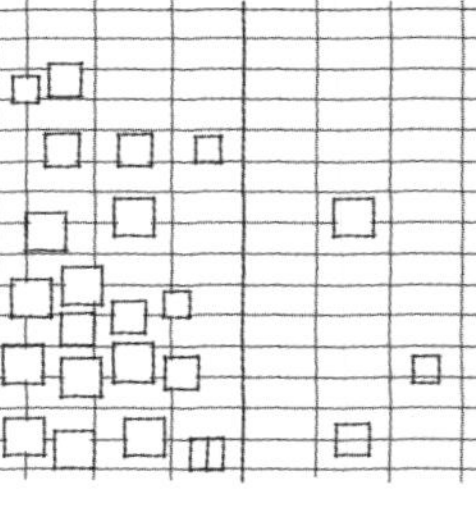

In other projects Sejima and Nishizawa have wrapped buildings in a separate uniform skin and pierced a regular skin with scattered openings.

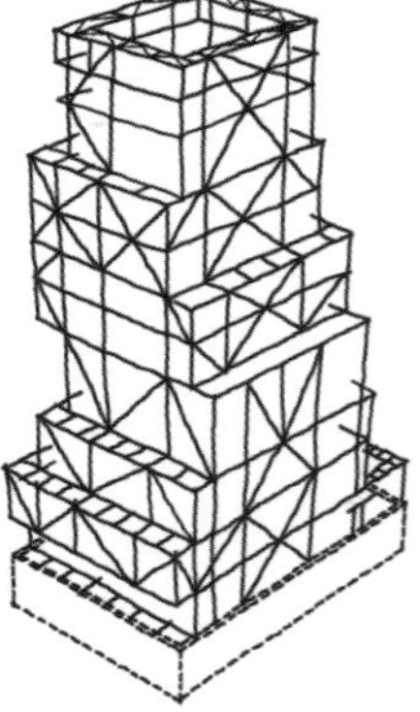

Zollverein School of Management, Essen, Germany (2003–6). Façade with pierced openings

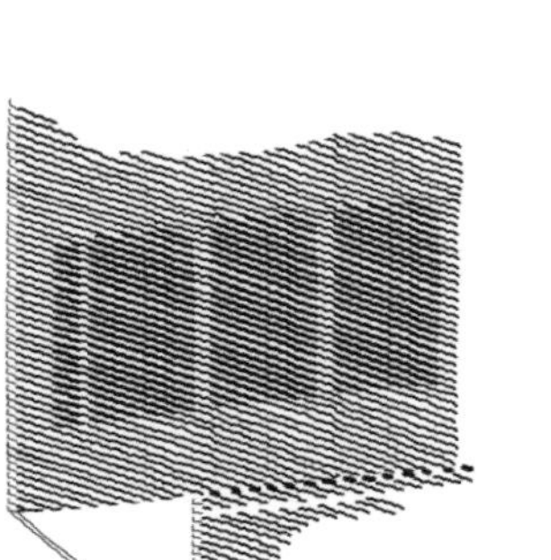

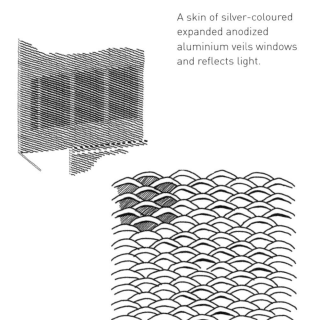

A skin of silver-coloured expanded anodized aluminium veils windows and reflects light.

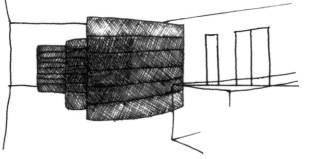

Mesh over the back of the shelves of the gallery shop blurs the view of displayed objects. The mesh side offers visual continuity with the building's exterior instead of with the smooth walls of the interior.

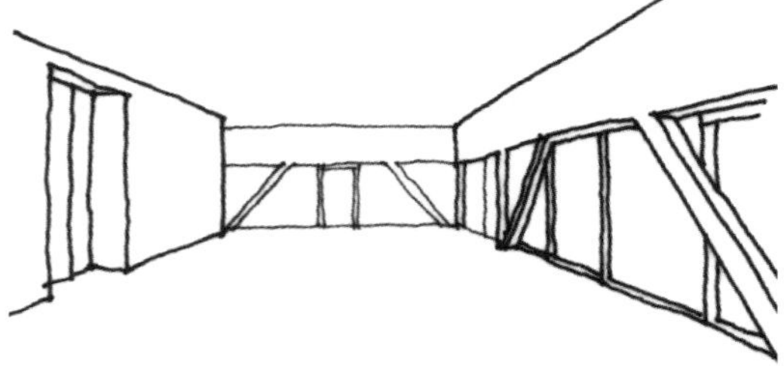

The structure is a steel frame braced cross members that are revealed at window openings. There are no internal columns to interrupt the gallery spaces.

Curves in a rectangular frame

The snaking curve of the shop shelves contrasts with the rectilinear box in which they sit. Sejima and Nishizawa have placed curves in or against a rectangular frame in other projects. In the Hayama villa, the form of the curve is similar but is placed outside, not inside, a box. At the Okurayama apartments the curves hollow into a straight-edged volume with strictly horizontal terraces and roofs. At the Rolex Learning Centre curves not only cut through the floor/ceiling sandwich but also distort the sandwich itself.

Response to climate

The building is highly serviced with two levels of plant at the top. The walls are shaded by the expanded aluminium screen and are well insulated, so the environmental strategy is a protected air-conditioned volume rather than interaction with the outside climate. There are few windows in the galleries, and those on the vulnerable west side are protected by continuing the screen over window openings. The terraces are located on the sunny south side of the building.

Straightforward industrial-type fluorescent tube lighting is ranged in rows alongside the ceiling structure. White walls diffuse the light. The component of natural light in the combined natural/artificial lighting system causes subtle changes in the lighting environment through the day.

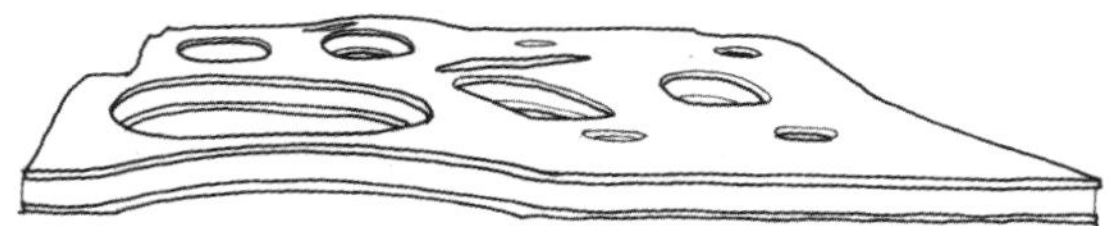

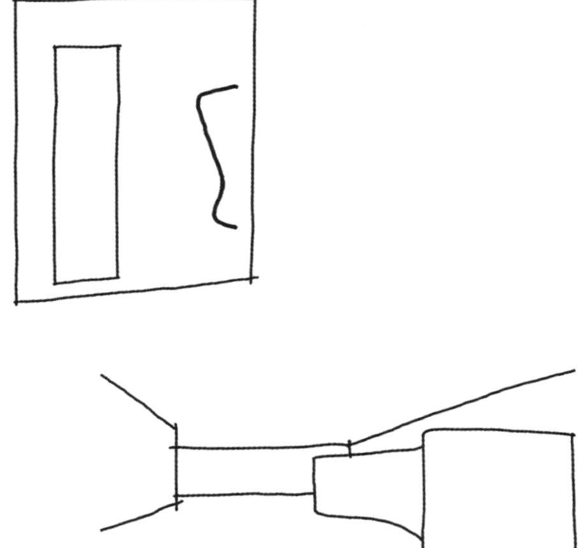

Shop and foyer at the New Museum

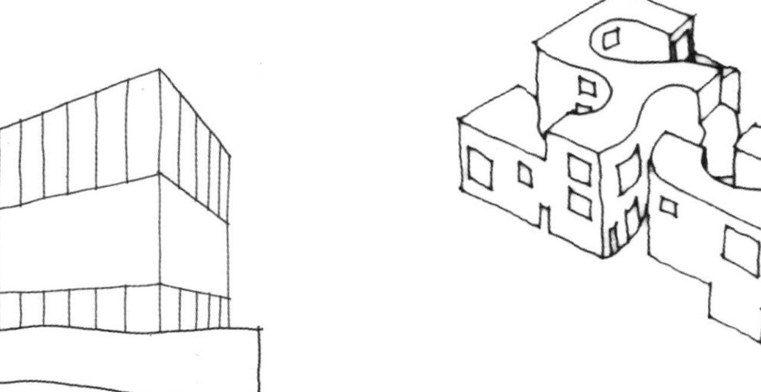

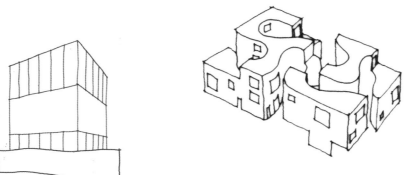

Villa, Hayama, Kanagawa, Japan (2007–10)

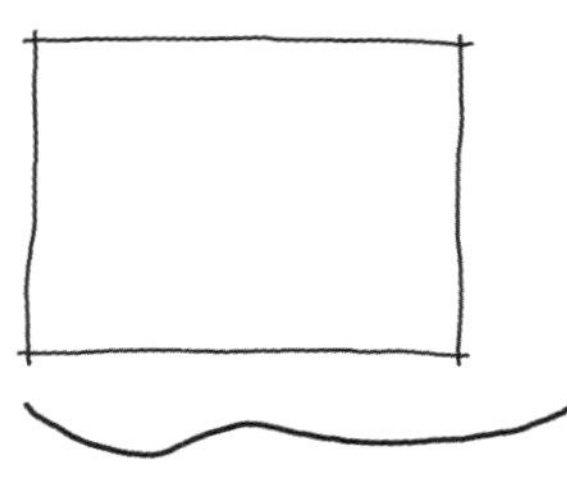

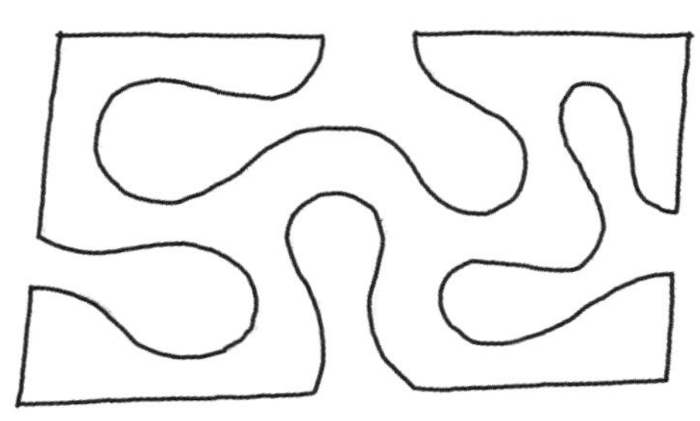

Okurayama apartments, Yokohama, Japan (2006–8)

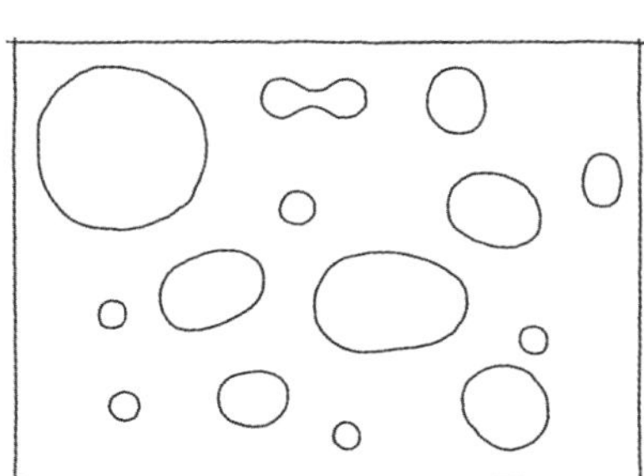

Rolex Learning Centre, Lausanne, Switzerland (2005–10)

Scottish Parliament Building | 1998–2002

EMBT / RMJM

Edinburgh, Scotland

SCOTLAND

Edinburgh

An expression of values and attitudes in a small democracy with a long history, the Scottish Parliament Building is the result of an international competition launched in 1998 and won by Barcelona-based architects EMBT (Enric Miralles from Spain and Benedetta Tagliabue from Italy) in association with the Scottish practice RMJM. The building is a collage of elements that respond locally to the small-scale medieval buildings of the World Heritage-listed Edinburgh Old Town, the bare grass slopes and cliffs of Holyrood Park and Salisbury Crags, and the neighbouring Holyrood Palace. At the same time, the building responds to its national context with poetic references to the Scottish landscape, people and culture. Enric Miralles died in 2000 before completion of the project.

Celia Johnston, Antony Radford and Lee Ken Ming Yi

36

Location and urban context

Edinburgh, the historic capital of Scotland, has distinctive areas of medieval, Georgian and Victorian developments with more recent infill of contemporary buildings. The site of the Scottish Parliament complex is opposite Holyrood Palace, the British monarch's official residence in Scotland.

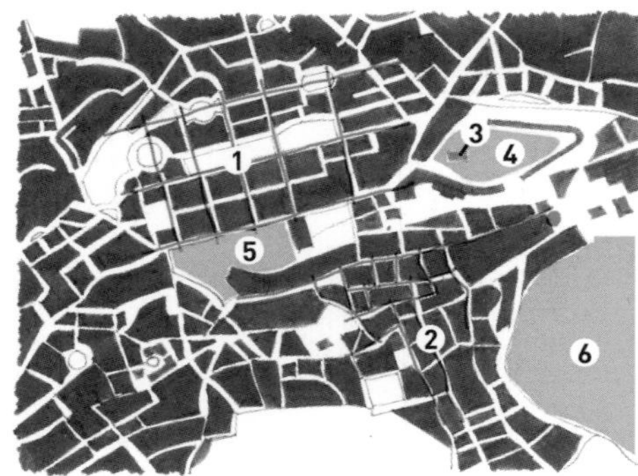

Key

1. Edinburgh New Town (Georgian, ordered, grid)
2. Edinburgh Old Town (medieval, organic, irregular)
3. National Monument of Scotland
4. Calton Hill
5. Princes Street Gardens
6. Arthur's Seat

The Royal Mile through Edinburgh Old Town links Holyrood Palace and Edinburgh Castle along a ridge. It is a processional route, visual axis and tourist attraction.

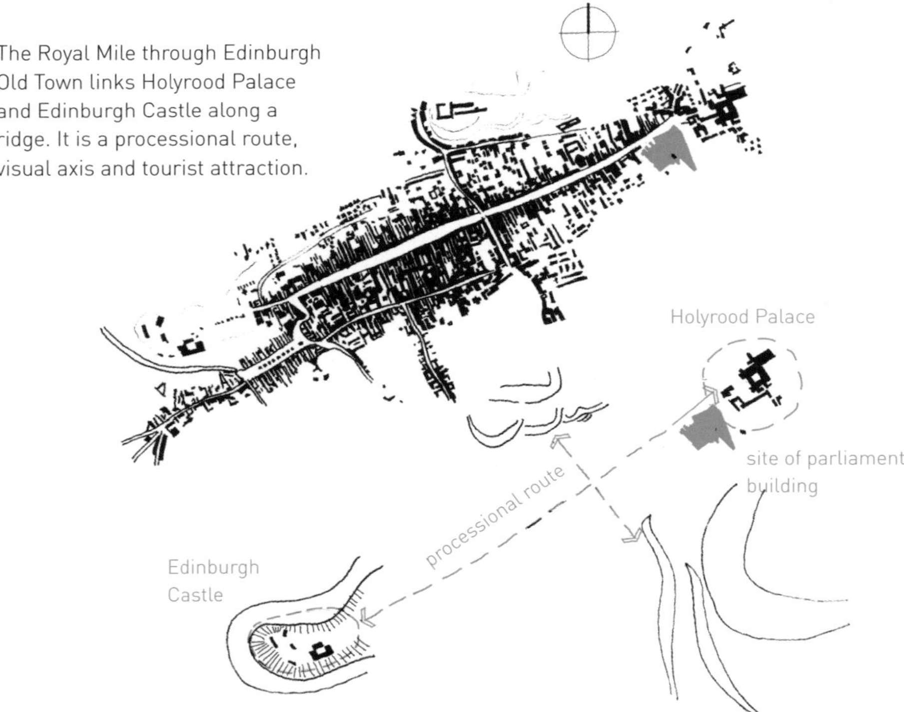

Approach and entrance

The main entrance is at the junction of three paths: from Edinburgh Castle along the Royal Mile (the main route), from Holyrood Park and from the park lands of Arthur's Seat. The public enter under a long pergola.

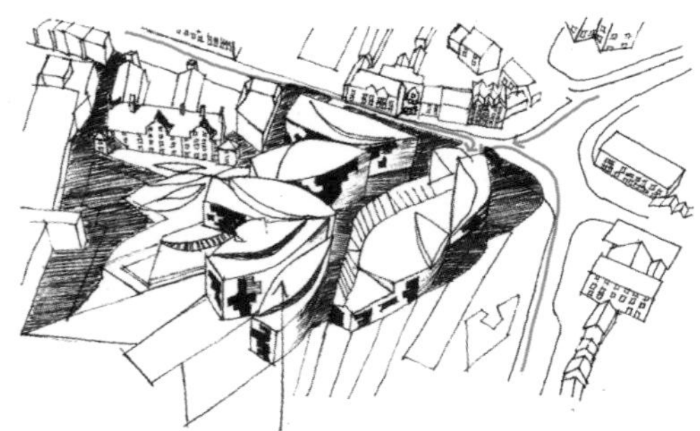

The side of the building along the Royal Mile maintains the historic street edge and sightlines. The side towards the park lands of Arthur's Seat is more rounded and organic.

The MSP (Members of the Scottish Parliament) entrance is slotted under a cantilevered wing of the Canongate Building at the end of the Royal Mile.

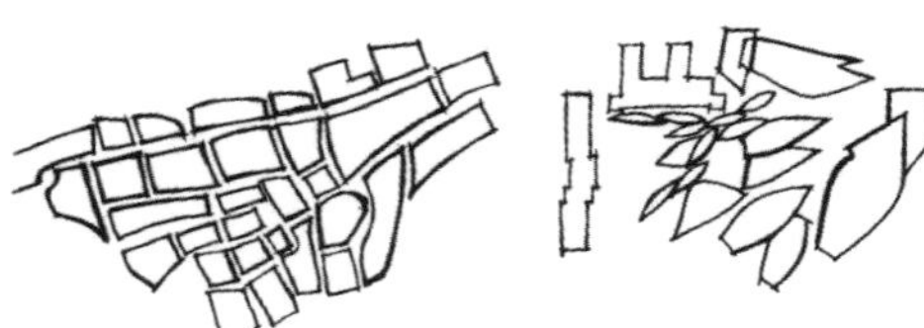

The close juxtaposition of spatial units within the building reflects the dense collection of buildings in the neighbouring medieval town.

Paths connect the building with the landscape, physically and visually leading to prominent landscape elements.

The Scottish Parliament complex is designed in a fragmented contemporary style with many references to diverse aspects of Scottish identity. The building respects the variety of its contexts, responding separately to them in a collage of design features.

Rectilinear elements (offices, Queensberry House, Canongate Building and entry portico) around the edge make a frame for the cluster of debating chamber and committee rooms. They lie like boats moored in a harbour.

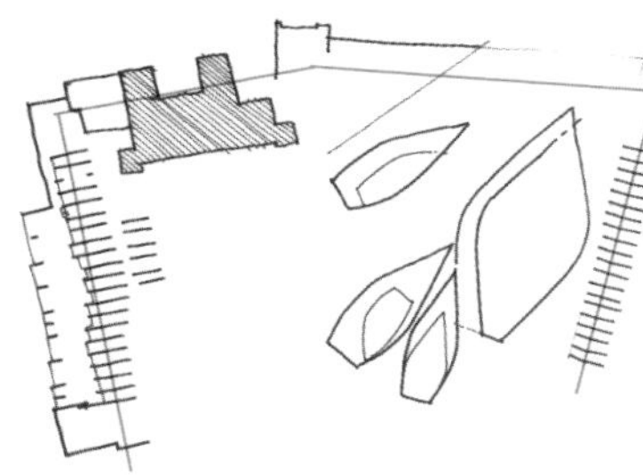

Between the 'soft' forms of the 'boats' and the rectilinear 'frame', angular lines with sharp corners are common.

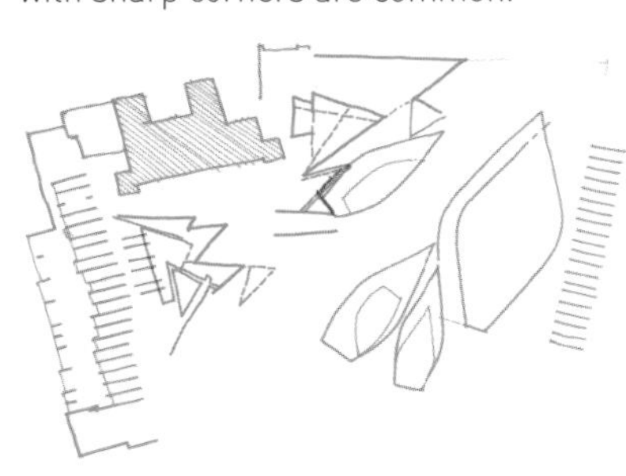

The roofs follow the rounded profile of Arthur's Seat and other hills behind the building.

The relationship between the Debating Chamber and the committee rooms is parent and children.

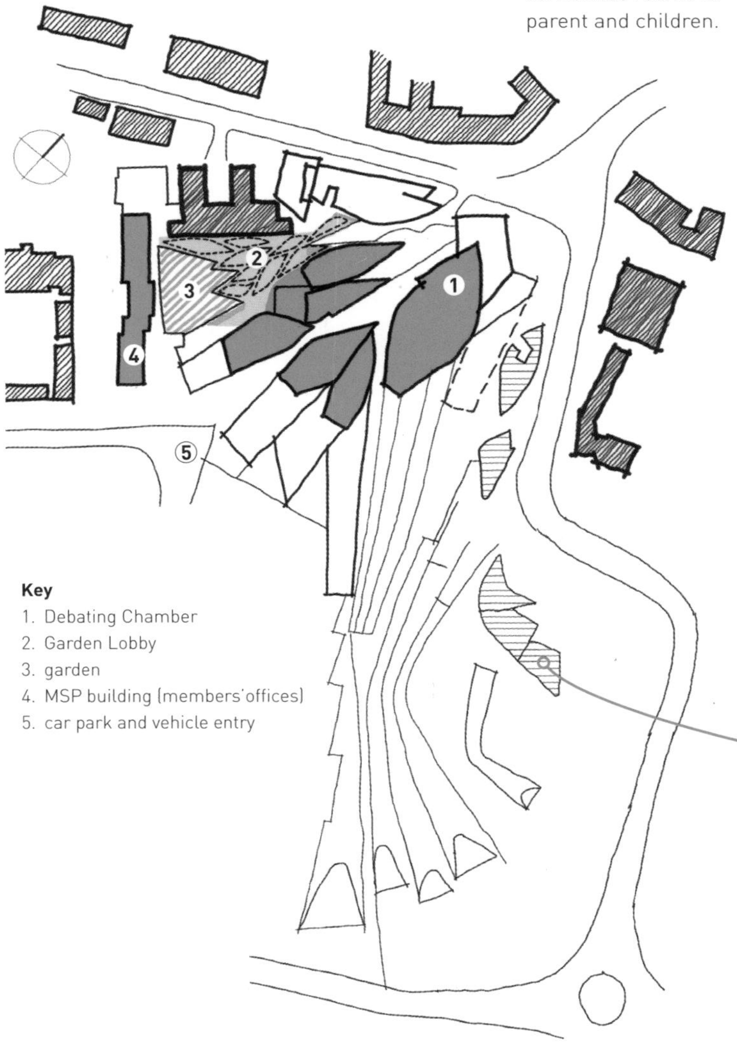

The scale of the new building responds to the scale of neighbouring buildings.

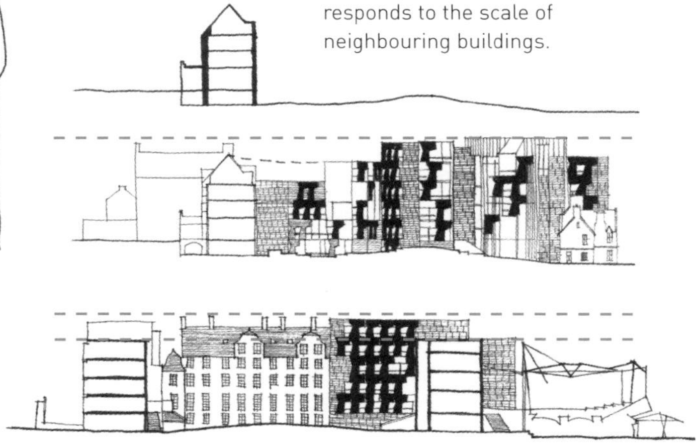

By contrast with the Scottish Parliament, Charles Barry's design for the Houses of Parliament in London (1870) adopts a medieval 'Gothic' style (symbolizing England) with a classical symmetrical plan (symbolizing order). The building enforces a unified architectural order on its context.

Key

1. Debating Chamber
2. Garden Lobby
3. garden
4. MSP building (members' offices)
5. car park and vehicle entry

Two ponds south-west of the building echo the shapes of the Debating Chamber and committee rooms. They are a transition to the natural landscape of Arthur's Seat.

Scottish Parliament Building | 1998–2002

EMBT / RMJM

Edinburgh, Scotland

The Garden Lobby has a complex ceiling surface following the exterior form. Numerous windows and skylights light the space, including a skylight that reveals the roof structure.

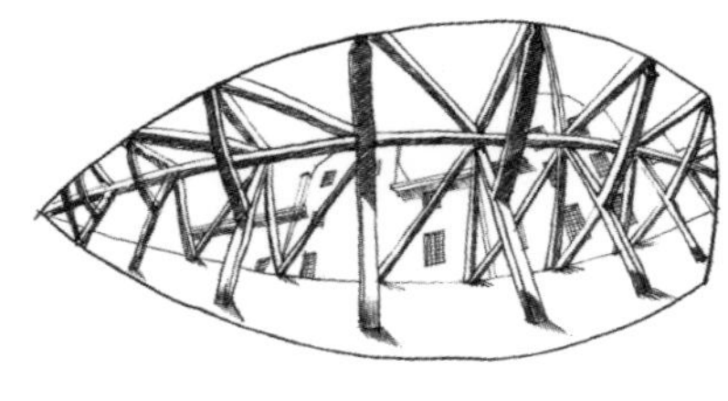

A view through a lobby skylight, with its contemporary design and structure, connects with historic built fabric.

The public entrance under a pergola leads to a hall under the debating chamber with an information desk, public seating and a permanent exhibition about the Scottish Parliament. The outline of the Saltire Cross from the national flag is cast into the concrete vaulted ceiling.

The Debating Chamber has views that connect with the landscape and city. Struts, beams and ties work together to hold up the roof, as members of the Scottish Parliament should work together to support their nation.

Members' offices have concrete vaulted ceilings that reference the monastic tradition of calm and reflective thought. The ceiling surface is inlaid with an abstracted design of the Saltire Cross from the flag of Scotland. Glass is slotted into the vault surface. The palette of materials for the offices is the same inside and outside: concrete, glass and oak.

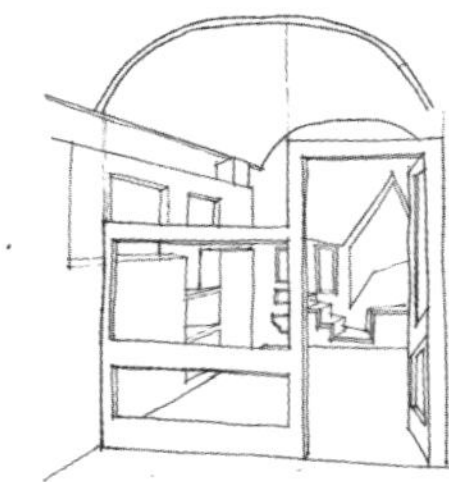

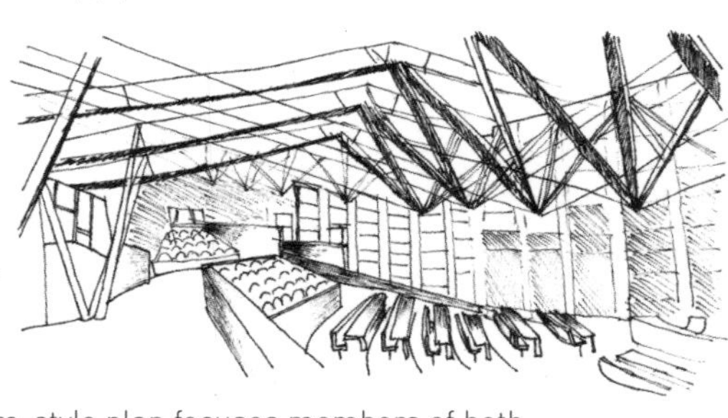

A theatre-style plan focuses members of both governing and opposition political parties on a common point backed by views to the exterior. The position of the Speaker is on the axis (symbolizing neutrality), and is not elevated, suggesting mediation rather than control.

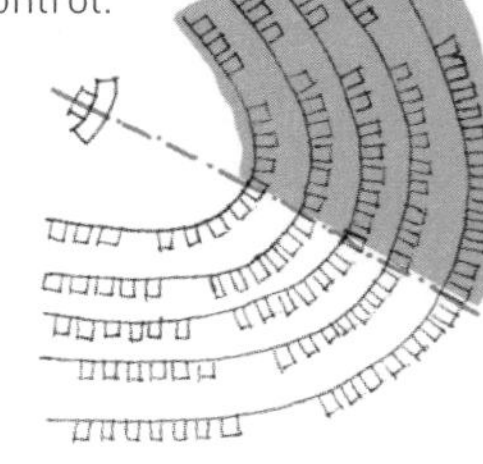

The garden contains indigenous Scottish plants and has a visual connection to Arthur's Seat over the neighbouring 'Our Dynamic Earth' exhibition building.

Committee rooms have a vaulted ceiling with suspended lights. There is a repeated pattern of two offset windows. Wood panels are part of the acoustic treatment. An oval instead of a rectangular table suggests inclusion and collaboration, rather than opposition.

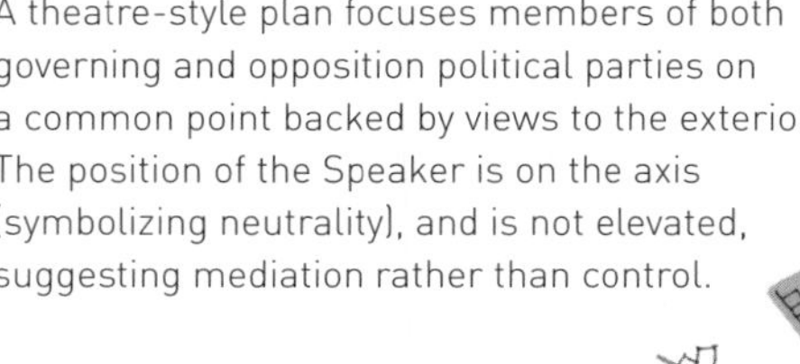

Screens of naturally bending wood rods on the exterior walls and the pergola resemble the stalks of plants, while the roof lights resemble leaves.

The exposed structural members of the roof lights are like ribs on a boat or veins on a leaf.

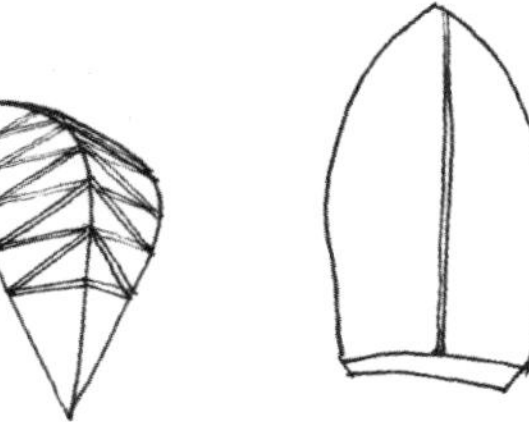

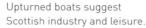

Scottish stones are inlaid into precast concrete elements. Some of the motifs have no inlay and create an interplay between positive and negative elements.

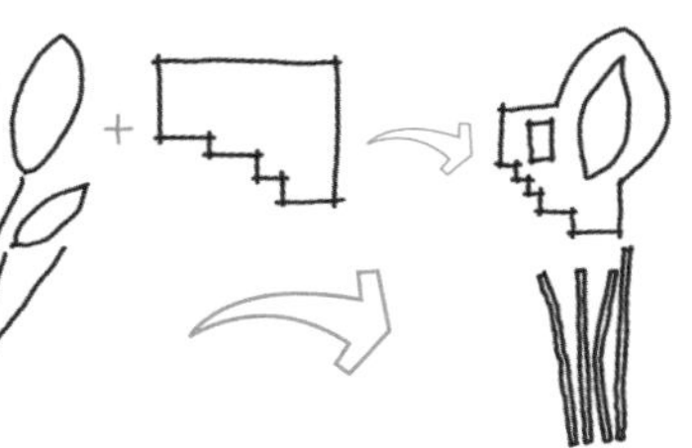

Upturned boats suggest Scottish industry and leisure.

Elements projecting from a wall surface are a part of traditional Scottish building.

Variation of the seat and window bays make up a 'façade of individuals', organized on a regular grid, like a façade of Georgian windows in Edinburgh's New Town but far more modelled and textured. Repetition with slight variation of motifs provides the building with coherence and reinforces key ideas without overuse of the same design.

The palette of materials – concrete, metal, timber and glass – is used in many projects designed by Enrique Miralles. The idea of collage is also apparent in his body of work.

The repetition of wall elements with dramatic shadow patterns has similarities to the earlier design for a wall by Enric Miralles and Carme Pinós at Igualada Cemetery, Spain (1985–94). Repeating elements in different configurations gives façade areas individual characters and recognizes the diversity in peoples' personalities.

The offices of the Members of the Scottish Parliament, housed in the MSP building, include a window seat in a sculptural bay window. The design is a combination of organic and rectilinear shapes and the materials are oak, concrete and glass. The bays are expressed outside as if pushed through the skin of the wall. A screen of rods partially covers some of the windows.

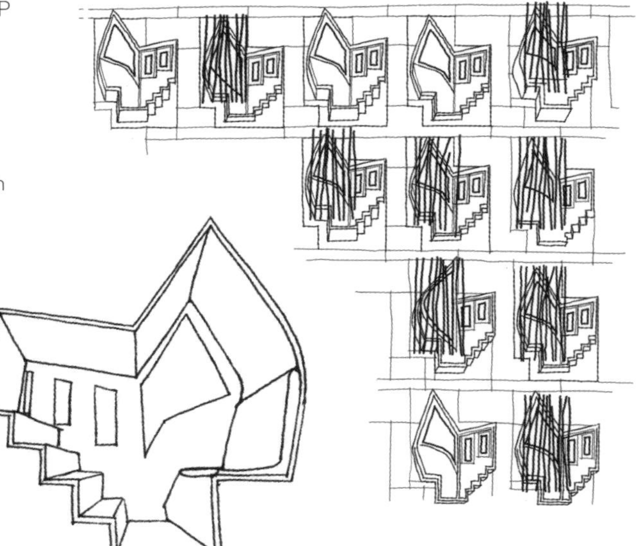

One of the window seats seen from inside the building (right) and a group of them in part of the façade of the MSP building seen from outside (far right)

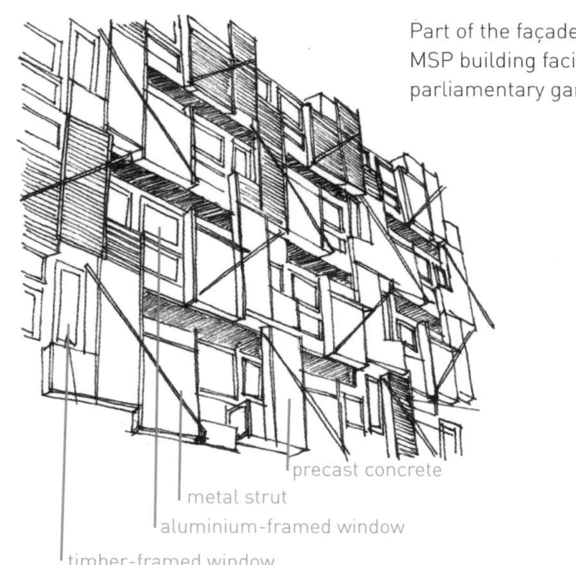

Part of the façade of the MSP building facing the parliamentary garden

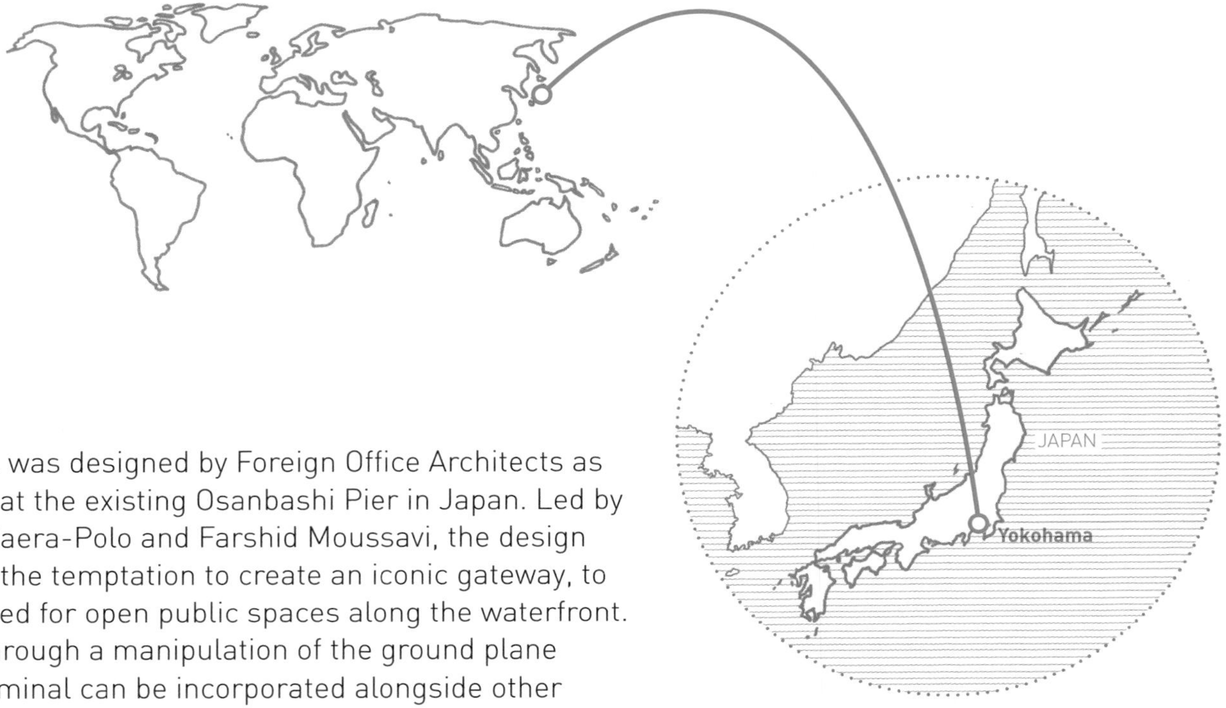

Yokohama Port Terminal | 1995–2002

Foreign Office Architects
Yokohama, Japan

37

The Yokohama Port Terminal was designed by Foreign Office Architects as a passenger cruise terminal at the existing Osanbashi Pier in Japan. Led by the architect duo Alejandro Zaera-Polo and Farshid Moussavi, the design response steered away from the temptation to create an iconic gateway, to focus instead on the city's need for open public spaces along the waterfront. The structure is developed through a manipulation of the ground plane whereby the needs of the terminal can be incorporated alongside other commercial and civic functions as a continuous extension of the city.

The design addresses the complexities of passenger movement through a terminal using architectural features that aid fluid movement. As a result, the form rethinks the distinctions between the floor, wall and roof planes, with a continuous surface structure that blurs the traditional separation of structure and envelope. This process helps to develop a non-differentiated continuous ramplike system that breaks down the separation between outside and inside, and offers open public plazas and internal private spaces as part of a single cohesive experience of space.

Ellen Hyo-Jin Sim, Wee Jack Lee and Amit Srivastava

JAPAN

Yokohama

37

Yokohama Port Terminal | 1995–2002
Foreign Office Architects
Yokohama, Japan

Response to urban context
The new terminal building is located on the Osanbashi Pier in Yokohama, which has strong connections with the surrounding urban context. The design acts as an extension of the urban ground. The project incorporates aspects of built form and landscape into one structure that addresses programmatic needs but also provides for a grand urban plaza.

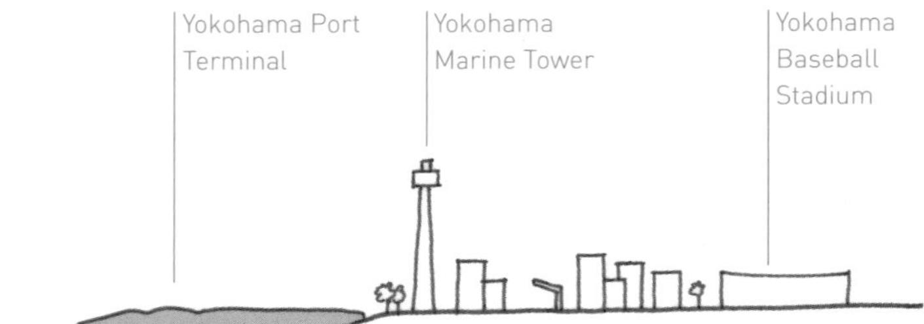

The notion of extending the urban ground plane is addressed in both overall scale and the interpretation of the built form. First, the overall height of the built form is very low, such that the entire terminal building acts as an extension of the ground level. Second, the building has an undulating roof form that serves as a fluid, multidirectional space for many activities, turning it into an urban playground.

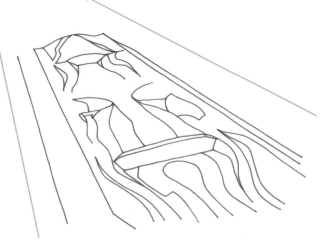

The pier has strong visual and physical connections with its surrounding urban fabric and is at the end of a main civic axis.

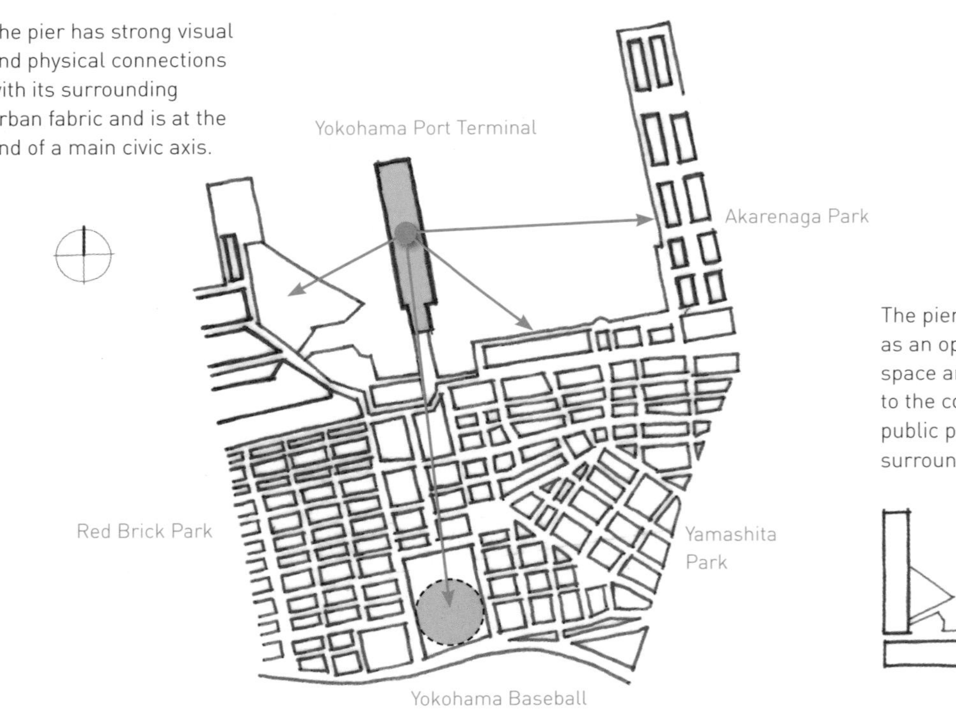

The low-lying building form juts out into the water, and the roof of the building acts as an urban playground that extends the civic realm into the ocean.

The pier is developed as an open public space and adds to the complex of public parks that surrounds it.

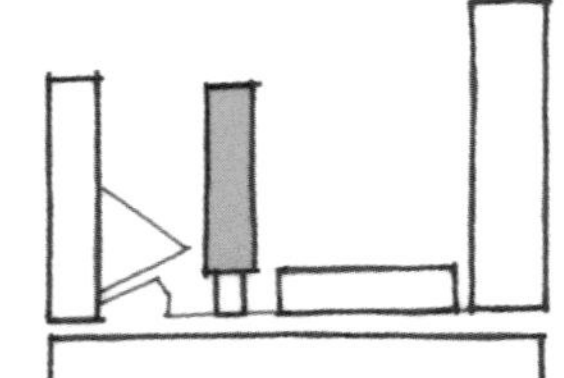

The undulating surface of the roof has a wavelike feel that forms a metaphoric connection between the land and the sea.

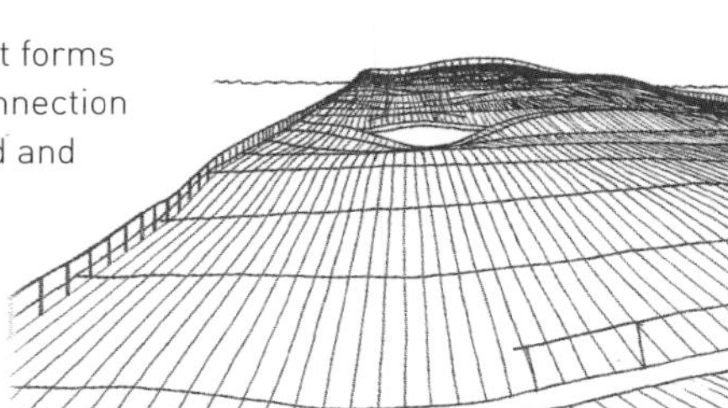

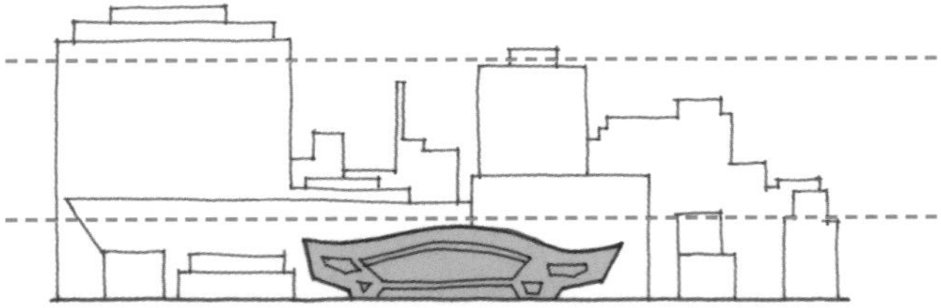
Yokohama Port Terminal (15m / 49ft)

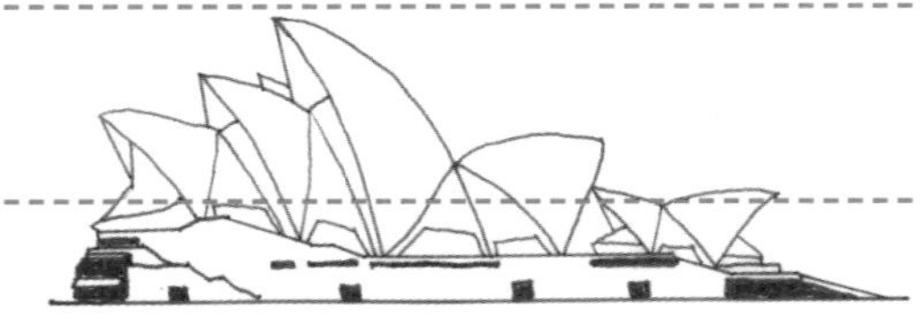
Sydney Opera House (65m / 213ft)

The design for the port terminal takes a different stance to the urban context from other waterfront structures. Instead of offering an iconic object, it underplays its symbolic presence as a gateway to the city and works to maximize public space by emphasizing its horizontality and allowing for an urban park.

Response to programme

The design of the building is a direct result of a rational approach to the programme and the resolution of the complex circulation pattern in a national and international port terminal. These problems were first reduced to a 'diagram of no-return', and a building design was then developed from that diagram.

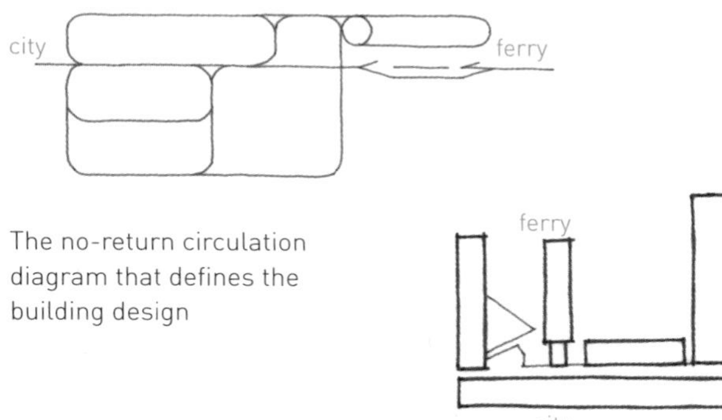

The no-return circulation diagram that defines the building design

The idea of the no-return diagram is based on the limitations of a dead-end pier, where people must retrace their steps to return back to the land. To avoid this dead-end experience, the designers sought to create alternative paths for approaching and returning, thereby increasing the number of events encountered on the way. This already breaks away from the conventional organization of a terminal space, which has a fixed orientation and specified flows. The no-return circulation diagram is thus transformed into a 'folded space' that allows for a smooth transition between all the interior programmes as well as a smooth connection between land and sea activities for residents and visitors. The removal of this barrier between the static and the dynamic allows for an uninterrupted, multidirectional space which fluidly connects all the programmatic needs and provides a range of alternative paths and experiences based on a continuous ramp system. The ramps further improve accessibility by reducing dependence on stairs and lifts.

To achieve the seamless transition of spaces, traditional floor plates are pushed and pulled to accommodate various functions in proximity to one another. This process of folding and bifurcation allows for certain depressions to become roof gardens or public plazas, while other pulled surfaces become covered areas to accommodate the functions of the terminal, shops and so on. The process further allows for a hybridization of the programme, forming a series of smooth connections between the floor plates and thereby the programmatic elements. These connections are slowly revealed as a visitor moves through the entire terminal.

The uninterrupted and multidirectional space allows for alternative paths and experiences.

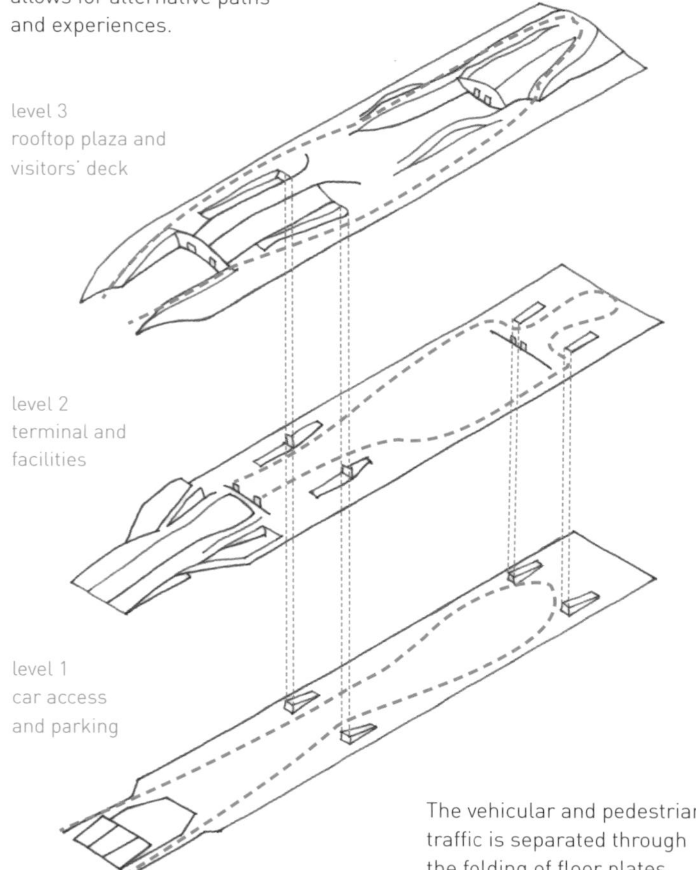

The vehicular and pedestrian traffic is separated through the folding of floor plates.

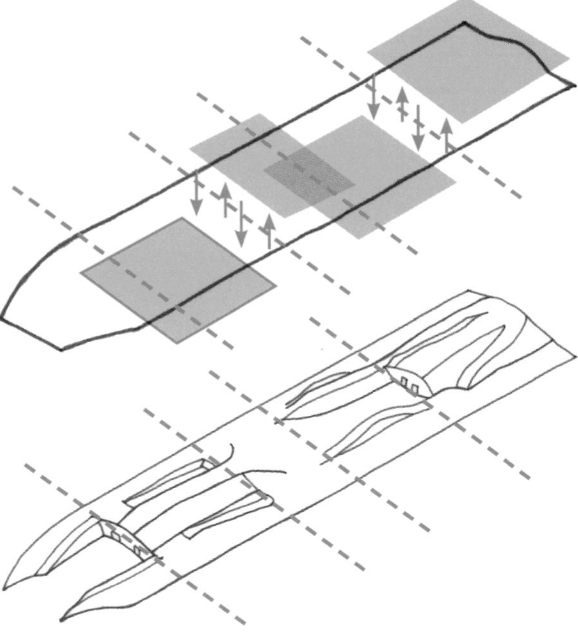

The process of pushing and pulling is carried out only along a single planar axis, and this allows for a series of symmetrical but differentiated spatial configurations.

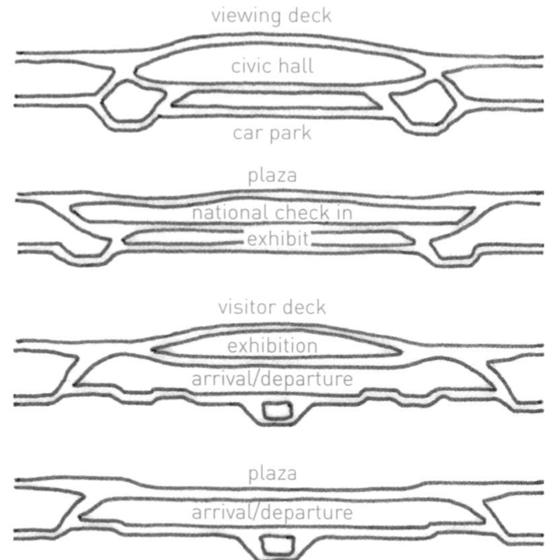

Response to disciplinary evolution

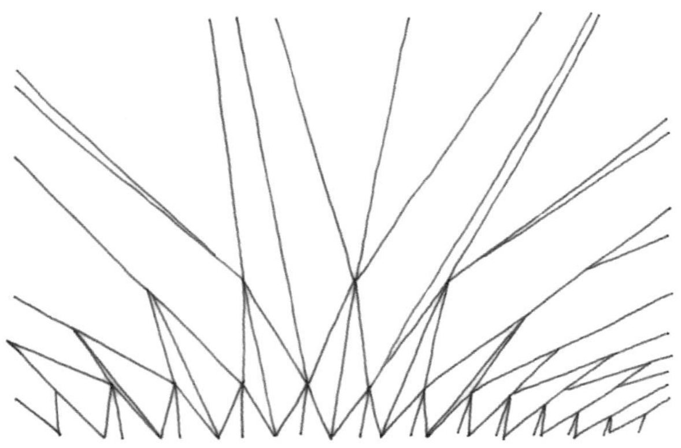

The roof surface is patterned by the use of a steel-trussed folded-plate system, suggesting Japanese paper origami.

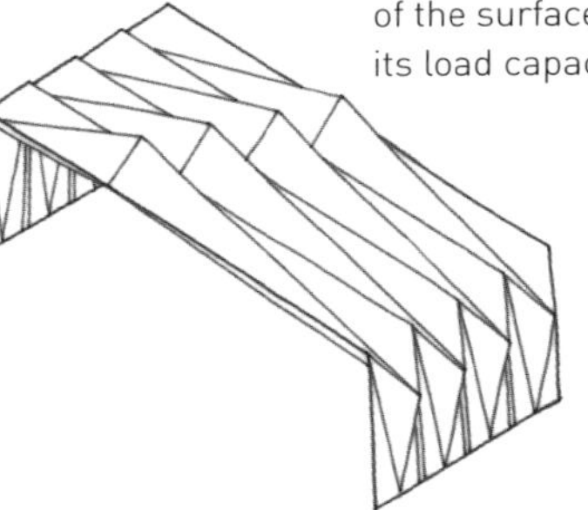

In a folded-plate structure the creasing of the surface increases its load capacity.

The process of folding creates diagonal surfaces that can absorb lateral forces generated by seismic activities and are thus well suited for Japan.

The structural systems and overall form of the project can be considered as part of an evolutionary process that maps the variations and developments of surfaces in architectural projects. The designers have developed a treelike matrix of the various typological attitudes to the treatment of surfaces, and use this as a basis to create modifications and generate a new prototype. This diagrammatic mapping of the system, known as a phylogram and more commonly used for mapping evolutionary (phylogenetic) relationships between groups of organisms in biology, becomes an instrument to chart growth in disciplinary knowledge, where each project is treated as a resource of techniques that can be referenced to produce a new architectural lineage. The generation of forms through this process allows for the new structure to respond to one or more of the existing patterns and to create a dialogue with the disciplinary history.

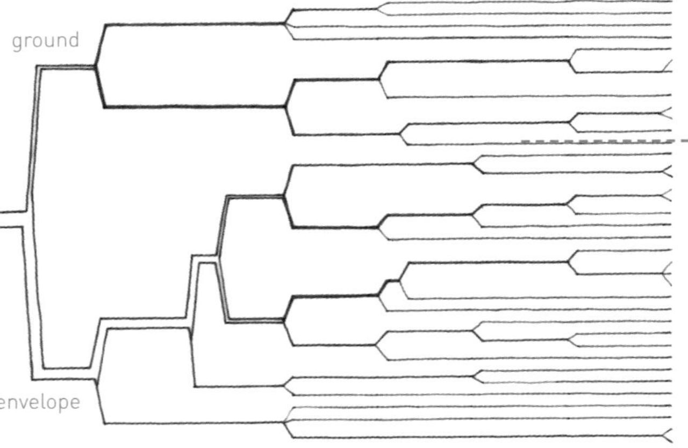

The phylogram based on a consideration of techniques employed for treatment of envelopes and ground planes allows the design of the new project to adopt from other systems and generate a hybrid. The Yokohama project thus engages a combination of steel-trussed folded plates for the envelope and folded concrete girders for the ground plane. Furthermore, the treatment of the ground plane itself develops from a Möbius strip, blurring the line between the floor, wall and roof planes. This hybrid prototype allows the traditional separation between structure and building envelope to disappear, creating a non-differentiated volume.

The ground plane is developed as a smooth transitory plane that is based on the idea of a Möbius strip, defining a continuous surface extending in all directions.

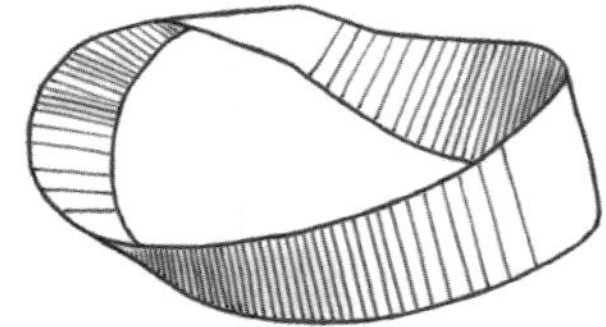

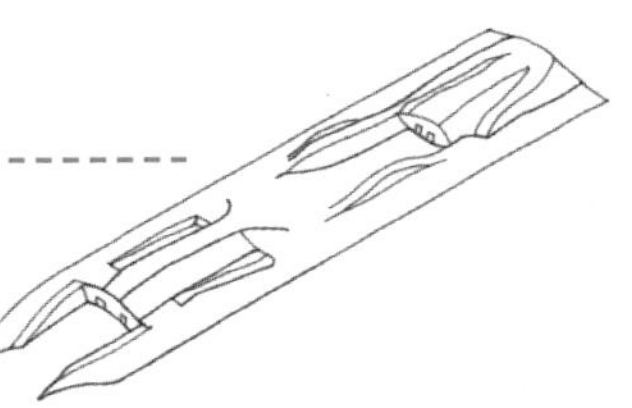

Yokohama Port Terminal
The folded and bifurcated forms of the building surfaces evolve from the ground plane as the result of a phylogenetic process.

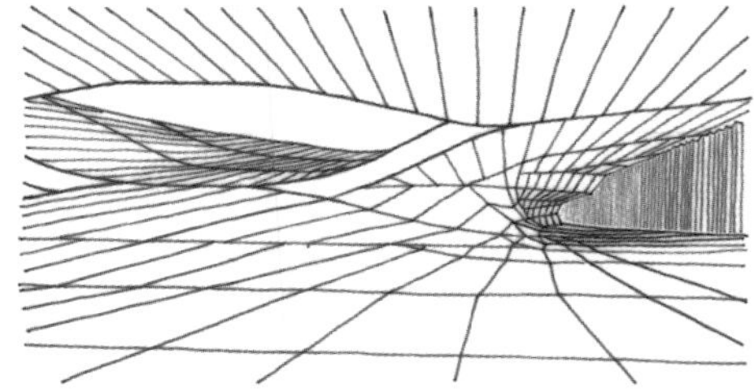

The floor plate is wrapped around the enclosed volume to dissolve the distinction between the floor and the wall, further allowing for a continuity of the interior and exterior spaces.

Response to user experience

The treatment of the structure through a series of folds creates interesting spaces for the use of local residents as well as visitors. The rooftop areas step up and down to create a series of flat public plaza-like spaces, as well as private areas that are shielded from public view. This variety of spaces on the rooftop attracts people to come out to this urban playground and engage with the form of the building. The muted palette of timber panels accentuates this undulating nature.

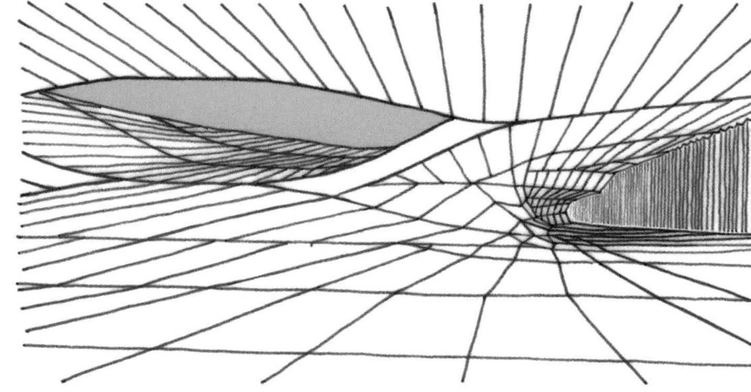

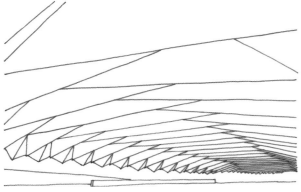

The undulating forms of the roof allow for varied spatial configurations above and below the surface.

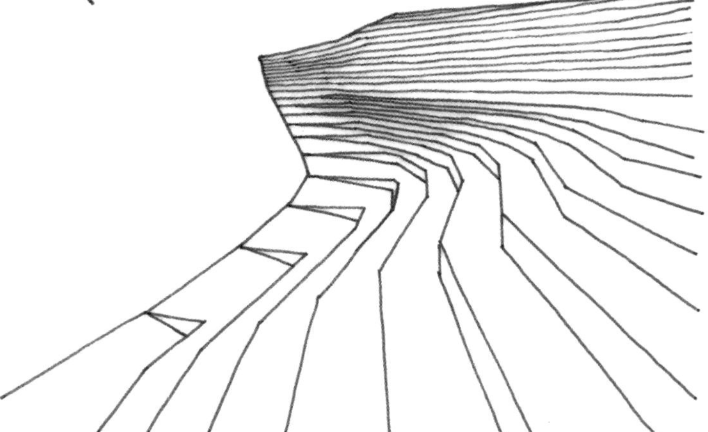

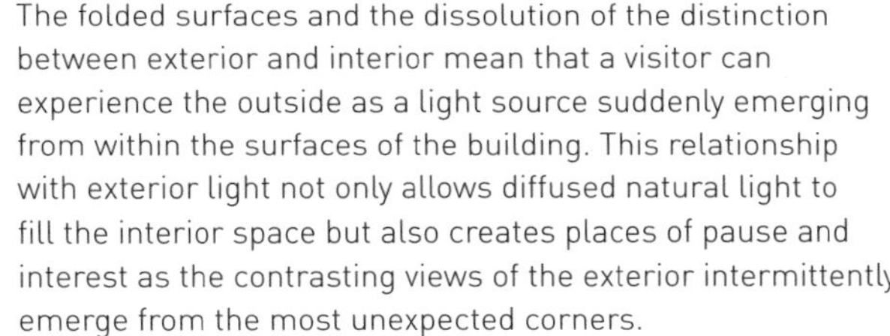

The folded surfaces and the dissolution of the distinction between exterior and interior mean that a visitor can experience the outside as a light source suddenly emerging from within the surfaces of the building. This relationship with exterior light not only allows diffused natural light to fill the interior space but also creates places of pause and interest as the contrasting views of the exterior intermittently emerge from the most unexpected corners.

The complexity of the roof form is reflected in the interior spaces, where the folded-plate system allows a large column-free space. The folds of the folded-plate system change in response to the undulating surface of the building itself and this creates an interesting pattern that guides the eye. The use of such a structural system also means that the building is extended longitudinally in one direction, creating a series of spaces that are symmetrical but continuously changing. The variations themselves result in the experience of space closing in and then opening up on the observers as they make their way from land to sea or vice versa.

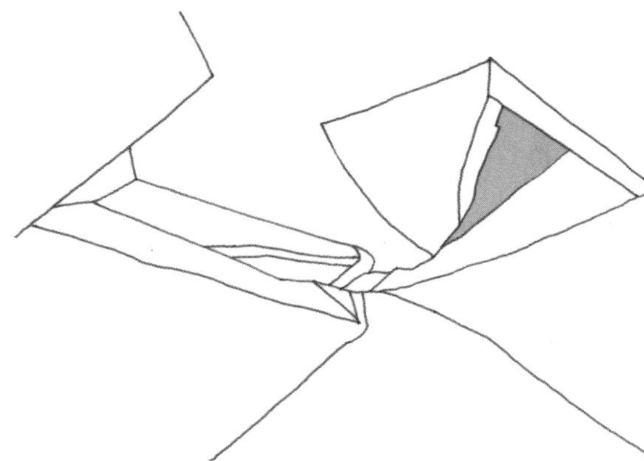

Interior view of one of the folded pathways and its opening to the exterior allowing daylight in.

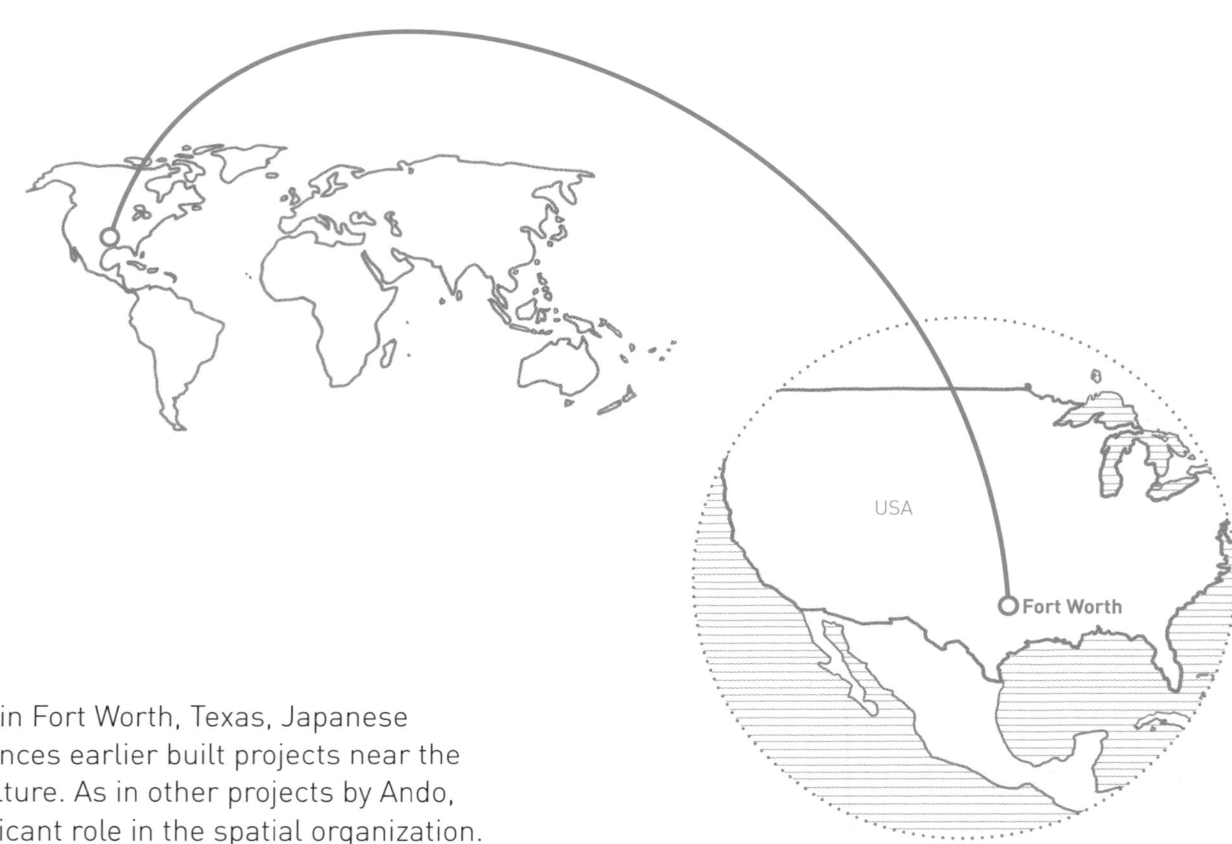

Modern Art Museum of Fort Worth | 1996–2002

Tadao Ando Architect & Associates
Fort Worth, Texas, USA

In the Modern Art Museum in Fort Worth, Texas, Japanese architect Tadao Ando references earlier built projects near the site as well as Japanese culture. As in other projects by Ando, light and water play a significant role in the spatial organization. His interest in the expressive possibilities of bare concrete is pursued with the distinct use of monumental columns and flat concrete roofs. The transparency and reflectivity of glass features throughout the project.

Ando was commissioned to design the museum after winning an international competition. His first major work in the United States and largest project outside Japan, the museum is an example of structural honesty and formal integrity coupled with richness of visual experience, further intensified through transparency.

Selen Morkoç, Tim Hastwell, Hui Wang and Alison Radford

38

Modern Art Museum of Fort Worth | 1996–2002
Tadao Ando Architect & Associates
Fort Worth, Texas, USA

Context

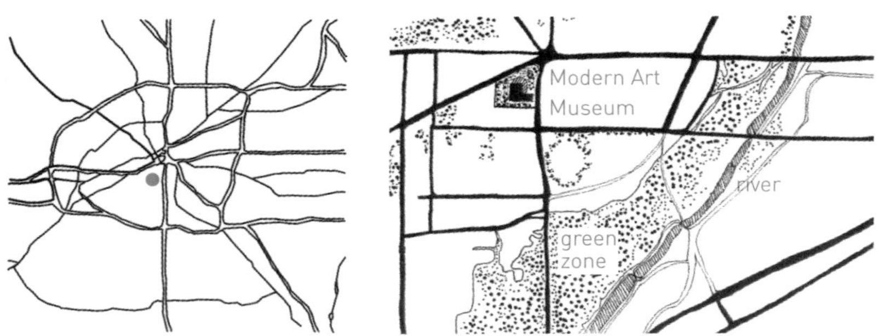

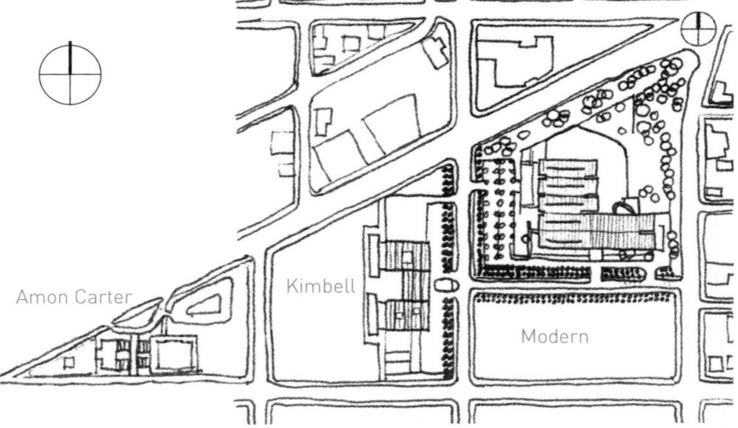

The Modern Art Museum is located at the heart of Fort Worth's cultural district, near Louis Kahn's Kimbell Art Museum (1972) and Philip Johnson's Amon Carter Museum (1962). The green zone of a nearby river is absorbed into the design through the use of water and plants.

Site plan The building site is surrounded by busy traffic and noisy highways. The building is protected by a landscape buffer.

Landscape and water

The building's roof responds to the flat landscape surrounding the site by seeming to reach out to the horizon. The large pond bounces light into the double-height transition spaces, with patterns of water movements seen on the walls.

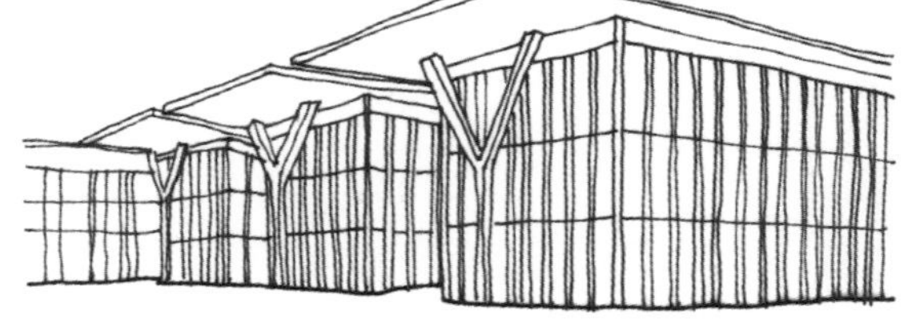

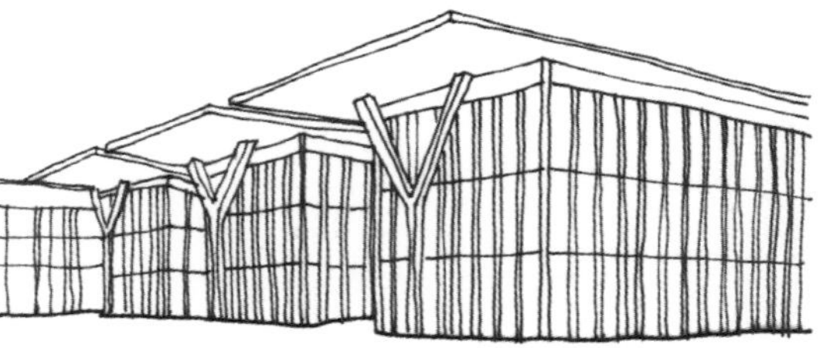

The edge of the site is enclosed by concrete walls to separate the building from noise and pollution.

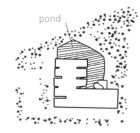

The only entrance is located on the south side of the building.

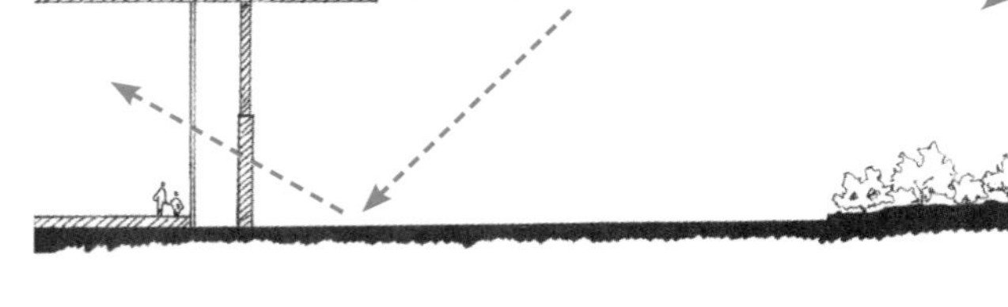

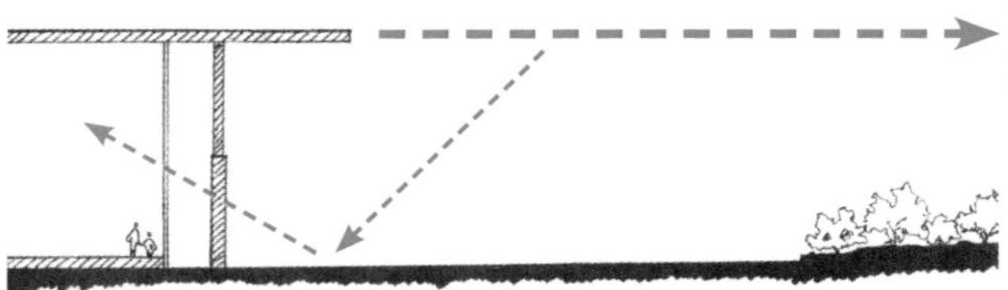

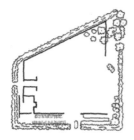

Trees planted along the sides of two busy roads are dense enough to act like a wall shielding the museum from the street.

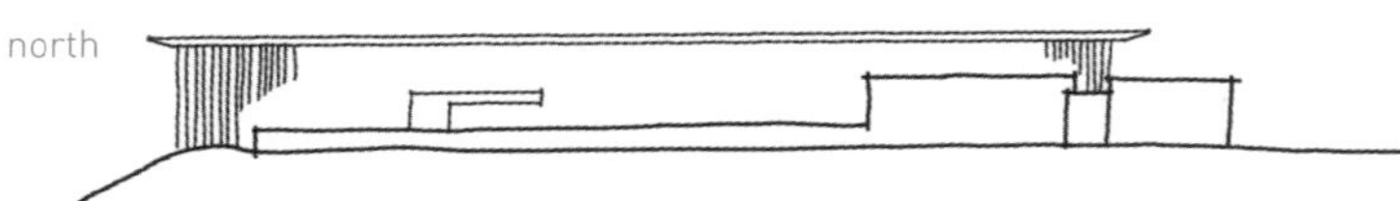

The west elevation overlooking the Kimbell is blocked by the loading park and concrete walls.

A raised bank increases the wall effect. Trees also work to frame the views.

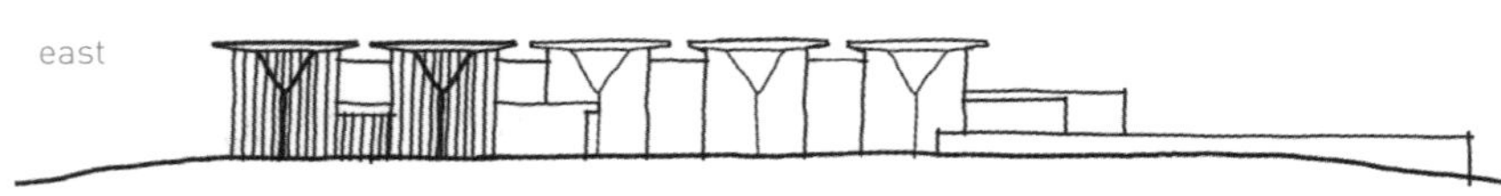

Movement

The building consists of two storeys, like most of the buildings in the cultural area. There is only one entrance to the whole museum. Gallery space occupies the majority of the rectangular volumes on both levels and visitors are encouraged to wander around them. Spaces for staff use are at the peripheries of the plan.

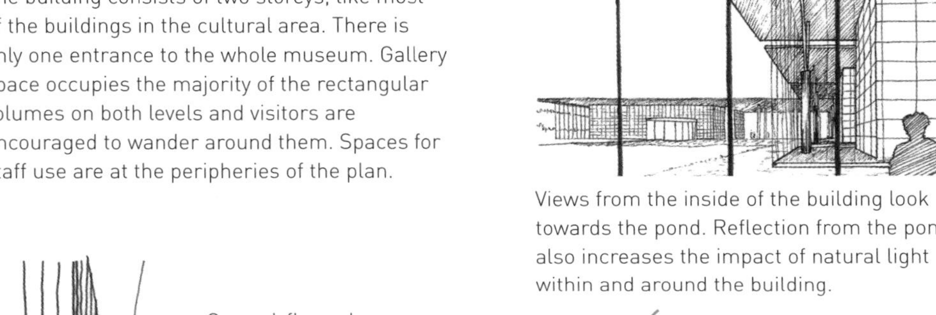

Views from the inside of the building look towards the pond. Reflection from the pond also increases the impact of natural light within and around the building.

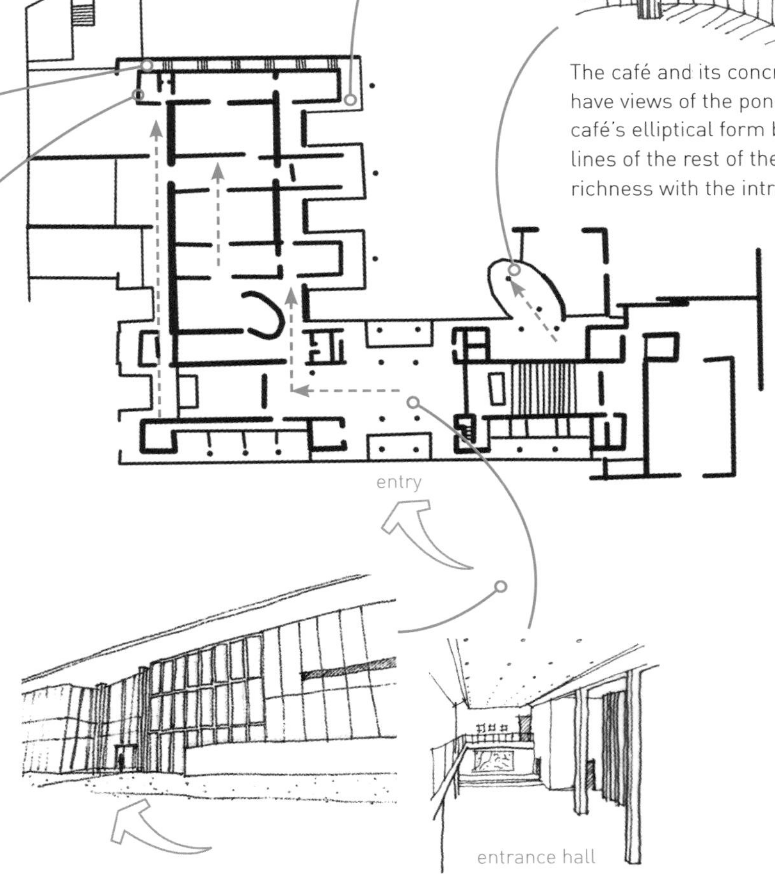

Tall transition spaces humble the visitor.

The café and its concrete-walled courtyard have views of the pond and galleries. The café's elliptical form breaks the orthogonal lines of the rest of the museum and provides richness with the introduction of curves.

The western part of the building is used as a studio forming the closest space to the adjacent road.

The entrance is through a stark glass door into a monumental hall with views of double-height glass walls and the pond. Visitors can see through the rectangular box: a visual connection is maintained with the outside, while people are encouraged to walk in.

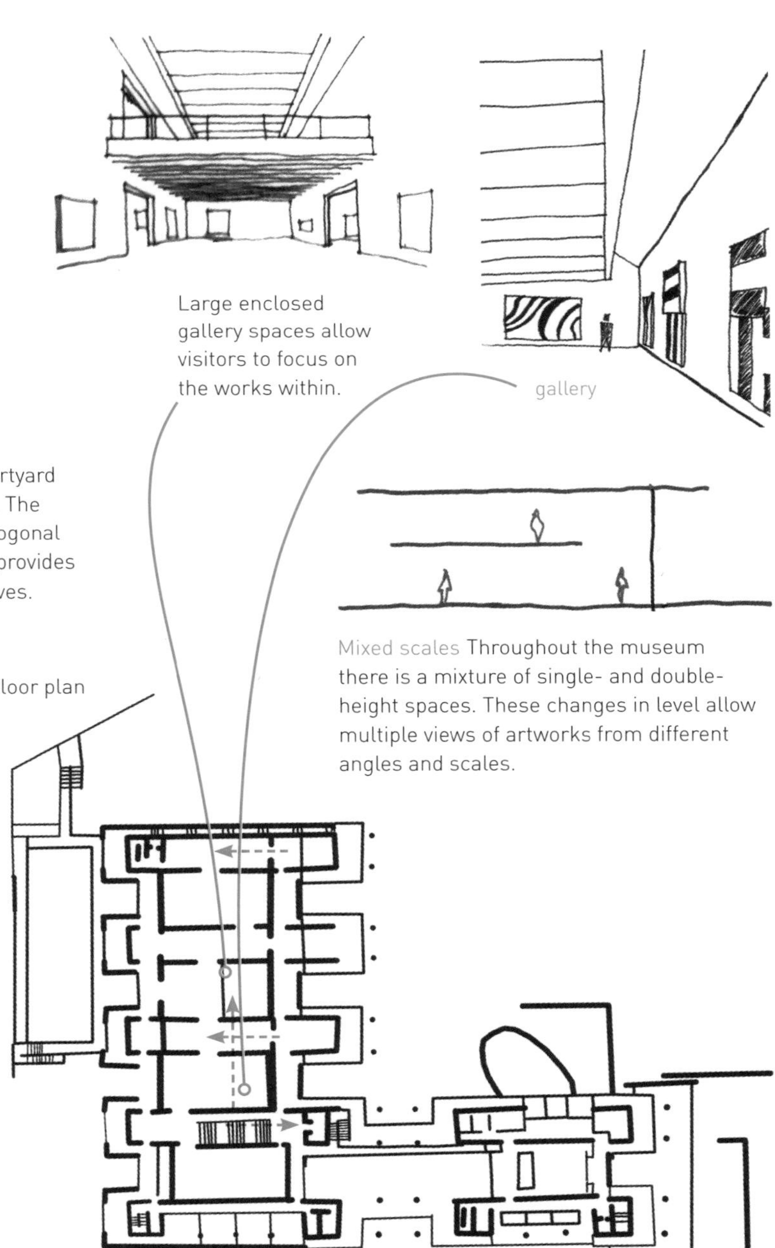

Large enclosed gallery spaces allow visitors to focus on the works within.

Mixed scales Throughout the museum there is a mixture of single- and double-height spaces. These changes in level allow multiple views of artworks from different angles and scales.

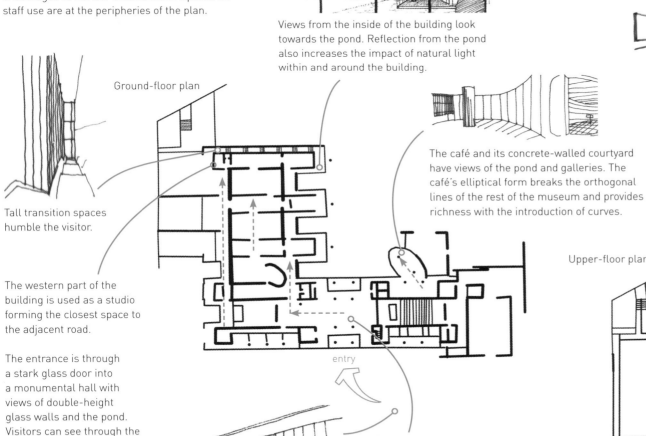

38 Modern Art Museum of Fort Worth | 1996–2002

Tadao Ando Architect & Associates
Fort Worth, Texas, USA

Form generation

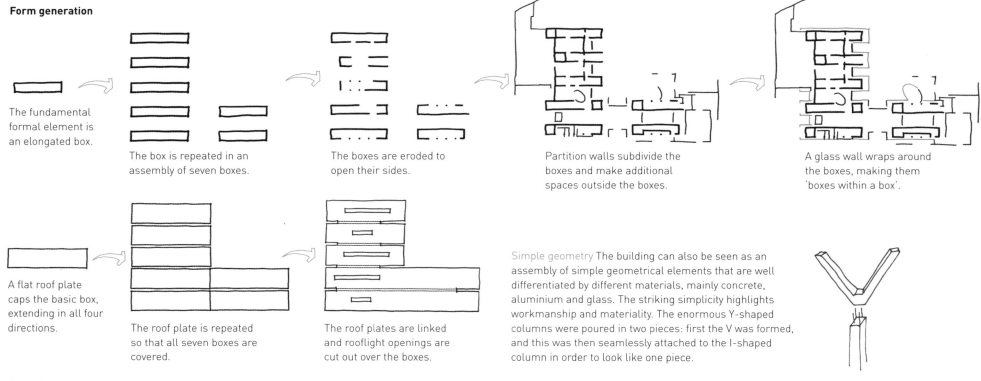

The fundamental formal element is an elongated box.

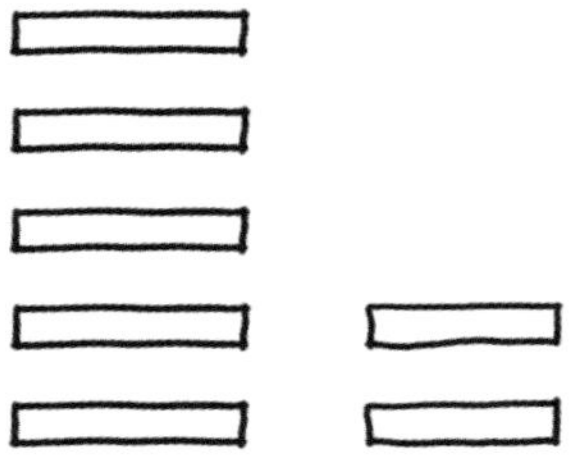

The box is repeated in an assembly of seven boxes.

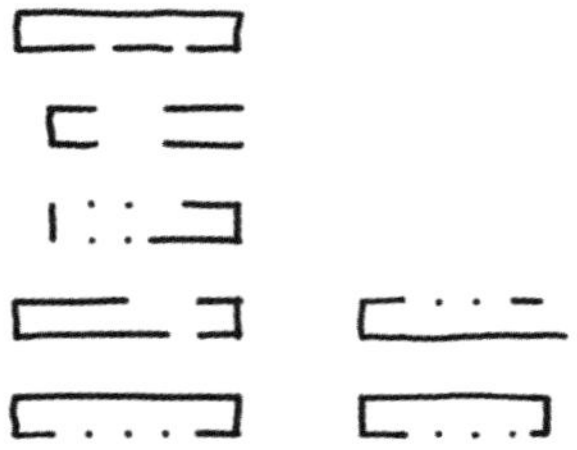

The boxes are eroded to open their sides.

Partition walls subdivide the boxes and make additional spaces outside the boxes.

A glass wall wraps around the boxes, making them 'boxes within a box'.

A flat roof plate caps the basic box, extending in all four directions.

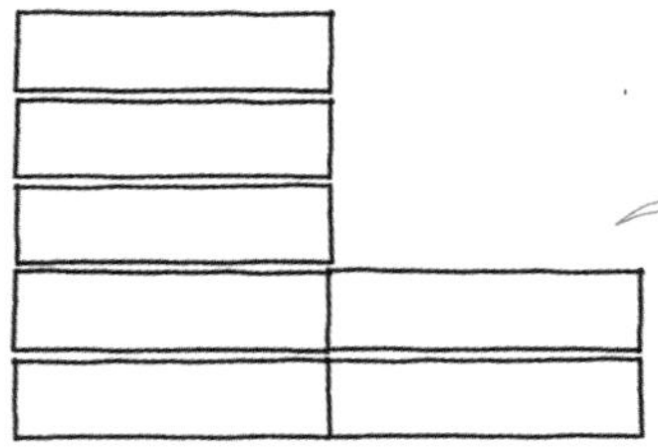

The roof plate is repeated so that all seven boxes are covered.

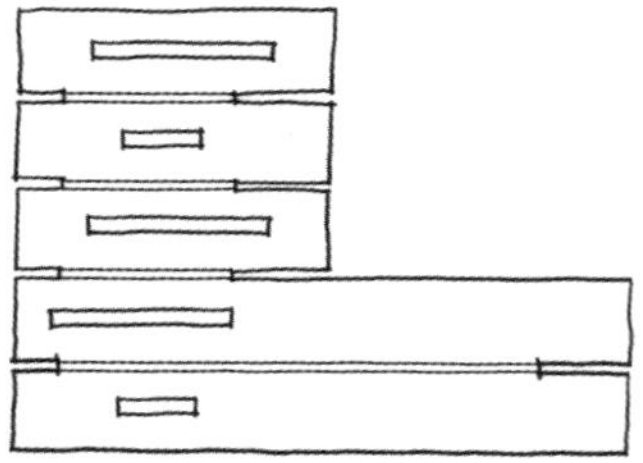

The roof plates are linked and rooflight openings are cut out over the boxes.

Simple geometry The building can also be seen as an assembly of simple geometrical elements that are well differentiated by different materials, mainly concrete, aluminium and glass. The striking simplicity highlights workmanship and materiality. The enormous Y-shaped columns were poured in two pieces: first the V was formed, and this was then seamlessly attached to the I-shaped column in order to look like one piece.

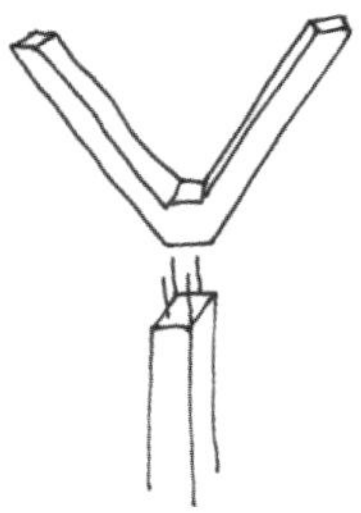

Precedents

The work of Louis Kahn has been an influence on Ando throughout his career. The Modern responds to Kahn's design of the Kimbell Museum with a similar series of elongated volumes on rectangular plans. However, the Modern turns its back to the Kimbell, with services and car park facing Kahn's building.

The fundamental design element in Kahn's museum, the half-ellipse profile of the vault, finds expression in the rectangular form Ando uses in his design. Extruding the basic 2D shapes creates the basic volumes in each design. The repetition of the basic volumes is then composited into the bodies of the both museums.

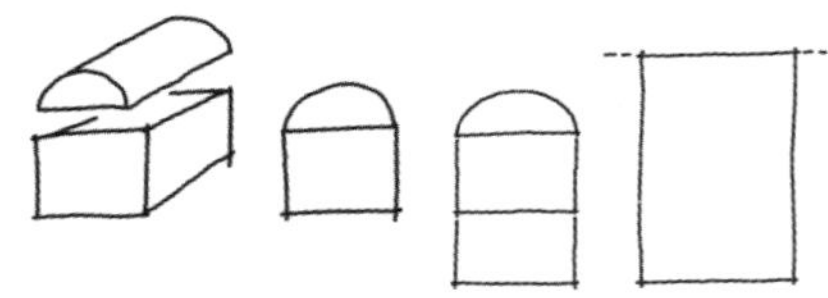

Japanese culture

As he has spent most of his life in Japan, Japanese culture has deep influences on Ando's architecture. It is possible to trace several references to Japanese culture and traditional Japanese architecture in the Modern.

Engawa Narrow glass-walled walkways around the outside of exhibition halls are reminiscent of the Japanese *engawa*, an open outer veranda around the outside of a building.

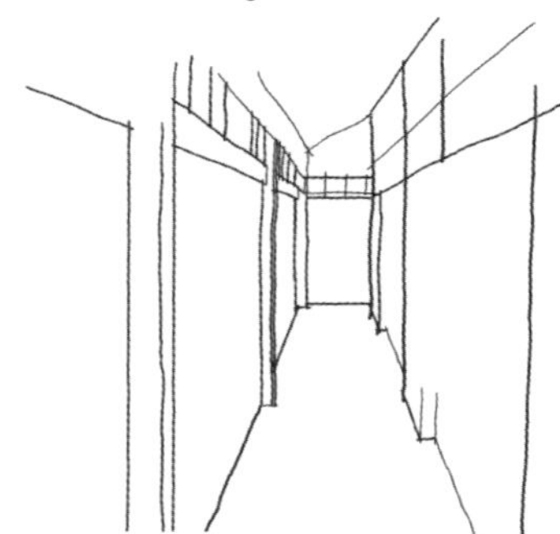

Hyogo Children's Museum The design of the Modern seems to be influenced by one of Ando's previous designs, the Hyogo Children's Museum in Himeji, Japan (1989). The influence is most evident in the concrete roofs that float on top of the large glass pavilions.

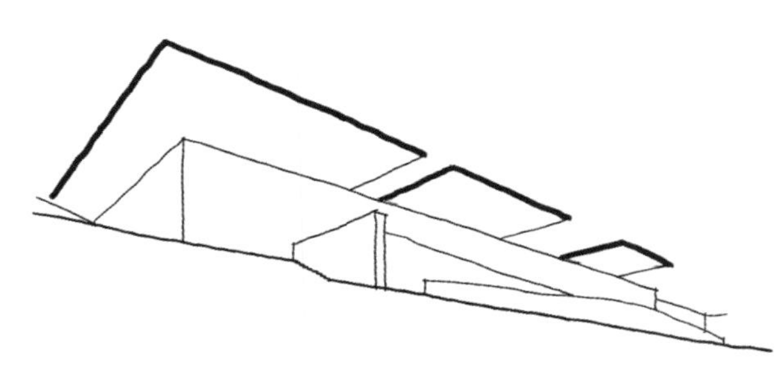

Form and meaning

Metaphors Heavy/light: There is a subtle balance between heavy and light elements in Ando's design. In all elevations, the heavy concrete roof sits gently on the glass walls. Together with the Y-shaped columns, this gives the effect that the roof is floating above the reflective pond.

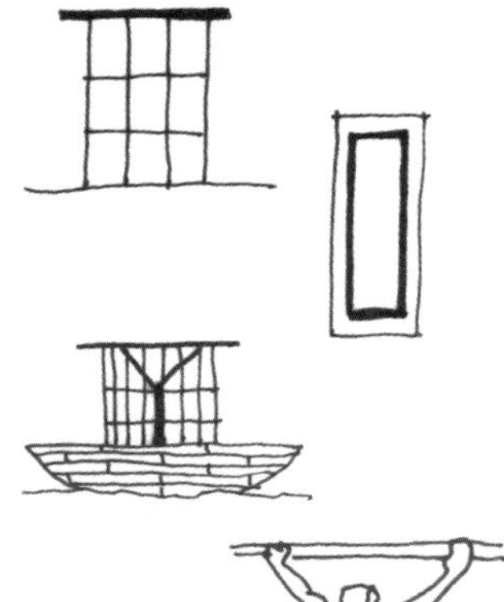

Strength Y-shaped concrete columns that support the flat concrete roofs give the building a sense of strength and monumentality, which is well balanced with the ephemeral qualities of glass and water.

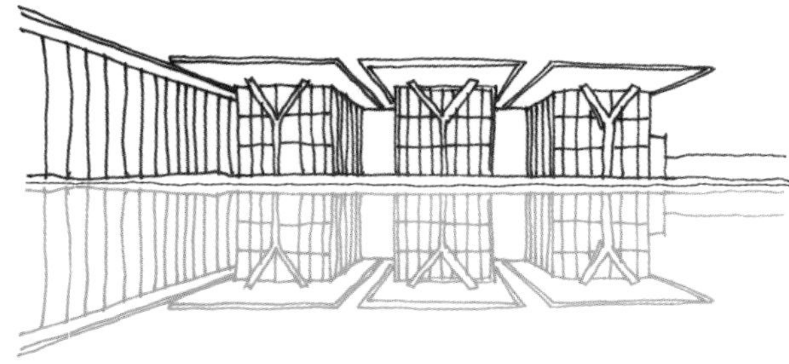

Symmetry and repetition Throughout the design there is local symmetry. There is repetition in plan and elevations. Repetition of materials, of structural elements and of certain forms is prevalent throughout the spaces.

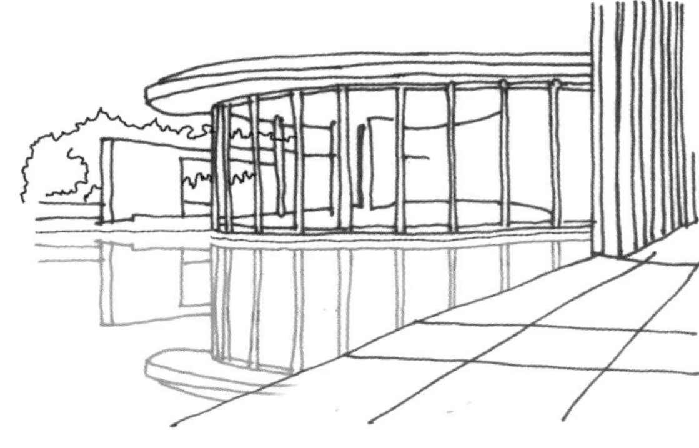

Transparency There is marked contrast between the enclosure of the windowless gallery walls and the transparency of the circulation-space outer walls. On a sunny day the window mullions and Y-shaped columns cast strong shadow patterns on the floors of the foyer and walkways.

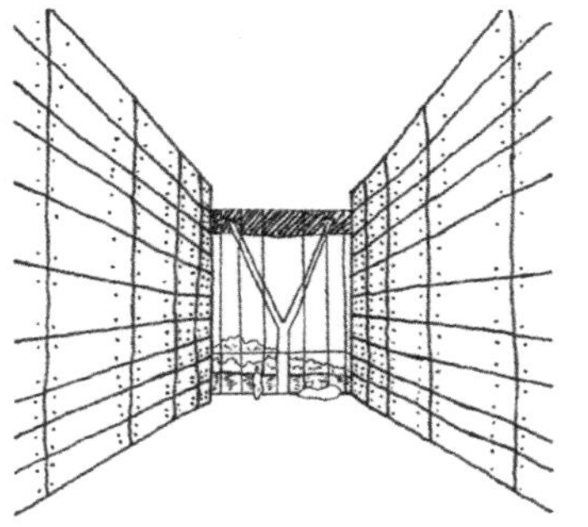

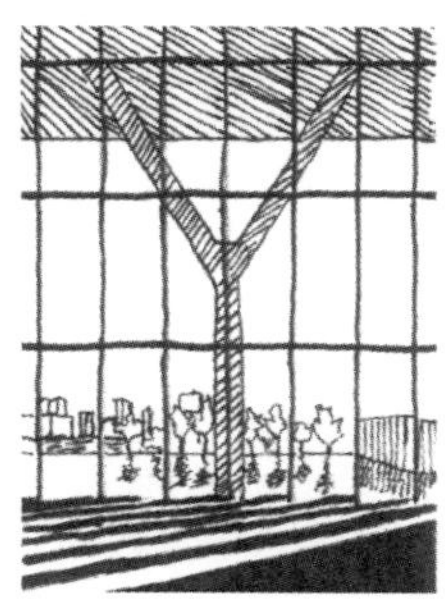

Use of light

Daylight is a crucial element in Ando's design. Indirect daylight is introduced into the galleries with no damaging effects on the artworks, and light serves as a functional element to enrich visitor experience.

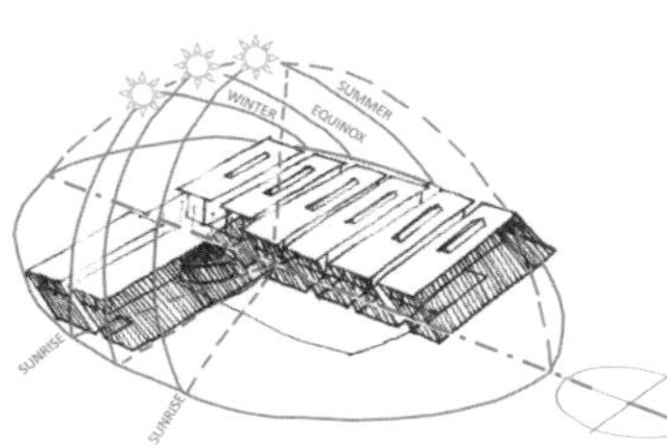

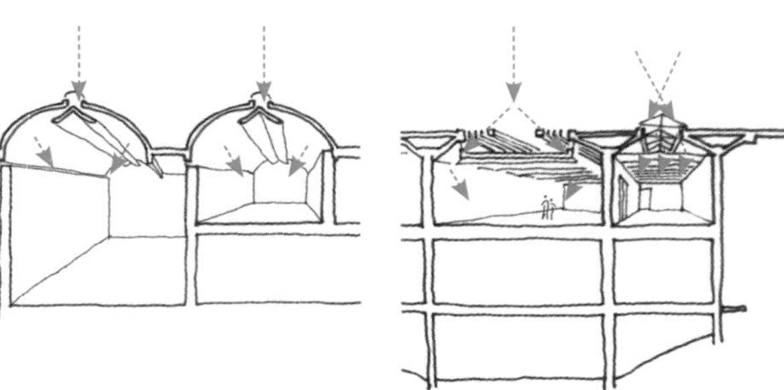

The Kimbell and the Modern use similar techniques for bringing light into the galleries. This is a major reason behind the similarity of their profiles in section. Both buildings use reflected light introduced through skylights. The Modern additionally uses adjustable louvres and translucent ceilings.

Japanese lantern

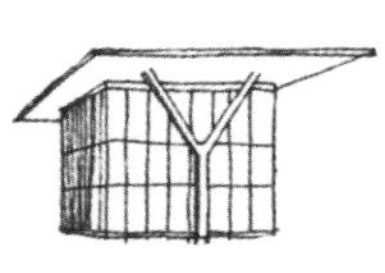

When illuminated at night, the Modern shines out across the reflecting pond like a traditional Japanese lantern.

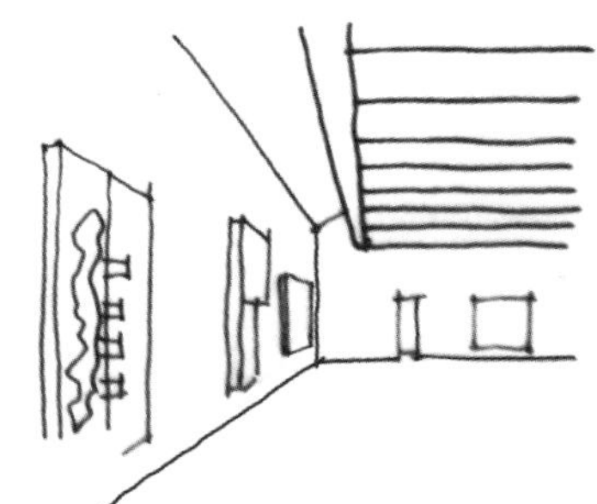

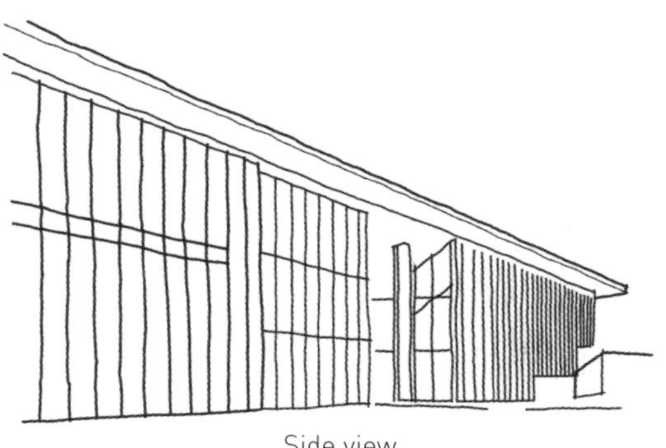

Side view

39

Kunsthaus Graz | 2000–3

Spacelab Cook-Fournier / ARGE Kunsthaus

Graz, Austria

The Kunsthaus is a museum for temporary exhibitions in Graz, Austria's second largest city. The 'friendly alien', as it was dubbed by its London architects Peter Cook and Colin Fournier, is a brave insertion into an old city that demonstrates identity and difference while at the same time showing respect for its built context. Intended to engage traditional Graz in the future, the building shows its origins in the Archigram movement from the 1960s and in the digital modelling of a twenty-first-century design process.

The new building is 'blob architecture', but this is a highly controlled and well-mannered blob. It is also highly evocative; it has been likened to a heart (because of its role in the culture of Graz as well as its form) and a spaceship, as well as to a friendly alien.

Lachlan Knox, Antony Radford and Douglas Lim Ming Fui

39

Kunsthaus Graz | **2000–3**
Spacelab Cook-Fournier / ARGE Kunsthaus
Graz, Austria

The urban context
The old city of Graz is a UNESCO World Heritage Site thanks to its harmony of architectural styles and history of artistic movements from the Middle Ages through to the nineteenth century. It is a demonstration of responsive cohesion in urban form.

The Kunsthaus enriches the urban scene by being alone among buildings that follow other more established rules. The biomorphic form and smooth materiality of the addition contrast vividly with the surrounding buildings. A street of similar blobs would not have the same attraction.

The building looks as if it has squeezed itself into the site, nestled between heritage buildings and the river.

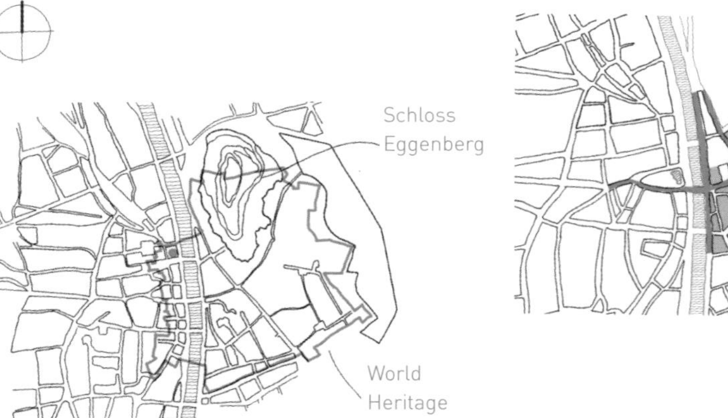

The Kunsthaus is accessed from one of the main pedestrian links, and is an icon of modernity attracting people from the popular and historic right bank of the river into the previously relatively neglected left bank.

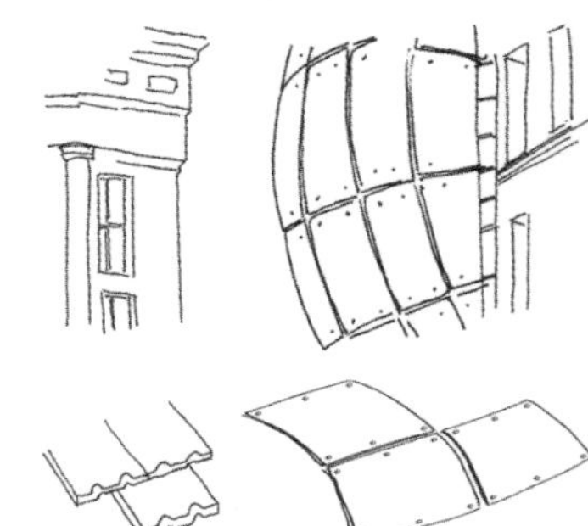

Instead of using the neighbouring buildings' skins of clay bricks and overlapping clay tiles, moulded acrylic panels are bolted to a steel frame.

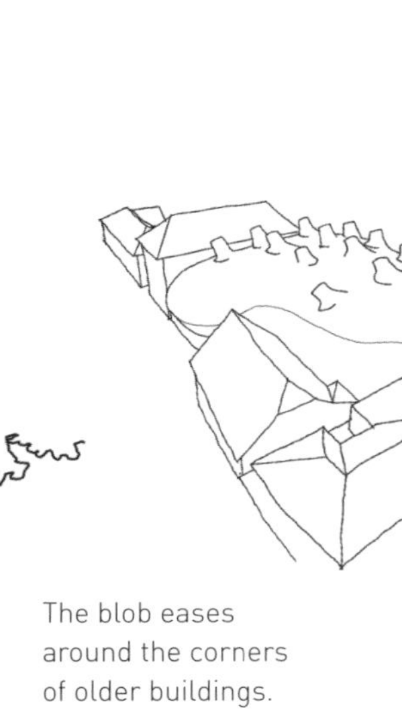

From across the Mur River, an exotic animal appears to crouch among the trees.

The blob eases around the corners of older buildings.

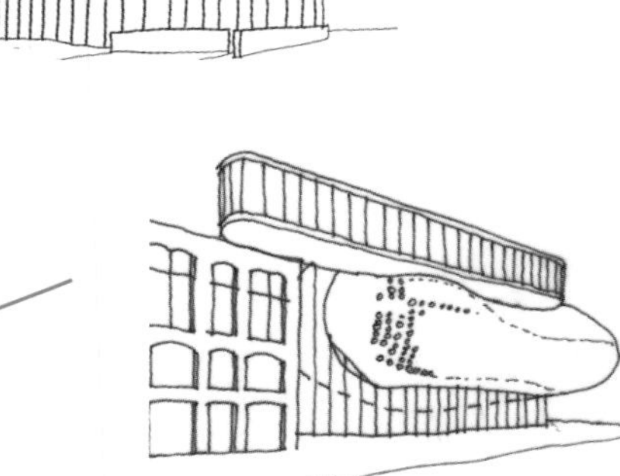

Eisernes Haus (Iron House), a building with a cast-iron structure designed by Graz architect Josef Benedict Withalm and completed in 1847, maintains the continuity of the street edge.

The design components

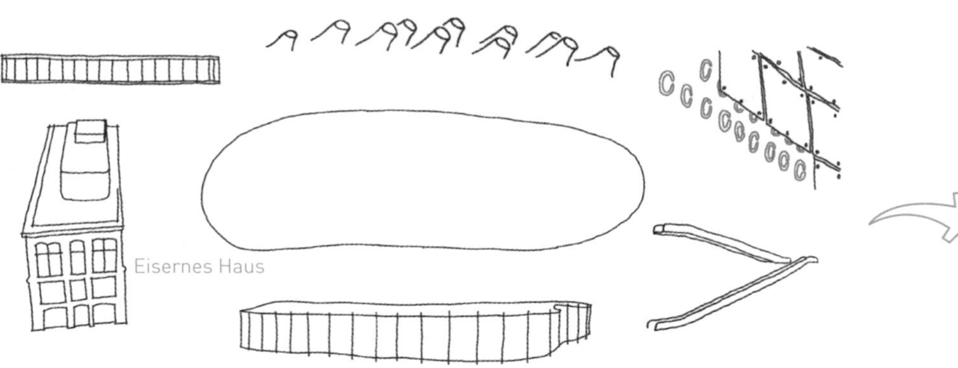

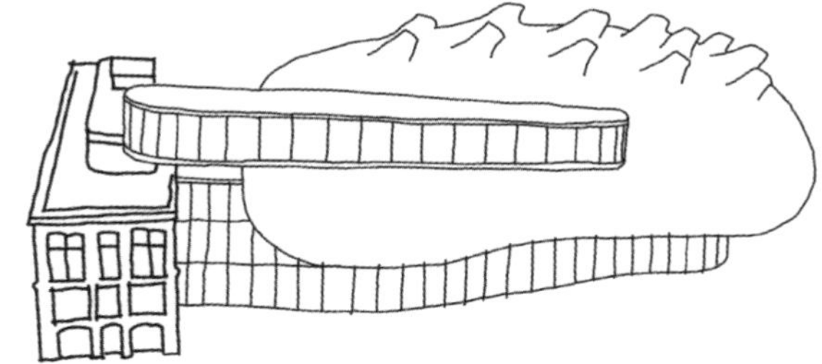

Eisernes Haus The rectilinear order of the nineteenth-century building, with its separate rooms and traditional windows, is an important part of the composition, highlighting the curves and spatial continuity of later work.

The blob The major part of the building is 'blob architecture', designed using computer digital modelling explored on-screen and in 3D-printed models. As well as the anthropomorphic analogies, the building has been likened to a spaceship in historic Graz.

The underbelly Under the belly of the blob, walls enclose a volume with a concave ceiling, like the underside of a balloon sitting in a bucket.

The needle A cantilevered glass corridor, later dubbed 'the needle', penetrates the organic blob and acts as a viewing platform overlooking the old city. Likening the blob to a creature, the needle is its eyes. The needle was designed to match the building heights of the adjacent buildings along the riverfront.

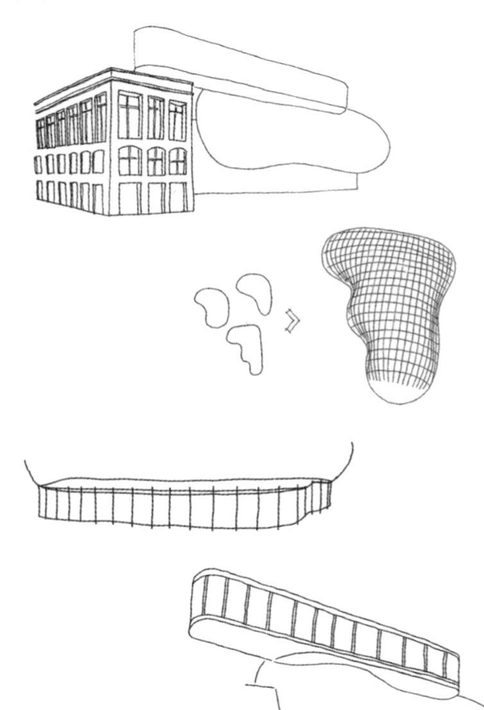

The nozzles The top surface of the blob erupts in fifteen nozzles that allow daylight to the second-floor exhibition space and add to the alien-like character of the building.

The pins Two long escalators inside the blob tie the three main floors of the building together.

The media façade: A large part of the blob's external surface doubles as a media screen. Nine hundred and thiry fluorescent rings are attached to the frame about 100mm (4in) behind the translucent skin. An integral part of the building, they can be individually controlled for intensity and duration to make displays of low-resolution still and moving images.

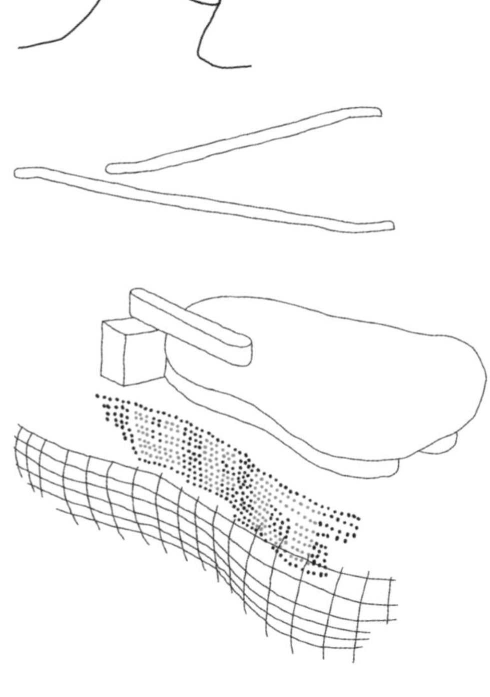

39 Kunsthaus Graz | 2000–3

Spacelab Cook-Fournier / ARGE Kunsthaus
Graz, Austria

Planning

Ground floor

The Kunsthaus is entered through a link from Eisernes House to a large foyer under the belly of the blob. The white curved surfaces of service and stair cores intrude on one side, volumes that penetrate the blob. On the other side, floor-to-ceiling glazing between perforated steel frames edges the foyer. An escalator leads up to the first gallery floor.

Middle floor

The middle floor, sandwiched between concrete floor slabs, has a hard, cold character. It is lit by rows of fluorescent tubes. Functionally, it offers adaptable exhibition space.

Turning round, visitors find a second escalator and ride up to the narrow end of the blob on the top floor.

Top floor

In a corner at the wide end of the blob, one nozzle breaks ranks with its north-facing colleagues and peers to the east. It brings the Clock Tower, the traditional landmark of Graz, into the Kunsthaus like an exhibit seen through a telescope.

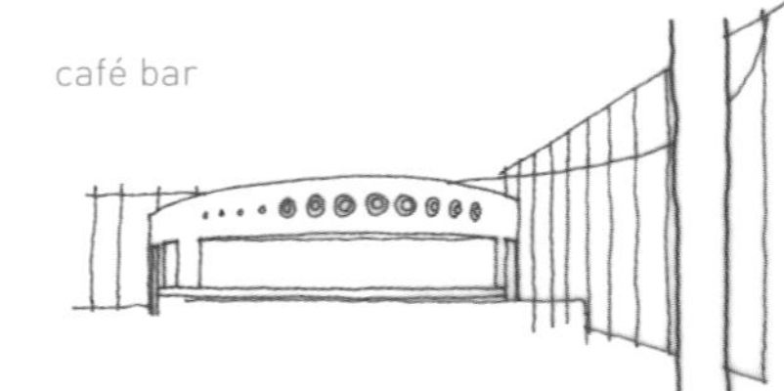

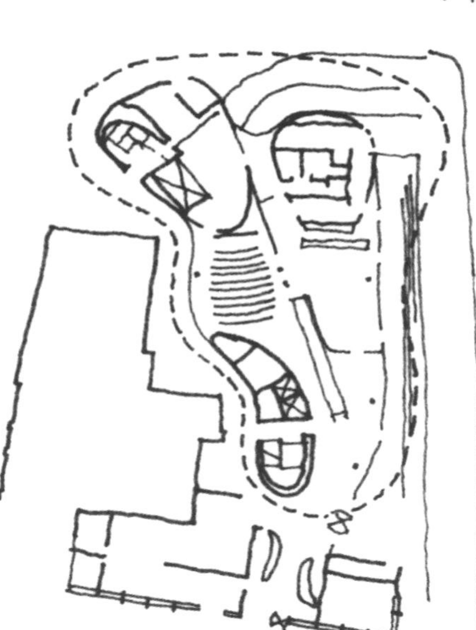

The gallery is entered from the pedestrian street through the old 'Iron House'.

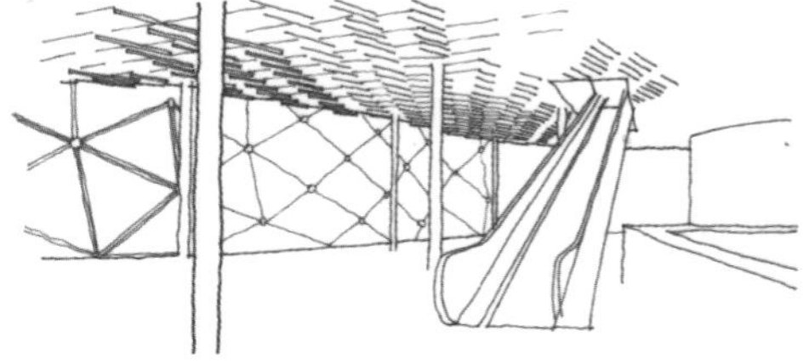

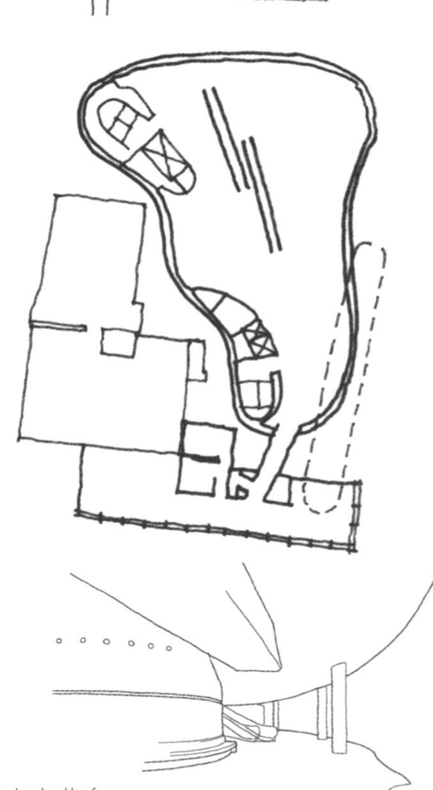

Underbelly foyer

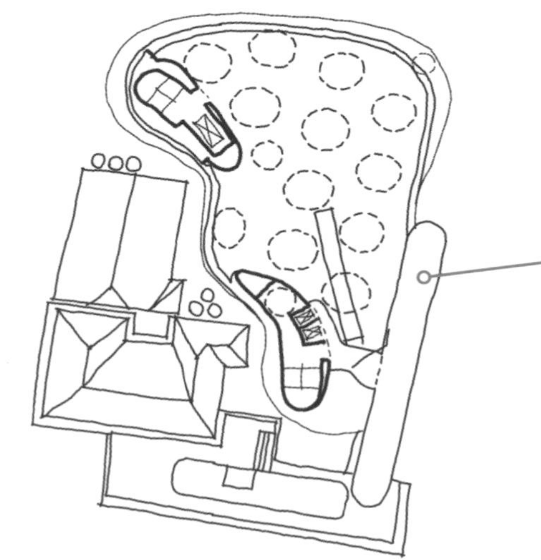

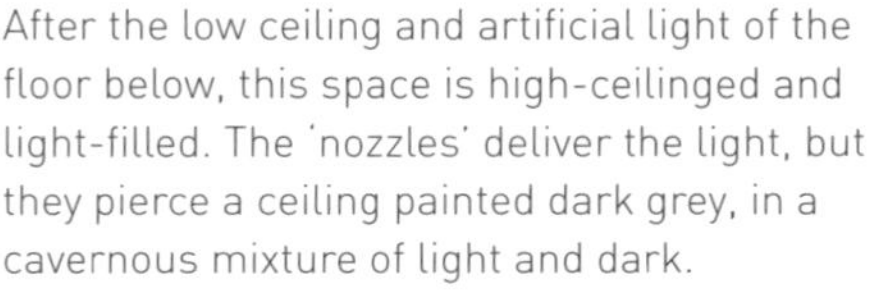

After the low ceiling and artificial light of the floor below, this space is high-ceilinged and light-filled. The 'nozzles' deliver the light, but they pierce a ceiling painted dark grey, in a cavernous mixture of light and dark.

Off to the left at the top of the escalator is the needle, a narrow corridor wrapped in floor-to-ceiling glass. The World Heritage city is the exhibit for an ultra-modern viewing platform.

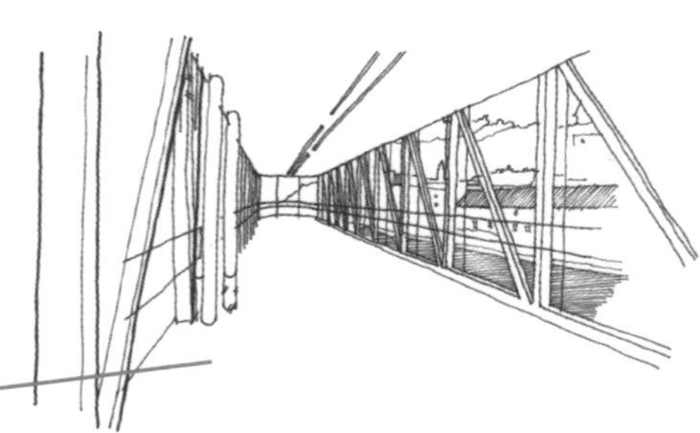

The needle viewing gallery is separated from the blob at both ends.

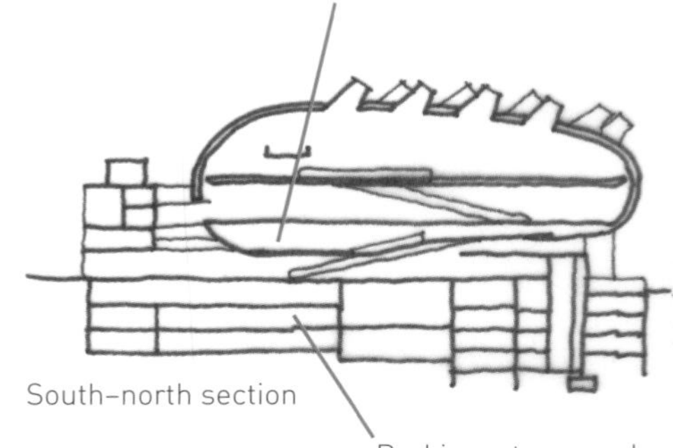

A small 'hidden' room fits into the belly of the blob.

Parking, stores and services are located on several basement levels.

South–north section

Construction

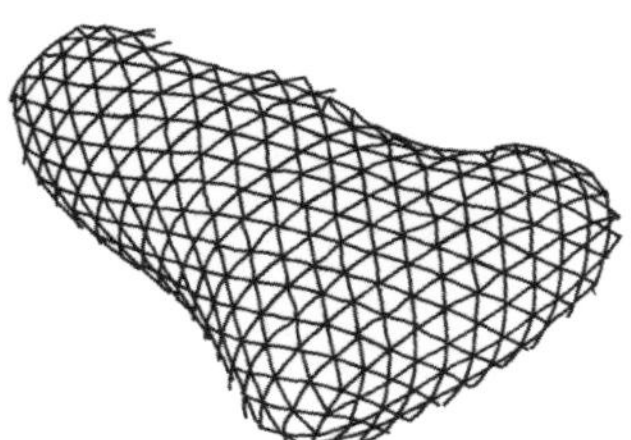

A triangulated steel space frame makes the biometric form of the blob structurally possible. It is self-supporting, enabling a column-free upper-level exhibition space with a 60m (197ft) roof span.

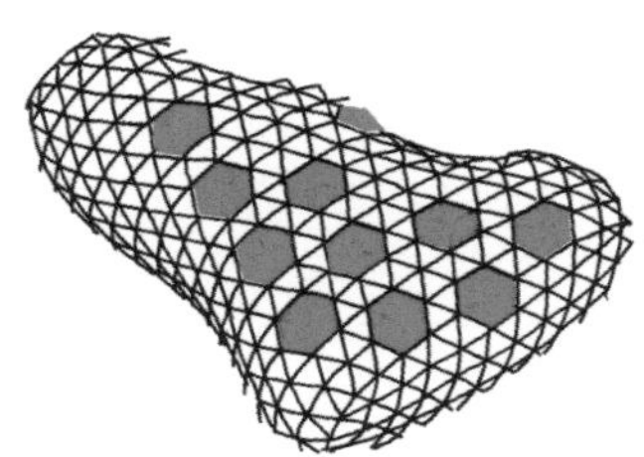

Hexagonal holes in the space frame allow for the nozzles.

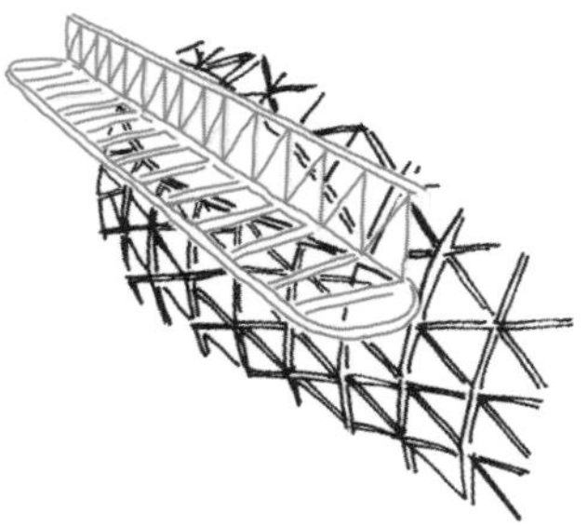

The lightweight steel frame of the needle is connected to the space frame and cantilevers over the roof of Eisernes Haus.

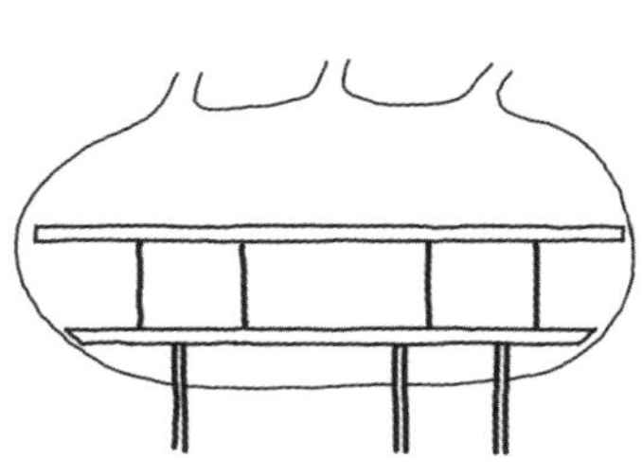

Reinforced-concrete columns support reinforced-concrete floor plates like two tables stacked on to each other. The top table has more (but thinner) columns than the bottom table.

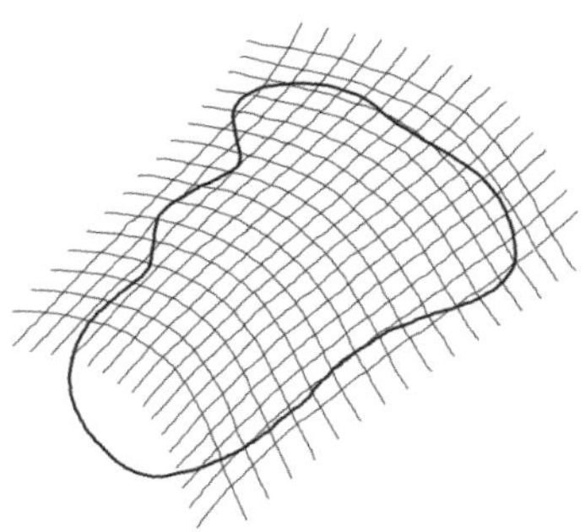

To set out the skin panels, a 2D grid was draped over the blob form using 3D digital modelling.

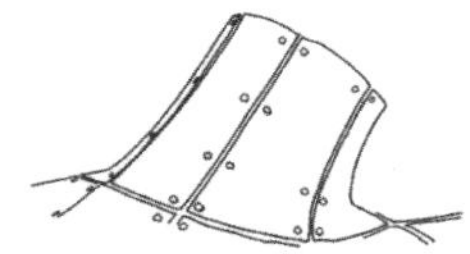

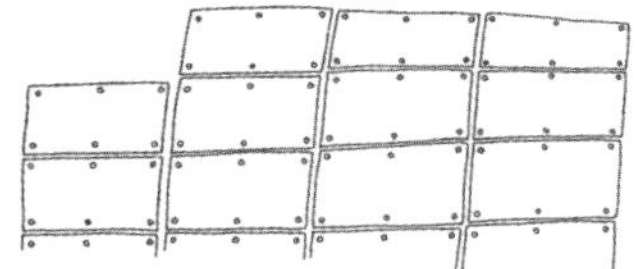

Individually moulded blue Plexiglas panels curve in two directions. A fire retardant was added in the panel construction to comply with fire regulations.

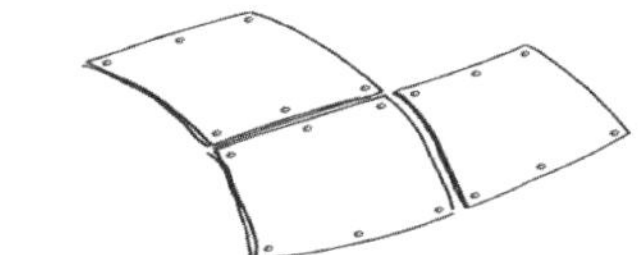

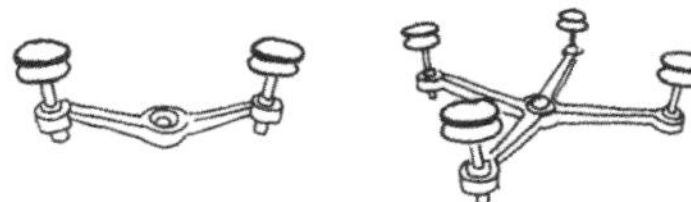

Each panel is 2m x 3m (6.6ft x 9.8ft) and attached to the space frame at six points by spider glazing fittings. A soft sealant is used to allow movement.

Response to climate

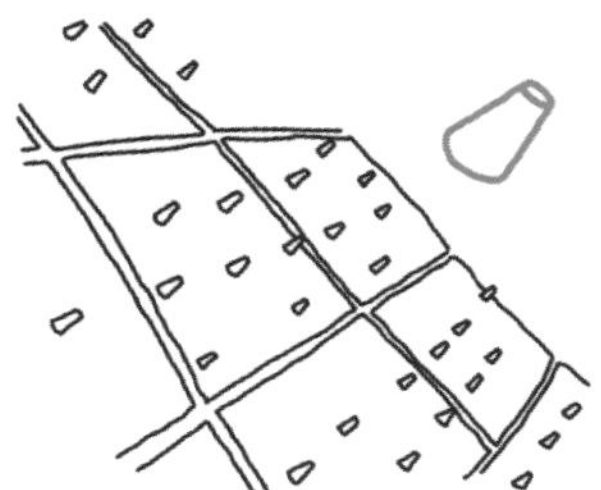

The nozzles point north, allowing daylight but avoiding direct sun penetration. The Plexiglas panels block UV light. The east-facing ground-level glass walls are deeply shaded by the overhanging blob and neighbouring trees. To cope with Graz's heavy winter snowfalls, acrylic nodes on the upper parts of the blob's skin help to retain snow – good for insulation as well as preventing blocks of snow and ice from falling on passers-by.

Archigram

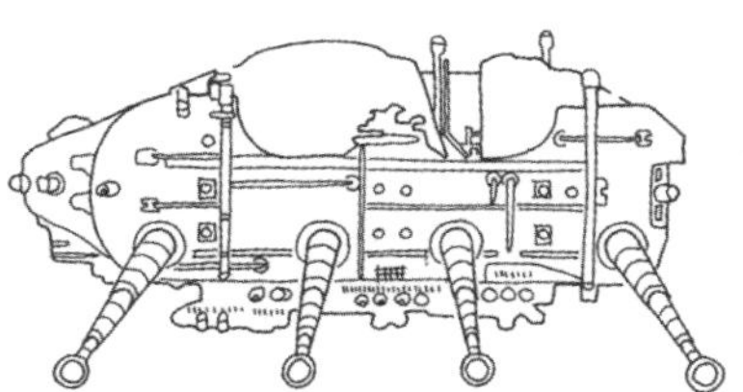

Peter Cook was a member of Archigram, an avant-garde group of London architects active from 1961 to 1974. The group created playful, Pop-inspired visions of a technological future. Cook proposed 'instant cities' (1969), mobile technological structures that would drift into drab towns via air balloons. If the Kunsthaus blob developed legs, it could fit into fellow Archigram member Ron Herron's 'walking city'.

40

Linked Hybrid | 2003–9
Steven Holl Architects
Beijing, China

The Linked Hybrid is a mixed-use development in the heart of modern Beijing. In response to the city's growing population density and commercial development, the design opens up to the urban realm to accommodate public and commercial facilities as well as housing. This hybrid building type is a break away from traditional Chinese developments and offers a model for future development.

The use of the term 'hybrid' distinguishes this project's aims from those of other mixed-use housing types that may be identified as 'social condensers' and aim to bring together disparate groups of people through the spatial manipulation of shared facilities. As an experiment in social engineering, social condensers fail to account for the consensus and shared interests that define the fine balance between private and community life, and thereby lead to problems concerning ownership of shared spaces. In contrast, the 'linked hybrid' allows for the various private and public programmatic needs to respond to 'free market' influences, and for a dynamic relationship between complementary functions to emerge from this process.

Wing Kin Yim, Amit Srivastava, Wen Ya and Marguerite Bartolo

40

Linked Hybrid | 2003-9
Steven Holl Architects
Beijing, China

Response to urban context
The rapid urbanization of the city of Beijing since the 1980s has inevitably led to the adoption of apartment blocks. Previous attempts to integrate the residential apartment block with commercial services have led only to social condensers that are the exclusive domain of the residents and form isolated clusters. The Linked Hybrid uses an interconnected loop to allow the public realm to infiltrate the residential block and integrate it into the urban fabric. Any future developments will extend along the commercial/public loop, allowing private residential blocks to coexist with the public domain.

The site along the Second Ring Road forms part of the new developments of modern Beijing.

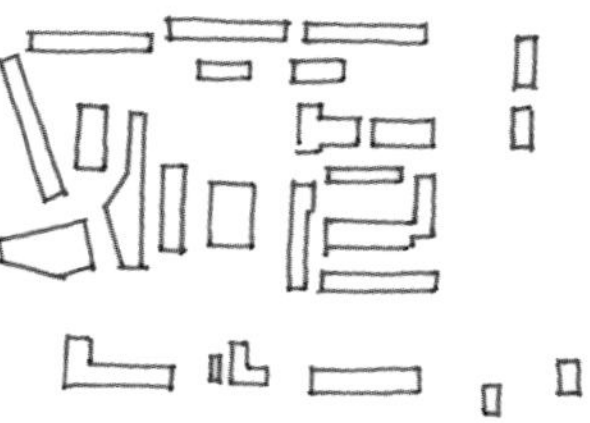

City of objects Existing residential developments with uncoordinated privatization result in isolated pockets or clusters.

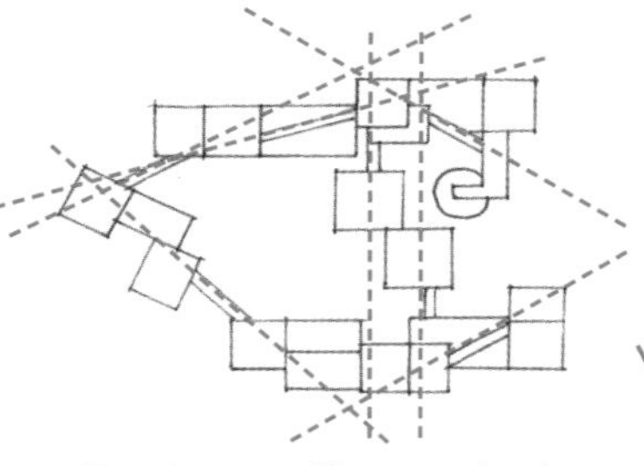

City of shapes The new development is an attempt to consolidate these objects into an interconnected community.

Site before new developments

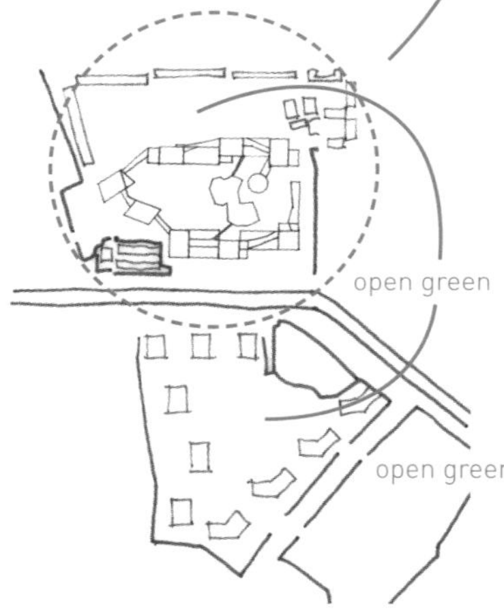

Site after new developments

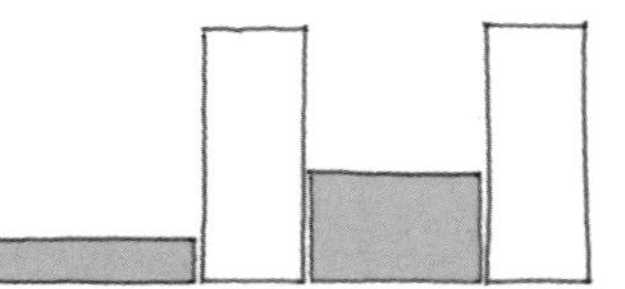

Isolated residential high-rise towers among low-rise public buildings

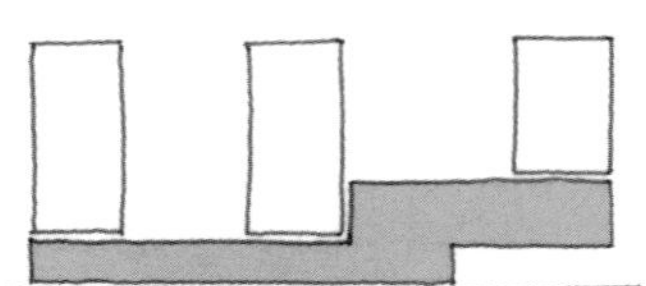

Residential apartments with integrated services – social condenser

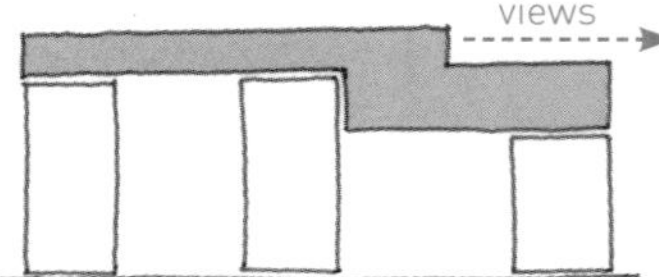

Upside-down social condenser with public amenities such as roof gardens

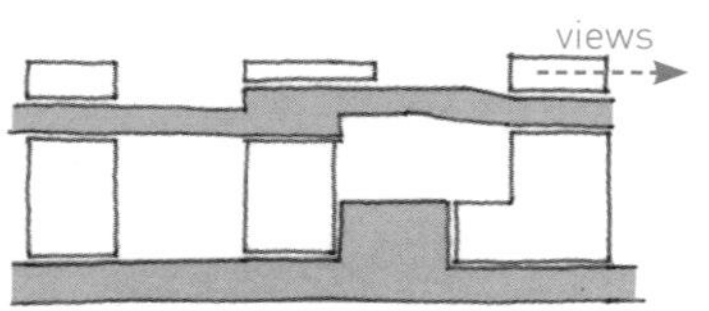

Linked Hybrid – extended public loop penetrating residential blocks

Open and built space

A series of landscaped mounds provides open green spaces for various age groups.

The adoption of the high-rise typology allows an increase in open green areas in the neighbourhood. The Linked Hybrid complex itself uses the earth extracted from the site to develop five recreational mounds, called the mounds of childhood, adolescence, middle age, old age, and infinity.

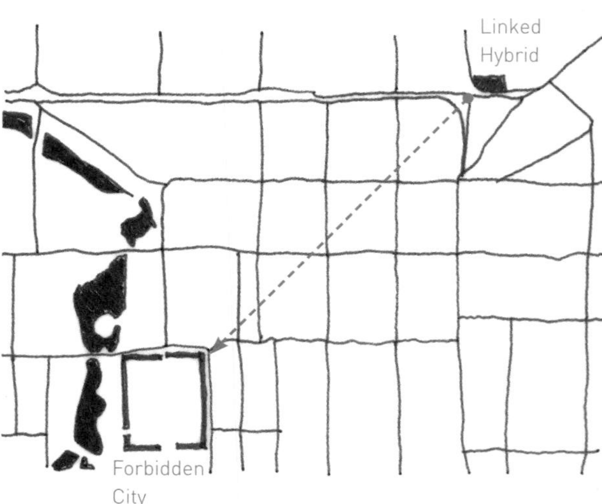

The public facilities along the upper levels provide unobstructed views to the heart of the Forbidden City.

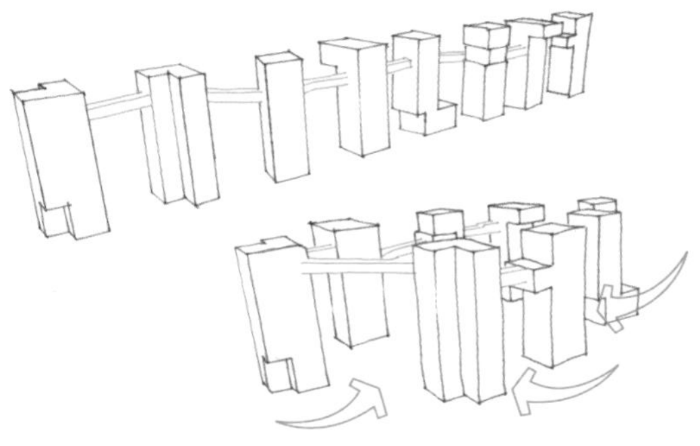

Response to programme

As a hybrid building type, the project includes numerous private and public functions, and the design allows for these various programmes to coexist. The residential towers are arranged around the cinema, which acts as a central orienting public space and allows for visual connections with urban life. The sky bridge on the twentieth floor brings other public functions even closer to the residential realm, allowing for greater social interaction to occur.

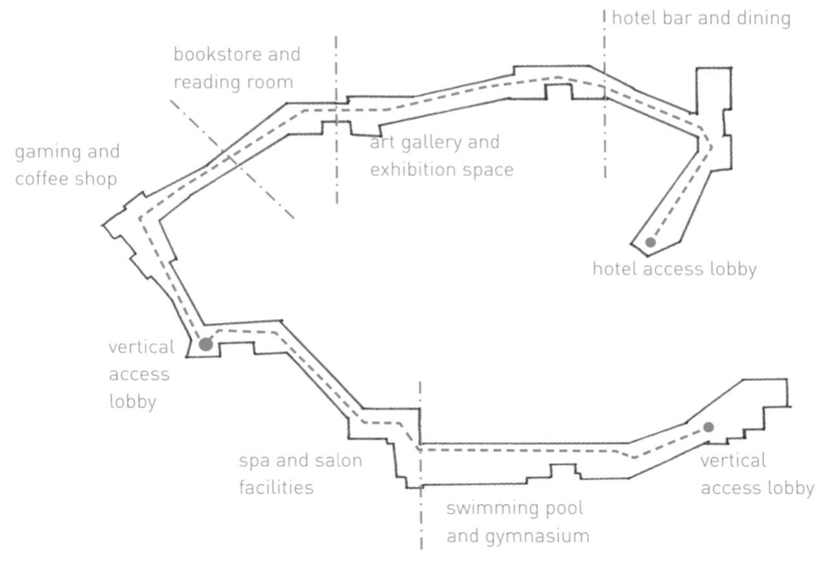

The connecting bridges are not considered as a linear series. Instead, the towers are organized in a loop to generate a central enclosure similar to those in traditional courtyard houses.

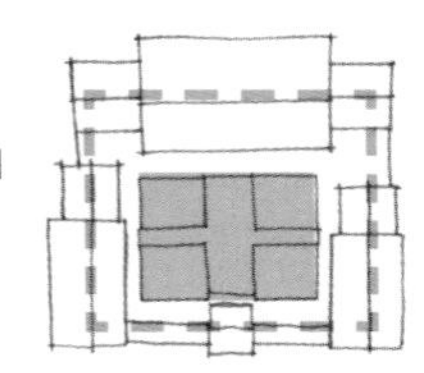

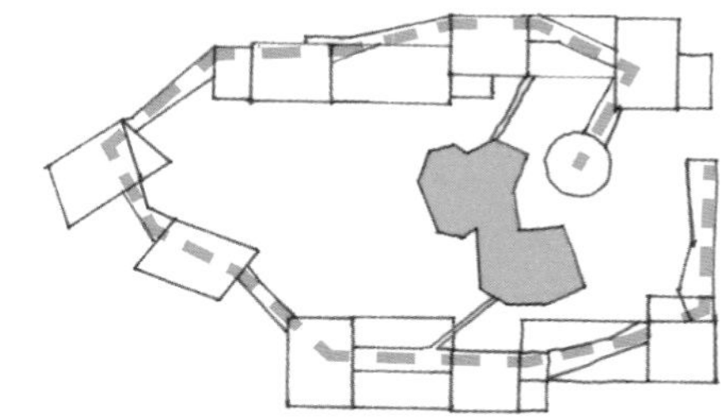

The central enclosure is activated by public buildings such as a cinema and a hotel; the roof of the cinema acts as a courtyard garden.

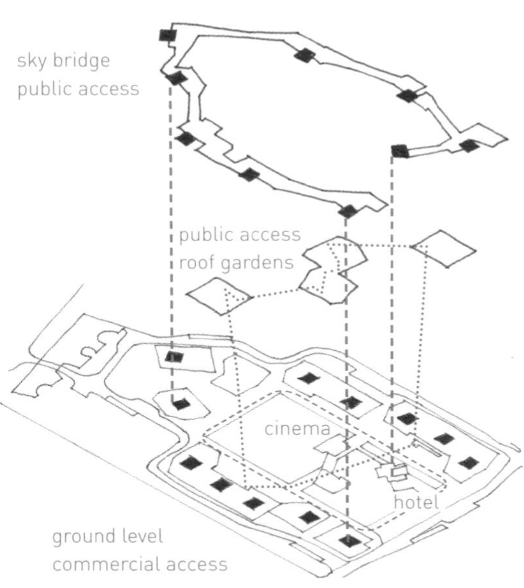

Various forms of community activities take place in the cinema's rooftop garden.

The organization of the blocks in a loop also allows for greater interaction between the two commercial/public levels situated on the ground and the twentieth floors. The vertical connections break the monotony of a linear experience. A parallel circulation network allows the public to access the roof garden atop the cinema hall. Since residents can look on to this complex central public space, the community activities are tied back to the private realm, thereby enhancing the feel of a cohesive community.

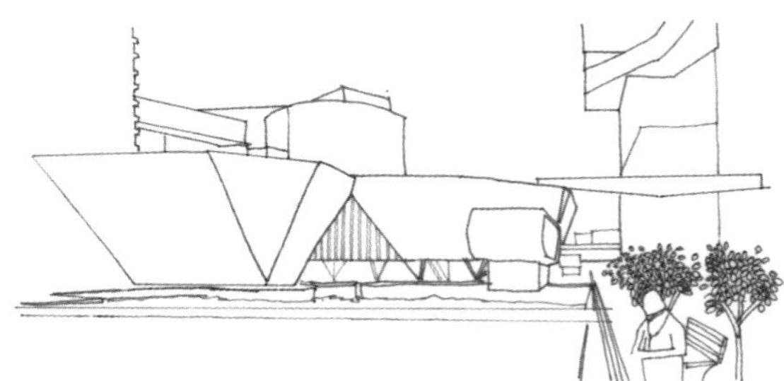

The sky bridge includes a series of public activities, including bar and dining for hotel guests and a public gymnasium, as well as shops. Their organization in the designs takes into account the residents' need for privacy, accommodating the most public activities on the bridges while using the sections through the built mass to serve supporting functions.

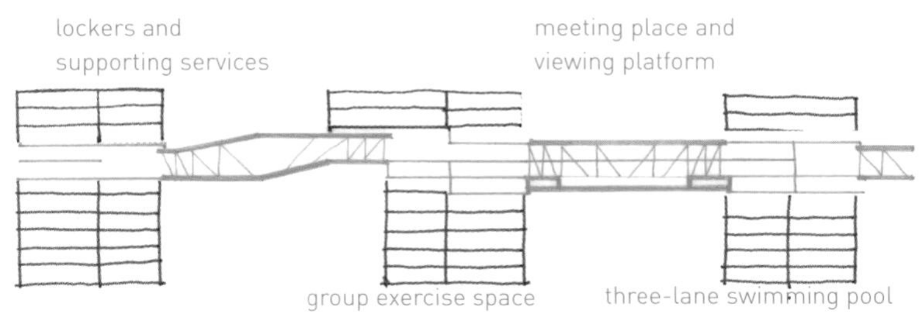

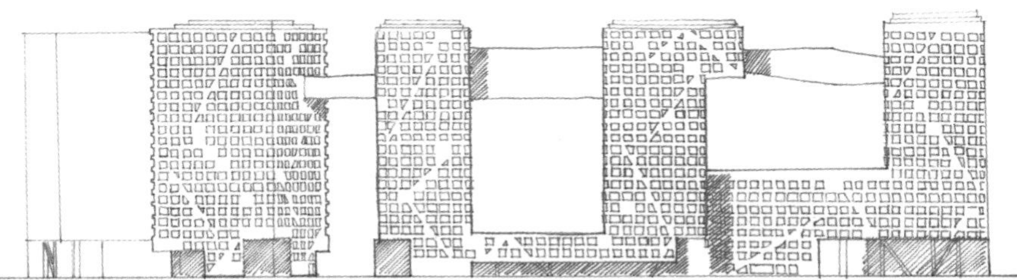

Linked Hybrid | 2003-9
Steven Holl Architects
Beijing, China

Form and analogy
The decision to organize the towers in a loop had practical benefits, but it was also developed out of a desire to represent the closely tied nature of the community. The simple rectilinear building blocks can be regarded as isolated members that are held together in this ring. They are designed to respond to their neighbours and seem to be in a dialogue with each other. An early sketch by the architect exploring this responsive relationship recreates the spirit of a group of people holding hands and dancing.

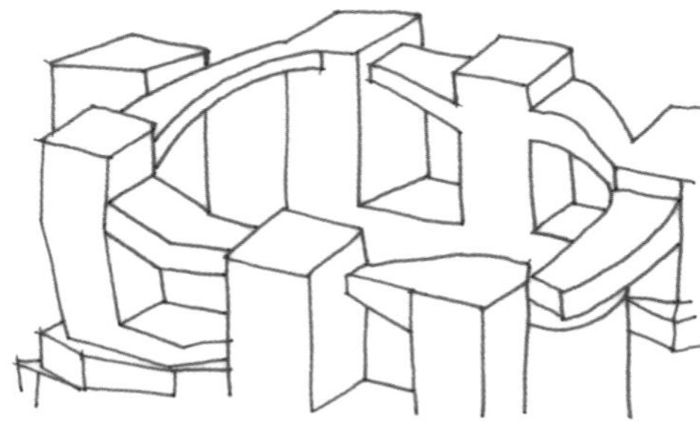

Sketch showing buildings as a gathering

The light and transparent bridges are contrasted against the solid mass of the building blocks to highlight their analogical relationship.

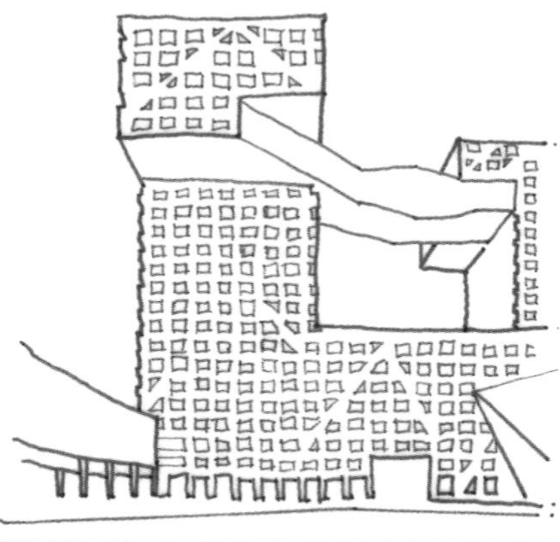

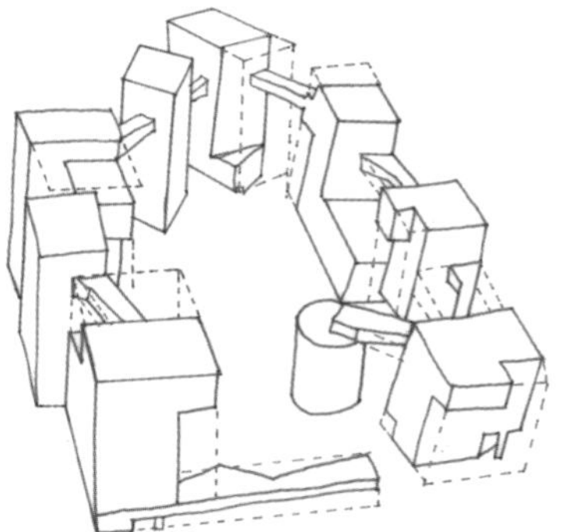

The geometric forms of the built blocks are modulated in response to neighbouring structures.

The Dance by Henri Matisse (1910)

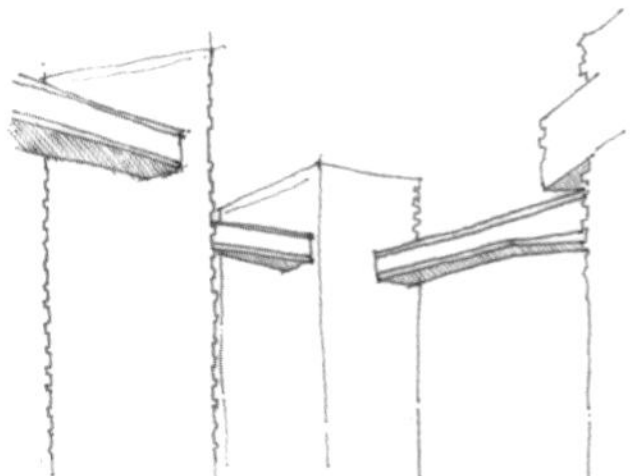

The idea of links is further explored through lighting of the underside of the bridges and linking strips on the skin of the buildings.

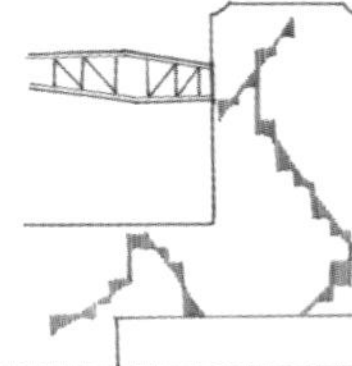

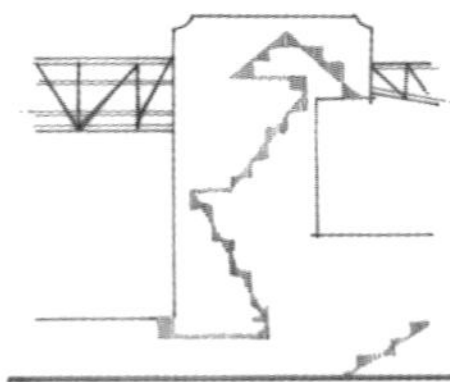

Response to local culture
While the overall look of the building corresponds to modern aesthetic principles, the design includes references to local cultures and beliefs. In the simplest sense the towers and the linking bridges provide a reference to the Great Wall of China as an important cultural symbol.

Other allusions to the local cultural practices include feng shui principles in the organization of the design elements, and the use of such elements as water and colour in accordance with local practices.

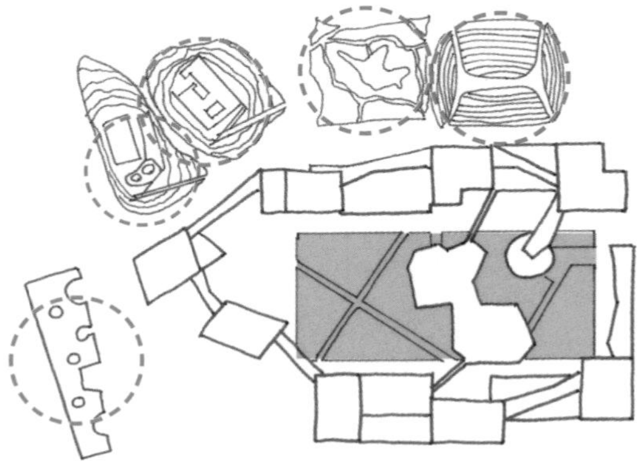

Following feng shui principles, a series of mounds developed on the northern side of the site corresponds to the idea of tall mountains and provides symbolic protection against bad energies. The large pool of water in the central enclosed courtyard is also a traditional design element intended to channel the flow of positive energy and bring prosperity and good health to the residents.

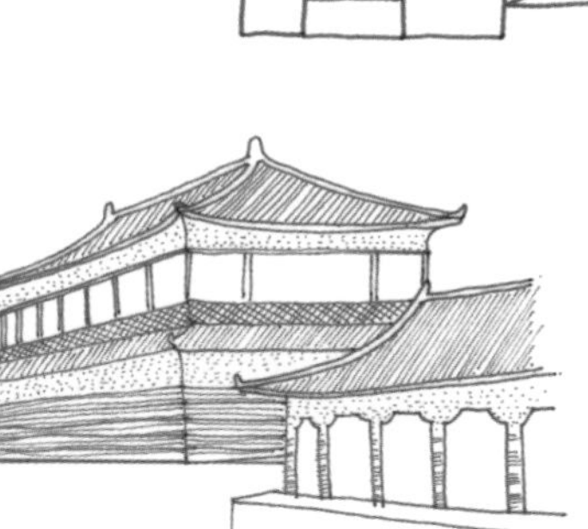

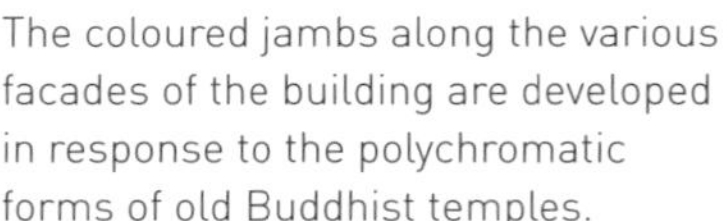

The coloured jambs along the various facades of the building are developed in response to the polychromatic forms of old Buddhist temples.

Response to user

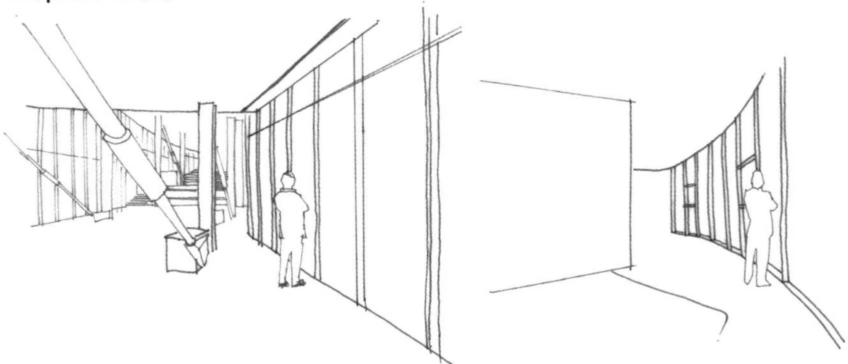

The transparent sky-bridge corridor functions as a space of public display.

A slight shift in the level of transparency transforms it into a viewing platform.

The design manipulates the level of transparency to create a smooth transition from the public functions housed in the sky-bridge corridors to the private realm of the residential apartments. Depending on its level of transparency, the sky bridge can itself change from a viewing platform for observing outdoor activity, to a showcase of activities on display for people outside.

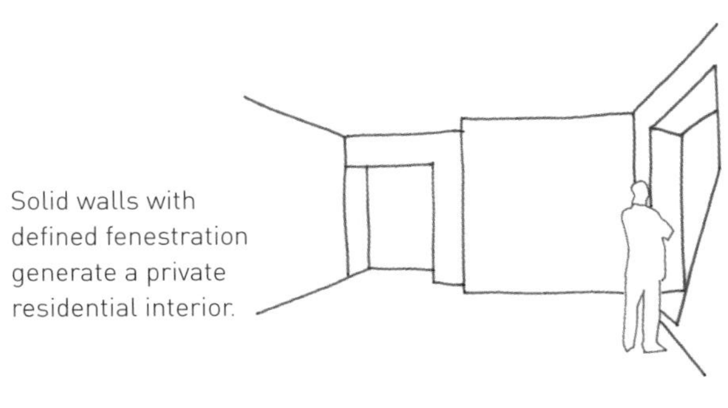

Solid walls with defined fenestration generate a private residential interior.

Public corridors have exaggerated scale and internal volume.

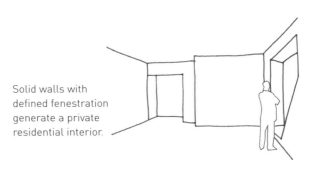

The design generates a series of experiences for the user through a play of scale and light, which helps users to orient themselves in the space. While the juxtaposition of smaller structures in the courtyard helps to break the scale of the high-rise towers, the internal volume of the commercial corridors is exaggerated to confirm their public nature. Similarly, the light-filled transparent nature of the sky-bridge corridors is contrasted against the solid walls and rectilinear openings of the more private residential interiors to mark the transition from the public to the private.

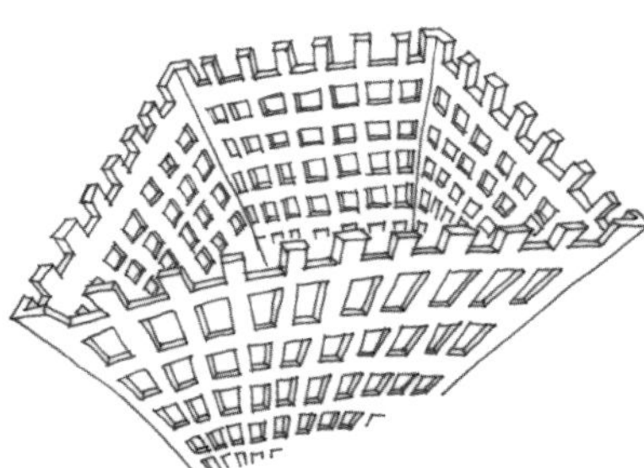

The structural exoskeleton allows freedom with the internal layouts, which are organized to take full advantage of the views and natural ventilation.

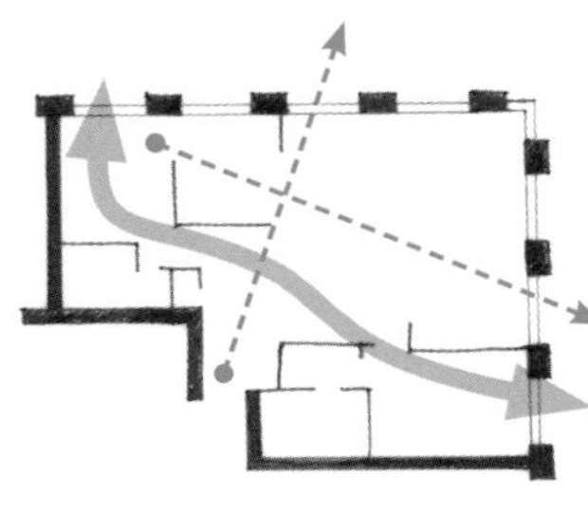

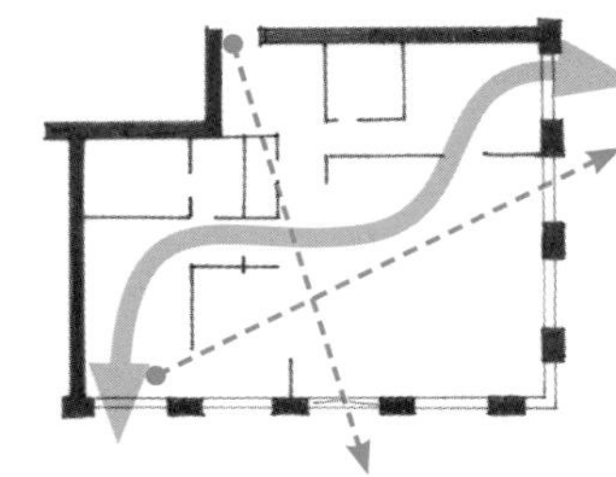

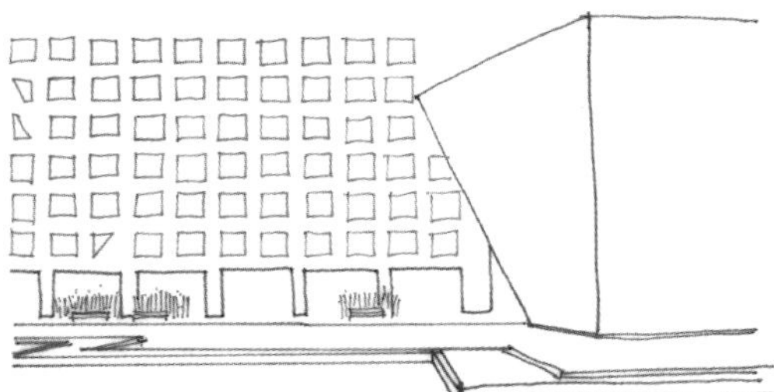

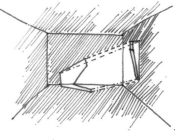

The relatively small cinema building situated in the courtyard breaks the scale of the high-rise towers.

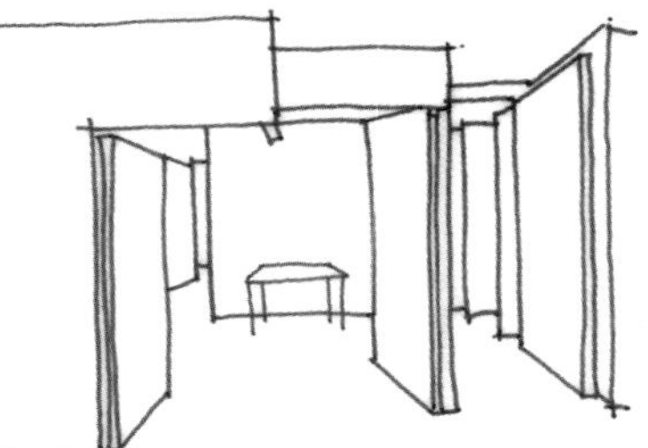

Movable walls in apartments allow for the transformation of space from private enclosures to an interconnected series of spaces depending on the needs of the occupants.

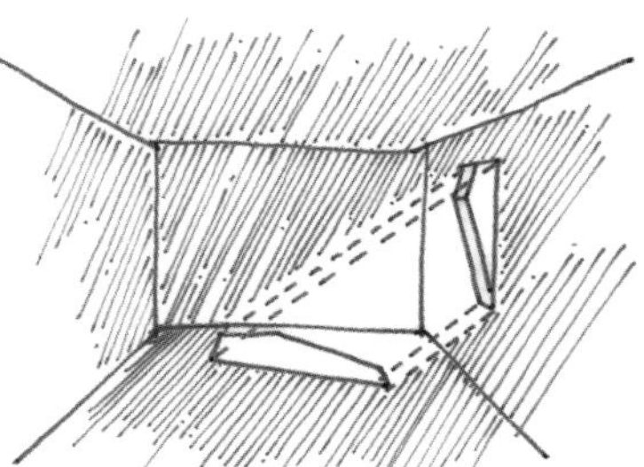

Irregular windows give patches of sunlight that change shape in unexpected ways across the room.

Santa Caterina Market | 1997–2005

EMBT

Barcelona, Spain

41

Santa Caterina Market is a rehabilitation project in a historical district of Barcelona. The Convent of Santa Maria was built in 1845 but after a fire in 1848 was converted into the first covered market in the city. For its renewal, architects EMBT retained three white masonry walls of the old market with their arched façades, while the fourth side was newly designed to open to a plaza. This is surrounded by social housing, which was part of the urban renewal proposal.

The market's distinctive new roof with its curving form and vibrant colour revitalizes the urban environment.

The project demonstrates a striving for responsive cohesion in urban design in several ways. The relationships between housing and public areas, between vehicles and pedestrians, between old and new, and between the overall building form and its details are all carefully considered to respond to one another.

Selen Morkoç, Mohammad Faiz Madlan, Zhe Cai Zack and Leona Greenslade

41

Santa Caterina Market | 1997–2005

EMBT
Barcelona, Spain

Context

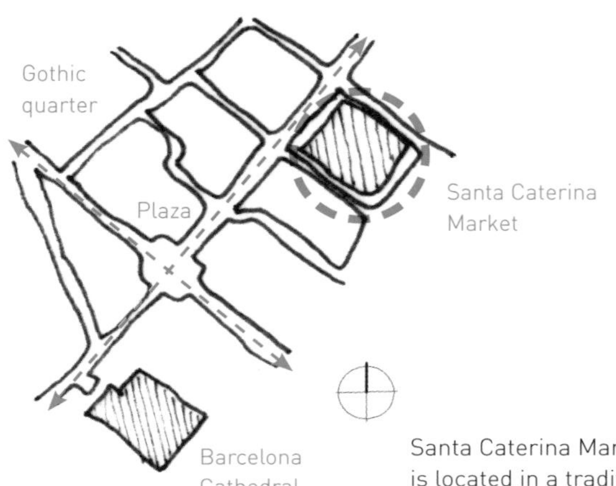

Santa Caterina Market is located in a traditional Gothic quarter of Barcelona.

In a high-density area, the market site as a rare open space is a significant node suitable for pedestrian activity.

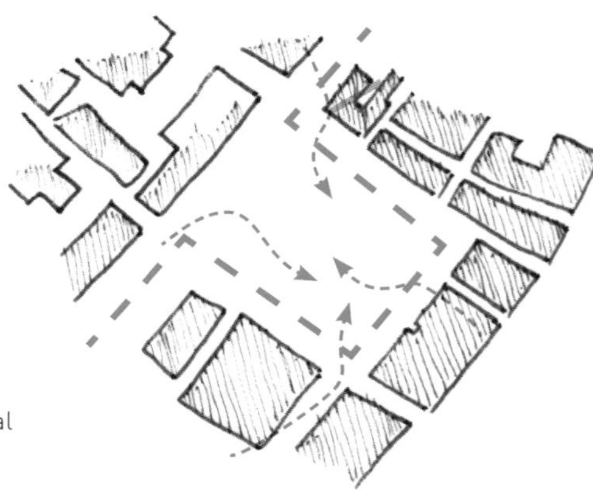

vehicular access

pedestrian street

site for redevelopment

pedestrian street

The market site is surrounded by five- to nine-level old residential blocks, and dim streets in a dense urban area with few open public spaces. It was known for high rates of poverty and crime.

Connectivity

Visual connectivity
The canopy extending to the street can be seen from the cathedral, strengthening the connection between the market and the cathedral.

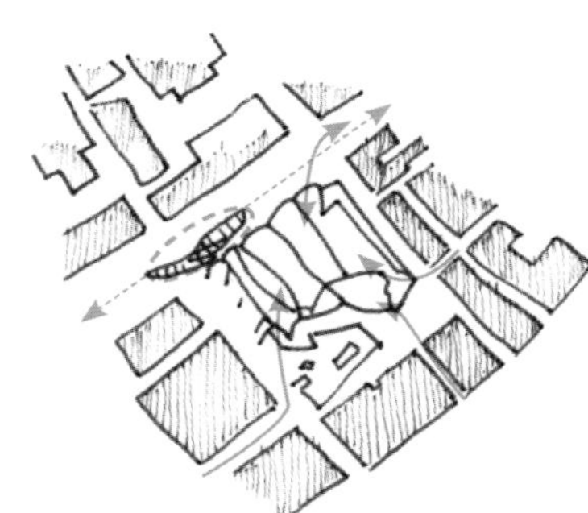

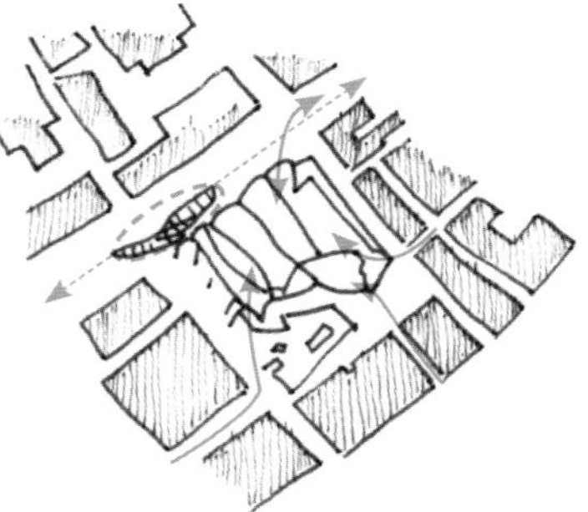

street canopy

cathedral

The market and the nearby cathedral both attract visitors. The cathedral is appropriately imposing, while the market's height and profile is low to keep in harmony with the surrounding buildings.

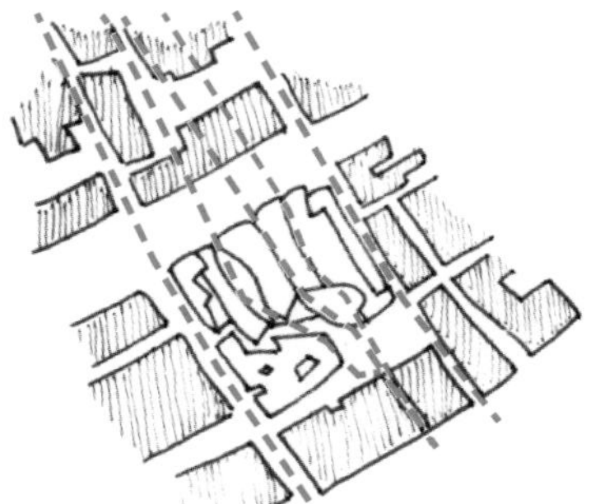

The connectivity of the district context The design of the roof layout responds to the existing building context and movement routes on both sides.

Airflow and natural light

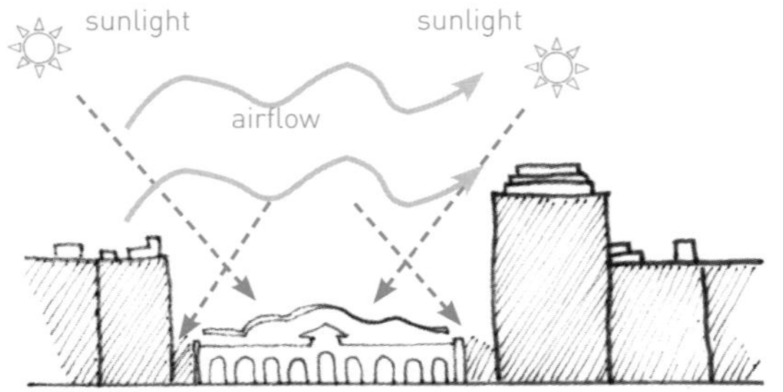

The low market form allows sunlight and air into this extremely dense part of the city.

Old market and streetscape

new façade
new apartment building
12 arches
7 arches
main façades of the old market

With its combination of new work and parts of the old market, the design increases the vibrancy of the precinct.

The old and the new

Old elevation

Back elevation of the new market

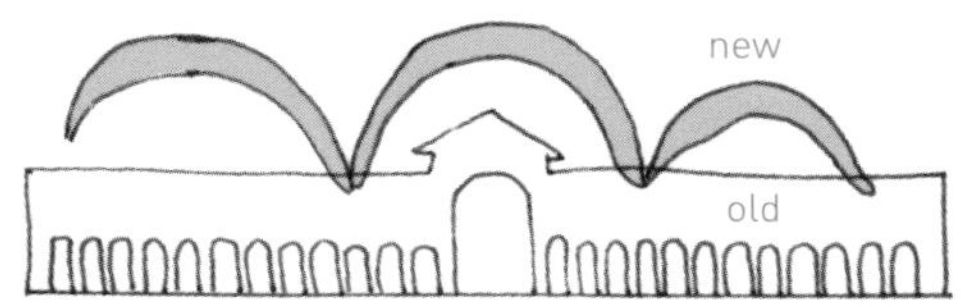

The orthogonal front has a classic style and is lined with arches in response to the buildings on the opposite side of the street. The back façade slightly curves but maintains the same rhythm as the old market elevation.

The new design responds to the old building through the roof structure. The projecting roof does not dominate the old façade but appears to hover gently above the walls.

Old market façade detail

In addition to a steel roof structure, the new design also uses timber. Use of timber is a reference to local building fenestration, and it forms a link between different building parts – the steel roof of the design and the masonry walls of the old structure.

Apartment house detail

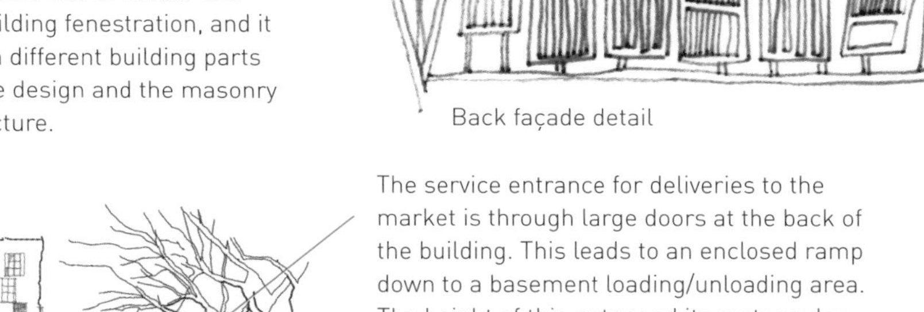

Back façade detail

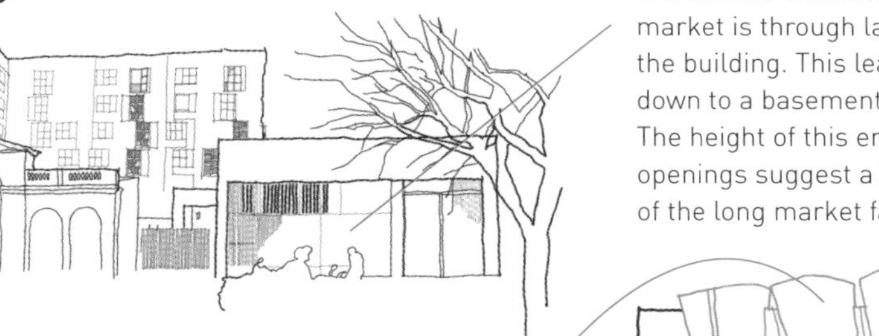

The service entrance for deliveries to the market is through large doors at the back of the building. This leads to an enclosed ramp down to a basement loading/unloading area. The height of this entry and its rectangular openings suggest a highly simplified version of the long market façade.

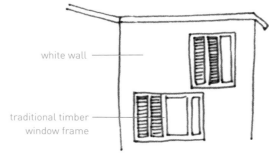

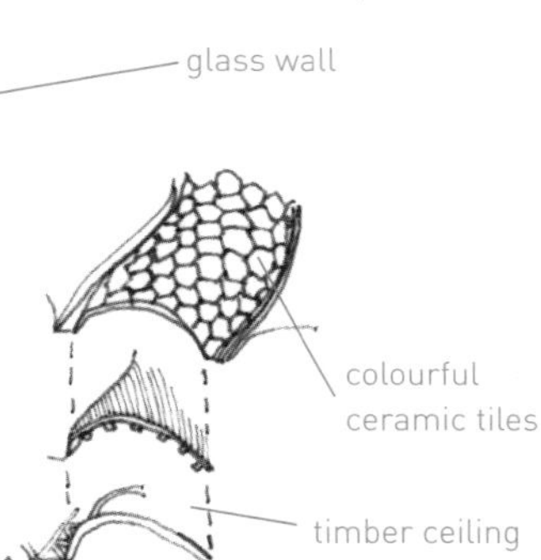

Material analysis

Various materials are used in the new additions to the market apart from existing materials. The main structure is steel. The colourful roof surface is composed of ceramic tiles as a local reference to other buildings in Barcelona. The market façade has timber and glass surfaces.

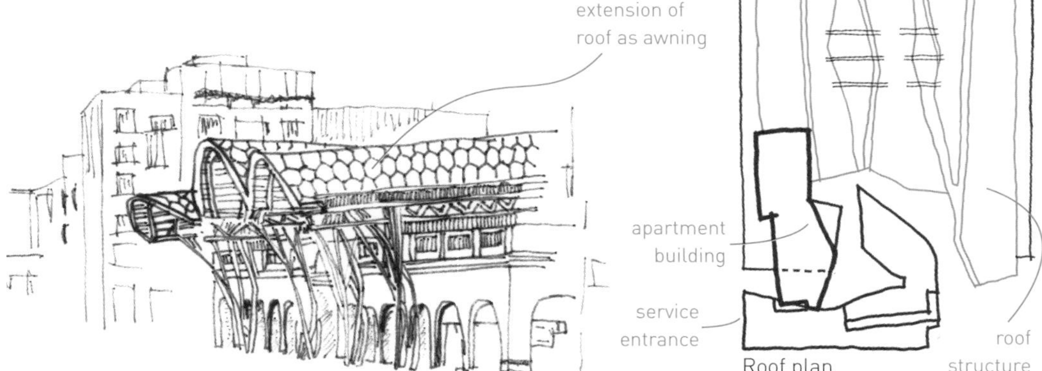

Roof plan

The roof extension reinforces connection between the new construction and the street.

The back wall responds to the new apartment building (which in turn responds to the market), while the roof form fits to the shape of the block.

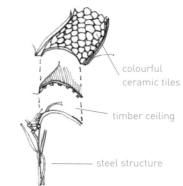

Santa Caterina Market | 1997–2005

EMBT

Barcelona, Spain

Approach and movement

The granite used in the footpath continues inside as the market floor, to emphasize the market being part of the public space.

The new rear plaza is a light-filled space in an area of narrow streets and dense housing.

Accesses to the market are redesigned to connect strategic points more efficiently. Staircases provide easy access to an underground car park.

Deliveries are made underground via a ramp from a side street. Car parking is also underground, but accessed from a wider street far from the market. Apartments occupy the south-west corner of the site.

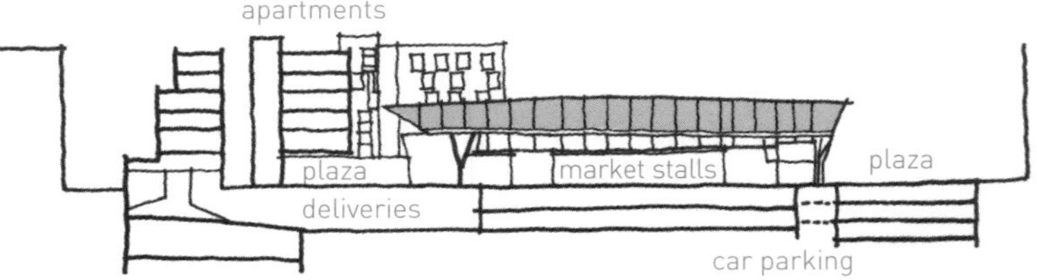

Structure and details

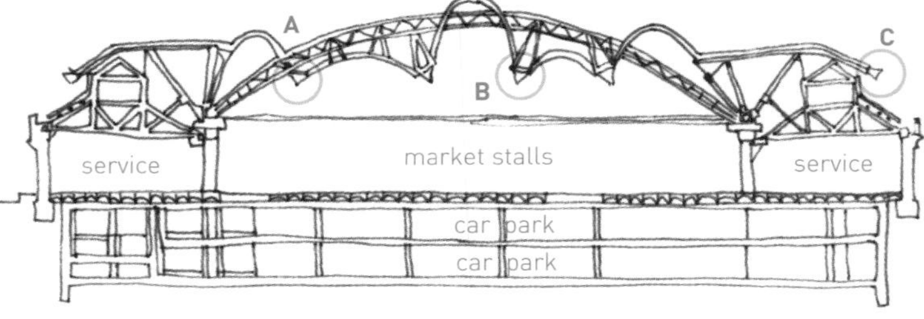

Plan and Use

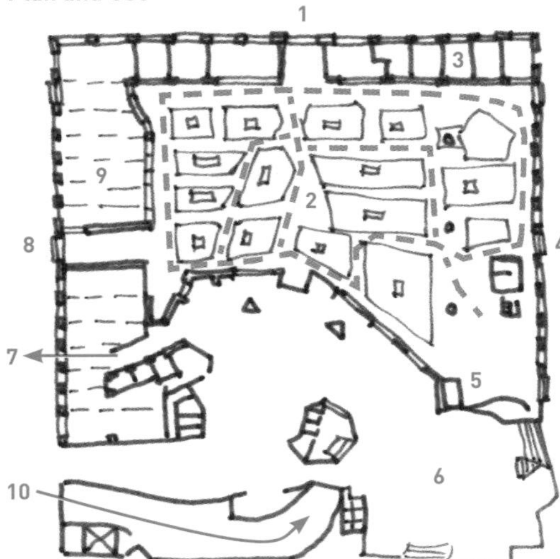

Key

1. main entrance
2. 60 stalls
3. stores
4. entry
5. area where excavated ruins are exposed below floor level
6. rear plaza
7. service
8. entry
9. restaurant
10. enclosed ramp down to delivery area

The market plan has public entrances on three sides. With places for shopping and eating, the planning encourages pedestrian movement through several route options.

Detail A

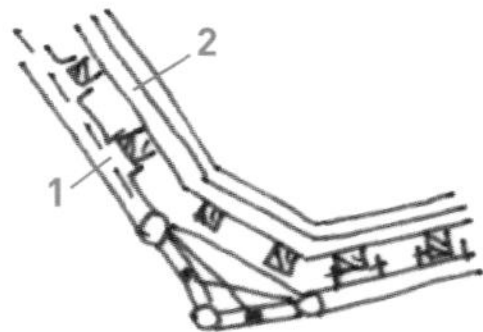

Detail B

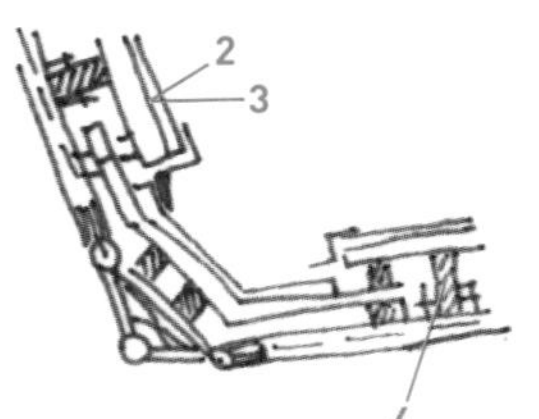

Detail C

Key

1. curved truss
2. laminated wood
3. colourful tiles
4. timber purlin
5. gutter

The long-span roof structure is supported by two concrete beams. The undulating vaults of steel change in height and profile as they run from the entry façade to the back.

Concrete beams and columns are the load-bearing system of the structure.

Reused original framing connects old market walls to a new concrete beam. Long-span timber arch trusses carry loads to these concrete beams through steel connections.

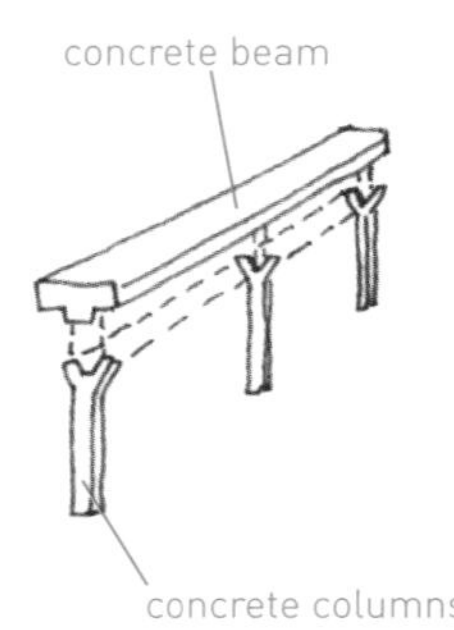

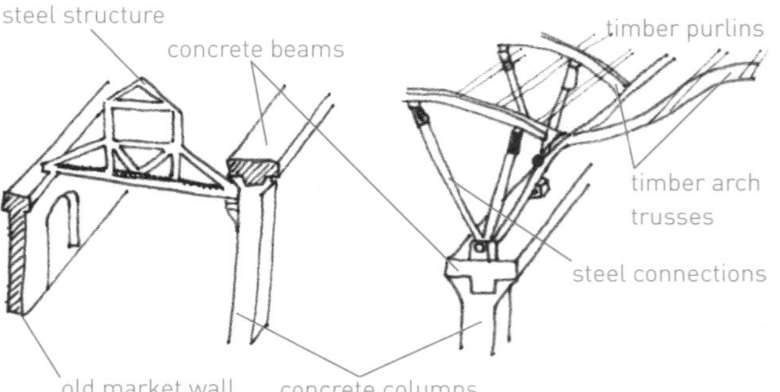

Roof form

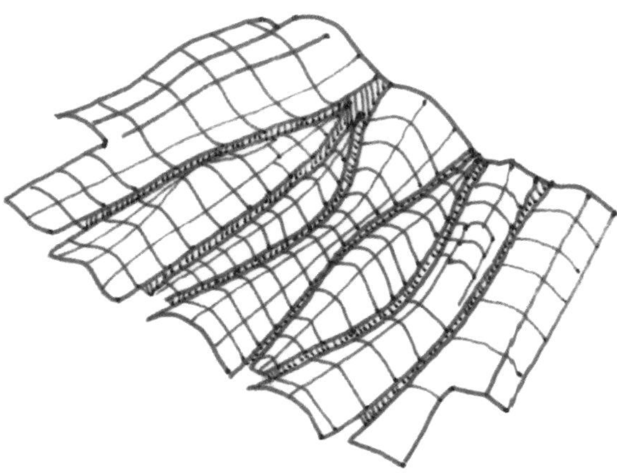

The undulating form of the roof with its diverse colours refers to the architectural heritage of Barcelona, in particular the work of architect Antoni Gaudí.

Casa Milá by Gaudí (1906–12)

Park Güell by Gaudí (1900–14). The colourful roof tiles recall Gaudi's park design.

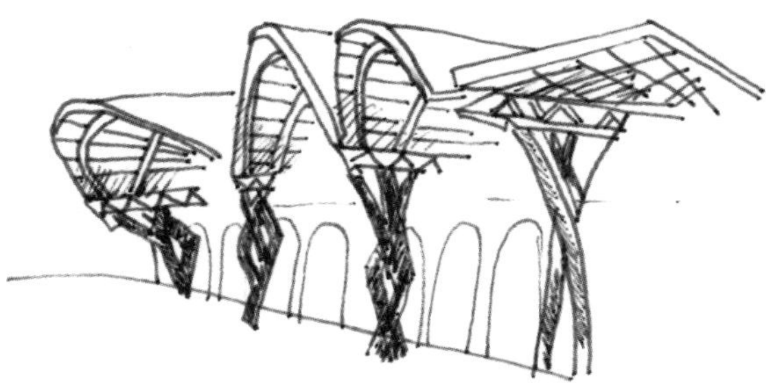

Arches and roof curve

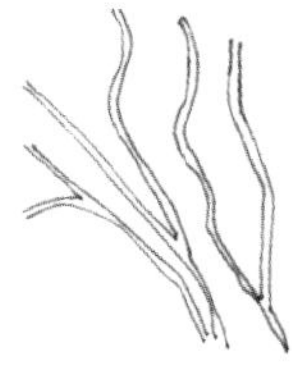

Pavers in the market

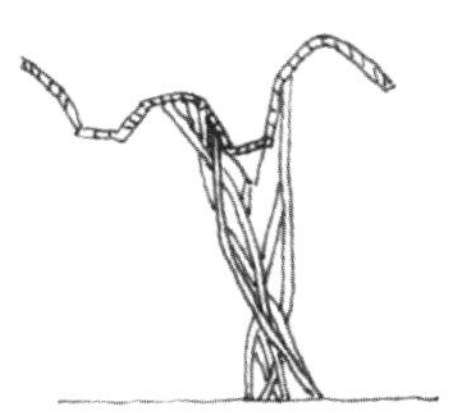

Tree-branch columns of main façade

There is formal correspondence between the roof structure and the plan layout and the existing façade; similar curves are repeated in pavers and in the columns of the façade, forming an organic unity of free-flowing curves.

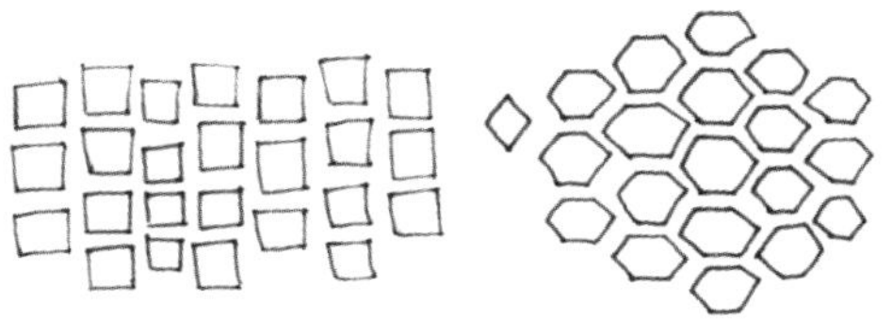

Tile design The metaphorical inspiration of the roof plane comes from the products of the market. Patterns of fruits and vegetables are abstracted into hexagonal tiles of sixty-six different colours, each with distinctive patterns.

Old market

New market

The rehabilitation of the old market through its innovative form and colours adds value to the existing structure, emphasizing its heritage quality. The colourful roof structure enriches the otherwise dull and marginal urban fabric around it while enhancing the use of public space.

New market with surrounding buildings

Upper roof structure and old façade

Modest scale of market and its undulating roof

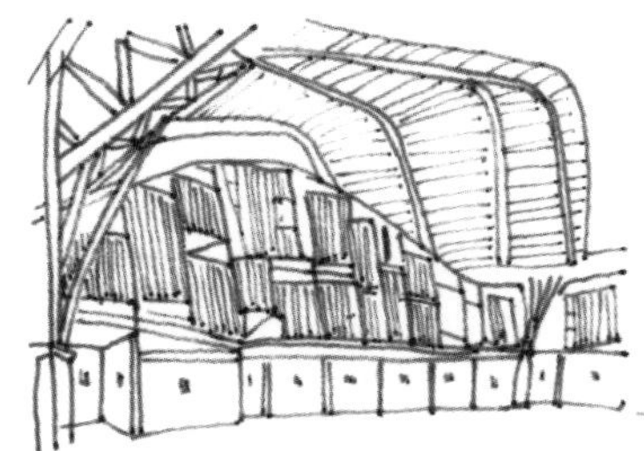

Back wall of new market

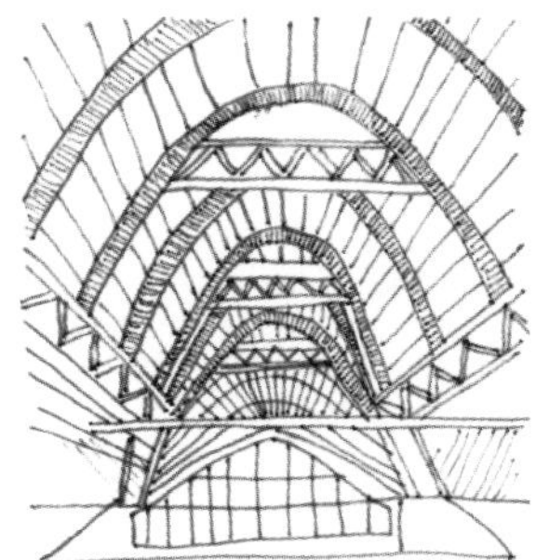

Interior perspective

42

Southern Cross Station | 2001–6

Grimshaw Architects / Jackson Architecture

Melbourne, Australia

AUSTRALIA

Melbourne

Southern Cross Station is a public transport node and civic beacon. The distinct dunelike roof structure responds to the sometimes wet, sometimes hot and humid climate of Melbourne by providing natural ventilation for cooling and for the extraction of fumes from diesel-powered trains. The roof also collects rainwater. The station is a part of redevelopment to revitalize the west end of the city of Melbourne.

Designed by London-based Grimshaw Architects in association with the Melbourne firm Jackson Architecture, the project displays a holistic approach to public space in which movement, scale, urban statement and response to environment work together.

Gabriel Ash and Selen Morkoc.

42

Southern Cross Station | 2001–6
Grimshaw Architects / Jackson Architecture
Melbourne, Australia

Urban context

Melbourne skyline

Southern Cross Station is at the west end of Melbourne city centre, providing links to the suburbs and to rural Victoria. It is located at the centre of a hub for public and private transport facilities, with interstate coach services and buses to the city's airport.

Melbourne CBD (central business district)

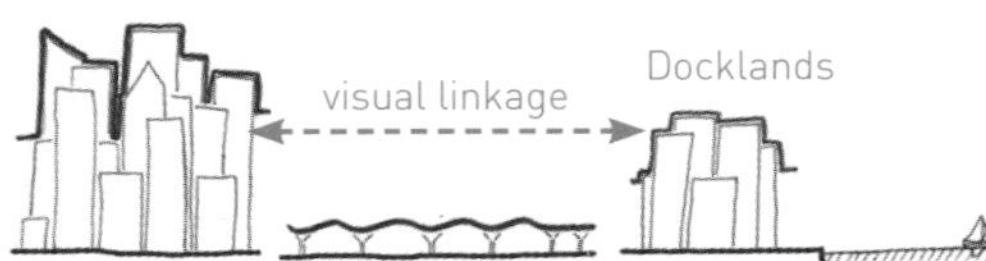

The design responds to the immediate context as a visual and literal link between downtown Melbourne and the new Docklands precinct, where docks are redeveloped into a residential, recreational and exhibition area.

Platforms and upper shell Each platform acts as an axis to the overhead structure, so that column supports are positioned on platform centre lines.

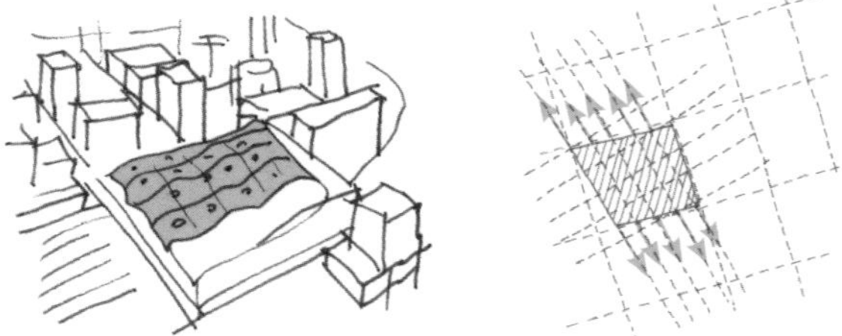

The station roof covers an entire city block and works as a linkage node between immediate and remote locations. The station grid is aligned with the railway lines, at a slight angle to the street grid. Its dune-like roof form provides a horizontal, organic contrast to the busy verticality of the city centre. A design priority was to upgrade the streetscape along Spencer Street in order to create a new dynamic urban space for the west end of Melbourne. A pedestrian link over the railway provides additional access to station platforms.

The outdated existing terminal was revitalized by the smooth, flowing curves of the new station, which created the largest covered civic space in the city centre.

Form generation

3D roof mesh

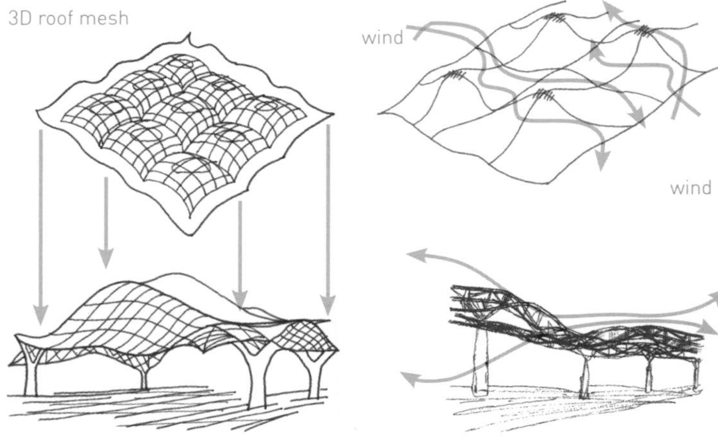

The three-dimensional roof mesh was designed to shelter a well-ventilated and comfortable urban space. Research into wind patterns in sand dunes influenced the roof design.

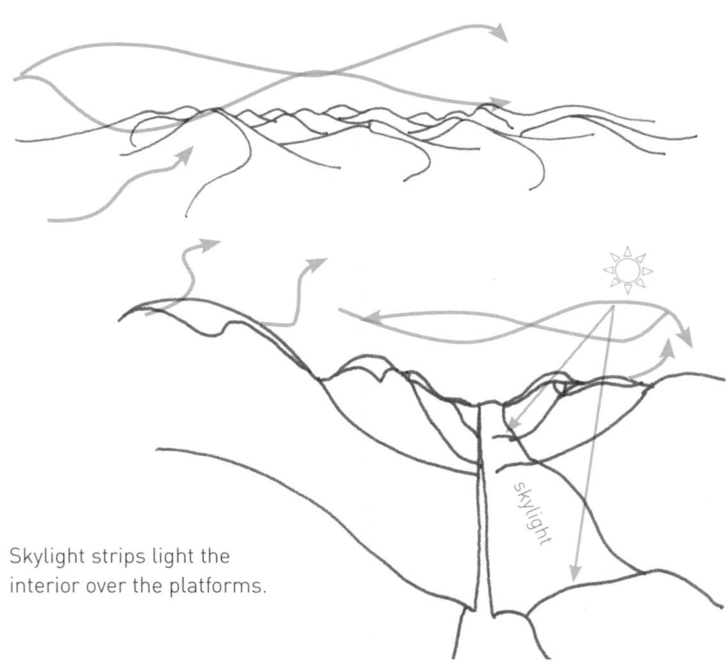

Skylight strips light the interior over the platforms.

Urban scale

Docklands frontage

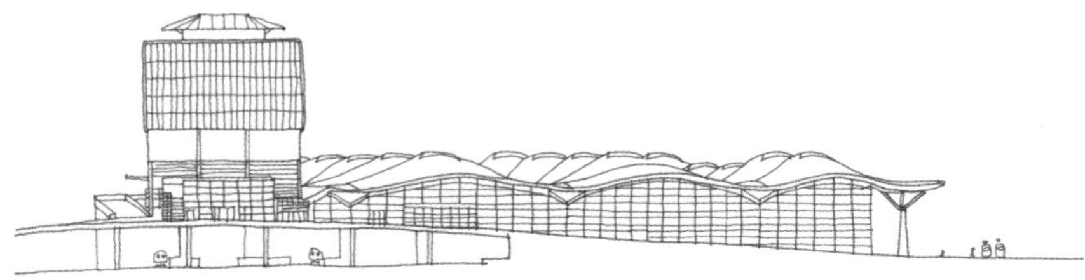

South façade

Compared with the array of high-rise structures lining Spencer Street, Southern Cross Station sits only three to four storeys high. The low-rise roof seems to float above the ground plane in its scale and transparency.

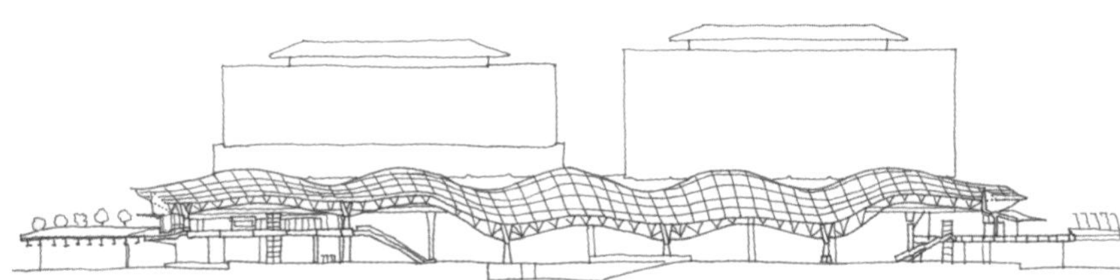

Spencer Street view

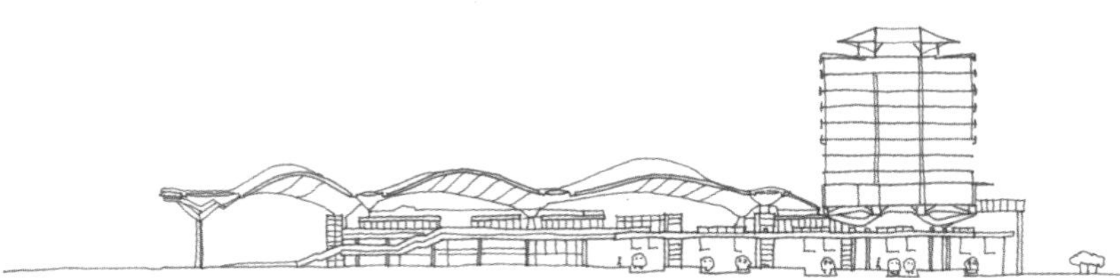

North façade

The building has a general 'light' feel to it, with its steel and polycarbonate roof lining. In comparison with the concrete and brick structures nearby, it sits modest yet modern in the urban context.

The interior elements create a hall-like atmosphere with views in every direction, helping to orient passengers. The impressive roof and the structure of the building respond to the raw engineering nature of trains and train tracks.

Structural integration

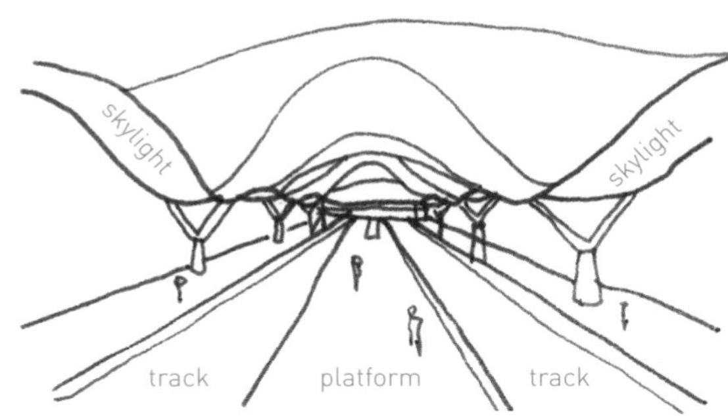

A view from the southern concourse shows how the roof structure is aligned with the platforms. The flexibility of materials in the skylight zones allows the steel roof to expand and contract with temperature changes.

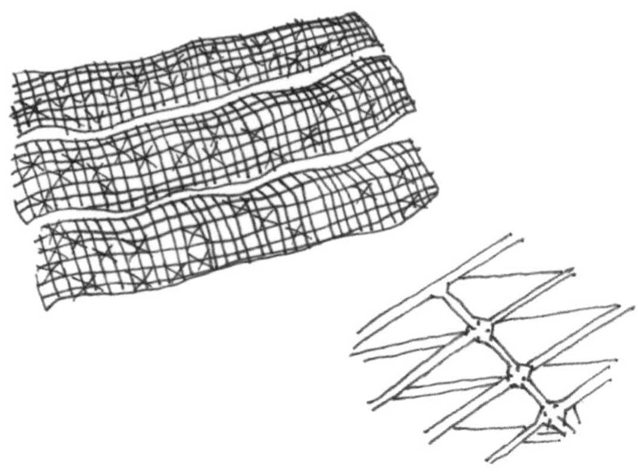

Precast-concrete columns support the lightweight roof shelter. The station continued to operate during the construction process. Roof modules were prefabricated and then raised to their place during off-peak periods.

Southern Cross Station | 2001–6

Grimshaw Architects / Jackson Architecture
Melbourne, Australia

Movement

The natural slope of the site is maintained in harmony with the flowing curves of the roof structure.

Anticipation and flexibility Routes into and through the building allow people to take many directions, with multiple places at which to stop between entry and exit. The long high-level roof spans offer flexibility for future changes.

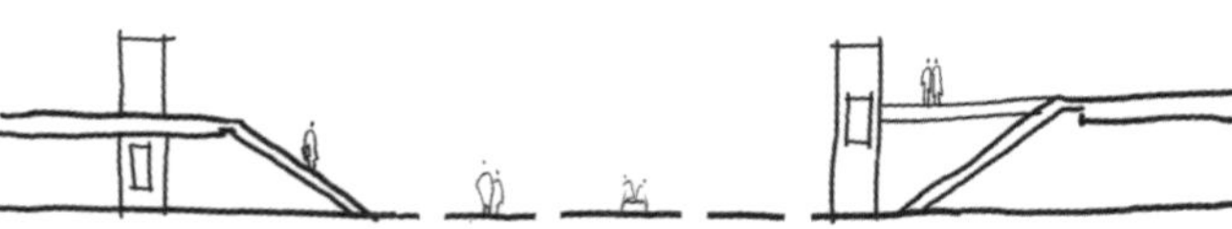

The form and plan offer clues for circulation, both vertically and horizontally.

sports stadium
long-distance trains
suburban trains
bus station
escalators and lifts from bridge
pods
escalators and lifts from upper level
entry to lower level
entry to upper level

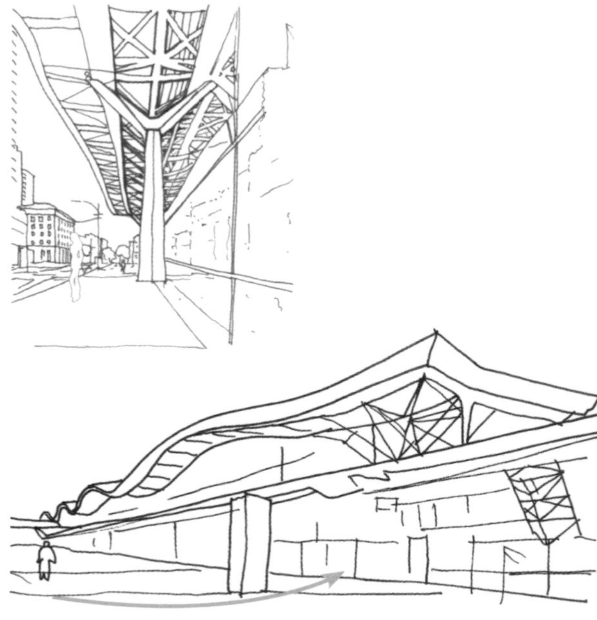

Entrance The large canopy structure defies the boundaries between inside and outside, emphasizing the strategic positioning of the entry points to the station.

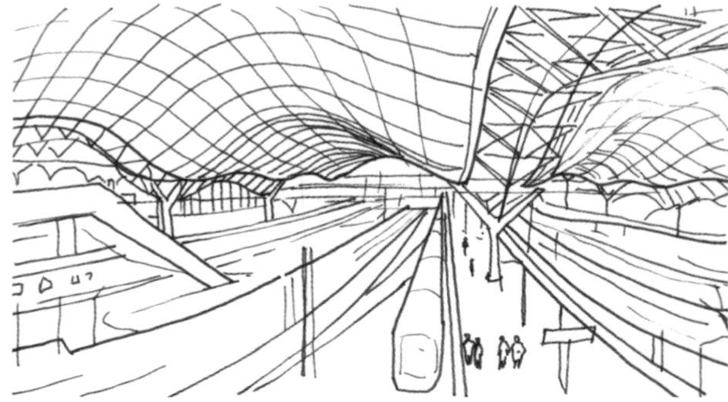

The interior space features manoeuvrable pods that house small retail outlets, offices and other public facilities. The vibrancy of these free-floating pods enhances the dynamism of the interior while not compromising its unity.

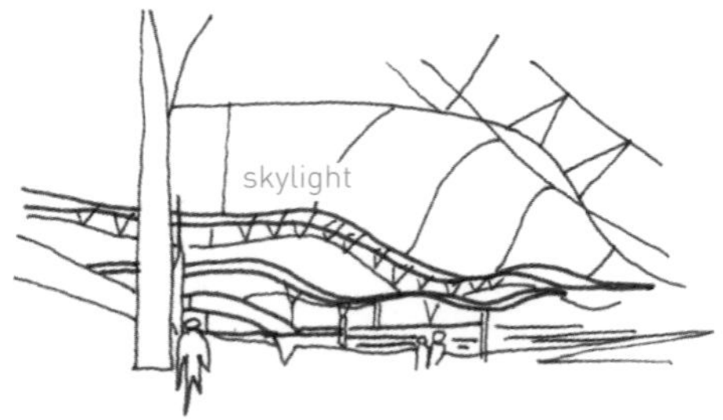

South-east platform and plaza

Climate/ventilation

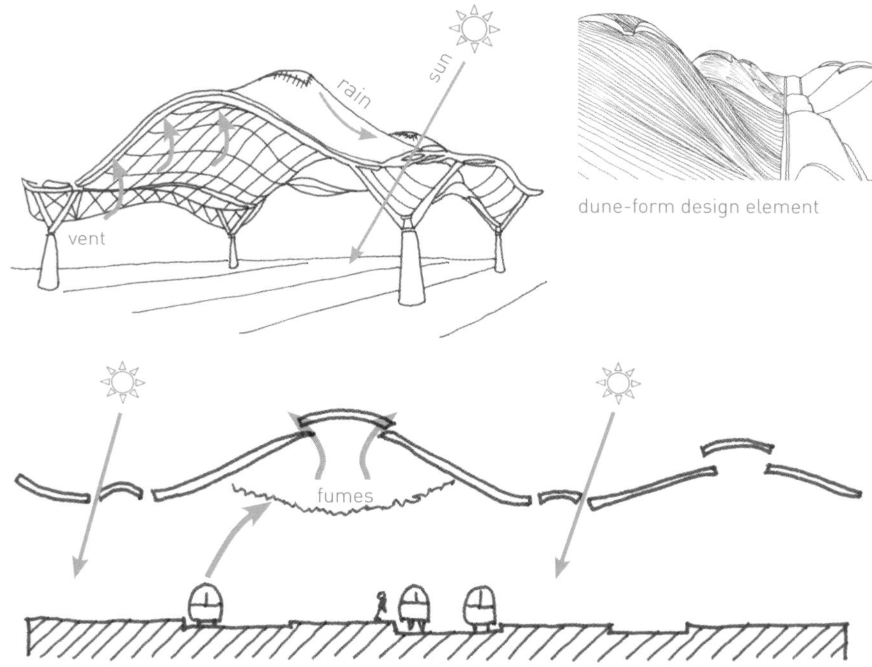

The dunelike roof structure allows natural ventilation. Diesel fumes from locomotives are drawn from platform level up through vented pockets at the highest point of each 'dune'.

Sustainability

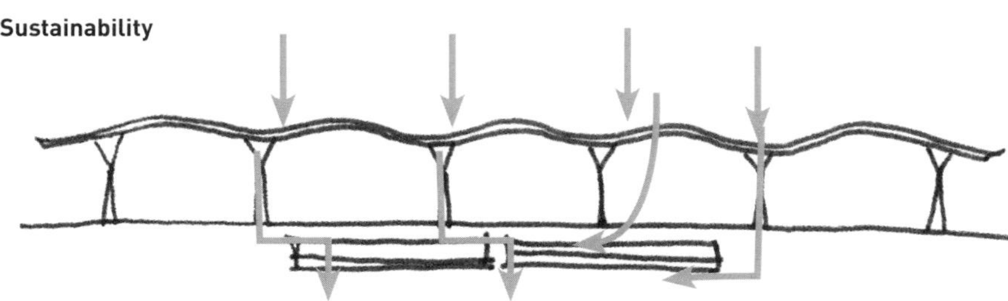

The building takes sustainability as a major design concern. The large roof area is exploited for rainwater harvesting. Water flows to the valleys and down to two underground tanks. The building is 50 per cent self-sufficient in water use.

By using passive systems provided by the roof and the structure, the design minimizes reliance on mechanical and electrical systems for ventilation and lighting.

The building is adaptable to accommodate future expansion over a 100-year life cycle.

Light

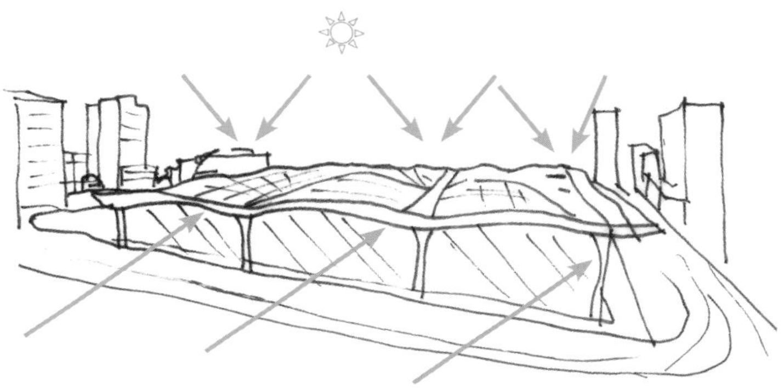

All façades of the station are glazed, providing both daylight and views for the internal spaces.

Design unity

All internal elements and the whole are related to one another. The flowing curves of the roof match the platform layout, allowing a contrast of visual elements. The platform layout works collaboratively with the nearby coach terminal to the south. Ease of access enables a smooth transition for interstate travellers. City commuters are easily dispersed from the terminal.

Meiso no Mori Crematorium | 2004–6

Toyo Ito & Associates

Kakamigahara, Gifu, Japan

The Meiso no Mori (Forest of Meditation) Crematorium is a contemporary example of Expressionist architecture. The organic whitewashed roof form is a lively response to the monolithic mass of the crematorium housed underneath. The curves of the roof structure mimic those of the nearby topography and serve as a connection between the hills and the lake. The public spaces of the building have full views of the impressive surrounding landscape. The accessible roof allows visitors a continuous walk from the landscape to the building.

The crematorium is an architectural example of blurring the boundaries between binary oppositions such as exterior/interior and natural/artificial.

Selen Morkoç, Kun Zhao and Simon Fisher

43

Meiso no Mori Crematorium | 2004–6
Toyo Ito & Associates
Kakamigahara, Gifu, Japan

Basic elements

Topography

The crematorium is located on the side of a hill overlooking a valley. A motorway tunnel runs beneath the hill.

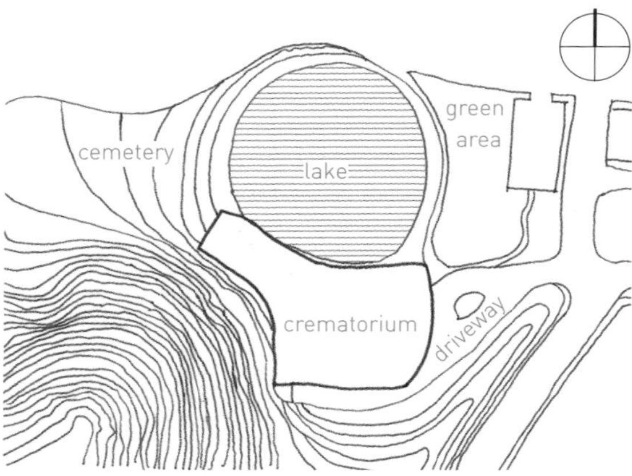

Site plan

The crematorium is part of a large cemetery district within a park nestled in mountains. There are mixed trees and plants in the south and a lake in the north. The surrounding area is mainly residential. The siting and design of the crematorium aim to minimize its presence in this sensitive area.

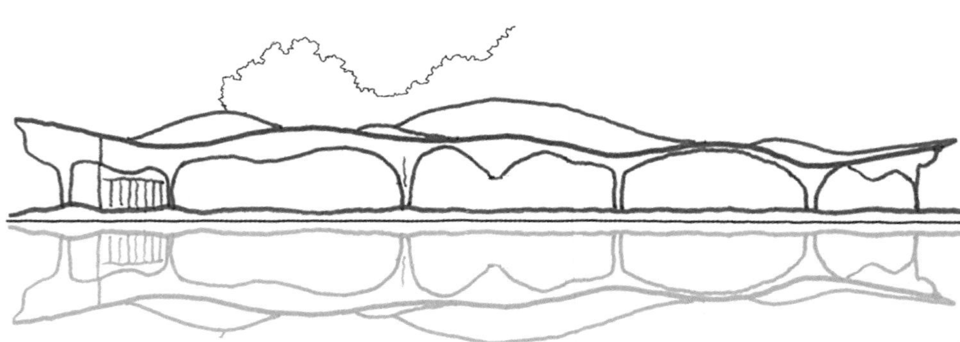

The building overlooks a lake to the north. Its large roof seems to extend from the hill rising behind it and acts as a connection between the hill and the lake. The building's footprint is designed to leave minimal impact on the surrounding natural shrublands.

The design of the building was inspired by nature. It is not a conventional massive crematorium. It is of modest height and consists of two elements: the roof, and the functional spaces hidden under the overarching roof structure. The roof with its white surface creates a serene atmosphere.

The site elevation demonstrates harmony with nature. The building follows the landscape in form and scale.

Roof analogy

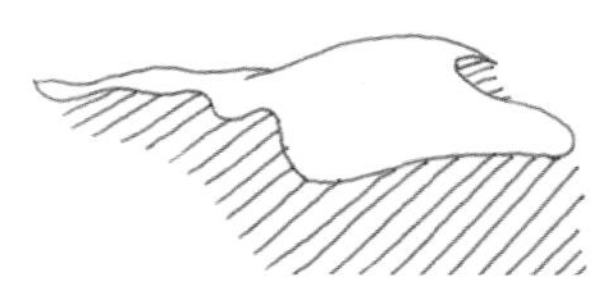

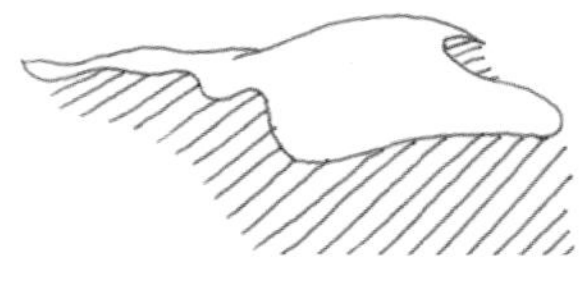

The egret is the symbol of a pure life in Japan. Toyo Ito aims to define the crematorium as the purification of life instead of death. The whitewashed roof structure, inspired by an egret's curves, symbolizes purity and peace.

People can reach the roof from the hill and walk on it to pay their last respects to the deceased. Although the roof follows the form of the hilltops, it is very different in colour and texture.

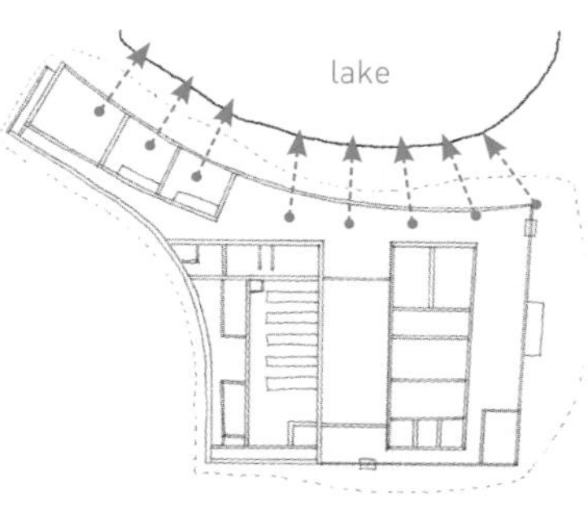

Views Waiting rooms and the entire lobby face the nearby lake through glass, a setting for quiet contemplation.

The building is partially two-storeyed and built of reinforced concrete. Seen from the sides, the free-form roof is offset and emphasized by the horizontal and vertical lines of the rectilinear walls.

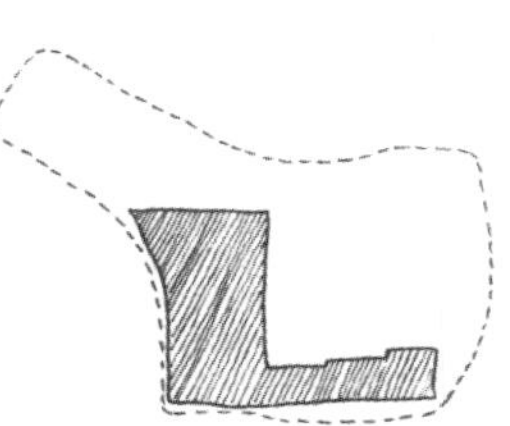

private spaces

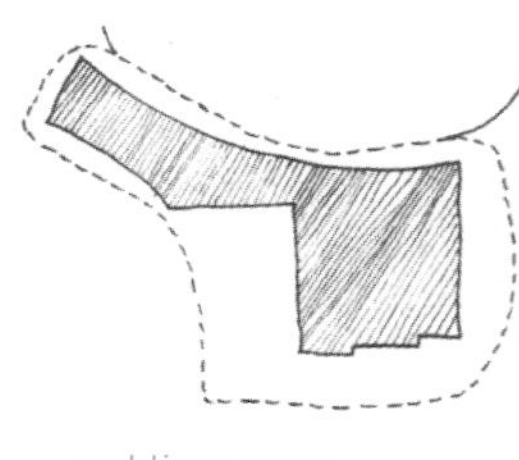

public spaces

Public spaces face the lake, while more private spaces face the hillside.

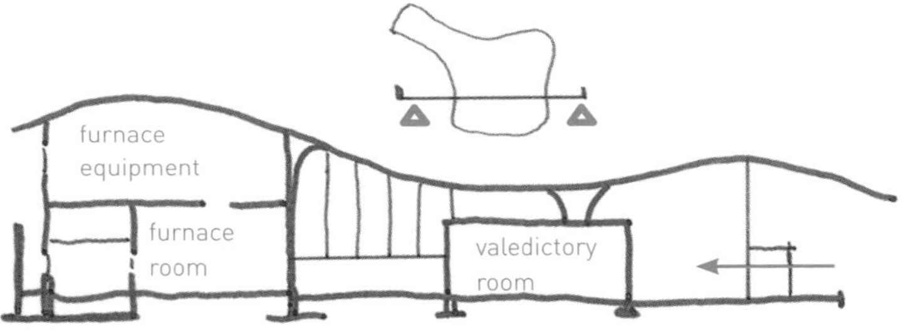

Beneath the roof, it is a typical building in which form follows function. The highest space is designed to accommodate the tall furnace equipment.

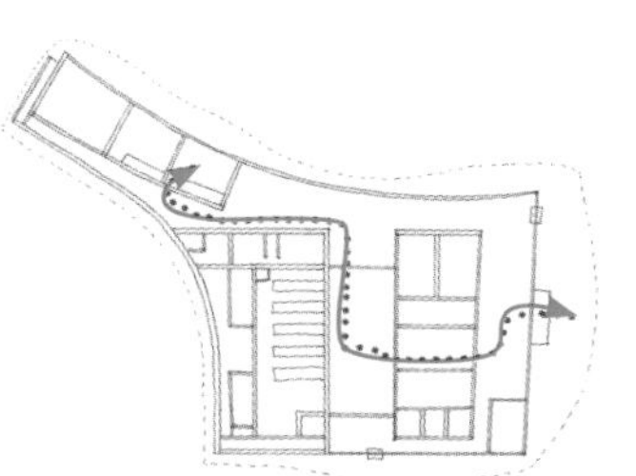

Visitors' path

Path of the deceased

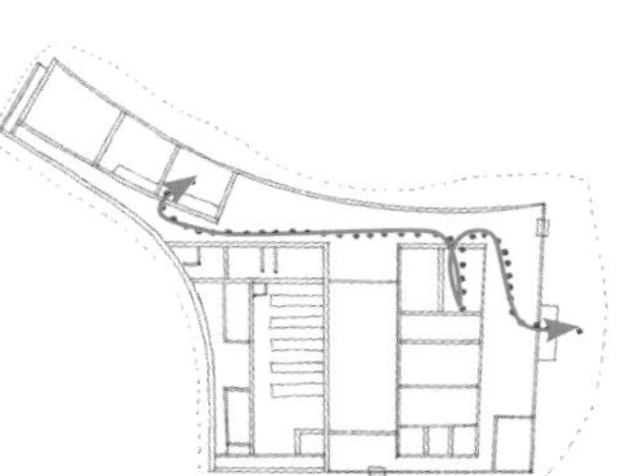

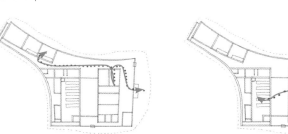

Circulation The route follows the process of Japanese cremation. The family follows the body through the main entrance. After the ceremony in the valedictory room, the family waits in the waiting room while the cremation takes place and then collects the ashes from the inurnment room.

Response to the site
The curves of the roof become part of the landscape, in harmony with the contours of the surrounding mountains and the water. People feel this connectedness to the site from the interior to the exterior and vice versa.

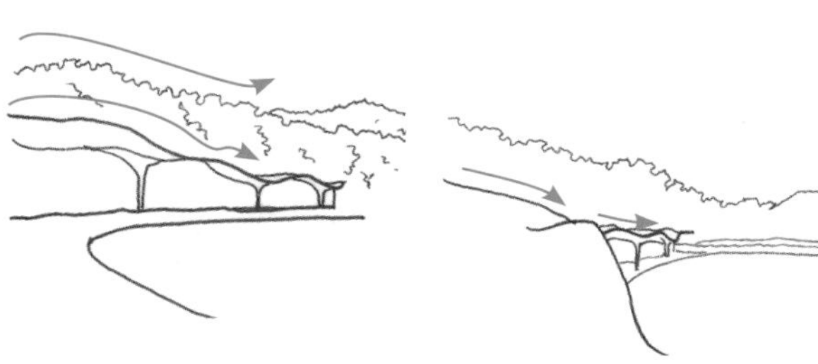

View from the bank of the lake

View from the roof

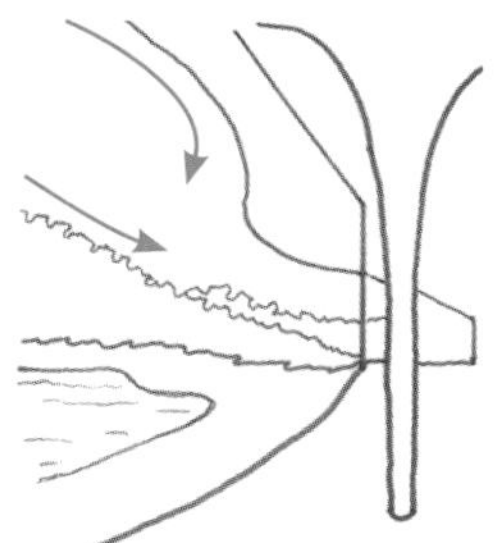

View from the lobby

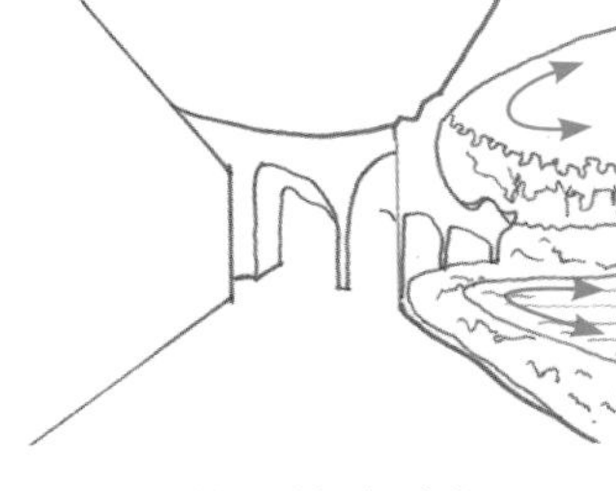

Relationship with the lake

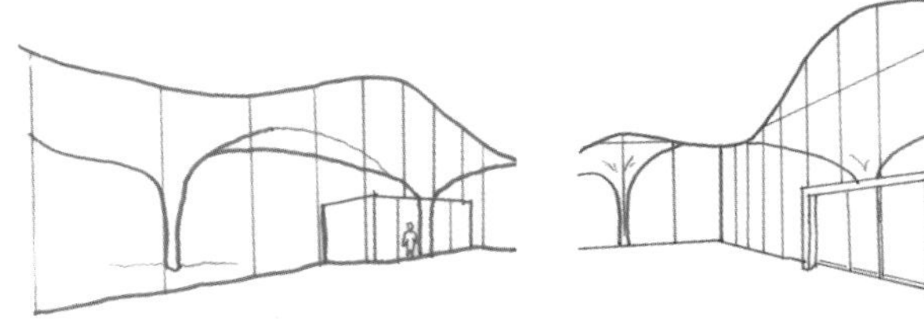

Entrance hall

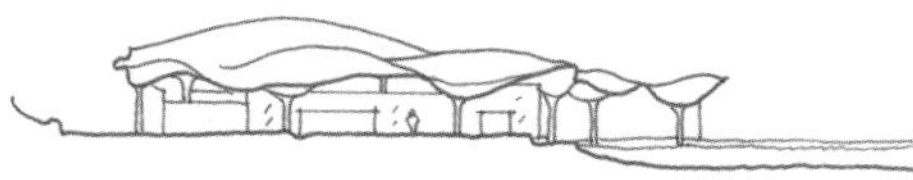

The east façade is extremely simple. It houses a glazed wall and two entrances.

On the south façade there is one sub-entrance. Half of the façade is concrete, allowing only partial daylight inside. In its solidity it is a link with the foot of the mountain.

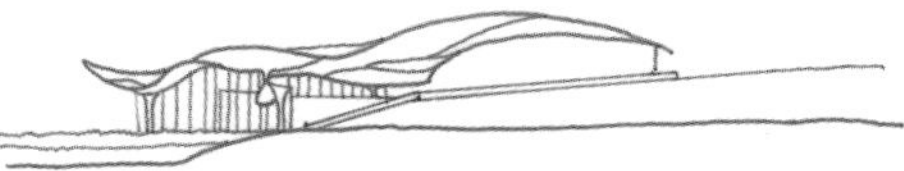

Most of the west façade is on the lower slope of the hill. There are no glazed surfaces on this wall. However, part of the curved glass wall facing the north protrudes through this façade as continuity with the rest of the façades.

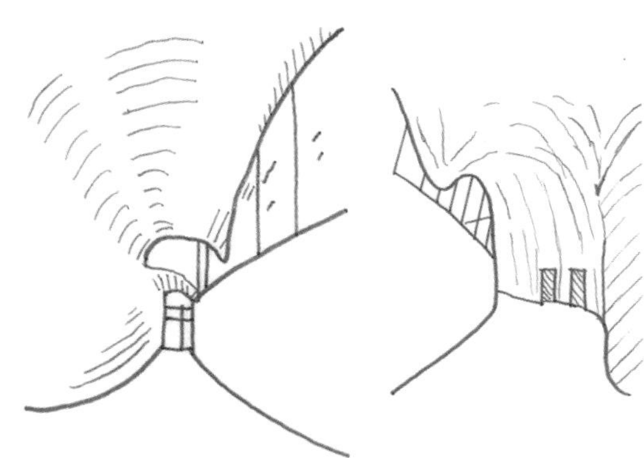

The high-level curved glass walls in the long corridor separate the double-curving ceiling from the single-curving wall and visually enrich the space.

Meiso no Mori Crematorium | 2004–6

Toyo Ito & Associates
Kakamigahara, Gifu, Japan

Boundaries

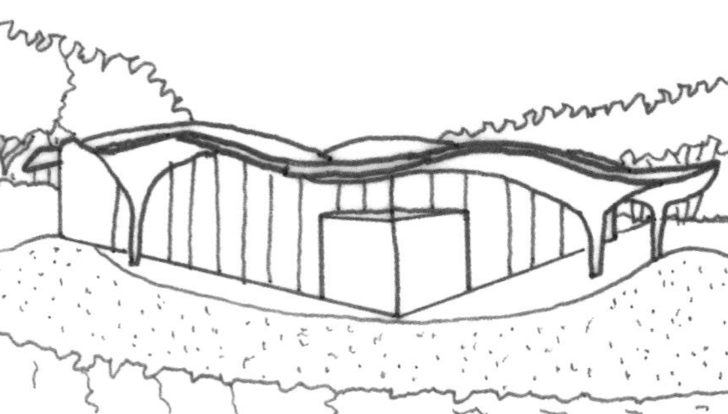

Boundaries between different spaces are indicated by changes in materials. Boundaries serve both to connect and to separate spaces.

The hall outside the furnaces has a ceremonial-monumental effect.

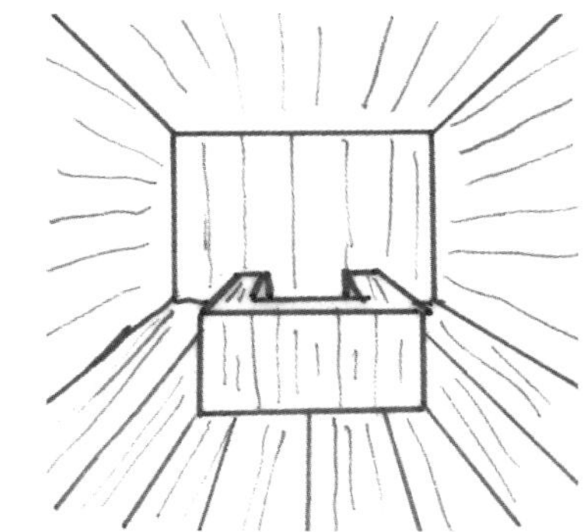

The small-scale inurnment room with its timber and marble surfaces creates an intimate atmosphere when families come to collect the ashes.

The minimalist boundary of glass connects the soft-shaped, light interiors to the lake and landscape outside with no visual interruption.

There are three waiting rooms in the crematorium. Respecting different funeral customs, one of them is traditional Japanese style and two are modern styles. The waiting rooms look out to the lake, facing the pond and trees with views, bringing the peaceful landscape into the interior and offering consolation.

Marble and concrete are mainly used in public spaces. In the hall outside the furnaces, marble floor and walls contrast with the curvilinear concrete wall on the opposite side. Glass and timber are transition materials between concrete and marble.

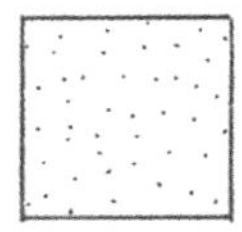

rendered concrete

cobble stones

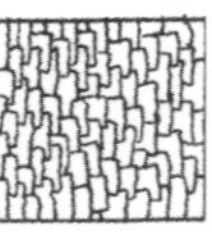

rough stackstone

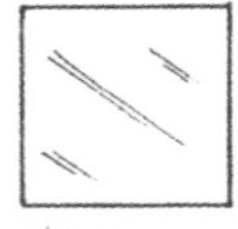

glass

marble

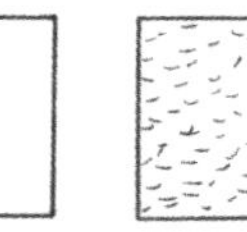

grass

Response to environment

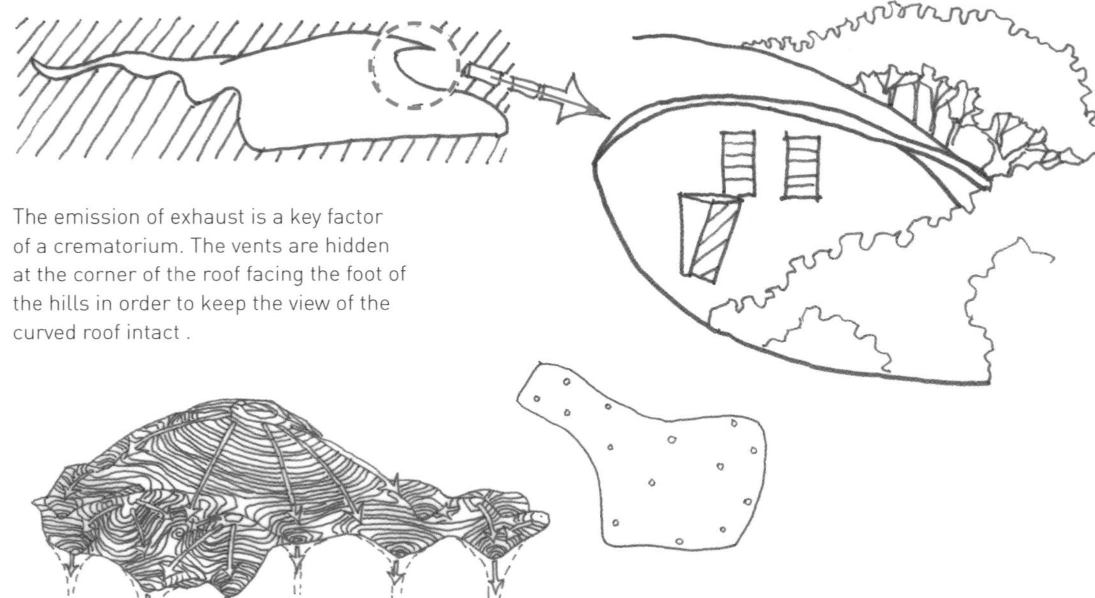

The emission of exhaust is a key factor of a crematorium. The vents are hidden at the corner of the roof facing the foot of the hills in order to keep the view of the curved roof intact .

The curved roof is built out of 200mm- (8in.-) thick reinforced concrete. The roof cantilevers past the glazed façade of the building, so that it appears to float on top of the tapered columns. The roof was poured on site and rendered.

The shape of the roof drains rainwater in the same way that rain runs off the surrounding hills. Four structural cores and eleven columns are positioned under the roof structure. The columns are shaped like spreading inverted cones so that their forms merge with the ceilings.

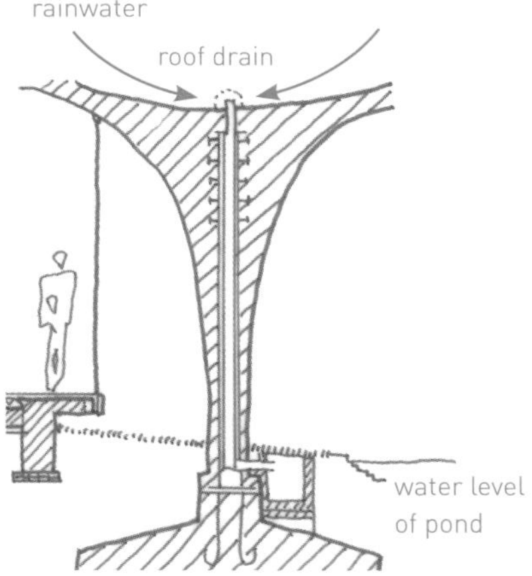

The cone-shaped columns have built-in rainwater collection pipes.

Use of light

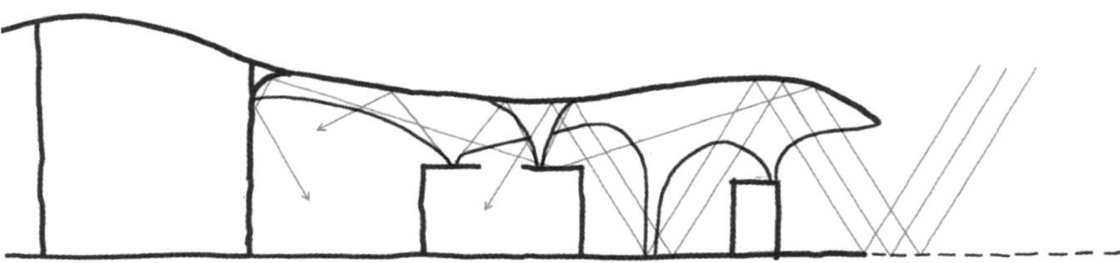

Natural light enlivens the main foyers and other large public spaces within the building. The main sources of light are direct sky and sunlight and reflected light from the lake. The light comes in through the north curtain wall and is reflected by the marble floor and clean white paint finish of the undulating ceiling. Light bounces around the building, penetrating deep into all public spaces and as indirect reflections in the more private spaces.

Indirect light softly illuminates the curved ceiling and spreads in all directions, giving the interior a subtle visual fluidity.

There are no windows in the valedictory rooms. When the door is closed, the ceiling skylight and artificial lights in the gaps between the ceiling and the walls create an atmosphere that is distinct from the hall outside. The soft light coming from the ceiling is reminiscent of a halo in the dark room and suits the spiritual function of the space.

Overall, the crematorium achieves responsive cohesion between its functional operation, its spiritual purpose and its landscape setting. For grieving visitors it provides a sensitive isolation from surrounding mundane activities and a calm setting for group and personal experiences.

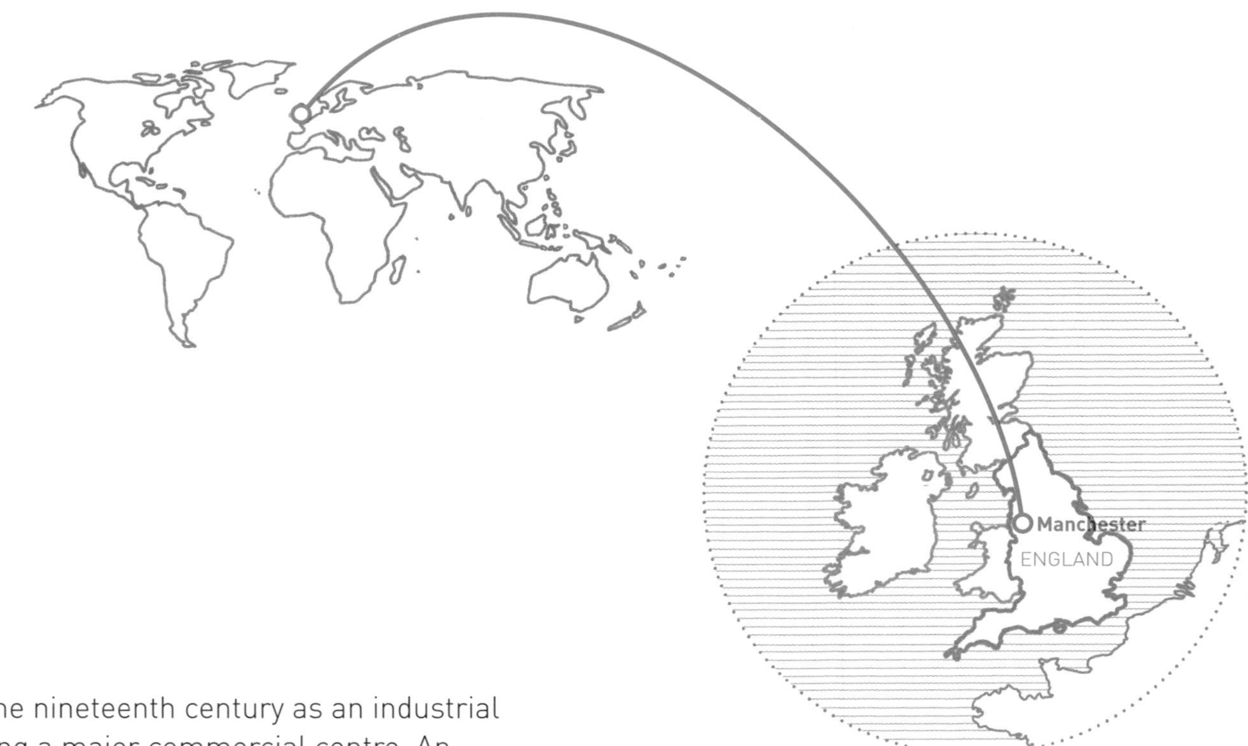

Civil Justice Centre | 2001–7

Denton Corker Marshall

Manchester, England

44

Manchester developed in the nineteenth century as an industrial city of textile mills, becoming a major commercial centre. An international design competition for the Civil Justice Centre was held in 2001–2 and won by Denton Corker Marshall, based in Melbourne, Australia. The building was completed in 2007.

The building is exceptional in the clarity of its planning, with separate public and professional sides, and circulation routes that come together in the courtrooms. It is also exemplary in the way that environmental features (double-skin glass wall, screen wall, light shelves and natural ventilation) are integrated in a crisp yet expressive architectural language.

Sam Lock and Antony Radford

Civil Justice Centre | 2001–7

Denton Corker Marshall

Manchester, England

Response to site

Spinningfields is a financial and business district around a legal precinct, at the western edge of central Manchester. The Civil Justice Centre is built on the site of a former multistorey car park next to existing court buildings. Much of the area has been redeveloped since 2000. The building is clad in glass and powder-coated aluminium, typical of new nearby office buildings. Its height and mass are appropriate for the area.

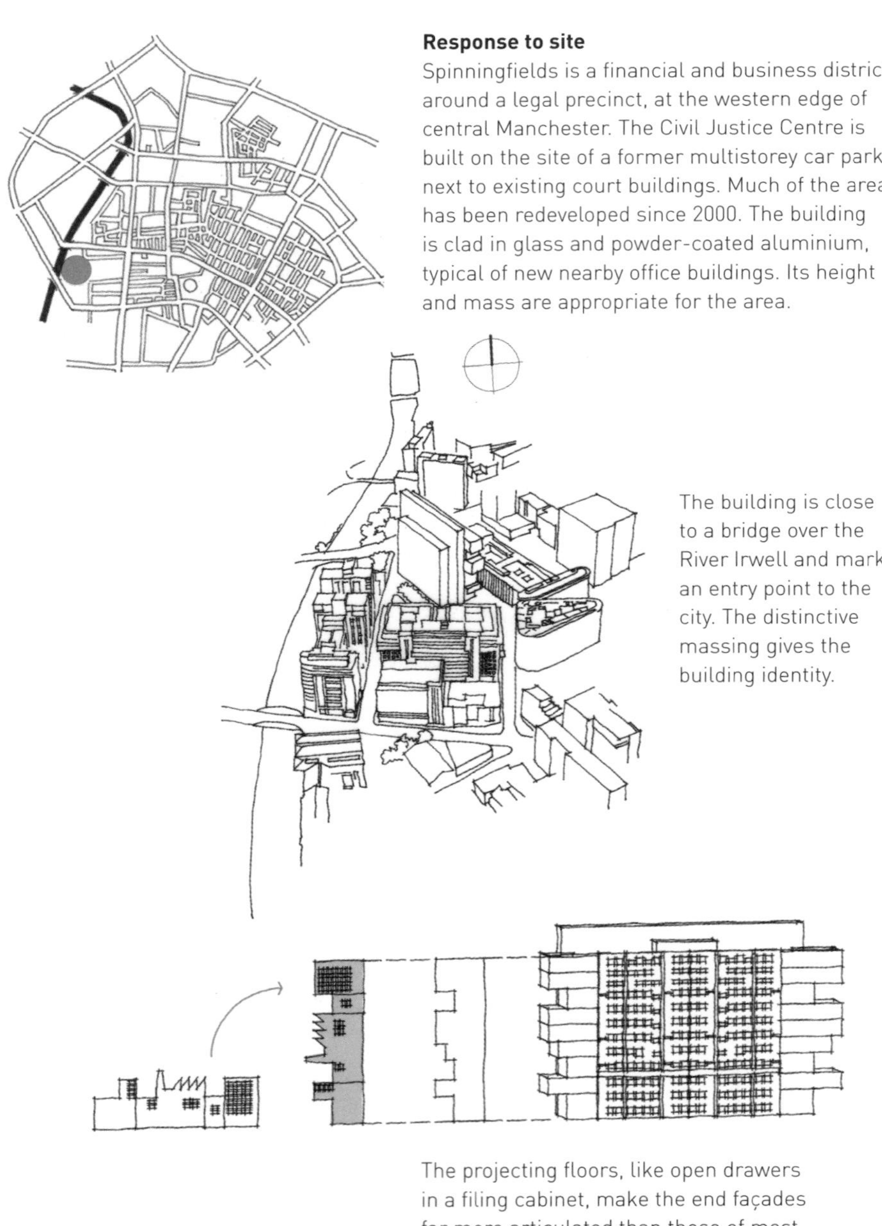

The building is close to a bridge over the River Irwell and marks an entry point to the city. The distinctive massing gives the building identity.

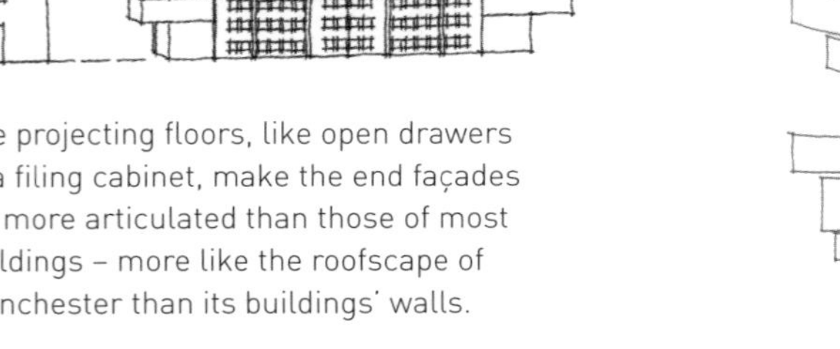

The projecting floors, like open drawers in a filing cabinet, make the end façades far more articulated than those of most buildings – more like the roofscape of Manchester than its buildings' walls.

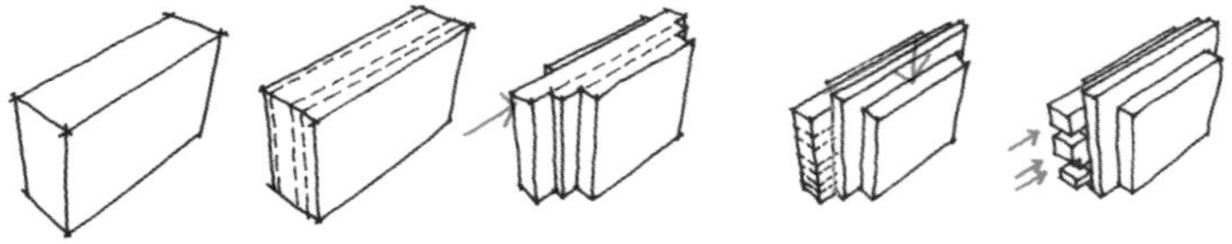

The building form can be described as deriving from transformations of a rectangular solid (above) and as an assembly of components (below).

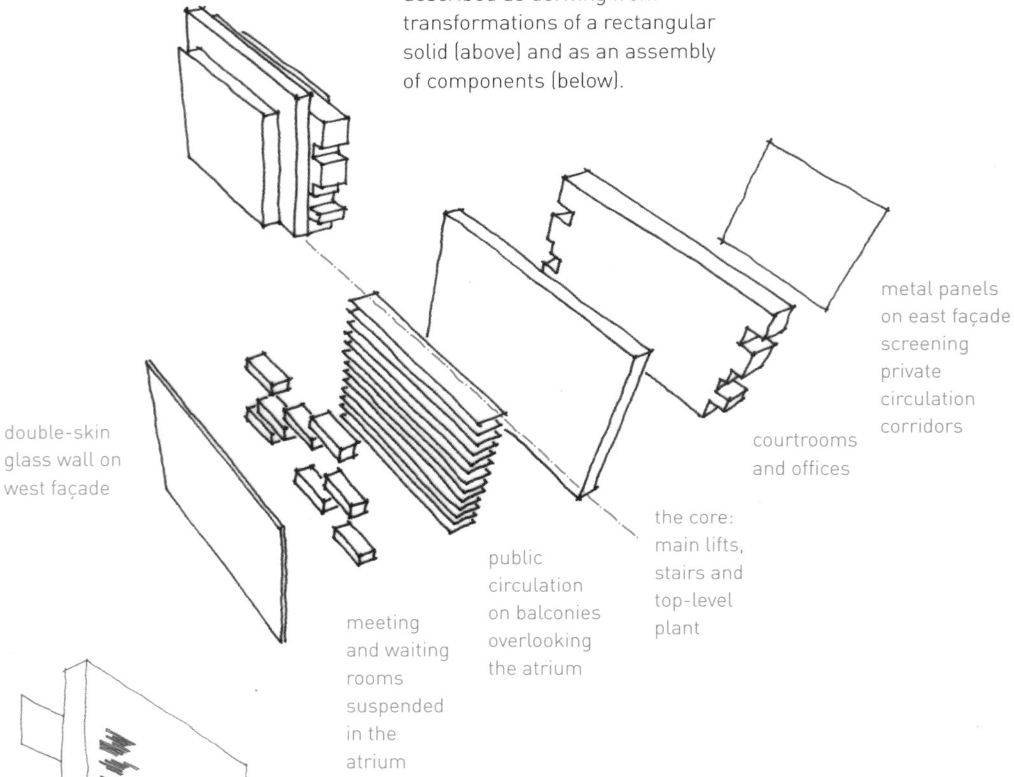

metal panels on east façade screening private circulation corridors

courtrooms and offices

double-skin glass wall on west façade

the core: main lifts, stairs and top-level plant

public circulation on balconies overlooking the atrium

meeting and waiting rooms suspended in the atrium

A strong juxtaposition of 'reference and action' can be seen in many aspects of the building. The leading edge of the building's spine acts as a reference for the movement and rhythm of the projecting floors, echoed at a smaller scale in the elongated window openings.

Courthouses typically express dignity, authority and order through symmetry and size. Entrances are imposing and alienating. The Civil Justice Centre suggests order and dignity but avoids oppressive authority. The justice system is positioned as a part of civil society.

United States Supreme Court, Cass Gilbert, Washington, DC, USA (1935)

Royal Courts of Justice, George Edmund Street, London, England (1882)

Supreme Federal Court, Oscar Niemeyer, Brasilia, Brazil (1958)

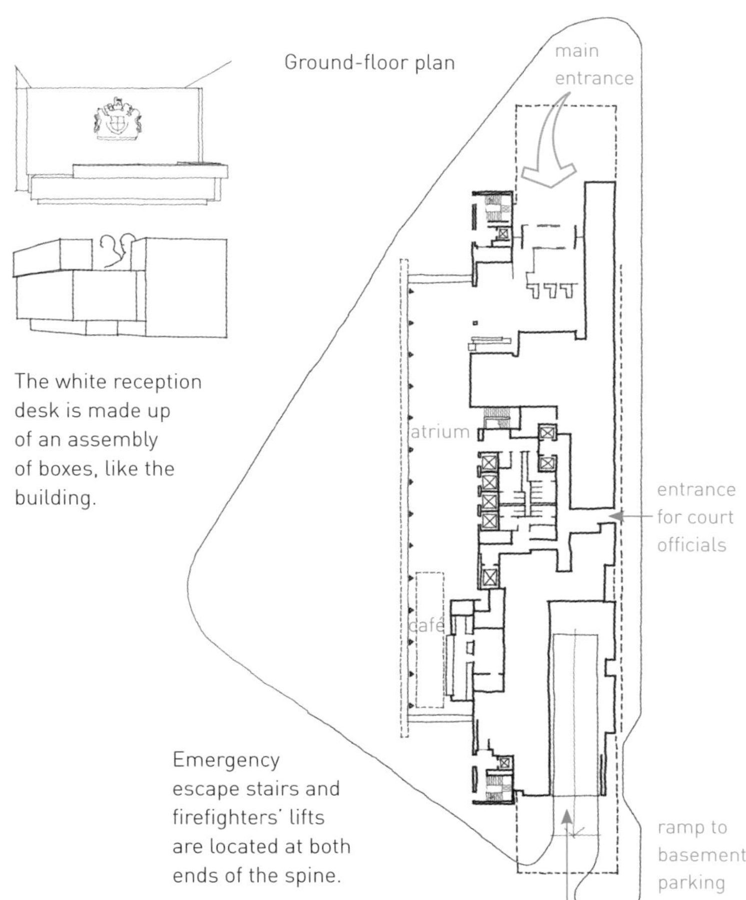

The white reception desk is made up of an assembly of boxes, like the building.

Emergency escape stairs and firefighters' lifts are located at both ends of the spine.

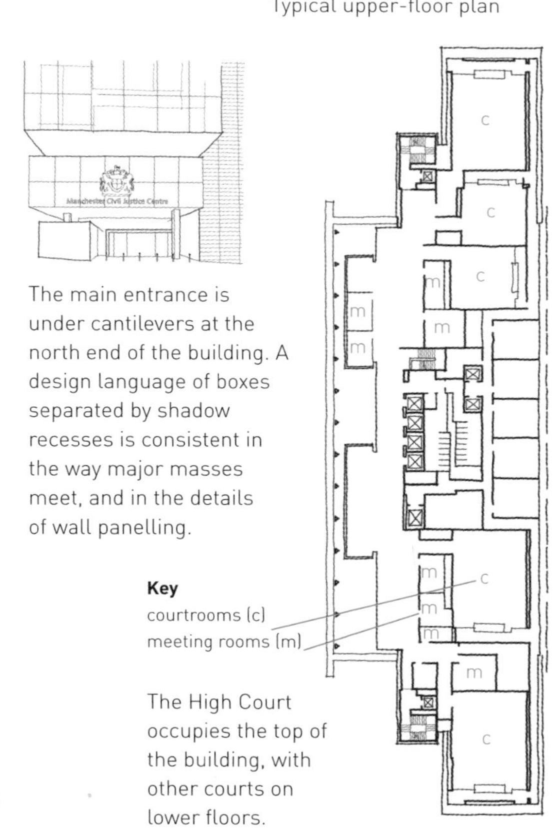

The main entrance is under cantilevers at the north end of the building. A design language of boxes separated by shadow recesses is consistent in the way major masses meet, and in the details of wall panelling.

The High Court occupies the top of the building, with other courts on lower floors.

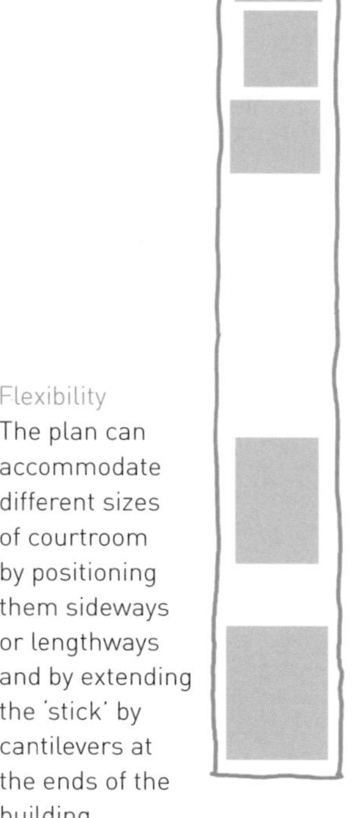

Flexibility
The plan can accommodate different sizes of courtroom by positioning them sideways or lengthways and by extending the 'stick' by cantilevers at the ends of the building.

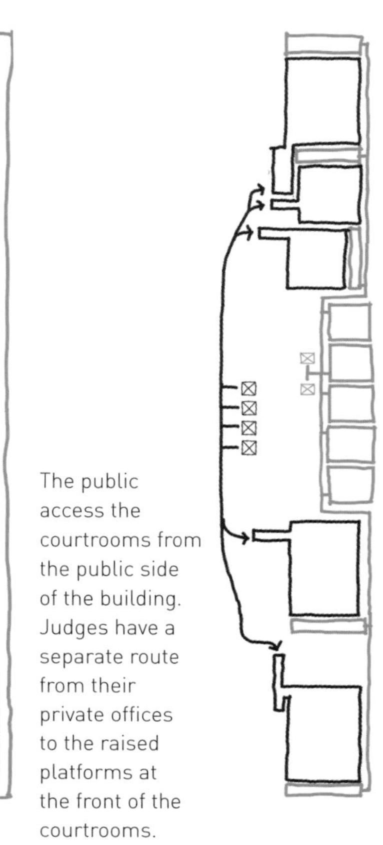

The public access the courtrooms from the public side of the building. Judges have a separate route from their private offices to the raised platforms at the front of the courtrooms.

44 Civil Justice Centre | 2001–7

Denton Corker Marshall

Manchester, England

Environmental response

The building is light and airy, with generous public spaces.

The height of the building resulted from decisions about its response to climate – the maximum width of a fully naturally ventilated building is 15–18 metres (49–59 feet). The Centre is naturally ventilated for about eight months of the year, supplemented by artificial cooling for the rest of the year.

Two boreholes tap into an aquifer about 75 metres (246 feet) beneath the building. Ground water with a temperature of 12°C (53.6°F) is pumped to the surface and run through pipes embedded in the atrium floor to directly cool the atrium. It also pre-cools supply air to the chillers, increasing their efficiency. After use, borehole water is returned to the aquifer, now with a temperature of 14°C (57.2°F).

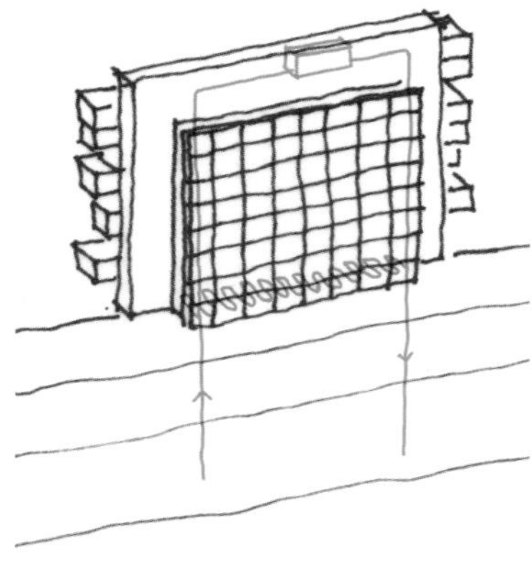

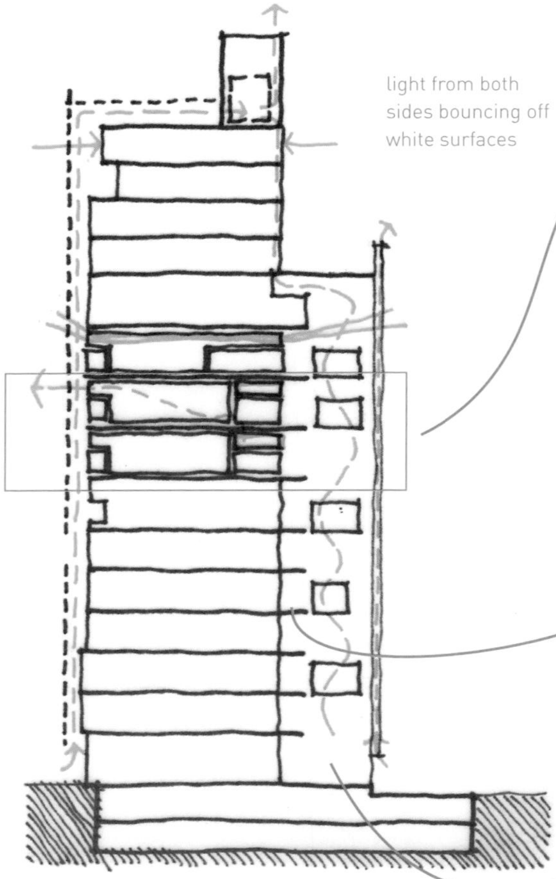

light from both sides bouncing off white surfaces

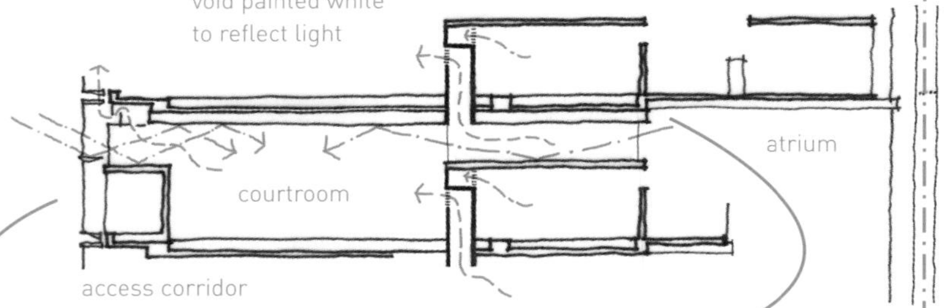

ducts run through building to vents at ends of the spine

void painted white to reflect light

atrium

courtroom

access corridor

glass

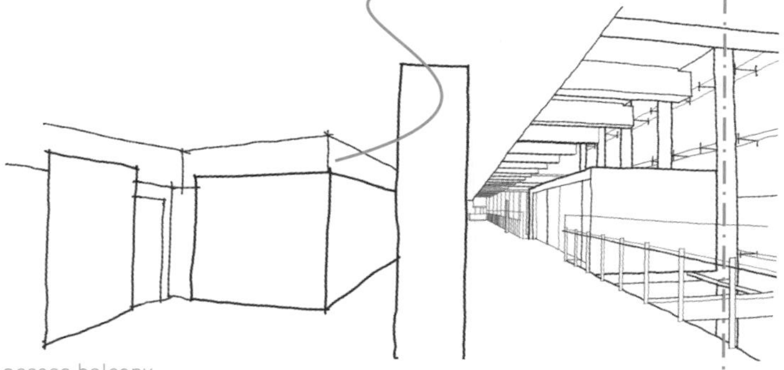

view along access balcony with meeting rooms supported by beams over the atrium

view along atrium with café ahead and meeting rooms above

triangular columns along edge of atrium

Outside air is drawn by stack effect over the faces of both east and west sides of the building, behind the metal screen panels on the east side and through the double-skin glass wall on the west side. Air is also drawn by stack effect up through the atrium and out via ducts to the top of the building.

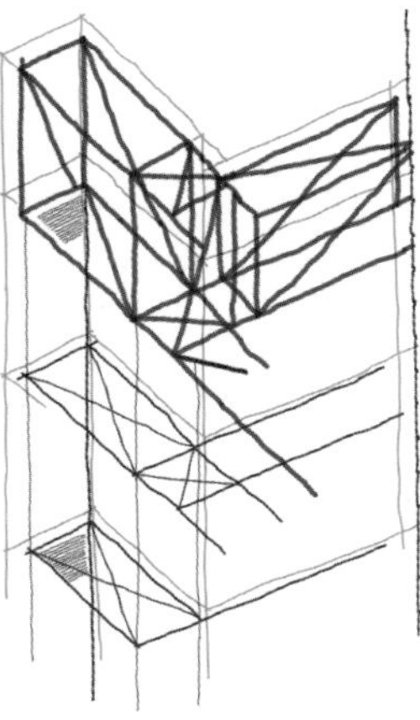

There is an accessible walkway every second floor.

West façade
A double-skin glass wall is hung from steel trusses with storey-height sheets of glass.

Adjustable glass louvres at the bottom of the double-skin wall allow air to circulate to reduce heat gain.

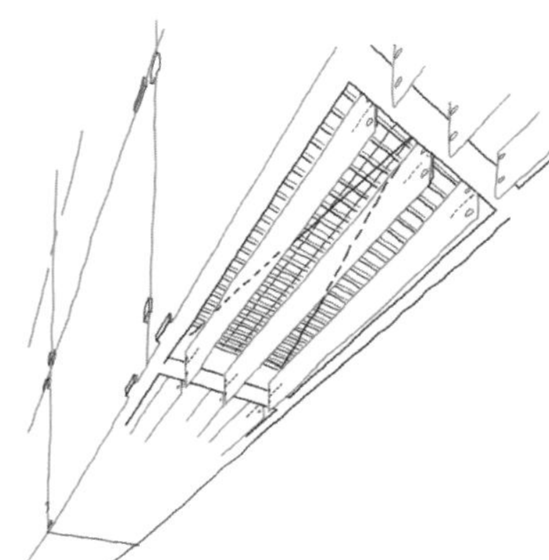

North and south façades
Where floors push out at the ends of the building, a second skin of glazing covers floor and roof structures as well as room heights, so that from outside the room is read as taller, with an impossibly thin floor and roof.

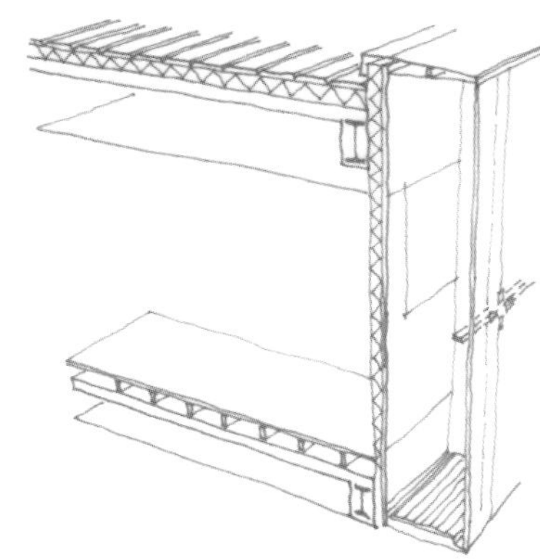

East façade Variations of a powder-coated aluminium panel are hung from a steel frame outside the actual building edge. The panels are arranged semi-randomly, taking into account views from rooms and corridors.

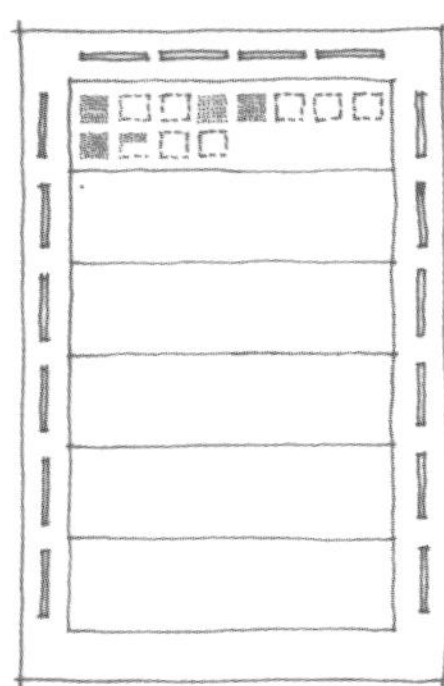

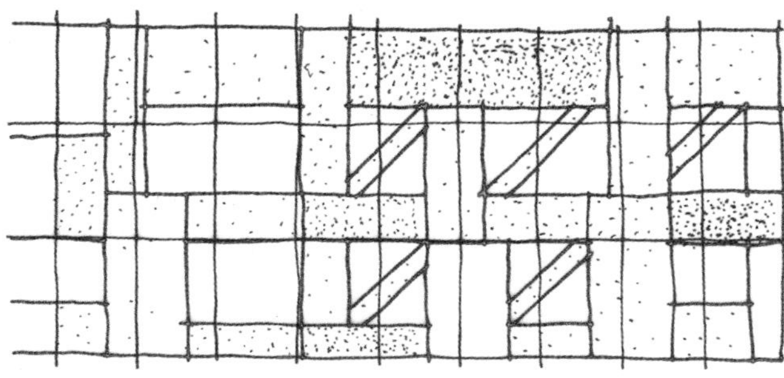

The cantilevered floors are braced by diagonal struts, visible inside and outside. The inner skin is powder-coated aluminium panels in subtle tones of yellow and grey.

On the top floors there are large 'super courts' for major cases. The courtrooms are finished internally in oak, with its connotations of tradition and permanence.

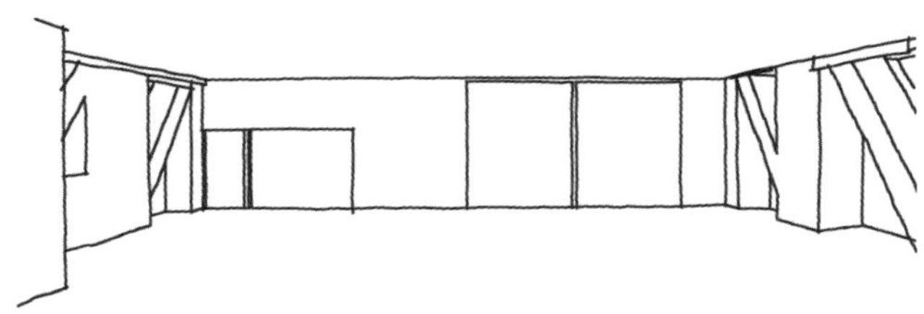

A dining room also projects out, with views over northern Manchester.

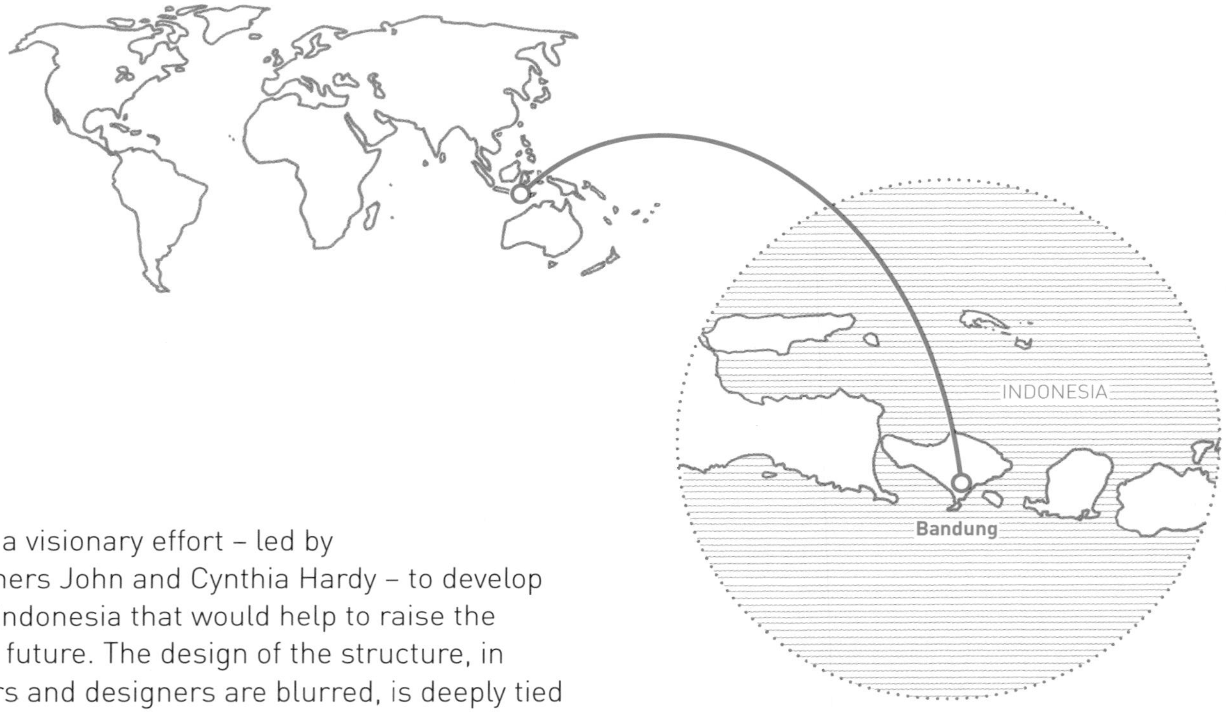

45 Green School | 2005–7

PT Bambu

Bandung, Bali, Indonesia

INDONESIA

Bandung

Green School is the result of a visionary effort – led by environmentalists and designers John and Cynthia Hardy – to develop an educational institution in Indonesia that would help to raise the environmental leaders of the future. The design of the structure, in which the lines between users and designers are blurred, is deeply tied to the educational values of the school. From the choice of the building materials to the incorporation of local techniques, its development has been guided by an ideological concern for natural and cultural sustainability. The project demonstrates the importance of responsive cohesion between the agencies involved.

Through the use of locally sourced bamboo and innovative and creative use of traditional knowledge, the design of this complex is an experiment that provides a delightful built example offering lessons for the future.

Amit Srivastava, Maryam Alfadhel and Siti Sarah Ramli

45

45 Green School | 2005–7

PT Bambu

Bandung, Bali, Indonesia

Response to local context

Green School should not be seen as a rigidly designed building complex, but instead as a collection of structures that are in dialogue with one another and the surrounding context. The various structures are bound together into a cohesive whole through a shared philosophical ideal: to build an educational institution that is based on and reinforces the values of local culture and respect for nature.

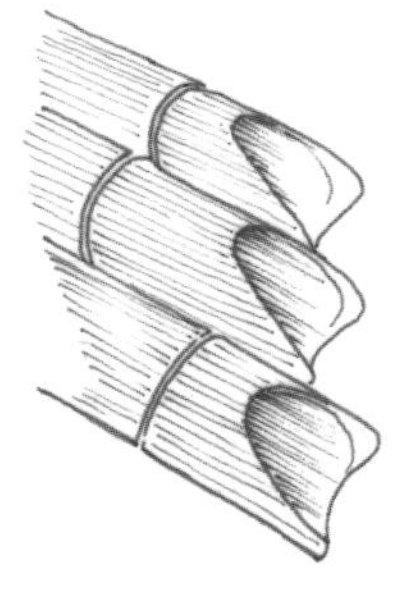

Locally produced bamboo is used instead of unsustainable materials.

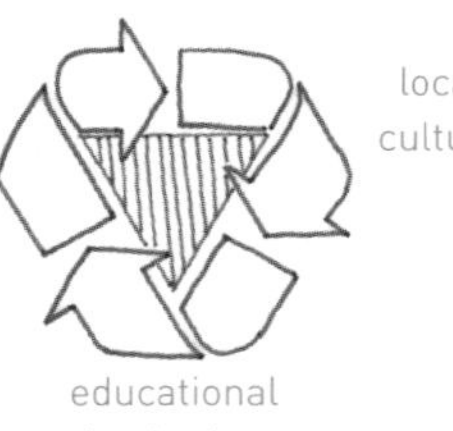

The school helps to institutionalize the ideological values and aid their dissemination.

Locally used crafts and tools are used instead of industrial materials.

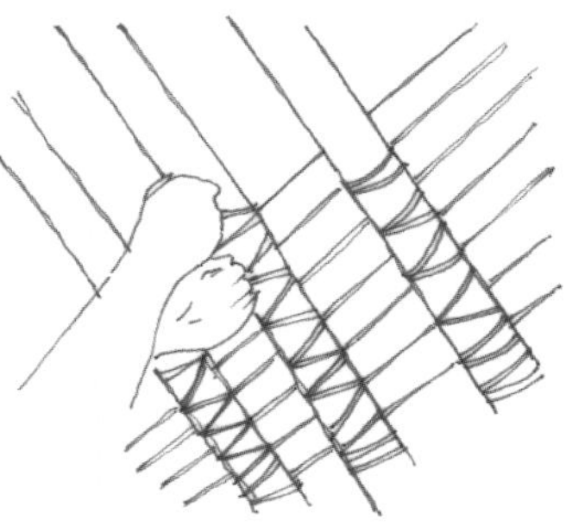

The surrounding fields are used to cultivate local produce and provide experiential learning for students.

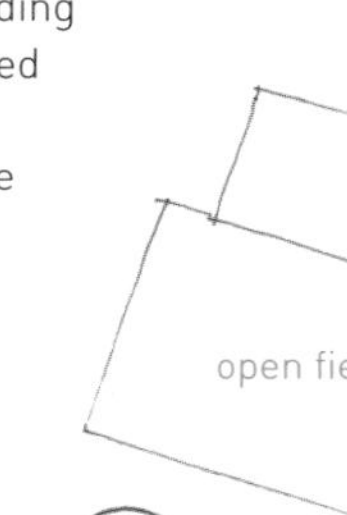

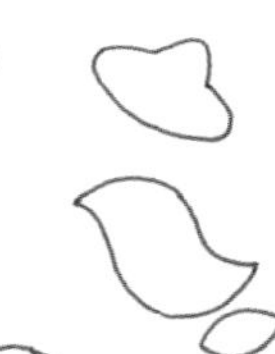

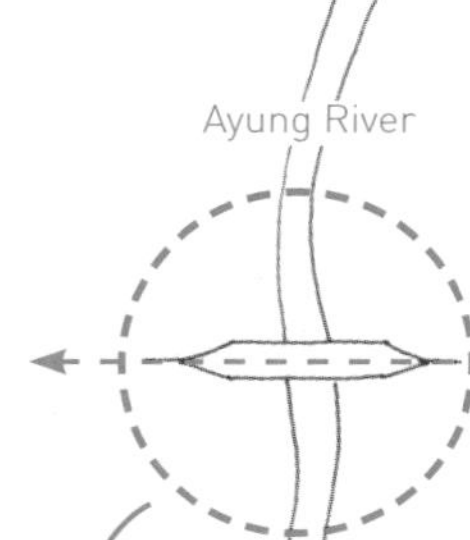

The design of the complex is guided by its response to the local cultural and natural context. In order to develop a sustainable relationship with the natural ecology, the various structures are constructed out of locally sourced materials such as bamboo instead of imported timber. The application of this local material is further informed by an engagement with local building cultures, which rely on simple techniques without use of heavy machinery. Following the Balinese tradition, the structures are developed by the community under the guidance of a master builder. This relationship with the local building tradition also guides the overall form of the structures as well as the clustering of buildings, which aggregate over time into a village-like grouping called 'banjar'. Students experience an integration with nature and culture that directly resonates with the educational principles.

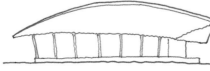

The hutlike structures recreate the building styles of the traditional Balinese villages.

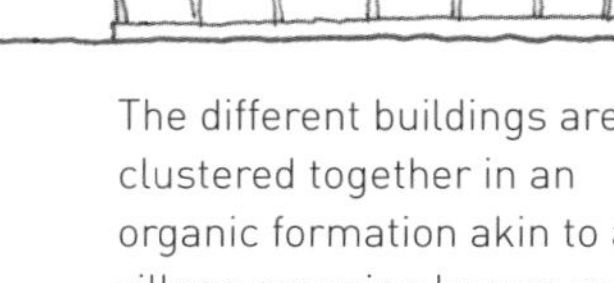

The different buildings are clustered together in an organic formation akin to a village grouping known as 'banjar'.

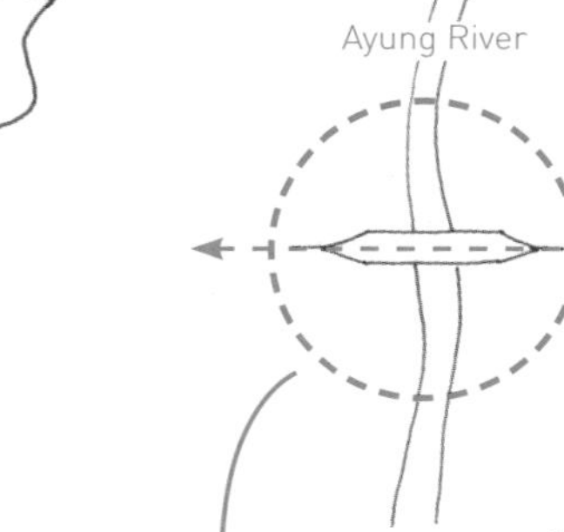

A bridge connects the school with the broader local community and allows for potential future expansion.

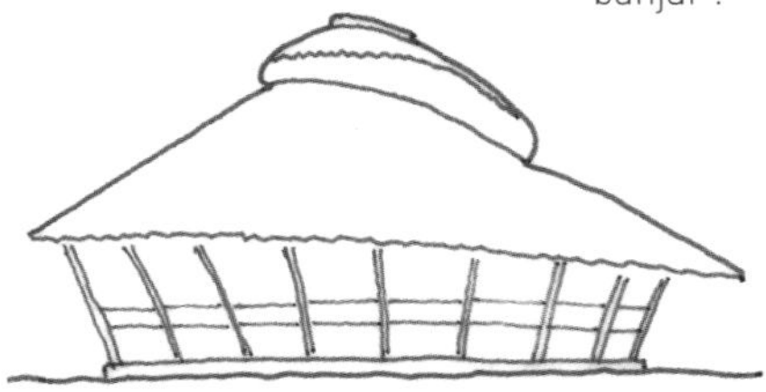

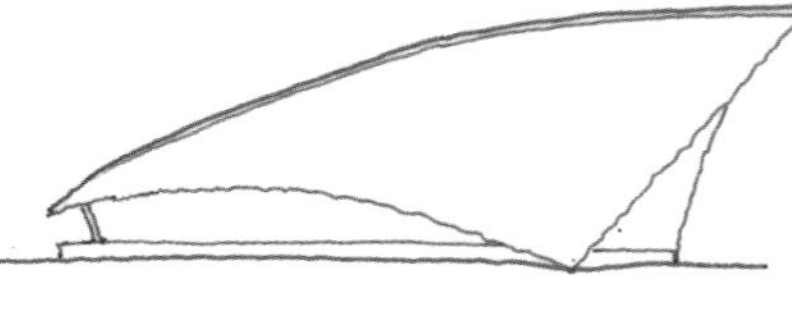

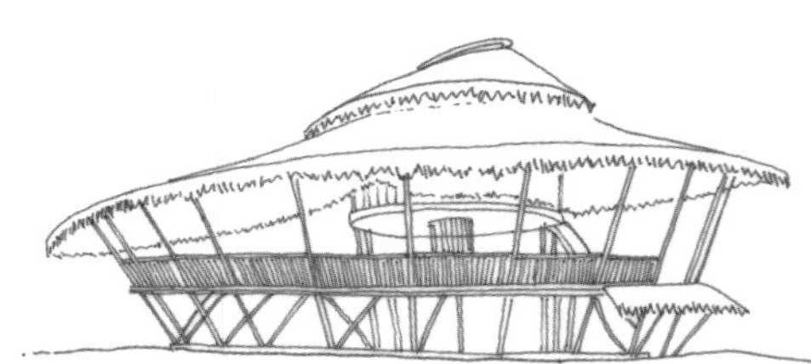

Marrying craft with pedagogy

The design of the school is the result of a responsive relationship between the educational principles that support the ideals of sustainability, and the process of construction that is based on culturally sustainable practices. Accordingly, the entire school serves as a laboratory to experiment with and promote the use of bamboo craft as a sustainable alternative to industrialized construction materials and processes.

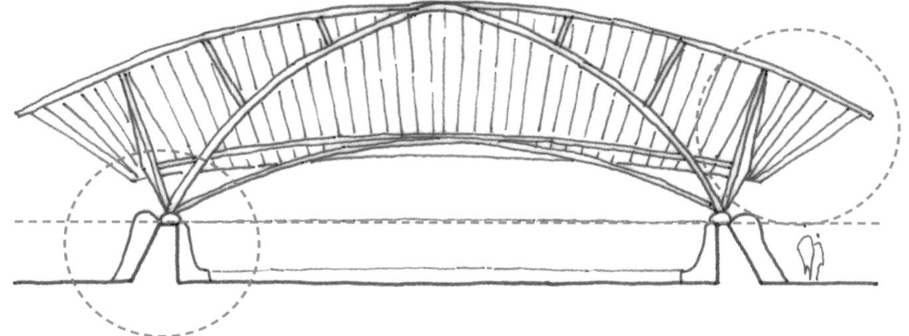

The structures are conceived as a sectional interplay between the flexible and long-spanning qualities of bamboo structure for the upper parts, and stable materials such as stone and mud for the lower parts that are in touch with the ground plane. Extra strength for wind loading is provided by some steel and concrete infill.

The construction processes use local creativity and skills to transform simple materials, often used only for temporary construction, into infinitely variable and complex structures. The large exposed bamboo structural members are connected to lighter bamboo systems and overlayed with organic covering material. All these materials are then tied together through the use of handicrafts, reminiscent of traditional weaving processes.

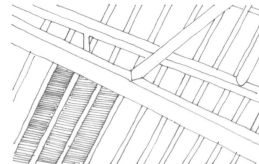

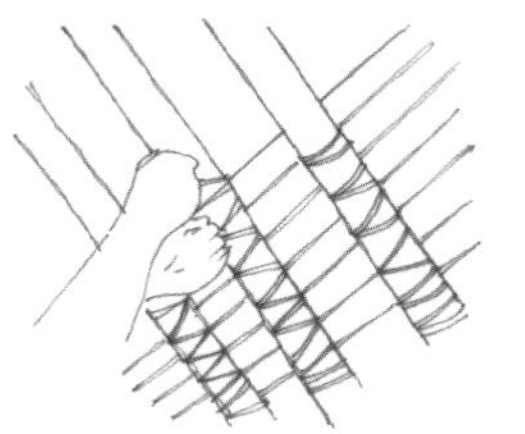

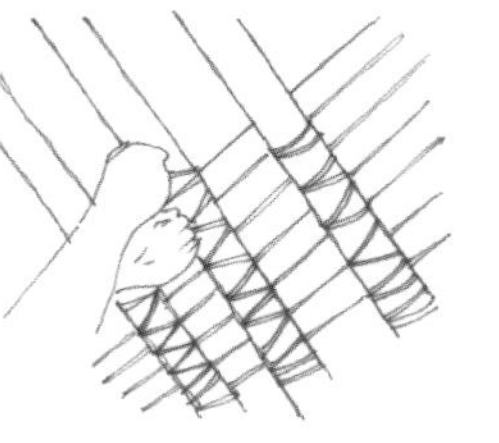

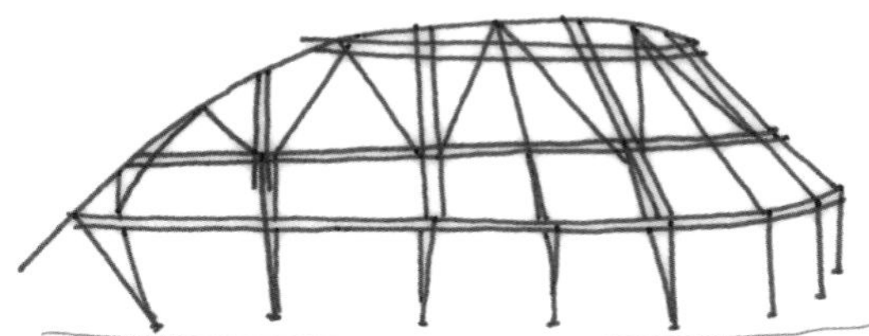

Almost all the elements of the school, from the structural framework to the furniture and other fixtures, are constructed from bamboo, where the bamboo is exposed and celebrated. Students learn about ecology as a larger concept but also get to build their own bamboo structures to continue with this spirit of experimentation.

The formal character of the structures is responsive to the natural properties of bamboo, and the natural flex and curve of the material results in organic shapes.

The seemingly complex roof form is developed out of straight lines allowing it to be covered with local alang-alang grass.

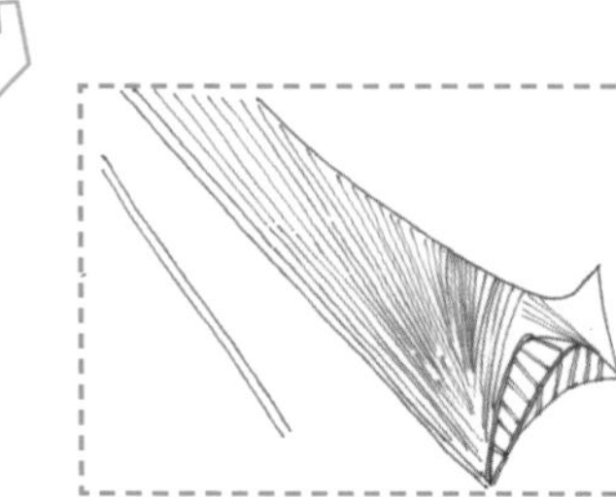

Even the furniture is made of bamboo.

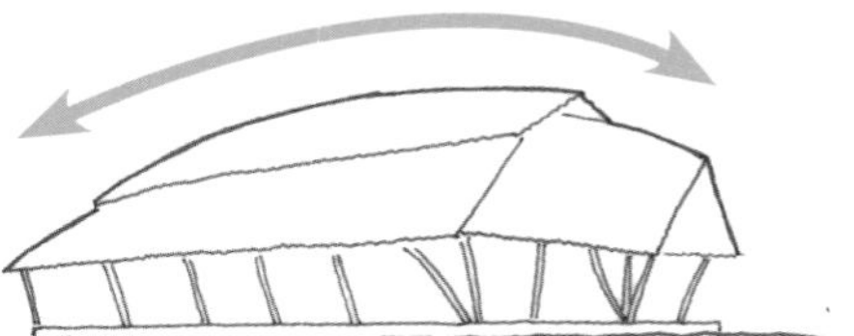

The roof forms reflect the flexibility of bamboo through their curves.

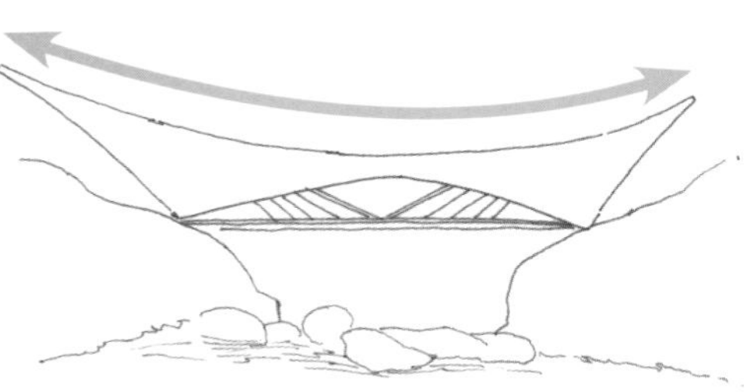

The bridge has a hyperbolic paraboloid profile.

Response to tropical climate

In response to the tropical climate, the design incorporates many features that allow for passive cooling of the building interiors and reduce dependence on mechanical or electrical systems. Most of the structures do not have any walls, and this allows for free movement of air through the building. The cross-ventilation is further assisted by the semi-detached skylights, which help to generate an upward draft.

The deep overhangs of the roof help to protect the users from the harsh tropical sun, and the shading of the surrounding area also reduces heat gain from radiation from the ground.

The helical thatched roof of the Heart of School building with its corkscrew profile drives the air inside into an upward draft.

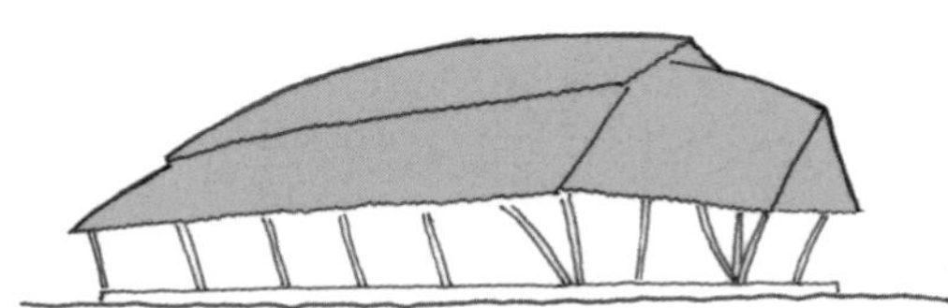

The thermal mass of the alang-alang roof helps to keep the interiors cool.

The largest structure, the Heart of School, is built around a series of supports developed out of clusters of bamboo. Central clusters support semi-detached skylights on top, while the rest of the structure leans outwards to generate an open yet shaded space.

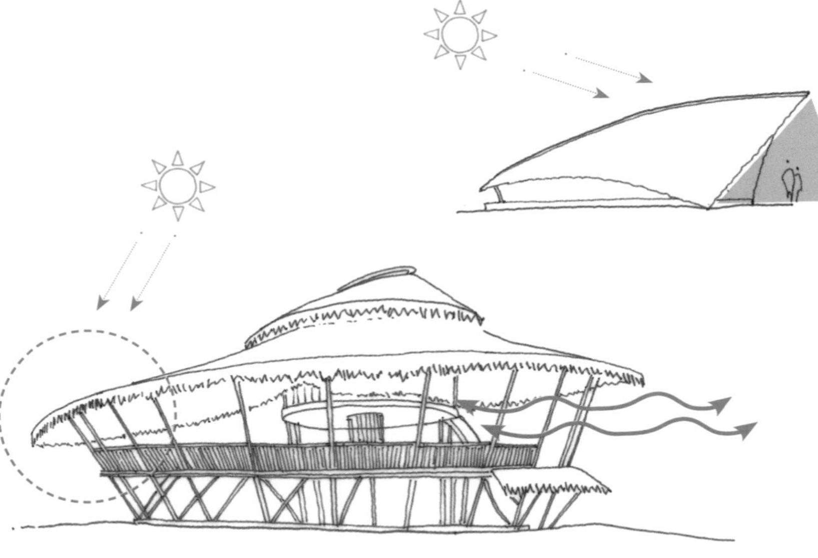

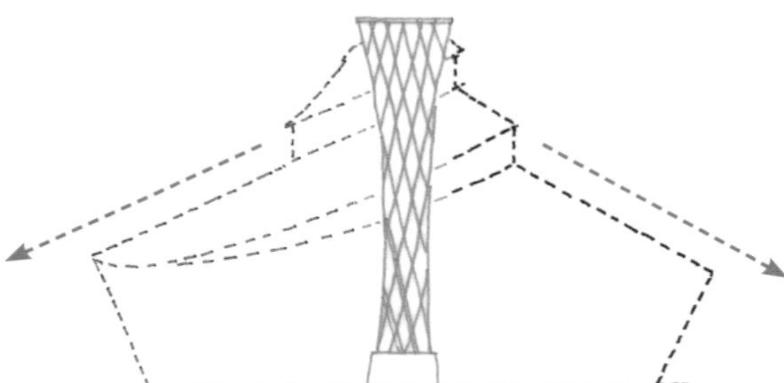

The structure radiates outwards from a central structural column with a semi-detached skylight.

The outward lean of the columns and the large overhangs create adequate shading from the harsh tropical sun.

Deep Overhang of Roofs

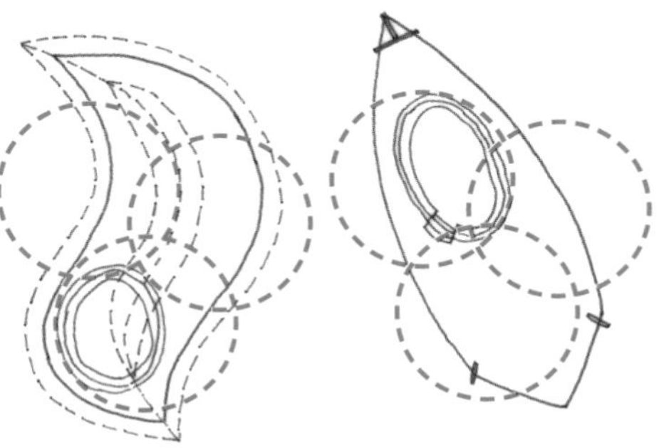

The multipurpose open-plan buildings offer opportunities for formal, informal and intimate spatial arrangements.

The themes of openness and flexibility are extended to the programmatic needs of running a school for children from kindergarten to high school. The lack of walls creates opportunities for different kinds of spatial conditions to develop, and each structure offers the possibility for formal classroom activities, informal meeting spaces for creative thinking, and intimate communal work gatherings. The lightweight bamboo furniture is easy to move around and supports the idea of flexible arrangements, while movable storage units serve as screens. The acoustic properties of the alang-alang roof further support teaching activities. The school's services and facilities reinforce the commitment to sustainable practices by using natural fuels, composting and recycling.

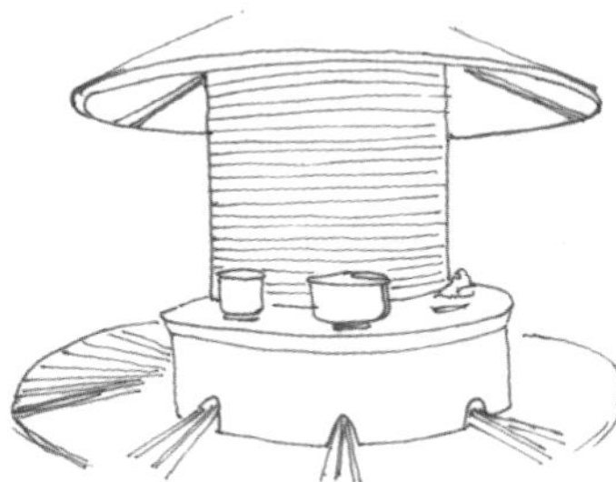

The communal kitchen uses bamboo sawdust and rice husks as fuel for cooking.

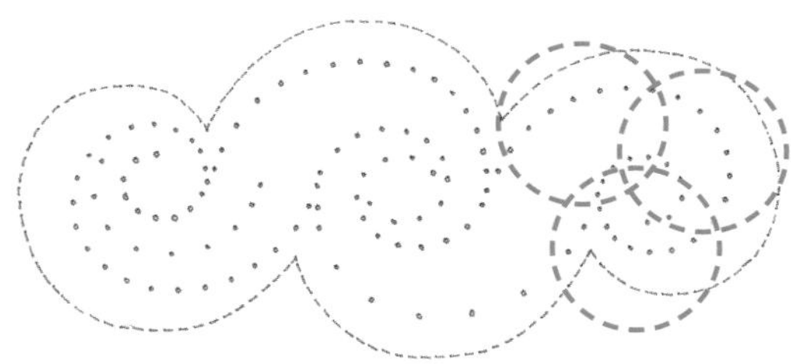

The Heart of School is the largest structure and houses various programmatic needs, including teaching facilities, library, display areas and offices.

In addition to the general openness and flexibility of programme, the school has special buildings such as the Mepantigan structure, which uses the large-span bamboo roof to provide gym facilities appropriate for Balinese martial arts training. The shape of its mud walls provides seating, transforming the gym into a public theatre.

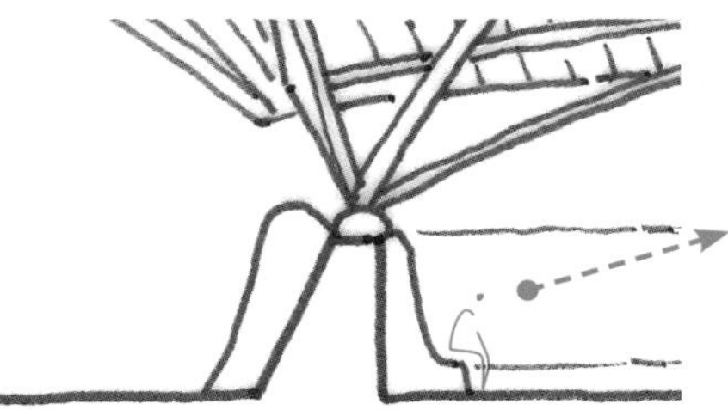

The mud walls serve as seating.

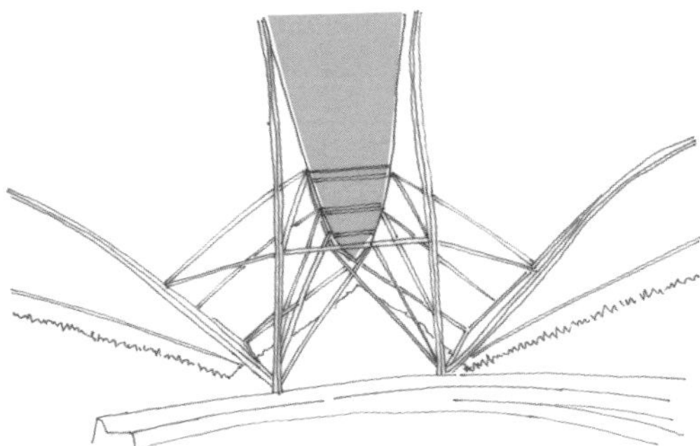

The large span of the Mepantigan structure with its exposed bamboo roof makes a grand arena.

Response to natural light/views

All structures are designed to make best use of the abundant natural light. The bamboo structural systems are developed so as to allow for a large central skylight that lets ample daylight into the depths of the interior. With a combination of the skylight and the lack of external walls there is no need for artificial lighting to conduct daily affairs.

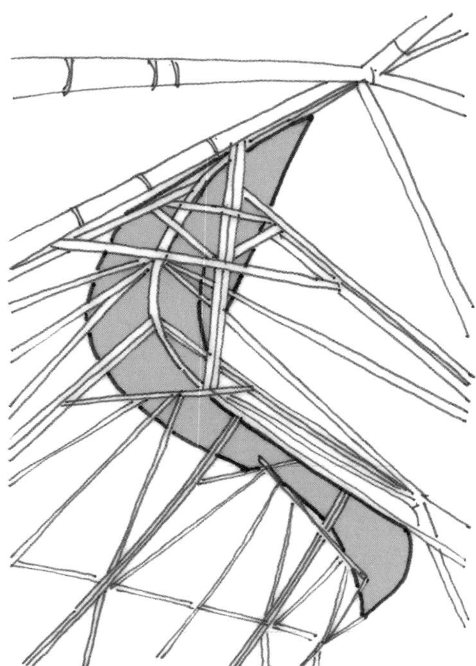

The organically shaped central skylights add to the sense of awe and excitement generated by the exposed bamboo structures.

The absence of walls also allows unrestricted views of the exterior. In the context of the educational principles espoused by the school, this continuous visual connection with the natural world reinforces the pedagogical intent of inspiring and educating children to live sustainably. This feature helps to blur the line between the interior and the exterior and creates a responsive relationship between the built mass and the natural landscape.

The intricate patterns of the mullions in the skylight merge with the criss-crossing bamboo columns.

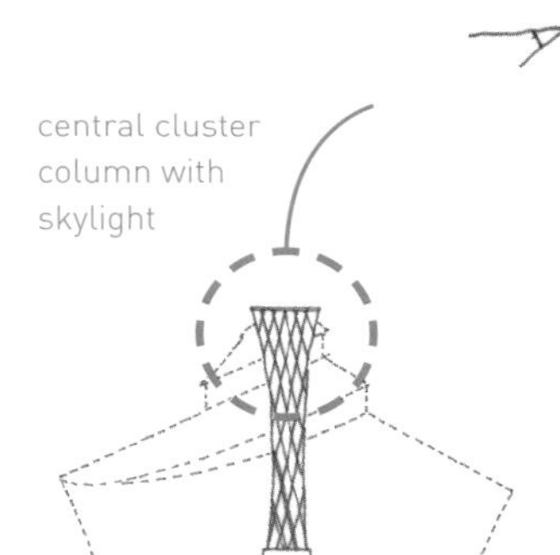

The skylight is provided not only for practical reasons of lighting but also to add wonder and amazement to the experience of the users. In the Heart of School the central circular skylight floats above a 19-metre (62-foot) high column structure made of clustered bamboos. The criss-crossing lines of the bamboo column extend into the intricate and ornate mullions of the skylight to form a mesmerizing pattern. As the sun moves through the sky, this tracery pattern casts a shadow on the floor that adds to the magical experience of this bamboo pantheon.

The lack of walls allows uninterrupted views of outside and helps to connect the user to the landscape.

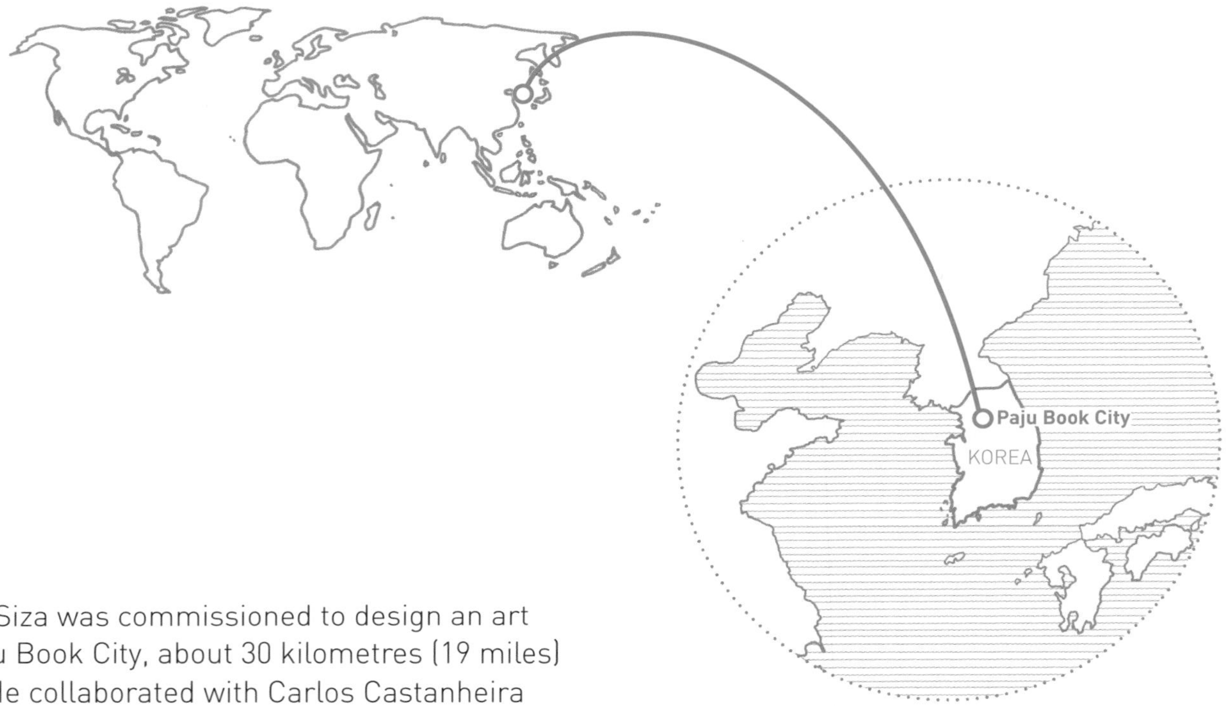

46

Mimesis Museum | 2007–9

Álvaro Siza / Castanheira & Bastai / Jun Sung Kim

Paju Book City, Republic of Korea

Portuguese architect Álvaro Siza was commissioned to design an art gallery and an archive in Paju Book City, about 30 kilometres (19 miles) from Seoul in South Korea. He collaborated with Carlos Castanheira and Jun Sung Kim for this project.

The Mimesis Museum is a contextual interpretation of Modernist aspirations. The playful curve of the courtyard is surrounded by concrete walls. There are few windows, with most of the light coming from rooflights.

The museum is a modest three-storey building. Services are grouped in the basement. The ground floor serves for reception and temporary exhibitions and is overlooked by a cafeteria and staff area on a mezzanine. The first floor contains the main exhibition spaces.

Enoch Liew Kang Yuen, Wan Iffah Wan Ahmad Nizar and Selen Morkoç

Paju Book City

KOREA

Mimesis Museum | 2007-9
Álvaro Siza / Castanheira & Bastai / Jun Sung Kim
Paju Book City, Republic of Korea

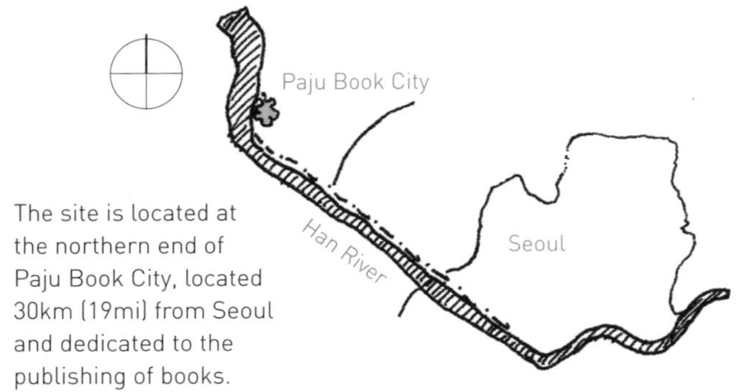

The site is located at the northern end of Paju Book City, located 30km (19mi) from Seoul and dedicated to the publishing of books.

Form generation (interior)
The idea of subtraction and addition of volumes can be seen on the exterior and interior of the building, creating a cohesive design language inside and outside.

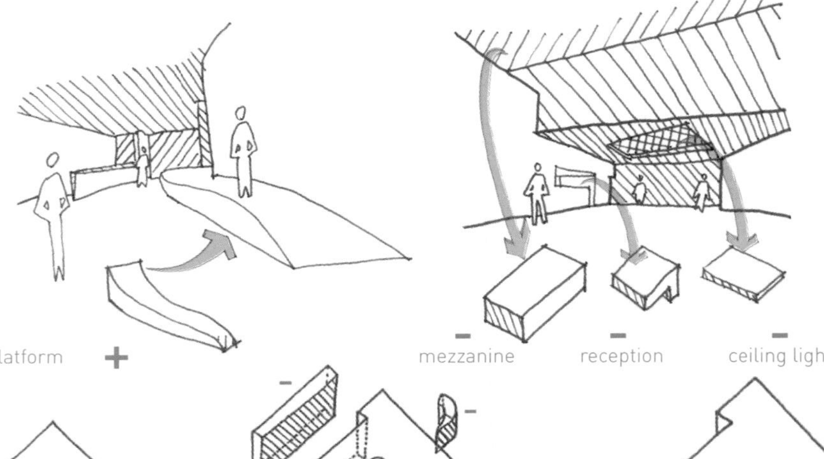

Form generation (exterior)

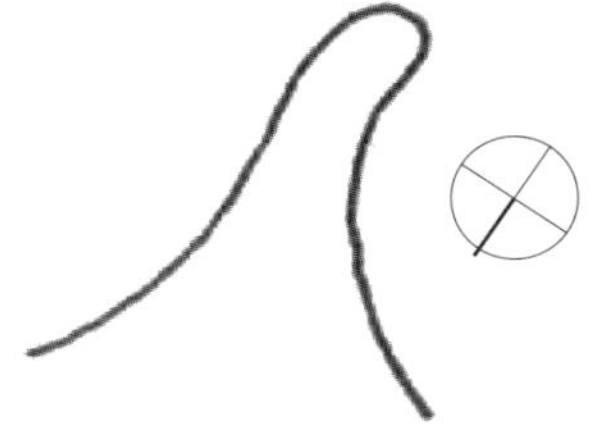

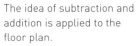

The design begins as just one stroke of a curvy line that reflects the nearby undulating creek.

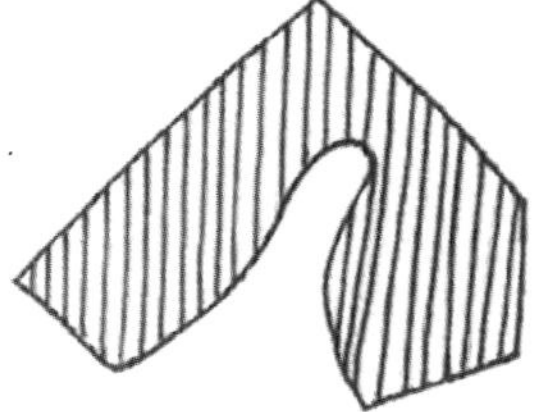

Straight lines then contrast with the curve to complete the floor plan.

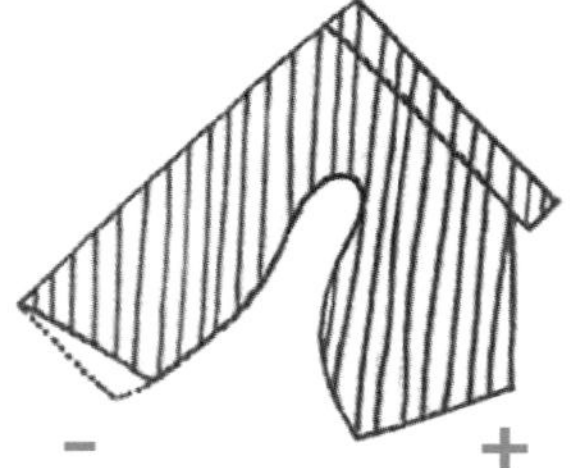

The idea of subtraction and addition is applied to the floor plan.

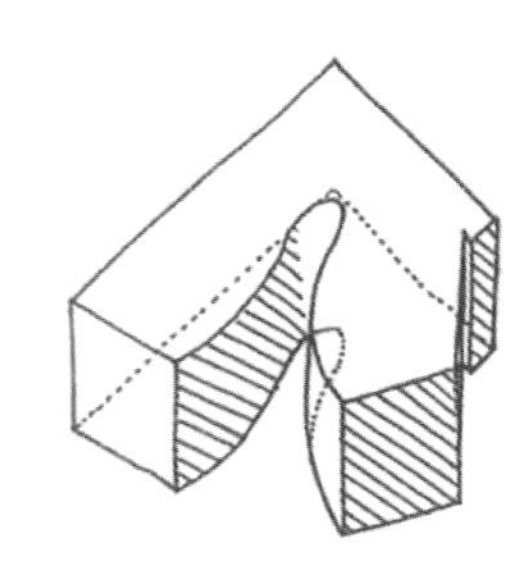

Extruding the basic 2D floor plan gives the basic form of the museum.

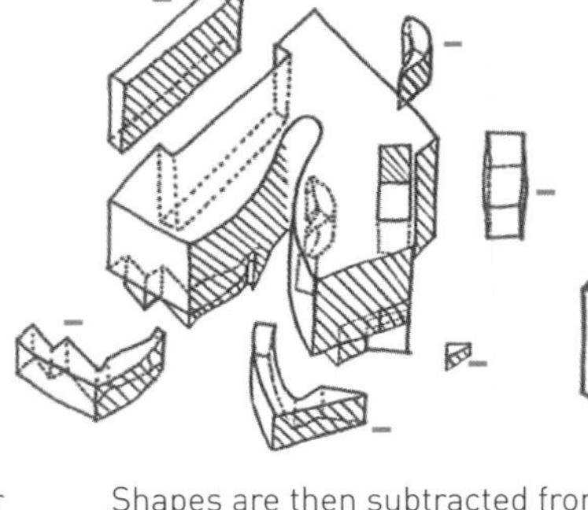

Shapes are then subtracted from the simple but dynamic form to create more dynamic spaces.

Abstraction of elements

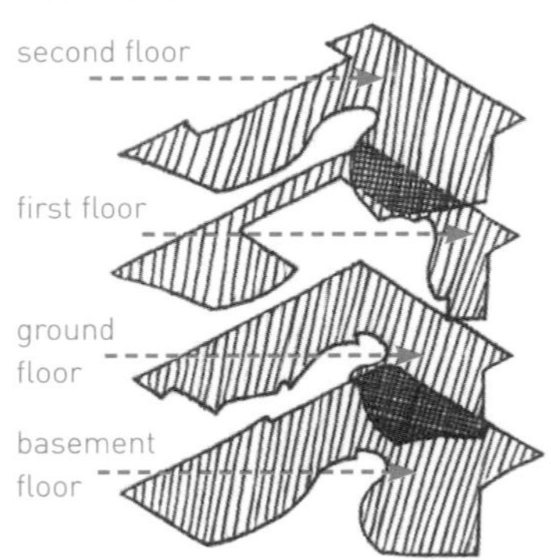

The varying floor plates take unexpected shapes that depart from the exterior form.

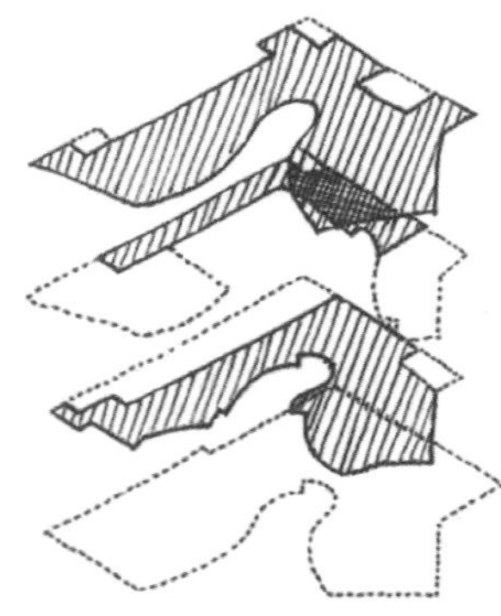

Areas of public access are mostly on the ground and second floors, forcing visitors to navigate through the building.

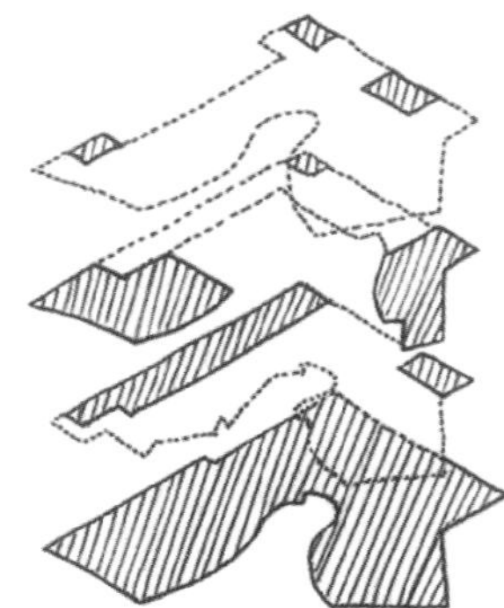

Services and areas of restricted access are located on the edges, allowing flexibility in the core of the building.

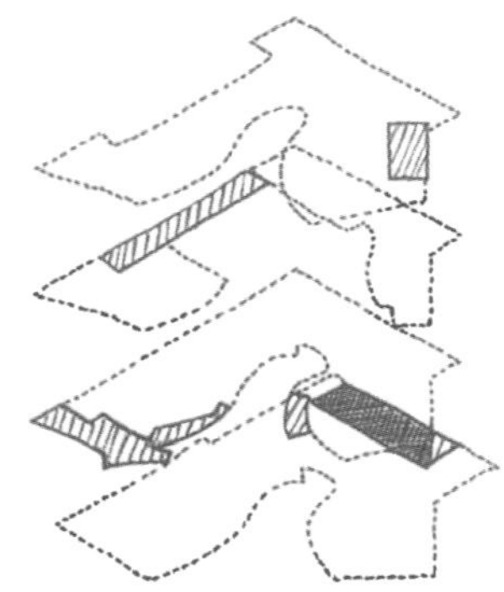

Different courtyard spaces punctuate every floor, creating an element of surprise.

Curved elements are relatively simple and are confined to one end of the building.

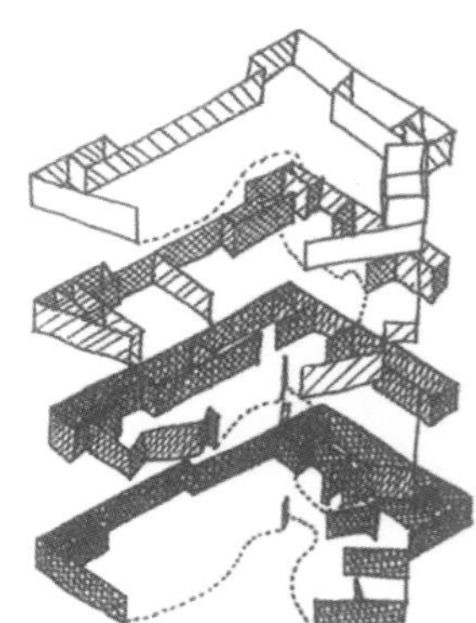

Straight elements are more complex, to create segments of usable space.

Response to nature

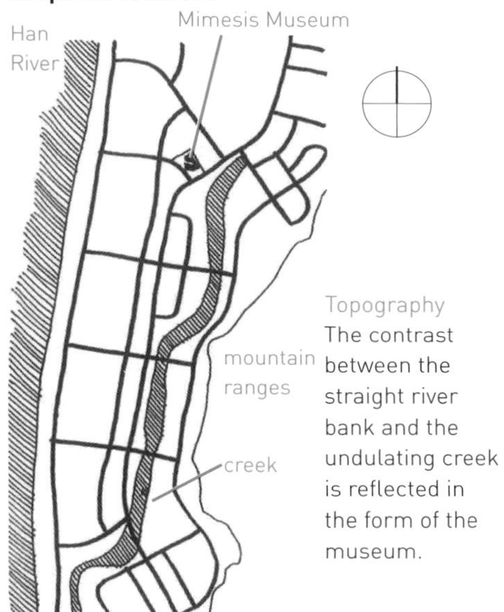

Topography The contrast between the straight river bank and the undulating creek is reflected in the form of the museum.

Climate Paju Book City has a wet climate most of the year. The areas outside the main entrance and the café are sheltered from the rain to create comfortable transitional spaces.

Relationship with the site The site had been highly adapted for farming. Consequently, the museum does not relate to its artificial surroundings, but creates its own artificial environment with limited openings.

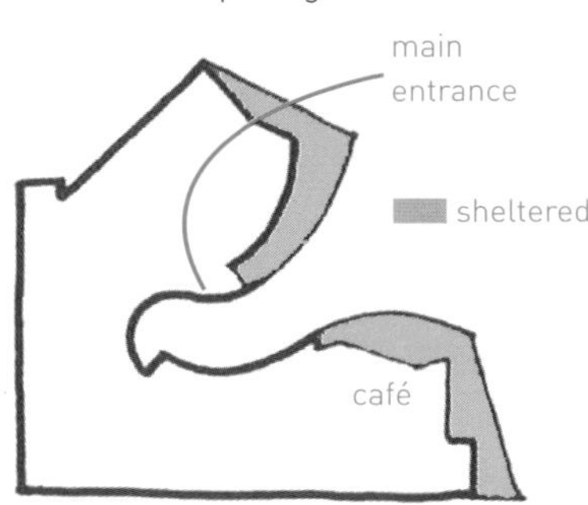

Landscape Cherry trees are significant in Korean culture, history and landscape. They have been chosen to frame the building and the site.

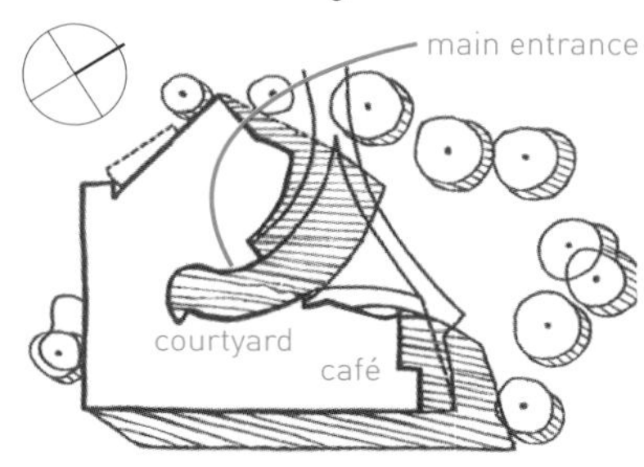

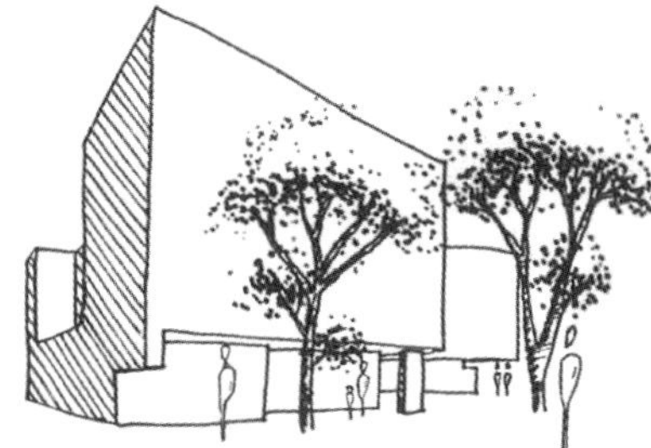

The monotonous grey concrete exterior walls are softened by the cherry trees, which change colour and lushness according to the season.

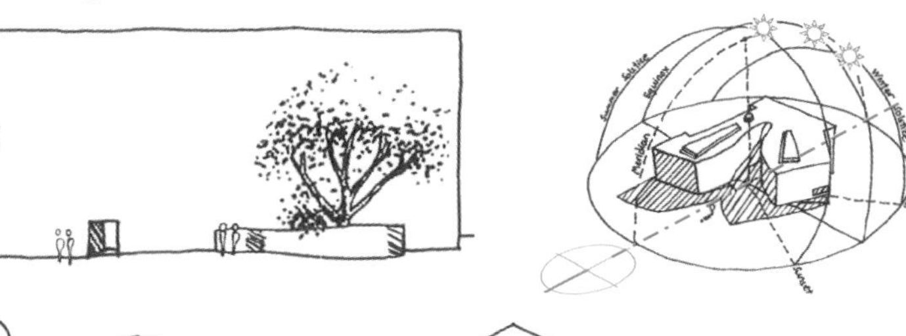

Light Álvaro Siza has a reputation for manipulating light to create interesting spaces. This museum uses light as a sculptural as well as functional element.

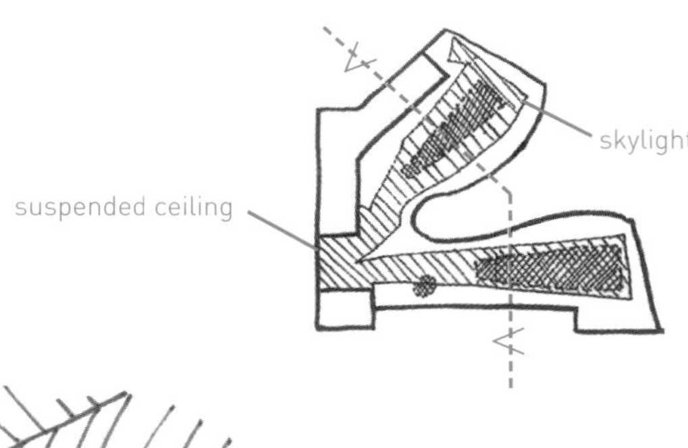

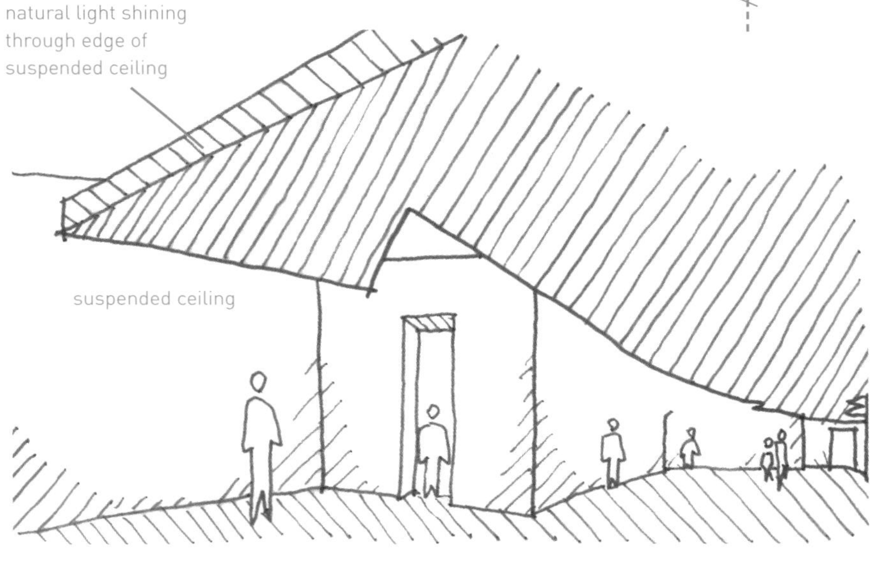

Light penetration from windows on the façade will depend on the angle of the sun and time of day, but the skylights mean there is consistent light penetration all day.

The use of reflected light prevents exhibition pieces from being damaged by direct sunlight.

Response to the artificial

Zoning The museum is located in the publishing district, away from the noise and pollution of the Jayu Highway, allowing the courtyard and the café to open to the west.

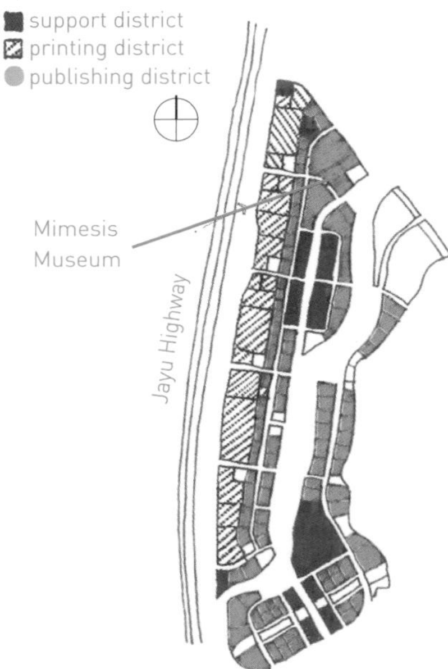

Materials The materials used for the Mimesis Museum are contemporary and have been used in many of Siza's past architectural projects, but there are also reminders of traditional Korean architecture.

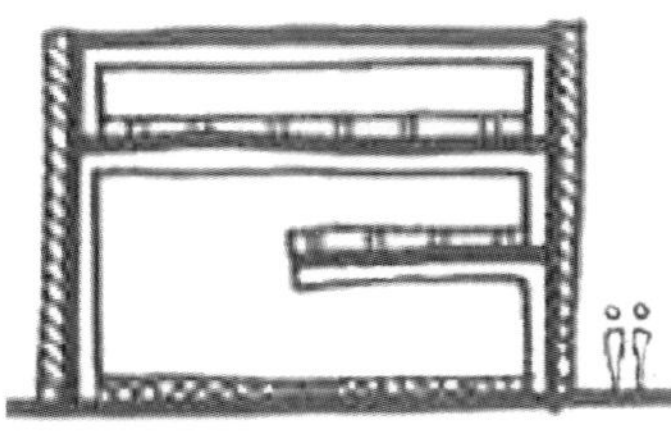

Introversion The interior and the exterior are detached to encourage users to be immersed in what is inside the building.

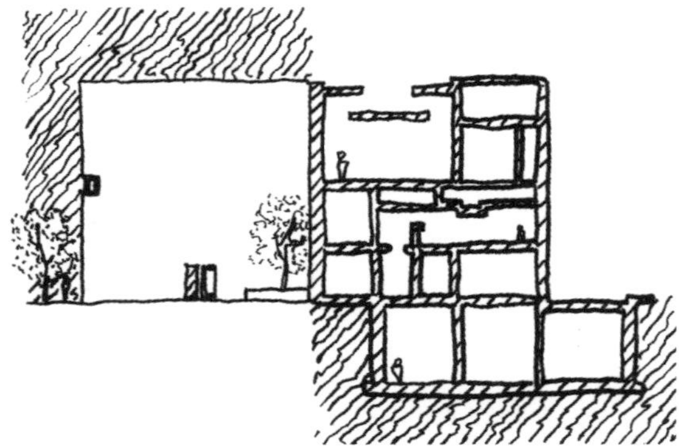

The exterior is bare, with not much to see, while the interior is complex and interesting, creating surprise with each turn.

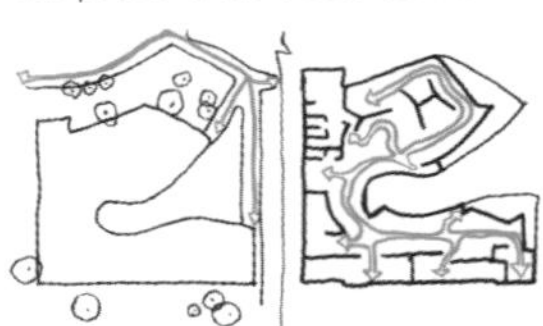

The exterior is simple and predictable, the interior is unpredictable.

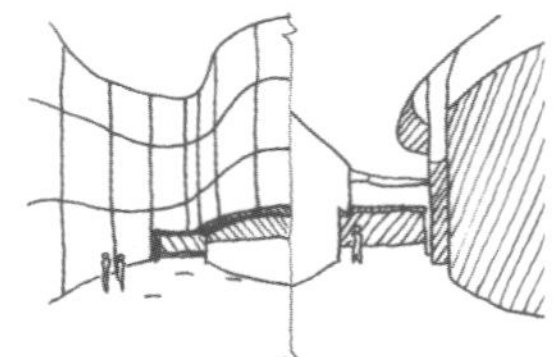

Windows connect the ground floor with the courtyard. From outside, they appear to be small openings in a mostly blank façade. From inside the windows appear large.

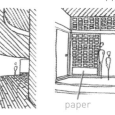

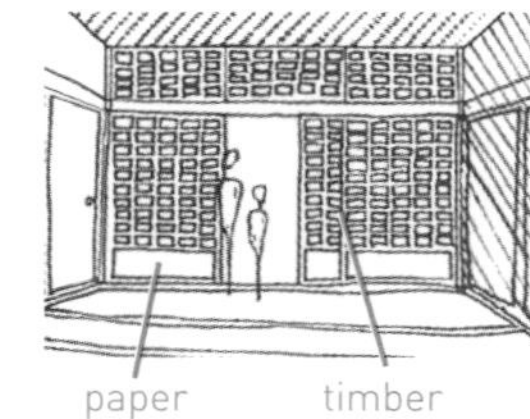

Timber is widely used in traditional Korean architecture. Although plaster is contemporary, it is similar to the colour and texture of paper and it contrasts with timber.

The added and subtracted planes on ceilings help direct users and contrast with their forms the curvy walls.

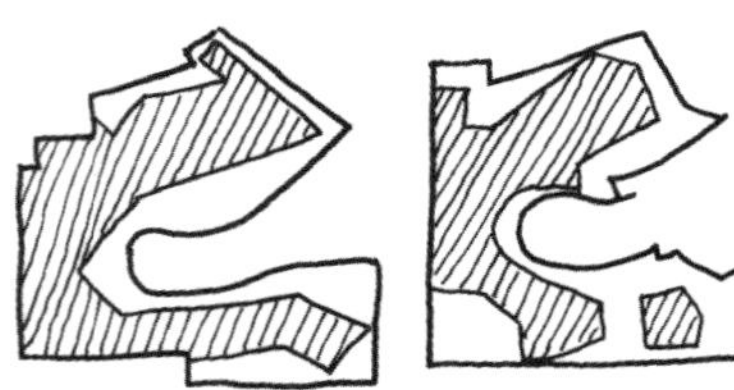

Wall surfaces step forward and backward to mark boundaries between public and private areas.

Immediate context The courtyard and café open to the west, away from the roads and the neighbouring buildings that are built close to the edges of the adjacent sites.

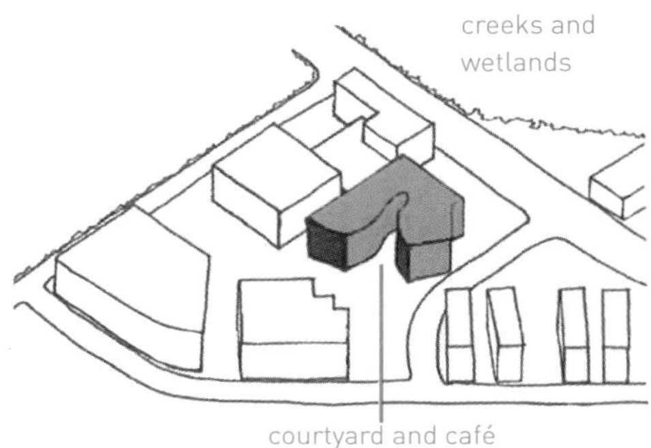

Jayu Highway also functions as a raised embankment for protection against flooding. Although views are not a concern for the museum, there is one window that overlooks the raised embankment.

Other buildings

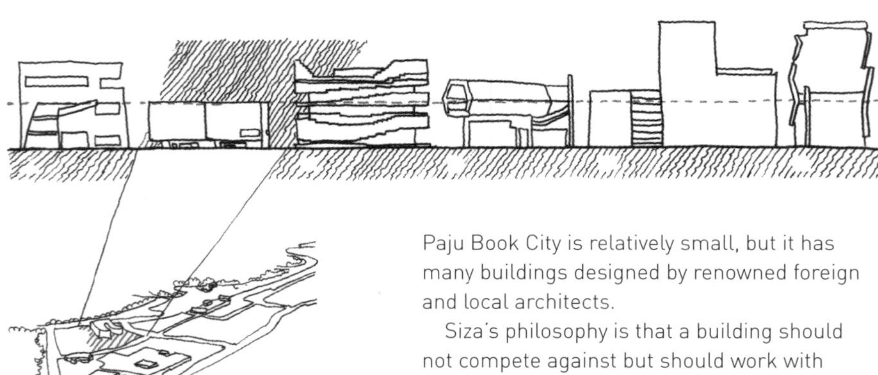

Paju Book City is relatively small, but it has many buildings designed by renowned foreign and local architects.

Siza's philosophy is that a building should not compete against but should work with neighbouring buildings. Hence the Mimesis Museum has a simple form and façade so as to complement its surroundings.

Scale The majority of public and commercial buildings in Paju Book City have three or four storeys, with some two-storey buildings. Although the large concrete walls have a sense of grandeur, the museum is similarly modest in scale. Joint lines in its concrete walls break down the mass, and there are enough windows and doors on the ground floor for human scale.

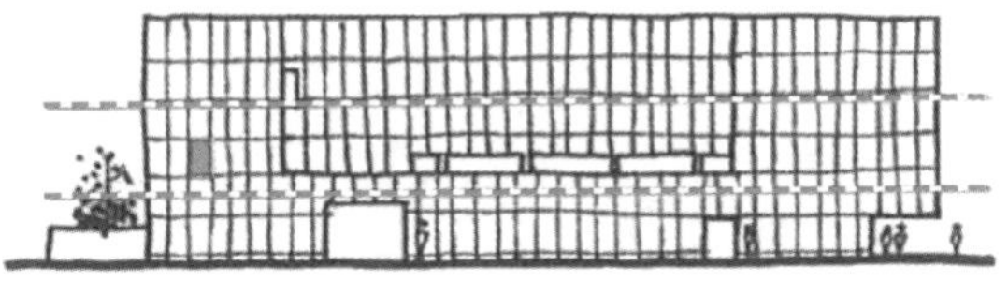

East elevation
Part of the ground floor is recessed, which is also effective in reducing the mass and giving it a human scale.

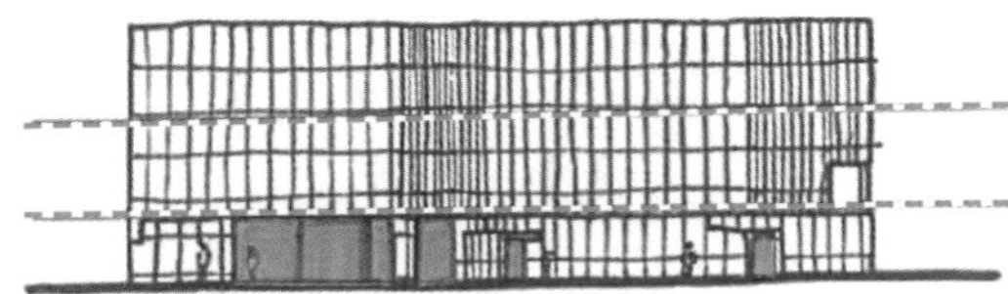

North elevation

West elevation

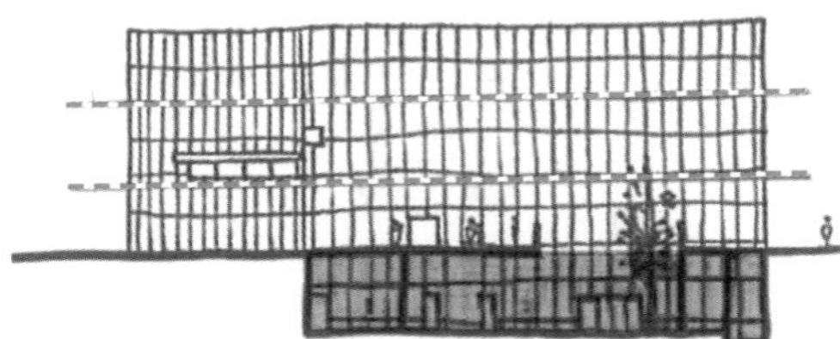

South elevation
The archive and storage facilities are placed underground to reduce the number of visible floors. This basement level extends beyond the south façade with a small courtyard open to the sky.

Response to the programme
The building is like a big box, with its high ceilings, limited openings and partition walls. It directs users to be immersed in the story of the exhibits.

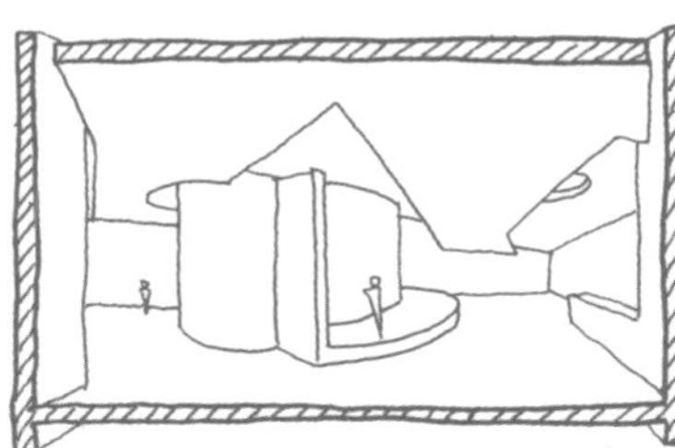

Storage and services Storage spaces and service stairs and lifts are located together at the corner of each level, easily accessible from the service road.

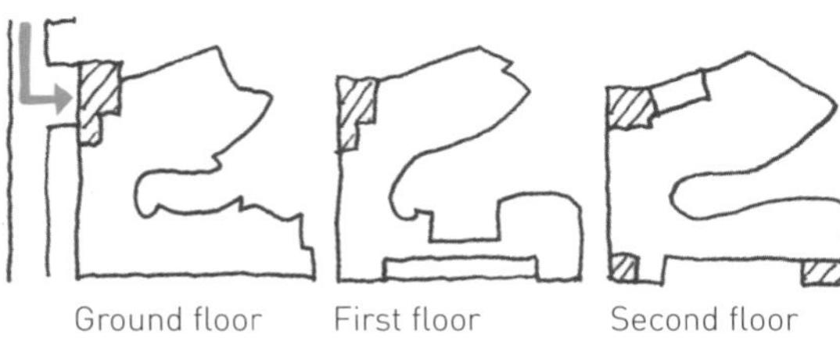

Poetic Modernism Siza's architecture is often described as 'Poetic Modernist', having Modernist qualities but still being contextual, influenced by such architects as Luis Barragán. The Modernist and simplified form and floor plans function well as large exhibition spaces but can be easily segmented into smaller usable spaces with partition walls.

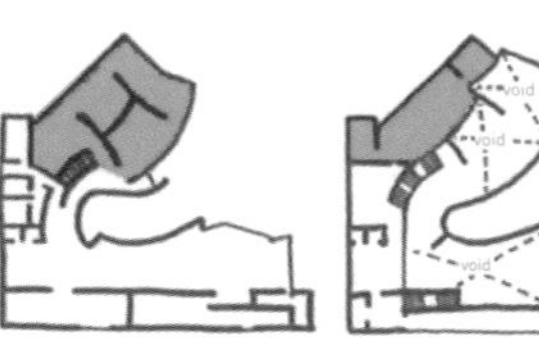

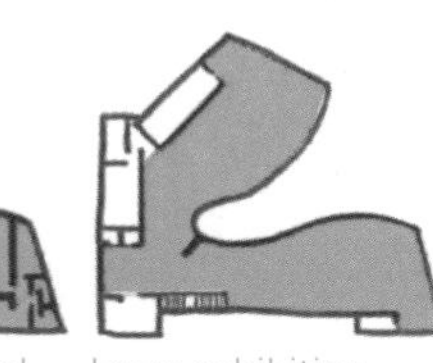

The *béton brut* rough concrete exterior walls contrast with the pristine white plaster walls of the interior that serve as backgrounds for exhibits.

The tightest curve of the museum, bounding the most dynamic space, is hidden from view when visitors enter through the main entrance.

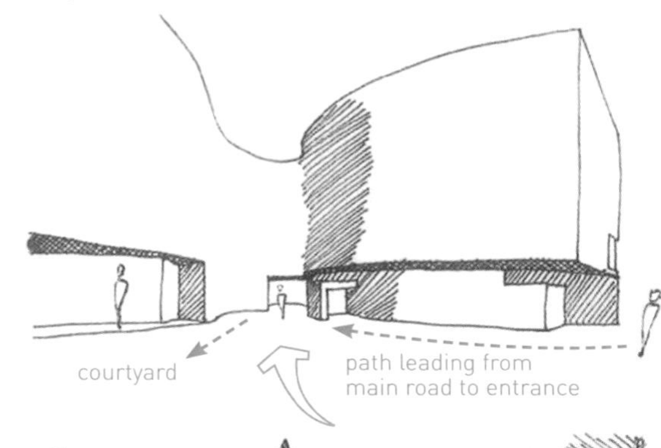

This curve can be viewed from the interior of the building. The distinctive curve allows visitors to orient themselves inside the museum, since there are few windows.

Mimesis Museum | 2007-9
Álvaro Siza / Castanheira & Bastai / Jun Sung Kim
Paju Book City, Republic of Korea

Courtyard spaces and sense of time Open space is provided on every floor, giving users a sense of time in a building with limited windows. However, the courtyards emphasize the isolation of the museum because they do not provide views of the surroundings. Courtyards are all designed with different ways of framing the sky (with limited openings). They grasp and reflect the essence of time on the canvas-like white walls and floors.

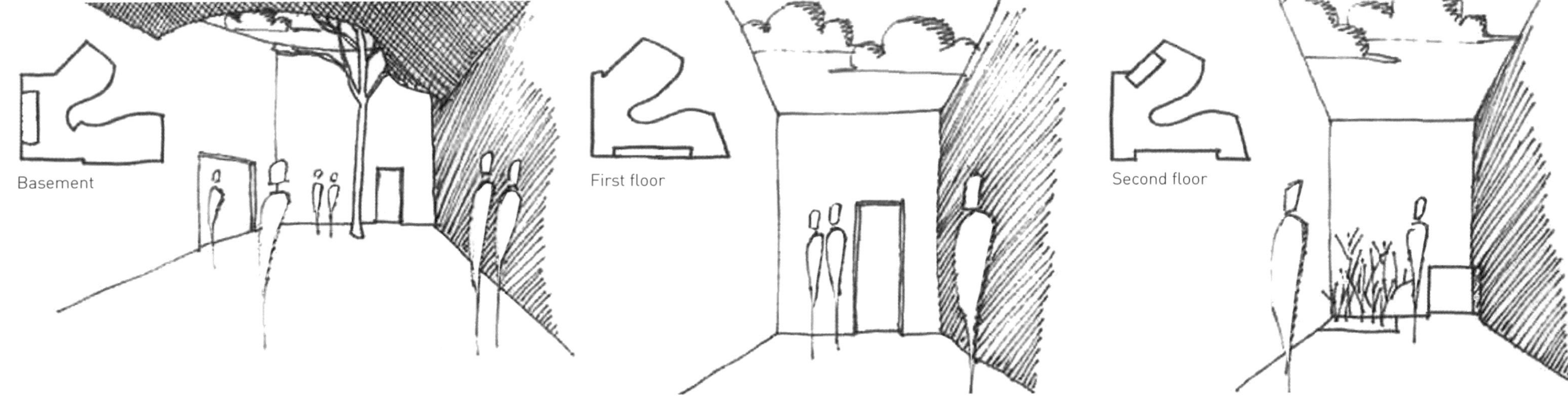

Linking spaces The main stairs linking the ground floor to the first floor and the first floor to the second are spaced apart, making visitors cross part of the building's first floor. There are also lifts and enclosed stairs.

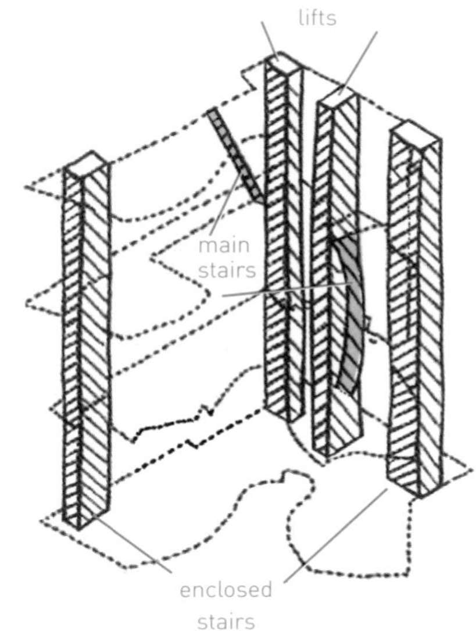

Creating anticipation
The exhibition spaces are small, but with strategically placed walls, a curved floor plan and exhibition spaces that are on separate levels, users are encouraged to explore.

A large void on the first floor offers a visual link to the ground floor.

Nodes of interest

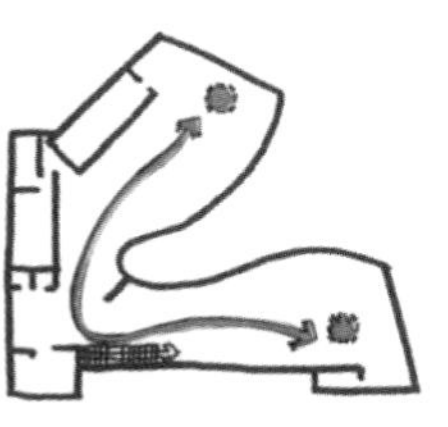
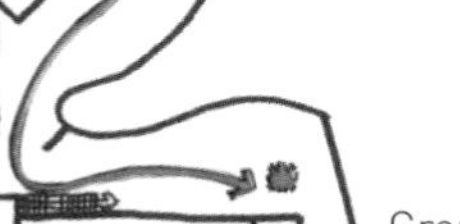

Ground floor

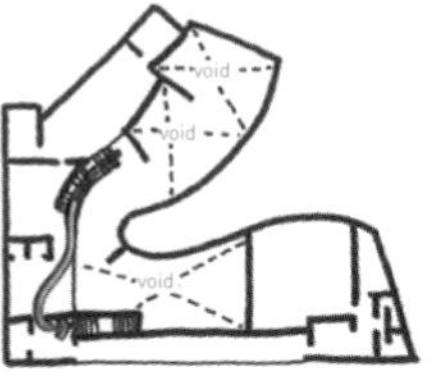

First floor

Second floor

Exterior view: courtyard

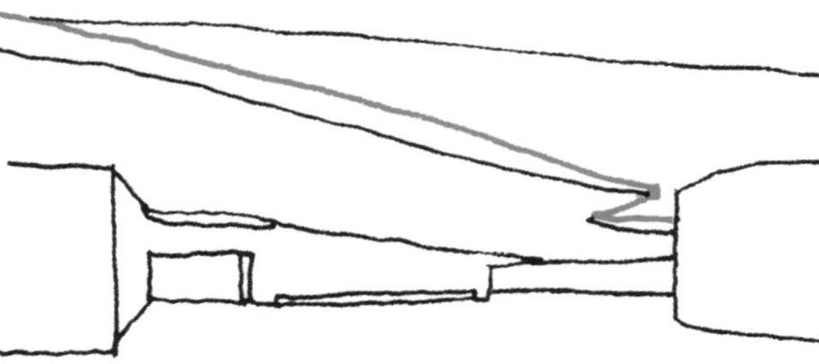

Interior view: second floor

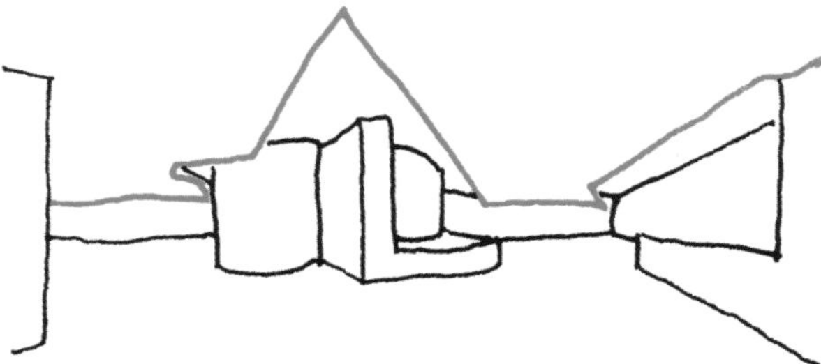

Interior view: first floor

Discontinuity of lines Internal spaces with jagged lines are in contrast with the main curvilinear line forming the courtyard.

Juilliard School & Alice Tully Hall | 2003–9

Diller Scofidio + Renfro / FXFOWLE

New York, USA

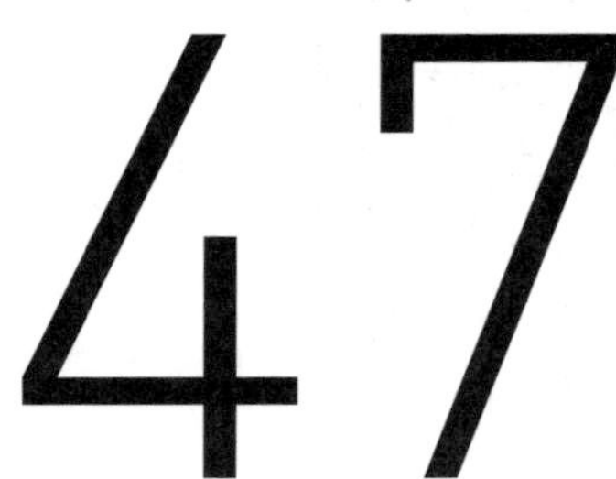

The design of the extension for the Juilliard School, part of New York's Lincoln Center for the Performing Arts, by architects Diller Scofidio + Renfro builds on the original design by Pietro Belluschi completed in the 1960s. The extension responds to the original building by engaging several elements from the existing façade as a starting point. This is mixed with a dynamic response to the street context to create an overall form that sits comfortably within its urban context and acts as a mediator between the public realm and the institutional facilities of the original building.

Subtle considerations about sightlines and transparency allow the design to turn this school of performance art into an urban grandstand, blurring the boundaries between private and public, real life and theatre.

William Rogers, Mark James Birch and Amit Srivastava

COLUMBUS AV
BROADWAY
ONE WAY

Juilliard School & Alice Tully Hall | 2003-9

Diller Scofidio + Renfro / FXFOWLE

New York, USA

Response to urban context

Lincoln Center was established in the 1950s as a centre for performing arts after slum clearance. The new precinct with several performing-art institutions was intended as a cultural centre for the Upper West Side of Manhattan. Over the years this precinct has maintained its identity against the high-rise corporate towers that surround it.

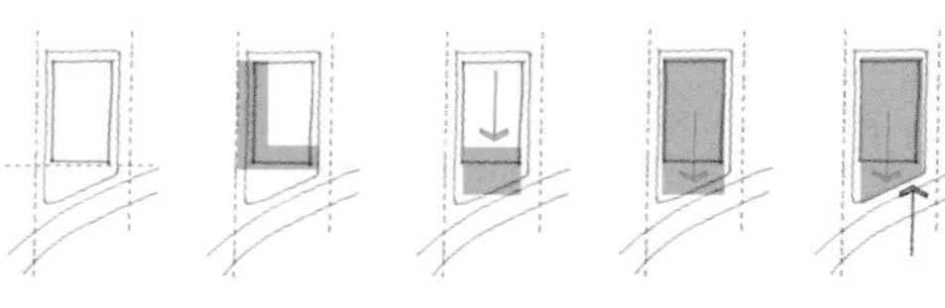

The extension is conceived as a responsive dialogue between the original building and Broadway. The existing mask is removed and a swelling of the internal volume is mediated in response to the diagonal axis of Broadway to generate the final form, which has a dynamic response towards the street context.

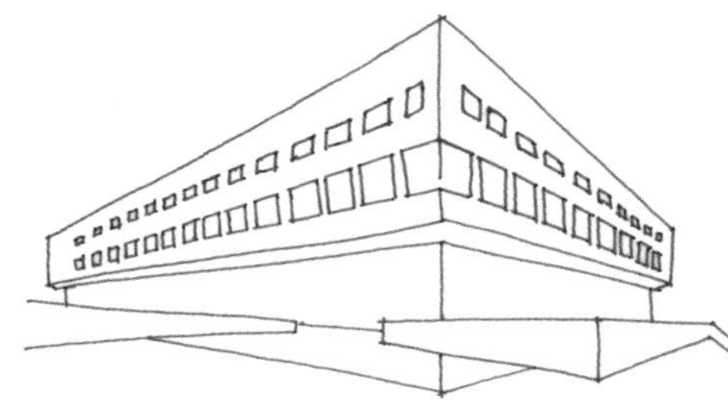

The existing building is maintained and the under-utilized outdoor space towards Broadway is incorporated to provide for new functions.

Wallace Harrison's Metropolitan Opera (1966)

Renewal of Lincoln Center

The extension and development of the Juilliard School building forms part of the overall renewal of Lincoln Center. The renewal project aims to (a) open up the centre, (b) unify the centre internally, (c) establish West 65th Street as a public spine, and (d) promote interaction through digital interface panels.

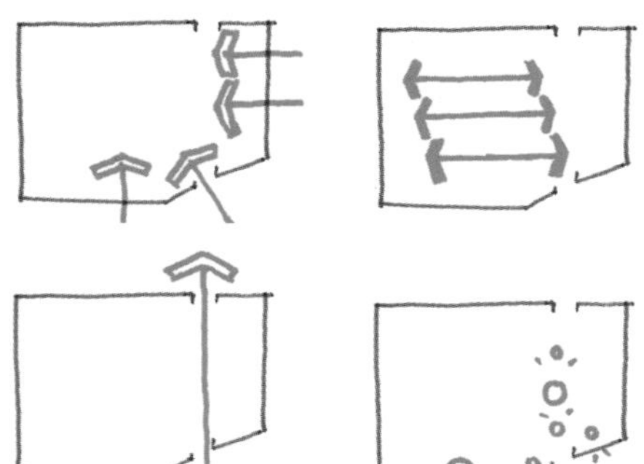

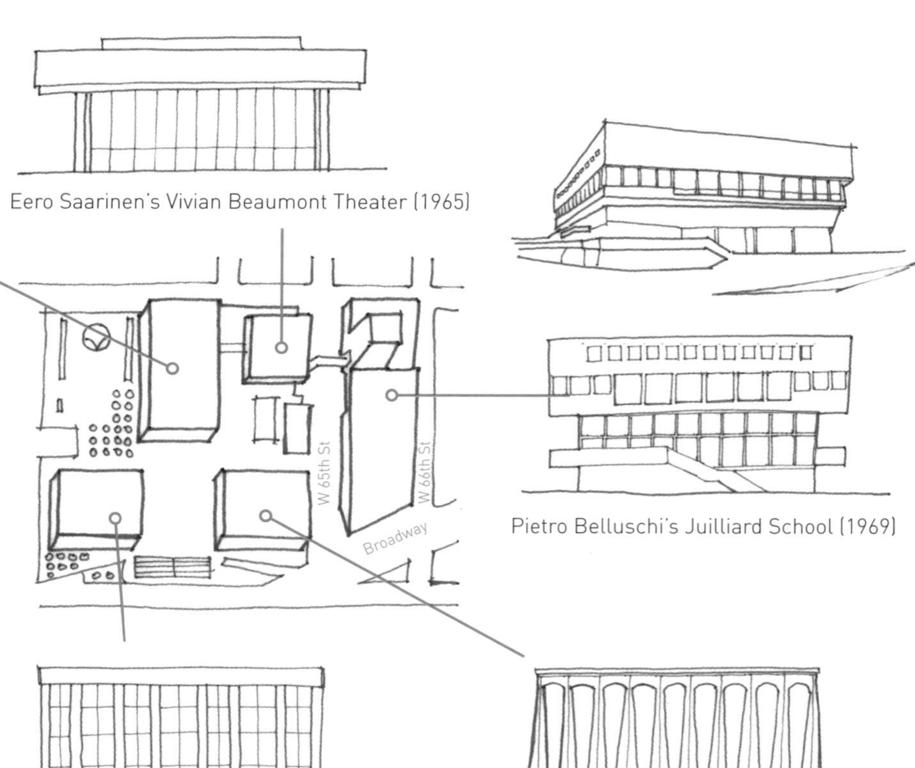

Eero Saarinen's Vivian Beaumont Theater (1965)

Pietro Belluschi's Juilliard School (1969)

Philip Johnson's New York State Theater (1964)

Max Abramovitz's Philharmonic Hall (1962)

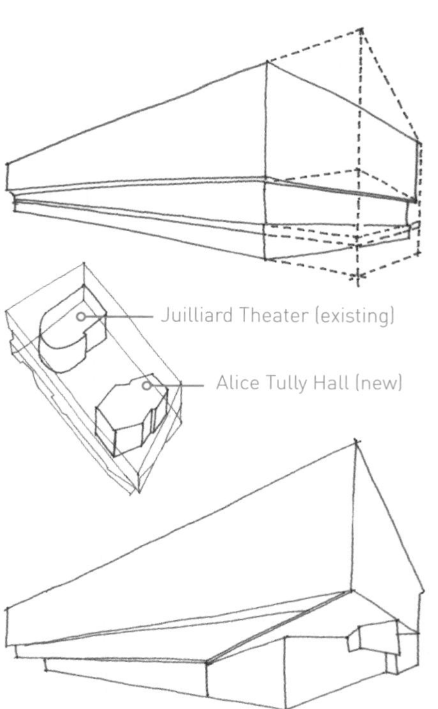

Integration of the old and the new

The new functions are incorporated into the existing structure, allowing old and new to work together as a cohesive whole. The building is extended over the space towards Broadway so as to better integrate the existing and the new functions with the public realm.

Integration with the existing

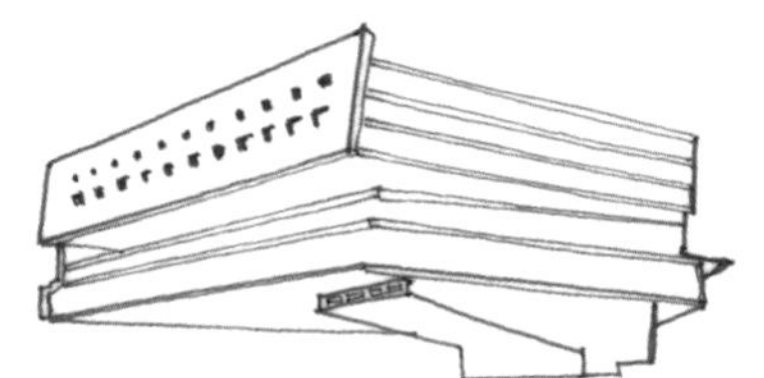

The original façade maintained a rigid distinction between the outside and the inside.

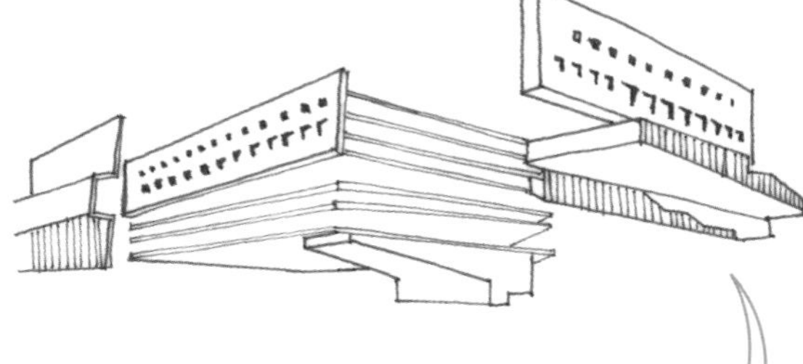

The original façade on the east side is removed to reveal the interior and allow for expansion.

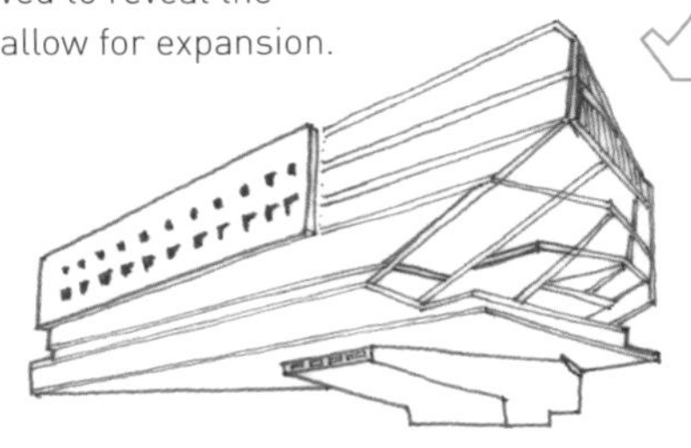

The existing floor plates extend to meet Broadway and lift in response to activities in the public realm.

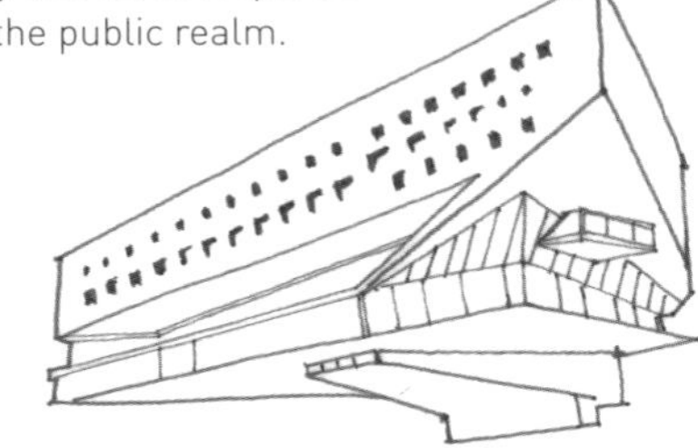

The new combined form integrates the new elements with the existing building.

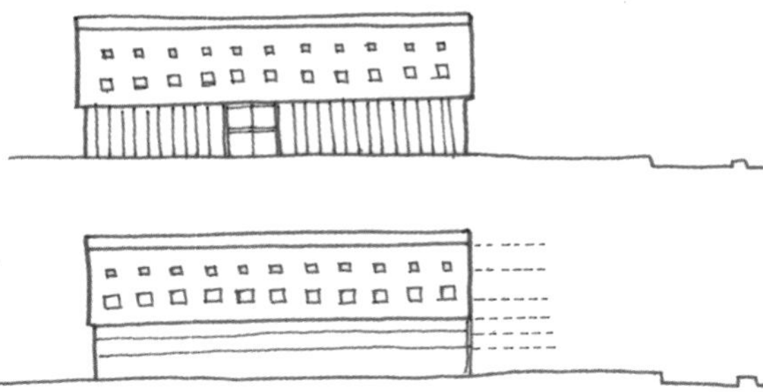

The original building, with its Modernist façade, creates a rigid distinction between inside and outside. So to increase responsiveness to the surrounding context this façade is removed and the internal spaces are allowed to expand. The extension of the existing floor plates towards Broadway is interrupted by the public realm along the street, and the new envelope is raised along the end to create a responsive and dynamic relationship with the exterior context.

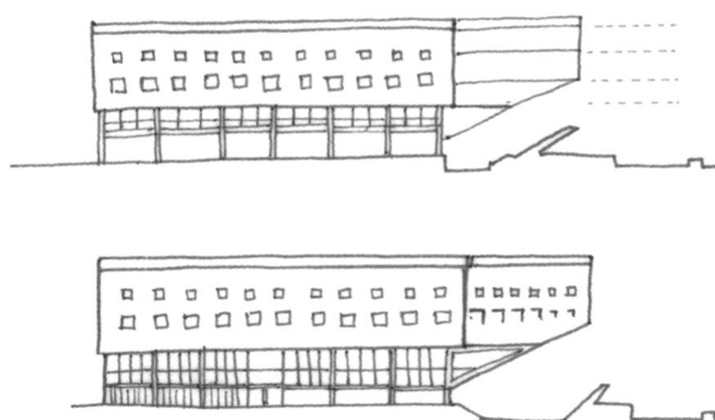

The dismembered façade is, however, not discarded and the elements of the old envelope continue to define the development of the new skin. The patterns and recesses of the old eastern façade find a new life on the extension along West 65th Street. These are supplemented with new materials and correspond to the new internal layouts. The integration of the new requirements with the architectural language of the existing building helps to create a cohesive whole.

Continuity and discontinuity

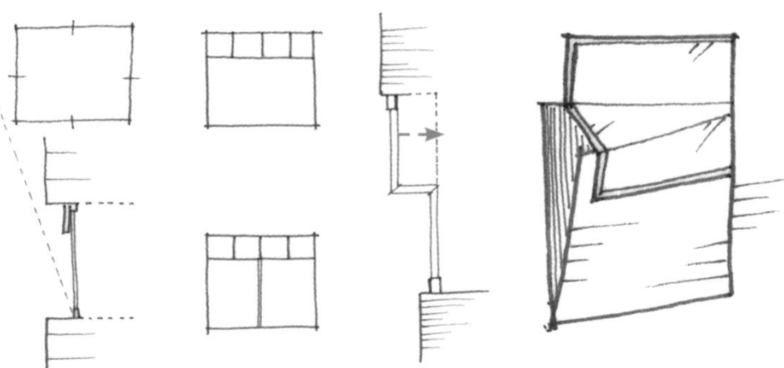

Fenestrations on old façade

Indented frames along new façade

The existing building was designed by Pietro Belluschi during the post-war era, and the exterior façade is developed as a series of repetitive window elements that are inset into the wall to provide for requisite shading and fixing details. The new façade does not require this inset detail for its fenestrations but acquires it as a part of the visual language, creating an interesting combination of openings and frames.

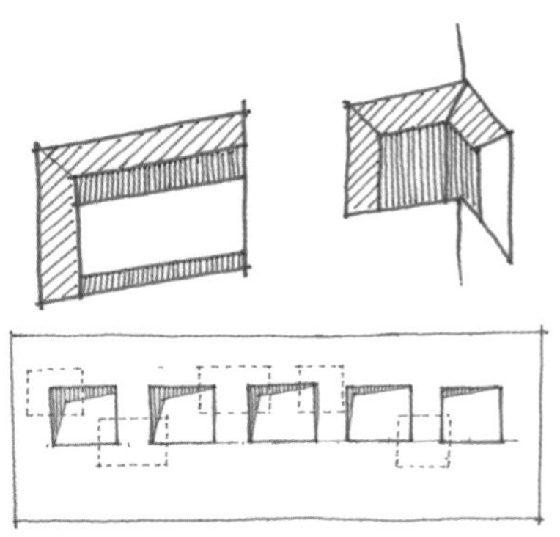

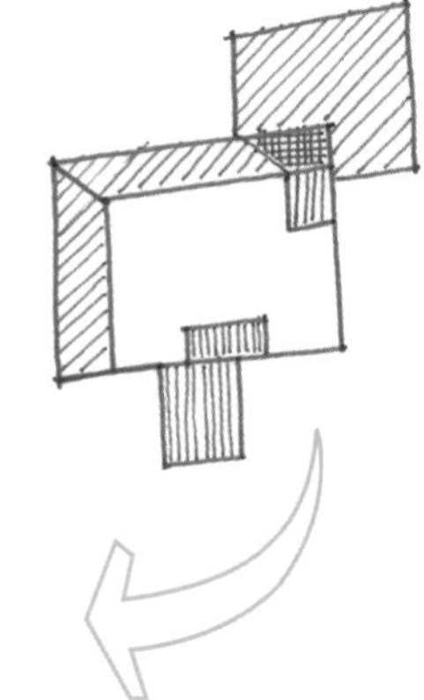

A combination of fenestrations and frames

The inset windows of the existing façade provide a visual complexity through a play of shadows. This language of chiaroscuro is replicated in the new façade by extending the series as inset frames. The actual fenestration for the extension then sits playfully within this series of frames and creates a rich experience for both external observers and occupiers of the building.

Performance and a school of dance

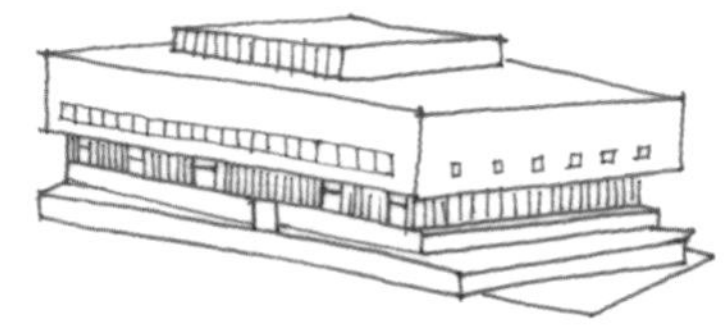

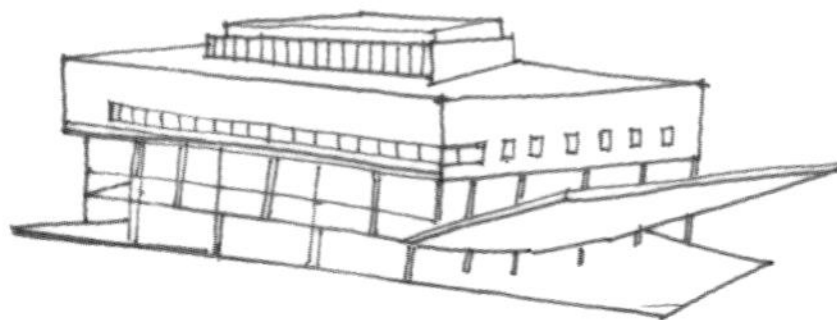

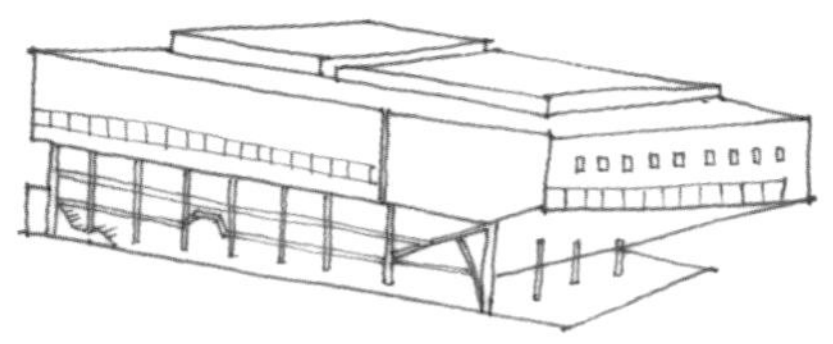

Sunken forecourt as grandstand

The entrance to the new extension is mediated with a sunken forecourt that acts as a point of pause in the transition from the public realm of Broadway to the more private interiors of the building. The experience of this transition is enhanced by the articulation of the space as a grandstand where the movement of people across the forecourt becomes a 'performance' for those seated on the steps facing the building. Furthermore, the people seated along the steps observe these performances conducted against the backdrop of the new building itself, making architecture an integral part of the show.

The analogy of dance can be used to define a particularly responsive relationship between two performers whose coordinated movements lead to a dynamic yet cohesive whole. The design of the extension for the Juilliard School exhibits a similar relationship with the existing building, where the dynamic and bold moves of the new part are balanced and anchored by the more stable entity of the original part to provide a unified performance in building aesthetics.

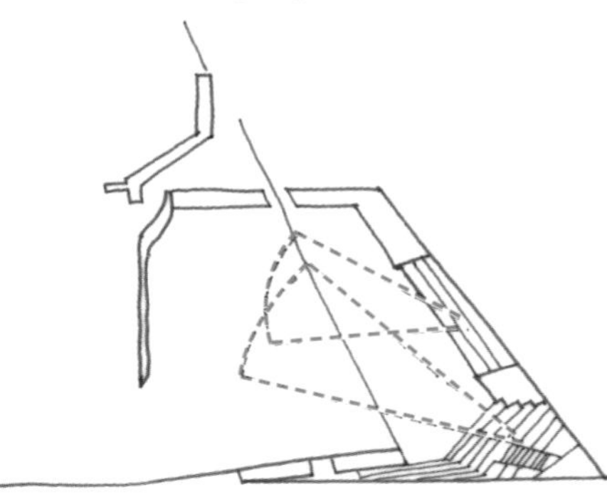

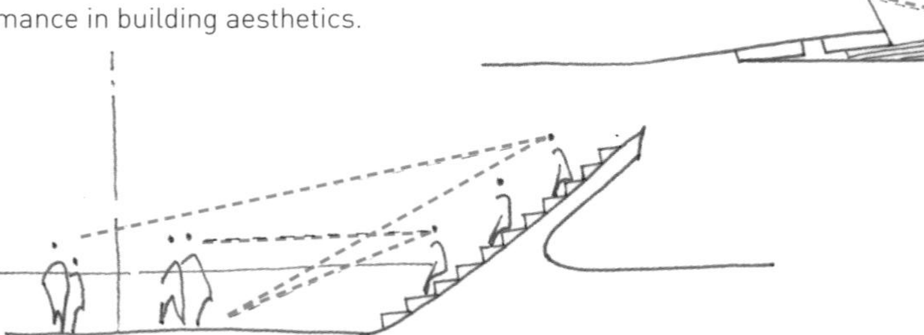

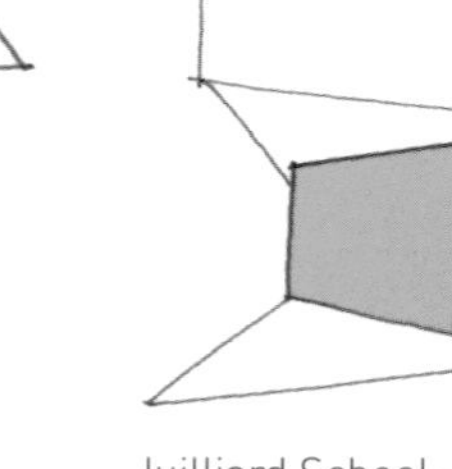

Performance, media and composing views

In the Juilliard School, Diller Scofidio + Renfro build on their previous experiments at Boston ICA (2001–6), in which the digital media centre hangs from the underside of a cantilevered gallery to frame a view of the harbour. In the Juilliard School the roles are reversed and the performers in the floating dance studio become the view, which is framed for observation by the audience in the street below.

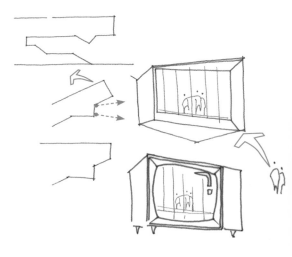

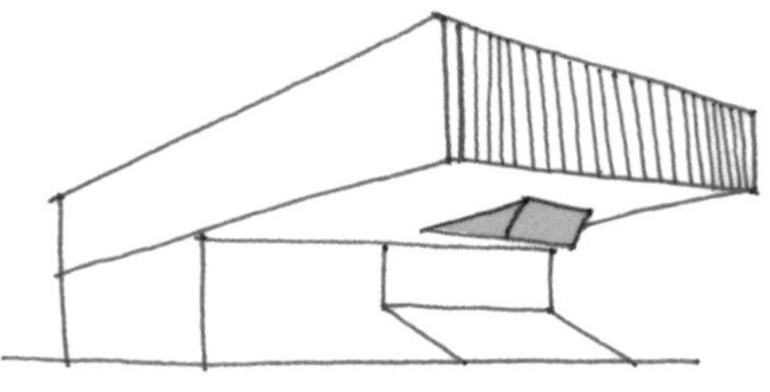

Boston ICA – digital media centre

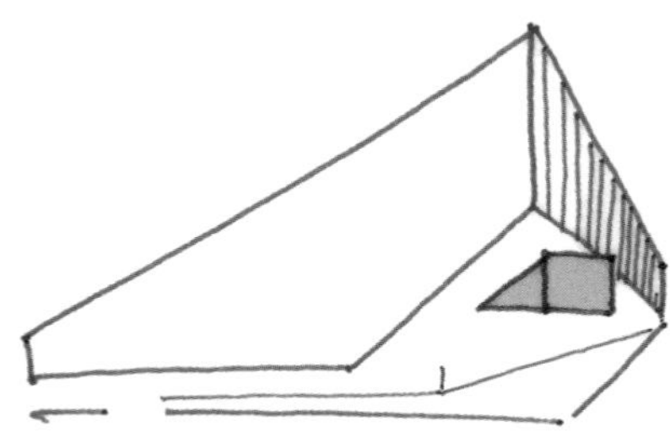

Juilliard School – dance studio

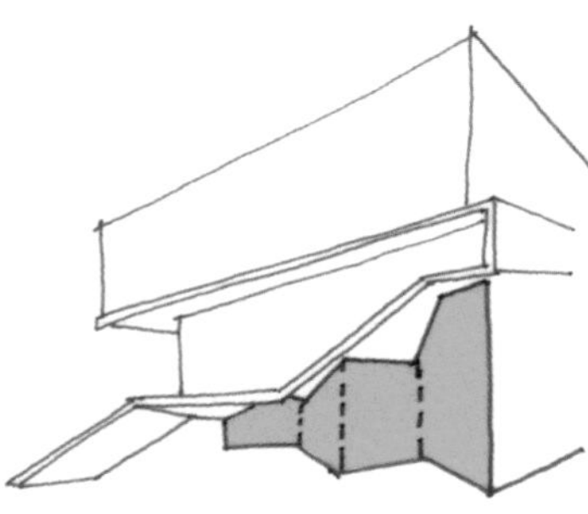

Boston ICA – grand staircase

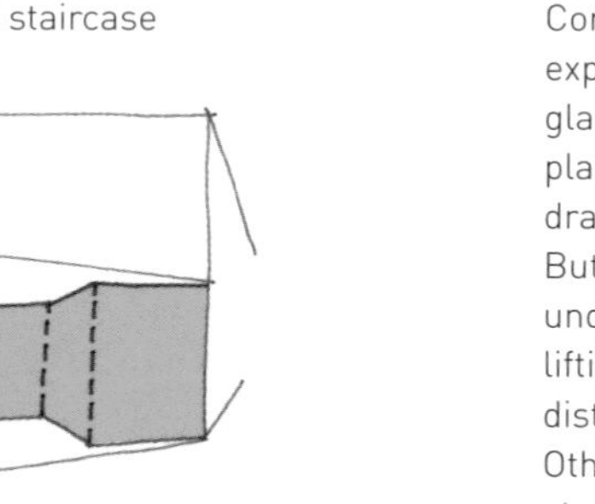

Juilliard School – Broadway cantilever

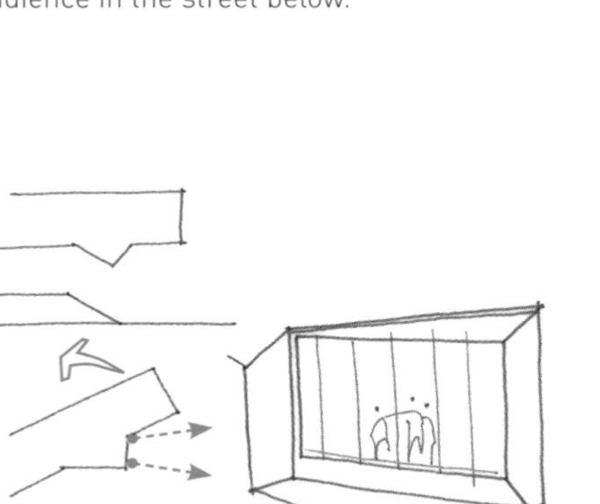

The deep bevel imitates the frame of an old television set.

Comparison with the Boston ICA project explains the Broadway entrance as a folded glass façade wedged underneath a sloping plane. The contrasting forms create a visual drama consistent with the idea of performance. But the articulation of the main entrance as an undercroft space revealed and made public by lifting the fabric of the building also blurs the distinction between the outside and the inside. Other features such as the framing of the dance studio or the sunken forecourt grandstand can also be seen as experiments with blurring.

Blurring of outside and inside, public and private

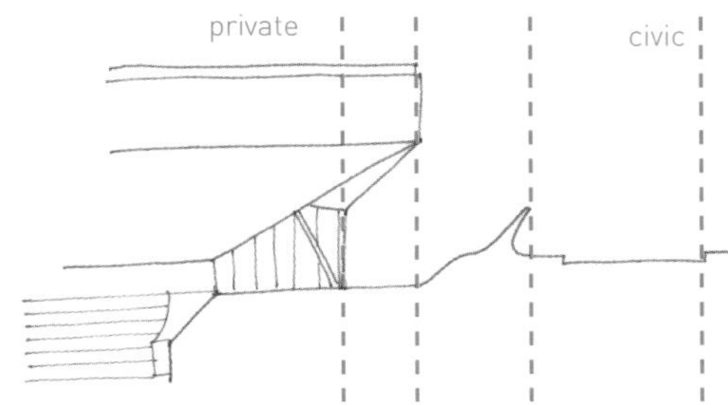

The sunken court blurs the concept of entry.

The desire to break the rigid distinction between inside and outside is continued through more subtle design features. The introduction of the sunken plaza blurs the sense of entry, relieving it from the building skin and articulating it as the physical act of descending into the otherwise open court. The semi-enclosed foyer area acts as an undefined zone between the public and the private, and the private dance studios project over the civic realm, offering a voyeuristic glimpse of the private.

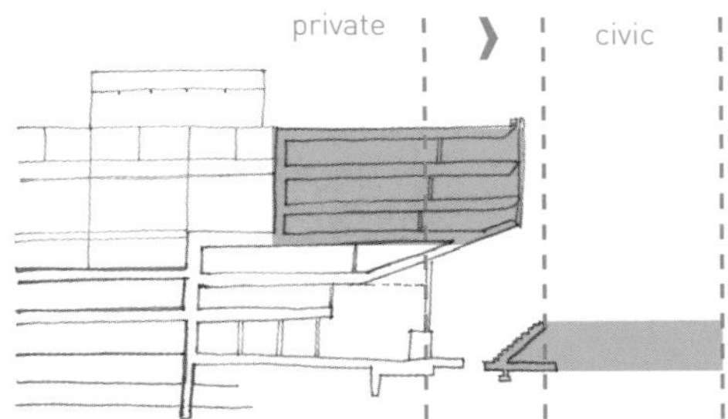

The private areas hover above the public civic realm.

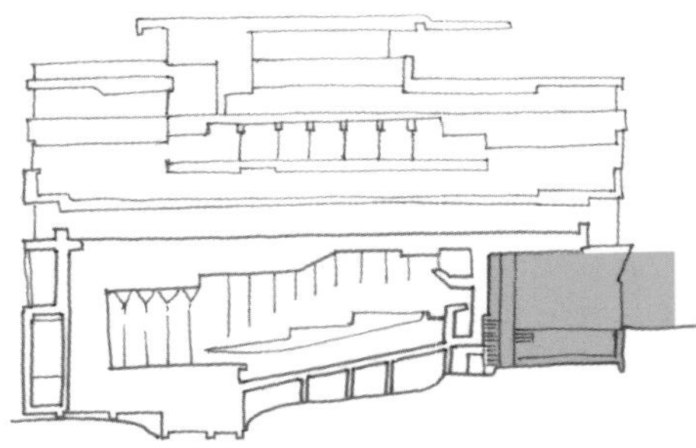
The semi-enclosed foyer forms a final transition.

A combination of benches and stairs in the sunken court forces a direct physical interaction with the building even before the visitor enters it, redefining the limits of outside and inside.

Even at the main entry, the entrance staircase incorporates spaces for other activities. The staircase has a built-in reception area, and a series of cuts and folds in the stairs provides benches for socializing or study. This blurring of the distinction between various functions facilitates greater interaction and results in the creation of the 'slow stairs'.

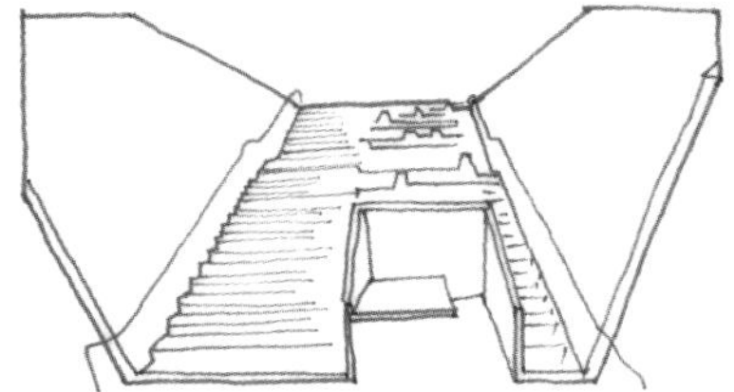

Cuts and folds and continuous surfaces

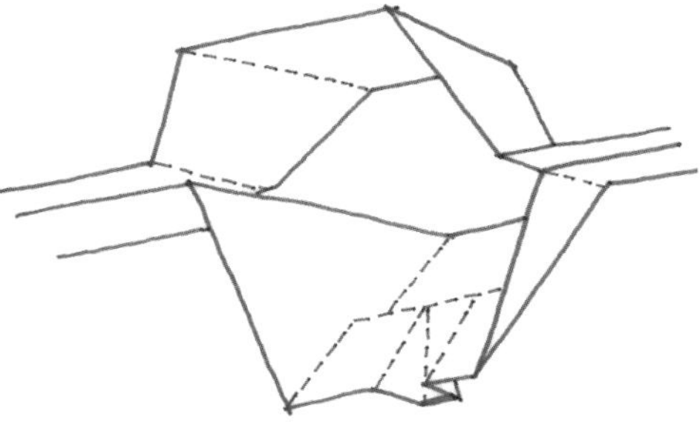
The overhang of the existing building is cut and folded down as the stairs.

The overarching desire to blur distinctions and to make different entities respond to one another leads to a particular design language in which cuts and folds are used to renegotiate the purpose of individual surfaces and to engage them in multiple ways.

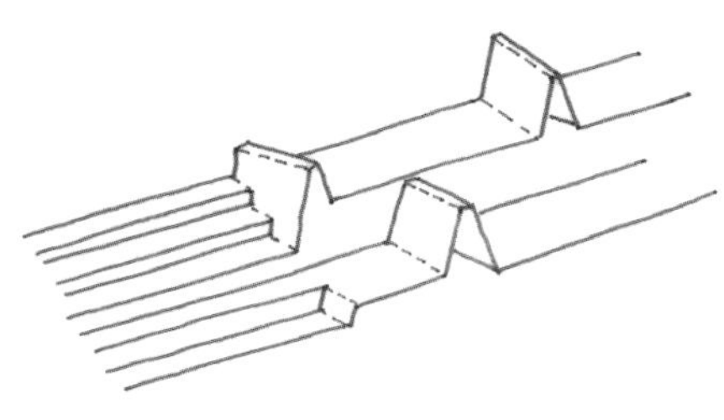
Cuts and folds also allow stairs to transform into benches.

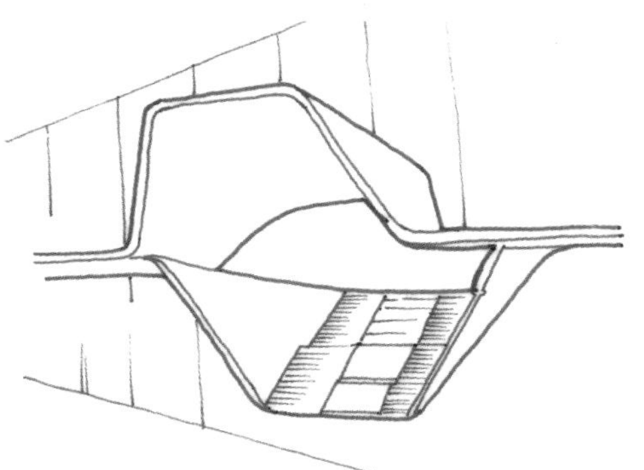

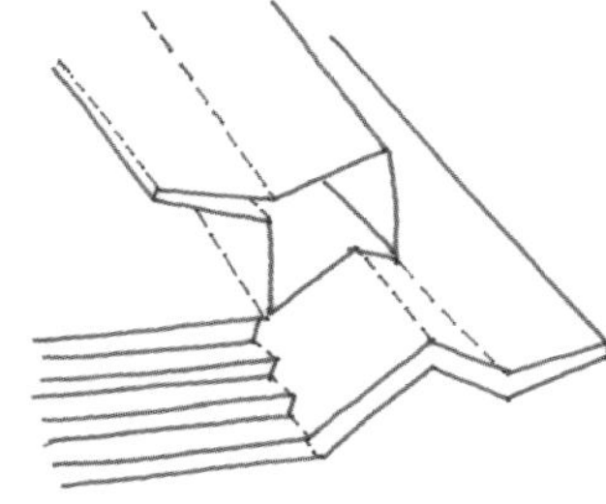

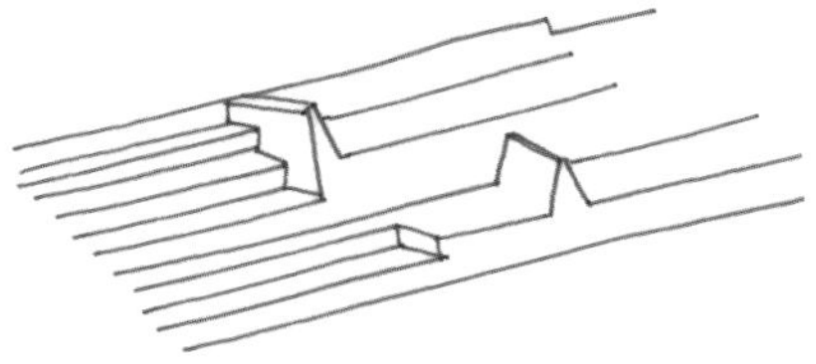
Walls, ceilings, floors, stairs and benches are no longer clearly delineated and one becomes the fold of another in a single continuous surface.

The combination of stairs and benches is particularly successful in the park bench/stairs developed for the open areas of the Lincoln Center. Here, the bottom step folds up to form a ground-level bench, which is further cut and folded to form a plinth-level bench.

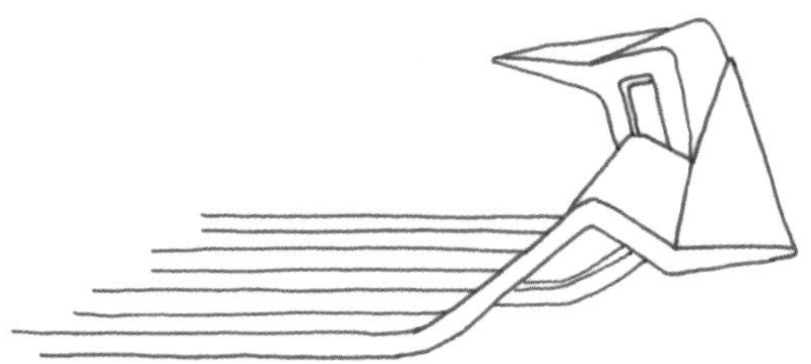

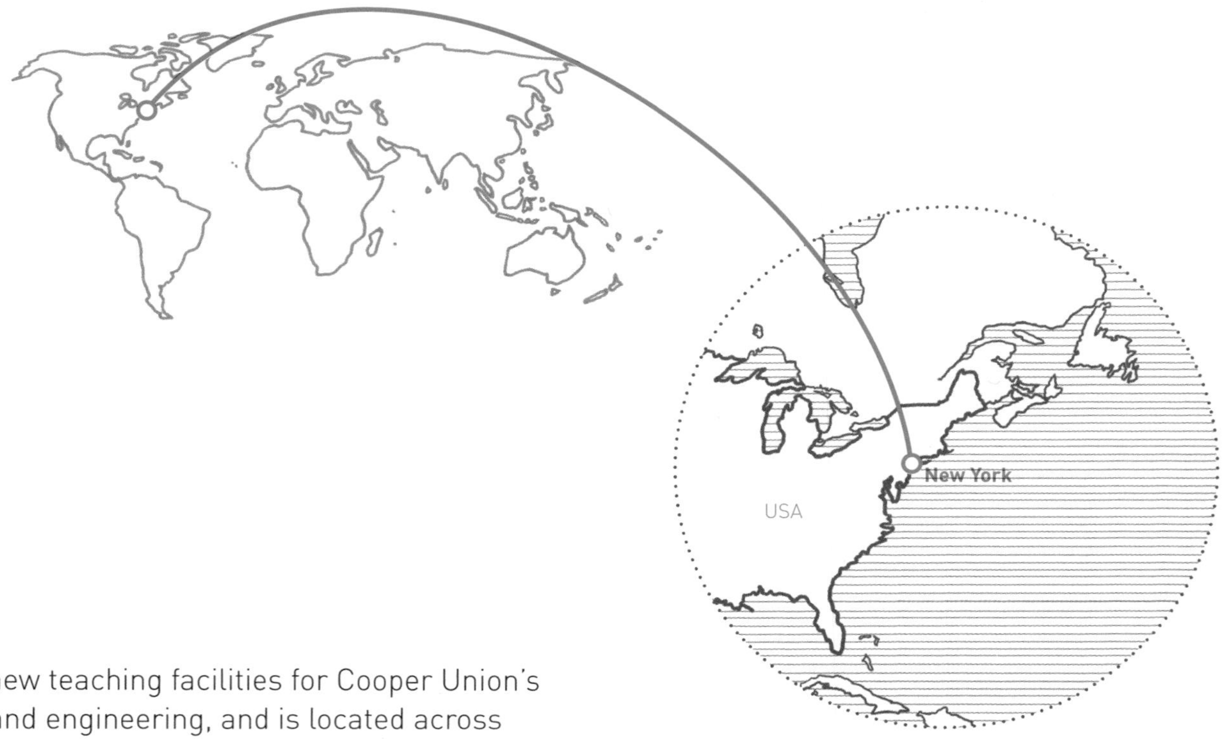

48

41 Cooper Square | 2004–9

Morphosis Architects
New York, USA

41 Cooper Square provides new teaching facilities for Cooper Union's schools of art, architecture and engineering, and is located across the street from the original Foundation Building and Cooper Square. The design by Thom Mayne of Morphosis Architects engages an architectural language of cuts and folds in order to respond to the larger urban context and help to develop a cohesive understanding of the entire institution. The language is continued inside, and a central atrium space is developed as a realm of public interaction that helps to tie together the three separate schools as a single entity. The end product contains some familiar and some unfamiliar volumes within a wrapper that warps and bends in response to the urban life around it.

Lewis Kevin Hardy Glastonbury, Blake Alexander and Amit Srivastava

48

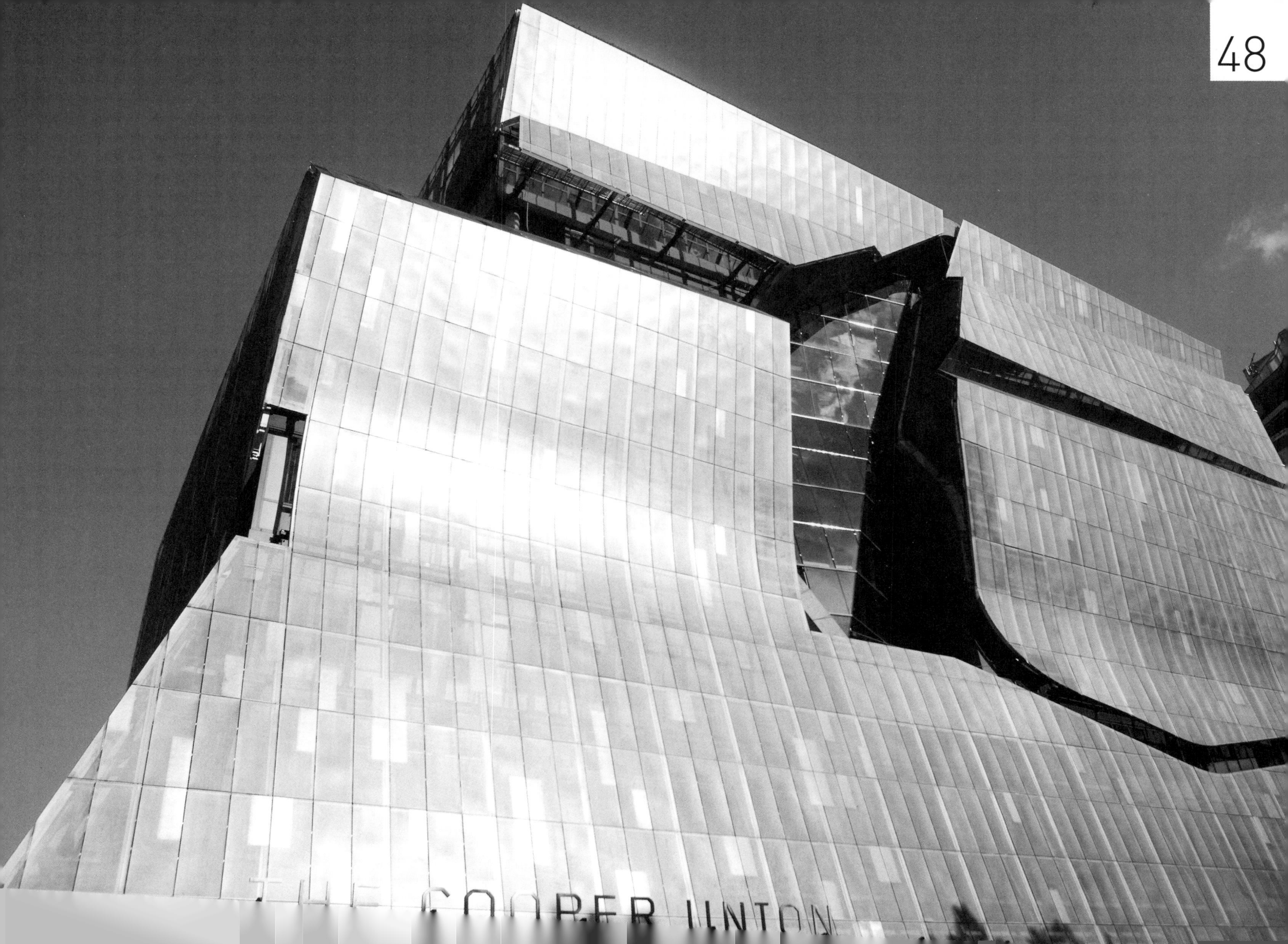

48

41 Cooper Square | 2004–9

Morphosis Architects

New York, USA

Response to Cooper Square site

As a part of the Cooper Union complex, the new academic building needed to respond to the Foundation Building of 1859 located across the street. The different architectural styles are obvious, but the new building maintains the massing and scale of the Foundation Building so as to make a cohesive experience of the entire complex, while new materials and technologies allow it to be a statement appropriate to its time.

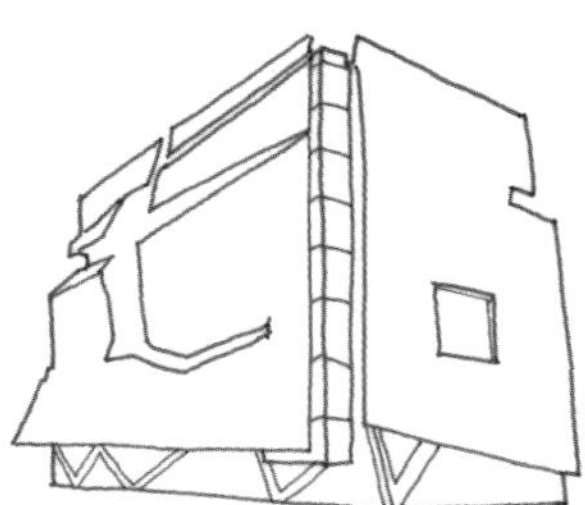

41 Cooper Square (2009)
New academic building

Cooper Union (1859)
Old Foundation Building

The façades of the two buildings have different treatments, which are responsive to their respective time and contexts.

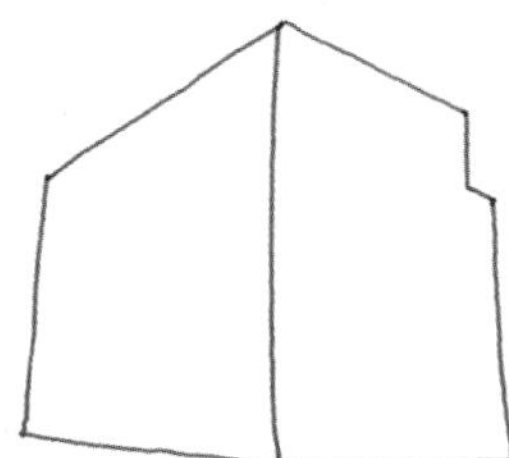

While a comparison of the two buildings exposes differences, they are very similar in massing and scale.

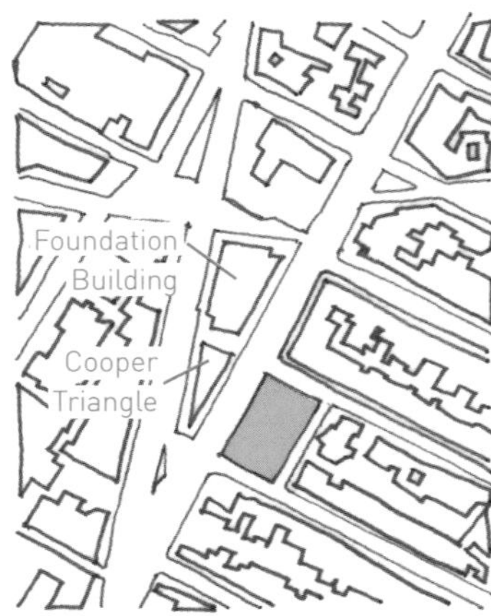

The site faces Cooper Triangle park in Lower Manhattan, and is surrounded by a range of old Neoclassical and new high-rise buildings.

Cooper Triangle and the Foundation Building, forming a sharp triangular shape, have a strong influence on the site. This is taken up in the design as an aggressive 'cut' into the façade. The 'cut' also allows the new building to open up and engage with the public square.

Response to surrounding context

The site is surrounded by buildings of different heights, making it difficult for the new development to sit harmoniously in its context. The broken façade allows the design to sit comfortably within the eclectic mix of low-rise and high-rise buildings, and helps to bind them together into a cohesive whole. The folds and cracks in the façade guide the sightline across the cityscape and connect the various neighbouring structures together.

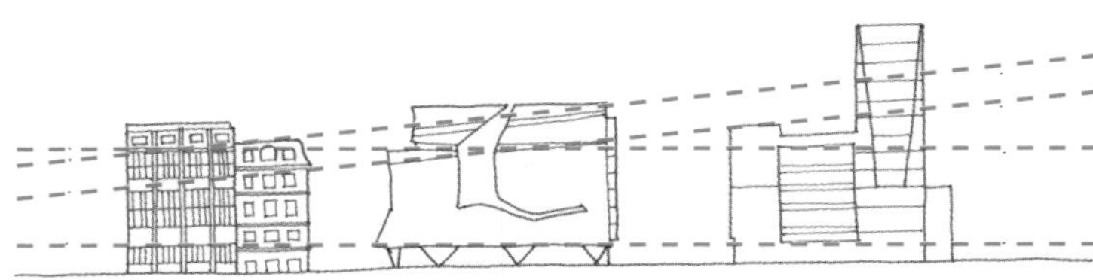

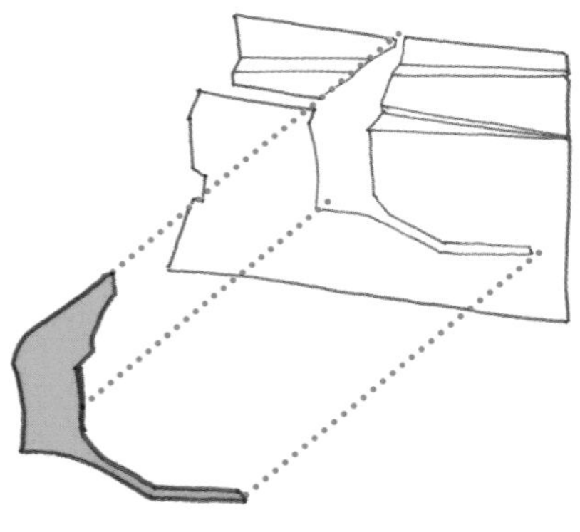

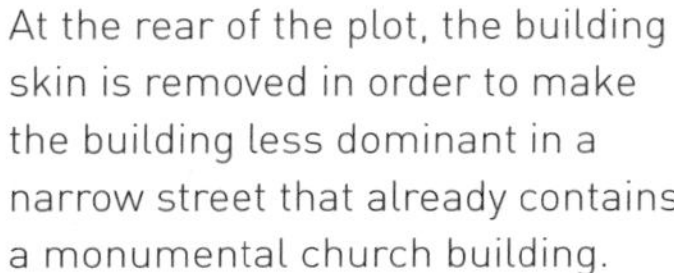

At the rear of the plot, the building skin is removed in order to make the building less dominant in a narrow street that already contains a monumental church building.

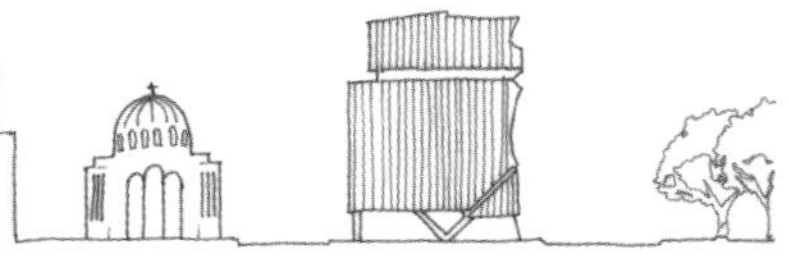

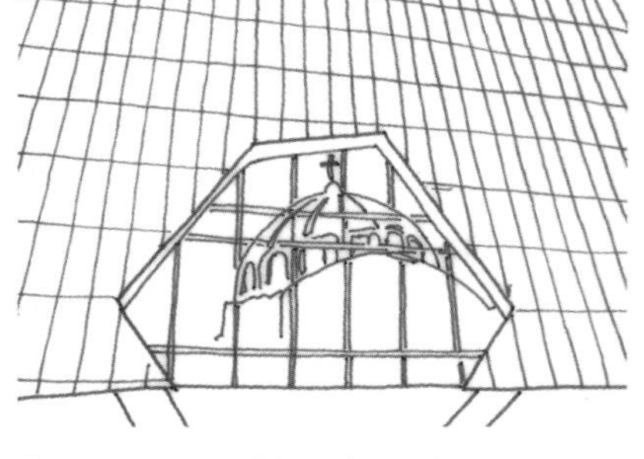

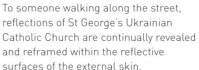

To someone walking along the street, reflections of St George's Ukrainian Catholic Church are continually revealed and reframed within the external skin.

Skin as external mediator

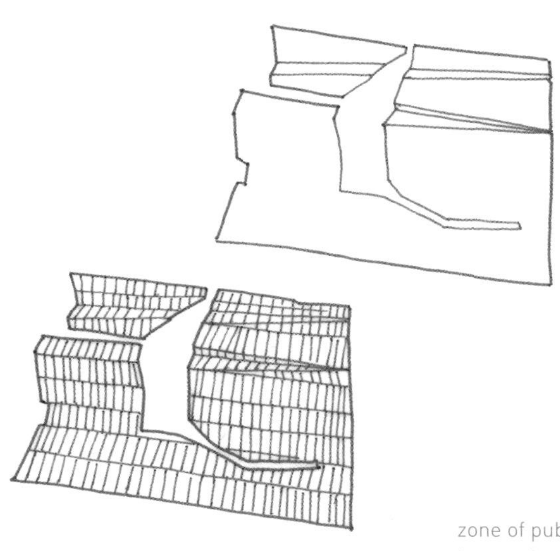

The ground floor of the new building allows for a zone of public interaction that opens up to the outside and blurs the strict boundary between the public and the private. This invitation to interact with the private space extends further into the external realm, where the angled columns and distorted glass walls convert the building into an urban playground.

Negotiating the social realm

The skin or building envelope is developed as a series of folds and cuts that respond to the energized city context and the public realm of Cooper Square. The façade is sculpted from a torus cut that corresponds to the flow of the public realm along Fourth Avenue, and the curve mediates the energy of the public realm by stepping back. The faceted mesh is an interference in this pattern in order to underscore the complex nature of public interaction.

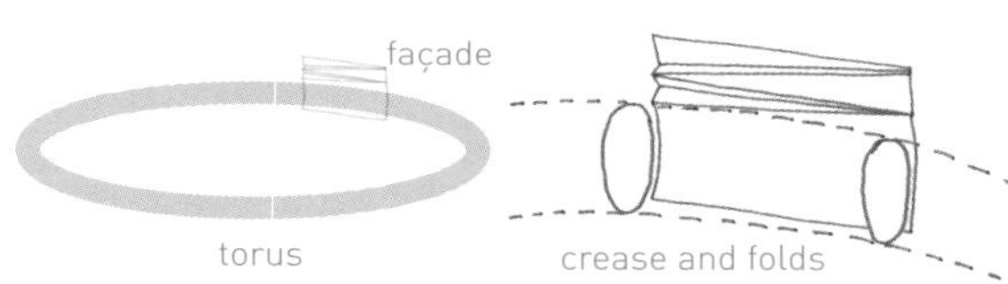

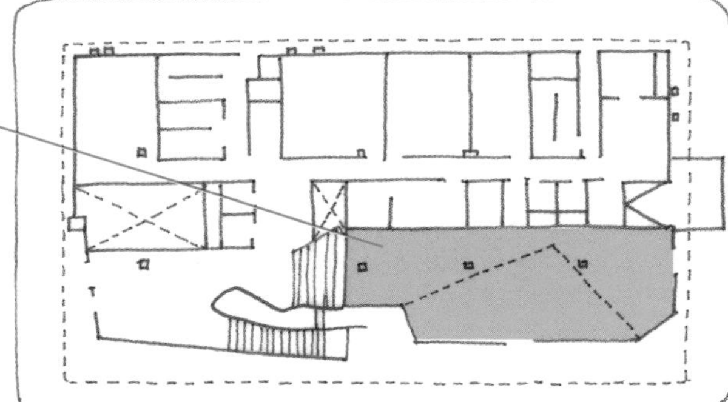

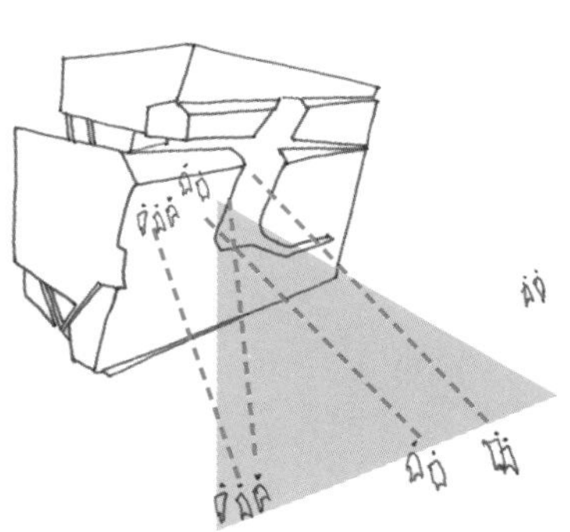

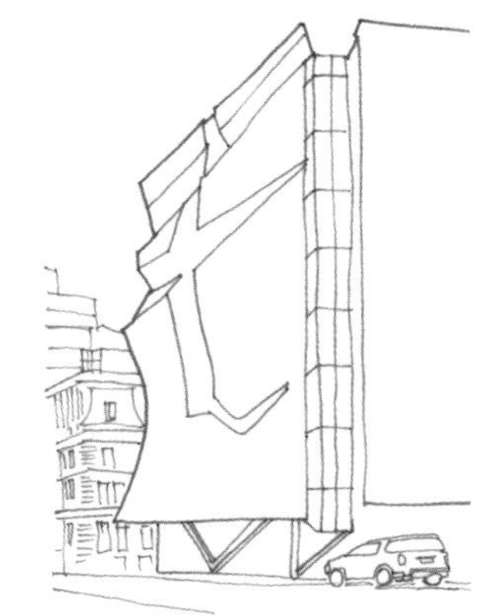

Visual connectivity

The building maintains visual connection with the street through its feature 'cut' façade and material transparency. This combination of literal and phenomenal transparency allows occupants to have a view of the outside and the public to have access to the semi-private realm. The blurring of boundaries between inside and outside reinforces the public nature of the institution and binds it to the social realm.

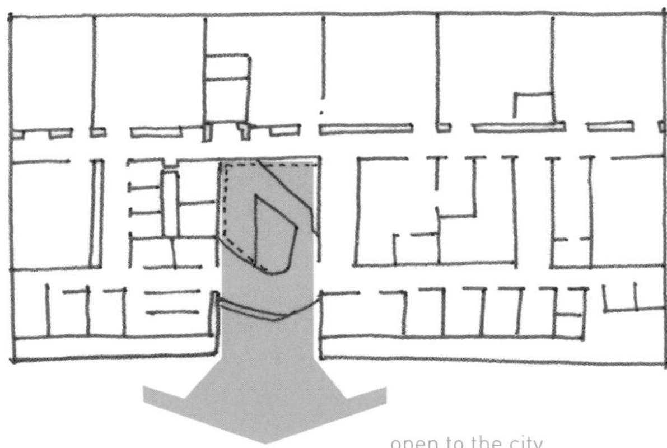

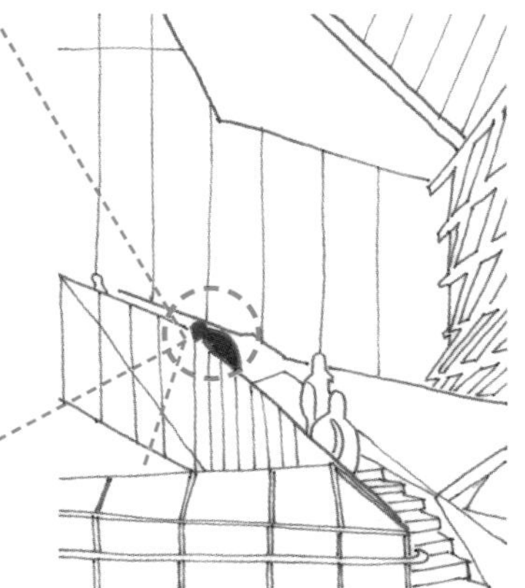

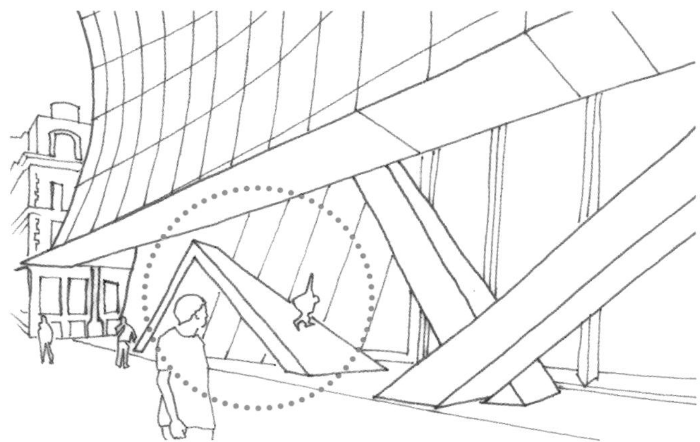

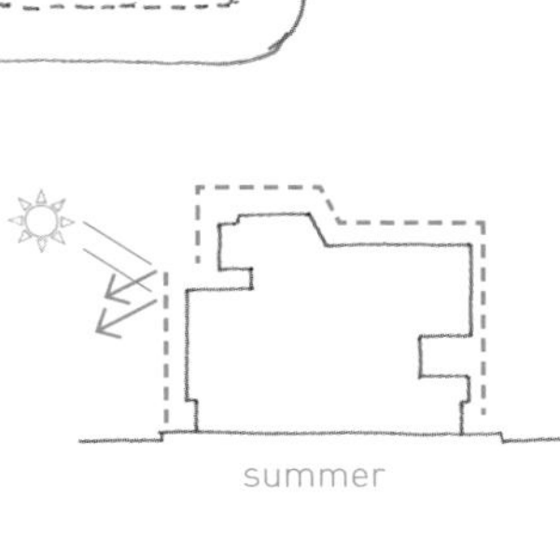

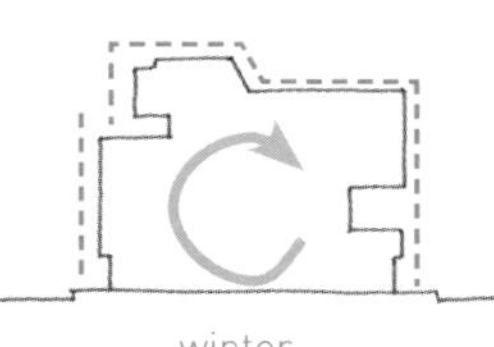

Response to climate

The double skin helps to mediate natural forces as well as social and cultural forces. The use of industrial materials combined with the architectonics of double-layered envelopes allows the building to moderate the gain and loss of heat over the summer and winter periods. The skin can halve summer heat gain and similarly helps to retain the heat produced in winter.

41 Cooper Square | 2004–9

Morphosis Architects
New York, USA

Response to programme

The intended programme was reconsidered and developed to promote cross-disciplinary exchange. The three schools of Art, Engineering and Architecture had previously operated as separate units. The new building houses them within a single envelope and uses the central staircase as a device to promote cross-disciplinary dialogue. Architect Louis Kahn once wrote about 'human institutions' and the desire to 'meet', explaining that learning extends beyond the classroom to corridors and in-between spaces that allow for chance encounters. The central staircase in the atrium at 41 Cooper Square acts as similar 'meeting place', a 'social heart' that promotes the overall cohesion of the student body by providing for such chance encounters.

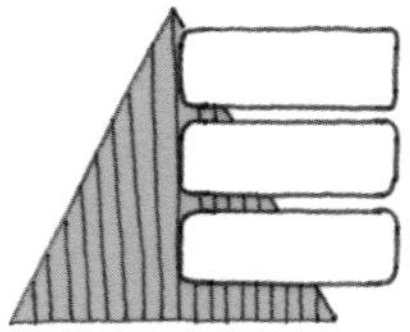

Original programme keeps disciplinary knowledge separate.

New programme allows for a cross-disciplinary institution.

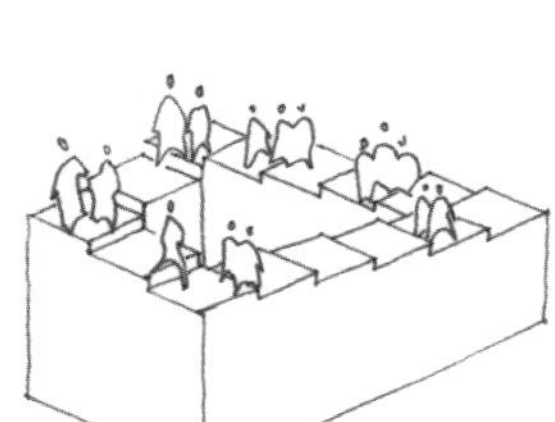

Separate disciplinary entities lead to a non-active corridor.

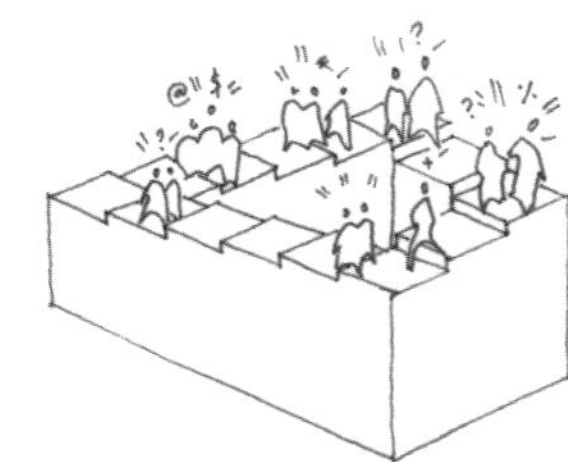

Cross-disciplinary programme leads to a reactive 'meeting place'.

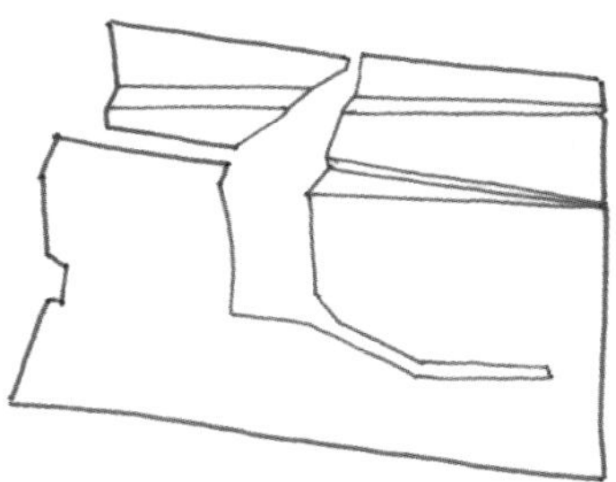

The 'cut' in the external façade is developed as a result of internal 'cuts'.

Skin as internal mediator

The design of the exterior skin closely responds to the development of the interior spaces, particularly in relation to the atrium that serves as the 'social heart' of the institution. The various volumetric cuts to accommodate the programme or the skylight are mimicked on the exterior façade, allowing the internal programme and the exterior envelope to be bound together in the design process and be developed as a cohesive whole. This responsiveness also extends to other aspects of the programme.

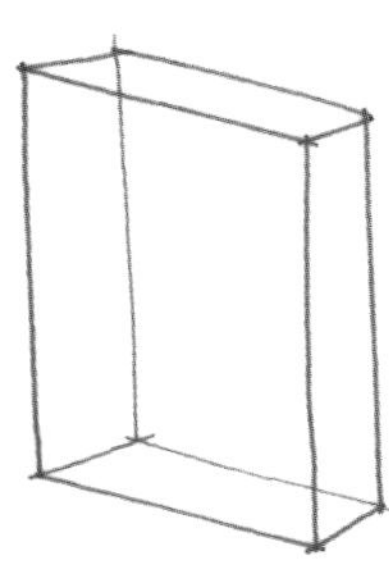

Original volume

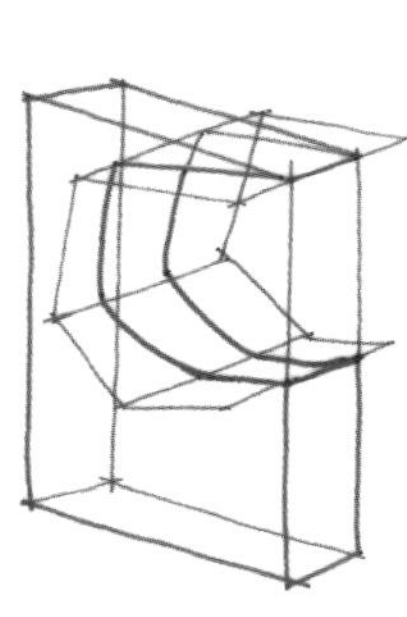

Programme cut

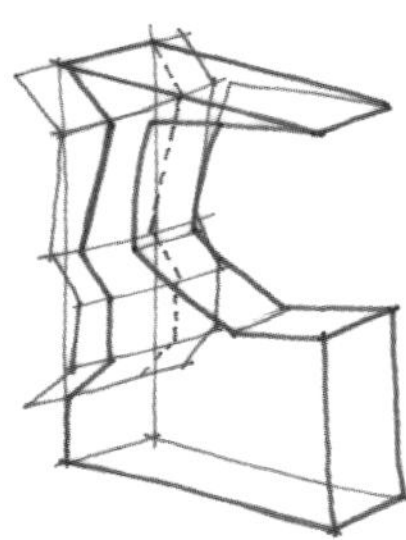

Skylight and bridge

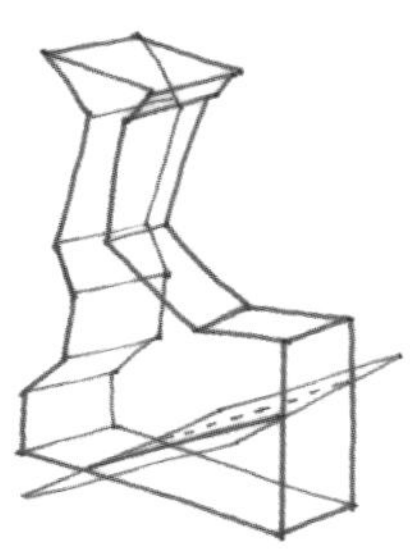

Grand stairs

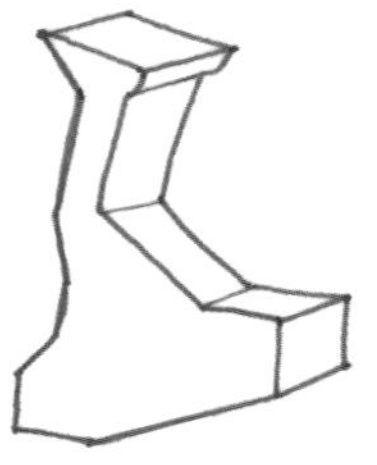

Final form

The programme and the envelope

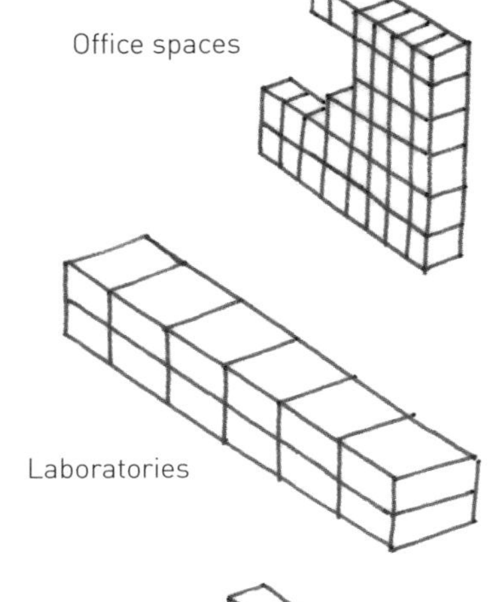

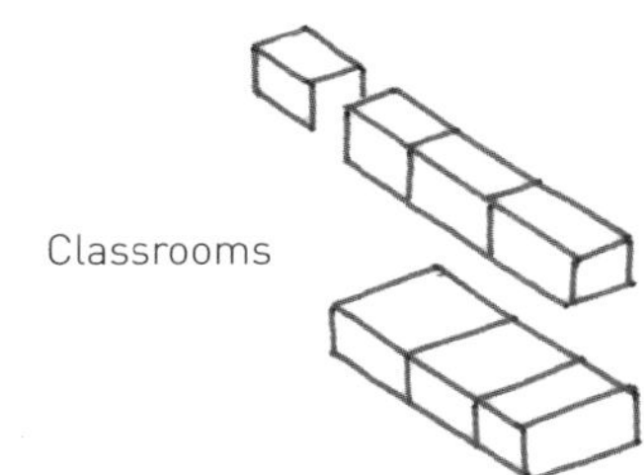

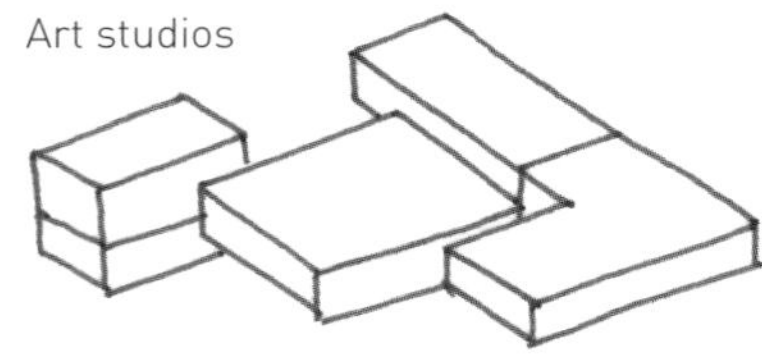

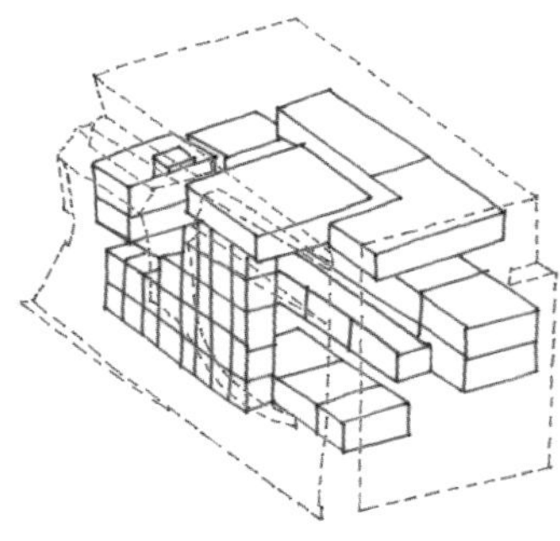

The various programmatic requirements are placed together in a manner that allows for internal cohesion between functions.

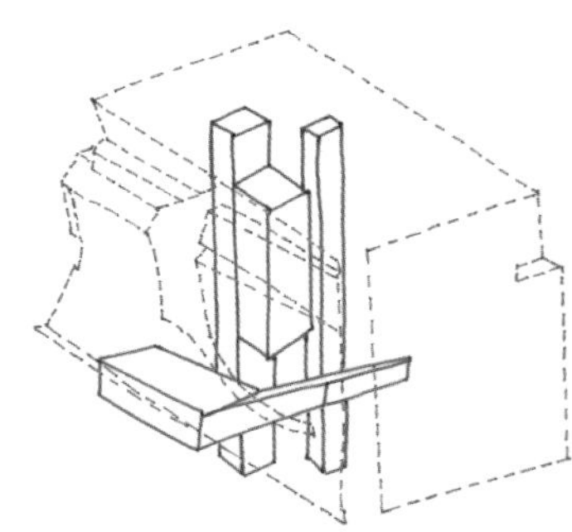

The atrium staircase provides an alternative to lifts.

Circulation and the envelope

The circulation within the building serves to tie the various programmatic elements together and allows the building to function as a single whole. The vertical circulation is designed around the atrium and the proximity allows for the stairs to be used as a preferred alternative to lifts. The circulation along the various floors is organized as a loop that works in response to this central atrium staircase, providing a sense of orientation in relation to the whole.

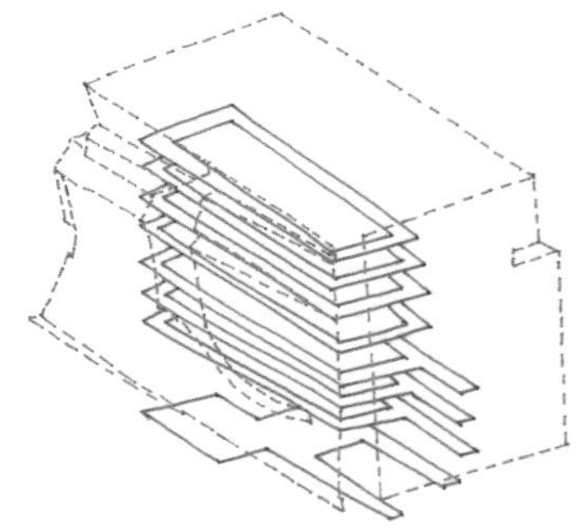

The planar circulation is organized as a loop around the central atrium staircase.

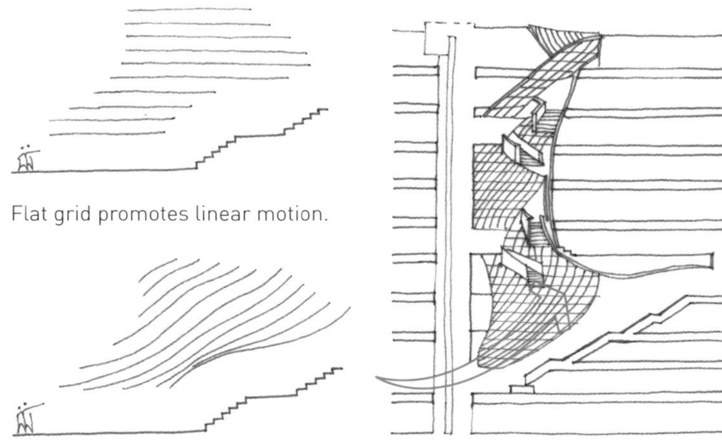

Flat grid promotes linear motion.

A curved lattice guides the eye upwards through the atrium.

The four-storey atrium creates a grand and dramatic volume.

The idea of engaging the central atrium and staircase as a social gathering and meeting space is developed through an understanding of the human scale. The transition from a low-height entrance area to a huge atrium over a short distance is a dramatic and engaging experience. This transition in scale is enhanced by the use of a curved and distorted lattice structure that envelopes the central atrium and guides the eye of the visitor. The experience of entering a larger and more dynamic space of human interaction is maintained in the development of the plan form, where the gradually widening staircase acts as a net and draws people into its folds.

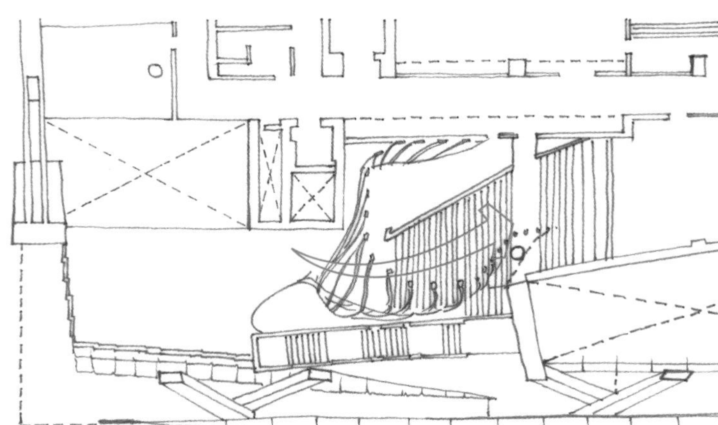

The central atrium staircase gradually widens out, drawing people in.

User experience

The various elements come together to create a new public space within the heart of the building. The central staircase as a gathering space replicates the scale and feel of established precedents in the city, such as the New York Public Library and Columbia University. The enclosing mesh that surrounds this space seems distorted and confusing at first, but the complexity of its form is vital to the performance of the space for public gathering, since it encourages people to pause and engage with the place rather than promoting a disengaged passage.

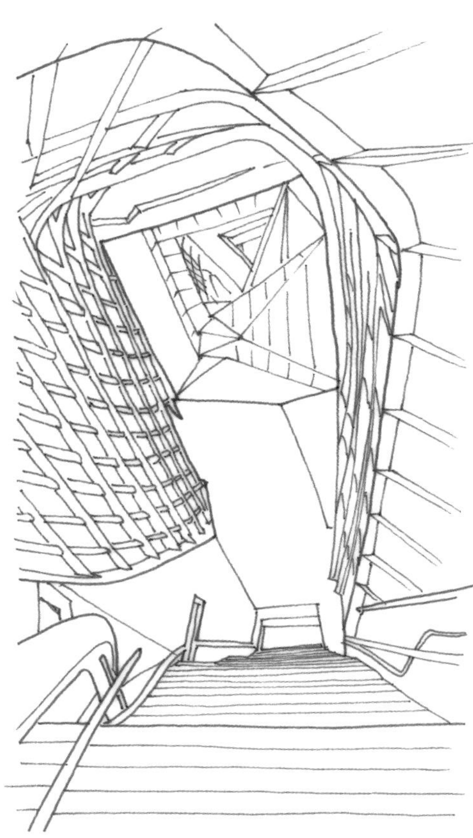

The distorted mesh binds the central atrium.

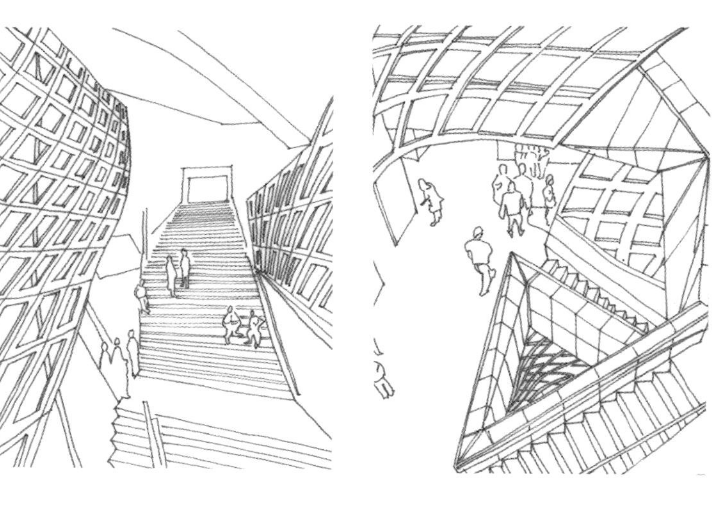

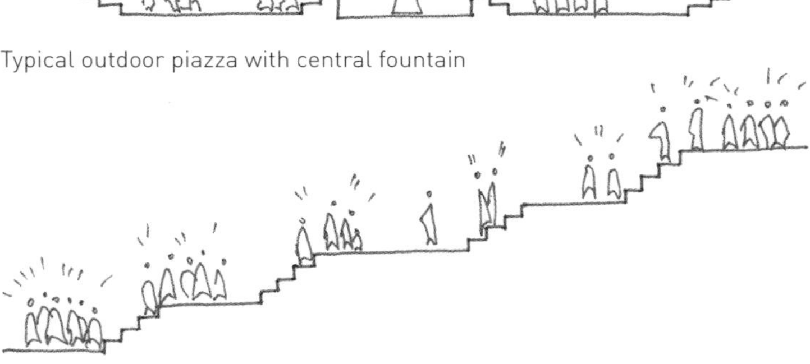

Typical outdoor piazza with central fountain

A vertical piazza acting as a stage for human interaction

The central atrium staircase replicates the precedent of a public piazza, which has been the basis of human gathering space for hundreds of years. The width of the staircase allows it to be used as more than a passageway, and the steps act as seating or a platform for discussions. The visual connectivity along the various levels means that the experience of seeing others encourages greater participation, and the space can be a realm for public debate.

The distorted mesh in the background serves a similar purpose as the central fountain in a typical piazza, helping the various user groups to orient themselves in relation to the other functions of the building complex.

49

Oslo Opera House | 2002–8

Snøhetta

Oslo, Norway

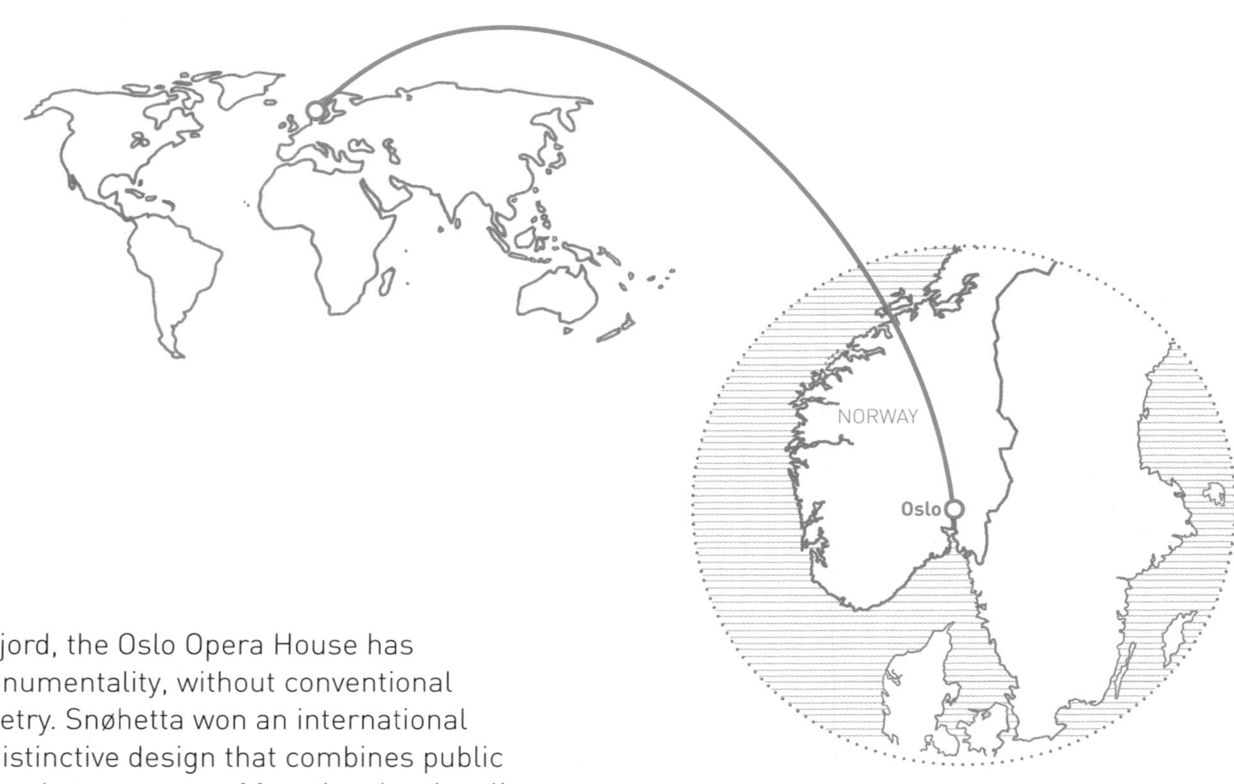

Like a pristine iceberg in a fjord, the Oslo Opera House has presence, even a kind of monumentality, without conventional devices of height and symmetry. Snøhetta won an international competition in 2002 with a distinctive design that combines public areas of lyrical beauty with backstage areas of functional rationality.

This is an inclusive building, an expression of Norwegian ideals as well as of place and culture. Anyone is welcome to explore the landscape of its roof, ponder views over the fjord and sunbathe on its slopes on a warm summer day, when the white marble paving sparkles and shimmers along with the rippling sea. Like the steps and promenades of Jørn Utzon's Opera House in Sydney's harbour on the other side of the world, Snøhetta's building has become a not-to-be-missed destination for tourists.

Antony Radford, Richard Le Messeurier, Jessica O'Connor and Enoch Liew Kang Yuen

49

Oslo Opera House | 2002–8

Snøhetta

Oslo, Norway

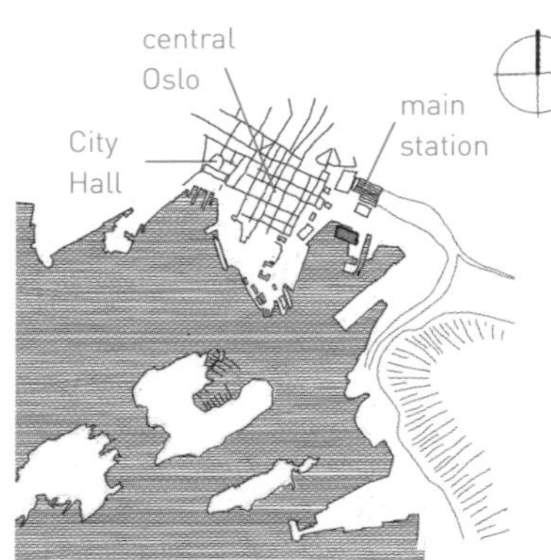

Context

Oslo is a city of bays, islands and promontories between mountains at the jagged end of a fjord that cuts deep into the south of Norway. The Bjorvika area east of central Oslo has been reconnected with this fjord by directing traffic through a tunnel and replacing its barren asphalt with pedestrian plazas and promenades. The Opera House is a focus for this new area of cultural development.

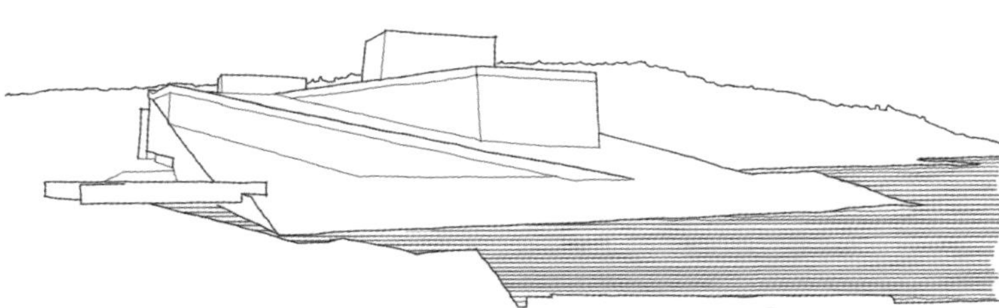

From the land, the broken mass and slope towards the fjord respond to the hills behind. In winter, both hills and building are draped in snow and the sharp angles of the building's faces echo shards of ice floating on the sea.

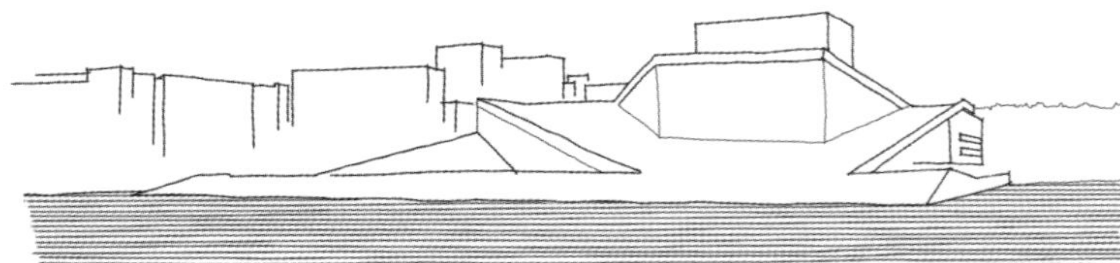

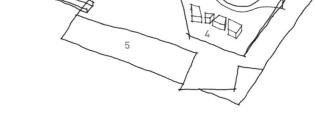

From the sea or from the shores of the bay to east and west, the slope from horizontal sea to the stage tower, upper foyer and blocky back of the building makes a transition to the rectilinear masses of the city backdrop.

Despite these responses to its urban and natural contexts, the building still looks as if it could float away, like the ferry to Copenhagen that moors nearby.

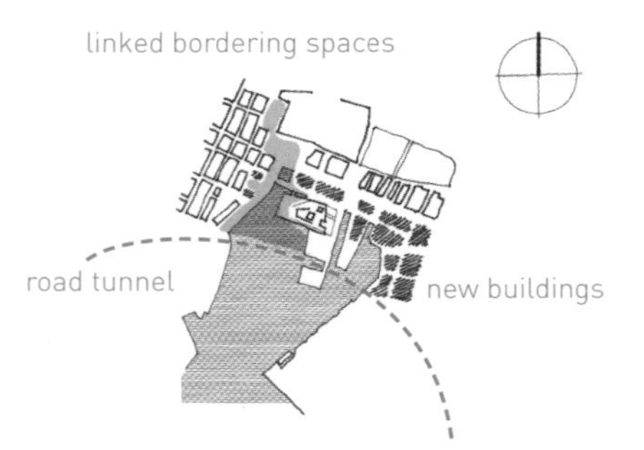

Key

1. subtraction: the courtyard
2. extrusion: the stage tower
3. kernel: the horseshoe theatre
4. angular shards
5. landscape carpet
6. free-form wave wall
7. rectilinear factory

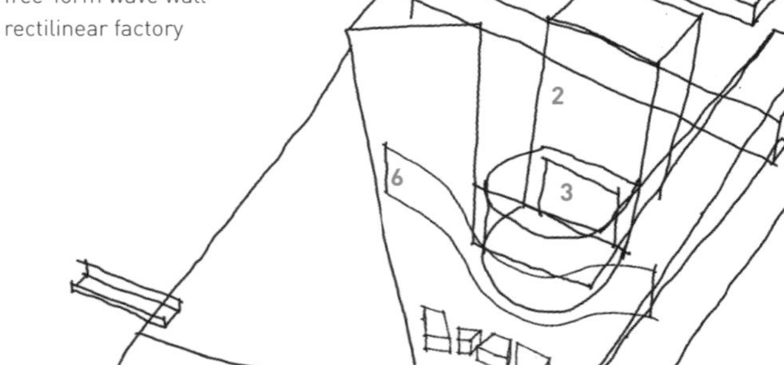

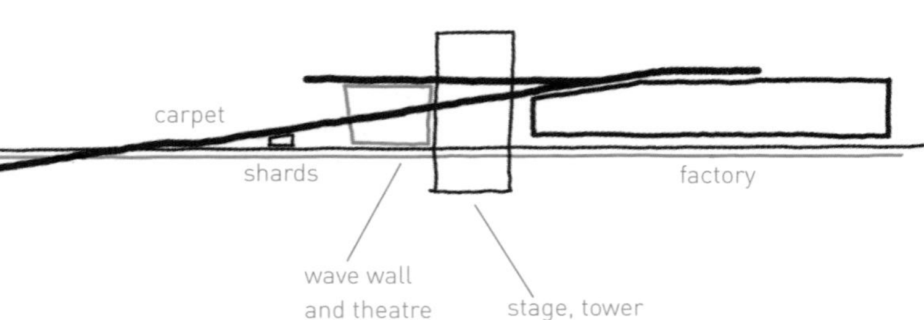

Components

The competition design, and the finished building, have three main components. The architects call these the wave wall, the factory and the carpet.

The wave wall is the edge between the open access and the ticketed parts of the opera house, a screen between the foyer and the auditorium. It also symbolizes an edge between sea and land, people and culture. The wall is not an oppressive barrier. It is softly curved, warm in tone and pierced by openings.

The factory is the production end of the building, where workshops, rehearsal rooms and offices are organized for efficiency in an economical rectilinear layout.

The carpet is the sculpted stone paving that is laid over much of the interior as a continuous surface from sea to roof. This is public space, transcending the division of the wall.

Under the low end of the carpet is a lesser fourth component: shards that occupy one edge of the foyer and contradict the softness of the wall.

These components are individually clear and assertive, yet they converse with one another in mutual responsive cohesion.

Planning
The building is split in two by a north–south corridor known as the 'opera street'. To the west are the public and stage areas. To the east are the production areas, the 'factory'.

The western part is split again by the wave wall that separates the foyer from the auditorium and stage.

The eastern part is split by a large east–west loading dock. On the north side are 'hard workshops' where scenery is made. Finished scenery is moved into the rear stage area through the loading dock. On the south side are smaller 'soft workshops' for costumes and make-up areas, plus administration and changing rooms. A courtyard lets light into this area, which the architects call a green lung deep inside the building.

The 'factory' has three to four storeys above ground and one basement level. The sub-stage area is a further three storeys deep, far below the surface of the fjord.

The main theatre seats approximately 1,370 in a classic horseshoe shape. An oval chandelier is made up of 5,800 hand-cast glass crystals through which 800 LED lights shine.

Built-in furniture is sculpted to respond to the building form.

Visitors arrive over a gangway, as if on to a ship.

Through the windows of the 'factory' can be seen the production processes inside: dancers rehearsing in upper-level rooms, workshops at street level.

There is direct access from ground and basement floors to the courtyard garden. This is a composition of timber decking, white marble and greenery, with a marble-clad stair connecting the two levels. Grasses, climbing plants and perennials are planted around clusters of cables, reaching up to the upper levels and providing shade to the façades.

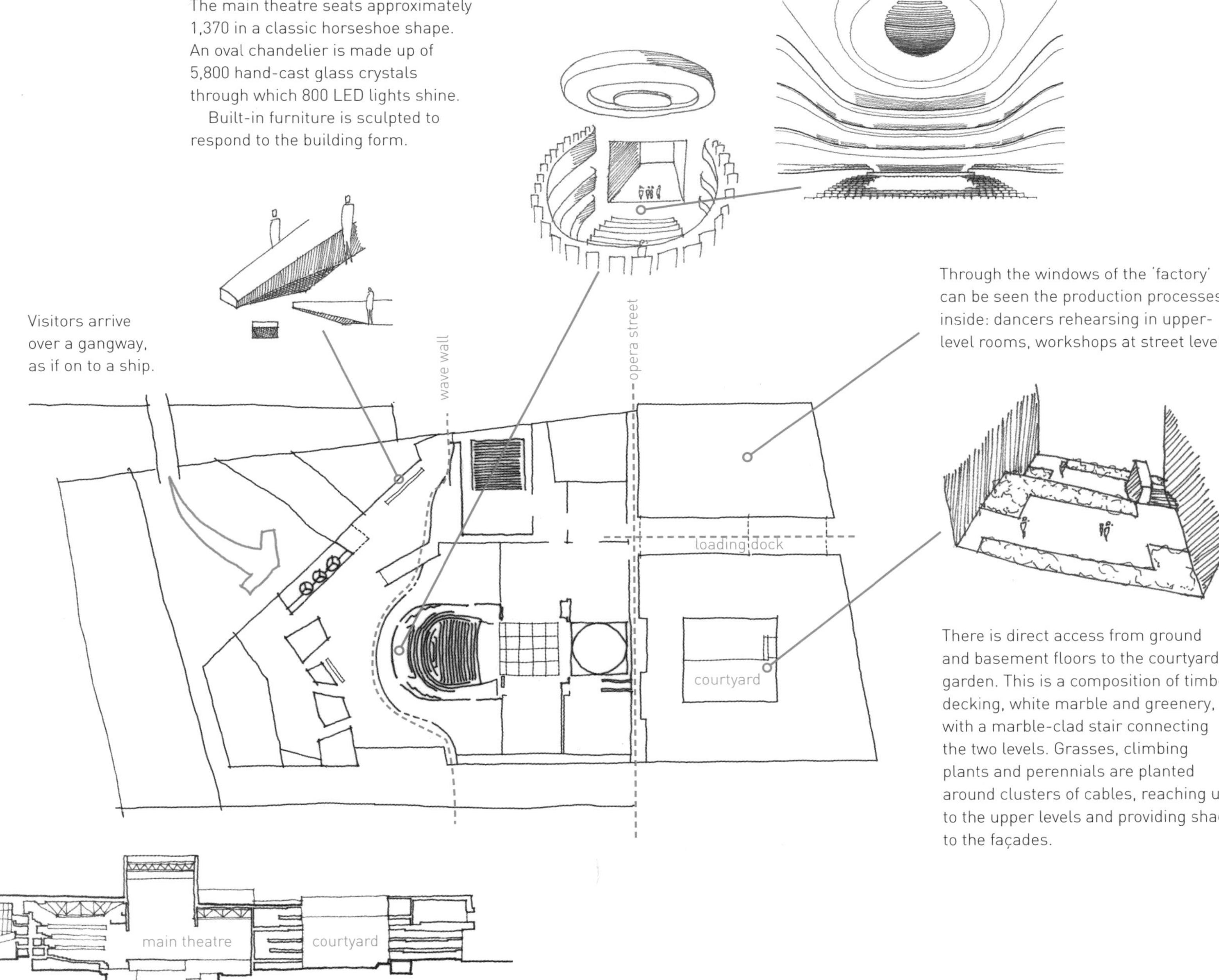

49

Oslo Opera House | 2002–8
Snøhetta
Oslo, Norway

Intermediate space
Visitors pass under a low-ceilinged doorway and then a lower edge zone before experiencing the full height of the intermediate space between the edge of the auditorium and its enclosing shelter.

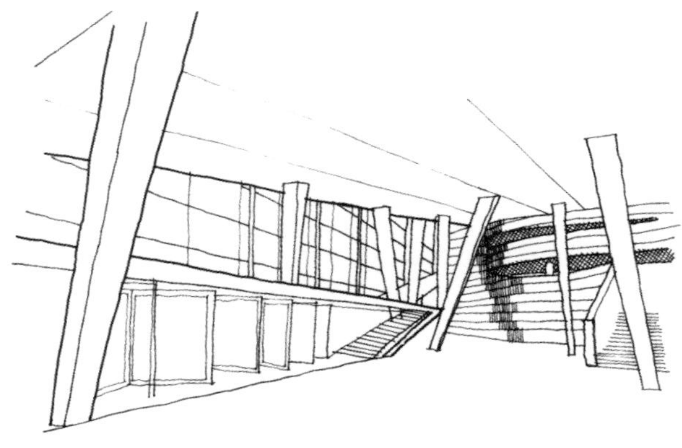

From this entrance visitors see the warm, wood surfaces of the wave wall on the left and the cold, angular edges of the slanting columns, glass wall and screens on the right.

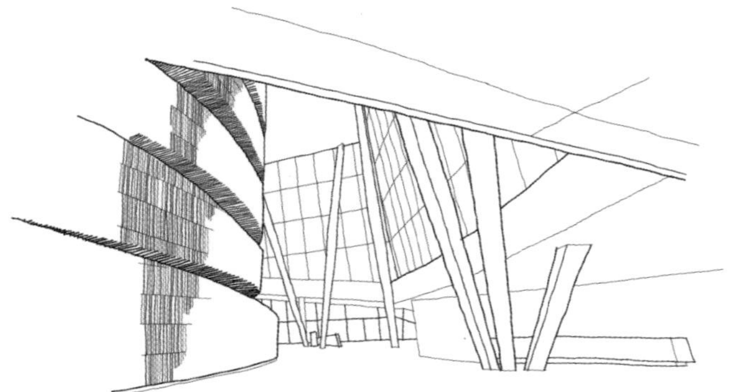

The slot between the balustrade and the ceiling of the balconies leading to the auditorium frames a panorama of the waterfront, seen through the glass walls of the foyer.

Glass The glass wall of the upper foyer is up to 15m (49ft) high. Laminated glass fins have minimal steel fixings sandwiched inside them. The glass has low iron content so it is clear, avoiding the greenish tones that are typical of thick glass.

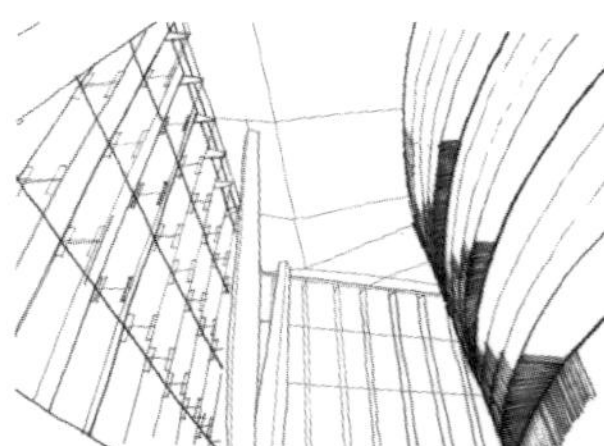

Wood The surface of the wave wall is a light and highly textured collage of strips of oak of various cross-sections, to deal with the curves and provide acoustic attenuation in a foyer where most surfaces are flat and hard. The auditorium interior is clad in oak treated with ammonia to give it a dark tone.

Stairs leading up to the auditorium appear as an outgrowth from the wave wall, with the same wood cladding.

Being behind the wave wall has been likened to being inside a violin. All the surfaces are wood. Lighting is indirect, gaining warmth from its reflection off wall and floor surfaces.

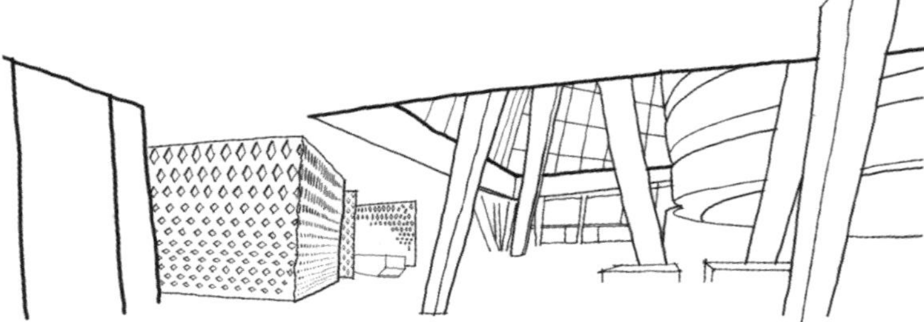

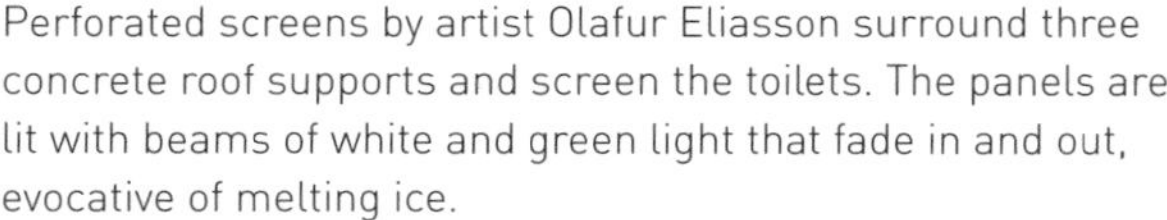

Perforated screens by artist Olafur Eliasson surround three concrete roof supports and screen the toilets. The panels are lit with beams of white and green light that fade in and out, evocative of melting ice.

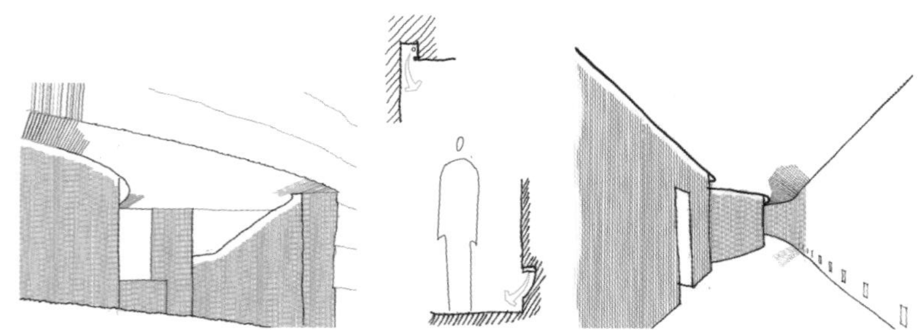

Public landscape
Designed by artists Kristian Blystad, Kalle Grude and Jorunn Sannes, the marble slabs form a complex, non-repetitive pattern of cuts, ledges, and textures.

The tower over the stage pushes through the 'carpet'. The paving is set back, leaving a slot around the bottom of the walls.

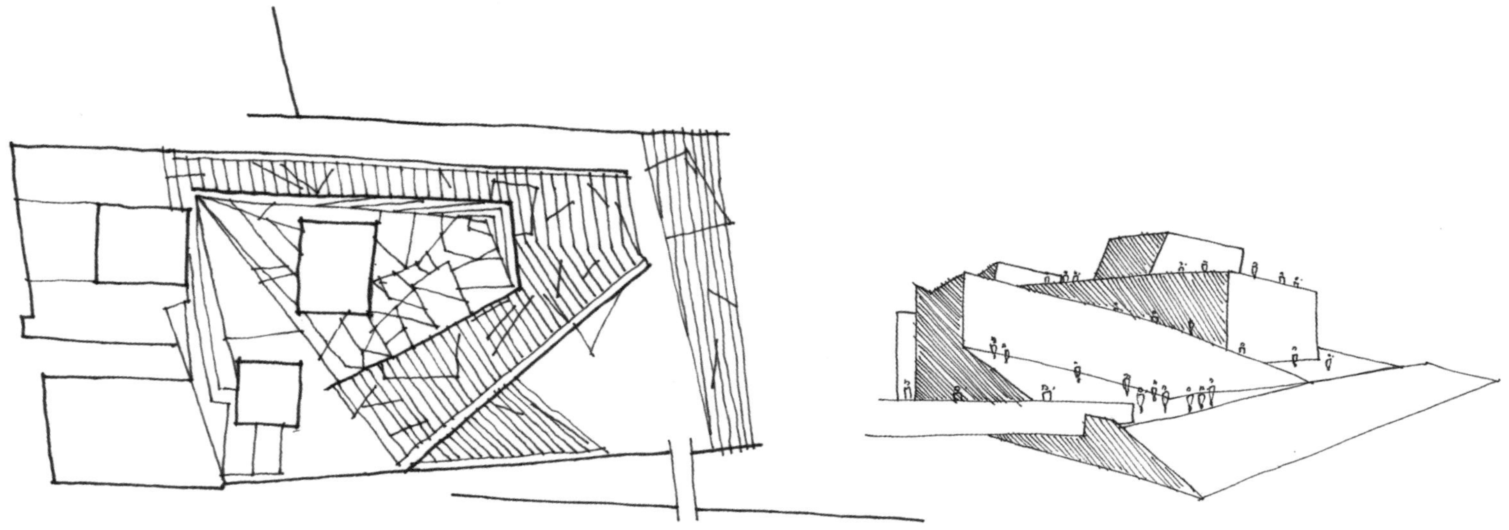

Stone The 'carpet' is paved in a white Italian marble from the La Facciata quarry. It looks good in sunlight and under a grey Oslo sky, and retains its brilliance and colour when wet.

Most of the paving is textured, but ledges are smooth, and subtle changes of level cast shadows across the surface.

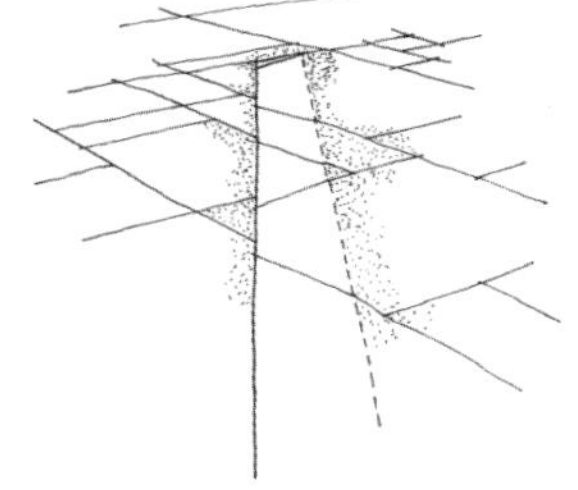

Metal External walls of the stage tower (and of the 'factory') are clad in panels of pressed aluminium sheet, chosen for aesthetics and longevity. In collaboration with artists Astrid Løvaas and Kirsten Wagle, the panels were punched with convex spherical segments and concave conical forms in a pattern based on old weaving techniques. Their appearance changes with the angle, intensity and colour of the light playing on their surfaces.

Ramps and steps recessed in channels along the roof edges allow balustrades to meet regulation height requirements without them appearing above the rising line of the roof. There are no handrails dividing the surface.

A background of bright white marble makes people and their colourful clothes stand out. Their movement animates the scene.

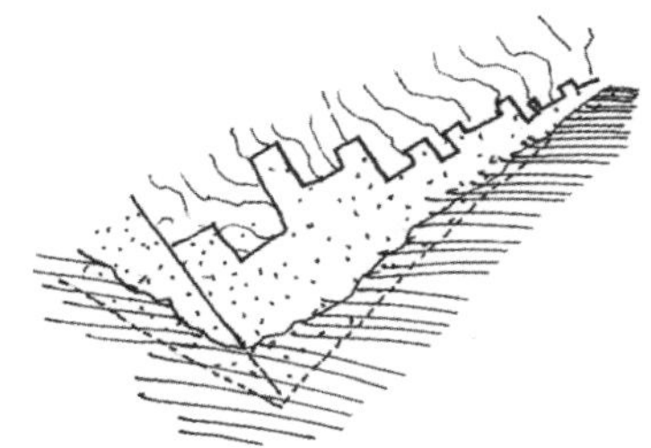

Where the paving meets the ocean, marble gives way to grey-brown Norwegian granite. The transition is a stepped line where slabs of granite interleaf with slabs of marble.

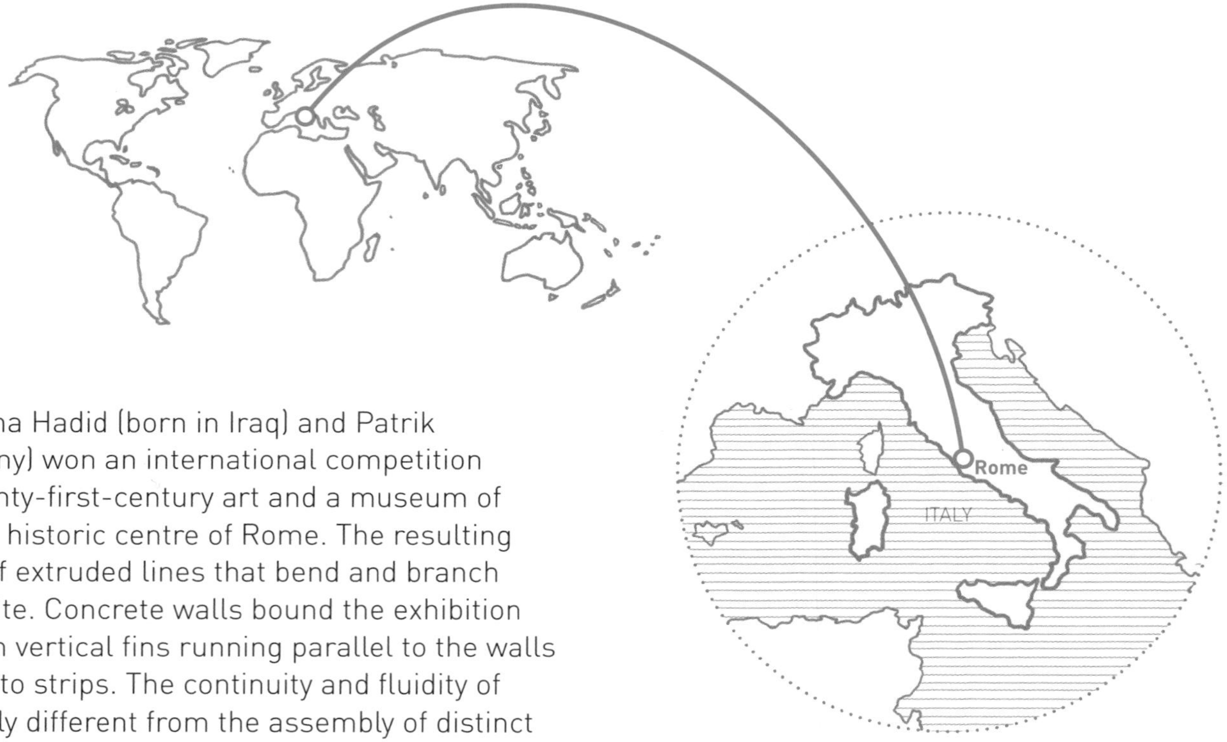

50 MAXXI | 1998–2009
Zaha Hadid Architects
Rome, Italy

London-based architects Zaha Hadid (born in Iraq) and Patrik Schumacher (born in Germany) won an international competition in 1998 for a museum of twenty-first-century art and a museum of architecture, just outside the historic centre of Rome. The resulting MAXXI museum is an array of extruded lines that bend and branch around an L-shaped urban site. Concrete walls bound the exhibition galleries. Between them, thin vertical fins running parallel to the walls divide the transparent roof into strips. The continuity and fluidity of this composition are markedly different from the assembly of distinct spaces that characterizes most buildings.

The MAXXI reveals itself gradually. It peeks over the wall on the north side, and squeezes around both sides of an old building on the south side. The entrance is withdrawn, under cantilevered volumes and behind screening columns. Once inside there are choices – the building has continuity, but there is no single obvious route. It has been called a field rather than an object. Like pathways in an Italian medieval hill town, there are narrow spaces, ramps and steps, long and short views, and wider places formed where galleries split.

Antony Radford, Natasha Kousvos and Lana Greer

Rome
ITALY

50

MAXXI | 1998–2009
Zaha Hadid Architects
Rome, Italy

Response to site
The project echoes the low-level, repetitive urban texture of the former army barracks that still occupy neighbouring sites, but rises to match the higher apartment blocks that line nearby streets. It hugs the southern and western edges of the L-shaped site, aligned with the urban grid of the block in which it is situated. Beyond the northern edge of the site the urban grid angles at 51 degrees. The building overlays this different grid, and the difference is mediated with curves. The highest gallery in the building aligns with the angled grid.

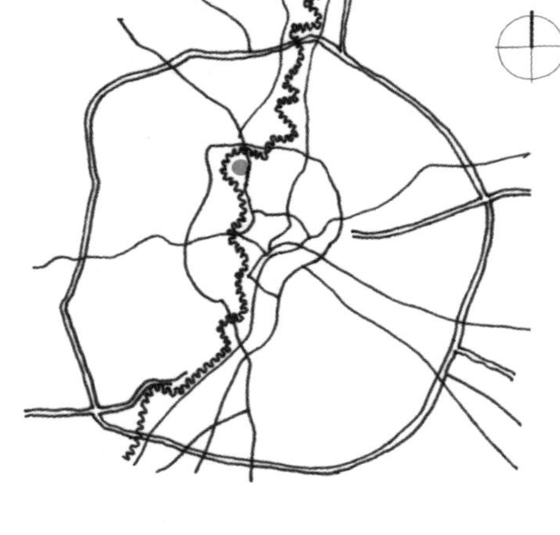

Flaminio district

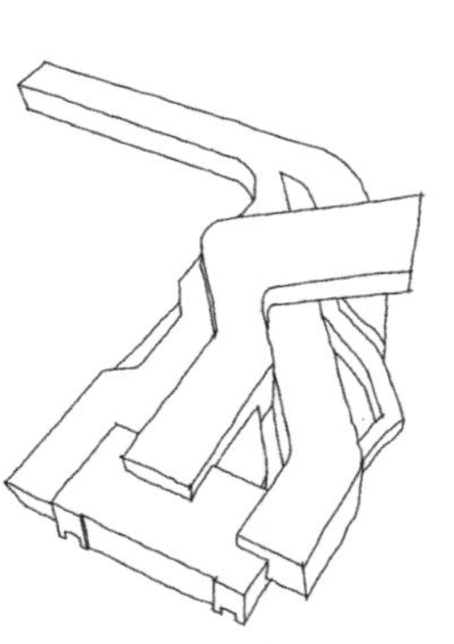

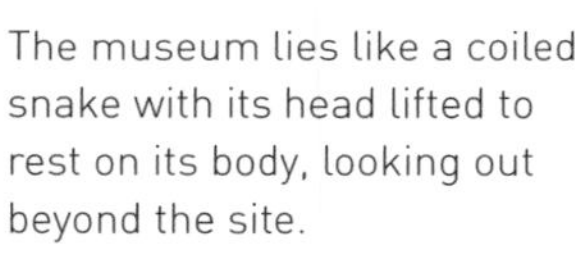

The museum lies like a coiled snake with its head lifted to rest on its body, looking out beyond the site.

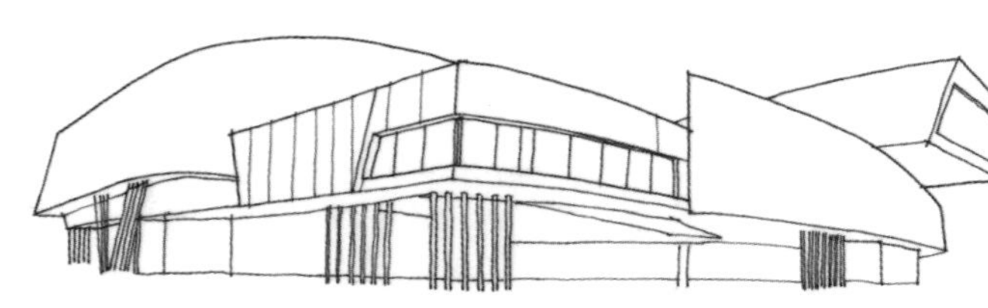

Looking along Via Guido Reni to the south, the streetscape is unchanged save for the new building peering over and around a retained building from the old barracks.

Looking west along Via Masaccio to the north, a wide window at the end of the top gallery peers over the boundary wall.

Structure and construction

Construction and technology are hidden behind wall and ceiling linings, keeping the form uncluttered. The basic structure is reinforced-concrete walls cast in place, supporting transverse steel beams. Thin trusses span between these transverse beams, parallel to the concrete walls and clad with a thin GRC (glass-fibre-reinforced concrete) shell. These make the array of sinuous fins that characterize the ceilings. The internal wall surface is white-painted plasterboard.

steel grating solar shading/walkway
sun filter glazing
line of fluorescent lamp
internal glazing
adjustable aluminium louvres
2.2m- (7.2ft-) deep steel trusses

Continuous rooflights

Rooflights are shielded from direct sun by an external metal sunshade that is also a walkway for maintenance. An outer layer of glass screens out ultraviolet and other solar rays that can damage artworks. Under the glass, a combination of louvres, screening blinds and blackout blinds can be adjusted to vary the lighting conditions.

Artificial light fittings are recessed into the side of the fins so that natural and artificial light come from the same direction, above the louvres. Additional fittings can be attached to a track on the underside of the fins to target specific items.

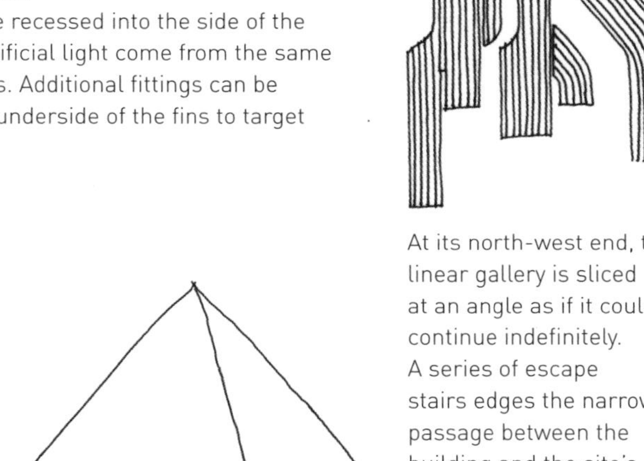

At its north-west end, the linear gallery is sliced at an angle as if it could continue indefinitely. A series of escape stairs edges the narrow passage between the building and the site's boundary wall.

The gallery entrance is recessed under projecting volumes and behind arrays of columns. The taller columns, supporting the upper floor, lean to the sides. A long window at the side and corner of the ramp to Gallery 3 allows those inside the building to see the forecourt and reorient themselves.

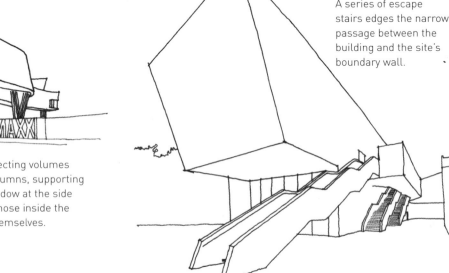

MAXXI | 1998–2009

Zaha Hadid Architects
Rome, Italy

Planning

On the ground floor the entrance area contains a reception desk at one end and a café at the other end. From reception there is direct access to the auditorium and shop, the gallery for temporary exhibitions and the sequence of main galleries. Gallery 1 next to the café houses the Museum of Architecture and its archives.

Gallery 1
the Architecture museum with three 'squeeze points' between sub-spaces

Gallery 2
160m (525ft) long, with a 39 degree bend

Gallery 3
on three levels linked by a ramp

Gallery 4
with a bifurcation

Gallery 5
at the top of the building, with two sections of sloping floor

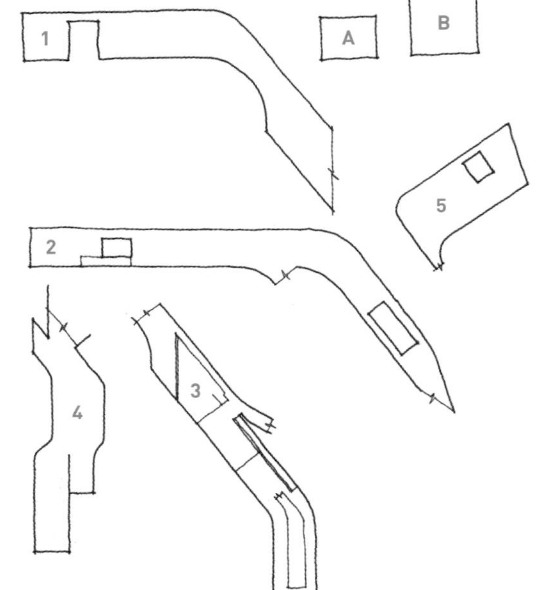

A. Gallery for print collection, in the old building

B. Gallery for temporary exhibitions, in the old building

If the galleries are extracted as separate spaces their shapes appear arbitrary. Visitors experience them as a sequence where boundaries are not important unless exhibition curators desire separation.

The thick external walls are layered to provide space for services.

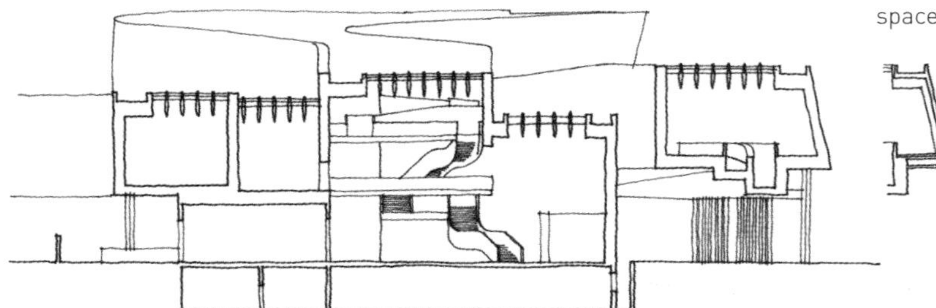

A section shows that the ground plane continues through the building and there is a lower basement level. The upper floors vary in levels, part of the ramp-and-platform system that rises through the building.

The glossy white reception desk is a ring of twisting surfaces. Only the desktop is planar. It is both an art object and a functional system.

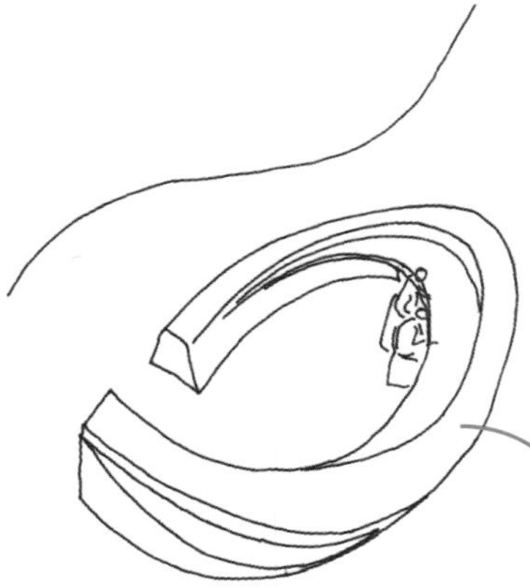

Key
1. Gallery 1
2. café
3. lecture room
4. shop
5. entry
6. prints
7. temporary exhibitions

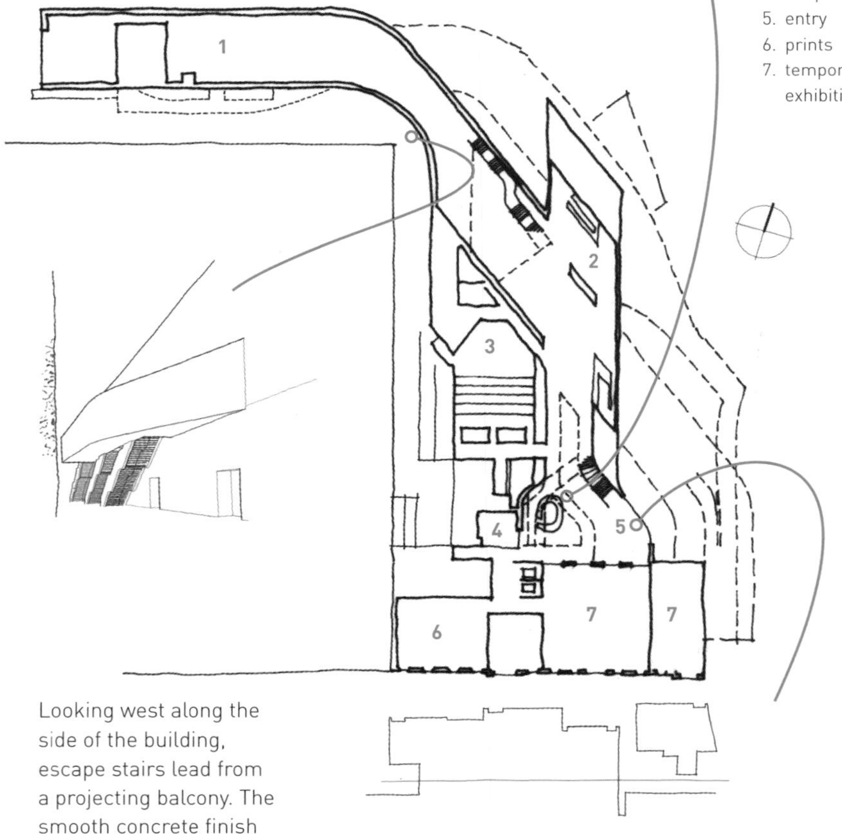

Looking west along the side of the building, escape stairs lead from a projecting balcony. The smooth concrete finish contrasts with the rough-finished render on the boundary wall.

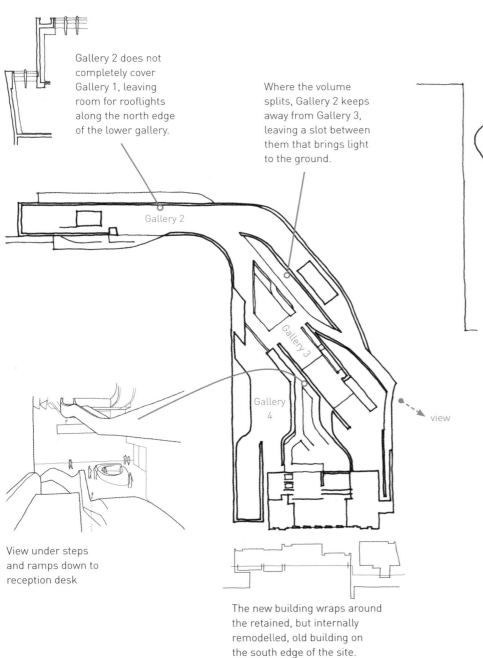

Gallery 2 does not completely cover Gallery 1, leaving room for rooflights along the north edge of the lower gallery.

Where the volume splits, Gallery 2 keeps away from Gallery 3, leaving a slot between them that brings light to the ground.

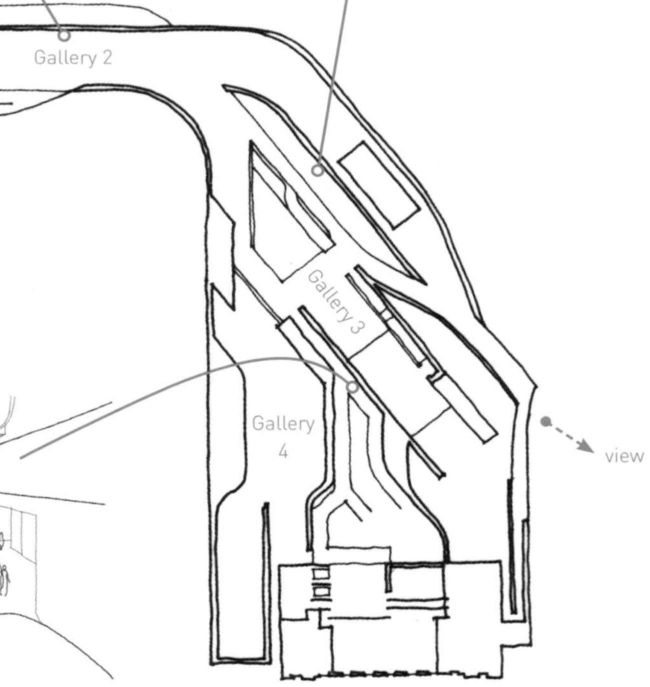

Gallery 2

Gallery 3

Gallery 4

view

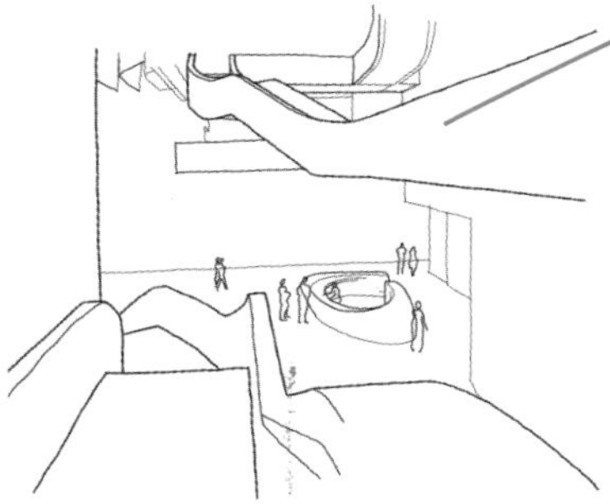

View under steps and ramps down to reception desk

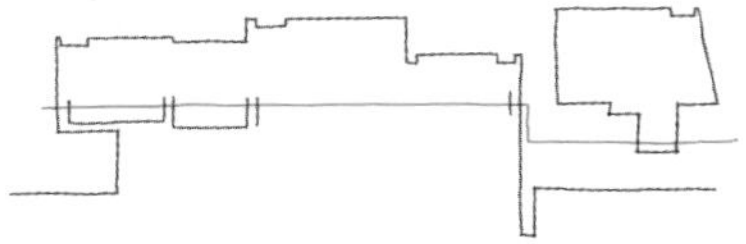

The new building wraps around the retained, but internally remodelled, old building on the south edge of the site.

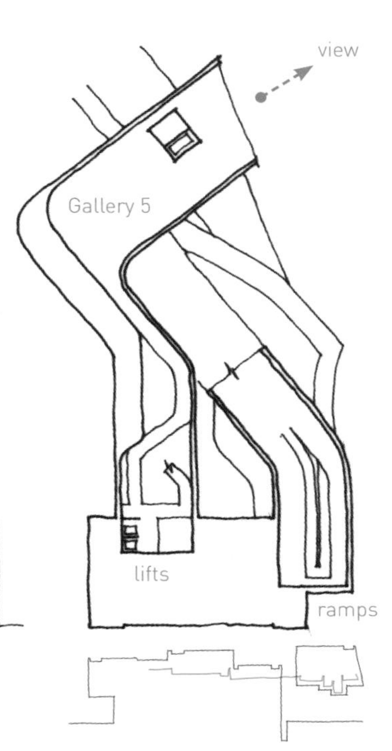

Lifts project beyond the top of the old building. On the way to the top gallery, the new building appears to rest on top of the old in order to access these lifts. A ramp to Gallery 3 cuts into the top of the old building.

A system of stairs and ramps leads from the entrance area to the upper floors and on to Gallery 5 at the top. A lift and fire-escape stairs connect directly back to ground level.

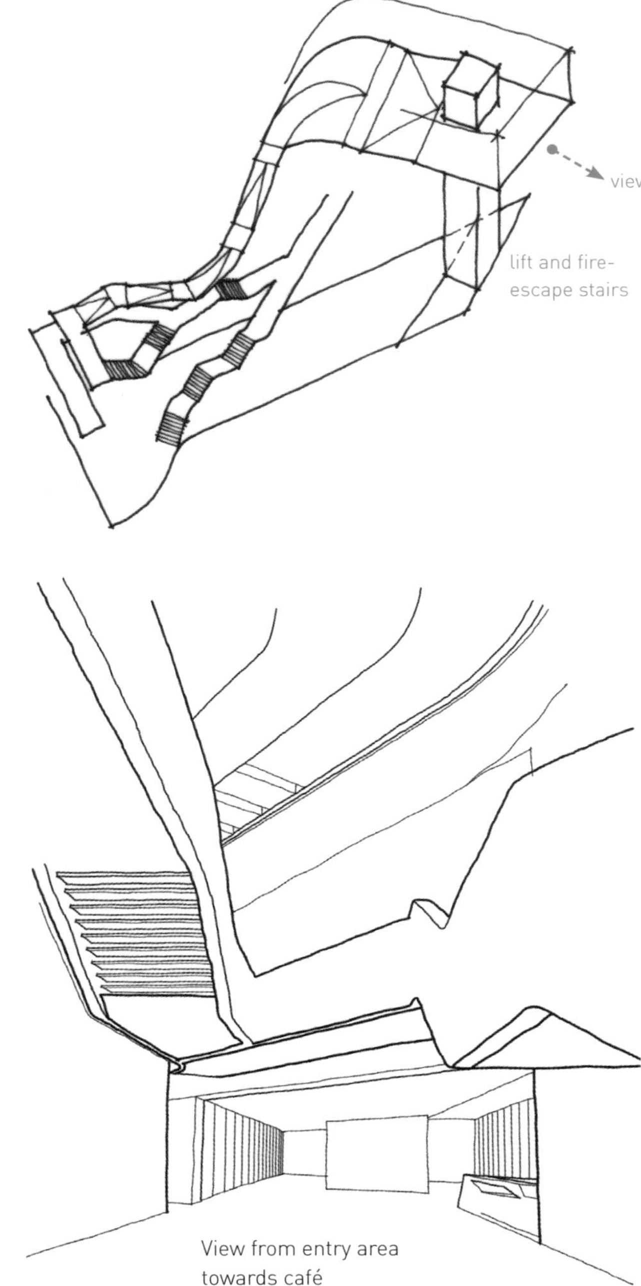

View from entry area towards café

Endnote: Some common themes

A collection of building analyses invites the comparison of one building with another to highlight common themes and what is special in each one. In this Endnote we draw attention to some recurring themes from the preceding pages. Although these themes will be familiar to those educated in architecture, we want to draw attention to a few buildings where their presence is particularly clear. Readers will find other examples. Our list is no more than a hint of very big topics.

Buildings are wholes Buildings examined individually and in detail reveal a complexity that is rarely acknowledged in the generalizing discourses of architecture. The buildings in this book are wholes, where (in the familiar adage) the whole is more than the sum of the parts. Mentally zooming in and out of the works reveals multifaceted assemblies hard to grasp in their wholeness. The way the diverse components of Snøhetta's Oslo Opera House [49] work together illustrates this reality.

Details reflect wholes If we played a game of identifying the buildings from a random collection of details in this book we would get most of them right. Details reflect the design style of the whole in concentrated form. Consider, for example, the window forms and the whole building form in Daniel Libeskind's extension to the Jewish Museum Berlin [31].

Details have multiple roles A single design element or strategy often responds to several different design requirements or contexts. For example, the curving shape of the ceiling of Jørn Utzon's Bagsvaerd Church [13] reflects sound, modulates light and symbolically expresses the soaring of spirits.

Form-patterns recur In all the buildings, we can see that form-patterns recur within them. We can see how their architects have developed a repertoire of patterns of built form, and how they respond to functional, environmental and other circumstances with built form. In the analysis of Alvar Aalto's Seinäjoki Town Hall [09] we show how the same form-patterns occur in different places and scales in the building.

Style is a loose label We are familiar with style labels such as 'organic' or 'high tech', but we can see from the buildings in this book that these are loose labels that may overlap. For example, Stirling & Gowan's Leicester Engineering Building [05] has characteristics of both Functionalism (in the way its component volumes reflect their functions) and Postmodernism (in the picturesque arrangement of those volumes). Ultimately, style is idiosyncratic to each building.

Order and variation is a common compositional device Many of the buildings in this book combine order (through grids, symmetry, repetition and other devices) with variation. Parts may belong to the same family but have individual identity, as in the three shells of Jørn Utzon's Sydney Opera House [03]. Rectilinear form may be offset by free form, as in the way a single curving volume is placed in front the planar south façade of Richard Meier's Barcelona Museum of Contemporary Art [21].

Good buildings are legible These buildings are legible; they can be 'read' and remembered by those who visit them. Entrances can be found without the need to follow signs. Routes inside the buildings are easily followed. Imagine arriving at Denton Corker Marshall's Civil Justice Centre in Manchester [44]. The entrance is obvious, we cannot miss the reception desk, and the atrium reveals the interior layout.

A clear identity does not need dominance All the buildings in this book stand out from the crowd. They do so through their individual identity, but without being overbearing. They do more than just merge into their local area; their presence improves their local area. Look, for example, at Richard Rogers's Lloyd's of London Office Building [19], Santiago Calatrava's Quadracci Pavilion in Milwaukee [32], and the Kunsthaus Graz by Spacelab Cook-Fournier/ARGE Kunsthaus [39], and how each of them relates to its neighbouring buildings and urban context.

Notable outcomes can result from cross-cultural interaction When architects from one country and culture operate in another with sensitivity, successful outcomes show responsive cohesion between the influences of the specific place and those of the architects' own backgrounds. For example, the skin of SANAA's New Museum in New York [35] adapts the transparency of Japanese architecture to the rugged context of a Lower Manhattan street.

Materiality and form are interlinked In Louis Khan's Indian Institute of Management [12] (brick), Future Systems' Lord's Media Centre [23] (aluminium), Peter Zumthor's Thermal Baths in Vals [27] (stone), Frank Gehry's Guggenheim Museum Bilbao [28] (titanium), and Toyo Ito's Meiso no Mori Crematorium [43] (concrete), the potential of materials is investigated and extended beyond the commonplace. This combination of expressing materiality and probing boundaries appears in many of the buildings.

New and old constructions can make a lively combination The juxtaposition of new and old construction offers an opportunity for an engaging dialogue between them. When new concrete platforms were inserted between medieval stone walls at Sverre Fehn's Hedmark Museum in Hamar, Norway [11], both old and new retained their integrity in equal partnership. Herzog and de Meuron's CaixaForum in Madrid [34] shows a very different kind of dialogue, in which the old is modified with less respect but is central to the building's identity.

Form and space come to life in light The play of sunlight over the exterior of a building and the dynamic interplay of different means of interior roof- and wall-lighting can radically change the character of surfaces and spaces. Examples include the rooflights of Carlo Scarpa's Canova Museum [02], the responsive perforated walls of Jean Nouvel's Arab World Institute in Paris [20], and the curving white external walls of the Mimesis Museum by Álvaro Siza with Castanheira & Bastai and Jun Sung Kim in Paju Book City, Republic of Korea [46].

Experiencing architecture embraces embodiment We cannot get a kinaesthetic experience of these buildings from drawings. We can, though, imagine our kinaesthetic pleasure and sense of embodiment (the interplay of our mind, our body and the world) that would result from walking up steps or along ramps, turning corners, passing between light and shadow, and moving from compressed to expanded space. Imagine exploring James Stirling's Neue Staatsgalerie in Stuttgart [16] or Zaha Hadid's MAXXI museum in Rome [50].

Buildings reveal ethics Buildings inevitably reflect the values of their clients and designers. Green School in Bali by PT Bambu [45] represents the client's ethical position in the way it responds to the local climate and culture in its open planning and choice of local, sustainable materials. Values can also be inferred from the ways a building respects its built neighbours and human occupants, or seeks environmental and cultural sustainability.

Buildings are collaborative works When we look at Norman Foster's HSBC Office Building in Hong Kong [15] or Pearce Partnership's Eastgate in Harare [26], we see the responsive cohesion between the structural and environmental behaviour of these buildings and their other design features. The buildings in this book result from the effective collaboration of teams that include architects, engineers, builders and clients, and often landscape architects, artists, planners and others. We have not named these teams in this book, but they can be found in publications listed under 'Further reading'.

Acknowledgments

This series of analyses began in a postgraduate course at the University of Adelaide, Australia, from 2008. The course explored a holistic view of building design as the integration of responses to many contexts. We are indebted to the students and others who have contributed to the project analyses through their work and drawings. They are named below and on the relevant project pages.

We thank our families for their patience while we spent many hours working on this book.

Finally, we thank the women and men who initiated, designed, made and maintain the buildings we show.

Antony Radford, Selen Morkoç
and Amit Srivastava
The University of Adelaide, Australia

We thank for their contributions Manalle Abiad, Blake Alexander, Maryam Alfadhel, Rumaiza Hani Ali, Gabriel Ash, Rowan Barbary, Marguerite Therese Bartolo, Mark James Birch, Hilal al-Busaidi, Zhe Cai, Brendan Capper, Sze Nga Chan, Ying Sung Chia, Sindy Chung, Alan L. Cooper, Leo Cooper, Gabriella Dias, Alix Dunbar, Philip Eaton, Brent Michael Eddy, Adam Fenton, Simon Fisher, Janine Fong, Douglas Lim Ming Fui, Saiful Azzam Abdul Ghapur, Lewis Kevin Hardy Glastonbury, Leona Greenslade, Lana Greer, Tim Hastwell, Simon Ho, Katherine Holford, Amy Holland, Celia Johnson, Felicity Jones, Rimas Kaminskas, Paul Anson Kassebaum, Sean Kellet, Lachlan Knox, Natasha Kousvos, Victoria Kovalevski, Verdy Kwee, Chun Yin Lau, Wee Jack Lee, Richard Le Messeurier, Megan Leen, Xi Li, Yifan Li, Huo Liu, Sam Lock, Hao Lv, Mohammad Faiz Madlan, Michelle Male, Matthew Bruce McCallum, Doug McCusker, Susan McDougall, Ben McPherson, Allyce McVicar, Mun Su Mei, Peiman Mirzaei, William Morris, Samuel Murphy, Michael Kin Pong Ng, Thuy Nguyen, Wan Iffah Wan Ahmad Nizar, Jessica O'Connor, Daniel O'Dea, Kay Tryn Oh, Tarkko Oksala, Sonya Otto, John Pargeter, Michael Pearce, Georgina Prenhall, Alison Radford, Siti Sarah Ramli, Nigel Reichenbach, William Rogers, Matthew Rundell, Ellen Hyo-Jin Sim, Katherine Snell, Wei Fen Soh, Sarah Sulaiman, Halina Tam, Daniel Turner, Hui Wang, Charles Whittington, Wen Ya, Lee Ken Ming Yi, Wing Kin Yim, Enoch Liew Kang Yuen, Stavros Zacharia, Xuan Zhang and Kun Zhao.

Picture credits

17 © View Pictures Ltd/SuperStock
23 Image from a rendered digital model of the Canova Museum by Peter Guthrie, © Peter Guthrie
29 © Selen Morkoc
37 © Brett Critchley/Dreamstime.com
43 © Antony Radford
49 © Amit Srivastava
55 Photoservice Electa/Universal Images Group/SuperStock
63 © David Cherepuschak/Alamy
69 © Antony Radford
75 © FocusJapan/Alamy
81 Photo Jan Haug, Hedmarksmuseet, Hamar, Norway
87 © Amit Srivastava
93 © Antony Radford
101 © Richard Powers/Arcaid/Corbis
105 © Paul Brown/Alamy
111 © Richard Bryant/Arcaid/Corbis
117 © Warchol Photography
121 © Ellen Liu, ellen's attic
129 © Lance Bellers/Dreamstime.com
135 © Isaxar/Dreamstime.com
141 © Edifice/Corbis
147 © Laurentiuz/Dreamstime.com
153 © View Pictures Ltd/SuperStock
159 © Amit Srivastava
165 © Pedro Antonio Salaverría Calahorra/Dreamstime.com
171 © Ken Wilson-Max/Alamy
177 © View Pictures Ltd/Alamy
185 © Juan Moyano/Dreamstime.com
191 © ESO/José Francisco Salgado (josefrancisco.org)
197 © Arcaid 2013
205 © Pixattitude/Dreamstime.com
211 Photograph by Steven Andrew Miller
219 © Cemal Emden/Aga Khan Trust for Culture
227 © Antony Radford
233 Mariano Rolando/AFP/Getty Images
239 © Stockcube/Dreamstime.com
245 © Photo Japan/Alamy
251 © Wes Thompson/Corbis
257 Photo Walter Bibikow. Getty Images
263 © Shu He/View/Corbis
269 © Antony Radford
275 © Antony Radford
281 © View Pictures Ltd/Alamy
287 © Antony Radford
293 © Aga Khan Award for Architecture/PT Bambu
299 © View Pictures Ltd/Alamy
307 © Luay Bahoora/Alamy
313 © Gerald Holubowicz/Alamy
319 © Serban Enache/Dreamstime.com
325 Photo Franco Origlia/Getty Images

Further reading

01 Sarabhai House

Curtis, W.J.R., *Le Corbusier, Ideas and Forms*, New York: Rizzoli, 1986

Frampton, K., *Le Corbusier*, London: Thames & Hudson, 2001

Masud, R., 'Language Spoken Around the World: Lessons from Le Corbusier' (thesis, Georgia Institute of Technology), 2010

Park, S., *Le Corbusier Redrawn: The Houses*, New York: Princeton Architectural Press, 2012

Serenyi, P., 'Timeless but of Its Time: Le Corbusier's Architecture in India', *Perspecta* 20, 1983: 91–118

Starbird, P., 'Corbu in Ahmadabad', *Interior Design*, February 2003: 142–49

Ubbelohde, S.M., 'The Dance of a Summer Day: Le Corbusier's Sarabhai House in Ahmedabad, India', *TDSR* 14, no. 2, 2003: 65–80

02 Canova Museum

Albertini, B. and Bagnoli, A., *Carlo Scarpa: Architecture in Details*, Cambridge MA: MIT Press, 1988

Beltramini, G. and Zannier, I., *Carlo Scarpa: Architecture and Design*, New York: Rizzoli, 2007

Buzas, Stefan, *Four Museums: Carlo Scarpa, Museo Canoviano, Possagno; Frank O. Gehry, Guggenheim Bilbao Museum; Rafael Moneo, the Audrey Jones Beck Building, MFAH; Heinz Tesar, Sammlung Essl, Klosterneuburg*, Stuttgart and London: Edition Axel Menges, 2004

Carmel-Arthur, J. and Buzas, S., *Carlo Scarpa, Museo Canoviano, Possagno* (photographs by Richard Bryant), Stuttgart and London: Edition Axel Menges, 2002

Los, Sergio, *Carlo Scarpa: 1906–1978: A Poet of Architecture*, New York: Taschen America 2009

Schultz, A., *Carlo Scarpa: Layers*, Stuttgart and London: Edition Axel Menges, 2007

03 Sydney Opera House

Drew, Philip, *Sydney Opera House: Jørn Utzon*, London: Phaidon, 1995

Fromonot, Françoise, *Jørn Utzon: The Sydney Opera House*, trans. Christopher Thompson, Corte Madera CA: Electa/Gingko, 1998

Moy, Michael, *Sydney Opera House: Idea to Icon*, Ashgrove Qld: Alpha Orion Press, 2008

Norberg-Schulz, Christian and Futagawa, Yukio, *GA: Global Architecture: Jørn Utzon Sydney Opera House, Sydney, Australia, 1957–73*, Tokyo: A.D.A. Edita, 1980

Perez, Adelyn, 'AD Classics: Sydney Opera House / Jørn Utzon', *ArchDaily*, http://www.archdaily.com/65218/ad-classics-sydney-opera-house-j%C3%B8rn-utzon/ (viewed 20 Sep 2013)

04 Solomon R. Guggenheim Museum

http://www.guggenheim.org/

Hession, J.K. and Pickrel, D., *Frank Lloyd Wright in New York: The Plaza Years 1954–1959*, Gibbs Smith, 2007

Laseau, P., *Frank Lloyd Wright: Between Principle and Form*, New York: Van Nostrand Reinhold, 1992

Levine, N., *The Architecture of Frank Lloyd Wright*, Princeton NJ: Princeton University Press, 1996

Quinan, J., 'Frank Lloyd Wright's Guggenheim Museum: A Historian's Report', *Journal of the Society of Architectural Historians* 52, 1993: 466–82

05 Leicester Engineering Building

Eisenman, Peter, *Ten Canonical Buildings 1950–2000*, New York: Rizzoli, 2008

Hodgetts, C., 'Inside James Stirling', *Design Quarterly* 100, no. 1, 1976: 6–19

Jacabus, John, 'Engineering Building, Leicester University', *Architectural Review*, April 1964

McKean, J., *Leicester University Engineering Building*, Architectural Detail Series, London: Phaidon, 1994. Republished in James Russell et al, *Pioneering British High-Tech*, London: Phaidon, 1999

Walmsley, Dominique, 'Leicester Engineering Building: Its Post-Modern Role', *Journal of Architectural Education* 42, no. 1, 1984: 10–17

06 Salk Institute for Biological Studies

Brownlee, David and De Long, David, *Louis I. Kahn: In the Realm of Architecture*, New York: Rizzoli, 1991

Crosbie, Michael J., 'Dissecting the Salk', *Progressive Architecture* 74, no. 10, Oct 1993: 40+

Goldhagen, Sarah Williams, *Louis Kahn's Situated Modernism*, New Haven CT and London: Yale University Press, 2001

Leslie, Thomas, *Louis I. Kahn: Building Art, Building Science*, New York: George Braziller, 2005

McCarter, Robert, *Louis I. Kahn*, London and New York: Phaidon, 2005

Steele, James, *Salk Institute Louis I Kahn*, London: Phaidon, 2002

Wiseman, C., *Louis I. Kahn: Beyond Time and Style, A Life in Architecture*, London: W.W. Norton, 2007

07 Louisiana Museum of Modern Art

Brawne, Michael, and Frederiksen, Jens, *Jorgen Bo, Vilhelm Wohlert: Louisiana Museum, Humlebaek*, Berlin: Wasmuth, 1993

Faber, Tobias, *A History of Danish Architecture*, Copenhagen: Danske Selskab, 1963

Pardey, John, *Louisiana and Beyond – The Work of Wilhelm Wohlert*, Hellerup: Bløndel, 2007

08 Yoyogi National Gymnasium

Altherr, Alfred, *Three Japanese Architects; Mayekawa ,Tange and Sakakura*, New York: Architectural Books, 1968

Boyd, R. *Kenzo Tange*, New York: Braziller, 1962

Kroll, Andrew, 'AD Classics: Yoyogi National Gymnasium / Kenzo Tange', *ArchDaily*, 15 Feb 2011, http://www.archdaily.com/109138 (viewed 25 Aug 2013)

Kultermann, U., *Kenzo Tange*, Barcelona: Gustavo Gili, 1989

Riani, P., *Kenzo Tange*, London: Hamlyn, 1970

Tagsold, Christian, 'Modernity, Space and National Representation at the Tokyo Olympics 1964', *Urban History* 37, 2010: 289–300

Tange, K. and Kultermann, U. (eds), *Kenzo Tange, 1946–1969: Architecture and Urban Design*, London: Pall Mall, 1970

09 Seinäjoki Town Hall

Baird, George, *Library of Contemporary Architects: Alvar Aalto*, New York: Simon and Schuster, 1971

Fleig, Karl, *Alvar Aalto: Volume II 1963–70*, London: Pall Mall, 1971

Radford, Antony, and Oksala, Tarkko, 'Alvar Aalto and the Expression of Discontinuity', *The Journal of Architecture* 12, no. 3, 2007: 257–80

Reed, Peter, *Alvar Aalto: Between Humanism and Materialism*, New York: MoMA, 1998
Schildt, Goran, *Alvar Aalto: The Complete Catalogue of Architecture, Design and Art*, London: Academy Editions, 1994
Weston, Richard, *Alvar Aalto*, London: Phaidon 1995

10 St Mary's Cathedral
Boyd, Robin, *Kenzo Tange*, New York: Braziller, 1962
Giannotti, Andrea, 'AD Classics: St. Mary Cathedral / Kenzo Tange', *ArchDaily*, 23 Feb 2011 http://www.archdaily.com/114435 (viewed 25 Aug 2013)
Riani, Paolo, *Kenzo Tange [translated from the Italian]*, London and New York: Hamlyn, 1970
Tange, Kenzo, *Kenzo Tange, 1946–1969: Architecture and Urban Design*, London: Pall Mall, 1970

11 Hedmark Museum
Fjeld, Per Olaf, *Sverre Fehn: The Art of Construction*, New York: Rizzoli 1983
Fjeld, Per Olaf, *Sverre Fehn: The Pattern of Thoughts*, New York: Random House 2009
Mings, Josh, *The Story of Building: Sverre Fehn's Museums*, San Fransciso: Blurb 2011, preview available at http://www.blurb.com/books/2537931-the-story-of-building-sverre-fehn-s-museums (viewed 12 May 2013)
Pérez-Gómez, Alberto, 'Luminous and Visceral. A comment on the work of Sverre Fehn', *An Online Review of Architecture*, 2009, http://www.architecturenorway.no/questions/identity/perez-gomez-on-fehn/ (viewed 27 Apr 2013)

12 Indian Institute of Management
Ashraf, Kazi Khaleed, 'Taking Place: Landscape in the Architecture of Louis Kahn', *Journal of Architectural Education* 61, no. 2, 2007: 48–58
Bhatia, Gautam, 'Silence in Light: Indian Institute of Management (Ahmedabad)' in *Eternal Stone: Great Buildings of India*, ed. Gautam Bhatia, New Delhi: Penguin Books, 2000: 29–39
Brownlee, David and De Long, David, *Louis I. Kahn: In the Realm of Architecture*, New York: Rizzoli, 1991
Buttiker, Urs, *Louis I. Kahn Light and Space*, New York: Watson-Guptill, 1994
Doshi, Balkrishna, Chauhan, Muktirajsinhji, and Pandya, Yatin, *Le Corbusier and Louis I. Kahn: The Acrobat and the Yogi of Architecture*, Ahmedabad: Vastu-Shilpa Foundation for Studies and Research in Environmental Design, 2007
Fleming, S., 'Louis Kahn and Platonic Mimesis: Kahn as Artist or Craftsman?' *Architectural Theory Review* 3, no. 1, 1998: 88–103
Ksiazek, S., 'Architectural Culture in the Fifties: Louis Kahn and the National Assembly Complex in Dhaka', *The Journal of the Society of Architectural Historians* 52, no. 4, 1993: 416–35
Srivastava, A., 'Encountering materials in architectural production: The case of Kahn and brick at IIM' (doctoral thesis, University of Adelaide, Adelaide), 2009

13 Bagsvaerd Church
Balters, Sofia, 'AD Classics: Bagsvaerd Community Church', *ArchDaily*, http://www.archdaily.com/160390/ad-classics-bagsvaerd-church-jorn-utzon/ (viewed 20 Sep 2013)
Norberg-Schulz, Christian, *Jørn Utzon: Church at Bagsvaerd*, Tokyo: Hennessey & Ingalls, 1982
Utzon, Jørn and Bløndal, Torsten, *Bagsvæd Church / Jørn Utzon*, Hellerup, Denmark: Edition Bløndal, 2005
Weston, Richard, *Jørn Utzon Logbook V II*, Copenhagen: Edition Blondel, 2005

14 Milan House
Bradbury, Dominic, 'La Maison Jardin', *AD – Architectural Digest* 98, France, 2011: 133–39
Marcos Acayaba Arquitetos, 'Milan House', *GA Houses* 106, 2008: 128–45
Marcos Acayaba Arquitetos, 'Residência na cidade jardim', http://www.marcosacayaba.arq.br/lista.projeto.chain?id=2 (viewed 22 Aug 2013)

15 HSBC Office Building
Jenkins, D. (ed), *Hongkong and Shanghai Bank Headquarters, Norman Foster Works 2*, Munich: Prestel, 2005: 32–149
Lambot, I. (ed), *Norman Foster – Foster Associates: Buildings and Projects Volume 3 1978–1985*, Hong Kong: Watermark, 1989:112–255
Quantrill, M., *Norman Foster Studio: Consistency Through Diversity*, New York: Routledge, 1999

16 Neue Staatsgalerie
Arnell, P. and Bickford, T. (eds), *James Stirling: Buildings and Projects: James Stirling, Michael Wilford and Associates*, London: Architectural Press,1984
Baker, Geoffrey, *The Architecture of James* Stirling and His Partners James Gowan and Michael Wilford: A Study of Architectural *Creativity in the Twentieth Century*, Burlington: Ashgate, 2011
Dogan, Fehmi and Nersessian, Nancy, 'Generic Abstraction in Design Creativity: The Case of Staatsgaleire by James Stirling', *Design Studies* 31, 2010: 207–36
Stirling, James, *Writings on Architecture*, Milan: Skira, 1998
Vidler, Anthony, 'Losing Face: Notes on the Modern Museum', *Assemblage* No. 9, June 1989: 40–57
Wilford, Michael, and Muirhead, Thomas, *James Stirling, Michael Wilford and Associates: Buildings & Projects, 1975–1992*, New York: Thames & Hudson, 1994

17 House at Martha's Vineyard
Holl, Steven, *Idea and Phenomena*, Baden, Switzerland: Lars Müller, 2002
Holl, Steven, *House: Black Swan Theory*, New York: Princeton Architectural Press, 2007
House at Martha's Vineyard (Berkowitz-Odgis House)' *El Croquis 78+93+108: Steven Holl 1986–2003*, 2003: 94–101

18 Church on the Water
Drew, Philip, *Church on the Water, Church of the Light*, Singapore: Phaidon, 1996
Frampton, Kenneth, *Tadao Ando/Kenneth Frampton*, New York: Museum of Modern Art, 1991
Futagawa, Yukio (ed.), *Tadao Ando. V: IV, 2001–2007*, Tokyo: A.D.A. Edita, 2012

19 Lloyd's of London Office Building
Burdett, Richard, *Richard Rogers Partnership*, New York: Monacelli Press, 1996

Charlie Rose: interview with Richard Rogers, PBS, 1999
Powell, Kenneth, *Lloyd's Building*, Singapore: Phaidon, 1994
Sudjic, Deyan, *Norman Foster, Richard Rogers, James Stirling: New Directions in British Architecture*, London: Thames & Hudson, 1986
Sudjic, Deyan, *The Architecture of Richard Rogers*, New York: Abrams, 1995

20 Arab World Institute
Baudrillard, Jean and Nouvel, Jean, *The Singular Objects of Architecture*, Minneapolis: Minnesota Press, 2002
Casamonti, Marco, *Jean Nouvel*, Milan: Motta, 2009
Jodidio, Philip, *Jean Nouvel: Complete Works, 1970–2008*, Cologne and London: Taschen, 2008
Morgan, C.L., *Jean Nouvel: The Elements of Architecture*, London: Thames & Hudson, 1998

21 Barcelona Museum of Contemporary Art
Frampton, Kenneth, *Richard Meier*, London: Phaidon Press, 2003
Frampton, Kenneth and Rykwert, Joseph, *Richard Meier, Architect: 1985–1991*, New York: Rizzoli, 1991
Meier, Richard, *Richard Meier: Barcelona Museum of Contemporary Art*, New York: Monacelli Press, 1997
Werner, Blaser, *Richard Meier: Details*, Basel: Birkhäuser, 1996

22 Vitra Fire Station
Ackerman, Matthias, 'Vitra; Ando, Gehry, Hadid, Siza: Figures of Artists at the Gates of the Factory', *Lotus International 85*, 1995: 74–99
Kroll, Andrew. 'AD Classics: Vitra Fire Station / Zaha Hadid', 19 Feb 2011, *ArchDaily*, http://www.archdaily.com/112681 (viewed 20 Sep 2013)
Monninger, Michael, 'Zaha Hadid: Fire Station, Weil am Rhein', *Domus 752*, 1993: 54–61
Woods, Lebbeus, 'Drawn into Space: Zaha Hadid', *Architectural Design 78/4*, 2008: 28–35

23 Lord's Media Centre
Buro Happold, 'NatWest Media Centre, Lord's Cricket Ground', *Architect's Journal*, 17 September 1998, http://www.architectsjournal.co.uk/home/natwest-media-centre-lords-cricket-ground/780405.article (viewed 15 Sep 2013)
Field, Marcus, *Future Systems*, London: Phaidon, 1999
Future Systems, *Unique Building (Lord's Media Centre)*, Chichester: Wiley-Academy, 2001
Future Systems, *Future Systems Architecture*, http://www.future-systems.com/architecture/architecture_list.html (viewed 28 May 2010)
Kaplicky, Jan, *Confessions*, Chichester: Wiley-Academy 2002

24 Menara UMNO
Gauzin-Muller, D., *Sustainable Architecture & Urbanism: Design, Construction, Examples*, Basel: Birkhäuser, 2002
Richards, I., *Groundscrapers + Subscrapers of Hamzah & Yeang*, Weinheim: Wiley-Academy, 2001
Yeang, K., *Tropical Urban Regionalism: Building in a South-east Asian City*, Singapore: Concept Media, 1987
Yeang, K., *Designing with Nature: The Ecological Basis for Architectural Design*, New York: McGraw-Hill, 1995
Yeang, K., *The Green Skyscraper*, London: Prestel, 2000
Yeang, K., *Ecodesign: A Manual for Ecological Design*, Chichester: Wiley-Academy, 2008

25 Dancing Building
Cohen, Jean-Louis and Ragheb, Fiona, *Frank Gehry, Architect*, New York: Guggenheim Museum and London: Thames & Hudson, 2001
Dal Co, Francesco, *Frank O. Gehry: The Complete Works*, New York: Monacelli Press, 1998
Gehry, Frank, 'Frank Gehry: Nationale Nederlanden Office Building, Prague', *Architectural Design 66/1–2*, 1996: 42–45

26 Eastgate
Baird, George, 'Eastgate Centre, Harare, Zimbabwe', in George Baird, *The Architectural Expression of Environmental Control Systems*, London and New York: Taylor and Francis, 2001: 164–80
Jones, D.L., *Architecture and the Environment: Bioclimatic Building Design*, Woodstock and New York: Overlook Press, 1998: 200–1

27 Thermal Baths in Vals
Binet, Hélène and Zumthor, Peter, *Peter Zumthor, Works: Buildings and Projects, 1979–1997*, Basel and Boston: Birkhäuser, 1999
Buxton, Pamela, 'Spas in their eyes', *RIBAJ (Magazine of the Royal Institute of British Architects)*, http://www.ribajournal.com/pages/pamela_buxton__zumthors_thermal_baths_204250.cfm (viewed 20 Sept 2013)
Hauser, Sigrid, *Peter Zumthor-Therme Vals / Essays*, Zürich: Scheidegger & Spiess, 2007
Zumthor, Peter, *Atmospheres: Architectural Environments; Surrounding Objects*, Basel and Boston: Birkhäuser, 2006

28 Guggenheim Museum Bilbao
Buzas, Stefan, *Four Museums: Carlo Scarpa, Museo Canoviano, Possagno; Frank O. Gehry, Guggenheim Bilbao Museum; Rafael Moneo, the Audrey Jones Beck Building, MFAH; Heinz Tesar, Sammlung Essl, Klosterneuburg*, Stuttgart and London: Edition Axel Menges, 2004
Eisenman, Peter, *Ten Canonical Buildings 1950–2000*, New York: Rizzoli, 2008
Hartoonian, Gevork, 'Frank Gehry: Roofing, Wrapping, and Wrapping the roof', *The Journal of Architecture* 7, no. 1, 2002: 1–31
Hourston, Laura, *Museum Builders II*, Chichester: Wiley-Academy, 2004
Mack, Gerhard, *Art Museums into the 21st Century*, Boston: Birkhäuser, 1999
Van Bruggen, Coosje, *Frank O. Gehry: Guggenheim Museum Bilbao*, New York: Guggenheim Museum Publications, 2003

29 ESO Hotel
Auer+Weber+Assoziierte, 'Eso Hotel -Auer und Weber', available online, http://www.auer-weber.de/eng/projekte/index.htm
LANXESS, *Colored Concrete Works: Case Study Project: ESO Hotel*, available online, http://www.colored-concrete-works.com/upload/Downloads/Downloads/Downloads_Case_Study_ESO_Hotel.pdf
Vickers, Graham, *21st Century Hotel*, London: Laurence King 2005

30 Arthur and Yvonne Boyd Education Centre

'Arthur and Yvonne Boyd Education Centre', *El Croquis* 163/164: *Glenn Murcutt 1980–2012: Feathers of Metal*, 2012: 282–313

Beck, Haigh and Cooper, Jackie, *Glenn Murcutt – A Singular Architectural Practice*, Melbourne: Images, 2002

Bundanon Trust, Riversdale Property, http://www.bundanon.com.au/content/riversdale-property (viewed 6 Oct 2013)

Drew, Philip, *Leaves of Iron: Glen Murcutt: Pioneer of an Australian Architectural Form*, Sydney: Law Book Company, 2005

Fromonot, F., *Glenn Murcutt – Buildings and Projects 1962–2003*, London: Thames & Hudson, 2003

Heneghan, Tom and Gusheh, Maryam, *The Architecture of Glenn Murcutt*, Tokyo: TOTO, 2008

Murcutt, Glenn, *Thinking Drawing, Working Drawing*, Tokyo: TOTO, 2008

31 Jewish Museum Berlin

Binet, Hélène, *A Passage Through Silence and Light*, London: Black Dog, 1997

Dogan, Fehmi and Nersessian, Nancy, 'Conceptual Diagrams in Creative Architectural Practice: The case of Daniel Libeskind's Jewish Museum', *Architectural Research Quarterly* 16, no. 1, 2012: 15–27

Kipnis, Jeffrey, *Daniel Libeskind: The Space of Encounter*, London: Thames & Hudson, 2001

Kroll, Andrew, 'AD Classics: Jewish Museum, Berlin / Daniel Libeskind', *ArchDaily*, 25 Nov 2010, http://www.archdaily.com/91273 (viewed 25 Aug 2013)

Libeskind, Daniel, *Between the Lines: The Jewish Museum. Jewish Museum Berlin: Concept and Vision*, Berlin: Judisches Museum, 1998

Schneider, Bernhard, *Daniel Libeskind: Jewish Museum Berlin*, New York: Prestel, 1999

32 Quadracci Pavilion

Jodidio, Philip, *Calatrava: Santiago Calatrava, Complete Works 1979–2007*, Hong Kong and London: Taschen, 2007

Kent, Cheryl, *Santiago Calatrava Milwaukee Art Museum Quadracci Pavilion*, New York: Rizzoli, 2006

Tzonis, Alexander, *Santiago Calatrava: The Complete Works – Expanded Edition*, New York: Rizzoli, 2007

Tzonis, Alexander and Lefaivre, Liane, *Santiago Calatrava's Creative Process: Sketchbooks*, Basel: Birkhäuser, 2001

33 B2 House

Aga Khan Award for Architecture, B2 House, 2004, http://www.akdn.org/architecture/project.asp?id=2763 (viewed 20 Sep 2013)

Bradbury, Dominic, *Mediterranean Modern*, London: Thames & Hudson, 2011

Lubell, Sam and Murdoch, James, '2004 Aga Khan Award for Architecture: Promoting Excellence in the Islamic World', *Architectural Record 192/12*, 2004: 94–100

Sarkis, Hashim, *Han Tümertekin – Recent Work*, Cambridge MA: Aga Khan Program, Harvard University Graduate School of Design, 2007

34 CaixaForum

Arroya, J.N., Ribas, I.M. and Fermosei, J.A.G., *Caixaforum Madrid*, Madrid: Foundacion La Caxia, 2004

'Caixaforum-Madrid', *El Croquis* 129/130: *Herzog & de Meuron 2002–2006*, 2011: 336–47

Cohn, D., 'Herzog & de Meuron Manipulates Materials, Space and Structure to Transform an Abandoned Power Station into Madrid's Caixaforum', *Architectural Record* 196, no. 6, 2008: 108

Mack, Gerhard (ed.) *Herzog & de Meuron 1997–2001. The Complete Works. Volume 4*, Basel, Boston and Berlin: Birkhäuser, 2008

Pagliari, F., 'Caixaforum', *The Plan: Architecture and Technologies in Detail* 26, 2008: 72–88

Richters, C., *Herzog & de Meuron: Caixaforum*, http://www.arcspace.com/features/herzog--de-meuron/caixa-forum/ (viewed 22 Apr 2013)

35 New Museum

'New Museum of Contemporary Art, New York', *El Croquis 139: SANAA 2004–2008, 2008*: 156–71

36 Scottish Parliament Building

Scottish Parliament, *Scottish Parliament Building*, http://www.scottish.parliament.uk/visitandlearn/12484.aspx (viewed 21 Apr 2013)

Jencks, Charles, *The Iconic Building*, London: Frances Lincoln, 2005

LeCuyer, Annette, *Radical Tectonics*, London: Thames & Hudson, 2001

'Scottish Parliament', *El Croquis* 144: *EMBT 2000–2009*, 2009: 148–95

Spellman, Catherine, 'Projects and Interpretations: Architectural Strategies of Enric Miralles', in Catherine Spellman (ed.), *Re-Envisioning Landscape/Architecture*, Barcelona: Actar, 2003: 150–63

37 Yokohama Port Terminal

AZ.PA 2011, Yokohama International Port Terminal, London, http://azpa.com/#/projects/465

Foreign Office Architects, Yokohama International Port Terminal http://www.f-o-a.net/#/projects/465

Fernando Marquez, Cecilia and Levene, Richard, *Foreign Office Architects, 1996–2003: Complexity and Consistency*, Madrid: El Croquis Editorial, 2003

Hensel, Michael, Menges, Achim and Weinstock, Michael, *Emergence: Morphogenetic design strategies*, Chichester: Wiley-Academy, 2004

Ito, Toyo, Kipnis, Jeffrey and Najle, Ciro, *2G N.16 Foreign Office Architects*, Barcelona: Gustavo Gili, 2000

Kubo, Michael and Ferre, Albert in collaboration with Foreign Office Architects, *Phylogenesis: FOA's Ark*, Barcelona: Actar, 2003

Machado, Rodolfo and el-Khoury, Rodolphe, *Monolithic Architecture*, Munich and New York: Prestel-Verlag, 1995

Melvin, Jeremy, *Young British Architects*, Basel and Boston: Birkhäuser, 2000

Scalbert, I., 'Public space – Yokohama International Port Terminal – Ship of State', in Rowan Moore (ed.), *Vertigo: The Strange New World of the Contemporary City*, Corte Madera CA: Gingko Press, 1999

38 Modern Art Museum of Fort Worth

Brettell, Richard R., 'Ando's Modern: Reflections on Architectural Translation' *Cite* 57, Spring 2003: 24–30, http://citemag.org/wp-content/uploads/2010/03/AndosModern_Brettell_Cite57.pdf (viewed 25 Aug 2013)

Dillon, David, 'Modern Art Museum of Fort Worth', *Architectural Record*, March 2003: 98–113
Frampton, Kenneth, *Tadao Ando/Kenneth Frampton*, New York: Museum of Modern Art, 1991
Futagawa, Yukio (ed.), *Tadao Ando. V: IV, 2001–2007*, Tokyo: A.D.A. Edita, 2012
'Modern Art Museum of Fort Worth', *El Croquis* 92: *Worlds Three: About the world, the Devil and Architecture*, 1998: 42–47
Morant, Roger, 'Boxing with Light', *Domus* 857, March 2003: 34–51

39 Kunsthaus Graz
Lubczynski, Sebastian and Karopoulos, Dimitri, *Plastic: Kunsthaus Graz, Analysis of the Use of Plastic as a Construction Material at the Kunsthaus Graz*, 2010, http://www.issuu.com/sebastianlubczynski/docs/kunsthaus_graz (viewed 22 Apr 2013)
Lubczynski, Sebastian, *Advanced Construction Case Study: Kunsthaus Graz, Further Study of the Kunsthaus Graz and its Construction Materials*, undated, http://www.issuu.com/sebastianlubczynski/docs/construction_case_study_project_2/10 (viewed 22 Apr 2013)
Morrill, Matthew, *Precedent Study: Kunsthaus Graz*, 2004, http://www-bcf.usc.edu/~kcoleman/Precedents/ALL%20PDFs/Spacelab_KunsthausGraz.pdf (viewed 22 Apr 2013)
Nagel, Rina, and Hasler, Dominique, *Kunsthaus Graz*, London: Spacelab, 2006
Richards, B., and Dennis, G., *New Glass Architecture*, London: Laurence King, 2006: 218–21
Slessor, Catherine, 'Mutant Bagpipe invades Graz', *Architectural review*, 213 (1282), Dec 2003: 24
Sommerhoff, Emilie W., 'Kunsthaus Graz, Austria', *Architectural Lighting* 19, no. 3, 2004: 20
LeFaivre, Liane, 'Yikes! Peter Cook's and Colin Fournier's Perkily Animistic Kunsthaus in Graz Recasts the Identity of the Museum and Recalls a Legendary Design Movement', *Architectural Record* 192, no. 1, 2004: 92
Universalmuseum Joanneum, *Kunsthaus Graz*, http://www.arcspace.com/features/spacelab-cook-fournier/kunsthaus-graz (viewed 22 Apr 2013)

40 Linked Hybrid
Fernández Per, Aurora, Mozas, Javier and Arpa, Javier, 'This is Hybrid', Vitoria-Gasteiz, Spain: a+t, 2011
Frampton, K., *Steven Holl Architect*, Milan: Electa Architecture, 2003
Futagawa, Y., *Steven Holl*, Tokyo: A.D.A. Edita, 1995
Holl, Steven, *Steven Holl: Architecture Spoken*, New York: Rizzoli, 2007
Holl, S., *Steven Holl*, Zürich: Artemis Verlags, 1993
Holl, S., Pallasmaa, J. and Perez, A., *Questions of Perception: Phenomenology of Architecture*, San Francisco: William Stout Publishers, 2006
Pearson, Clifford A., 'Connected Living', *Architectural Record* 1, 2010: 48–55

41 Santa Caterina Market
Cohn, David, 'Rehabilitation of Santa Caterina Market, Spain', *Architectural Record* V 194/2, 2006: 99-105
Miralles, Enric and Tagliabue, Benedetta, *Architecture and Urbanism*, Tokyo: A+U Publishing, V 416, 2005: 88–99
'Renovations to Santa Caterina Market', *El Croquis* 144: *EMBT 2000–2009*, 2009: 124–47

42 Southern Cross Station
Dorrel, Ed, 'Grimshaw set to create waves in Melbourne Rail Station Redesign', *Architects' Journal* 219/1–8, 2004: 7–8
Roke, Rebecca, 'Southern Skies', *Architectural Review* 221/1319-24, 2007: 28–36
Southern Cross Station Redevelopment Project, Melbourne, Australia, *Railway-Technology* undated, http://www.railway-technology.com/projects/southern-cross-station-redevelopment-australia/ (viewed 24 Aug 2013)

43 Meiso no Mori Crematorium
C+A, 'Meiso no Mori Crematorium Gifu, Japan', *C+A Online* 12: 12–24 Cement Concrete and Aggregates Australia, http://www.concrete.net.au/CplusA/issue10/Meiso%20no%20Mori%20Issue%2010.pdf (viewed 24 Aug 2013)
'Meiso no Mori Municipal Funeral Hall', *El Croquis 147: Toyo Ito 2005–2009*, http://www.elcroquis.es/Shop/Project/Details/891 (viewed 20 Sep 2013)
Web, Michael, 'Organic Architecture', *Architectural Review 222/1326*, 2007: 74–78
Yoshida, Nobuyuki, *Toyo Ito: Architecture and Place: Feature*, Tokyo: A + U Publishing, 2010

44 Civil Justice Centre
Allied London, *The Manchester Civil Justice Centre*, London: Alma Media International, 2008
Bizley, Graham, 'In Detail: Civil Justice Centre, Manchester', *bdonline*, 14 September 2007, http://www.bdonline.co.uk/buildings/in-detail-civil-justice-centre-manchester/3095199.article (viewed 5 Jun 2013)
Denton Corker Marshall, *Manchester Civil Justice Centre*, London: Denton Corker Marshall, 2011
Tombesi, Paolo, 'Raising the Bar', *Architecture Australia*, 97:1, Jan 2008, http://architectureau.com/articles/raising-the-bar/ (viewed 5 Jun 2013)

45 Green School
http://www.ecology.com/2012/01/24/balis-green-school/
Hazard, Marian, Hazzard, Ed and Erickson, Sheryl, 'The Green School Effect: An Exploration of the Influence of Place, Space and Environment on Teaching and Learning at Green School, Bali, Indonesia', http://www.powersofplace.com/pdfs/greenschoolreport.pdf
James, Caroline, 'The Green School : Deep within the jungles of Bali, a School Made Entirely of Bamboo Seeks to Train the Next Generations of Leaders in Sustainability', *Domus*, 2012, http://www.domusweb.it/en/architecture/2010/12/12/the-green-school.html
Saieh N, 'Green School PT Bambu', *ArchDaily*, http://www.archdaily.com/81585/the-green-school-pt-bambu/

46 Mimesis Museum
El Croquis 140: *Álvaro Siza 2001–2008*, 2008
Figueira, Jorge, *Álvaro Siza: Modern Redux*, Ostfildern: Hatje Cantz, 2008

Gregory, Rob, 'Mimesis Museum by Álvaro Siza, Carlos Castanheira and Jun Saung Kim, Paju Book City, South Korea', *Architectural Review*, 2010, http://www.architectural-review.com/mimesis-museum-by-alvaro-siza-carlos-castanheira-and-jun-saung-kim-paju-book-city-south-korea/8607232.article (viewed 20 Sep 2013)

Jodidio, Philip, *Álvaro Siza: Complete Works 1952–2013*, Cologne: Taschen, 2013

Leoni, Giovanni, *Álvaro Siza*, Milan: Motta Architettura, 2009

47 Juilliard School and Alice Tully Hall

Guiney, Anne, 'Alice Tully Hall, Lincoln Center, New York', *Architect*, April 2009: 101–9

Incerti G., Ricchi D., Simpson D., *Diller + Scofidio (+ Renfro): The Cilliary Function*, New York: Skira, 2007

Kolb, Jaffer, 'Alice Tully Hall by Diller Scofidio + Renfro, New York, USA', *Architectural Review* 225, no. 1346, 2009: 54–59

Merkel, Jayne, 'Alice Tully Hall, New York', *Architectural Design* 79, no. 4, 2009: 108–13

Otero-Pailos, Jorge, Diller, Elizabeth and Scofidio, Ricardo, 'Morphing Lincoln Center', *Future Anterior* 6, no. 1, 2009: 84–97

48 41 Cooper Square

Goncharm Joann, '41 Cooper Square, New York City, Morphosis', *Architectural Record* 197, no. 11, 2009: 97

Doscher, Martin, 'New Academic Building for the Cooper Union for the Advancement of Science and Art – Morphosis', *Architectural Design* 79, no. 2, 2009: 28–31

Morphosis Architects, *Cooper Union*, http://morphopedia.com/projects/cooper-union

Mayne, Thom, *Fresh Morphosis: 1998–2004*, New York: Rizzoli, 2006

Mayne, Thom, *Morphosis; Buildings and Projects, 1993–1997*, New York: Rizzoli, 1999

Merkel, Jayne, 'Morphosis Architects' Cooper Union Academic Building, New York', *Architectural Design* 80, no. 2, 2010: 110–13

Millard, Bill, *Meta Morphosis: Thom Mayne's Cooper Union*, http://www.designbuild-network.com/features/feature75153

'41 Cooper Square', *arcspace*, 2009, http://www.arcspace.com/features/morphosis/41-cooper-square/

49 Oslo Opera House

Craven, Jackie, 'Oslo Opera House in Oslo, Norway', undated, http://architecture.about.com/od/greatbuildings/ss/osloopera.htm (viewed 8 Jun 2013)

GA Document, 'Snøhetta: New Opera House Oslo', *GA document* (102), 2008: 8

Gronvold, Ulf, 'Oslo's New Opera House – Roofscape and an Element of Urban Renewal', *Detail* (English edn), 3 274, May/June 2009

'Oslo Opera House / Snøhetta', *ArchDaily*, 07 May 2008, http://www.archdaily.com/440 (viewed 8 Jun 2013)

50 MAXXI

MAXXI, http://www.fondazionemaxxi.it/?lang=en (viewed 22 Apr 2013)

Zaha Hadid Architects, http://www.zaha-hadid.com/architecture/maxxi/ (viewed 22 Apr 2013)

Anon, 'Zaha Hadid MAXXI Museum', *Architectuul*, http://architectuul.com/architecture/maxxi-museum (viewed 22 Apr 2013)

C+A, '*MAXXI Roma*', *C+A* 13: 12-28 Cement Concrete and Aggregates Australia, http://www.concrete.net.au/CplusA/issue13/ (viewed 24 Aug 2013)

Janssens, M., and Racana G. (eds), *MAXXI: Zaha Hadid Architects*, New York: Rizzoli, 2010

Mara, F. 'Zaha Hadid Architects', *Architect's Journal* 232, no. 12, 2010: 62–68

Schumacher, Patrik, 'The Meaning of MAXXI – Concepts, Ambitions, Achievements' in Janssens and Racana, 2010: 18–39. Also available online at http://www.patrikschumacher.com/Texts/The%20Meaning%20of%20MAXXI.html (viewed 22 Apr 2013)

Index

Page references in italic are to full-page illustrations